CCIE Professional Development

Network Security Technologies and Solutions

Yusuf Bhaiji, CCIE No. 9305

Cisco Press

Cisco Press
201 West 103rd Street
Indianapolis, IN 46290 USA

CCIE Professional Development

Network Security Technologies and Solutions

Yusuf Bhaiji

Copyright© 2008 Cisco Systems, Inc.

Published by:
Cisco Press
800 East 96th Street
Indianapolis, IN 46240 USA

Printed in the United States of America

First Printing   March 2008

Library of Congress Cataloging-in-Publication Data:

Bhaiji, Fahim Hussain Yusuf.

  Network security technologies and solutions / Yusuf Bhaiji.

      p. cm.

  ISBN 978-1-58705-246-0 (pbk.)

1. Computer networks--Security measures. I. Title.

  TK5105.59.B468 2008

  005.8--dc22

   2008003231

ISBN-13: 978-1-58705-246-6

ISBN-10: 1-58705-246-6

Warning and Disclaimer

Trademark Acknowledgments

All terms mentioned in this book that are known to be trademarks or service marks have been appropriately capital-ized. Cisco Press or Cisco Systems, Inc., cannot attest to the accuracy of this information. Use of a term in this book should not be regarded as affecting the validity of any trademark or service mark.

Corporate and Government Sales

The publisher offers excellent discounts on this book when ordered in quantity for bulk purchases or special sales, which may include electronic versions and/or custom covers and content particular to your business, training goals, marketing focus, and branding interests. For more information, please contact:

U.S. Corporate and Government Sales   1-800-382-3419   corpsales@pearsontechgroup.com

For sales outside the United States please contact: **International Sales**   international@pearsoned.com

Feedback Information

At Cisco Press, our goal is to create in-depth technical books of the highest quality and value. Each book is crafted with care and precision, undergoing rigorous development that involves the unique expertise of members from the professional technical community.

Readers' feedback is a natural continuation of this process. If you have any comments regarding how we could improve the quality of this book, or otherwise alter it to better suit your needs, you can contact us through e-mail at feedback@ciscopress.com. Please make sure to include the book title and ISBN in your message.

We greatly appreciate your assistance.

Publisher	Paul Boger
Associate Publisher	Dave Dusthimer
Cisco Representative	Anthony Wolfenden
Cisco Press Program Manager	Jeff Brady
Executive Editor	Brett Bartow
Managing Editor	Patrick Kanouse
Development Editor	Betsey Henkels
Project Editor	San Dee Phillips
Copy Editor	Barbara Hacha
Technical Editors	Nairi Adamian, Kevin Hofstra, Gert DeLaet
Editorial Assistant	Vanessa Evans
Book and Cover Designer	Louisa Adair
Composition	Mark Shirar
Indexer	Tim Wright
Proofreader	Karen A. Gill

About the Author

Yusuf Bhaiji, CCIE No. 9305 (Routing and Switching and Security), has been with Cisco for seven years and is currently the program manager for the Cisco CCIE Security Certification and CCIE proctor in Cisco Dubai Lab. Prior to this, he was technical lead for the Sydney TAC Security and VPN team.

Yusuf's passion for security technologies and solutions has played a dominant role in his 17 years of industry experience, from as far back as his initial master's degree in computer science, and has since been reflected in his numerous certifications.

Yusuf prides himself in his knowledge-sharing abilities, which are evident in the fact that he has mentored many successful candidates, as well as having designed and delivered a number of Network Security solutions around the globe.

Yusuf is an advisory board member of several nonprofit organizations for the dissemination of technologies and promotion of indigenous excellence in the field of internetworking through academic and professional activities. Yusuf chairs the Networkers Society of Pakistan (NSP) and IPv6 Forum Pakistan chapter.

Yusuf has also authored a Cisco Press publication titled *CCIE Security Practice Labs* (ISBN 1587051346), released in early 2004. He has been a technical reviewer for several Cisco Press publications and written articles, white papers, and presentations on various security technologies. He is a frequent lecturer and well-known speaker presenting in several conferences and seminars worldwide.

About the Technical Reviewers

Nairi Adamian, CCIE Security No. 10294, has been with Cisco since 1999 and currently is a technical support manager at Cisco, Australia. She leads a team of customer support engineers at the Cisco Technical Assistance Center (TAC). She holds a bachelor's degree in computing science from University of Technology, Sydney, and has an MBA from Macquarie Graduate School of Management.

Kevin Hofstra, CCIE No. 14619, CCNP, CCDP, CCSP, CCVP, manages a network engineering unit within the Air Force Communications Agency of the U.S. Department of Defense. Mr. Hofstra is responsible for designing, implementing, and optimizing DoD networks and has deployed as a civilian engineer to Iraq, Kuwait, and Qatar in support of Operation Iraqi Freedom. Mr. Hofstra has a computer science degree from Yale University and a master of engineering degree in telecommunications and a master of engineering management degree from the University of Colorado.

Gert DeLaet, CCIE No. 2657, is a product manager for the CCIE team at Cisco. Gert was a contributing author to *CCIE Security Exam Certification Guide* and *CCDA Exam Certification Guide* from Cisco Press. He resides in Brussels, Belgium.

Dedications

This book is dedicated to my beloved wife, Farah. Without her support and encouragement, I could not have completed this book.

Acknowledgments

I would like to thank my family for all their continuous support and encouragement, and especially my father, Asghar Bhaiji, for his wisdom. Last but not least, I reminisce about my mother, Khatija Bhaiji, whose love is ever shining on me.

I would like to especially thank the technical reviewers, Nairi Adamian, Gert DeLaet, and Kevin Hofstra, who have done an amazing job in contributing to this book. Their valuable feedback and efforts to research each topic are greatly appreciated in the accomplishment of this project.

I extend my sincere gratitude to Brett Bartow and the entire development team—Betsey Henkels, Dayna Isley, Barbara Hacha, San Dee Phillips, Chris Cleveland, and members of the Cisco Press team working on this project, whose expert guidance has been a determining factor in the completion of this book.

I would like to take this opportunity to thank my manager, Sarah DeMark, the leadership team of Learning@Cisco group, and my colleagues at Cisco for their support in writing this book and every other project. I have benefited greatly from working with them and am honored to be a member of this team.

Finally, I would like to thank you, the reader of this book, for helping me to make this book a success.

This Book Is Safari Enabled

The Safari® Enabled icon on the cover of your favorite technology book means the book is available through Safari Bookshelf. When you buy this book, you get free access to the online edition for 45 days.

Safari Bookshelf is an electronic reference library that lets you easily search thousands of technical books, find code samples, download chapters, and access technical information whenever and wherever you need it.

To gain 45-day Safari Enabled access to this book:

- Go to http://www.ciscopress.com/safarienabled
- Complete the brief registration form
- Enter the coupon code SJGV-KMZF-ENN5-ITFN-EYIT

If you have difficulty registering on Safari Bookshelf or accessing the online edition, please e-mail customer-service@safaribooksonline.com.

Contents at a Glance

Contents

Icons Used in This Book

 PC

 Router

 Workgroup Switch

 Hub

 File Server

 Multilayer Switch

 Router with Firewall

 IOS Firewall

 PIX Firewall

 CS-MARS

 Access Server

 Secure Switch

 Wireless Access Point

 IP Phone

 VPN Concentrator

 Optical Services Router

 Detector

 Web Cluster

 Secure Endpoints

 Cisco ASA 5500

 Secure Switch

 Secure Router

 NAC Appliance

 Wireless Signal

 Serial Line

 Circuit Switched Line

Line: Ethernet

Command Syntax Conventions

The conventions used to present command syntax in this book are the same conventions used in the IOS Command Reference. The Command Reference describes these conventions as follows:

- **Boldface** indicates commands and keywords that are entered literally as shown. In actual configuration examples and output (not general command syntax), boldface indicates commands that are manually input by the user (such as a **show** command).

- *Italic* indicates arguments for which you supply actual values.

- Vertical bars (|) separate alternative, mutually exclusive elements.

- Square brackets ([ ]) indicate an optional element.

- Braces ({ }) indicate a required choice.

- Braces within brackets ([{ }]) indicate a required choice within an optional element.

Foreword

With the explosion of the Internet economy, the continuous availability of mission-critical systems has never been more important. Network administrators through to business managers are expected by their customers, employees, and suppliers to provide constant network resource availability and access to critical applications and data in a completely secure environment. Not only is this a challenge, the stakes in breaching network security have never been higher.

Network Security Technologies and Solutions is a comprehensive, all-in-one reference for managing Cisco networks. It was written to help network security professionals understand and implement current, state-of-the-art network security technologies and solutions. Whether you are an expert in networking and security or a novice, this book is a valuable resource.

Many books on network security are based primarily on concepts and theory. *Network Security Technologies and Solutions*, however, goes far beyond that. It is a hands-on tool for configuring and managing Cisco market-leading dynamic links between customer security policy, user or host identity, and network infrastructures. The foundation of this book is based on key elements from the Cisco security solution. It provides practical, day-to-day guidance on how to successfully configure all aspects of network security, covering topics such as perimeter security, identity security and access management, and data privacy, as well as security monitoring and management.

Yusuf Bhaiji has been with Cisco for seven years and is currently the product manager for the Cisco CCIE Security certification track and a CCIE Proctor in Cisco Dubai Lab. Yusuf's passion for security technologies and solutions is evident in his 17 years of industry experience and numerous certifications. Yusuf's extensive experience as a mentor and advisor in the security technology field has honed his ability to translate highly technical information into a straightforward, easy-to-understand format. If you're looking for a truly comprehensive guide to network security, this is the one!

Steve Gordon
Cisco Systems, Inc.
Vice President, Technical Services
Remote Operations Services and Learning@Cisco

Introduction

The Internet was born in 1969 as the ARPANET, a project funded by the Advanced Research Projects Agency (ARPA) of the U.S. Department of Defense. The Internet is a worldwide collection of loosely connected networks that are accessible by individual computers in varied ways, such as gateways, routers, dial-up connections, and through Internet service providers (ISP). Anyone today can reach any device/computer via the Internet without the restriction of geographical boundaries.

As Dr. Vinton G. Cerf states, "The wonderful thing about the Internet is that you're connected to everyone else. The terrible thing about the Internet is that you're connected to everyone else."

The luxury of access to this wealth of information comes with its risks, with anyone on the Internet potentially being the stakeholder. The risks vary from information loss or corruption to information theft and much more. The number of security incidents is also growing dramatically.

With all this happening, a strong drive exists for network security implementations to improve security postures within every organization worldwide. Today's most complex networks require the most comprehensive and integrated security solutions.

Security has evolved over the past few years and is one of the fastest-growing areas in the industry. Information security is on top of the agenda for all organizations. Companies need to keep information secure, and there is an ever-growing demand for the IT professionals who know how to do this.

Point products are no longer sufficient for protecting the information and require system-level security solutions. Linking endpoint and network security is a vital ingredient in designing the modern networks coupled with proactive and adaptive security systems to defend against the new breed of day-zero attacks.

Security is no longer simply an enabling technology or a one-time affair; it has become an essential component of the network blueprint. Security technologies and solutions need to be fundamentally integrated into the infrastructure itself, woven into the fabric of the network. Security today requires comprehensive, end-to-end solutions.

Goals and Methods

Cisco Network Security Technologies and Solutions is a comprehensive all-in-one reference book that covers all major Cisco Security products, technologies, and solutions. This book is a complete reference that helps networking professionals understand and implement current, state-of-the-art security technologies and solutions. The coverage is wide but deep enough to provide the audience with concepts, design, and implementation guidelines as well as basic configuration skills.

With an easy-to-understand approach, this invaluable resource will serve as a central warehouse of security knowledge to the security professionals with end-to-end security implementations.

The book makes no assumption of knowledge level, thereby ensuring that the readers have an explanation that will make sense and be comprehendible at the same time. It takes the reader from the fundamental level of each technology to more detailed descriptions and discussions of each subject.

With this definitive reference, the readers will possess a greater understanding of the solutions available and learn how to build integrated secure networks in today's modern, heterogeneous infrastructure.

This book is comprehensive in scope, including information about mature as well as emerging technologies, including the Adaptive Security Appliance (ASA) Firewall Software Release 8.0, Cisco Intrusion Prevention System (IPS) Sensor Software Release 6.0, Host IPS, Cisco Group Encrypted Transport VPN (GETVPN), MPLS VPN technology, Cisco Distributed Denial-of-Service (DDoS) Anomaly Detection and Mitigation Solutions, Cisco Security Monitoring, Analysis, and Response System (CS-MARS), and Security Framework, Standards and Regulatory Compliance, to name a few.

Who Should Read This Book

Whether you are a network engineer or a security engineer, consultant, or andidate pursuing security certifications, this book will become your primary reference when designing and building a secure network.

Additionally, this book will serve as a valuable resource for candidates preparing for the CCIE Security certification exam that covers topics from the new blueprints.

The book will serve as a reference for any networking professional managing or considering exploring and implementing Cisco network security solutions and technologies.

How This Book Is Organized

This book is meant to complement the information already available on Cisco.com and in the Cisco security products documentation.

The book is divided into five parts, mapping Cisco security technologies and solutions into five key elements.

Part I, "Perimeter Security": This element provides the means to control access to critical network applications, data, and services so that only legitimate users and information can pass through the network. Part I includes the following chapters:

- Chapter 1, "Overview of Network Security," introduces principles of network security, security models, and a basic overview of security standards, policies, and the network security framework.

- Chapter 2, "Access Control," describes the capability to perform traffic filtering using access control lists (ACL). It covers numerous types of ACL, such as standard and extended ACL, Lock-and-key, Reflexive, Time-based, Receive ACL, Infrastructure ACL, and Transit ACL. The chapter addresses traffic filtering based on RFC standards and best common practices.

- Chapter 3, "Device Security," covers some of the most common techniques used for device hardening and securing management access for routers, firewall appliances, and the intrusion prevention system (IPS) appliance.

- Chapter 4, "Security Features on Switches," provides a comprehensive set of security features available on the switches. The chapter covers port-level security controls at Layer 2 and security features and best practices available on the switch.

- Chapter 5, "Cisco IOS Firewall," introduces the software-based IOS firewall features, including the legacy Context-Based Access Control (CBAC) and the newly introduced Zone-Based Policy Firewall (ZFW) feature available on the router.

- Chapter 6, "Cisco Firewalls: Appliance and Module," covers the complete range of hardware-based Cisco firewall products, including Cisco PIX, Cisco ASA Firewall appliance, and Cisco Firewall Services Module (FWSM). The chapter provides comprehensive coverage of firewall operating systems (OS), software features, and capabilities.

- Chapter 7, "Attack Vectors and Mitigation Techniques," is a uniquely positioned chapter covering details of common types of attacks, and providing details of how to characterize and classify various attacks. The chapter provides mitigation techniques for a wide range of attacks at Layer 2 and Layer 3.

Part II, "Identity Security and Access Management": Identity is the accurate and positive identification of network users, hosts, applications, services and resources. Part II includes the following chapters:

- Chapter 8, "Securing Management Access," covers details of the authentication, authorization, and accounting (AAA) framework and implementation of AAA technology. The chapter covers implementing the two widely used security protocols in access management: RADIUS and TACACS+ protocols.

- Chapter 9, "Cisco Secure ACS Software and Appliance," provides details of Cisco Secure Access Control Server (ACS) software that supports the AAA technology and security protocols covered in Chapter 8. The chapter highlights the commonly use ACS software functions and features.

- Chapter 10, "Multifactor Authentication," describes the identification and authentication mechanism using the multifactor authentication system. The chapter introduces common two-factor mechanisms.

- Chapter 11, "Layer 2 Access Control," covers the Cisco trust and identity management solution based on the Identity-Based Networking Services (IBNS) technique. The chapter provides details of implementing port-based authentication and controlling network access at Layer 2 using IEEE 802.1x technology.

- Chapter 12, "Wireless LAN (WLAN) Security," provides an overview of wireless LAN (WLAN) and details of securing WLAN networks. The chapter covers various techniques available to protect WLAN and expands on the various EAP protocols, including EAP-MD5, EAP-TLS, EAP-TTLS, EAP-FAST, PEAP, and Cisco LEAP. The chapter also provides coverage of common WLAN attacks and mitigation techniques.

- Chapter 13, "Network Admission Control (NAC)" provides details of Cisco Self-Defending Network (SDN) solution using the Cisco Network Admission Control (NAC) appliance-based and framework-based solutions. The chapter covers implementing the Cisco NAC appliance solution as well as the NAC-L3-IP, NAC-L2-IP, and NAC-L2-802.1x solutions.

Part III, "Data Privacy": When information must be protected from eavesdropping, the capability to provide authenticated, confidential communication on demand is crucial. Employing security services at the network layer provides the best of both worlds. VPN solutions can secure communications using confidentiality, integrity, and authentication protocols between devices located anywhere on an untrusted or public network, particularly the Internet. Part III includes the following chapters:

- Chapter 14, "Cryptography," lays the foundation of data privacy and how to secure communication using crypto methodology and cryptographic solutions. The chapter gives a basic overview of various cryptographic algorithms, including hash algorithms, symmetric key, and asymmetric key algorithms.

- Chapter 15, "IPsec VPN," is a comprehensive chapter covering a wide range of IPsec VPN solutions. The chapter provides various types of VPN deployment with focus on IPsec VPN technology covering IPsec protocols, standards, IKE, ISAKMP, and IPsec profiles. The chapter provides comprehensive coverage of implementing IPsec VPN solutions using various methods.

- Chapter 16, "Dynamic Multipoint VPN (DMVPN)," covers the dynamic multipoint VPN (DMVPN) solution architecture and describes the design, components, and how DMVPN works. The chapter provides coverage of implementing various types of DMVPN hub-and-spoke and spoke-to-spoke solutions.

- Chapter 17, "Group Encrypted Transport VPN (GET VPN)," covers the innovative tunnel-less VPN approach to provide data security. The chapter describes the newly introduced GET VPN technology, solution architecture, components, and how GET VPN works.

- Chapter 18, "Secure Sockets Layer VPN (SSL VPN)," describes the SSL-based VPN approach covering SSL VPN solution architecture and various types of SSL VPN. The chapter also covers the newly introduced Cisco AnyConnect VPN.

- Chapter 19, "Multiprotocol Label Switching VPN (MPLS VPN)," provides coverage of Multiprotocol Label Switching (MPLS)-based VPN technology to provide data security across MPLS networks. The chapter provides MPLS VPN solution architecture and various types of MPLS VPN technologies available. The chapter covers implementing Layer 2 (L2VPN) and Layer 3 (L3VPN)–based MPLS VPN solutions.

Part IV, "Security Monitoring": To ensure that a network remains secure, it's important to regularly test and monitor the state of security preparation. Network vulnerability scanners can proactively identify areas of weakness, and intrusion detection systems can monitor and respond to security events as they occur. Using security monitoring solutions, organizations can obtain unprecedented visibility into both the network data stream and the security posture of the network. Part IV includes the following chapters:

- Chapter 20, "Network Intrusion Prevention," covers network security monitoring using the network-based appliance sensor technology, Intrusion Prevention System (IPS). The chapter provides a comprehensive coverage of the sensor operating system (OS) software functions and features.

- Chapter 21, "Host Intrusion Prevention," covers network security monitoring using the host-based technology, Host Intrusion Prevention System (HIPS). The chapter provides comprehensive details of Cisco Security Agent (CSA) technology providing solution architecture, components, and CSA deployment using CSA MC.

- Chapter 22, "Anomaly Detection," provides coverage of anomaly-based security monitoring using Cisco Anomaly Detection and Mitigation Systems. The chapter covers Cisco Traffic Anomaly Detector and Cisco Guard products to provide DDoS mitigation.

- Chapter 23, "Security Monitoring and Correlation," covers the innovative Security Monitoring, Analysis, and Response System (CS-MARS) based on the Security Threat Mitigation (STM) System. The chapter provides key concepts of CS-MARS and deployment guidelines.

Part V, "Security Management": As networks grow in size and complexity, the requirement for centralized policy management tools grow as well. Sophisticated tools that can analyze, interpret, configure, and monitor the state of security policy, with browser-based user interfaces, enhance the usability and effectiveness of network security solutions. Part V includes the following chapters:

- Chapter 24, "Security and Policy Management," provides comprehensive coverage of the security management solutions using the Cisco Security Manager (CSM) software and various device manager xDM tools including SDM, ASDM, PDM, and IDM.

- Chapter 25, "Security Framework and Regulatory Compliance," provides an overview of security standards, policy and regulatory compliance, and best practices frameworks. The chapter covers the two commonly used security frameworks: ISO/IEC 17799 and COBIT. The chapter covers regulatory compliance and legislative acts including GLBA, HIPAA, and SOX.

å*Network Security Technologies and Solutions* is a complete reference book, like a security dictionary, an encyclopedia, and an administrator's guide—all in one.

Perimeter Security

CHAPTER 1

Overview of Network Security

At the same time networks are growing exponentially, they are becoming complex and mission critical, bringing new challenges to those who run and manage them. The need for integrated network infrastructure comprising voice, video, and data (all-in-one) services is evident, but these rapidly growing technologies introduce fresh security concerns. Therefore, as network managers struggle to include the latest technology in their network infrastructure, network security has become a pivotal function in building and maintaining today's modern high-growth networks.

This chapter presents a broad description of network security in the context of today's rapidly changing network environments. The security paradigm is changing, and security solutions today are solution driven and designed to meet the requirements of business. To help you face the complexities of managing a modern network, this chapter discusses the core principles of security—the CIA triad: confidentiality, integrity, and availability.

In addition to discussing CIA, this chapter discusses security policies that are the heart of all network security implementations. The discussion covers the following aspects of security policies: standards, procedures, baselines, guidelines, and various security models.

The chapter takes a closer look at the perimeter security issue and the multilayered perimeter approach. The chapter concludes with the Cisco security wheel paradigm involving five cyclical steps.

Fundamental Questions for Network Security

When you are planning, designing, or implementing a network or are assigned to operate and manage one, it is useful to ask yourself the following questions:

1 What are you trying to protect or maintain?

2 What are your business objectives?

3 What do you need to accomplish these objectives?

4 What technologies or solutions are required to support these objectives?

5 Are your objectives compatible with your security infrastructure, operations, and tools?

6   What risks are associated with inadequate security?

7   What are the implications of not implementing security?

8   Will you introduce new risks not covered by your current security solutions or policy?

9   How do you reduce that risk?

10   What is your tolerance for risk?

You can use these questions to pose and answer some of the basic questions that underlie fundamental requirements for establishing a secure network. Network security technologies reduce risk and provide a foundation for expanding businesses with intranet, extranet, and electronic commerce applications.

Solutions also protect sensitive data and corporate resources from intrusion and corruption.

Advanced technologies now offer opportunities for small and medium-sized businesses (SMB), as well as enterprise and large-scale networks to grow and compete; they also highlight a need to protect computer systems against a wide range of security threats.

The challenge of keeping your network infrastructure secure has never been greater or more crucial to your business. Despite considerable investments in information security, organizations continue to be afflicted by cyber incidents. At the same time, management aims for greater results with fewer resources. Hence, improving security effectiveness remains vital, if not essential, while enhancement of both effectiveness and flexibility has also become a primary objective.

Without proper safeguards, every part of a network is vulnerable to a security breach or unauthorized activity from intruders, competitors, or even employees. Many of the organizations that manage their own internal network security and use the Internet for more than just sending/receiving e-mails experience a network attack—and more than half of these companies do not even know they were attacked. Smaller companies are often complacent, having gained a false sense of security. They usually react to the last virus or the most recent defacing of their website. But they are trapped in a situation where they do not have the necessary time and resources to spend on security.

To cope with these problems, Cisco has developed the SAFE Blueprint, a comprehensive security plan that recommends and explains specific security solutions for different elements of networks.

Cisco also offers the integrated security solution, which delivers services above and beyond the "one size fits all" model. In addition, Cisco services are designed to deliver value throughout the entire network life cycle that includes the stages of prepare, plan, design, implement, operate, and optimize (PPDIOO). the Cisco PPDIOO model, as shown in Figure 1-1, encompasses all the steps from network vision to optimization, enabling Cisco to provide a broader portfolio of support and end-to-end solutions to its customers.

Figure 1-1   *The Cisco PPDIOO Model*

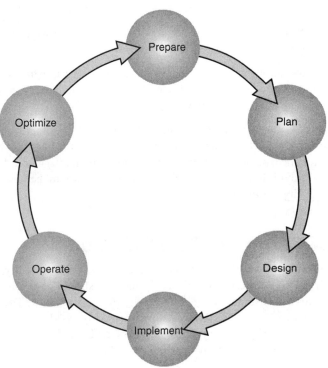

Transformation of the Security Paradigm

As the size of networks continues to grow and attacks to those networks become increasingly sophisticated, the way we think about security changes. Here are some of the major factors that are changing the security paradigm:

- **Security is no longer about "products":** Security solutions must be chosen with business objectives in mind and integrated with operational procedures and tools.

- **Scalability demands are increasing:** With the increasing number of vulnerabilities and security threats, solutions must scale to thousands of hosts in large enterprises.

- **Legacy endpoint security Total Cost of Ownership (TCO) is a challenge:** Reactive products force deployment and renewal of multiple agents and management paradigms.

- **Day zero damage:** Rapidly propagating attacks (Slammer, Nimda, MyDoom) happen too fast for reactive products to control. Therefore, an automated, proactive security system is needed to combat the dynamic array of modern-day viruses and worms.

With modern-day distributed networks, security cannot be enforced only at the network edge or perimeter. We will discuss perimeter security in more detail later in this chapter.

Zero-day attacks or new and unknown viruses continue to plague enterprises and service provider networks.

To attempt to establish protection against attacks, enterprises try to patch systems as vulnerabilities become known. This clearly cannot scale in large networks, and this situation can be addressed only with real-time proactive-based systems.

Security *now* is about management and reduction of risk in a rapidly evolving environment. Maximum risk reduction is achieved with an integrated solution built on a flexible and intelligent infrastructure and effective operations and management tools. Business objectives should drive security decisions. Today, we are in the new era that forces us to rethink security and outbreak prevention.

Principles of Security—The CIA Model

A simple but widely applicable security model is the confidentiality, integrity, and availability (CIA) triad. These three key principles should guide all secure systems. CIA also provides a measurement tool for security implementations. These principles are applicable across the entire spectrum of security analysis—from access, to a user's Internet history, to the security of encrypted data across the Internet. A breach of any of these three principles can have serious consequences for all parties concerned.

Figure 1-2 *The CIA Triad*

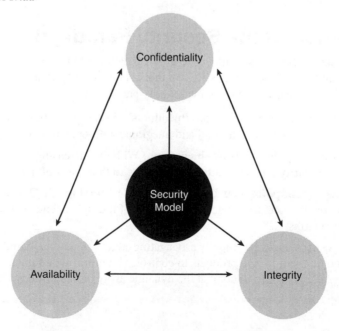

Confidentiality

Confidentiality prevents unauthorized disclosure of sensitive information. It is the capability to ensure that the necessary level of secrecy is enforced and that information is concealed from unauthorized users. When it comes to security, confidentiality is perhaps the most obvious aspect of the CIA triad, and it is the aspect of security most often attacked. Cryptography and encryption methods are examples of attempts to ensure the confidentiality of data transferred from one computer to another. For example, when performing an online banking transaction, the user wants to protect the privacy of the account details, such as passwords and card numbers. Cryptography provides a secure transmission protecting the sensitive data traversing across the shared medium.

Integrity

Integrity prevents unauthorized modification of data, systems, and information, thereby providing assurance of the accuracy of information and systems. If your data has integrity, you can be sure that it is an accurate and unchanged representation of the original secure information. A common type of a security attack is man-in-the-middle. In this type of attack, an intruder intercepts data in transfer and makes changes to it.

Availability

Availability is the prevention of loss of access to resources and information to ensure that information is available for use when it is needed. It is imperative to make sure that information requested is readily accessible to the authorized users at all times. Denial of service (DoS) is one of several types of security attacks that attempts to deny access to the appropriate user, often for the sake of disruption of service.

Policies, Standards, Procedures, Baselines, Guidelines

A *security model* is a multilayered framework made of many integrated entities and logical and physical protection mechanisms, all working together to provide a secure system that complies with industry best practices and regulations.

Security Policy

A *security policy* is a set of rules, practices, and procedures dictating how sensitive information is managed, protected, and distributed. In the network security realm, policies are usually point specific, which means they cover a single area. A security policy is a document that expresses exactly what the security level should be by setting the goals of what the security mechanisms are to accomplish. Security policy is written by higher management and is intended to describe the "whats" of information security. The next section gives a few examples of security policies. Procedures, standards, baselines, and guidelines are the "hows" for implementation of the policy. Information security policies underline the security and well-being of information resources; they are the foundation of information security within an organization.

Trust is one of the main themes in many policies. Some companies do not have policies because they trust in their people and trust that everyone will do the right thing. But, that is not always the case, as we all know. Therefore, most organizations need policies to ensure that everyone complies with the same set of rules.

In my experience, policies tend to elevate people's apprehension because people do not want to be bound by rules and regulations. Instead, people want freedom and non-accountability. A policy should define the level of control users must observe and balance that with productivity goals. An overly strict policy will be hard to implement because compliance will be minimal or ignored. On the contrary, a loosely defined policy can be evaded and does not ensure accountability and responsibility. A good policy has to have the right balance.

Examples of Security Policies

Depending on the size of the organization, potentially dozens of security policy topics may be appropriate. For some organizations, one large document covers all facets; at other organizations, several smaller, individually focused documents are needed. The sample list that follows covers some common policies that an organization should consider.

- **Acceptable use:** This policy outlines the acceptable use of computer equipment. The rules are established to protect the employee and the organization. Inappropriate use exposes the company to risks including virus attacks, compromise of network systems and services, and legal issues.

- **Ethics:** This policy emphasizes the employee's and consumer's expectations to be subject to fair business practices. It establishes a culture of openness, trust, and integrity in business practices. This policy can guide business behavior to ensure ethical conduct.

- **Information sensitivity:** This policy is intended to help employees determine what information can be disclosed to nonemployees, as well as the relative sensitivity of information that should not be disclosed outside an organization without proper authorization. The information covered in these guidelines includes but is not limited to information that is either stored or shared via any means. This includes electronic information, information on paper, and information shared orally or visually (such as by telephone, video conferencing, and teleconferencing).

- **E-mail:** This policy covers appropriate use of any e-mail sent from an organization's e-mail address and applies to all employees, vendors, and agents operating on behalf of the company.

- **Password:** The purpose of this policy is to establish a standard for creation of strong passwords, the protection of those passwords, and the frequency of change.
- **Risk assessment:** This policy is used to empower the Information Security (InfoSec) group to perform periodic information security risk assessments (RA) for the purpose of determining areas of vulnerability and to initiate appropriate remediation.

TIP   Examples of policies listed previously and other templates can be found at the SANS website:

https://www2.sans.org/resources/policies/#template

NOTE   Policies need to be concise, to the point, and easy to read and understand. Most policies listed previously are on average two to three pages.

Standards

Standards are industry-recognized best practices, frameworks, and agreed principles of concepts and designs, which are designed to implement, achieve, and maintain the required levels of processes and procedures.

Like security policies, standards are strategic in nature in that they define systems parameters and processes.

Standards vary by industry. There are two notable standards in security information management—ISO 17799 and COBIT. These are discussed in Chapter 25, "Security Framework and Regulatory Compliance."

Procedures

Procedures are low-level documents providing systematic instructions on how the security policy and the standards are to be implemented in a system. Procedures are detailed in nature to provide maximum information to users so that they can successfully implement and enforce the security policy and apply the standards and guidelines of a security program.

Employees usually refer to procedures more often than other policies and standards because procedures provide the actual details of the implementation phase of a security program.

Baselines

A *baseline* is the minimum level of security requirement in a system. Baselines provide users the means to achieve the absolute minimum security required that is consistent across all the systems in the organization. For example, a company might have a baseline for Windows 2000 servers to have Service Pack 4 installed on each server in the production environment. The procedure document would supplement the baseline by spelling out step-by-step instructions on where to download Service Pack 4 and how to install it to comply with this security level.

Guidelines

Guidelines are recommended actions and operational guides for users. Similar to procedures, guidelines are tactical in nature. The major difference between standards and guidelines is that guidelines can be used as reference, whereas standards are mandatory actions in most cases.

Figure 1-3 depicts the fundamental relationship among security policies, standards, baselines, guidelines, and procedures.

Figure 1-3   *Relationships Among Security Policies, Standards, Procedures, Baselines, and Guidelines*

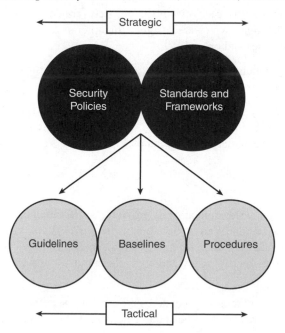

Security Models

An important element in the design and analysis of secure systems is the security model, because it integrates the security policy that should be enforced in the system. A *security model* is a symbolic portrayal of a security policy. It maps the requirements of the policy makers into a set of rules and regulations that are to be followed by a computer system or a network system. A *security policy* is a set of abstract goals and high-level requirements, and the security model is the do's and don'ts to make this happen.

You should know about several important security models even though describing them in detail is beyond the scope of this book:

- The Bell-LaPadula Model (BLM), also called the multilevel model, was introduced mainly to enforce access control in government and military applications. BLM protects the confidentiality of the information within a system.

- The Biba model is a modification of the Bell-LaPadula model that mainly emphasizes the integrity of the information within a system.

- The Clark-Wilson model prevents authorized users from making unauthorized modification to the data. This model introduces a system of triples: a subject, a program, and an object.

- The Access Control Matrix is a general model of access control that is based on the concept of subjects and objects.

- The Information Flow model restricts information in its flow so that it moves only to and from approved security levels.

- The Chinese Wall model combines commercial discretion with legally enforceable mandatory controls. It is required in the operation of many financial services organizations.

- The Lattice model deals with military information. Lattice-based access control models were developed in the early 1970s to deal with the confidentiality of military information. In the late 1970s and early 1980s, researchers applied these models to certain integrity concerns. Later, application of the models to the Chinese Wall policy, a confidentiality policy unique to the commercial sector, was developed. A balanced perspective on lattice-based access control models is provided.

Perimeter Security

Opinions on perimeter security have changed a great deal over the past few years. Part of that change is that the very nature of perimeter security is becoming increasingly uncertain, and everyone has a different view of just what it is. The limits of the perimeter itself are becoming broad and extensive, with no geographic boundaries, and remote access is becoming part of the integral network.

Is Perimeter Security Disappearing?

In essence, the perimeter has been transformed and extended to the various levels within the network. In other words, networks today do not have a single point of entrance; they are multi-entry open environments where controlled access is required from anywhere within the network. This transformation leads us to start thinking in terms of multiperimeter networks.

The Difficulty of Defining Perimeter

Traditional networks are growing with the merging of remote network access. Wireless networks, laptops, mobile phones, PDAs, and numerous other wireless gadgets need to connect from outside the enterprise into the corporate network. To fulfill these needs, the concept of inside versus outside becomes rather complicated. For example, when you connect to the corporate network using a virtual private network (VPN), you are no longer on the outside the network. You are now on the inside of the network, and so is everything that is running on your computer.

Globally networked businesses rely on their networks to communicate with employees, customers, partners, and suppliers. Although immediate access to information and communication is an advantage, it raises concerns about security and protecting access to critical network resources.

Network administrators need to know who is accessing which resources and establish clear perimeters to control the access. An effective security policy balances accessibility with protection. Security policies are enforced at network perimeters. Often people think of a perimeter as the boundary between an internal network and the public Internet, but a perimeter can be established anywhere within a private network, or between your network and a partner's network.

A Solid Perimeter Security Solution

A comprehensive perimeter security solution enables communications across it as defined by the security policy, yet protects the network resources from breaches, attacks, or unauthorized use. It controls multiple network entry and exit points. It also increases user assurance by implementing multiple layers of security.

The Cisco wide range of Cisco perimeter security solutions provides several levels of perimeter security that can be deployed throughout your network as defined by your security policy. These solutions are highly flexible and can be tailored to your security policy.

Security in Layers

As discussed earlier, security in layers is the preferred and most scalable approach to safeguard a network. One single mechanism cannot be relied on for the security of a system. To protect your infrastructure, you must apply security in layers. This layered approach is also called *defense in depth*. The idea is that you create multiple systems so that a failure in one does not leave you vulnerable, but is caught in the next layer. Additionally, in a layered approach, the vulnerability can be limited and contained to the affected layer because of the applied security at varying levels.

Multilayer Perimeter Solution

As stated previously, today's solutions are shifting toward the approach of placing safeguard mechanisms at various layers of the network, not just at the boundary or edge devices. Today, it is recommended to deploy Intrusion Prevention System (IPS) devices on both the inside and outside boundaries of private networks. Firewalls, on the other hand, are placed between various business segments or departments within the same organization, dividing the network into logical groupings and applying perimeter defense at each segment or department. In this multiperimeter model, each segment can have different layers of defense within it.

Effective perimeter security has become increasingly important over recent years. Perimeter security cannot be trusted to only the traditional defense mechanisms of firewalls and IDS. Web applications, wireless access, network interconnectivities, and VPNs have made the perimeter a much more complicated concept than it was a couple of years ago.

A layered approach requires implementing security solutions at different spectrums of the network. Another similar concept is *islands of security*. To implement islands of security, do not restrict your thinking to perimeter security. Do not depend on just one method for your security. You should, instead, have layers of protection—perimeter, distribution, core, and access layer. Figure 1-4 illustrates a basic multilayered security mechanism, which is designed to protect the data flow in the system.

Figure 1-4 *Layers of Defense*

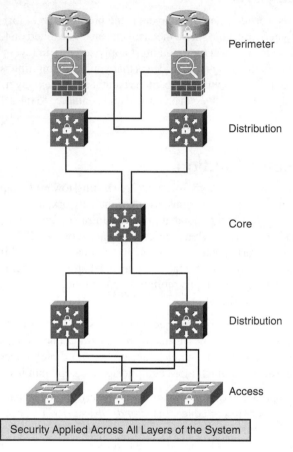

This layered approach is related to the technology of an environment and the complexity of each of the technologies at each layer. The complexity comes from different protocols, applications, hardware, and security mechanisms that work at one or more of the seven layers in the OSI model. Just as there are different levels within an environment, different types of attacks can occur at each level and would require respective countermeasures.

The Domino Effect

- The OSI reference model was built to enable different layers to work independently of each other. The layered approach was developed to accommodate changes in the evolving technology. Each OSI layer is responsible for a specific function within the networking stack, with information flowing up and down to the next subsequent layer as data is processed. Unfortunately, this means that if one layer is hacked, communications are compromised without the other layers being aware of the problem. For example, as shown in Figure 1-5, if the physical layer (Layer 1) was compromised, it could cause all other layers to be compromised in succession. Security is only as strong as the weakest link. When it comes to networking, any layer can be the weakest link.

Figure 1-5   *The Domino Effect*

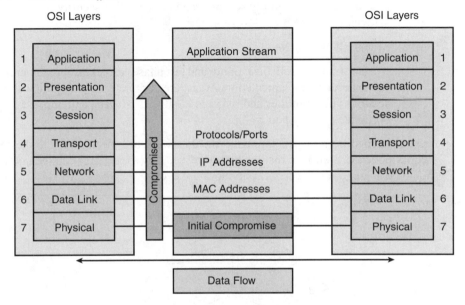

Security Wheel

Network security is a continuous process built around the corporate security policy. The security wheel depicted in Figure 1-6 shows a recursive, ongoing process of striving toward perfection—to achieve a secured network infrastructure. The paradigm incorporates the following five steps:

Step 1   Develop a security policy

A strong security policy should be clearly defined, implemented, and documented, yet simple enough that users can easily conduct business within its parameters.

Step 2   Make the network secure

Secure the network by implementing security solutions (implement authentication, encryption, firewalls, intrusion prevention, and other techniques) to stop or prevent unauthorized access or activities and to protect information and information systems.

Step 3   Monitor and respond.

This phase detects violations to the security policy. It involves system auditing and real-time intrusion detection and prevention solutions. This also validates the security implementation in Step 2.

Step 4   Test.

This step validates the effectiveness of the security policy through system auditing and vulnerability scanning and tests existing security safeguards.

Step 5   Manage and improve.

Use information from the monitor and test phases to make improvements to the security implementation. Adjust the corporate security policy as security vulnerabilities and risks are identified. Manage and improve corporate security policy.

Lessons learned from Steps 2 through 5 should always be reflected back to the corporate security policy in Step 1, so that the high-level security expectations are being met. This should be an ongoing process, a continuous life cycle!

Figure 1-6   *The Security Wheel*

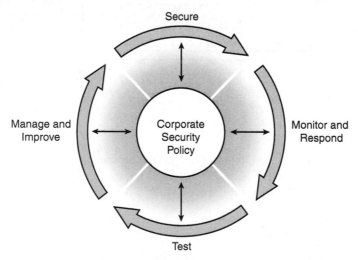

Summary

This chapter gave an overview of network security and discussed the challenges of managing a secured network infrastructure. The chapter discussed how the security paradigm is changing and that security solutions today are no longer product based. Instead, they are more solution oriented and designed with business objectives in mind. The chapter also discussed the core principles of security—the CIA triad of confidentiality, integrity, and availability—followed by brief discussion of aspects of security policies: standards, procedures, baselines, guidelines, and various security models. The chapter takes a detailed look at the perimeter security issue and the multilayered security approach. The chapter concludes with the Cisco security wheel paradigm involving five cyclical steps.

References

Harris, Shon. *CISSP All-in-One Exam Guide*, Second Edition. McGraw-Hill Osborne Media, 2003.

https://www2.sans.org/resources/policies/#template

http://www.cisco.com/go/securityconsulting

http://www.doc.ic.ac.uk/~ajs300m/security/CIA.htm

http://portal.acm.org/citation.cfm?id=619980

http://www.gammassl.co.uk/topics/chinesewall.html

http://www.devx.com/security/Article/20472

Guel, Michele. "A Short Primer for Developing Security Policy," Cisco Systems, http://www.sans.org/resources/policies/#primer

CHAPTER 2

Access Control

The use of technology continues to expand in this digital age with the ever-increasing volume of data. An exponential amount of data is crossing the networks today. Without any security mechanism in place, each network has complete access to the other with no way of differentiating between authorized and unauthorized activity.

One of the fundamental steps necessary to control network access is the capability to control the data flow within a network. One of the many ways to achieve this is to use an ACL, or access control list (commonly referred to as ACL). ACLs are effective, easy to configure, and available across all major Cisco products.

This chapter focuses primarily on the use and configuration of ACLs available on Cisco IOS and other devices for traffic filtering. The chapter also gives an overview of IP addressing, IP classes, subnets, and masks.

Traffic Filtering Using ACLs

Cisco IOS provides traffic-filtering capabilities for ACLs with the capability to prevent traffic from entering or exiting the network. The use of an ACL is also sometimes referred to as *filtering*, because it regulates traffic by allowing or denying network access.

ACL Overview

An *ACL* is essentially a list of permit or deny statements that control network access to enforce a security policy. ACLs are an integral part of the end-to-end security solution. Products and technologies such as firewalls, encryption and authentication, and intrusion detection and prevention solutions, however, should be part of an integrated approach to implementing any corporate security policy.

ACL Applications

ACLs have many applications (available across all Cisco platforms), including traffic filtering; however, ACLs cannot be used as a replacement or substitute for context-based stateful firewalls, which will be discussed further in Chapter 5, "Cisco IOS Firewall," and Chapter 6, "Cisco Firewalls: Appliance and Module."

ACLs are used in numerous ways. Some common applications of ACLs include the following:

- Filtering routing information received from or sent to the adjacent neighbor(s)
- Controlling interactive access to prevent unauthorized access to the devices in the network—for example, Console, Telnet, or SSH access
- Controlling traffic flow and network access through devices
- Securing the router by limiting access to services on the router such as Hypertext Transfer Protocol (HTTP), Simple Network Management Protocol (SNMP), and Network Time Protocol (NTP)
- Defining interesting traffic for dial-on-demand routing (DDR)
- Defining interesting traffic for IPsec virtual private network (VPN) encryption
- Several applications in IOS quality of service (QoS) features
- Extensive use in security techniques and technologies (for example, TCP Intercept and IOS Firewall)

ACLs can be used to provide a basic level of security for all traffic accessing or traversing the network. If ACLs are not configured, all packets passing through the router would be allowed onto all parts of the network.

For example, ACLs can allow one host to access the Internet and prevent another host from accessing the Internet, as shown in Figure 2-1. Host A can access resources on the Internet, whereas access for Host B is denied. ACLs can also be used to determine what type of traffic is forwarded or blocked at the router interfaces. For example, all HTTP traffic can be permitted, while FTP traffic is blocked. This is just a simple example; much more complex scenarios can be achieved by using ACLs.

Figure 2-1 *Secure Router Using ACL*

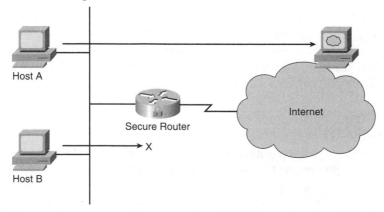

When to Configure ACLs

ACLs can be used on a device as the first line of defense for the network. This can be achieved using an ACL on routers, switches, or firewalls that are placed between an internal network (protected zone) and an external network (unprotected zone), such as the Internet. ACLs can also be used on a device placed between two parts of the network, to control traffic entering or exiting a specific part of the network. Another alternative is to use ACLs to filter inbound traffic or outbound traffic on a device, or both for that matter. ACLs should be defined on a per-protocol and per source/destination/port basis to achieve more granularity and control on various types of traffic.

To better understand the use of ACLs, the next sections provide an overview of basic IP addressing, subnets and masks, and IP classes.

IP Address Overview

The IP address is the address assigned to a particular network and the host within the network.

There are two basic types of IP addresses:

- **IP Version 4 (IPv4):** IPv4 was initially deployed in January 1983 and is commonly used in today's networks in general deployment. IPv4 addresses are 32-bit numbers displayed as four octets in dotted decimal notation (for example, 10.1.1.1). RFC 1166 specifies the IPv4 address format.

- **IP Version 6 (IPv6) or IPng:** IPv6, also known as IPng, is a next-generation Internet protocol, with a new version designed to be an evolutionary move in Internet addressing. Growth is the basic issue because the IPv4 address is becoming increasingly strained. This scarce has laid the foundation for the next generation IP. IPv6 addresses are 128-bit numbers and are typically displayed in hexadecimal strings (for example, 2080:0:0:2:8:400:20AC:217B). Cisco Systems announced IPv6 support in Cisco IOS 12.2(2)T on May 14, 2001.

NOTE	For more information on IPv6, refer to http://www.cisco.com/go/ipv6.

NOTE	This chapter focuses only on the IPv4 addresses, which are referred to as IP addresses.

Classes of IP Addresses

The Internet Assigned Numbers Authority (IANA) grouped IP addresses into the following classes. Each class has its own requirements and purpose:

- Class A
- Class B
- Class C
- Class D
- Class E

Understanding IP Address Classes

- Class A—0NNNNNNN.HHHHHHHH.HHHHHHHH.HHHHHHHH

  First octet represents the network address and the remaining three octets represent the host address.

  First high order bit is set to 0.

  7 network bits.

  24 host bits.

  First byte range: 0–127.

  126 Class A ranges exist (0 and 127 are reserved).

  16,777,214 hosts are on each Class A.

  Example: Host 10.0.0.1 on network 10.0.0.0

- Class B—10NNNNNN.NNNNNNNN.HHHHHHHH.HHHHHHHH

  First two octets represent the network address and the remaining two octets represent the host address.

  First two high order bits are set to 1 and 0, respectively.

  14 network bits.

  16 host bits.

  First byte range: 128–191.

  16,384 Class B ranges exist.

  65,532 hosts are on each Class B.

  Example: Host 128.10.1.5 on network 128.10.0.0

- Class C—110NNNNN.NNNNNNNN.NNNNNNNN.HHHHHHHH

  First three octets represent the network address, and the remaining octet represents the host address.

  First three high-order bits are set to 1, 1, and 0, respectively.

  21 network bits.

  8 host bits.

  First byte range: 192–223.

  2,097,152 Class C ranges exist.

  254 hosts are on each Class C.

  Example: Host 192.15.1.1 on network 192.15.1.0

- Class D—1110MMMM.MMMMMMMM.MMMMMMMM.MMMMMMMM

  Mainly reserved as multicast addresses.

  First four high-order bits are set to 1, 1, 1, and 0, respectively.

  28 multicast address bits.

  First byte range: 224–247 (first octet of a Class D address has a minimum value of 224 and a maximum value of 239).

  Class D range is used for multicast addresses—see RFC 1112.

  Example: 225.1.100.100

- Class E—1111RRRR.RRRRRRRR.RRRRRRRR.RRRRRRRR

  Mainly reserved for experimental and future use.

  First four high bits are set to 1, 1, 1, and 1, respectively.

  28 reserved address bits.

  First byte range: 248–255 (first octet of a Class E address starts with 240).

  In addition to being used for experimentation, Class E addresses are reserved for future use.

NOTE   N denotes the network ID bits.
H denotes the host ID bits.
M denotes the multicast address bits.
R denotes the reserved bits.

The class of an IP address can be established from the first four bits of the first byte of the IP address. The value of the first octet in the IP address resolves to the class within the range of which the IP address falls. Table 2-1 summarizes the possible range of IP addresses for the different IP address classes that were previously discussed.

Table 2-1   *Range of IP Addresses per Class*

Class	Possible Range of Addresses
A	0.0.0.0 through 127.255.255.255
B	128.0.0.0 through 191.255.255.255
C	192.0.0.0 through 223.255.255.255
D	224.0.0.0 through 239.255.255.255
E	240.0.0.0 through 247.255.255.255

Table 2-2 shows the maximum number of networks and hosts that can be derived within each class.

Table 2-2   *Networks and Hosts per Class*

Class	Max Number of Networks	Max Number of Hosts per Network
A	126 (2^7–2)	16777214 (2^24–2)
B	16384 (2^14)	65534 (2^16–2)
C	2097152 (2^21)	254 (2^8–2)
D	—	—
E	—	—

NOTE   Class A—The maximum number of networks is reduced by 2 to account for the reserved network IP address of 0.xxx.xxx.xxx and 127.xxx.xxx.xxx.

The maximum number of hosts per network is also reduced by 2 to account for the reserved host IP address in which all the host ID address bits are either 1 or 0—that is, the network address and the broadcast address.

Private IP Address (RFC 1918)

Under the present IPv4 addressing scheme, the IP address space is divided into two types: public IP address space and private IP address space. The public IP address space is routable via the Internet and is managed by one of the Regional Internet Registries (RIR).

A small part of the address range, shown in Table 2-1, has been set aside and designated as a "reserved" or "private" IP address range, as documented in RFC 1918. These addresses are reserved for use by private networks and are not routed on the Internet. These private IP address ranges must be filtered on border routers so that no traffic with a private address as source is allowed from the Internet. Table 2-3 includes the details of the private address ranges.

Table 2-3   *RFC 1918 Address Ranges Reserved for Private Use*

Class	Range of Addresses
A	10.0.0.0 through 10.255.255.255
B	172.16.0.0 through 172.32.255.255
C	192.168.0.0 through 192.168.255.255

In addition to the previously described RFC 1918-based private addresses range, the IANA has blocked a special Class B private address range and reserved it for automatic private IP addressing (APIPA). For example, when using Dynamic Host Configuration Protocol (DHCP), if the DHCP server cannot be found for an assigned IP address, the operating system will automatically assign addresses from this special block to enable communication.

NOTE   The RIRs are nonprofit organizations charged to manage the role of management for allocating Internet number resources distribution, such as globally unique IP addresses (IPv4 and IPv6) and autonomous system numbers (within their assigned regions). For more information, visit the RIR of your region:

APNIC   http://www.apnic.net
ARIN   http://www.arin.net
LACNIC   http://www.lacnic.net
RIPE NCC   http://www.ripe.net
AfriNIC   http://www.afrinic.net

Subnet Mask Versus Inverse Mask Overview

The IP address has two basic components: the network address and the host address. A mask is used to partition the network address from the host address within the IP address. The following section describes two types of masks—the subnet mask and the inverse mask.

Subnet Mask

As mentioned earlier, an IP address consists of two parts: a network address and a host address. The subnet mask is used to establish where the network number in an IP address ends and the host number begins. It is a method used for splitting IP networks into a series of subgroups or subnets as documented in RFC 950. The mask is a 32-bit binary pattern that is matched up with the IP address to turn part of the host ID address field into a field for subnets. (Table 2-4 shows an example.)

Inverse Mask

Masks for IOS IP ACLs are the reverse (for example, mask 0.0.0.255) and are referred to as the inverse mask, also commonly known as a wildcard mask. (The terms *wildcard* and *inverse* are used interchangeably.) When the value of the mask is broken down into binary numbers (0s and 1s), the results determine which address bits are to be considered in processing the traffic. A 0 indicates that the address bits must be considered (exact match); a 1 in the mask is a "don't care." Table 2-4 explains the concept further.

Table 2-4   *Mask Example*

Network address (traffic that is to be processed)	10.1.1.0
Network address (binary)	00001010.00000001.00000001.00000000
Subnet mask (decimal)	255.0.0.0
Subnet mask (binary)	11111111.00000000.00000000.00000000
Wildcard/inverse mask (decimal)	0.0.0.255
Wildcard/inverse mask (binary)	00000000.00000000.00000000.11111111

Based on the inverse mask shown in binary, the first three sets (octets) must match the given binary network address exactly (00001010.00000001.00000001). The last set of numbers represents "don't care" (.11111111).

Therefore, all traffic that begins with 10.1.1. matches because the last octet is not considered. With this mask, network addresses 10.1.1.1 through 10.1.1.255 (10.1.1.x) are processed.

The ACL inverse mask can also be determined by subtracting the normal mask from 255.255.255.255. See Example 2-1.

Example 2-1   *ACL Inverse Mask*

```
The inverse mask for network address 172.16.1.0 with a subnet mask of 255.255.240.0
is;
255.255.255.255 - 255.255.240.0 (subnet mask) = 0.0.15.255 (inverse mask)
```

NOTE	When configuring an ACL, you can substitute long dotted numbers with special keywords that represent the same equivalents, as shown in the following examples:

- Source/source-wildcard of 0.0.0.0/255.255.255.255 can also be represented with the keyword "any" within the ACL.

- Source/wildcard of 10.1.1.2/0.0.0.0 can also be represented as "host 10.1.1.2."

ACL Configuration

There are two basic steps in configuring an ACL:

Step 1   Create an ACL.

Step 2   Apply an ACL list to an interface.

These are explained further in the sections that follow.

Creating an ACL

The first step in the configuration process is to create an ACL for each protocol to be filtered, per interface. For some protocols, one ACL can be created to filter inbound traffic and another to filter outbound traffic.

To create an ACL, specify the protocol to be filtered by assigning a unique name or number to the ACL and defining the filtering criteria. Each individual filtering rule that is part of an ACL is called an *access control entry* (ACE). A single ACL can have multiple ACEs, and a group of ACEs forms an ACL.

Assigning a Unique Name or Number to Each ACL

Each ACL must be uniquely identified by using either a name or a number. A device could have several ACLs configured; therefore, the device must have a way to distinguish one ACL from another. Assigning a name or a number to an ACL serves this objective along with binding the ACL entries together. The ACL name or number also tells the device which type of ACL it is. (Various ACL types are discussed later in this chapter.)

Tables 2-5 and 2-6 show a list of protocols that can be defined using either the named or numbered ACL. The table also lists the range of ACL numbers that is valid for each protocol.

Examples for creating an ACL are shown later under each type of ACL.

Table 2-5 *Protocols with ACL Specified by Name*

Protocol
Apollo Domain
IP
IPX
ISO CLNS
Network BIOS
Source-route bridging network

Table 2-6 *Protocols with ACL Specified by Number*

Protocol	Range
IP Standard	1 to 99 and 1300 to 1999
IP Extended	100 to 199 and 2000 to 2699
Protocol type-code	200 to 299
48-bit MAC address ACL	700 to 799
Extended 48-bit MAC address ACL	1100 to 1199

Applying an ACL to an Interface

The second step of the configuration process involves applying the ACL to an interface. ACLs can be defined without applying them to an interface on a device. However, the ACL will have no effect until it is applied to the device's interface. ACLs can also be used for various other services in addition to applying to interfaces, such as in route-map, SNMP, or traffic-classification techniques.

ACLs can be applied on various interfaces and devices in a network, but you should consider a number of intricate factors before deciding where to apply them. Figure 2-2 shows a requirement that is blocking traffic that is entering the network from Router A from reaching the source Host A to destination Host B. When deciding where to apply an ACL, such as that shown in Figure 2-2, consider the following:

- When using a standard ACL, apply the ACL filter closest to the destination Router C within the traffic flow. This is recommended because standard ACL filter packets, which are based on the source address only, are dropped closer to the ingress point

Router A. A potential danger exists in blocking Host A entirely for all other traffic—for example, Host C or Host D in the network. Hence, applying the ACL on Router C is more appropriate than on Router A or Router B.

- When using an extended ACL, apply the ACL filter closest to the source Router A ingress point into the network. This is recommended because with extended ACL, filter packets are based on the source/destination IP address and source/destination ports, and so on, and are much more granular in nature than standard ACL. Therefore, dropping the packet closer to the ingress point into the network is more appropriate. Although dropping the packet closer to the destination will achieve the same result, it will cause unnecessary resource consumption on the traversing routers. The packet is traversing the entire network, chewing up resources and eventually being dropped at the destination Router C. Hence it is best to drop the packet closer to the source (ingress) within the network by applying the ACL on Router A instead of Router B or Router C.

Figure 2-2   *Where to Apply ACL—Considerations*

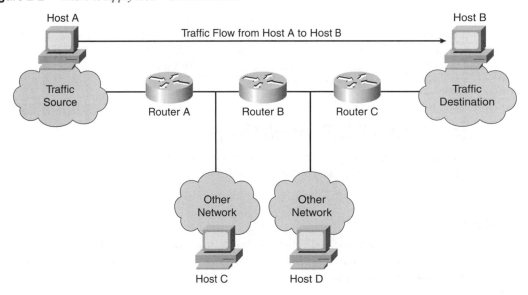

For some protocols, up to two ACLs can be applied to an interface: one inbound ACL and one outbound ACL. With other protocols, only one ACL is allowed, and this list checks both inbound and outbound packets.

NOTE   Outbound ACLs that are applied to router interfaces do not filter traffic that originates from the router.

Direction of the ACL

The terms *in*, *out*, *source*, and *destination* are used as referenced by the device in the context of the flow of the traffic. As an analogy, traffic on the router can be compared to a passenger flying from Sydney to San Francisco. If the immigration department wants to stop this passenger traveling from Sydney (source) to San Francisco (destination), there are two possibilities for interception:

- The passenger could be stopped at the Sydney airport at the immigration control (out) departing outbound.

- The passenger could be stopped at the San Francisco airport at the immigration control (in) arriving inbound.

When referring to a device where an ACL is applied, these terms are defined as follows:

- **Out:** Traffic that has already been processed through the router and is exiting the router interface (also called *egress traffic*). The source is where the traffic originated (on the other side of the router), and the destination is where it is going (beyond this router).

- **In:** Traffic that arrives on the router interface (also called *ingress traffic*) and will be processed by the router for its destination traversing through this router. The source is where it has arrived from (before this router), and the destination is where it is going (on the other side of the router).

Understanding ACL Processing

This section helps you to understand ACL processing by explaining inbound and outbound ACLs, packet flow rules, and guidelines for implementing ACLs.

Inbound ACL

Examine the pseudocode that follows to understand packet processing. When an inbound ACL is applied on an interface, the router checks the received packet against the ACL's statements for a match.

```
if {a match is found} then
  if {the action is to permit) then
    {router continues to process the packet}
  else {the action is to deny} then
      {router discards the packet sending an ICMP Unreachable message to the
        source address in the packet - assuming this is not disabled}
  endif
else {a match is not found} then
    {with the default 'implicit deny' statement—the router discards the packet,
        sending an ICMP Unreachable message}
endif
```

Outbound ACL

Examine the pseudocode that follows to understand packet processing. When an outbound ACL is applied on an interface, the router first performs a route lookup for the destination address in the routing table to determine the exit (egress) interface.

```
if {valid path found in routing table} then
  if {a match is found} then
   if {the action is to permit) then
       {router continues to process the packet}
   else {the action is to deny} then
       {router discards the packet sending an ICMP Unreachable message to the source
        address in the packet - assuming this is not disabled}
   endif
  else {a match is not found} then
       {with the default 'implicit deny' statement—the router discards the packet,
        sending an ICMP Unreachable message}
  endif
else {valid path not found in routing table, the router drops the packet}
endif
```

Figure 2-3 shows the logical flowchart for how a packet is processed against an inbound or outbound ACL.

Packet Flow Rules for Various Packet Types

The packet flowchart shown in Figure 2-4 demonstrates how ACL rules are applied to various packet types such as nonfragments, initial fragments, and noninitial fragments that are checked against an ACL.

RFC 1858 covers security considerations for IP fragment filtering and highlights two attacks with two defending mechanisms involving an IP fragment attack.

NOTE   The noninitial fragment packet contains only Layer 3 information, not Layer 4 information, although the ACL may contain both Layer 3 and Layer 4 information.

Figure 2-3 *Life of a Packet Undergoing the ACL Process*

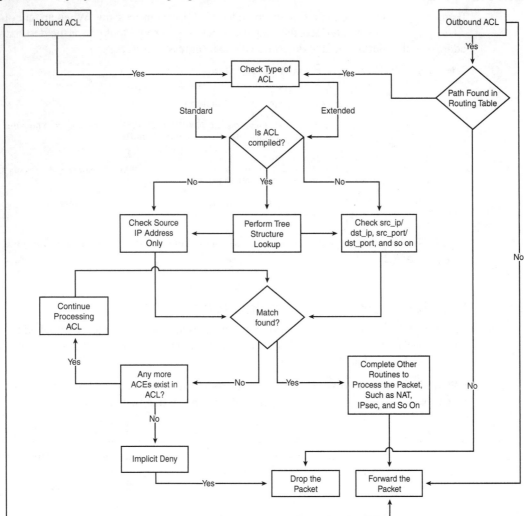

Figure 2-4 *ACL Flow for Non-fragments, Initial Fragments, and Non-initial Fragments*

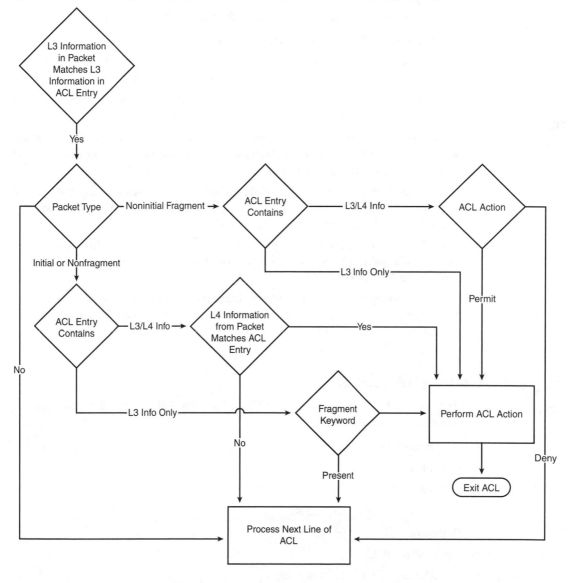

NOTE   Figure 2-4 is taken from the Cisco documentation URL listed here. For more details on ACLS and IP Fragments, visit http://www.cisco.com/warp/public/105/acl_wp.html.

Guidelines for Implementing ACLs

Following are some general guidelines to consider when implementing ACLs:

- ACLs can be applied to multiple interfaces on a device.

- Only *one* ACL is allowed per protocol per interface per direction. This means that you can have two ACLs per interface—one inbound and one outbound.

- ACLs are processed from the top down. The order of the access-list entries needs to be planned carefully. More specific entries *must* appear first.

- When entering the ACL, the router appends the access control entries (ACEs) at the bottom. In newer IOS versions that have sequencing function, it is possible to insert ACE entries between current entries.

- There is an "implicit deny" for traffic that is not permitted. A single-entry ACL with only one deny statement has the effect of denying all traffic. An ACL must have at least one permit statement; otherwise, all traffic is blocked.

- Always create an ACL before applying it to the interface. When modifying or editing an ACL, always remove the ACL from the interface, make the changes, and then reapply the ACL to the interface.

- An outbound (egress) ACL applied to a router interface checks only for traffic traversing through the router—that is, traffic going through the router and *not* traffic originating from the router.

Types of Access Lists

Many types of ACLs can be configured in Cisco IOS. The following lists are the most commonly known and used:

- Standard ACLs
- Extended ACLs
- IP named ACLs
- Lock and key (Dynamic ACLs)
- Reflexive ACLs
- Established ACLs
- Time-based ACLs using time ranges
- Distributed time-based ACLs

- Turbo ACLs
- Receive ACLs
- Infrastructure protection ACLs
- Transit ACLs
- Classification ACLs
- Debugging traffic using ACLs

Standard ACLs

Standard ACLs are the oldest and one of the most basic types of ACLs. Standard ACLs inspect traffic by comparing the source address of the IP packets to the addresses configured in the ACL. A standard ACL can be defined to permit or deny specific source IP addresses only.

The command syntax format to define a numbered standard ACL is the following:

```
access-list access-list-number {deny | permit} source [source-wildcard] [log]
```

The keyword **log** causes an informational logging message when the packet matches the access-list statement. For all matched packets, a message is sent to the console, the buffer, or to a syslog server. The message includes the ACL number, a notification of whether the packet was permitted or denied, the source address, and the number of packets.

NOTE   Fields represented by { } brackets are mandatory in the command syntax. Fields represented by [] brackets are optional.

In all Cisco IOS Software releases, the standard *access-list-number* can be anything from 1 to 99 or the expanded range 1300 to 1999, as shown in Table 2-6. Example 2-2 shows a standard numbered ACL allowing access to hosts on the two specified networks. The wildcard bits apply to the host portions of the network addresses. Traffic from any host with a source address that does not match the ACL criteria will be dropped because of the implicit deny.

Example 2-2   *Standard Numbered ACL Example*

```
Router(config)# access-list 1 permit 192.16.1.0  0.0.0.255
Router(config)# access-list 1 permit 139.65.0.0  0.0.255.255
(Note: implicit deny)
```

TIP
A *source/source-wildcard* setting of 0.0.0.0/255.255.255.255 can be specified as **any**. The wildcard can be omitted if it is all zeros. Therefore, 10.1.1.1 0.0.0.0 is the same as **host 10.1.1.1**.

After the ACL is defined, it must be applied to the interface (inbound or outbound direction).

```
Router(config)# interface <interface-name>
Router(config-if)# ip access-group {access-list-number|name} {in|out}
```

The following is another example showing the use of a standard ACL to block all traffic except that from source 10.1.1.0/24. Note that the example has one permit statement followed by an implicit deny, which will block all other traffic.

Step 1 Define a standard ACL.

```
Router(config)# access-list 1 permit 10.1.1.0 0.0.0.255
```

Step 2 Apply the ACL to an interface.

```
Router(config)# interface Serial0
Router(config-if)# ip access-group 1 in
```

Extended ACLs

Extended ACLs are used to filter more-specific traffic based on the source address, the destination address, and specific protocols, ports, and flags. A sample command syntax format for various types of extended ACLs for each protocol is shown in the list that follows:

- To define an extended IP ACL:

```
access-list access-list-number [dynamic dynamic-name [timeout minutes]] {deny |
  permit} protocol source source-wildcard destination destination-wildcard
  [precedence precedence] [tos tos] [log | log-input] [time-range time-range-name]
  [fragments]
```

- To define an extended TCP ACL:

```
access-list access-list-number [dynamic dynamic-name [timeout minutes]] {deny |
  permit} tcp source source-wildcard [operator [port]] destination destination-
  wildcard [operator [port]] [established] [precedence precedence] [tos tos] [log
  | log-input] [time-range time-range-name] [fragments]
```

- To define an extended User Datagram Protocol (UDP) ACL:

```
access-list access-list-number [dynamic dynamic-name [timeout minutes]] {deny |
  permit} udp source source-wildcard [operator [port]] destination destination-
  wildcard [operator [port]] [precedence precedence] [tos tos] [log | log-input]
  [time-range time-range-name] [fragments]
```

- To define an extended Internet Control Message Protocol (ICMP) ACL:

```
access-list access-list-number [dynamic dynamic-name [timeout minutes]] {deny |
  permit} icmp source source-wildcard destination destination-wildcard [icmp-type
  [icmp-code] | icmp-message] [precedence precedence] [tos tos] [log | log-input]
  [time-range time-range-name] [fragments]
```

- To define an extended Internet Group Management Protocol (IGMP) ACL:

```
access-list access-list-number [dynamic dynamic-name [timeout minutes]] {deny |
  permit} igmp source source-wildcard destination destination-wildcard [igmp-
  type] [precedence precedence] [tos tos] [log | log-input] [time-range time-
  range-name] [fragments]
```

In all Cisco IOS Software releases, the *access-list-number* for extended access lists can be 101 to 199 or the expanded numbers 2000 to 2699, as shown in Table 2-6.

The following example permits Simple Mail Transfer Protocol (SMTP) (e-mail) traffic to host 172.16.1.1, Domain Name System (DNS) traffic, and ICMP echo and echo reply packets sourced from all hosts:

Step 1   Define an extended ACL.

```
Router(config)# access-list 101 permit tcp any host 172.16.1.1 eq smtp
Router(config)# access-list 101 permit tcp any any eq domain
Router(config)# access-list 101 permit udp any any eq domain
Router(config)# access-list 101 permit icmp any any echo
Router(config)# access-list 101 permit icmp any any echo-reply
```

Step 2   Apply the ACL to an interface.

```
Router(config)# interface Serial0
Router(config-if)# ip access-group 101 in
```

IP Named ACLs

Cisco IOS Software also added the capability to use a *name* in the ACL. This allows standard and extended ACLs to be given *names* instead of *numbers*. All other parameters remain the same. This is an additional feature added to the normal ACL convention. The command syntax format you use to define a *named* ACL is the following:

```
Router(config)# ip access-list {standard | extended} access-list-name
  (Followed by permit/deny criteria statements)
```

Example 2-3 shows the configuration of a standard named ACL called myacl that allows all traffic sourced from network 192.16.1.0/24 and host 172.65.1.1.

Example 2-3   *Standard Named ACL Example*

```
ip access-list standard myacl
  permit 192.16.1.0 0.0.0.255
  permit host 172.65.1.1
  (Note: implicit deny)
```

Example 2-4 shows configuration of an extended named ACL called myacl that allows SMTP connections to host 172.16.1.1 and DNS packets and all ICMP packets.

Example 2-4   *Extended Named ACL Example*

```
ip access-list extended myacl
 permit tcp any host 172.16.1.1 eq smtp
 permit tcp any any eq domain
 permit udp any any eq domain
 permit icmp any any
 (Note: implicit deny)
```

Lock and Key (Dynamic ACLs)

Lock and key (also known as Dynamic ACL) allows you to set up a dynamic access that will allow per-user access control to a particular source/destination using an authentication mechanism. The lock-and-key feature depends on the following items: the Telnet protocol, an authentication process, and an extended ACL.

The following process elaborates the operation of lock-and-key access.

1   Configure an extended ACL to block traffic through the router, except the ability to telnet to the router from any host. This is important, as the user needs to telnet to the router to open the dynamic access entry. If the ACL is denying everything, the whole process will fail.

2   Users who want to pass traffic through the lock-and-key router must initiate a Telnet to the router and authenticate successfully with valid credentials; dynamic entries are populated accordingly.

3   Either the local router or remote authentication performs the authentication process using TACACS+ or Radius. (Cisco recommends using a TACACS+ server.)

4   When the Telnet process completes, the router then disconnects the Telnet connection, and a dynamic entry is populated in the extended ACL that was configured earlier. This dynamic entry permits traffic for a particular period.

Follow the steps shown to configure lock-and-key access. Note this example uses local router authentication.

Configure a local username for authentication:

```
username test password test123
```

Under the vty lines, configure login local; this will trigger the authentication process.

```
line vty 0 4
 login local
```

To automatically invoke the **access-enable** command and set the timeout parameter, configure a username by using one of the following methods:

1 Configure the **access-enable** command and associate the timeout with the user allowing control on a per-user basis.

```
username test autocommand access-enable host timeout 10
```

2 Configure a global timeout value for all users who telnet in, so that they all have the same timeout.

```
line vty 0 4
  login local
  autocommand access-enable host timeout 10
```

NOTE   The value 10 in the previous example is the idle-timeout for the ACL. Absolute-timeout in the Dynamic ACL will always supersede this value.

Then configure an extended ACL that is applied when a user (any user) logs in to the router and the **access-enable** command is invoked. The maximum absolute time for this "hole" in the filter is set to 15 minutes; 15 (minutes) is the absolute timeout, and 10 (minutes) is the idle timeout. After 15 minutes, the dynamic entry is removed, regardless of the usage and whether anyone is connected. Limit the networks to which the user needs access by configuring the source or destination address and/or protocol/port details. The following example allows the user to connect to the SMTP server 192.168.1.1 after a successful authentication.

```
access-list 102 dynamic myacl timeout 15 permit tcp any host 192.168.1.1 eq smtp
```

The ACL should explicitly ensure that the capability for the host to telnet into the router is allowed, as shown in the example that follows. The IP address used in this example is the Ethernet IP address of the router where the user would telnet to authenticate and open the dynamic hole.

```
access-list 102 permit tcp any host 172.16.1.2 eq telnet
```

Apply this ACL to the interface on which the user is connected:

```
interface Ethernet0
  ip address 172.16.1.2 255.255.255.0
  ip access-group 102 in
```

The ACL will show as follows after a user has successfully authenticated, and a dynamic entry will be populated in the extended ACL with the source address of the host. In the

sample output that follows, the user host address is 172.16.1.5, and the user is allowed to
connect to the SMTP server at 192.168.1.1. All other traffic from this host is blocked.

```
Router# show access-lists
Extended IP access list 102
    10 Dynamic myacl permit tcp any host 172.16.1.1 eq smtp
       permit ip host 172.16.1.5 permit tcp any host 192.168.1.1 eq smtp (time left
       160)
    20 permit tcp any host 172.16.1.2 eq telnet (104 matches)
```

The dynamic entry is appended in the ACL for every user who passes authentication, based
on the source IP address.

Reflexive ACLs

Reflexive ACLs allow IP packets to be filtered based on upper-layer session information.
Reflexive ACLs are generally used to allow outbound traffic and to limit inbound traffic in
response to sessions originating inside the router. A reflexive ACL is similar to the Context-
Based Access Control (CBAC), which will be discussed in Chapter 5.

Reflexive ACLs have an important restriction—that is, they can be used only in conjunction
with an extended-named IP ACL. They cannot be defined with a numbered or standard-
named IP ACL, or with any other non-IP protocol ACLs. Reflexive ACLs can be used in
combination with other standard and static extended ACLs.

With the extended ACL in Example 2-5, all ICMP traffic statically and all TCP traffic
originating from source 10.0.0.0/24 going to destination 172.16.1.0/24 through the
reflexive router is permitted on the return path through the use of a dynamic mechanism in
the inbound ACL. In essence, the reflexive process permits only the return traffic that has
been initiated from inside. (All other traffic is denied.)

Example 2-5 *Reflexive ACL Example*

```
interface Ethernet0
 ip address 172.16.1.2 255.255.255.0
 ip access-group inbound_acl in
 ip access-group outbound_acl out
!
ip access-list extended inbound_acl
permit icmp any any
evaluate tcp_reflect
!
ip access-list extended outbound_acl
permit icmp any any
  permit tcp 10.0.0.0 0.0.0.255 172.16.1.0 0.0.0.255 reflect tcp_reflect
```

The context binding the outbound_acl ACL called tcp_reflect is linked with the evaluate
tcp_reflect reference in the inbound_acl ACL. Hence, traffic originating from 10.0.0.0/24
to destination 172.16.1.0/24 will be permitted, and it will return when it hits the
inbound_acl.

Established ACLs

The established keyword in a TCP extended ACL validates that a packet belongs to an existing connection from an ongoing TCP session initiated earlier and checks whether the TCP datagram has the acknowledgment (ACK) or reset (RST) bit set. This mechanism allows only internal networks to initiate a TCP session outbound through the device. Any TCP connections originated from the external network inbound are dropped.

The configuration in Example 2-6 for Figure 2-5 shows TCP traffic sourced from Network A (10.2.2.0/24) destined to Network B (10.1.1.0/24) being permitted, while denying TCP traffic from Network B destined to Network A.

ACL 101 in Example 2-6 permits all inbound TCP packets to pass through the router interface Ethernet1 only when the TCP datagram has the acknowledged (ACK) or the reset (RST) bit set, validating an established TCP session originated from inside. When a host from Network B (10.1.1.0/24) initiates a TCP connection by sending the first TCP packet in the three-way handshake with the SYN bit set, it will be denied, and the TCP session will not succeed. Any TCP sessions initiated from Network A (10.2.2.0/24) destined to Network B (10.1.1.0/24) will be allowed because they will have the ACK/RST bit set for all the returning packets. Any datagram with an ACK/RST bit not set will be dropped.

Figure 2-5   *Established ACL Example*

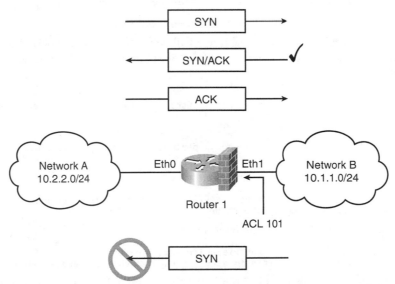

Example 2-6 *Established ACL Example*

```
interface Ethernet1
 ip address 10.1.1.2 255.255.255.0
 ip access-group 101 in
!
access-list 101 permit tcp any any established
```

Time-Based ACLs Using Time Ranges

Time-based ACLs are similar to the extended ACLs in function; they provide the additional feature of controlling access based on the time. The time range relies on the router's system clock. However, this feature works best with Network Time Protocol (NTP) synchronization. IP and IPX numbered or named extended ACLs are the only functions that can use time ranges.

To configure time-based ACLs, a time range is created that defines specific times of the day and week. The time range is identified by a name and then referenced within the extended ACL allowing control when the permit or deny statements in the ACL are in effect. Both named and numbered ACLs can reference a time range.

Step 1 Assign a name to the time range to be configured and enter time-range configuration mode for subcommands.

```
Router(config)# time-range time-range-name
```

Step 2 Specify when this time range will be in effect. Multiple periodic statements are allowed; only one absolute statement is allowed.

Define an absolute time.

```
Router(config-time-range)# absolute [start time date] [end time date]
```

Or define a periodic time.

```
Router(config-time-range)# periodic days-of-the-week hh:mm to [days-of-the-
    week] hh:mm
```

Step 3 Reference the time range in the extended ACL.

```
Router(config)# access-list number {permit | deny} source destination time-
    range name_of_time_range
```

Step 4 Apply the ACL to an interface.

```
Router(config)# interface {interface-name}
Router(config-if)# ip access-group {access-list-number|name} {in | out}
```

Example 2-7 shows that all IP traffic is being permitted through the network on weekdays (Monday through Friday) during normal business hours.

Example 2-7   *Time-Based ACL Example*

```
interface Ethernet0
 ip address 172.16.1.2 255.255.255.0
 ip access-group 101 in
access-list 101 permit ip any any time-range mytime
time-range mytime
 periodic weekdays 9:00 to 17:00
```

Distributed Time-Based ACLs

Distributed time-based ACLs were introduced primarily for the high-end routers. Distributed time-based ACLs were designed to be implemented on the VPN-enabled Cisco 7500 series routers. As discussed earlier, time-based ACLs were not initially supported on the line cards in the Cisco 7500 series. If an interface on a 7500 line card was configured with a time-based ACL, the packets switched into the interface were not "distributed switched" through the line card. Instead, they were forwarded to the route processor for processing and therefore did not take advantage of the distributed switching capability. The distributed time-based ACLs feature allows packets destined for an interface that are configured with time-based ACLs to be "distributed-switched" through the line card.

Distributed time-based ACLs leverage the performance benefits of distributed switching and the flexibility provided by time-based ACLs. The software clock must remain synchronized between the Route Processor (RP) and the line card for the distributed time-based ACL to function properly.

Configuring Distributed Time-Based ACLs

Because this feature is enabled automatically when the normal time-range ACL is configured on a line card interface, there is no command syntax to enable this feature. The command syntax is the same as for the time-based ACL. The function is only a software code integration in the IOS; no additional commands are required. Use the following commands to monitor the status and display statistics for the Interprocessor Communication (IPC) messages between the RP and line card:

```
clear time-range ipc
```

Used to clear the time-range IPC message statistics and counters between the RP and the line card.

```
debug time-range ipc
```

Used to enable debugging output for monitoring the time-range IPC messages between the RP and the line card.

```
show time-range ipc
```

Used to display the statistics about the time-range IPC messages between the RP and the line card.

Turbo ACLs

Traditional ACLs are searched sequentially (top-down) to find matching criteria. As the ACLs grow, a significant amount of time and memory can be consumed for lookups when packets are being processed. This adds a variable latency to the packet forwarding and results in performance issues. The Turbo ACL feature is designed to process ACLs more efficiently to improve router performance. This feature is available on high-end platforms such as the Cisco 7200 and 7500 series routers and the Cisco 12000 series Gigabit Switch Routers (GSR).

The Turbo ACLs feature compiles the ACLs into a group of lookup tables while maintaining the first match requirements. Packet headers are used to access these tables in a small, fixed number of lookups, independent of the existing number of ACL entries. This tremendously improves the performance and saves ACLs lookup cycles.

NOTE　　ACLs configured with time-range or reflexive ACL are *not* supported and are excluded from Turbo ACL acceleration.

To enable the Turbo ACL feature, use the **access-list compiled** command from the global configuration mode to compile all ACLs. This command should be applied after the normal ACLs have been configured and are ready to be compiled.

The Turbo ACL feature is disabled by default. When Turbo ACL is not enabled, the normal ACL processing is enabled, with no occurrence of ACL acceleration.

Use the **show access-list** and the **show access-list compiled** commands to verify that the Turbo ACL feature has taken effect and ACLs have been compiled for acceleration. The ACLs will be flagged as (Compiled), indicating they are operating as an accelerated ACL.

Receive ACLs (rACL)

Cisco 12000 series Gigabit Switch Routers (GSR) and 7500 platforms support Receive ACL (rACL) to increase security and thereby protect the router from unnecessary and potentially nefarious traffic. High volumes of data sent to the GRP can be overwhelming, resulting in an effective denial-of-service (DoS) attack. GSRs need to be protected against such scenarios, which may result from DoS attacks directed at the GRP of the router. There are few techniques available to alleviate DoS, such as rate-limiting traffic destined to the GRP from the line cards. Unfortunately, this approach comes with a trade-off and some limitations. The rate limiting for normal-priority traffic destined to the GRP does not guarantee protection to high-priority traffic, such as routing protocol data in the event of an attack channeled via several line cards.

Receive ACL can be configured using the following global configuration command and distributed to each line card in the router. Standard and extended ACL numbers are supported for rACL.

```
ip receive access-list <access-list-number>
```

Infrastructure Protection ACLs (iACL)

Infrastructure ACL (iACL) is a conceptual view, and no special configuration is required. It is mainly used to minimize the risk of direct infrastructure attacks by explicitly permitting only authorized traffic to the infrastructure equipment (such as the routers, switches, and firewalls). This technique secures network devices by denying access from valid external sources to all infrastructure device addresses that do not require direct access. When configuring an iACL, be careful to ensure that that iACL allows all transit traffic traversing the router and maintaining an uninterrupted packet flow, thereby complying with basic RFCs such as RFC 1918, RFC 3330, and RFC 2827 ingress filtering and anti-spoofing guidelines.

Because they are armed with a number of techniques and solutions that safeguard networks from both accidental and malicious risks, you should seriously consider using infrastructure protection ACLs for deployment at all network ingress points.

Transit ACLs

Transit ACLS are similar to infrastructure protection ACLs in two ways: transit ACLS give you a conceptual view, and they do not require special configuration. Transit ACLs represent one of the many ways to increase network security by explicitly allowing legitimate traffic into the network. For most network environments, filtering should be applied to control inbound traffic into the network and to block any unauthorized attempt at the edge of the network. Service provider networks, for example, often control traffic entering or exiting customer networks by using edge or transit filtering. This protects unwanted traffic from one customer to another because unwanted traffic is dropped at the service provider edge.

A transit ACL is developed using the following guidelines:

- Using antispoofing protection based on best practices from the following three RFCs:
    — RFC 1918—Private address space not routable on the Internet
    — RFC 3330—Special use addresses that might require filtering
    — RFC 2827—Antispoofing guidelines
- Explicitly permitting return traffic for all connections originating from the internal network to the Internet

- Explicitly permitting externally sourced traffic that is originating from the external network destined to the protected internal network
- Explicitly using a **deny** statement toward the end of the ACL

Visit the Cisco documentation URL shown in the Tip that follows for an example of transit ACL.

TIP   For further details on transit ACLs and basic configuration templates, refer to

http://www.cisco.com/en/US/tech/tk648/tk361/technologies_white_
paper09186a00801afc76.shtml

Classification ACLs

Another common type of ACL is the classification, also commonly known as characterization ACL. It is initially composed with all **permit** statements for the various protocols, ports, flags, and so on that could be sent to any of these three destinations: an infrastructure device, a public server in the protected zone, or any other device in the network. In some cases, a classification ACL can also have any source and the destination IP address using the keyword **any** in the ACL. This type of ACL is useful in classifying and categorizing a denial-of-service (DoS) attack and identifying the type of traffic and its source. Logging can be used to develop a list of source addresses that match the protocol permit statements. A last line permitting **ip any any** is required to permit all other traffic flow.

Example 2-8 shows a sample ACL that characterizes a suspected DoS attack. The first line checks for possible ICMP Smurf attacks. The second line checks for any sort of TCP SYN attack. The third, fourth, and fifth lines check for any sort of fragment attack. Finally, the last four lines check for general protocol types. This ACL is a very basic generic example and can be configured for virtually any protocol, ports, flags, and so on in a classification ACL.

Example 2-8 *Example of DoS Characterization ACL*

```
access-list 101 permit icmp any any eq echo
access-list 101 permit tcp any any syn
access-list 101 permit tcp any any fragment
access-list 101 permit udp any any fragment
access-list 101 permit ip any any fragment
access-list 101 permit tcp any any
access-list 101 permit udp any any
access-list 101 permit icmp any any
access-list 101 permit ip any any
```

After applying this ACL on the suspected ingress interface, enter the **show access-list** command repeatedly and check for the line that shows the highest hit counts, indicating the possible cause of the attack. Continue to tune this ACL to further narrow down the type of traffic until a closer match is found. This is a very useful technique to implement under a DoS attack, particularly when you are unsure what type of DoS attack is underway.

Debugging Traffic Using ACLs

ACLs can be used to debug traffic on a router. Running debugs on a router is resource consuming and could potentially use almost all system resources, such as memory and processing power. Excessive debugging under high load conditions may cause unexpected interruptions or in some cases cause the device to crash. Therefore, debugging commands need to be used with extreme caution. Before enabling debugging, inspect the CPU load by using the **show processes cpu** command and verify that sufficient CPU is available before running the debugs.

One way of reducing the impact of the debug command on a device is to use an ACL to selectively define the traffic criteria that needs to be examined. This concept does not do any packet filtering; it is used only for controlled monitoring. Example 2-9 shows a configuration that enables debugging only for packets between the hosts 10.1.1.1 and 192.168.1.1 using the **debug ip packet [detail] <ACL-number>** command.

Example 2-9 *Debugging Traffic Using ACL Example*

```
Router(config)# access-list 101 permit ip host 10.1.1.1 host 192.168.1.1
Router(config)# access-list 101 permit ip host 192.168.1.1 host 10.1.1.1
Router(config)# end
Router# debug ip packet detail 101
  IP packet debugging is on (detailed) for access list 101
```

CAUTION   On the router console, when debugs are running, usually the router prompt is not seen because debugs tend to scroll very fast on the console screen, especially when the debug is intensive. However, use the **no debug all** or **undebug all** commands to stop the debugs (Type this command as blind-folded.) For more information on safely using debugs, visit

http://www.cisco.com/en/US/tech/tk801/tk379/technologies_tech_
note09186a008017874c.shtml

Summary

ACLs are the most common and inexpensive method available for filtering traffic across the network. This chapter primarily focused on the use of ACLs for traffic filtering. An overview of IP addressing, subnets, and masks was also presented to help you better understand the implementation of ACL. A major part of this chapter was devoted to several types of ACLs and their applications. All Cisco IOS software versions are capable of supporting ACLs.

References

http://www.iana.org/ipaddress/ip-addresses.htm

http://www.freesoft.org/CIE/Topics/26.htm

http://www.isoc.org/briefings/021/

http://www.cisco.com/en/US/products/ps6350/
products_configuration_guide_chapter09186a00800ca7c0.html

http://www.cisco.com/en/US/products/sw/secursw/ps1018/
products_tech_note09186a00800a5b9a.shtml

http://www.cisco.com/en/US/tech/tk827/tk369/
technologies_white_paper09186a00800949b8.shtml

http://www.cisco.com/en/US/tech/tk583/tk822/
technologies_tech_note09186a0080094524.shtml

http://www.cisco.com/en/US/products/sw/iosswrel/ps1835/
products_configuration_guide_chapter09186a008030c799.html#wp1001647

http://www.cisco.com/en/US/products/sw/iosswrel/ps1834/
products_feature_guide09186a0080080374.html

http://www.cisco.com/en/US/tech/tk648/tk361/
technologies_white_paper09186a00801a1a55.shtml

http://www.cisco.com/en/US/products/ps6350/
products_configuration_guide_chapter09186a0080431056.html

http://www.cisco.com/en/US/tech/tk648/tk361/
technologies_white_paper09186a00801afc76.shtml

CHAPTER 3

Device Security

Securing devices in a network is one of the most important tasks in network security. This chapter describes general principles for protecting the device itself, beginning with a device security policy. In describing these general principles, the chapter focuses on routers, switches, firewalls, concentrators, and intrusion-detection devices. The chapter describes a number of important security tasks, including accessing methods and controls, hardening configuration, identifying unwanted services, managing devices, and monitoring and auditing services. Device-specific features available for administration devices such as firewalls, concentrators, and Intrusion Prevention Systems (IPS) are also discussed. The last part of the chapter presents a basic checklist for device security.

Device Security Policy

As discussed in Chapter 1, "Overview of Network Security," security policies are of utmost importance. They are a set of rules, practices, and procedures that dictate how sensitive information is managed, protected, and distributed. Among several types of policies, one is developed to establish the rules for protecting devices.

Cisco devices such as routers, switches, firewalls, and concentrators are an integral part of the network, and securing these devices is an essential part of the overall network security policy.

An organization must have a device security policy that dictates the rules to protect device access and access control. The device security policy can also outline the minimal security configuration for all devices in the network they serve.

Figure 3-1 shows a conceptual layered view of device security. The security of each layer depends on the security of the layers within. For example, if physical security is compromised (the inner layer), all other layers above will also be affected, resulting in a domino effect.

Figure 3-1 *Conceptual Layered View of Device Security*

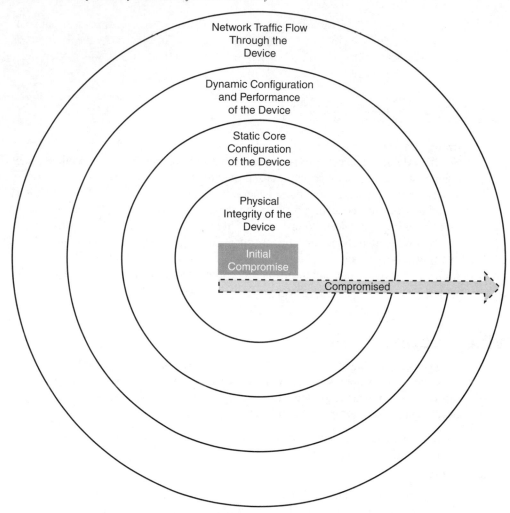

A device security policy should define rules that spell out who, where, and how these devices will be accessed, in terms of both administrative roles and network services. The device security policy must blend into the overall framework of the high-level requirements of the network security policy.

Hardening the Device

Device hardening is one of the fundamental security modules that should be put into practice to protect the device from unauthorized users and activity. An intruder gaining unauthorized access to a device relinquishes complete access to the networks, and all other security measures taken become redundant.

This chapter describes several security features that are applicable in Cisco IOS Software. Some of these features may also be applicable to other Cisco platforms such as Firewall and IDS. The later section of this chapter describes specific features available on these non-IOS Cisco devices.

Physical Security

The facility (physical location) where devices are housed is in most cases the first and last barrier encountered by an intruder. Physical security prevents intruders from gaining physical access to the devices, and this means hands-on contact. Physical security is more critical than network security but is often overlooked by network administrators. Despite all the high-level safeguard measures, a compromise in physical access will almost always result in a complete compromise. Having a secured physical facility that is accessible only to authorized personnel is extremely important.

Passwords

Identification is mainly based on a combination of the username and the password. A password is a protected string of characters that is used to authenticate a user. There are three types of password protection schemes in Cisco IOS.

- **Clear-text passwords:** These are the most insecure because they have no encryption. Passwords are viewable in the device configuration in clear text.

- **Type 7 passwords:** These use the Cisco proprietary encryption algorithm and are known to be weak. Several password utilities are available to decipher Type 7 encrypted passwords. Type 7 encryption is used by the **enable password**, **username**, and **line password** commands.

- **Type 5 passwords:** These use MD5 hashing algorithm (one-way hash) and are therefore much stronger because they are considered irreversible. The only way to crack the Type 5 password is by using brute force or dictionary attacks. It is highly recommended that you use Type 5 encryption instead of Type 7 where possible. Type 5 encryption is used by the **enable secret** command to specify an additional layer of security over the **enable password** command. The **enable secret** command takes preference over the **enable password** command. The **username secret** command also uses Type 5 encryption.

| TIP | The following URL is an index of password recovery procedures for most Cisco products:
http://www.cisco.com/en/US/products/sw/iosswrel/ps1831/products_tech_
note09186a00801746e6.shtml |

Creating Strong Passwords

Creating strong passwords is one of the most important issues in device security. Users at times create very simple passwords using their pet names, maiden name, birth dates, or other similar known terms. These passwords are easily crackable using dictionary or brute force attacks. An alternative would be to use a completely random combination of numbers and symbols, but that is not very practical and very difficult to remember. To help remember passwords, users write them down and keep them under their keyboard or save them in a text file on their computers. These practices are counter to good security practices.

A strong password is one that is at least eight to ten characters and includes a combination of letters (uppercase and lowercase combination), numbers, and special symbols (example: !@#$%^&,.*). Here again, combining characters and symbols can create a password that is difficult to remember. Therefore, security administrators often favor using pass phrases.

Pass-Phrase Technique

One of the common techniques used today to create strong passwords that are easy to remember is to use a pass phrase. A pass phrase is a sentence or a word that is easy to remember. A strong password can be derived by using the first letter of each word from the pass phrase. In addition, passwords can be made even stronger by using a combination of upper- and lowercase letters, numbers, and using substitute techniques to replace a character that looks like a letter; for example, i=1, i=!, s=5, S=5, o=0. Another good technique is to replace any numbers with the uppercase of that number on the keyboard, for example, 1=!, 2=@, 3=#, and 4=$. Users can create different ideas to develop pass-phrase-based passwords resulting in a cipher text. What follows are some examples of pass phrases:

- I can never remember my password = !cNrmp
- Quarter pounder with cheese = .25#erwchz
- How many times do I need to change my password? = hmtd!n2cmp?
- All people seem to need data processing = Ap$2Ndp!ng
- Take a long walk off a short pier = taLw0a5P
- Sticks and stones will break my bones! = S&5wBmB!
- Skilift = Sk1l1ft or Sk!l!ft

TIP	In Cisco IOS Software Release 12.3(1) and later, the **security passwords min-length** command is available to set the minimum character length for all passwords. The **security passwords min-length** command provides enhanced security access by specifying the minimum password length, thereby eliminating common passwords that are prevalent on most networks, such as "admin" or "cisco." This command affects user passwords, enable passwords, enable secret, and line passwords. After this command is enabled, any new password that is less than the specified length will fail, but the existing passwords will function. In Cisco IOS Software Release 12.3(1) and later, the **security authentication failure rate** command is available to configure the number of allowable unsuccessful login attempts. The **security authentication failure rate** command provides enhanced security access to the router by generating syslog messages after the number of unsuccessful login attempts exceeds the configured threshold rate. This command ensures that there are no continuous failures to access the router—for example, to combat a brute force type attack.

Password Encryption

The **service password-encryption** command in global configuration mode is used to encrypt passwords in the configuration and prevents unauthorized users from viewing the password in the configuration. Therefore, if someone executed **show run** during a clear-text Telnet session, the protocol analyzer would display the password. However, if **service password-encryption** is used, the password would be encrypted even during the same clear-text Telnet session.

NOTE	Passwords configured prior to configuring the **service password-encryption** command will not be encrypted. For the passwords to be encrypted, they must be reentered into the configuration after the **service password-encryption** command is issued.

ROMMON Security

Bypassing device configuration and allowing complete access to the device can be achieved following a very simple and well-documented procedure. Physical or console access is required to the device so it can reboot or power cycle to perform the procedure. Cisco IOS software provides a password recovery procedure that relies on gaining access to ROMMON. To access ROMMON mode, the break key sequence needs to be entered on the keyboard within 60 seconds of reboot.

In ROMMON mode, the router software can be reloaded, at which time a new system configuration is prompted that includes a new password.

The password recovery procedure enables anyone with console access the ability to access the router and its network. The **no service password-recovery** is a security enhancement feature that prevents the completion of the break key sequence and the entering of ROMMON mode. It prevents users with console access from accessing the router configuration and clearing the password. It also prevents changes to the configuration register values and access to nonvolatile RAM (NVRAM).

The following message is seen during startup when the **no service password-recovery** command is configured:

```
PASSWORD RECOVERY FUNCTIONALITY IS DISABLED

System Bootstrap, Version 11.1(19)AA, EARLY DEPLOYMENT RELEASE SOFTWARE (fc1)
Copyright  1998 by cisco Systems, Inc.
C3600 processor with 65536 Kbytes of main memory
Main memory is configured to 64 bit mode with parity enabled

PASSWORD RECOVERY FUNCTIONALITY IS DISABLED
program load complete, entry point: 0x80008000, size: 0x10ce394
Self decompressing the image : ###################################
####################################################################
####################################################################
##################################################  [OK]
Smart Init is disabled. IOMEM set to: 10

Using iomem percentage: 10

 Restricted Rights Legend

Use, duplication, or disclosure by the Government is
subject to restrictions as set forth in subparagraph
 of the Commercial Computer Software—Restricted
Rights clause at FAR sec. 52.227-19 and subparagraph
 (1) (ii) of the Rights in Technical Data and Computer
Software clause at DFARS sec. 252.227-7013.

Cisco Systems, Inc.
170 West Tasman Drive
San Jose, California 95134-1706

Cisco Internetwork Operating System Software
IOS (tm) 3600 Software (C3640-IS-M), Version 12.3(3), RELEASE SOFTWARE (fc2)
Copyright  1986-2003 by Cisco Systems, Inc.
Compiled Mon 18-Aug-03 19:03 by dchih
Image text-base: 0x60008950, data-base: 0x61B3E000
```

The following list outlines a few methods for recovering from a lost password when the **no service password-recovery** command is configured. These methods involve destroying the startup configuration; hence all configurations will be lost.

- Devices that have NVRAM chips can be removed and reseated. The NVRAM is implemented using battery-backed up static RAM (SRAM). Removing the SRAM erases the contents of NVRAM, which contain the **no service password-recovery** configuration.

- Other devices use an electrically erasable programmable read-only memory (EEPROM) to hold the configuration. The EEPROM is not erased when removed and is reseated; hence, recovery is not possible. (Contact the Cisco TAC support center for further assistance.)

- Another way to recover the lost password when the **no service password-recovery** command is configured becomes possible during the rebooting process of the router. (You must have console access to perform this task.) During the rebootubf process, press the break-key sequence combination within five to ten seconds of the image decompressing (when you see the message **Image text-base:**.... on the console screen). At this point, the software will prompt you to reset the router to the factory default configuration. See the sample output captured for this process that follows.

```
System Bootstrap, Version 11.1(19)AA, EARLY DEPLOYMENT RELEASE SOFTWARE (fc1)
Copyright  1998 by Cisco Systems, Inc.
C3600 processor with 65536 Kbytes of main memory
Main memory is configured to 64 bit mode with parity enabled

PASSWORD RECOVERY FUNCTIONALITY IS DISABLED
program load complete, entry point: 0x80008000, size: 0x10ce394
Self decompressing the image :
###########################################################
################################################################################
######
######################################################################   [OK]

Smart Init is disabled. IOMEM set to: 10

Using iomem percentage: 10

Restricted Rights Legend

Use, duplication, or disclosure by the Government is
subject to restrictions as set forth in subparagraph
 of the Commercial Computer Software—Restricted
Rights clause at FAR sec. 52.227-19 and subparagraph
 (1) (ii) of the Rights in Technical Data and Computer
Software clause at DFARS sec. 252.227-7013.

Cisco Systems, Inc.
170 West Tasman Drive
San Jose, California 95134-1706
Cisco Internetwork Operating System Software
IOS (tm) 3600 Software (C3640-IS-M), Version 12.3(3), RELEASE SOFTWARE (fc2)
Copyright  1986-2003 by Cisco Systems, Inc.
Compiled Mon 18-Aug-03 19:03 by dchih
Image text-base: 0x60008950, data-base: 0x61B3E000  ← hit CTRL-BREAK sequence here

PASSWORD RECOVERY IS DISABLED
Do you want to reset the router to factory default
configuration and proceed [y/n] ? y
Reset router configuration to factory default.
Cisco 3640 (R4700) processor (revision 0x00) with 59392K/6144K bytes of memory.
Processor board ID 09196037
R4700 CPU at 100Mhz, Implementation 33, Rev 1.0
Bridging software.
X.25 software, Version 3.0.0.
SuperLAT software (copyright 1990 by Meridian Technology Corp).
2 Ethernet/IEEE 802.3 interface(s)
2 Voice FXO interface(s)
```

```
2 Voice FXS interface(s)
DRAM configuration is 64 bits wide with parity enabled.
125K bytes of non-volatile configuration memory.
8192K bytes of processor board System flash (Read/Write)
8192K bytes of processor board PCMCIA Slot0 flash (Read/Write)
20480K bytes of processor board PCMCIA Slot1 flash (Read/Write)
[OK][OK]
SETUP: new interface Ethernet0/0 placed in "shutdown" state
SETUP: new interface Ethernet1/0 placed in "shutdown" state

Press RETURN to get started!

Router>
```

NOTE   Use the following link for standard break-key sequence combinations for most
applications, operating systems, and platforms, and to get some tips on how to troubleshoot
related problems: http://www.cisco.com/warp/public/701/61.html.

TIP   Use the following links to recover a device when the **no service password-recovery**
feature has been enabled:

http://www.cisco.com/en/US/products/sw/iosswrel/ps5413/
products_feature_guide09186a00802a1e76.html#wp1027258

http://www.cisco.com/en/US/products/hw/routers/ps274/
products_configuration_example09186a00801d8113.shtml

User Accounts

User identification can best be achieved with a combination of the username and password
parameters. The previous section discussed how to create strong passwords that can be used
to authenticate a user. This section elaborates on the combination of the two.

To establish a credential-based authentication system, you can create usernames on a device
for all device operators. Usernames configured from global configuration mode are stored
in device's local database. Give each operator a login username for the device. This allows
you to track which user makes changes to the configuration and can be useful for billing
and accounting purposes. The login accounts are created with the **username** command and
can be assigned different privilege levels and passwords. (Privilege levels are discussed in
more detail later in the chapter.) Also note that when using the **username secret** command,
the password will be encrypted as an MD5 hash.

```
Router(config)# username {username} password {password}
Router(config)# username {username} secret {password}
Router(config)# username {username} privilege {priv_level}
```

User accounts can be used for several applications—for example, console or vty lines, VPN users, and remote dial-in users. Accounts that are no longer required should be removed from the configuration.

A more scalable and preferred approach is to use the authentication, authorization, and accounting (AAA) technology, which is discussed in detail in the second part of this book, "Identity Security and Access Management."

Privilege Levels

Cisco IOS provides 16 privilege levels ranging from 0 to 15. By default, there are three predefined user levels in IOS:

- Privilege level 0 includes the **disable**, **enable**, **exit**, **help**, and **logout** commands.
- Privilege level 1 is the **User EXEC mode**. This is the normal level on Telnet and includes all user-level commands at the **Router>** prompt.
- Privilege level 15 is the **Privileged EXEC mode** (also known as enabled mode). It includes all enable-level commands at the **Router#** prompt.

All Cisco IOS commands are pre-assigned to levels 0, 1, or 15. Levels 2 through 14 are available as user-defined (customized) modes.

The global configuration **privilege** {*mode*} **level** {*level*} command is available to change, move, or set a privilege for a command to any of these levels. The {mode} refers to different modes on the router, such as exec or configure.

The line configuration mode **privilege level** {*level*} command is used to change the default privilege level for a given line or a group of lines.

Example 3-1 shows a user account "yusuf" created with privilege level 5, and several IOS (privilege 15) commands are moved to level 5 to be available for this user.

Example 3-1 *Configuring Privilege Level*

```
Router(config)# username yusuf privilege 5 password cisco
Router(config)# privilege exec level 5 show run
Router(config)# privilege exec all level 5 clear
Router(config)# privilege exec level 5 write memory
Router(config)# privilege exec level 5 configure terminal
Router(config)# privilege configure level 5 interface
```

Although the previous example shows local authentication, more granularities in control of the device can be achieved with the implementation of TACACS+ Command authorization using the AAA paradigm (discussed in Part II of this book). RADIUS does not support Command authorization.

The command **show privilege** displays the current privilege level. The **enable password level** command can be used to set the password for a particular privilege level.

Infrastructure ACL

As discussed in Chapter 2, "Access Control," Infrastructure ACLs are applied to explicitly filter traffic destined to the device addresses. The ACL is applied inbound on all externally facing connections (such as peering connections and customer connections) to minimize the risk of direct infrastructure attack by explicitly permitting only authorized traffic to the infrastructure equipment.

NOTE   For more details and a configuration example of Infrastructure ACLs, refer to http://www.cisco.com/en/US/tech/tk648/tk361/technologies_white_paper09186a00801a1a55.shtml.

Interactive Access Methods

To gain access to a device for administrative purposes, you can use three basic methods: the console port, VTY ports, and the auxiliary port, each discussed in detail in the sections that follow.

Console Port

The console port is the default access method for device management and configuration. This type of connection is used to physically connect to the console port of a device via the TTY line 0. By default, the console port is not password configured. The connection to the console port should not be left logged in. Therefore, it's recommended to configure the timeout for EXEC sessions on the console line, so that if a user forgets to log out or leaves the session idle for an extended period, the device will log out the idle sessions automatically. Example 3-2 shows how to set up the console line for a password and enforcing automatic logout if the session is idle for more than ten minutes. The **transport input none** command prevents remote access to the TTY lines via reverse Telnet.

Example 3-2 *Configuring Console Port Password and Idle Time*

```
Router(config)# line console  0
Router(config-line)# exec-timeout 10 0
Router(config-line)# transport input none
Router(config-line)# password <password>
Router(config-line)# login
Router(config-line)# end
Router#
```

VTY Ports

Cisco IOS supports multiple remote interactive access connections serviced by a logical vty line to connect to the device. Cisco IOS supports more than 100 vty lines (depending on the IOS version and feature set). By default, five vty lines (0 to 4) are available using the **line vty 0 4** command. Similar to the console port, vty lines have no passwords preconfigured. It is imperative to secure these lines with strong passwords and an access-control mechanism. Note that although the vty lines do not have a password set by default, they are still inaccessible until the **login** command is entered to allow remote logon. An ACL can also be used optionally to further secure access control to authorized users, thereby allowing access only from a restricted set of IP addresses.

You can use two common methods to access the vty lines: the Telnet and SSH protocols.

VTY Access Using Telnet

Example 3-3 shows you three procedures. First, it shows you how to configure VTY lines for Telnet access with a password. Second, it shows you how to apply an access list explicitly listing the hosts or networks from which remote administration will be permitted. And third, it shows how to set an exec session timeout.

Example 3-3   *Configuring VTY Access Using Telnet and Access List*

```
Router(config)# access-list 10 permit host 10.1.1.1
Router(config)# access-list 10 permit host 10.1.1.2
Router(config)# access-list 10 permit 192.168.1.1 0.0.0.255
Router(config)# access-list 10 deny any log
Router(config)# line vty 0 4
Router(config-line)# access-class 10 in
Router(config-line)# exec-timeout 10 0
Router(config-line)# transport input telnet
Router(config-line)# password <password>
Router(config-line)# login
Router(config-line)# end
Router#
```

The IP access-list number 10 in Example 3-3 is used to identify the hosts that are allowed to connect to the device through the VTY ports. Good practice is to have these IP addresses on an internal or trusted network. Be careful, though, when allowing IP addresses from external networks via the Internet. For more details on access lists, see Chapter 2. The **transport input telnet** command restricts the management interface to Telnet protocol only. (Telnet protocol uses TCP port 23.) If required, configure **transport input all** or selective protocols, which will allow for all supported protocols (for example, X.3 PAD, Async over ISDN v120, DEC MOP, TCP/IP Telnet, UNIX rlogin, UDPTN async via UDP, and TCP/IP SSH protocol).

VTY Access Using SSH

Telnet is the most popular protocol used to access a router for administrative purposes, yet it is important to understand that it is the most insecure. All communications in the Telnet session are in clear text, and there are many attacks known to capture the Telnet session and view and/or capture the session information. A more reliable and secure method for device administration is to use Secure Shell (SSH) protocol.

SSH provides strong authentication and encryption using strong cryptographic algorithms. SSH uses TCP port 22. Two versions of SSH are available: SSH protocol Version 1 and Version 2. SSH Version 1 is an improvement over using clear-text Telnet. However, some fundamental flaws exist in the SSHv1 protocol. SSH Version 2 is a rework and stronger version of SSH.

SSH coupled with the AAA authentication mechanism using TACACS+ or RADIUS provides the best solution for a secure, scalable access mechanism. Example 3-4 shows how to configure SSH for vty lines. (AAA configuration examples are available in Part II of this book.)

Example 3-4 *Configuring VTY Access Using SSH and Access List*

```
Router(config)# hostname R1
R1(config)# username cisco password cisco
R1(config)# ip domain-name syd.cisco.com
R1(config)# crypto key generate rsa
R1(config)# access-list 10 permit 10.1.1.1
R1(config)# access-list 10 permit 10.1.1.2
R1(config)# access-list 10 permit 192.168.1.1
R1(config)# access-list 10 deny any log
R1(config)# line vty 0 4
R1(config-line)# access-class 10 in
R1(config-line)# exec-timeout 10 0
R1(config-line)# transport input ssh
R1(config-line)# password <password>
R1(config-line)# login
R1(config-line)# end
R1#
```

The **transport input ssh** command stipulates that only the SSH protocol may be used for interactive logins to the router. Any sessions using Telnet protocol will be denied.

NOTE   SSH requires having a Crypto IOS image.

Auxiliary Port

Some devices have an auxiliary (aux) port available for remote administration via a dialup modem connection. In most cases, the aux port should be disabled by using the **no exec** command under **line aux 0**.

A modem should be connected to the aux port with no alternatives for backup or remote access methods to the device only if it is absolutely necessary. Through a simple war-dialing technique, an intruder can find a rogue modem; hence it is necessary to apply authentication for access control to the aux port. As discussed earlier, all connections to the device (including aux port) must require authentication (using individual user accounts) for access, either using local authentication or via AAA servers using TACACS+ or RADIUS.

For enhanced security, IOS callback features can be implemented. Refer to Cisco documentation for information about connecting modems on aux ports and configuring callback features.

Banner Messages

Banners are informational messages that can be displayed to users who connect to the device. Banners are important messaging tools used to warn the unauthorized users of their activity and most importantly to warn them they are being monitored and logged. Banner messages are very useful for law enforcement.

There are five types of banner messages:

- **Message-of-the-day banner (MOTD):** A message-of-the-day (MOTD) banner is displayed when a user connects to the router on all connected terminals. This banner is displayed at login and is useful for sending messages that affect all network users. The **banner motd** command in global configuration mode can be used to configure a MOTD banner message.

- **Login banner:** A login banner is configured to be displayed on all connected terminals. This banner is displayed after the MOTD banner appears and before the login prompt. The **banner login** command in global configuration mode can be used to configure a login banner message.

- **EXEC banner:** Depending on the type of the connection, an EXEC banner is displayed after the user successfully logs in to the router. An EXEC banner is configured to be displayed whenever an EXEC process is initiated. For example, this banner is displayed to users telneting to the system after entering their usernames and passwords, but before the user EXEC mode prompt is displayed. The **banner exec** command in global configuration mode can be used to configure an EXEC banner message.

- **Incoming banner:** An incoming banner is displayed on terminals connected to reverse Telnet lines, usually initiated from the network side of the router. This banner is useful for providing instructions to users. The **banner incoming** command in global configuration mode can be used to configure an incoming banner message.

- **SLIP-PPP banner message:** Default banner messages have been known to cause connectivity problems in some non-Cisco Serial Line Internet Protocol (SLIP) and Point-to-Point Protocol (PPP) dialup software connections. The SLIP-PPP banner message can now be customized to make Cisco SLIP and PPP compatible with non-Cisco dialup software. The **banner slip-ppp** command in global configuration mode can be used to configure an incoming banner message.

An example of a login banner follows:

```
********************************************************************
*   WARNING: This is a controlled access system with login        *
*   restricted to authorized personnel. Unauthorized access       *
*   is a criminal offense under the Computer Misuse Act of 1990.   *
*     Any unauthorized access attempt will be investigated and     *
*   prosecuted to the full extent of the law.                      *
*   ------------------------------------------------------------   *
*       YOUR LOGIN DETAILS HAVE BEEN CAPTURED AND LOGGED           *
*   ------------------------------------------------------------   *
*   If you are not an authorized user, disconnect now.             *
********************************************************************
```

Banners can be customized by using banner tokens. Tokens are keywords in the form **$(*token*)** that, when used in a banner message, display the currently configured value of the token argument (for example, the router hostname, domain name, or IP address). By using these tokens, you can allow customized banners to be designed that display current Cisco IOS configuration variables. Only Cisco IOS-supported tokens may be used. There is no facility to define user-defined tokens. Table 3-1 lists the tokens supported by the different **banner** commands.

Table 3-1 *Tokens Allowed by Banner Type*

Token	Description	motd banner	login banner	exec banner	incoming banner	slip-ppp banner
$(hostname)	Router hostname	Yes	Yes	Yes	Yes	Yes
$(domain)	Router domain name	Yes	Yes	Yes	Yes	Yes
$(peer-ip)	IP address of the peer machine	No	No	No	No	Yes
$(gate-ip)	IP address of the gateway machine	No	No	No	No	Yes
$(encap)	Encapsulation type (SLIP or PPP)	No	No	No	No	Yes
$(encap-alt)	Encapsulation type displayed as SL/IP instead of SLIP	No	No	No	No	Yes

Table 3-1   *Tokens Allowed by Banner Type (Continued)*

Token	Description	motd banner	login banner	exec banner	incoming banner	slip-ppp banner
$(mtu)	Maximum transmission unit (MTU) size	No	No	No	No	Yes
$(line)	VTY or TTY line number	Yes	Yes	Yes	Yes	No
$(line-desc)	User-specified description of the line	Yes	Yes	Yes	Yes	No

Cisco IOS Software has a number of services and protocols available on a device. Many of them are unnecessary in normal operation and can be susceptible to information gathering or network attacks. It is important to identify all the services on each device and ensure that they are configured appropriately (with hardened security). Only required services should be enabled on devices, and unnecessary services and protocols should be disabled. Limiting these unnecessary and unwanted services and protocols running on the device greatly enhances the device security and prevents it from being exploited by the known and unknown vulnerabilities.

The sections that follow outline some of the common services and protocols available in IOS and other Cisco devices such as firewalls. Some of these services are used for management (for example, Cisco Discovery Protocol [CDP], Simple Network Management Protocol [SNMP], Network Time Protocol [NTP], Hypertext Transfer Protocol [HTTP]). These management services must be tightly configured to allow access to authorized users only. Careful consideration should be taken to activate these services and protocols with hardened configuration.

Cisco IOS Resilient Configuration

In IOS Version 12.3T, a new feature was introduced to maintain at all times a secure working copy of the router IOS image and the startup configuration. In the event of a network downtime due to a compromise or any other disaster, the last thing to worry about is finding a valid copy of the IOS image and the configuration file. Time spent on recovering from such a catastrophe is critical, and speedy recovery is of utmost priority. The Cisco IOS Resilient Configuration feature enables a router to secure a working copy of the running image and configuration so that those files can withstand malicious attempts to erase the contents of persistent storage (NVRAM and flash). These secure files are protected by the IFS (IOS File System) and cannot be removed by the user. This set of IOS image and router running configuration is referred to as the *primary bootset*.

To enable the IOS Resilient Configuration feature, use the **secure boot-image** command from the global configuration mode to enable IOS image resilience. Use the **secure boot-config** command to store a secure copy of the primary bootset in the persistent storage.

The **dir** command will not list these secured files, because the IFS shields the secured files from being listed in a directory output. There is no restriction in the ROM monitor (ROMMON) mode, and files can be listed and used to boot from the secured files. To display the IOS resilience configuration and the primary bootset filename, use the **show secure bootset** command to verify archive existence.

Cisco Discovery Protocol (CDP)

CDP is a Cisco proprietary protocol for device discovery (media and protocol independent) that runs over OSI Layer 2 (the data link layer) on most Cisco devices (routers, bridges, access and communication servers, and switches). CDP displays information about other directly connected Cisco devices. Network management applications and intruders can map the network and retrieve valuable information of neighboring Cisco devices leveraging CDP.

CDP is enabled by default at the global level and on each supported interface to send and receive CDP information. However, on some interfaces, CDP is disabled by default (for example, on async interfaces).

CDP can be disabled globally for the device or on selected interfaces. The **no cdp run** command from the global configuration mode can be used to disable CDP for the entire device, as shown in Example 3-5.

Example 3-5 *Disable CDP Globally*

```
Router# configure terminal
Router(config)# no cdp run
```

Alternatively, CDP can be disabled on a particular interface. The **no cdp enable** command from the interface configuration mode can be used to disable CDP per interface, as shown in Example 3-6.

Example 3-6 *Disable CDP per Interface*

```
Router# configure terminal
Router(config)# interface <interface-id>
Router(config-if)# no cdp enable
```

The **show cdp neighbors [detail]** command can be used to display information about directly connected Cisco devices.

TCP/UDP Small-Servers

TCP and UDP small-servers can be used to access minor services from hosts on the network. TCP small-servers access the minor TCP services such as echo, chargen, discard, and daytime. UDP small-servers access minor UDP services such as echo, chargen, and discard.

By default, TCP and UDP small-services are disabled on all IOS versions except in Cisco IOS Software Version 11.2 and earlier. If these services have been enabled, they can be disabled using the **no service tcp-small-servers** and the **no service udp-small-servers** command from the global configuration mode.

Finger

The Finger protocol enables network users to obtain a list of all users currently using a device. The Finger service allows remote users to view the output equivalent to the **show users** [**wide**] command. The information displayed includes the processes running on the system, the line number, the connection name, the idle time, and the terminal location. Finger protocol uses TCP port 79. This information can be very useful for an intruder in the reconnaissance phase, because it gathers information about remote hosts and networks by examining such network services. As with all other minor services, the Finger service should be disabled if not required in the network.

By default, Finger protocol is disabled on all IOS versions beginning with Cisco IOS Software Version 12.1(5) and 12.1(5)T and later. (Finger protocol was enabled by default in previous versions.) If this service has been enabled, it can be disabled using the **no ip finger** or the **no service finger** command from the global configuration mode.

Identification (auth) Protocol

Identification (auth) protocol (Identd) allows any host to ask the router to identify itself. Identd can be used as a reconnaissance tool.

By default, identification support is disabled on all IOS versions. If this service has been enabled, it can be disabled using the **no ip identd** command from the global configuration mode.

DHCP and BOOTP Service

The Dynamic Host Configuration Protocol (DHCP) server and client are integrated in Cisco IOS. DHCP is based on BOOTP and shares the well-known UDP server port 67 (per RFC 951, RFC 1534, and RFC 2131). When the BOOTP server and DHCP servers are disabled, all incoming packets on UDP port 67 are discarded, and ICMP port-unreachable messages are sent out in response.

The **no ip bootp server** and **no service dhcp** commands can be used to disable BOOTP and DHCP, respectively, from the global configuration mode.

Trivial File Transfer Protocol (TFTP) Server

Cisco routers or the flash memory device on the router can act as a TFTP server. The system sends a copy of the system image contained in ROM or one of the system images contained in flash memory to any client that issues a TFTP Read Request with this filename. This service must be disabled to prevent unauthorized reading and writing from the router flash memory.

By default, TFTP support is disabled on all IOS versions. If this service has been enabled, it can be disabled using the **no tftp-server flash:[filename]** command from the global configuration mode.

File Transfer Protocol (FTP) Server

Similarly, Cisco routers can act as FTP servers. FTP service is used to transfer files to and from the router. For example, system image files, backup configs, and syslog data can be transferred to or from the router. This service must be disabled to prevent unauthorized reading and writing from the router.

By default, FTP server service is disabled on all IOS versions. If this service has been enabled, it can be disabled using the **no ftp-server enable** command from the global configuration mode.

Autoloading Device Configuration

Cisco IOS offers the facility to autoload device configuration directly from a server on the network to the device. There are several methods to achieve this, but none of them are recommended, because the process of passing the configuration file down to the device is in clear text and subject to unauthorized viewing in transition. Example 3-7 shows how to disable autoloading of configuration files from a network server.

Example 3-7   *Disable Autoloading Device Configuration*

```
Router(config)# no service config
Router(config)# no boot network
```

PAD

PAD service is used to enable all packet assembler/disassembler (PAD) commands and connections between PAD devices and access servers. By default, all PAD commands and associated connections are enabled.

To disable PAD, use the **no service pad** command from the global configuration mode.

IP Source Routing

The Cisco IOS software examines IP header options on every packet and supports the IP header options, including Strict Source Route, Loose Source Route, Record Route, and Time Stamp, defined in RFC 791. The IOS takes respective action as per RFC standards when encountering a packet with one of these options enabled. When the IOS encounters a packet with an invalid option, it sends out an Internet Control Message Protocol (ICMP) Parameter Problem message to the source of the packet and discards the packet.

IP protocol allows the source IP host to specify a route through the IP network. This provision is known as *source routing*. Source routing is specified as an option in the IP header. Source routing allows (or requires) the source of a packet to supply information with the message that will influence the route of that message as it passes through the network. When source routing is specified, the IOS forwards the packet according to the specified source route found in the message. This feature is employed to force a packet to take a certain route through the network and not follow the route in the routing table.

IP source routing can be used by an intruder to gain unauthorized path access by rerouting packets originally destined to use other network paths to itself. To prevent this and other forms of spoofing attacks, all devices should have this feature turned off. Various types of spoofing attacks and mitigation techniques are covered in Chapter 7, "Attack Vectors and Mitigation Techniques."

IP source route is enabled by default in all IOS as per RFC 1812, "Requirements for IP Version 4 Routers," which specifies that a router must support the source route option in the IP header and forward the packets accordingly, unless otherwise explicitly disabled. The command **no ip source-route** can be used to disable the IP source-route header options from the global configuration mode.

Proxy Address Resolution Protocol (ARP)

Proxy ARP is the technique in which a device, usually a router, replies for incoming ARP requests intended for other hosts.

By "faking" its identity, the router accepts responsibility for routing these packets to the "real" destination. All interfaces on Cisco devices are enabled to accept and respond to proxy ARP requests.

Proxy ARP, which is defined in 1027, is enabled by default on all interfaces.

The interface configuration mode command **no ip proxy-arp** can be used to disable Proxy ARP on a per-interface basis.

Although the intricacies, advantages, and disadvantages of using Proxy ARP are beyond the scope of this book, you should explore them on your own.

NOTE   For more details on Proxy ARP, visit http://www.cisco.com/en/US/tech/tk648/tk361/
technologies_tech_note09186a0080094 adb.shtml.

Gratuitous ARP

Gratuitous Address Resolution Protocol (gARP) is an unsolicited ARP broadcast
containing the IP address of the client host and the router's MAC address. A Cisco router
will send out a gARP message when a client connects and negotiates an address over a PPP
connection. This transmission occurs even when the client receives the address from a local
address pool.

Gratuitous ARP is enabled by default on all interfaces. To disable gARP, use the **no ip
gratuitous-arps** command from the global configuration mode.

IP Directed Broadcast

By default, IP directed broadcast is disabled under all the interfaces in all Cisco IOS
Software Version 12.0 and later. In earlier IOS versions, the **no ip directed-broadcast**
command was required to be applied on every interface known to forward broadcast
packets. When an interface is configured with the **no ip directed-broadcast** command, all
directed broadcast packets are dropped at the interface.

IP Mask Reply

IP mask reply service is used to send an Internet Control Message Protocol (ICMP) mask
reply message with subnet mask information for a particular network in response to the
ICMP mask requests. An attacker can use this technique to aid in mapping a network.

By default, IP mask reply is disabled on all IOS versions. IP mask reply can be enabled on
a per-interface basis using the **ip mask-reply** command under the interface configuration
mode.

If this service has been enabled, the command **no ip mask-reply** under the interface
configuration mode can be used to disable it.

IP Redirects

When a packet received on an interface is required to exit out through the same interface on
which it was received, an ICMP redirect message is sent to the host indicating the default
gateway address to be used for subsequent forwarding. In earlier versions of IOS, if Hot
Standby Router Protocol (HSRP) was configured on an interface, ICMP redirect messages

were disabled by default for the interface. With Cisco IOS Release 12.1(3)T and later, ICMP redirect messages are enabled by default if HSRP is configured.

The **no ip redirects** command under the interface configuration mode can be used to disable IP redirect. This service should be disabled especially on untrusted network interfaces because it can be used to map the network.

ICMP Unreachable

When an IOS device receives a nonbroadcast packet destined for itself that uses a protocol it does not recognize, it sends an ICMP unreachable message to the source. In addition, an ICMP unreachable message is used to send a response to a host to inform it that the device cannot deliver the packet to the requested destination because it does not have a route to the destination address.

One of several common attacks an intruder can launch involves sending crafted packets to the device spoofing random source IP addresses for which the device has no route. This results in the device replying with an *ICMP unreachable* packet to all those spoofed hosts. In some cases, a reply to a large number of these requests containing unknown or invalid IP addresses can result in degradation in performance. To prevent such an occurrence and many other types of attacks, the ICMP unreachable message can be disabled under the interface mode shown in Example 3-8.

Example 3-8 *Configuring ICMP Unreachable*

```
Router(config)# interface <interface-id>
Router(if-config)# no ip unreachables
```

CAUTION   In some configurations, such as certain types of tunnel structures, the use of **ip unreachables** is required. If the device must use the ICMP Unreachable feature, an alternative that alleviates performance degradation is to rate limit the number of replies using the **ip icmp rate-limit {milliseconds}** command in global configuration mode. In Cisco IOS 12.0 and later, the default rate limit is set to two packets per second.

HTTP

One of the features Cisco IOS offers to manage the device is the HTTP protocol. The integrated web server in Cisco IOS allows for basic management using the web browser. If HTTP is not required, it is highly recommended that you disable it.

HTTP server is enabled using the **ip http server** command from the global configuration mode. The secure HTTP (HTTPS) server feature was also added from IOS version 12.2(15)T and later. Secure HTTP (HTTPS) can be enabled using the **ip http secure-server** command from the global configuration mode. The standard HTTP server and the secure

HTTP server can run concurrently on a device. For increased security, it is recommended that you use the Secure HTTP (HTTPS) server and disable the standard HTTP server using the **no ip http server** command. This will ensure that secure data cannot be accessed through the standard HTTP connection. The **show ip http server** command can be used for detailed status information about the HTTP server.

By default, the HTTP server uses the standard TCP port 80, and Secure HTTP (HTTPS) uses the standard TCP port 443. These ports can be changed to user-defined ports by using the **ip http port {port}** command and the **ip http secure-port {port}** command, respectively. Only values above 1024 are accepted.

For more granular security, an authentication mechanism can be used for login when a client connects to HTTP server, coupled with an access list to restrict the access of HTTP service to authorized users only. The **ip http access-class {access-list-number}** command can be used to define sets of IP addresses and networks that are permitted or denied access. The **ip http authentication** command can be used to enable authentication using the **AAA**, **enable**, **local**, and **tacacs** methods.

If HTTP and HTTPS services are not required, they can be disabled by using the **no ip http server** command and **no ip http secure-server** commands, respectively, from the global configuration mode.

Network Time Protocol (NTP)

The heart of the time service is the system clock. The system clock starts at the beginning of every system startup keeping track of the current date and time. The system clock keeps track of time internally based on UTC, also known as Greenwich Mean Time (GMT). Local time zone and daylight savings time must be configured to reflect the correct time relative to the local time zone.

NOTE   On the high-end routers such as the 7500 and 12000 Series, the system keeps time on an internal clock, thus time is not lost during a reboot.

NTP is designed to synchronize the time on the device clock. An NTP network usually gets its time from an authoritative time source, such as a radio clock or an atomic clock attached to a time server.

NTP is essential for syslog messages, and for troubleshooting and correlation activities. NTP uses UDP port 123 as both the source and destination and can be secured using an authentication mechanism that uses the MD5 algorithm. The **ntp** command from the global configuration mode can be used for all NTP-related configurations in the Cisco IOS.

Simple Network Management Protocol (SNMP)

SNMP is a widely used management protocol and defined set of standards for communication with devices connected to a TCP/IP network that are defined by the Internet Engineering Task Force (IETF). SNMP provides a means to monitor and control network devices and to manage configurations, statistics collection, and performance monitoring. *SNMP* is an application layer protocol that facilitates the exchange of management information between network devices. SNMP uses UDP ports 161 and 162.

Like other management protocols, SNMP is vulnerable to a variety of security threats. Numerous guidelines exist for configuring SNMP. If SNMP is not required in the network, it should be disabled on all devices.

Auto-Secure Feature

There are a number of services available on Cisco devices, as discussed in earlier sections. It is a very difficult task to monitor and maintain the security level and to identify each service. To help with this task, Cisco IOS introduced a single CLI command, called **Auto-Secure**, which performs the following functions:

- Disables common IP services that can be exploited for network attacks
- Enables IP services and features that can aid in the defense of a network when under attack

In addition, this feature simplifies the security configuration of a router and hardens the router configuration. Auto-Secure is a valuable feature for people without special security operations applications, because it allows them to quickly secure their network without thorough knowledge of all the Cisco IOS security features.

The Auto-Secure feature is available in Cisco IOS Release 12.3(1) and later. The **auto secure** command in privileged EXEC mode can be used to secure the management and forwarding planes of the router. When executed, an interactive wizard prompts the user, unless the **no-interact** keyword is used, in which case the user is not prompted for interactive configurations.

The **show auto secure config** command can be used to display all configuration commands that have been added as part of the Auto-Secure process.

NOTE   For more information on the Auto-Secure feature, visit http://www.cisco.com/en/US/products/sw/iosswrel/ps5187/products_feature_guide09186a008017d101.html.

CAUTION	Prior to Cisco IOS Release 12.3(8)T, rollback of the Auto-Secure configuration is not available. The rollback feature is available in IOS Release 12.3(8)T and later. Rollback enables a router to revert back to its pre-autosecure configuration state, if the Auto-Secure configuration fails.

Securing Management Access for Security Appliance

This section discusses the various system management security features available for security appliances such as the Cisco PIX 500 series, ASA 5500 Series Adaptive Security Appliances, and IPS 4200 series appliance sensors.

PIX 500 and ASA 5500 Security Appliance—Device Access Security

This section describes how to secure the Cisco PIX 500 and ASA 5500 Series Adaptive Security Appliances for system management through Telnet, SSH, and HTTPS, and authentication mechanism using AAA.

Telnet Access

Cisco PIX 500 and ASA 5500 Series Adaptive Security Appliances allow Telnet connections for management purposes. For security reasons, users cannot telnet to the lowest security interface unless Telnet is encapsulated in an IPsec tunnel. Security appliance allows a maximum of five concurrent Telnet connections per context, if available, with a maximum of 100 connections divided among all contexts. For Telnet access to the Security appliance, IP addresses need to be configured for hosts from which the appliance accepts connections, as shown in Example 3-9. The **telnet** command from the global configuration mode can be used to define the IP address/network and the interface from which the hosts are allowed to telnet.

Example 3-9 *Configuring Telnet Access for PIX*

```
Pix(config)# telnet <source_IP_address> mask <source_interface>
```

SSH Access

Telnet protocol in general is the most popular protocol used to perform device management, but it is highly insecure because communications in the Telnet session are in clear text. A more reliable approach is to use the SSH protocol. Security appliance supports SSH connections for management purposes. Security appliance supports the SSH remote shell functionality provided in SSH Versions 1 and 2 and supports DES and 3DES ciphers. To configure SSH, generate an RSA key pair, which is required for SSH, and then identify the IP addresses/networks from which the appliance accepts connections by using the **ssh** command from the global configuration mode. Other requirements need to be fulfilled to configure SSH, such as configuring the domain name and creating the RSA key pair.

The most secure and highly recommended device management access control combination is obtained by using SSH with AAA authentication with either TACACS+ or RADIUS. (AAA authentication is discussed in Chapter 8, "Securing Management Access.")

HTTPS Access for ADSM

Cisco Adaptive Security Device Manager (ASDM) is a security management and monitoring application for Cisco PIX 500 and ASA 5500 Series Adaptive Security Appliances that is used through an intuitive, easy-to-use, web-based management interface. ADSM will be discussed more in Chapter 24, "Security and Policy Management."

To use ASDM, the HTTPS server needs to be enabled to allow SSL connections to the security appliance. A step-by-step setup wizard is available to configure all these tasks using the **setup** command. An alternative is to configure all steps manually. Example 3-10 shows how to enable the HTTPS server and allow hosts on the 10.1.1.0/24 network from the inside interface to access ASDM.

Example 3-10 *Configuring HTTPS Access for ASDM*

```
Pix(config)# crypto key generate rsa modulus 1024
Pix(config)# write mem
Pix(config)# http server enable
Pix(config)# http 10.1.1.0 255.255.255.0 inside
```

The appliance allows a maximum of five concurrent ASDM instances per context, if available, with a maximum of 32 ASDM instances among all contexts.

NOTE Security contexts will be discussed in detail in Chapter 6, "Cisco Firewalls: Appliance and Module."

Authenticating and Authorizing Using Local and AAA Database

The security appliance supports authentication, authorization, and accounting capabilities using the AAA servers and a local database stored on the appliance. AAA provides an extra level of protection, scalability, and better control for user access.

AAA services are available using TACACS+, Radius, and the local database type on the security appliance. Note that accounting with a local database is not supported, and Radius command authorization is not supported. This is not a limitation within the appliance but is protocol inherent.

AAA technology will be discussed in depth in Part II of this book.

IPS 4200 Series Appliance Sensors (formerly known as IDS 4200)

The IPS sensor appliance system management can be performed in two ways:

- **Console access:** The IPS Sensor software provides a command-line interface (CLI), which is a full-featured Cisco IOS software-like CLI that provides device configuration. Although using the CLI allows the user to configure most of the configuration and administrative tasks, a web-based graphical interface is more intuitive and easy to navigate.

- **Web-based GUI interface using HTTP or HTTPS:** After the sensor is initialized using the console, the administrator can use the HTTP or HTTPS web-based user-interface application to perform configuration, administration, and monitoring tasks. HTTPS is enabled by default.

A step-by-step setup wizard is available to configure basic initialization tasks using the **setup** command. The **setup** command allows configuring basic sensor settings, including the hostname, IP interfaces, Telnet server, web server port, ACLs, time settings, and assigning and enabling interfaces. After the sensor is initialized, it can communicate over the network using the IDM, VMS, or Cisco Intrusion Prevention System Device Manager. Use the **show configuration** command or the **more current-config** command to verify sensor settings. Cisco IPS Sensor is covered in detail in Chapter 20, "Network Intrusion Prevention."

IPS Device Manager (IDM)

IDM is a web-based Java application to configure and manage the sensor. The web server for IDM resides on the sensor. IDM can be accessed through the common web browsers such as Internet Explorer, Netscape, or Mozilla. IDM is suitable for managing small deployments such as 3 to 5 sensors in the network. For large-scale sensor deployments, Cisco Security Manager is used. Both IDM and Cisco Security Manager are discussed in Chapter 24.

HTTP/HTTPS Access

By default, sensor appliance has built-in web server service enabled with HTTPS on the standard TCP port 443 and enabled to use Transport Layer Security (TLS) and Secure Socket Layer (SSL) protocols.

SSL enables encrypted communications between a client web browser and the sensor appliance. If required, TLS/SSL can be disabled, and the standard HTTP port can be used instead, but this is not recommended because HTTP is insecure. The web server port can be changed from its default.

NOTE   If the web services are changed from HTTPS to HTTP or if the web server port is changed, you should specify the port in the URL address in the browser when connecting to the IDM in the format https://*sensor_ip_address:port* or http://*sensor_ip_address:port* (for example, https://10.1.1.254:8080 or http://10.1.1.254:8080, respectively).

Telnet and SSH Access

As discussed earlier, Telnet protocol is not a secure access method and therefore is disabled by default on the sensor appliance. However, SSH is enabled by default on the sensor and is a secure access method. If required, Telnet protocol can be enabled by using the **telnet-option enabled** command under the network settings in the service host mode or can be enabled when using the **setup** wizard.

Access Control List

Sensor appliance uses the ACL to enforce authorized access to the appliance via HTTP, HTTPS, FTP, Telnet, SSH, or SCP. If you use an ACL, you need to configure a list of authorized IP addresses and networks that are allowed to log in to the sensor (for example, hosts that need to Telnet/SSH to the sensor or access via IDM, or management workstations). By default, the Class A subnet 10.0.0.0/8 is permitted. When a host with an IP address that is not defined in the ACL attempts to log in to the sensor appliance, the sensor will drop the connection automatically.

The **access-list [ip_address / netmask]** command in the **network-settings** submode in **service host** mode can be used to configure the list of hosts or networks requiring sensor access.

User Accounts

User accounts can be managed on the local sensor because there is no support for AAA servers on sensor appliance. Each user is associated with a role that controls what that user can and cannot modify. There are four basic user roles:

- **Administrator:** The highest level of privileges with unrestricted view and can perform all operations.
- **Operator:** The second highest level of privileges and can view everything, but perform limited operations.
- **Viewer:** The lowest level of privileges and can view configuration and events, but cannot modify any configuration data except their user passwords.
- **Service:** A special role that allows a user to bypass the sensor CLI and directly log in to a bash shell. Service account is mainly created for support and troubleshooting purposes. (There is no supported user configuration from within the service account.) Only one user with service privileges can be configured on a sensor. The service user cannot be used to log in to the IDM.

CAUTION   User access in the service account is not supported except under direct supervision of Cisco TAC or Cisco development engineering.

Device Security Checklist

A security checklist is an important document containing a summary of various guidelines and instructions for secure implementations. Device security checklists can be viewed as templates for device lockdown and security implementation guidelines. You can use the following checklist as a quick summary and working guide to the device security configuration topics discussed in this chapter.

- ✓ Device security policy written, approved, distributed, and reviewed on regular basis.
- ✓ Facilities (room, building, area) housing the devices secured—physical security.
- ✓ Password policies to ensure that good passwords are created that cannot be easily guessed or hacked.
- ✓ Password encryption used so that passwords are not visible when device configuration is viewed.
- ✓ Access methods such as Console, VTY, AUX using ACLs, and authentication mechanisms secured.
- ✓ Access methods such as SSH with AAA authentication chosen wisely.
- ✓ Unneeded services and protocols to be disabled.

✓ Unused interfaces shut down or disabled.

✓ Configuration hardened for network services and protocols in use (for example, HTTP and SNMP).

✓ Port and protocol needs of the network and use access lists to limit traffic flow identified.

✓ Access list for anti-spoofing and infrastructure protection and for blocking reserved and private addresses considered.

✓ Routing protocols established that use authentication mechanisms for integrity.

✓ Appropriate logging enabled with proper time information.

✓ Device's time of day set accurately, maintained with NTP.

Summary

The chapter focused on the essentials of securing device and management access. Security implementation is not possible without a policy, and correspondingly, device hardening is not possible without a device security policy. The chapter begins with a brief overview of a device security policy followed by key factors in device security, such as access methods, access control, device hardening, and identifying unneeded services. The chapter then concentrates on a discussion of various system management security features specifically available on security appliances, such as Cisco PIX 500 and ASA 5500 Series Adaptive Security Appliances, VPN3000 Concentrator, and IPS 4200 series appliance sensors. The chapter ends with a device security checklist that is developed as a summary.

References

http://www.nsa.gov/snac/

http://www.ntp.org/ntpfaq/NTP-s-def.htm

http://www.cisco.com/en/US/tech/tk648/tk361/
technologies_tech_note09186a0080120f48.shtml

http://www.cisco.com/en/US/products/ps6350/
products_configuration_guide_chapter09186a008044036d.html

http://www.cisco.com/en/US/products/ps6350/
products_configuration_guide_chapter09186a008030c799.html

http://www.cisco.com/en/US/tech/tk869/tk769/
technologies_white_paper09186a0080117070.shtml

http://www.cisco.com/en/US/products/sw/iosswrel/ps5207/
products_feature_guide09186a008022a7ce.html

Security Features on Switches

This chapter describes Layer 2 security basics and security features on switches available to combat network security threats. These threats result from weaknesses in Layer 2 of the OSI model—the data-link layer. Switches act as arbiters to forward and control all the data flowing across the network. The current trend is for network security to be solidified through the support of switch security features that build feature-rich, high-performance, and optimized networks. The chapter examines the integrated security features available on Cisco catalyst switches to mitigate threats that result from the weaknesses in Layer 2 of the OSI model. The chapter also provides guidelines and recommendations intended to help you understand and configure the Layer 2 security features available on Cisco switches to build robust networks.

A summary of Layer 2 best practices is provided toward the end of the chapter.

Securing Layer 2

With the rapid growth of IP networks in the past years, high-end switching has played one of the most fundamental and essential roles in moving data reliably, efficiently, and securely across networks. Cisco Catalyst switches are the leader in the switching market and major players in today's networks.

The data-link layer (Layer 2 of the OSI model) provides the functional and procedural means to transfer data between network entities with interoperability and interconnectivity to other layers, but from a security perspective, the data-link layer presents its own challenges. Network security is only as strong as the weakest link, and Layer 2 is no exception. Applying first-class security measures to the upper layers (Layers 3 and higher) does not benefit your network if Layer 2 is compromised. Cisco switches offer a wide range of security features at Layer 2 to protect the network traffic flow and the devices themselves.

Understanding and preparing for network threats is important, and hardening Layer 2 is becoming imperative. Cisco is continuously raising the bar for security, and security feature availability at Layer 2 is no exception. The sections that follow highlight the Layer 2 security features available on Cisco Catalyst switches.

NOTE The configuration examples shown in this chapter are based on Cisco IOS Software syntax only (also known as native mode). Catalyst Operating System (CatOS) software-based examples are not covered.

Port-Level Traffic Controls

Port-based traffic control features can be used to provide protection at the port level. Catalyst switches offer Storm Control, Protected Ports, Private Virtual Local Area Network (PVLAN), Port Blocking, and Port Security features.

Storm Control

A LAN storm typically occurs when hostile packets are flooded on the LAN segment, creating unnecessary and excessive traffic resulting in network performance degradation. Several factors can cause a storm on a network; examples include errors in the protocol-stack implementation or a loophole that is exploited in a device configuration.

The Storm Control feature prevents regular network traffic from being disrupted by a broadcast, multicast, or unicast packet storm on any of the physical interfaces.

The traffic storm control (also known as a *traffic suppression feature*) monitors inbound packets over a 1-second interval and compares it to the configured storm-control suppression level by using one of the following methods to measure activity:

- The percentage of total available bandwidth of the port allocated for the broadcast, multicast, or unicast traffic
- Traffic rate over a 1-second interval in packets per second at which broadcast, multicast, or unicast packets are received on an interface

With either method, the port blocks traffic when a threshold is reached, filtering out all subsequent packets. As the port remains in a blocked state, the traffic continues to be dropped until the traffic rate drops below the suppression level, at which point the port resumes normal traffic forwarding.

To enable the traffic storm-control feature, use the **storm-control {broadcast | multicast | unicast}** command from the global configuration mode. By default, storm-control is disabled.

The **storm-control action** {**shutdown | trap**} command is used to specify the action to be taken when a storm is detected. By default, the storm traffic is suppressed when no action is configured.

To verify the storm-control suppression levels configured on an interface, use the **show storm-control [interface] [broadcast | multicast | unicast]** command.

Protected Ports (PVLAN Edge)

In some network environments, there is a requirement for no traffic to be seen or forwarded between host(s) on the same LAN segment, thereby preventing interhost communications. The PVLAN edge feature provisions this isolation by creating a firewall-like barrier, thereby blocking any unicast, broadcast, or multicast traffic among the protected ports on the switch. Note that the significance of the protected port feature is limited to the local switch, and there is no provision in the PVLAN edge feature to isolate traffic between two "protected" ports located on different switches. For this purpose, the PVLAN feature can be used. (This feature is discussed in more detail later in this chapter.)

The PVLAN edge offers the following features:

- The switch will not forward traffic (unicast, multicast, or broadcast) between ports that are configured as protected. Data traffic must be routed via a Layer 3 device between the protected ports.

- Control traffic, such as routing protocol updates, is an exception and will be forwarded between protected ports.

- Forwarding behavior between a protected port and a nonprotected port proceeds normally per default behavior.

By default, no ports are configured as protected. Example 4-1 shows how to enable and verify switch ports that are configured for the protected port feature.

Example 4-1 *Configuring the Protected Port Feature*

```
Switch(config)# interface Fastethernet0/1
Switch(config-if)# switchport protected
Switch(config-if)# end

Switch# show interfaces FastEthernet 0/1 switchport
Name: Fa0/1
Switchport: Enabled
Administrative Mode: static access
...
Protected: true
```

Private VLAN (PVLAN)

As discussed in the "Protected Ports (PVLAN Edge)" section, the PVLAN feature prevents interhost communications providing port-based security among adjacent ports within a VLAN across one or more switches. PVLAN provides Layer 2 isolation to quarantine hosts from one another among ports within the same PVLAN.

Access ports in a PVLAN are allowed to communicate only with the certain designated router ports. In most cases, this is the default gateway IP address. Private VLANs and normal VLANs can coexist on the same switch. The PVLAN feature allows segregating traffic at Layer 2, thereby transforming a broadcast segment into a nonbroadcast multi-access-like segment. To prevent interhost and interserver communication, PVLAN can be used efficiently because the number of subnets or VLANs is greatly reduced, although the segmented approach within a single network segment is still achieved. The number is reduced because there is no need to create extra subnet/VLANs.

NOTE   The PVLAN feature is *not* available on all Cisco switches. Refer to Table 4-1 for a list of supported platforms.

The list that follows describes three types of PVLAN ports, as shown in Figure 4-1a:

- **Promiscuous:** A promiscuous port can communicate with all interfaces, including the isolated and community ports within a PVLAN. The function of the promiscuous port is to move traffic between ports in community or isolated VLANs. It can use access lists to identify which traffic can pass between these VLANs. Only one promiscuous port is allowed per single PVLAN, and it serves all the community and isolated VLANs in the Private VLAN.

- **Isolated:** An isolated PVLAN port has complete Layer 2 segregation from all the other ports within the same PVLAN, but not from the promiscuous ports. Traffic from the isolated port is forwarded only to the promiscuous ports and none other.

- **Community:** Community ports are logically combined groups of ports in a common community and can pass traffic among themselves and with promiscuous ports. Ports are separated at Layer 2 from all other interfaces in other communities or isolated ports within their PVLAN.

It is possible for isolated and community port traffic to enter or leave the switch through a trunk interface because trunks support VLANs carrying traffic among isolated, community, and promiscuous ports. Hence, PVLAN ports are associated with a separate set of VLANs that are used to create the PVLAN structure. A PVLAN uses VLANs in following three ways:

- **As a primary VLAN:** Carries traffic from a promiscuous port to isolated, community, and other promiscuous ports in the same primary VLAN.

- **As an isolated VLAN:** Carries traffic from isolated ports to a promiscuous port. Ports in the isolated VLAN cannot communicate at Layer 2 with any other port within the Private VLAN (either another community VLAN port or a port in the same isolated VLAN). To communicate with other ports, it must go through the promiscuous port.

- **As a community VLAN:** Carries traffic between community ports within the same community VLAN and to promiscuous ports. Ports in the community VLAN can communicate at Layer 2 with each other (only within the same community VLAN) but cannot communicate with ports in other community or isolated VLANs. To communicate with other ports, they must go through the promiscuous port. Multiple community VLANs can be configured in a PVLAN.

Figure 4-1a depicts the basic PVLAN components and the different types of PVLAN ports.

Figure 4-1a *PVLAN Components*

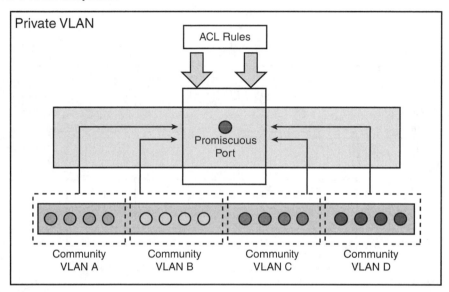

The isolated and community VLANs are also called *secondary VLANs*. PVLANs can be extended across multiple devices by trunking the primary, isolated, and community VLANs to other devices that support PVLANs.

In summary, a Private VLAN contains three elements: the Private VLAN itself, the secondary VLANs (known as the community VLAN and isolated VLAN), and the promiscuous port.

Figure 4-1b summarizes the PVLAN components and traffic flow policies among the PVLAN ports.

Figure 4-1b *PVLAN Traffic Flow Policies*

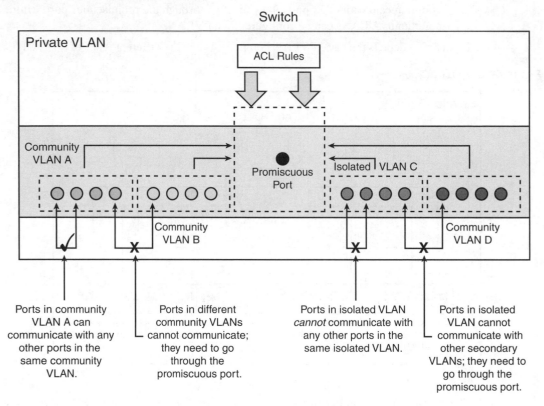

Table 4-1 shows a list of Cisco switches that support the PVLAN feature with the respective software version.

Table 4-1 *VLAN Support on Catalyst Switches*

Platform	Software Version	Isolated VLAN	PVLAN Edge (Protected Port)	Community VLAN
Catalyst 8500	Not Supported	—	—	—
Catalyst 6500/6000 — CatOS on Supervisor and Cisco IOS on MSFC	5.4(1) on Supervisor and 12.0(7)XE1 on MSFC	Yes	N/A	Yes
Catalyst 6500/6000 — Cisco IOS System software	12.1(8a)EX, 12.1(11b)E1	Yes	N/A	Yes

Table 4-1 *VLAN Support on Catalyst Switches (Continued)*

Platform	Software Version	Isolated VLAN	PVLAN Edge (Protected Port)	Community VLAN
Catalyst 5500/5000	Not Supported	—	—	—
Catalyst 4500/4000 — CatOS	6.2(1)	Yes	N/A	Yes
Catalyst 4500/4000 — Cisco IOS	12.1(8a)EW	Yes	N/A	12.2(20)EW
Catalyst 3750	12.2(20)SE—EMI	Yes	12.1(11)AX	Yes
Catalyst 3750 Metro	12.1(14)AX	No	Yes	No
Catalyst 3560	12.2(20)SE—EMI	Yes	12.1(19)EA1	Yes
Catalyst 3550	12.1(4)EA1	No	Yes	Not Currently Supported
Catalyst 2970	12.1(11)AX	No	Yes	No
Catalyst 2955	12.1(6)EA2	No	Yes	No
Catalyst 2950	12.0(5.2)WC1, 12.1(4)EA1	No	Yes	Not Currently Supported
Catalyst 2900XL/3500XL	12.0(5)XU (on 8MB switches only)	No	Yes	No
Catalyst 2948G-L3 / 4908G-L3	Not Supported	—	—	—
Catalyst 2948G/2980G	6.2	Yes	N/A	Yes
Catalyst 2940	12.1(13)AY	No	Yes	No
Catalyst 1900	Not Supported	—	—	—

Configuring PVLAN

NOTE   When enabling PVLAN, it is important to remember to configure the switch as VTP transparent mode before you can create a PVLAN. PVLANs are configured in the context of a single switch and cannot have members on other switches.

Perform the following steps to configure the PVLAN feature:

Step 1   Create the primary and secondary PVLANs. For example, configure VLAN 101 as a primary VLAN, VLANs 201 to 202 as community VLANs, and VLAN 301 as an isolated VLAN.

```
Hostname(config)# vlan 101
Hostname(config-vlan)# private-vlan primary
Hostname(config)# vlan 201
Hostname(config-vlan)# private-vlan community
Hostname(config)# vlan 202
Hostname(config-vlan)# private-vlan community
Hostname(config)# vlan 301
Hostname(config-vlan)# private-vlan isolated
```

Step 2   Associate the secondary VLANs to the primary PVLAN. For example, associate community VLANs 201 to 202 and isolated VLAN 301 with the primary VLAN 101.

```
Hostname(config)# vlan 101
Hostname(config-vlan)# private-vlan association 201-202,301
Hostname(config-vlan)# exit
```

NOTE   Only one isolated VLAN can be mapped to a primary VLAN, but multiple community VLANs can be mapped to a primary VLAN.

Step 3   Map secondary VLANs to the SVI (Switched Virtual Interface), which is the Layer 3 VLAN interface of a primary VLAN to allow Layer 3 switching of PVLAN ingress traffic.

For example, permit routing of secondary VLAN ingress traffic from VLANs 201 to 202 and 301 to the private VLAN 101 SVI (Layer 3 interface).

```
Hostname(config)# interface vlan 101
Hostname(config-if)# private-vlan mapping add 201-202,301
```

Step 4   Configure a Layer 2 interface as an isolated *or* community port, and associate the Layer 2 port to the primary VLAN and selected secondary VLAN pair. For example, configure interface FastEthernet 1/1 as a PVLAN host port in community VLAN 201, map it to a private-secondary PVLAN pair, configure FastEthernet 1/2 as a PVLAN host port in isolated VLAN 301, and map it to a private-secondary PVLAN pair.

```
Hostname(config)# interface Fastethernet 1/1
Hostname(config-if)# switchport mode private-vlan host
Hostname(config-if)# switchport private-vlan host-association 101 201
Hostname(config)# interface Fastethernet 1/2
Hostname(config-if)# switchport mode private-vlan host
Hostname(config-if)# switchport private-vlan host-association 101 301
```

Step 5 Configure a Layer 2 interface as a PVLAN promiscuous port and map the PVLAN promiscuous port to the primary VLAN and to the selected secondary VLAN pair. For example, configure interface FastEthernet 1/10 as a PVLAN promiscuous port, and map it to a private-secondary PVLAN pair.

```
Hostname(config)# interface Fastethernet 1/10
Hostname(config-if)# switchport mode private-vlan promiscuous
Hostname(config-if)# switchport private-vlan mapping 101 201-202,301
```

Use the **show interface private-vlan mapping** command and the **show interface [interface-id] switchport** command to verify the configuration.

Port Blocking

When a packet arrives at the switch, the switch performs a lookup for the destination MAC address in the MAC address table to determine which port it will use to send the packet out to send on. If no entry is found in the MAC address table, the switch will broadcast (flood) unknown unicast or multicast traffic out to all the ports in the same VLAN (broadcast domain). Forwarding an unknown unicast or multicast traffic to a protected port could raise security issues.

Unknown unicast or multicast traffic can be blocked from being forwarded by using the port blocking feature.

To configure port blocking for unknown unicast and multicast flooding, use the following procedures:

- The **switchport block multicast** interface configuration command to block unknown multicast forwarding to a port

- The **switchport block unicast** interface configuration command to block unknown unicast forwarding to a port

- The **show interfaces {*interface*} switchport** command to validate the port blocking configuration

By default, ports are not configured in blocking mode. Example 4-2 shows how to enable and verify switch ports configured for the port blocking feature.

Example 4-2 *Configuring the Port Blocking Feature*

```
Switch(config)# interface Fastethernet0/1
Switch(config-if)# switchport block multicast
Switch(config-if)# switchport block unicast
Switch(config-if)# end
Switch# show interfaces FastEthernet 0/1 switchport
Name: Fa0/1
Switchport: Enabled
Administrative Mode: static access
...
Protected: true
Unknown unicast blocked: enabled
Unknown multicast blocked: enabled
Appliance trust: none
```

Port Security

Port security is a dynamic feature that prevents unauthorized access to a switch port. The port security feature can be used to restrict input to an interface by identifying and limiting the MAC addresses of the hosts that are allowed to access the port. When secure MAC addresses are assigned to a secure port, the switch does not forward packets with source MAC addresses outside the defined group of addresses. To understand this process, think of the analogy of a secure car park facility, where a spot is reserved and marked with a particular car registration number so that no other car is allowed to park at that spot. Similarly, a switch port is configured with the secure MAC address of a host, and no other host can connect to that port with any other MAC address.

Port security can be implemented in the following three ways:

- Static secure MAC addresses are manually configured using the switchport **port-security mac-address [source-mac-address]** command and stored in the MAC address table and in the configuration.

- Dynamic secure MAC addresses are dynamically learned, stored in the MAC address table, but removed when the switch is reloaded or powered down.

- Sticky secure MAC addresses are the combination of items 1 and 2 in this list. They can be learned dynamically or configured statically and are stored in the MAC address table and in the configuration. When the switch reloads, the interface does not need to dynamically discover the MAC addresses if they are saved in the configuration file.

In the event of a violation, an action is required. A violation occurs when an attempt is made to access the switch port by a host address that is not found in the MAC address table, or when an address learned or defined on one secure interface is discovered on another secure interface in the same VLAN.

An interface can be configured for one of the following three security violation modes, based on the action to be taken when a violation occurs:

- **Protect:** This puts the port into the protected port mode, where all unicast or multicast packets with unknown source MAC addresses are dropped. No notification is sent out in this mode when security violation occurs.

- **Restrict:** Packets with unknown source addresses are dropped when the number of secure MAC addresses reaches the set limit allowed on the port. This continues until a sufficient number of secure MAC addresses is removed or the number of maximum allowable addresses is increased. Notification is sent out in this mode that a security violation has occurred. An SNMP trap is sent, a syslog message is logged, and the violation counter is incremented.

- **Shutdown:** When a port security violation occurs, the port is placed in error-disabled state, turning off its port LED. In this mode, an SNMP trap is sent out, a syslog message is logged, and the violation counter is incremented.

To enable the port security feature, use the **switchport port-security** interface configuration command. The command has several options.

Example 4-3 shows how to configure a static secure MAC address on a port and enable sticky learning.

Example 4-3   *Port Security Configuration Example 1*

```
Switch(config)# interface Fastethernet0/1
Switch(config-if)# switchport mode access
Switch(config-if)# switchport port-security
Switch(config-if)# switchport port-security mac-address 0009.6B90.F4FE
Switch(config-if)# switchport port-security mac-address sticky
Switch(config-if)# end
```

Example 4-4 shows how to configure a maximum of 10 secure MAC addresses on VLAN 5 on port interface FastEthernet 0/2. The **[vlan]** option in this command sets a maximum value per VLAN for the specified VLAN or range of VLANs.

Example 4-4   *Port Security Configuration Example 2*

```
Switch(config)# interface Fastethernet0/2
Switch(config-if)# switchport mode access
Switch(config-if)# switchport port-security maximum 10 vlan 5
Switch(config-if)# end
```

In addition to the configuration shown in Example 4-4, a port-security aging mechanism can be configured. By default the secure MAC addresses will not be aged out, and in normal port security configuration, the entries will remain in the MAC table until the switch is powered off. When using the sticky option, these MAC addresses will be stored until cleared manually.

There are two types of aging mechanisms:

- **Absolute:** The secure addresses on the port age out after a fixed specified time, and all references are flushed from the secure address list.

- **Inactivity:** Also known as *idle time*, the secure addresses on the port age out if they are idle, and no traffic from the secure source addresses passes for the specified time period.

Example 4-5 shows how to configure the aging time to 5 minutes for the inactivity aging type. In this example, aging is enabled for statically configured secure addresses on the port.

Example 4-5   *Port Security Aging Configuration Example*

```
Switch(config)# interface Fastethernet0/1
Switch(config-if)# switchport mode access
Switch(config-if)# switchport port-security aging time 5
Switch(config-if)# switchport port-security aging type inactivity
Switch(config-if)# switchport port-security aging static
```

Access Lists on Switches

The switch supports the following four types of ACLs for traffic filtering:

- Router ACL
- Port ACL
- VLAN ACL
- MAC ACL

Router ACL

As the name implies, Router ACLs are similar to the IOS ACL discussed in Chapter 2, "Access Control," and can be used to filter network traffic on the switched virtual interfaces (SVI). (SVI interfaces are Layer 3 interfaces on VLANs, on Layer 3 physical interfaces, and on Layer 3 EtherChannel interfaces.) Both standard and extended ACLs are supported. For more details to configure Router ACL, refer to Chapter 2.

Port ACL

Port ACLs are similar to Router ACLs but are supported on physical interfaces and configured on Layer 2 interfaces on a switch. Port ACL supports only inbound traffic filtering. Port ACL can be configured as three type access lists: standard, extended, and MAC-extended.

Processing of the Port ACL is similar to that of the Router ACLs; the switch examines ACLs associated with features configured on a given interface and permits or denies packet forwarding based on packet-matching criteria in the ACL.

When applied to a trunk port, the ACL filters traffic on all VLANs present on the trunk port. When applied to a port with voice VLAN, the ACL filters traffic on both data and voice VLANs.

The main benefit with Port ACL is that it can filter IP traffic (using IP access lists) and non-IP traffic (using MAC access list). Both types of filtering can be achieved—that is, a Layer 2 interface can have both an IP access list and a MAC access list applied to it at the same time.

NOTE   Port ACLs are not supported on EtherChannel interfaces.

VLAN ACL (VACL)

VLAN ACL (also called *VLAN map*) provides packet filtering for *all* types of traffic that are bridged within a VLAN or routed into or out of the VLAN. Unlike Router ACL, VACL is not defined by a direction (input or output). All packets entering the VLAN (bridged or routed) are checked against the VACL. It is possible to filter traffic based on the direction of the traffic by combining VACLs and Private VLAN features.

VACLs are processed in hardware, so there is no performance penalty in processing them. Therefore, they are also referred to as *wire-speed ACLs*. The forwarding rate remains unchanged regardless of the size of the access list because the lookup of VACLs is performed in hardware.

VACL on a Bridged Port

Figure 4-2 illustrates where the VACL is processed when VACL is applied on a bridged port for traffic from Host A in VLAN 5 that is communicating to Host B in VLAN 10 through the switch.

Figure 4-2   *VACL on a Bridged Port*

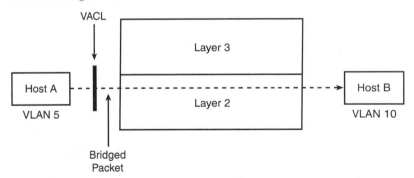

VACL on a Routed Port

Figure 4-3 illustrates how IOS ACL and VACL are applied on routed packets and Layer 3 switched packets. Following is the order of processing:

1 VACL for input VLAN

2 Input IOS ACL

3 Output IOS ACL

4 VACL for output VLAN

Figure 4-3 *VACL on a Routed Port*

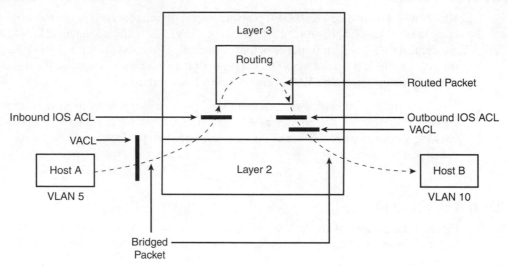

Configuring VACL

Perform the following steps to configure and apply a VACL (VLAN access map) on the switch:

1 Define the standard or extended access list to be used in VACL.

2 Define a VLAN access map.

3 Configure a match clause in a VLAN access map sequence.

4 Configure an action clause in a VLAN access map sequence.

5 Apply the VLAN access map to the specified VLANs.

6 Display VLAN access map information.

Example 4-6 shows how to define and apply a VACL to drop packets matching access list 1 from network 192.168.1.0/24; all other packets matching access list 2 are forwarded. The VACL is applied to VLANs 5 through 10.

Example 4-6 *VACL Configuration Example*

```
Switch(config)#access-list 1 permit 192.168.1.0 0.0.0.255
Switch(config)#access-list 2 permit any
Switch(config)#vlan access-map mymap 10
Switch(config-access-map)#match ip address 1
Switch(config-access-map)#action drop
Switch(config-access-map)#exit
Switch(config)#vlan access-map mymap 20
Switch(config-access-map)#match ip address 2
```

Example 4-6   *VACL Configuration Example (Continued)*

```
Switch(config-access-map)#action forward
Switch(config-access-map)#exit
Switch(config)# vlan filter mymap vlan-list 5-10
Switch(config-access-map)#end

Switch# show vlan access-map
Vlan access-map "mymap"  10
  Match clauses:
    ip address: 1
  Action:
    drop
Vlan access-map "mymap"  20
  Match clauses:
    ip address: 2
  Action:
    Forward

Switch# show vlan filter
VLAN Map mymap is filtering VLANs:
  5-10
```

MAC ACL

MAC ACL, also known as *Ethernet ACL*, can filter non-IP traffic on a VLAN and on a physical Layer 2 interface by using MAC addresses in a named MAC extended ACL. The steps to configure a MAC ACL are similar to those of extended named ACLs. MAC ACL supports only inbound traffic filtering.

To define the MAC Extended ACL, use the **mac access-list extended** command. Several non-IP protocols are supported.

After the MAC ACL is created, it can be applied to a Layer 2 interface using the **mac access-group [acl-name] in** command to filter non-IP traffic received on the interface.

Example 4-7 shows how to define and apply a MAC ACL to drop all (non-IP) AppleTalk Address Resolution Protocol (AARP) packets, allowing all other types of traffic.

Example 4-7   *MAC ACL Configuration Example*

```
Switch(config)# mac access-list extended my-mac-acl
Switch(config-ext-macl)# deny any any aarp
Switch(config-ext-macl)# permit any any
Switch(config-ext-macl)# exit
Switch(config)# interface Fastethernet0/10
Switch(config-if)# mac access-group my-mac-acl in
Switch(config-if)# end
Switch#
```

Spanning Tree Protocol Features

Spanning Tree Protocol (STP) resolves redundant topologies into loop-free, treelike topologies. When switches are interconnected via multiple paths, STP prevents loops from being formed. An STP loop (or forwarding loops) can occur when the entire network fails because of a hardware failure, a configuration issue, or a network attack. STP loops can be costly, causing major network outages. The following STP features can be used to improve the stability of the Layer 2 networks.

Bridge Protocol Data Unit (BPDU) Guard

Bridge protocol data units (BPDU) are data messages exchanged between bridges using spanning tree protocol to detect loops in a network topology. BPDU contains management and control data information that is used to determine the root bridge and establish the port roles—for example: root, designated, or blocked port.

The BPDU Guard feature is designed to keep the active topology predictable and to enhance switch network reliability by enforcing the STP domain borders.

The guard can be enabled globally on the switch or enabled on a per-interface basis. In a valid configuration, ports with port fast enabled do not receive BPDUs. Receiving a BPDU on a port with port fast enabled signals an invalid configuration, such as the connection of an unauthorized device, and the BPDU Guard feature puts the interface in the error-disabled state.

At the global level, BPDU Guard can be enabled on a port with port fast enabled using the **spanning-tree portfast bpduguard default** global configuration command. Spanning tree shuts down interfaces that are in a port fast operational state.

At the interface level, BPDU Guard can be enabled on an interface by using the **spanning-tree bpduguard enable** interface configuration command without also enabling the port fast feature. When the interface receives a BPDU, the switch assumes that a problem exists and puts the interface in the error-disabled state.

The BPDU Guard feature provides a secure response to invalid configurations because you must manually put the interface back in service. In a service-provider network environment, the BPUD Guard feature can be used to prevent an access port from participating in the spanning tree.

Root Guard

In a switched network environment with shared administrative control or in a service provider (SP) environment where there are many connections to other switches (into customer networks), it is important to identify the correct placement of the root bridge. If possible, it is also important to identify a specific predetermined location to achieve an optimal forwarding loop-free topology. There is no mechanism in the standard STP to enforce the position of the root bridge, as any bridge in a network with a *lower* bridge ID can assume the role of the root bridge. Sometimes because of a misconfiguration, a spanning tree may converge incorrectly by selecting an imprecise switch to be the root switch. This situation can be prevented by enabling the Root Guard feature. For example, you could enable Root Guard on SP-side switch interfaces that connect to a customer-side switch. With the Root Guard feature implemented, if a switch outside the SP network becomes the root switch, the interface is put in a blocked state, and spanning tree will select a new root switch. The customer's switch does not become the root switch and is not in the path to the root.

With the Root Guard feature, a Layer 2 interface is set as the designated port, and if any device through this port becomes the root bridge, the interface is placed into the blocked (root-inconsistent) state. The Root Guard feature can be enabled by using the **spanning-tree guard root** command in interface configuration mode.

EtherChannel Guard

The EtherChannel Guard feature is used to detect EtherChannel misconfigurations between the switch and a connected device. An example of a misconfiguration is when the channel parameters are not identical and do not match on both sides of the EtherChannel. Another example could be when only one side is configured with channel parameters. EtherChannel parameters must be the same on both sides for the guard to work.

When the switch detects an EtherChannel misconfiguration, the EtherChannel Guard places the switch interface in the error-disabled state and displays an error message.

The EtherChannel Guard feature can be enabled by using the **spanning-tree etherchannel guard misconfig** global configuration command.

Loop Guard

The Loop Guard feature provides an additional layer of protection against the Layer 2 forwarding loops (STP loops) by preventing alternative or root ports from becoming designated ports because of a failure resulting in a unidirectional link. This feature works best when enabled on all switches across a network. By default, the spanning tree does not send BPDUs on root or alternative ports.

The Loop Guard feature can be enabled by using the **spanning-tree loopguard default** global configuration command.

Dynamic Host Configuration Protocol (DHCP) Snooping

The DHCP Snooping feature provides network protection from rogue DHCP servers. It creates a logical firewall between untrusted hosts and DHCP servers. The switch builds and maintains a DHCP snooping table (also called DHCP binding database), shown in Figure 4-4a. In addition, the switch uses this table to identify and filter untrusted messages from the network. The switch maintains a DHCP binding database that keeps track of DHCP addresses that are assigned to ports, as well as filtering DHCP messages from untrusted ports. For incoming packets received on untrusted ports, packets are dropped if the source MAC address does not match MAC in the binding table entry.

Figure 4-4a *DHCP Snooping Table*

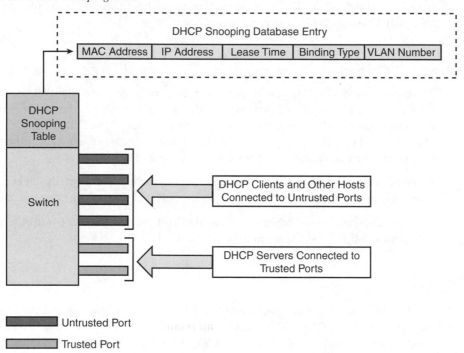

Figure 4-4b illustrates the DHCP Snooping feature in action, showing how the intruder is blocked on the untrusted port when it tries to intervene by injecting a bogus DHCP response packet to a legitimate conversation between the DHCP client and server.

Figure 4-4b *DHCP Snooping in Action*

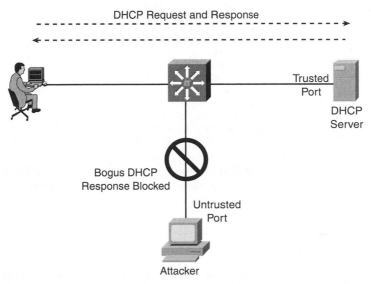

The DHCP Snooping feature can be configured for switches and VLANs. When enabled on a switch, the interface acts as a Layer 2 bridge, intercepting and safeguarding DHCP messages going to a Layer 2 VLAN. When enabled on a VLAN, the switch acts as a Layer 2 bridge within a VLAN domain.

For DHCP Snooping to function correctly, all DHCP servers connected to the switch must be configured as trusted interfaces. A trusted interface can be configured by using the **ip dhcp snooping trust** interface configuration command. All other DHCP clients connected to the switch and other ports receiving traffic from outside the network or firewall should be configured as untrusted by using the **no ip dhcp snooping trust** interface configuration command.

To configure the DHCP Snooping feature, first enable DHCP Snooping on a particular VLAN by using the **ip dhcp snooping vlan [vlan-id]** command in global configuration mode. (Repeat this command for multiple VLANs.) Next, enable DHCP Snooping globally by using the **ip dhcp snooping** command from the global configuration mode. Both options must be set to enable DHCP snooping.

In Example 4-8, the DHCP server is connected to the FastEthernet0/1 interface and is configured as a trusted port with a rate limit of 100 packets per second. The **rate limit** command ensures that a DHCP flood will not overwhelm the DHCP server. DHCP Snooping is enabled on VLAN 5 and globally activated.

Example 4-8 *DHCP Snooping Configuration Example*

```
Switch(config)# interface Fastethernet0/1
Switch(config-if)# ip dhcp snooping trust
Switch(config-if)# ip dhcp snooping limit rate 100
Switch(config-if)# exit
Switch(config)# ip dhcp snooping vlan 5
Switch(config)# ip dhcp snooping
Switch(config)# ip dhcp snooping information option
```

Use the **show ip dhcp snooping** command to display DHCP snooping settings. Use the **show ip dhcp snooping binding** command to display binding entries corresponding to untrusted ports.

IP Source Guard

IP Source Guard is a security feature that restricts IP traffic on untrusted Layer 2 ports by filtering traffic based on the DHCP snooping binding database or manually configured IP source bindings. This feature helps prevent IP spoofing attacks when a host tries to spoof and use the IP address of another host. Any IP traffic coming into the interface with a source IP address other than that assigned (via DHCP or static configuration) will be filtered out on the untrusted Layer 2 ports.

The IP Source Guard feature is enabled in combination with the DHCP snooping feature on untrusted Layer 2 interfaces. It builds and maintains an IP source binding table that is learned by DHCP snooping or manually configured (static IP source bindings). An entry in the IP source binding table contains the IP address and the associated MAC and VLAN numbers. The IP Source Guard is supported on Layer 2 ports only, including access and trunk ports.

Example 4-9 shows how to enable the IP Source Guard with dynamic source IP and MAC address filtering.

Example 4-9 *IP Source Guard Configuration Example 1*

```
Switch(config)#interface GigabitEthernet1/0/1
Switch(config-if)#ip verify source port-security
```

Example 4-10 shows how to enable the IP Source Guard with a static source IP address and MAC address filtering mapped on VLAN 5.

Example 4-10 *IP Source Guard Configuration Example 2*

```
Switch(config)# ip source binding 0011.0011.0011 vlan 5 10.1.1.11 interface
GigabitEthernet1/0/2
```

Use the **show ip verify source** command to display the IP Source Guard configuration and the **show ip source binding** command to display the IP source bindings on the switch.

Dynamic ARP Inspection (DAI)

Address Resolution Protocol (ARP) provides IP-to-MAC (32-bit IP address into a 48-bit Ethernet address) resolution. ARP operates at Layer 2 (the data-link layer) of the OSI model. ARP provides the translation mapping the IP address to the MAC address of the destination host using a lookup table (also known as the ARP cache).

Several types of attacks can be launched against a host or devices connected to Layer 2 networks by "poisoning" the ARP caches. A malicious user could intercept traffic intended for other hosts on the LAN segment and poison the ARP caches of connected systems by broadcasting forged ARP responses. Several known ARP-based attacks can have a devastating impact on data privacy, confidentiality, and sensitive information. To block such attacks, the Layer 2 switch must have a mechanism to validate and ensure that only valid ARP requests and responses are forwarded.

Dynamic ARP inspection is a security feature that validates ARP packets in a network. Dynamic ARP inspection determines the validity of packets by performing an IP-to-MAC address binding inspection stored in a trusted database, (the DHCP snooping binding database) before forwarding the packet to the appropriate destination. Dynamic ARP inspection will drop all ARP packets with invalid IP-to-MAC address bindings that fail the inspection. The DHCP snooping binding database is built when the DHCP snooping feature is enabled on the VLANs and on the switch.

NOTE   Dynamic ARP inspection inspects *inbound* packets only; it does not check *outbound* packets.

Figure 4-5a shows an example of an attacker attempting to spoof and hijack traffic for an important address (a default gateway in this example) by broadcasting to all hosts spoofing the MAC address of the router (using a gratuitous ARP). This will poison ARP cache entries (create an invalid ARP entry) on Host A and Host B, resulting in data being redirected to the wrong destination. Because of the poisoned entries, when Host A sends data destined for the router, it is incorrectly sent to the attacker instead. Dynamic ARP inspection locks down the IP-MAC mapping for hosts so that the attacking ARP is denied and logged.

Figure 4-5a *Dynamic ARP Inspection*

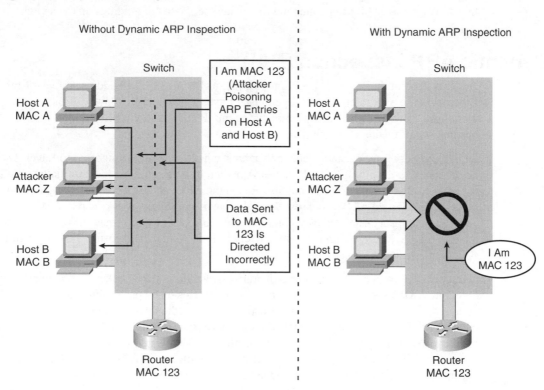

The dynamic ARP Inspection (DAI) feature safeguards the network from many of the commonly known man-in-the-middle (MITM) type attacks. Dynamic ARP Inspection ensures that only valid ARP requests and responses are forwarded.

Figure 4-5b illustrates the DAI feature in action and shows how the intruder is blocked on the untrusted port when it is trying to poison ARP entries.

Figure 4-5b *DAI-in Action*

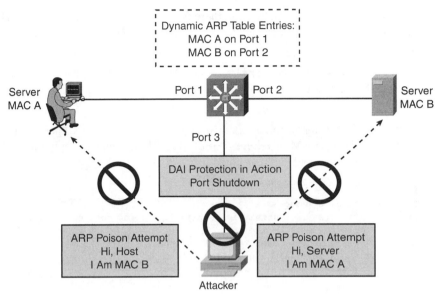

DAI in a DHCP Environment

As mentioned earlier, DAI relies on the entries in the DHCP snooping binding database to verify IP-to-MAC address bindings. Configure each secure interface as trusted using the **ip arp inspection trust** interface configuration command. The trusted interfaces bypass the ARP inspection validation checks, and all other packets are subject to inspection when they arrive on untrusted interfaces.

Enable DAI on a per-VLAN basis by using the **ip arp inspection vlan [*vlan-range*]** command from the global configuration command.

Example 4-11 shows how to configure an interface as trusted and how to enable DAI for VLANs 5 through 10.

Example 4-11 *DAI in a DHCP Environment Configuration Example*

```
Switch(config)# interface GigabitEthernet1/0/1
Switch(config-if)# ip arp inspection trust
Switch(config)# ip arp inspection vlan 5-10
```

DAI in a Non-DHCP Environment

In non-DHCP environments, because there is no DHCP snooping binding database, the DAI can validate ARP packets against a user-defined ARP ACL to map hosts with a statically configured IP address to their MAC address.

Use the **arp access-list [*acl-name*]** command from the global configuration mode on the switch to define an ARP ACL and apply the ARP ACL to the specified VLANs on the switch.

Example 4-12 shows how to configure an ARP ACL to permit ARP packets from host IP address 10.1.1.11 with MAC address 0011.0011.0011 and how to apply this ACL to VLAN 5 with the interface configured as untrusted.

Example 4-12 *DAI in a Non-DHCP Environment Configuration Example*

```
Switch(config)# arp access-list arpacl
Switch(config-arp-acl)# permit ip host 10.1.1.11 mac host 0011.0011.0011
Switch(config-arp-acl)# exit
Switch(config)# ip arp inspection filter arpacl vlan 5
Switch(config)# interface GigabitEthernet1/0/2
Switch(config-if)# no ip arp inspection trust
```

Use the **show ip arp inspection vlan [vlan# or range]** command to verify the configuration.

Rate Limiting Incoming ARP Packets

Because the switch CPU performs the DAI, there is a potential for an ARP flooding denial-of-service (DoS) attack resulting in performance degradation. To prevent this, ARP packets can be rate limited using the **ip arp inspection limit** command from the interface configuration mode to limit the rate of incoming ARP requests and responses. By default, 15 pps (packets per second) is allowed on untrusted interfaces; however, there is no limit on trusted interfaces. The burst interval is 1 second.

When the rate of incoming ARP packets exceeds the configured thresholds, the port is placed in the error-disabled state. The port will remain in this state until the user intervenes or the **errdisable recovery cause arp-inspection interval [seconds]** command is enabled, so that ports can automatically recover from this state after a specified timeout period.

Use the **show ip arp inspection interfaces** to display the trust state, the rate limit (pps stands for packets per second), and the burst interval configured for the interfaces.

Use the **show ip arp inspection vlan [vlan# or range]** command to display the DAI configuration and the operation state of the VLANs configured on the switch.

ARP Validation Checks

Specific additional checks can be performed on incoming ARP packets to validate the destination MAC address, the sender IP address in ARP requests, the target IP address in ARP responses, or the source MAC address. Use the **ip arp inspection validate {[src-mac] [dst-mac] [ip]}** command from the global configuration mode to enable these additional ARP validation checks.

Use the **show ip arp inspection statistics** command to display packet statistics on DAI-configured VLANs.

Advanced Integrated Security Features on High-End Catalyst Switches

In addition to the features previously discussed, several integrated security features are available on high-end catalyst switches such as the Catalyst 6500 series and the Catalyst 7600 series switches. These features provide protection from excessive or unnecessary traffic and against various types of DoS attacks.

The Cisco Catalyst series switches offer a strong set of integrated security features, including the following: hardware- and software-based CPU rate limiters (for DoS protection), user-based rate limiting, hardware-based MAC learning, uRPF check in hardware, TCP intercept hardware acceleration, and most important, the Control Plane Policing (CoPP) feature. CoPP is also supported on all Cisco Integrated Services Routers (ISRs). One of the main advantages is that most of these integrated security features are based on hardware and can be enabled concurrently with no performance penalty.

Control Plane Policing (CoPP) Feature

The traffic managed by a device can be divided into three functional components or planes:

- Data plane
- Management plane
- Control plane

The vast majority of traffic flows through the device via the data plane; however, the route processor handles certain traffic, such as routing protocol updates, remote-access services, and network management traffic such as SNMP. This type of traffic is referred to as the *control and management plane*. The route processor is critical to network operation. Therefore any service disruption or security compromise to the route processor, and hence the control and management planes, can result in network outages that impact regular operations. For example, a DoS attack targeting the route processor typically involves high bursty traffic resulting in excessive CPU utilization on the route processor. Such attacks can be devastating to network stability and availability. The bulk of traffic managed by the route processor is handled by way of the control and management planes.

The CoPP feature is used to protect the aforementioned control and management planes; to ensure stability, reachability, and availability and to block unnecessary or DoS traffic. CoPP uses a dedicated control plane configuration through the modular QoS CLI (MQC) to provide filtering and rate limiting capabilities for the control plane packets.

As mentioned earlier, the CoPP feature is available on all major Cisco router series including ISR. Table 4-2 provides a complete list of compatible hardware and software support.

Table 4-2 *CoPP Support on Cisco Routers*

Router Models	Cisco IOS Software Release
Cisco 12000 Series	Release 12.0(29)S and later
Cisco 7600 Series	Release 12.2(18)SXD1 and later
Cisco 6500 Series	Release 12.2(18)SXD1 and later
Cisco 7200 Series Cisco 7500 Series	Release 12.2(18)S and later
Cisco 1751 Router Cisco 2600/2600-XM Series Cisco 3700 Series Cisco 7200 Series	Release 12.3(4)T and later
Cisco 1800 Series Cisco 2800 Series	Release 12.3(8)T and later
Cisco 3800 Series	Release 12.3(11)T and later

Perform the following steps to configure and apply the CoPP feature:

Step 1 Define a packet classification criterion. There are a number of ways to categorize the type of traffic—for example, by using an access list or protocol or IP precedence values.

```
Hostname(config)# class-map {traffic_class_name}
Hostname(config-cmap)# match {access-list | protocol | ip prec | ip dscp | vlan}
```

Step 2 Define a service policy. Note that flow policing is the only valid option available (as of this writing) in the policy map for CoPP.

```
Hostname(config-pmap)# policy-map {service_policy_name}
Hostname(config-pmap)# class {traffic_class_name}
Hostname(config-pmap-c)# police <rate> conform-action <action> exceed-action
  <action>
```

Step 3   Enter control plane configuration mode using the **control-plane** global command. In this CP submode, the service policies are attached to the control plane.

```
Hostname(config)# control-plane
```

Step 4   Apply QoS policy configured to the control plane.

```
Hostname(config-cp)# service-policy {input | output} {service_policy_name}
```

NOTE   The CoPP feature is also available as part of the integrated Network Foundation Protection (NFP) security features on the Cisco ISR (Integrated Services Router) platforms.

CPU Rate Limiters

The Supervisor Engine 720 (SUP720) is available for high-end Catalyst 6500/7600 series switches and supports several integrated security features, including one that is important to mention. SUP720 has built-in "special case" CPU rate limiters to classify traffic that cannot be categorized otherwise. The built-in special case CPU rate limiters use an access list (examples include IP options cases, time to live [TTL] and maximum transmission unit [MTU] failure cases, and packets with errors). The CPU rate limit is mainly used for DoS protection.

Layer 2 Security Best Practices

To conclude this chapter, a list of best practices is presented here for implementing, managing, and maintaining secure Layer 2 network:

- Manage the switches in a secure manner. For example, use SSH, authentication mechanism, access list, and set privilege levels.
- Restrict management access to the switch so that untrusted networks are not able to exploit management interfaces and protocols such as SNMP.
- Always use a dedicated VLAN ID for all trunk ports.
- Be skeptical; avoid using VLAN 1 for anything.
- Disable DTP on all non-trunking access ports.
- Deploy the Port Security feature to prevent unauthorized access from switching ports.
- Use the Private VLAN feature where applicable to segregate network traffic at Layer 2.
- Use MD5 authentication where applicable.
- Disable CDP where possible.

- Prevent denial-of-service attacks and other exploitation by disabling unused services and protocols.

- Shut down or disable all unused ports on the switch, and put them in a VLAN that is not used for normal operations.

- Use port security mechanisms to provide protection against a MAC flooding attack.

- Use port-level security features such as DHCP Snooping, IP Source Guard, and ARP security where applicable.

- Enable Spanning Tree Protocol features (for example, BPDU Guard, Loopguard, and Root Guard).

- Use Switch IOS ACLs and Wire-speed ACLs to filter undesirable traffic (IP and non-IP).

Summary

This chapter presents a basic overview of Layer 2 security. The chapter gives you configuration examples and brings together the integrated-security features available on Cisco switches, such as port-level controls, port blocking, port security Private VLAN (PVLAN), and many more. The chapter discusses the various configurable ACLs that can be used on the switches, including the wire-speed ACLs. The chapter takes a quick look at the Spanning Tree Protocol features and safeguard mechanisms available to prevent STP attacks. Cisco switches offer unique features to mitigate common attacks on the services such as DHCP, DNS, and ARP-cache poisoning attacks. The chapter briefly outlines some platform-specific integrated security features available on the high-end switch platforms. The chapter concludes with the summary of Layer 2 security best practices to implement, manage, and maintain a secure Layer 2 network.

References

http://www.cisco.com/en/US/products/hw/switches/ps700/
products_tech_note09186a008013565f.shtml

http://www.cisco.com/en/US/products/hw/switches/ps5528/
products_configuration_guide_chapter09186a00802b7c35.html

http://www.cisco.com/en/US/products/hw/switches/ps5528/
products_configuration_guide_chapter09186a00803a9a88.html

http://www.cisco.com/en/US/products/hw/switches/ps708/
products_configuration_guide_chapter09186a00804357b1.html

http://www.cisco.com/en/US/products/hw/switches/ps5528/
products_configuration_guide_chapter09186a00803a9a24.html

http://www.cisco.com/en/US/products/hw/switches/ps5528/
products_configuration_guide_chapter09186a00803a9a23.html

http://www.cisco.com/en/US/products/hw/switches/ps708/
products_configuration_guide_chapter09186a0080435872.html

http://www.cisco.com/en/US/products/ps6642/
products_white_paper0900aecd804fa16a.shtml

CHAPTER 5

Cisco IOS Firewall

Security is no longer a straightforward product or technology enabler, but a core system in a network design. The innovative flagship Cisco IOS Software provides an array of security solutions including the flagship IOS Firewall feature set. This set provides integrated firewall and intrusion detection technology for the Cisco IOS Software. The Cisco IOS Firewall feature is a stateful-inspection software component of Cisco IOS Software.

The Cisco IOS Firewall feature set provides a single point of protection at the network perimeter, making security policy enforcement an inherent component of the network.

Cisco IOS Firewall consists of several major subsystems: an advanced firewall engine for stateful-packet inspection (SPI), Context-Based Access Control (CBAC), Zone-Based Policy Firewall (ZFW), Intrusion Prevention Systems (IPS), Authentication Proxy, Port-to-Application Mapping (PAM), Multi-VRF firewall, Transparent firewall, and several others.

This chapter focuses mainly on the SPI and Classic Firewall CBAC, illustrating fundamental concepts and functions of how stateful inspection works and a step-by-step process to configure the Cisco IOS Firewall in the classical CBAC format.

The chapter also highlights some of the Advanced IOS Firewall features introduced in the newer IOS Software versions.

The chapter also covers the new Zone-Based Policy Firewall (ZFW) model, providing an overview of the new zone-based concept and a configuration example that uses the new Cisco Policy Language (CPL) commands.

Router-Based Firewall Solution

The Cisco IOS Firewall feature set provides network security with integrated, inline security solutions. The IOS Firewall feature set is a suite of security services provisioning a single point of protection at the network perimeter. In addition, the IOS Firewall feature is widely available on a range of IOS software-based devices, thereby offering sophisticated security and policy enforcement for network connections.

The Cisco IOS Firewall feature is a stateful-inspection firewall engine with application-level intelligence. This provides dynamic control to permit or deny traffic flow, thereby providing enhanced security. In the simplest form, the principal function of a firewall is to monitor and filter traffic. Cisco routers can be configured with the IOS Firewall feature in one of the following deployment scenarios:

- A firewall router facing the Internet.
- A firewall router to protect the internal network from the external network. An external network can be any network outside the organization (for example, a customer or a partner network).
- A firewall router between groups of networks in the internal network.
- A firewall router that provides secure connections to or from remote or branch offices.

Cisco IOS Software provides an extensive set of security features to design customized firewall solutions to fit an organization's security policy. A Cisco networking device running Cisco IOS Software can be configured to function as a firewall by using several solutions available in the IOS Firewall feature set.

The Cisco IOS Firewall consists of several major subsystems:

- **Cisco IOS Firewall stateful packet inspection (SPI):** SPI provides true firewall capabilities to protect networks against unauthorized traffic and to control legitimate business-critical data.

- **Context-Based Access Control (CBAC):** CBAC (now known as Classic Firewall) is a stateful-inspection firewall engine that provides dynamic traffic filtering functionality.

- **Intrusion Prevention System (IOS IPS) (formerly known as IOS IDS):** Cisco IOS IPS offers integrated IPS functionality as part of the Cisco IOS Software. From IOS Version 12.3T, Cisco IOS IPS replaces the previous IOS IDS functionality by implementing a large part of classic sensor functionality as part of the IOS-based device. IOS IPS is an inline intrusion detection sensor that scans packets and sessions flowing through the router to identify any of the Cisco IOS IPS signatures that protect the network from internal and external threats.

- **Authentication proxy:** The authentication proxy feature (also known as Proxy Authentication) allows security policy enforcement on a per-user basis. Earlier, user access and policy enforcement was associated with a user's IP address or a single global policy applied to an entire user group. With the authentication proxy feature, users can now be authenticated and authorized on a per-user policy with access control customized to an individual level.

- **Port-to-Application Mapping (PAM):** PAM allows you to customize TCP or User Datagram Protocol (UDP) port numbers for network services or applications to nonstandard ports (for example, HTTP service using TCP port 8080 instead of the default port 80). CBAC inspection leverages this information to examine nonstandard application-layer protocols.

- **Network Address Translation (NAT):** NAT hides internal IP addresses from networks that are external to the firewall. NAT was designed to provide IP address conservation and for internal IP networks that use the unregistered private address space per RFC 1918. NAT translates these private IP addresses into legal registered addresses as packets traverse through the NAT device. This provides a basic low-level security by effectively hiding the internal network from the outside world.

- **Zone-Based Policy Firewall (ZFW):** ZFW is a new enhanced security tool available in the Cisco IOS Software-based firewall feature set. ZFW offers a completely revamped configuration syntax that offers network protection that uses intuitive policies and increased granularity to control unauthorized network access.

Several other security solutions are available on Cisco IOS. These include Lock-and-Key, Reflexive access list, TCP Intercept, IPsec, and AAA support. This chapter focuses primarily on the CBAC and ZFW solutions available in the IOS Firewall feature set.

Context-Based Access Control (CBAC)

CBAC is the Cisco IOS Firewall feature set—an advanced firewall engine that provides traffic-filtering functionality and can be used as an integral part of the network. The main features of CBAC include the following:

- CBAC protects internal networks from external intrusion.

- CBAC provides denial of service (DoS) protection.

- CBAC provides a per-application control mechanism across network perimeters.

- CBAC examines the transport layer, network layer, and upper-layer application-protocol information, keeping track of the flows and the state of each session (for example, HTTP, Simple Mail Transfer Protocol (SMTP), and FTP).

- CBAC maintains state information for every connection passing through the firewall in a session table (also called the state table). The connection information from the state table is used to make intelligent decisions about whether packets should be permitted or denied, thereby dynamically creating temporary openings in the firewall.

- CBAC generates real-time event alerts and audit trails. Alerts and audit trail information can be configured on a per-application protocol basis.

- Upon detecting suspicious activity, the real-time event alert feature sends SYSLOG error messages to central management consoles for notification.

- Enhanced audit trail features use SYSLOG to track all network transactions used for advance analysis and reporting.

NOTE   CBAC is being replaced with the new ZFW configuration model in the new Cisco IOS
         Software releases. ZFW will also be covered in this chapter. All new features will be offered
         in the new ZFW configuration model. There is no end-of-life plan (as of this writing) for
         CBAC, but there will be no new features added into CBAC.

CBAC Functions

CBAC provides networkwide protection by using the following functions:

- Traffic filtering
- Traffic inspection
- Alerts and audit trails

Traffic Filtering

CBAC is a software-based firewall feature that offers dynamic traffic filtering capabilities
to filter TCP and UDP packets based on upper-layer application protocols such as HTTP,
SMTP, and FTP to name a few. For CBAC to function, the network must be divided in two
logical segments: "trusted or protected" and "untrusted or unprotected." The principal of
CBAC traffic filtering is to allow any traffic that originates from the trusted network and
goes out to the untrusted network through the firewall.

Traffic Inspection

CBAC inspects traffic that traverses through the firewall and manages state information for
all the TCP and UDP sessions. This state information is used to create temporary openings
through the firewall to allow return traffic and additional data connections for permissible
sessions.

With the application-level awareness, CBAC maintains TCP and UDP connections, which
provide all the necessary information to perform deep packet inspection in the data payload
for any malicious activity. For example, as shown in Figure 5-1, an intruder could craft a
malicious, unauthorized, non-SMTP activity packet encapsulated in an SMTP packet
destined on TCP port 25. In conventional access list filtering, this packet would be allowed
because it would check only the Layer 3 and Layer 4 information in the packet. With CBAC
packet inspection, the packet is further examined for known SMTP operations as per RFC
standards, and any noncompliance operation (illegal commands) in the payload is blocked.

Based on this inspection method, several types of network attacks that use the embedding
technique to pass malicious traffic encapsulating in known application protocol packets can
be prevented.

Figure 5-1   *Application-Aware Traffic Inspection*

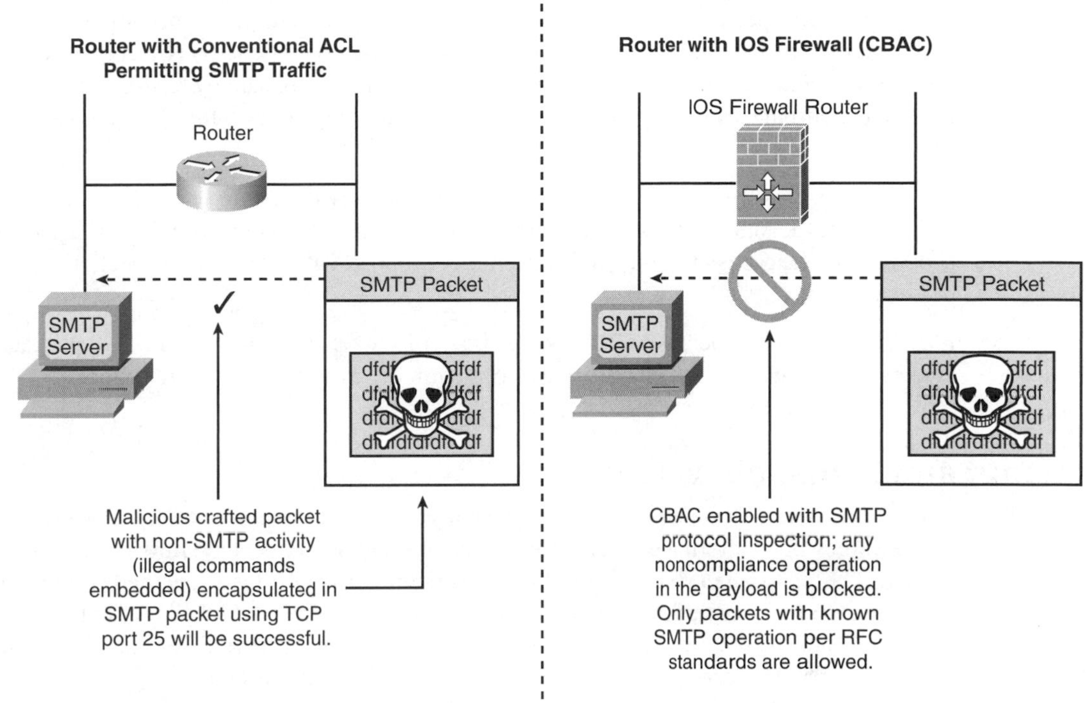

Alerts and Audit Trails

In addition to traffic inspection, CBAC can generate real-time event alerts and audit trails for all the session information maintained in the state table. The enhanced audit trail feature uses SYSLOG to track all network transactions, recording information such as source/destination host addresses, ports used, and the total number of transmitted bytes with time stamps. This information can be valuable for advanced session-based reporting, anomaly identification, or the charting of network baselines. For any suspicious activity, CBAC can send real-time event alerts using SYSLOG notification messages to a management console. CBAC inspection rules can be configured for reporting event alerts and audit trail information on a per-application-protocol basis.

How CBAC Works

The following sections highlight the fundamental concepts of how CBAC inspects packets and maintains state information for all the connections, thereby providing intelligent filtering.

Packet Inspection

CBAC performs per-protocol inspection. Each protocol that requires inspection is individually enabled, and an interface and interface direction (in or out) is specified where inspection originates. Only the specified protocols will be inspected by CBAC. All other protocols continue uninterrupted, subject to other router processes—for example, NAT, routing, and ACL.

Packets entering the firewall are subject to inspection only if they first pass the inbound access list at the input interface and outbound access list at the output interface. If a packet is denied by the access list, the packet is simply dropped without CBAC inspection performed.

For TCP protocol inspection, CBAC keeps track of sequence numbers in all TCP packets. Packets with sequence numbers that are not within the expected ranges are dropped.

Timeout and Threshold Values

CBAC uses several timeout and threshold values to manage session state information. These values help determine when to drop sessions that do not become fully established. This also helps to free up system resources, dropping sessions after a specified amount of idle time. CBAC sends a reset message for all dropped sessions to both sides (source and destination) of the session. The system receiving the reset message releases the incomplete connection from its process, thereby clearing the resource allocation table.

CBAC monitors the thresholds in the following three ways:

- The total number of half-open TCP or UDP sessions
- The number of half-open sessions based on time
- The number of per-host half-open TCP sessions

The Session State Table

CBAC maintains a session state table with connection information, such as the source/destination IP addresses, source/destination port numbers, and the application protocol information. For every incoming packet that CBAC inspects, the state table is updated with all the information. This information is used to punch a dynamic hole in the firewall access list for the return traffic. Return traffic will be permitted back through the firewall only if an entry in the state table indicates that the packet belongs to a permissible session. Example

5-1 shows sample session state table information, and Example 5-2 shows the dynamic ACL entry that corresponds to the information in this state table.

Example 5-1 *Connection Information in the State Table*

```
Router# show ip inspect session
Established Sessions
  Session 25A4E53 (10.1.1.1:11006)=>(20.1.1.1:23) tcp SIS_OPEN
```

UDP Connections

UDP is a connectionless transport-layer protocol; hence, there is no state information available to track the flow of the connections. CBAC deals with UDP sessions by examining the information in the packet and determining whether the packet is similar to the UDP packet exited earlier. Returning UDP packets are checked within the idle timeout period to ensure that they have the corresponding source/destination IP addresses and port numbers.

Dynamic ACL Entries

As discussed earlier, CBAC uses the connection information from the session table to open dynamic holes in the firewall access list for the returning traffic (that would normally be blocked). CBAC dynamically adds and removes access list entries at the firewall interfaces. These temporary openings are created in accordance with the state table for all inspected traffic that originates from an internal (protected) network outbound toward the unprotected zone through the firewall. The purpose of these access list entries is to examine traffic flowing back into the internal network. These entries create temporary openings in the firewall to permit only traffic that is part of a permissible session. Example 5-2 shows a dynamic ACL entry (corresponding to Example 5-1) that permits returning Telnet traffic initiated by a host from the internal network.

Example 5-2 *Dynamic ACL Entry Corresponding to the State Table*

```
Router# show ip access-lists
Extended IP access list 101
    permit tcp host 20.1.1.1 eq telnet host 10.1.1.1 eq 11006 (16 matches)
    permit tcp any host WebServer eq http
    deny ip any any (12 matches)
```

NOTE   The dynamically created access list entries that allow returning traffic are temporary and are not saved to the nonvolatile random-access memory (NVRAM).

Embryonic (Half-Open) Sessions

CBAC provides DoS detection and prevention. An excessive number of half-open sessions (either absolute or measured as the arrival rate) could indicate the possible occurrence of a denial-of-service attack. Traffic patterns can be established for a TCP SYN-flood type attack. TCP is a connection-oriented transport protocol that requires completing a three-way handshake mechanism. Incomplete (half-open) connections mean that the session has not completed the TCP three-way handshake; hence, the session is not established. Because UDP is a connectionless protocol, there is no handshake mechanism; incomplete sessions (half-open) in UDP context indicate that the firewall has detected no return traffic.

CBAC monitors the total number of half-open connections and the rate of session establishment attempts for both TCP and UDP half-open connections. CBAC monitors these values several times per minute. Adjusting threshold values for network connections helps prevent DoS attacks by controlling the number of half-open sessions, thereby freeing up system resources occupied by half-open sessions.

Example 5-3 shows a CBAC session table with few half-open (incomplete) TCP connections.

Example 5-3   *Sample Half-Open Connections*

```
Router# show ip inspect session
Half-open Sessions
  Session 63938D28 (10.1.1.2:11000)=>(20.1.1.2:23) tcp SIS_OPENING
  Session 63938EB8 (10.1.1.2:11001)=>(20.1.1.2:25) tcp SIS_OPENING
  Session 639C2343 (10.1.1.20:11012)=>(20.0.0.20:23) tcp SIS_OPENING
  Session 63976A22 (10.1.1.20:11013)=>(20.0.0.20:80) tcp SIS_OPENING
```

When the number of half-open connections exceeds the specified threshold (using the **ip inspect max-incomplete high** or **ip inspect one-minute high** number), CBAC will delete subsequent half-open sessions as required to accommodate new incoming connections. CBAC continues to delete the half-open connection requests as required until the number of existing half-open sessions drops below another specified threshold (using the **ip inspect max-incomplete low** or **ip inspect one-minute low** number). See Table 5-1 for more details on these commands and threshold values.

Per-Host DoS Prevention

CBAC provides a more aggressive TCP-based host-specific DoS prevention. CBAC monitors the total number of half-open connections initiated to the same destination host address. When the number of incomplete (half-open) TCP connections exceeds the configured threshold, CBAC blocks all subsequent connections to the host for the specified block-time, thereby preventing the flood. To configure per-host CBAC monitoring, use the **ip inspect tcp max-incomplete host** command. Refer to Table 5-1 for more details on this command.

Example 5-4 shows how to change the max-incomplete host to 100 half-open sessions, with block-time timeout to 5 minutes.

Example 5-4 *Per-Host CBAC Monitoring for DoS Prevention*

```
Router(config)# ip inspect tcp max-incomplete host 100 block-time 5
```

CBAC-Supported Protocols

CBAC can be enabled to inspect all TCP and UDP sessions, regardless of the application-layer protocol. This method is called *single-channel*, or *generic*, TCP/UDP inspection. For TCP/UDP generic inspection to work, the return traffic must have the same source/ destination IP address and port numbers. It must also be within the sequence number window. If the port number changes, the packet will be dropped.

In addition, CBAC can specifically inspect individual application-layer protocols to maintain the connection information for each session. Application-layer protocol inspection takes precedence over the TCP or UDP protocol inspection. The following application-layer protocols are supported and can be configured for CBAC inspection:

- CU-SeeMe
- FTP
- H.323 (such as NetMeeting)
- HTTP (Java blocking)
- ICMP
- Microsoft NetShow
- RealAudio
- RTSP (Real-Time Streaming Protocol)
- RPC (Sun RPC, not DCE RPC)
- SMTP (Simple Mail Transport Protocol)
- ESMTP (Extended Simple Mail Transport Protocol)
- SQL*Net
- StreamWorks
- TFTP
- UNIX R-commands (such as rlogin, rexec, and rsh)
- VDOLive

Configuring CBAC

To configure CBAC, perform the following steps:

Step 1   Select an interface: internal or external.

Step 2   Configure an IP access list.

Step 3   Define an inspection rule.

Step 4   Configure global timeouts and thresholds (optional).

Step 5   Apply the access list and the inspection rule to an interface.

Step 6   Verify and monitor CBAC.

Step 1—Select an Interface: Internal or External

CBAC can be configured either on an internal or external interface of the firewall.

- *Internal* refers to the trusted/protected side where sessions must originate for traffic to be permitted through the firewall.

- *External* refers to the untrusted/unprotected side where sessions cannot originate. Sessions originating from the external side will be blocked.

Figure 5-2   *Internal Versus External Interface*

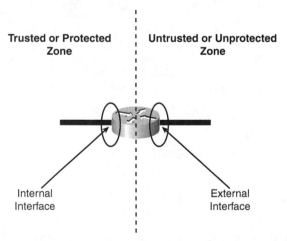

Although CBAC is recommended to be configured in one direction per interface, it can be configured in two directions (also known as bidirectional CBAC) at one or more interfaces when the networks on both sides of the firewall require protection, such as with extranet or intranet configurations, and for protection against DoS attacks.

Step 2—Configure an IP Access List

For CBAC to work, an IP access list is configured to create temporary openings through the firewall to allow return traffic. It is important to remember that the access list must be an extended access list.

There is no basic template for configuring the access list. Configuration depends on the security policy of an organization. The access list should be kept simple, starting with a basic initial configuration. Making the access list complex and cluttered could unintentionally introduce security risks by allowing unwanted traffic through the firewall, thereby putting the protected network at risk. It is essential to understand and verify the access list before applying it in a production environment.

Follow these general guidelines to create an access list:

- Explicitly block all network traffic that originates from the unprotected zone and moves to the protected zone, unless required. For example, when hosting a web server in the protected zone, it is explicitly required to permit HTTP (TCP port 80) that originates from the unprotected zone.

Step 3—Define an Inspection Rule

CBAC requires defining an inspection rule to specify which IP traffic (application-layer protocols) will be inspected by the firewall engine.

An inspection rule should specify each desired application-layer protocol as well as the generic TCP or UDP if required. The inspection rule consists of a series of statements, each listing a protocol that specifies the same inspection rule name, as shown in Example 5-5. Inspection rule statements can include other options, such as controlling alert and audit trail messages and checking IP packet fragmentation.

Use the **ip inspect name** global configuration command to create a CBAC inspection rule set for the required application-layer protocol. Example 5-5 shows how to enable inspection for HTTP, FTP, SMTP, and generic TCP and UDP protocols. Other application protocols (not defined here) can be enabled as required.

Example 5-5 *Define CBAC Inspection Rules*

```
Router(config)# ip inspect name myfw http
Router(config)# ip inspect name myfw ftp
Router(config)# ip inspect name myfw smtp
Router(config)# ip inspect name myfw tcp
Router(config)# ip inspect name myfw udp
```

Step 4—Configure Global Timeouts and Thresholds

CBAC uses several timeout and threshold values to determine the state of the session and the duration for which it is maintained. At times, connections are continually maintained for abruptly terminated sessions that occupy unnecessary resources. Incomplete sessions, idle (unused) sessions, or abruptly terminated sessions can be cleared using the timeout and threshold values.

The timeout and threshold values can be used either with default values or can be tuned to suit the network requirement. Table 5-1 shows the available CBAC timeout and threshold commands and their default values. Use the commands listed in the table to modify global timeout or threshold values as required.

Table 5-1   *Global Timeout and Threshold Values*

Timeout or Threshold Values	Command	Default
The length of time the software waits for a TCP session to reach the established state before dropping the session	**ip inspect tcp synwait-time** *seconds*	30 seconds
The length of time a TCP session will still be managed after the firewall detects a FIN-exchange	**ip inspect tcp finwait-time** *seconds*	5 seconds
The length of time a TCP session will still be managed after no activity (the TCP idle timeout)	**ip inspect tcp idle-time** *seconds*	3600 seconds (1 hour)
The length of time a UDP session will still be managed after no activity (the UDP idle timeout)	**ip inspect udp idle-time** *seconds*	30 seconds
The length of time a DNS name lookup session will still be managed after no activity	**ip inspect dns-timeout** *seconds*	5 seconds
The number of existing half-open sessions that will cause the software to start deleting half-open sessions	**ip inspect max-incomplete high** *number*	500 existing half-open sessions
The number of existing half-open sessions that will cause the software to stop deleting half-open sessions	**ip inspect max-incomplete low** *number*	400 existing half-open sessions
The rate of new unestablished sessions in 1-minute intervals that will cause the software to start deleting half-open sessions	**ip inspect one-minute high** *number*	500 half-open sessions per minute
The rate of new unestablished sessions in 1-minute intervals that will cause the software to stop deleting half-open sessions	**ip inspect one-minute low** *number*	400 half-open sessions per minute
The number of existing half-open TCP sessions with the same destination host address that will cause the software to start dropping half-open sessions to the same destination host address	**ip inspect tcp max-incomplete host** *number* **block-time** *minutes*	50 existing half-open TCP sessions; 0 minutes

The information in Table 5-1 is taken from "Configuring Context-Based Access Control" at http://www.cisco.com/en/US/docs/ios/12_0/security/configuration/guide/sccbac.html#wp4154.

Step 5—Apply the Access List and the Inspection Rule to an Interface

For CBAC to take effect, the access list and the inspection rules configured earlier need to be applied to the interface.

Deciding where CBAC should be configured (internal or external interface) is subjective. As shown in Figure 5-3, CBAC inspection can be configured on either internal or external interfaces—a decision that depends entirely on the security policy. When making that decision, consider which segment is required to be protected:

- Apply CBAC inspection to the external (outbound) interface when configuring CBAC for outbound traffic.

- Apply CBAC inspection to the internal (inbound) interface when configuring CBAC for inbound traffic.

To apply an inspection rule to an interface, use the **ip inspect** *inspection-name* {**in** | **out**} command in interface configuration mode.

Figure 5-3   *Applying ACL and CBAC Inspection*

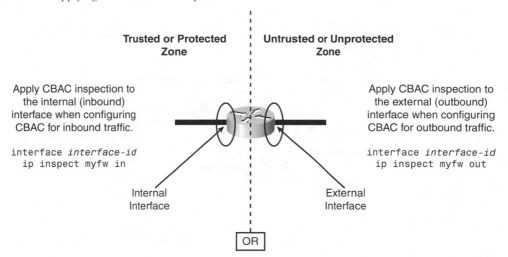

Step 6—Verifying and Monitoring CBAC

Use the **show ip inspect [config | interface]** command or the **show ip inspect all** command to verify CBAC configuration settings. To view the statistics and session information table with all the established and half-open connections for all session flow through the firewall, use the **show ip inspect session [detail]** command. In addition, use the **show ip access lists** command to verify the dynamic access list entries populated in the firewall access list, as shown in Example 5-1 and Example 5-2.

Putting It All Together

Figure 5-4 depicts a simple CBAC scenario for protecting a web server in the internal network. CBAC inspection can be applied on internal or external interfaces. Access list 101 shows that HTTP traffic that originates from an external network that is external to the web server is permitted. All other traffic is explicitly denied. Traffic originating from the internal network (protected zone) will pass through. Maintaining session table and a corresponding dynamic ACL entry will be punched in ACL 101 to allow all returning traffic.

Figure 5-4 *Putting It All Together*

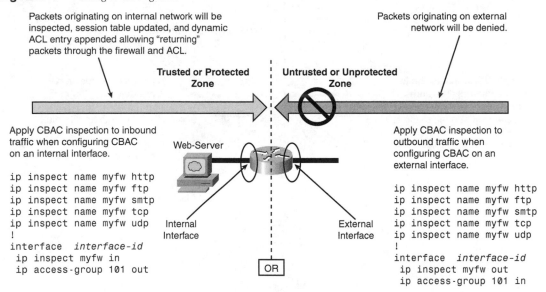

IOS Firewall Advanced Features

Several new enhancements and advanced capabilities have been added in the IOS Firewall feature set in IOS Software 12.3T and 12.4 mainline versions. The following section highlights some of the commonly used advanced features.

HTTP Inspection Engine

The HTTP inspection engine in the IOS Firewall has been enhanced with the introduction of Advanced Application Inspection and Control. For HTTP port 80 web traffic passing through the conventional firewalls, there is a possibility that non-HTTP traffic can be embedded or tunneled in the HTTP traffic (for example, Instant Messaging (IM) or any malicious traffic), thereby bypassing the firewall. Using this embedding technique, malformed packets can be crafted to carry viruses, worms, Trojans, or any other malicious activity. With deep packet inspection, IOS Firewall inspects the data streams to ensure that traffic that is assumed to be HTTP is legitimate web browsing and not IM or illegitimate traffic that is trying to gain unauthorized access through the firewall.

As shown in Figure 5-5, the HTTP Inspection Engine gives IOS Firewall engine more granular control and the intelligence to block non-HTTP traffic by challenging its legitimacy and conformance to standards. The HTTP inspection performs packet inspection to detect whether any applications are being tunneled through port 80.

Packets not conforming to the standards in HTTP protocol are dropped. A reset message is sent out, and a SYSLOG message is generated accordingly.

This feature was introduced in IOS Version 12.3(14)T.

Figure 5-5 *HTTP Inspection Engine with Advanced Application Inspection*

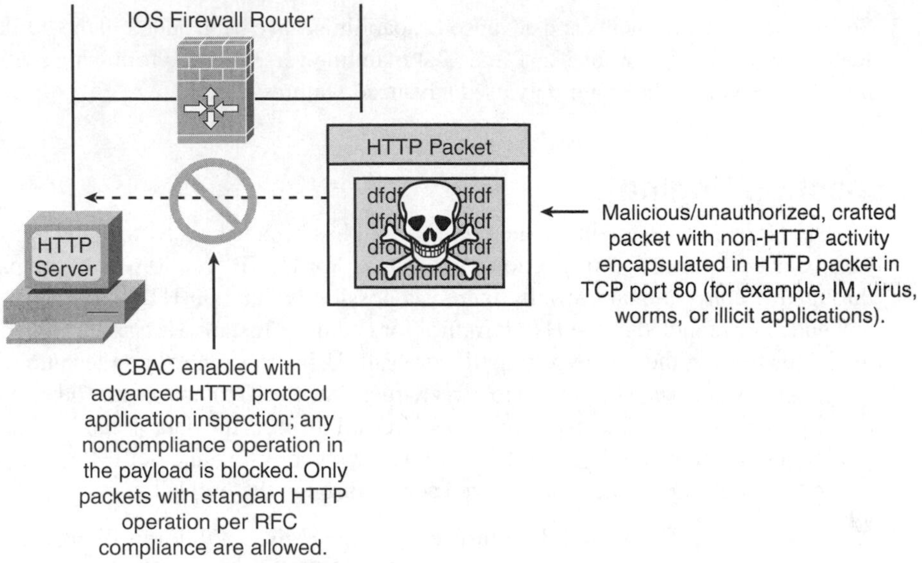

NOTE For a configuration template, visit www.cisco.com/en/US/products/ps6350/ products_configuration_guide_chapter09186a0080455927.html#wp1027188.

E-Mail Inspection Engine

Similar to the SMTP protocol, the ESMTP protocol provides a basic method for exchanging e-mail messages. ESMTP specifies service extensions to the original SMTP protocol for sending e-mail messages that support graphics, audio, and video files, and text in various national languages. Although an ESMTP session is similar to SMTP, there is one difference—the **EHLO** command. An ESMTP client supporting ESMTP protocol starts a connection by issuing the **EHLO** command instead of the **HELO** command used in standard SMTP. (Refer to RFC 1869, "SMTP Service Extensions," for further details.)

The enhanced SMTP inspection engine adds support for ESMTP, Post Office Protocol 3 (POP3), and Internet Message Access Protocol (IMAP) in addition to the standard SMTP protocol. Advanced application inspection prevents protocol masquerading and enforcing strict RFC compliance.

To configure SMTP/ESMTP inspection, use the **ip inspect name** *inspection-name* {**smtp** | **esmtp**} command from the global configuration mode along with other required parameters. (Refer to steps defined earlier in the section "Configuring CBAC.") This feature was introduced in IOS Version 12.3(14)T.

Firewall ACL Bypass

Before the implementation of the Firewall ACL Bypass feature, a packet was subject to processing for three searches (inbound ACL, outbound ACL, and the session table of the firewall). As discussed earlier, the dynamic ACL entry is a result of the corresponding connection information found in the session table that validates the session as being legitimate; therefore, checking the packet against the inbound and outbound ACL entries was deemed redundant and no longer necessary. The extra checks can be eliminated to save CPU cycles. Bypassing the ACL check enhancement subjects the packet to one search only (the session table) during the packet processing path through the router. Figure 5-6 shows how this works. The primary benefit in this feature is that the performance of the packet throughput is improved by approximately 10%.

Because the firewall ACL bypassing is performed by default, you can configure CBAC inspection as normal. This feature is transparent to the user, and no additional commands are required to enable or disable it.

This feature was introduced in IOS Version 12.3(4)T.

Figure 5-6   *Firewall ACL Bypass—Order of Packet Processing*

Order of Packet Processing

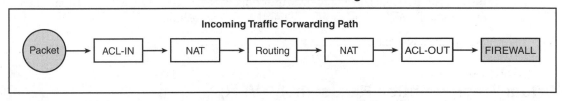

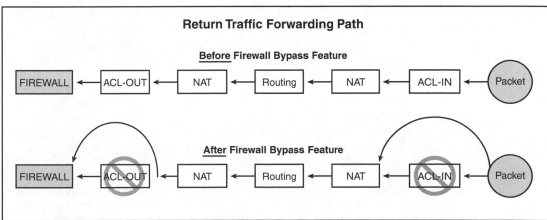

Transparent IOS Firewall (Layer 2)

The transparent IOS Firewall feature (also known as Layer 2 firewall) acts as a Layer 2 transparent bridge with CBAC inspection configured on the Bridged Virtual Interface (BVI).

A Layer 3 IOS Firewall implementation requires two logical zones—trusted and untrusted—both on different IP subnets (existing subnets). A network implementation not designed to accommodate this subnetted architecture would require the redesign of IP subnets to accommodate the firewall. Placing a Layer 3 firewall would be difficult in such scenarios and is considered resource intensive and could be unfeasible for most deployment scenarios.

Traditional firewalls operate in either a Layer 3 or Layer 2 (transparent) mode. The Cisco IOS Firewall is designed to simultaneously interoperate in both modes, providing scalability and ease of integration. This enhanced functionality allows a Cisco IOS Firewall to be implemented concurrently for both the Layer 2 transparent firewall operating on the bridged packets and a Layer 3 firewall operating on routed packets on the same device.

The transparent firewall configuration is no different from the Layer 3 firewall using the **ip inspect** command from the global configuration mode. The CBAC inspection rule **ip inspect in/out** command is applied to the bridged interfaces for Layer 2 protection, whereas other routed interfaces are configured for Layer 3 protection.

This feature was introduced in IOS Version 12.3(7)T.

Virtual Fragmentation Reassembly (VFR)

Before the implementation of the Virtual Fragmentation Reassembly (VFR) feature, the IOS Firewall (CBAC) could not identify the contents of the IP fragments or gather any port information from the fragmented packets. This shortcoming allowed all fragmented packets to bypass the firewall checks and get through the network without being inspected.

Before the VFR feature was available, several known fragment-type attacks could succeed. (Examples include Tiny Fragment attack, Overlapping Fragment attack, and the Buffer Overflow attack that sends a large number of incomplete IP fragments to thwart the firewall.) The VFR feature provides the capability to scan into the fragmented packets to check the connection information and create the corresponding dynamic ACL entries, hence protecting the network from various fragmentation attacks.

To enable VFR, use the **ip virtual-reassembly** command from the interface configuration mode. Example 5-6 shows how to configure VFR with a maximum number of 100 IP datagrams to be reassembled at any given time and a maximum number of 20 fragments allowed per IP datagram (fragment set). The timeout of 5 seconds specifies that if all the fragment packets are not received within the specified time, the IP datagram and all its fragments will be dropped.

This feature was introduced in IOS Version 12.3(8)T.

Example 5-6   *Virtual Fragmentation Reassembly (VFR) Configuration Example*

```
interface Fastethernet0/0
 ip inspect <name> in | out
 ip virtual-reassembly max-reassemblies 100 max-fragments 20 timeout 5
 !
```

VRF-Aware IOS Firewall

The Multiprotocol Label Switching Virtual Private Network (MPLS VPN) feature allows several sites to interconnect transparently through a service provider network. A service provider network can support several IP VPNs. Each of these appears as a separate private network. VRF is an IP routing table instance for connecting sites in a VPN network. Each VPN has its own set or sets of VRF instances, thereby allowing each site to send IP packets to any other site in the same VRF instance.

The Cisco IOS Firewall feature is enhanced to support inspection for VRF instances in a MPLS VPN network. CBAC can inspect packets on a per-VRF basis for packets sent and received within a VRF. VRF-aware CBAC implementation can include multiple firewall instances (with VRF instances) that are allocated to separate VPN customers. VRF-aware CBAC provides scalability and low-cost integration without the need for separate firewall devices for each VPN network. In effect, a single physical router running multiple virtual routing instances (emulating multiple routers) can now run multiple virtual IOS Firewalls in a single device.

This feature was introduced in IOS Version 12.3(14)T.

Inspection of Router-Generated Traffic

The Cisco IOS Firewall feature is enhanced to support inspection for traffic that was originated by or destined to the CBAC-configured device. Inspection of router-generated traffic augments CBAC functionality to inspect TCP, UDP, and H.323 connections that have the firewall as one of the connection endpoints. CBAC dynamically opens temporary holes for TCP, UDP, and H.323 control channel connections to and from the router, and for the data and media channels negotiated over the H.323 control channels. For example, CBAC can be configured to inspect a Telnet initiated from the CBAC-enabled router to a device in the unprotected zone, allowing return traffic dynamically without needing to explicitly permit in the access list.

To enable the Router-Generated Traffic inspection feature, use the **router-traffic** keyword in the **ip inspect name** command when configuring CBAC inspection rules. This option is available for H.323, TCP, and UDP protocols only.

This feature was introduced in IOS Version 12.3(14)T.

Zone-Based Policy Firewall (ZFW)

The new ZFW feature was introduced in Cisco IOS Software Release 12.4(6)T for the enhanced Cisco IOS Firewall feature set.

All features from prior to IOS Software Release 12.4(6)T are inclusive in this new implementation and are supported in the new zone-based inspection.

ZFW supports the following features:

- Stateful packet inspection (SPI)
- VRF-aware Cisco IOS Firewall
- URL filtering
- Denial-of-service (DoS) mitigation

More ZFW features were added into Cisco IOS Software Release 12.4(9)T for per-class session/connection and throughput limits, as well as application inspection and control:

- HTTP
- Post Office Protocol (POP3)
- Internet Mail Access Protocol (IMAP)
- Simple Mail Transfer Protocol and Enhanced Simple Mail Transfer Protocol (SMTP/ESMTP)
- Sun Remote Procedure Call (RPC)
- Instant Messaging (IM) applications, including Microsoft Messenger (MSN), Yahoo Messenger, and AOL Instant Messenger
- Peer-to-peer (P2P) file sharing, including Bittorrent, KaZaA, Gnutella, and eDonkey

---

NOTE   Stateful inspection for multicast traffic is not supported in ZFW or legacy classic Firewall CBAC.

Zone-Based Policy Overview

Before the ZFW was introduced, the Cisco IOS Firewall offered stateful inspection using the CBAC feature. CBAC was covered in detail in the previous sections of this chapter.

In the recent releases of Cisco IOS Software from Version 12.4(6)T and later, the CBAC model is being replaced with the new configuration model that uses ZFW.

This new feature was added mainly to overcome the limitations of the CBAC that was employing stateful inspection policy on an interface-based model. To be specific, the limitation was that all traffic passing through the interface was subject to the same inspection policy, thereby limiting the granularity and policy enforcement, particularly in scenarios where multiple interfaces existed.

With ZFW, stateful inspection can now be applied on a zone-based model. Interfaces are assigned to zones, and policy inspection is applied to traffic moving between zones. This enhancement provides more granularity, flexibility, scalability, and an easy-to-use zone-based security approach. With a zone-based inspection model, varying interzone policies can be applied to multiple hosts or groups of hosts connected to the same interface.

TIP   The following Cisco whitepaper URL provides more details on the conceptual difference between Cisco IOS Classic and ZFW features: www.cisco.com/en/US/products/sw/secursw/ps1018/products_white_paper0900 aecd806f31f9.shtml.

Security Zones

Security Zones establish the security boundaries of the network where traffic is subjected to policy restrictions as it crosses to another region within the network.

Figure 5-7   *Basic Security Zone*

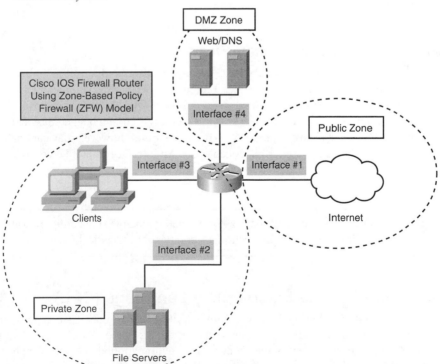

As shown in Figure 5-7, a zone can have one or more interface(s) assigned to it. This example shows a Cisco IOS Firewall router with four interfaces and three zones:

- Interface #1 connected to the Public Internet zone
- Interfaces #2 and #3 connected to a Private zone connecting file servers and clients on a LAN (on separate physical interfaces, but in the same security zone), which must not be accessible from the public Internet
- Interface #4 connected to the DMZ zone, connecting a web server and Domain Name System (DNS) server, which must be accessible to the public Internet

In the example illustrated by Figure 5-7, the IOS Firewall will typically have three main security policies:

- Private zone connectivity to the Internet
- Private zone connectivity to DMZ
- Public zone connectivity to DMZ

Devices connected in the private zone would be able to pass traffic to all other devices between interface #2 and #3 because they are in the same Private zone. If an additional new interface is added to the Private zone, inter-interface and intra-interface traffic is allowed within the same zone. Additionally, the hosts' traffic to hosts in other zones would be similarly affected by existing policies.

Configuring Zone-Based Policy Firewall

ZFW does not use the classical CBAC **ip inspect** command set. ZFW policies are configured with the new Cisco Policy Language (CPL), which employs a hierarchical structure to define inspection for network protocols and the groups of hosts to which the inspection will be applied. Note that the two configuration models (Classical CBAC and new ZFW) can be used concurrently on the same router; however, they cannot be combined on the same interface overlapping each other. An interface cannot be configured as a zone member and be configured for **ip inspect** simultaneously.

NOTE   It is important to understand that ZFW completely changes the configuration syntax for Cisco IOS Firewall stateful inspection, as compared to Classical CBAC.

Configuring ZFW Using Cisco Policy Language (CPL)

ZFW is configured using the new command set of Cisco Policy Language (CPL). CPL is the new format to enable ZFW. The format is similar to the Modular QoS CLI (MQC) in using **class-map** to identify the traffic and the action applied in a policy map.

Several steps are required to complete the configuration. Although the sequence of tasks that follows is not important, some tasks depend on each other. For example, **class-map** must be configured before it can be used in the policy-map. Similarly, the policy-map cannot be assigned to a zone-pair before configuring the policy-map itself, and so on.

The following tasks are required to complete the ZFW configuration using the CPL:

- Define zones
- Define zone-pairs
- Define class-map(s) that identify the traffic that must have policy applied as it traverses a zone-pair
- Define a policy-map to apply action to the traffic in a class-map
- Apply a policy-map to a zone-pair
- Assign interface(s) to zones

NOTE   By default, traffic between the zones is blocked unless an explicit policy dictates the permission.

Based on Figure 5-8, Example 5-7 shows a very basic ZFW configuration that uses the new CPL command set in two zones.

Figure 5-8   *Basic ZFW for Two-Zone Setup*

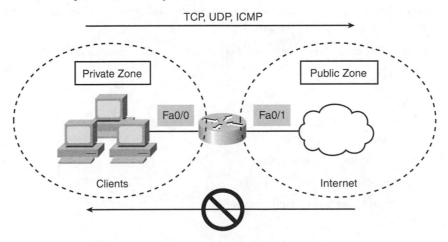

Example 5-7 *Basic ZFW Configuration Using CPL*

```
<omit>
class-map type inspect match-any myclass
 match protocol tcp
 match protocol udp
 match protocol icmp
!
policy-map type inspect mypolicy
 class type inspect myclass
  inspect
!
zone security private
zone security public
!
zone-pair security mypair source private destination public
 service-policy type inspect mypolicy
!
Interface FastEthernet0/0
 zone-member security private
!
interface FastEthernet0/1
 zone-member security public
!
<omit>
```

Application Inspection and Control (AIC)

In addition to the extensive ZFW features and capabilities, ZFW extends the function of application inspection and control (AIC) engine by providing additional capabilities to the ZFW. AIC policies are applied at Layer 7 of the OSI model, performing deep packet inspection at the application-protocol level.

ZFW offers application inspection and control for the following application services:

- HTTP
- SMTP
- POP3
- IMAP
- Sun remote procedure call
- Peer-to-peer application traffic
- Instant Messaging applications

NOTE   AIC is configured as an additional set of application-specific class-maps and policy-maps, which are then applied to existing inspection class-maps and policy-maps.

Summary

This chapter discussed the router-based IOS Firewall technology and focused mainly on one of the several subsystems—the SPI technology that uses the classical firewall that in turn uses CBAC and the new ZFW structures. SPI is an advanced firewall engine for stateful inspection providing traffic-filtering functionality on a Cisco IOS–based device as a single point of protection.

The chapter described CBAC functions and how they work using step-by-step configuration processes with examples.

The chapter also covered the new ZFW concept using security zones and exemplified the required steps to configure the ZFW.

The chapter also provided an overview of some of the advanced IOS Firewall features introduced in the newer IOS Software versions.

References

www.cisco.com/en/US/products/ps6441/
products_configuration_guide_book09186a008049e249.html

www.cisco.com/en/US/products/sw/iosswrel/ps1835/
products_configuration_guide_chapter09186a00800ca7c5.html

www.cisco.com/en/US/products/sw/secursw/ps1018/
products_implementation_design_guide09186a00800fd670.html

www.cisco.com/en/US/products/sw/iosswrel/ps5207/
prod_bulletin09186a00801abfda.html

www.cisco.com/en/US/products/ps6441/prod_bulletin09186a00804a8728.html

www.cisco.com/en/US/products/ps6350/prod_bulletin09186a0080457a84.html

www.cisco.com/en/US/products/ps6350/products_feature_guide09186a008072c6e3.html

www.cisco.com/en/US/products/sw/secursw/ps1018/
products_white_paper0900aecd806f31f9.shtml

CHAPTER 6

Cisco Firewalls: Appliance and Module

The firewall has become a common entity and is a necessary and integral part of every network infrastructure. The most critical requirement in most security solutions today is implementing a firewall. Networks today have grown both in size and complexity, with the environment becoming increasingly hostile. This chapter brings together Cisco industry-leading innovative firewall technology with flagship products uniquely positioned to deliver purpose-built, feature-rich firewall technology.

The previous chapter focused on a router-based IOS Firewall solution, whereas this chapter mainly focuses on the hardware-based, purpose-built Cisco Firewall technology.

The chapter discusses various types of Cisco Firewalls available and includes a brief overview of each model. The chapter is divided into two segments—features and configuration based on the following:

- Firewall appliance software for PIX 500 and ASA 5500 platforms
- Firewall module software for Firewall Services Module (FWSM)

The chapter takes a closer look at core concepts, such as firewall modes, security contexts, stateful inspection, the Adaptive Security Algorithm, IP routing, various types of Network Address Translation (NAT), the control of traffic flow and network access through the firewall, the Modular Policy Framework (MPF), and the provisioning of high-availability and resilient networks.

Firewalls Overview

A firewall is a hardware or software solution implemented within the network to enforce security policies by controlling network access. The traditional function of firewalls has evolved from the original function of protecting a network from unauthorized external access. Besides protecting the perimeter of a network, today's firewalls implement the following: access control, virtual private network (VPN) services, quality of service (QoS) features, redundancy mechanisms, and much more. In general, firewalls can offer data privacy, integrity, and availability.

A firewall is often seen as the first step toward a network security solution. Network security needs to be architected as a foundation for success, and firewalls are an integral part of this architecture.

Firewall deployment requires charting network boundaries between security domains. A network security domain is a contiguous zone of a network that operates under a uniform security policy. A policy enforcement mechanism is required where these domains interconnect. This is where firewall technology comes into play. Firewalls ensure protection by acting as the first line of network defense.

Hardware Versus Software Firewalls

The primary differentiator between a hardware- and software- based firewall is the underlying dependency on the operating systems they run on. Both can prove equally secure if the network design and configuration are impeccable. As seen in the previous chapter, the software-based Cisco IOS Firewall technology is integrated functionality inside the Cisco IOS Software, thereby providing a stateful inspection firewall engine with application-level intelligence. There are a couple of reasons why hardware firewalls are better than software firewalls: hardware firewalls are robust and built specifically for the purpose of "firewalling," and they are less vulnerable than software firewalls. Hence, hardware firewalls have an edge over software-based firewalls.

The Cisco Firewall technology provides a wealth of advanced security and networking services for small-to-medium enterprise and service provider networks, in a modular, purpose-built solution. Cisco hardware-based firewall technology comes in three flavors:

- PIX 500 Series Security Appliances
- ASA 5500 Series Adaptive Security Appliances
- Catalyst 6500 Series and Cisco 7600 Series Firewall Services Module (FWSM)

Cisco Firewall technology solutions provide application-aware and protocol inspection, access control and flow-based policy enforcement, multi-vector attack protection, and secure connectivity services through a wide range of rich security and networking services. The following sections will briefly highlight features of each platform.

Cisco PIX 500 Series Security Appliances

Cisco flagship and industry-leading PIX 500 Series Security Appliance provides comprehensive security, performance, and reliability for network environments of all sizes, offering an array of multitiered solutions. It is a family of specialized appliances that provide robust integrated network security services, including stateful inspection firewalling, VPNs, and inline intrusion detection.

The dedicated software engine incorporates the state-of-the-art Cisco Adaptive Security Algorithm, which provides stateful inspection firewall services by monitoring the state of all authorized network communications while preventing unauthorized network access. Cisco PIX Security Appliances offer an additional layer of security by integrating more than two dozen purpose-built inspection engines that perform in-depth packet examination for the most common applications and protocols used today. The Cisco PIX Security Appliance provides a wide range of integrated security services in an easy-to-deploy, high-performance solution.

THe Cisco PIX 500 Series range from desktop appliances for small and home offices to modular gigabit appliances for enterprise and service-provider environments, as shown in Table 6-1. (Note that photos are not available for the Cisco PIX 506E and Cisco PIX 515E.)

Table 6-1   *Cisco PIX 500 Series Devices*

Device	Description
Cisco PIX 501	Compact, plug-n-play Security Appliance for small office/home office environments. PIX 501 appliances provide an integrated 4-port Fast Ethernet (10/100) switch and a Fast Ethernet (10/100) interface.
Cisco PIX 506E	Cost-effective, high-performance Security Appliance for remote office/branch office environments. PIX 506E provides two auto-sensing Fast Ethernet (10/100) interfaces.
Cisco PIX 515E	Modular, high-performance Security Appliance for small-to-medium and enterprise network environments. PIX 515E appliance is a modular one-rack-unit design supporting up to six 10/100 Fast Ethernet interfaces.
Cisco PIX 525	Gigabit Ethernet connectivity, modular Security Appliance for medium-to-large enterprise network environments. PIX 525 appliance is a modular two-rack-unit design supporting up to eight 10/100 Fast Ethernet interfaces or three Gigabit Ethernet interfaces.
Cisco PIX 535	Highly modular, high-performance Gigabit Ethernet connectivity Security Appliance for enterprise and service provider network environments. PIX 535 appliance is a modular three-rack-unit design supporting up to ten 10/100 Fast Ethernet interfaces or nine Gigabit Ethernet interfaces and redundant power supplies.

NOTE   Cisco PIX 506, 515, and 520 Firewall models have reached end of sale (EOS).

Cisco ASA 5500 Series Adaptive Security Appliances

The Cisco ASA 5500 Series Adaptive Security Appliance (Figure 6-1) is the newest member in the group of Cisco Firewall technology products. The ASA 5500 series includes multifunction Security Appliances delivering converged firewall, Intrusion Prevention System (IPS), advanced adaptive threat defense services including Anti-X defenses, application security, and VPN services simplifying network security solutions.

Figure 6-1   *Cisco ASA 5500 Series Appliance i*

The ASA 5500 Series is one of the key components in the Cisco Self-Defending Network initiative. At the heart of the ASA 5500 Series design is the Adaptive Identification and Mitigation (AIM) architecture that provides proactive threat mitigation, thereby stopping attacks before they spread through the network, network activity controls, and application traffic. The AIM architecture delivers flexible, high-performance site-to-site VPN, remote access VPN, and SSL VPN solutions.

In a single platform, the Cisco ASA 5500 Series offers the following:

- Market-proven firewall, IPS, adaptive threat defense, and VPN capabilities
- Adaptive identification and mitigation services architecture, thereby delivering granular policy control and future services extensibility
- Saving overall deployment and operational costs and reduced complexity

The Cisco ASA 5500 Series is an innovative appliance that builds on the depth and breadth of security features, combining the following three industry-leading security and VPN technologies:

- Firewall technology
- IPS (inline) technology
- VPN technology—IPsec, SSL (WebVPN), and AnyConnect VPN

Blending these multiple functions, the Cisco ASA 5500 Series delivers an unmatched best-of-breed in network protection solutions. The Cisco ASA 5500 Series brings together a wide range of security and VPN technologies to provide rich application security, Anti-X defenses, network containment and control, and secure connectivity tightening the network security posture.

Cisco ASA 5500 Series offer five high-performance purpose-built appliances that span small- and medium-sized to large enterprise and service provider environments. Concurrent security services architecture lowers operational complexity and reduces the overall deployment and operation costs.

- **ASA 5505:** Cost-effective, easy-to-deploy appliance for small business, branch office, and enterprise teleworkers environments with integrated 8 port 10/100 Fast Ethernet switch (includes two Power over Ethernet [PoE] ports)

- **ASA 5510:** Cost-effective, easy-to-deploy appliance for medium-sized business, remote/branch, and enterprise environments with advanced security and networking services

- **ASA 5520:** High-availability Active/Active services and Gigabit Ethernet connectivity appliance for medium-sized enterprise networks, in a modular, high-performance network

- **ASA 5540:** High-density, with Active/Active high-availability services and Gigabit Ethernet connectivity with greater reliability, high-performance appliance for medium-to-large enterprises and service-provider networks

- **ASA 5550:** Gigabit-class offering up to 1.2 Gbps firewall throughput, with Active/Active high-availability services, and Fiber and Gigabit Ethernet connectivity; high-performance appliance for large enterprise and service-provider networks

Cisco Firewall Services Module (FWSM)

Cisco Firewall Services Module (FWSM), pictured in Figure 6-2, is a high-speed, high-performance integrated firewall module that is installed in Cisco Catalyst 6500 switches and Cisco 7600 Series routers.

Figure 6-2   *Cisco Firewall Services Module (FWSM)*

The FWSM provides large enterprises and service providers with unparalleled security, reliability, scalability and performance. Some of the key features in FWSM are the following:

- **Integrated module:** Installs inside a Cisco Catalyst 6500 Series Switch or Cisco 7600 Series Router. The FWSM integrates firewall security inside the network infrastructure.

- **Superior performance and scalability:** The FWSM offers the fastest firewall solution in the industry, with unprecedented data rates. FWSM can handle up to 5 Gbps of traffic, 100,000 connections per second (cps), and 1 million concurrent connections, thereby providing unsurpassed performance to meet future requirements. With the capacity to install up to four FWSMs in a single chassis, throughput performance is enhanced to 20 Gbps per chassis to meet growing demands.

- **Proven technology:** The FWSM software is based on Cisco PIX technology and uses the same time-tested Cisco PIX Operating System, a secure, real-time operating system.

- **Lower TCO (total cost of ownership):** Virtualized FWSM delivers multiple firewalls on one physical hardware platform. Virtualization reduces the number of physical devices required in a network, thereby significantly minimizing the complexity of managing network infrastructure and operational efficiency.

- **ROI (return on investment):** Higher ROI with flexible deployment leveraging existing infrastructure investments.

Firewall Appliance Software for PIX 500 and ASA 5500

Cisco Firewall Appliance provides integrated hardware and software delivering full stateful firewall protection and VPN capabilities. It provides in-depth packet inspection and flow-specific monitoring, improved network integration, resiliency, and scalability. Unlike typical CPU-intensive proxy servers, the Cisco Firewall Software uses a non-UNIX secure, real-time, embedded system.

Both appliances (PIX 500 and ASA 5500 series) are based on the industry-leading Cisco Firewall Software currently on version 8.0 as of this writing. The majority of the functions are the same on both appliances, with the exception that in comparison to the PIX 500 series, the ASA 5500 series has the additional support of SSL VPN technology (WebVPN), VPN Load Balancing, the Security Services Module (SSM)—IPS module, Compact Flash (CF) card support, and Aux port support.

NOTE   PIX 501 and 506E models do not support the new firewall software versions. They are capable of running up to version 6.3 only.

Firewall Appliance OS Software

Cisco Security Appliance software for firewalls delivers the latest firewall and VPN capabilities, enhanced performance, and security improvements, as well as a list of new features. Version 7.0 and the latest release, version 8.0, introduce significant enhancements to all major functional areas. These areas include firewalling and inspection services such as transparent (Layer 2) firewall or routed (Layer 3) firewall operation and multiple security contexts (virtualized firewalls), Enhanced Interior Gateway Routing Protocol (EIGRP) support, Application-Aware Inspection Services, enhanced VPN services, Dynamic Access Policies (DAP), browser-based SSL VPN, network integration, high availability (Active/ Active) and enhanced management and monitoring services.

Some of the advanced features include TCP stream reassembly, which assists in detecting attacks that are spread across multiple packets (fragmented) by reassembling packets into a full packet stream and performing analysis on the entire stream.

Another feature, TCP normalization, provides improved techniques to detect TCP-based attacks and is designed to drop packets that do not appear normal. A strict inspection is performed to confirm RFC compliance on the TCP header (advanced header examination for flags and checking option, window variation, checksum verification and detection of data tampering in retransmitted packets). Several other advanced features and enhancements are available in the more recent software version releases.

The Security Appliance combines in one device advanced stateful firewall, VPN concentrator functionality, and advanced protection features to intercept and respond to network attacks.

The Security Appliance software supports an intuitive, easy-to-use GUI-based application called Adaptive Security Device Manager (ASDM). ASDM is a browser-based Java applet used to configure, monitor, and manage the Security Appliances. ASDM is covered in Chapter 24, "Security and Policy Management."

With the brief introduction and product overviews, sections to follow will discuss the features and the configuration details.

Firewall Modes

The Security Appliance runs in two firewall modes:

- Routed firewall mode
- Transparent firewall mode (stealth firewall)

Routed Firewall Mode

In this mode, the Security Appliance is considered to be a router hop in the network. (This is the regular mode that everyone is familiar with.) Network Address Translation and dynamic routing protocol capabilities using Routing Information Protocol (RIP) and Open Short Path First (OSPF) can be performed in this mode. Note that routing protocols RIP and OSPF are supported in single context mode only. Multimode context does not support routing. In addition, routed mode supports use of multiple interfaces. Each interface must be on a different subnet, and interfaces can be shared between contexts. By default, routed mode is set as the default mode.

Transparent Firewall Mode (Stealth Firewall)

Firewall Software Version 7.0 and later introduces the capability to deploy the Security Appliance in a secure bridging mode, as a Layer 2 device, to provide rich Layer 2 through 7 firewall services. In a transparent mode, the Security Appliance acts like a "bump in the wire" and is not a router hop. There is no need to redesign the IP network (Layer 3 addressing scheme). The Security Appliance connects the same network (IP subnet) on its inside and outside interfaces. The inside and outside interfaces are put on different Layer 2 segments if they are connected on the same switch (use unique VLAN numbers or use separate switches).

In essence, the network is split into two Layer 2 segments and the appliance is placed in between, thereby acting in bridge mode, and Layer 3 remains unchanged. Alternatively, clients can be connected on either side into two separate switches that are independent of each other (and not connected to each other in any way).

Figure 6-3 illustrates this further. Even though the firewall is in the bridge mode, an ACL is still required to control and allow all Layer 3 traffic that is passing through the firewall, with the exception of ARP traffic, which does not need an ACL. ARP traffic can be controlled with ARP inspection on the firewall.

Transparent mode does not support IP routing protocols for traffic passing through the router, because the firewall is in bridge mode. Static routes are used for traffic originating from the appliance and not for traffic traversing the appliance. However, IP routing protocols through the firewall are supported, as long as the access lists on the firewall permit the protocols to pass through. OSPF, RIP, EIGRP, and Border Gateway Protocol (BGP) adjacencies can be established through the firewall in the transparent mode.

While running in transparent mode, the Security Appliance continues to perform the stateful inspection with application-layer intelligence and perform all regular firewalling capabilities, including NAT support. NAT configuration is supported in software version 8.0 and later. Prior to version 8.0, NAT was not supported in transparent mode.

The egress interface for the outgoing packets is determined by performing a MAC address lookup instead of a route lookup. The only Layer 3 addressing required on the firewall is the management IP address. The management IP address is also used as the source IP address for packets originating from the Security Appliance, such as system messages or communications with AAA or SYSLOG servers. The management IP address must be on the same subnet as the connected network.

Transparent mode is a good technique to protect the network passively (camouflage) without the intruder/attacker detecting the existence of the firewall.

Figure 6-3 shows an example of transparent firewall implementation. The example shows three client workstations with the default gateway set to upstream router 10.1.1.1. Note that all PCs, the upstream router, and the management IP address are in the same IP subnet 10.1.1.0/24, but they have been split in different Layer 2 VLANs because all the devices in the diagram are connected into the same switch. Client workstations and the inside interface of Security Appliance are set in VLAN 10, and the upstream router and outside interface are set to VLAN 20. Note that if clients and all devices on both sides are connected to separate switches, and the switches are not connected to each other in any way, the VLAN numbers can be the same, or anything for that matter, because they are independent and do not interconnect.

Figure 6-3   *Transparent Firewall Setup*

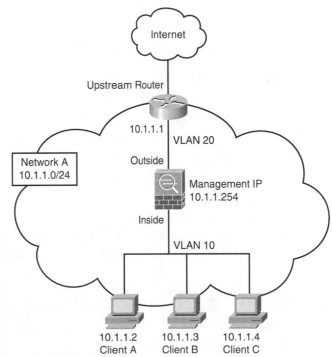

Illustration assumes
all devices in this
diagram are connected
to the same switch.

<u>By Default, the Mode Is Set to Routed</u>
Firewall# **show firewall**
Firewall Mode: Router

<u>Change to Transparent Mode</u>
Firewall(config)# **firewall transparent**
Switched to transparent mode
Hostname# **show firewall**
Firewall Mode: Transparent

Stateful Inspection

Every inbound packet is inspected against the adaptive security algorithm and the connection state information to decide whether to allow or deny the packet. Like the PIX and ASA Security Appliance, a stateful firewall checks the state of a packet as follows:

1   Is this a new connection?

    If the arriving packet is part of a new connection, the Adaptive Security Algorithm checks the packet against access lists and performs other routine tasks (such as route lookup) to determine whether the packet is allowed or denied. The session management path is responsible for performing the following:

    • Perform the access list checks

    • Perform route lookups

    • Allocate NAT translations (xlate table)

    • Establish the session in the "fast path"

    Packets are further passed to the control plane path to examine the payload for application-level (Layer 7) inspection.

2   Is this an established connection?

    If the arriving packet is part of an existing connection, the Adaptive Security Algorithm does not reexamine the packet, and matching packets in the established connection table can go through the fast path in both directions. The fast path is responsible for performing the following checks:

    • IP checksum verification

    • Session lookup

    • TCP sequence number check

    • NAT translations based on existing sessions

    • Layer 3 and Layer 4 header adjustments

    In some instances, established session packets must continue to go through the session management path or the control plane path for protocols that require Layer 7 inspection. For example, HTTP packets requiring content filtering need to go through the session management path.

Application Layer Protocol Inspection

In addition to the stateful-inspection previously discussed, the Adaptive Security Algorithm is enhanced with powerful capabilities and is built with application-layer intelligence that assists in detecting and preventing protocol and application-layer attacks. It performs deep packet inspection of application-layer protocol traffic (such as HTTP) by checking the packet IP header and the payload contents. Conventional firewalls maintain the session information details up to Layer 4, whereas the Security Appliance adds another tier of security by extending its inspection in the data payload at Layer 7.

With the application-layer awareness, Security Appliance performs deep packet inspection in the data payload for any malicious activity. As shown in Figure 6-4, when the Security Appliance receives a packet that is of well-known application protocol (such as HTTP), it further examines the packet for respective application operation to check for adherence to RFC standards and compliance operations to ensure there is no malicious intent. If the packet is crafted maliciously with unauthorized, nonstandard activity and found to be performing noncompliance operations (illegal commands), the packet is blocked. In a conventional access-list filtering, this packet would be allowed, because only the Layer 3 and Layer 4 information in the packet would be checked.

The Security Appliance armed with the application intelligence provides protection from several types of network attacks that use the embedding technique to pass malicious traffic encapsulating in well-known application protocols.

Figure 6-4   *Application Layer Intelligence*

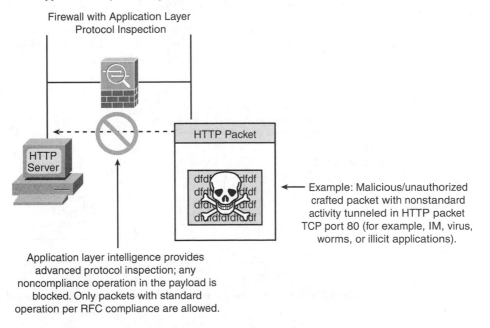

Application inspection is enabled by default for most standard well-known protocols with specific TCP or UDP port numbers. See Table 6-2 for a complete list of supported protocols, with their respective standard compliance enforcement. Security Appliance can be tuned to inform the inspection engine to listen on nonstandard ports. For example, the HTTP port can be changed from a standard TCP/80 to a nonstandard TCP/8080 port. Some protocols cannot be changed; Table 6-2 identifies which protocols can be modified to inspect for nonstandard ports. The Modular Policy Framework Command Line Interface (CLI) is used to change the default settings for application inspection for any application layer inspection (discussed further in this chapter). The MPF is similar to the Cisco IOS Software technique called Modular QoS CLI (MQC).

Adaptive Security Algorithm Operation

Figure 6-5 illustrates how the stateful-inspection and application intelligence works in the Security Appliance. Conceptually, three basic operational functions are performed:

- **Access lists:** Controlling network access based on specific networks, hosts, and services (TCP/UDP port numbers).

- **Connections (xlate and conn tables):** Maintaining state information for each connection. This information is used by the Adaptive Security Algorithm and cut-through proxy to effectively forward traffic within established connections.

- **Inspection Engine:** Perform stateful inspection coupled with application-level inspection functions. These inspection rule sets are predefined to validate application compliance as per RFC and other standards and cannot be altered.

Figure 6-5 *Adaptive Security Algorithm Operations*

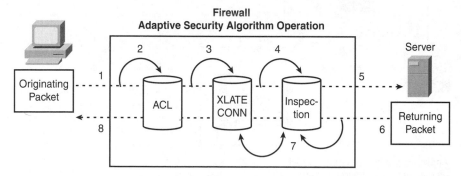

Figure 6-5 is numbered with the operations in the order they occur and are detailed as follows:

1 An incoming TCP SYN packet arrives on the Security Appliance to establish a new connection.

2 The Security Appliance checks the access list database to determine whether the connection is permitted.

3 The Security Appliance creates a new entry in the connection database (XLATE and CONN tables) using the necessary session information.

4 The Security Appliance checks the predefined rule sets in the inspection engine and in case of well-known applications, further performs application-level inspection.

5 At this point, Security Appliance makes a decision whether to forward or drop the packet according to the findings of the inspection engine. The Security Appliance forwards the packet to the desired destination subject to clearance from the application inspection engine.

6 The destination system responds to the initial request returning the packet.

7 The Security Appliance receives the reply packet, performs the inspection, and looks up the connection in the connection database to determine whether the session information matches an existing connection.

8 The Security Appliance forwards the packet belonging to an existing established session.

Table 6-2 lists all the application protocols and details for which the Security Appliance provides application layer inspection capability.

Table 6-2 *Application Inspection Engines*

Application	PAT?	NAT (1-1)?	Ports Can Be Modified to Nonstandard?	Default Port	Standards Compliance
CTIQBE	Yes	Yes	Yes	TCP/2748	—
DNS	Yes	Yes	No	UDP/53	RFC 1123
FTP	Yes	Yes	Yes	TCP/21	RFC 959
GTP	Yes	Yes	Yes	UDP/3386 UDP/2123	—
H.323	Yes	Yes	Yes	TCP/1720 UDP/1718 UDP (RAS) 1718-1719	ITU-T H.323, H.245, H225.0, Q.931, Q.932
HTTP	Yes	Yes	Yes	TCP/80	RFC 2616
ICMP	Yes	Yes	No	—	—
ICMP ERROR	Yes	Yes	No	—	—
ILS (LDAP)	Yes	Yes	Yes	—	—
MGCP	Yes	Yes	Yes	2427, 2727	RFC 2705bis-05
NBDS / UDP	Yes	Yes	No	UDP/138	—
NBNS / UDP	No	No	No	UDP/137	—

continues

Table 6-2 *Application Inspection Engines (Continued)*

Application	PAT?	NAT (1-1)?	Ports Can Be Modified to Nonstandard?	Default Port	Standards Compliance
NetBIOS over IP3	No	No	No	—	—
PPTP	Yes	Yes	Yes	1723	RFC 2637
RSH	Yes	Yes	Yes	TCP/514	Berkeley UNIX
RTSP	No	No	Yes	TCP/554	RFC 2326, RFC 2327, RFC 1889
SIP	Yes	Yes	Yes	TCP/5060 UDP/5060	RFC 2543
SKINNY (SCCP)	Yes	Yes	Yes	TCP/2000	—
SMTP/ESMTP	Yes	Yes	Yes	TCP/25	RFC 821, 1123
SQL*Net	Yes	Yes	Yes	TCP/1521 (v.1)	—
Sun RPC	No	Yes	No	UDP/111 TCP/111	—
XDCMP	No	No	No	UDP/177	—

The information in Table 6-2 is taken from "Cisco Security Appliance Command Line Configuration Guide, Version 7.0" at http://www.cisco.com/en/US/docs/security/asa/asa70/configuration/guide/inspect.html#wp1250375.

Security Context

Software Version 7.0 introduced the capability to create multiple virtual firewalls, which are also referred to as security contexts within a single appliance. Multiple contexts are similar to having multiple standalone devices. Each virtualized partition is an independent device and has its own set of security policies (NAT, access list, routing, and so on), logical interfaces, and administrative domain. Multiple contexts mode supports almost all the options that are configurable on a standalone device, such as NAT, firewall features, routing tables, IPS, and management features. Some features, such as VPN and dynamic routing protocols, are not supported in multiple context mode. In addition, interfaces can be shared between contexts but supported in routed mode only. For example, the outside interface can be shared to conserve interfaces, or Inside and demilitarized zone (DMZ) interfaces can be used to share resources between contexts.

There are a number of ways to set up a Security Appliance in multiple mode. The following sections illustrate two common ways for the implementation, including sharing an interface between the contexts.

Multiple Contexts—Routed Mode (with Shared Resources)

Figure 6-6 shows an admin context plus two multiple contexts for multiple departments within an organization, each with three segments: an Inside, an Outside, and a shared segment. Each department has its own security context (virtual firewall) so that it can have its own security policy (NAT, access list, routing, and so on). Several servers are shared across both departments. Hence these servers are placed on a shared network using the shared interface concept.

Figure 6-6   *Multiple Contexts—Routed Mode (with Shared Resources)*

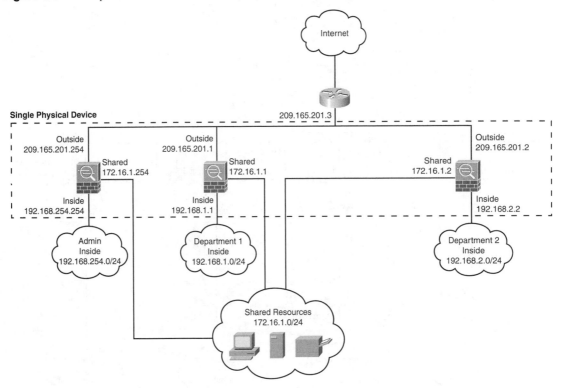

Multiple Contexts—Transparent Mode

Figure 6-7 shows an admin context plus three multiple contexts for multiple customers in a transparent mode. Each customer has its own security context with its own security policy (NAT, access list, static routes, and so on). A transparent firewall is in a secure bridging mode and connects the inside and outside interfaces to the same network (Net A). Each security context is assigned a management IP address of 10.1.x.2 on the same connected (Net A) IP subnet.

Figure 6-7   *Multiple Contexts—Transparent Mode*

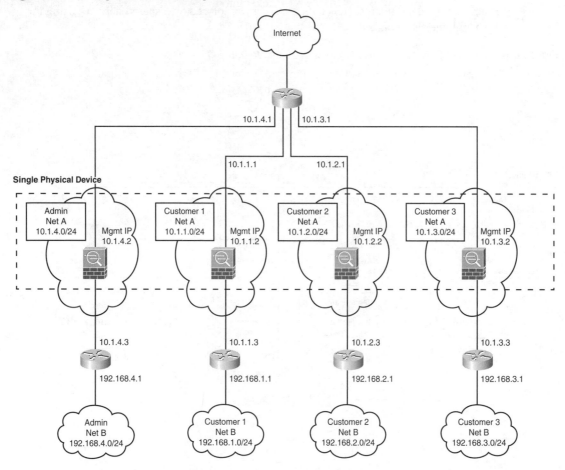

How does the Security Appliance classify which context to send a packet to?

All packets entering the appliance must be classified to determine which context to send a packet to. The classifier uses the following policy to assign the packet to a context:

1 Unique Interface: If only one context is associated with the ingress interface, the Security Appliance classifies the packet into that context. Note that when using the transparent mode, use unique interfaces only because transparent mode requires unique interface allocation for each context. For routed mode, the following methods also apply.

2 Unique MAC Address: If multiple contexts are associated with the ingress interface, the appliance classifies the packet into a context by matching interface MAC addresses. By default, shared interfaces in a context do not have a unique MAC address, and it uses the default physical MAC address in every context. This can cause ARP issues as an upstream device cannot send the packet to the correct context due to the duplicate MAC address across multiple context interfaces. The solution is to assign a unique MAC address to the shared interface within each context. This can be done using the mac-address mac_address [standby mac_address] command under the interface configuration mode. Alternatively, you can use the global command mac-address auto to automatically generate MAC addresses to each shared context interface.

3 Address Translation: If you are not using unique MAC addresses as just explained, then Security Appliance classifies the packet into a context by matching the destination address to one of the following context configurations. The classifier relies on the NAT configuration and matches the destination IP address in either a static command or global command and looks at the following:

   a Global address in a **static** NAT statement where the global interface matches the ingress interface of the packet

   b Global NAT pool for IP addresses identified by a **global** pool for the ingress interface.

Configuring Security Context

To define a context mode, add, or change a context in the system configuration, perform the following steps:

Step 1 Define the context mode (single or multiple). Use the **mode {single | multiple}** command from the global configuration. The appliance will require a reboot. Note that the mode configuration is not stored in the configuration file.

Step 2 To add or modify a context in the system execution space or the admin context, use the **context {*name*}** command from the global configuration mode to enter the context submode. The prompt changes to the following to indicate it is still in the system execution space and is modifying parameters for the specific context:

```
hostname(config-ctx)#
```

Step 3 Specify the interface(s) allocated to a context. Enter the command appropriate for a physical interface or for one or more subinterfaces using the **allocate-interface** command from the context submode. Repeat these commands multiple times to specify different ranges. Note that the transparent firewall mode allows for only two interfaces to pass through traffic. Same interfaces can be assigned to multiple contexts in routed mode, if desired. Transparent mode does not allow shared interfaces.

Step 4 Identify the URL from which the system downloads the context configuration by using the **config-url** command. Context configuration can be downloaded via several methods, such as internal flash, HTTP/HTTPS, TFTP, or using FTP server.

Step 5 Change between contexts to perform configuration and monitoring tasks within each context by using the **changeto context {*name*}** command. The prompt changes to the following:

hostname/context-*name*#

Step 6 To view the context information, use the **show context [*name* | detail| count]** command.

Example 6-1 shows how to enable multiple contexts mode. The example sets the **admin-context** to be **administrator**, creates a context called "**administrator**" on the internal flash memory, and adds another two contexts: a context called **customerA** from an FTP server, and another context called **customerB** from internal flash. Note that the context names are case sensitive.

Example 6-1 *Configuring Multiple Contexts*

```
hostname(config)# mode multiple
hostname(config)# admin-context administrator
hostname(config)# context administrator
hostname(config-ctx)# allocate-interface Ethernet0.1
hostname(config-ctx)# allocate-interface Ethernet1.1
hostname(config-ctx)# allocate-interface Management0/0
hostname(config-ctx)# config-url flash:/admin.cfg

hostname(config-ctx)# context customerA
hostname(config-ctx)# allocate-interface Ethernet0.100 int1
hostname(config-ctx)# allocate-interface Ethernet0.102 int2
hostname(config-ctx)# allocate-interface Ethernet0.103-Ethernet0.108 int3-int8
hostname(config-ctx)# config-url ftp://joe:password@10.1.1.1/configs/
customerA.cfg

hostname(config-ctx)# context customerB
hostname(config-ctx)# allocate-interface Ethernet1.200 int1
hostname(config-ctx)# allocate-interface Ethernet1.202-Ethernet1.203 int2-int3
hostname(config-ctx)# allocate-interface Ethernet1.205-Ethernet1.210 int5-int10
hostname(config-ctx)# config-url flash:/customerB.cfg
```

Example 6-2 shows how to change between contexts and the system execution space in privileged EXEC mode to perform configuration and monitoring tasks within each context. The system execution space is the admin context from where you can switch between the contexts. Ensure the location, because the configuration changes made are applicable to the current position (within the context). For example, when the **show running-config** command is executed, it will display only the current configuration of that context and not the running configurations of all contexts (system plus all contexts).

Example 6-2 *Changing Between Contexts*

```
hostname/admin# changeto system
hostname# changeto context customerA
hostname/customerA#
OR
hostname# changeto context customerB
hostname/customerB#
```

Security Levels

The Adaptive Security Algorithm permits connections from one firewall network interface to another by using a security level mechanism. Each interface must be assigned with a security level ranging between 0 (lowest) to 100 (highest). By default, the Security Appliance assigns the internal network (the inside network) security level 100, whereas the external network (outside network) connected to the Internet is assigned with level 0. Other networks, such as DMZ, can be assigned any number in between.

By default, the Security Appliance allows traffic to flow freely from an internal network (higher security level 100) to an external network (lower security level 0).

For traffic to flow between the interfaces through the Security Appliance, basic parameters need to be configured. These include the interface name, security level, an IP address, and the dynamic or static routing and enabling of the interface as physical interfaces are shut down by default.

Example 6-3 shows how to configure physical interface parameters in single mode.

Example 6-3 *Configuring Interface Parameters in Single Mode*

```
hostname(config)# interface Ethernet1
hostname(config-if)# nameif inside
hostname(config-if)# security-level 100
hostname(config-if)# ip address 10.1.1.1 255.255.255.0
hostname(config-if)# no shutdown
```

Example 6-4 shows how to configure interface parameters in multiple contexts mode for the system configuration. The example creates a subinterface Ethernet1.100, by putting it in VLAN 100 allocating the Ethernet1.100 subinterface to contextA.

Example 6-4 *Configuring Interface Parameters in Multiple Mode*

```
hostname(config)# interface Ethernet1
hostname(config-if)# speed 100
hostname(config-if)# duplex full
hostname(config-if)# no shutdown
hostname(config-if)# interface Ethernet1.100
hostname(config-subif)# vlan 100
hostname(config-subif)# no shutdown
hostname(config-subif)# context contextA
hostname(config-ctx)# ...
hostname(config-ctx)# allocate-interface Ethernet1.100
```

By default, the Adaptive Security Algorithm does not permit interfaces on the same security level to communicate with each other. To explicitly permit this, use the following command from the global configuration mode to enable traffic flow between same security level interfaces without access lists.

```
hostname(config)# same-security-traffic permit inter-interface
```

Redundant Interface

Software Version 8.0 introduces the capability to create redundant interface pairs that group multiple physical interfaces into a logical group to provide an active/standby environment. When the active interface fails, the standby interface becomes active and starts passing traffic. This feature offers increased reliability and ensures traffic will pass when there is a problem with a physical interface. Note that this feature is separate from device-level failover. Redundant interfaces can be configured along with regular failover configuration. The Security Appliance supports up to eight redundant interface pairs.

Perform the following steps to configure a redundant interface on the Security Appliance.

Step 1 Enable the logical redundant interface by using the following commands from the global configuration mode. The *number* argument is an integer value between 1 and 8.

firewall(config)# **interface redundant** *number*

Step 2 Add the first member interface to the redundant interface logical group.

firewall(config-if)# **member-interface** *1st_physical_interface*

Step 3 Add the second member interface to the redundant interface logical group.

firewall(config-if)# **member-interface** *2nd_physical_interface*

Use the **show interface redundant***number* **detail** command to view the redundant interface settings and also to determine which interface is currently active. By default, the first member interface in the configuration is active. However, this can be changed by using the **redundant-interface redundant***number* **active-member** *physical_interface command.*

IP Routing

IP Routing is one of the basic initialization steps used when configuring the Security Appliance. Routing is the process of deciding the path for each packet that a Security Appliance handles. The routing table contains a list of IP network addresses for which the Security Appliance is intended to provide IP routing services. After the address translation and other routines are completed, a route identifies the interface and the gateway used to forward packets for a specific destination network. Using the destination IP address in the packet header, the routing mechanism decides whether the packet is to be forwarded if a valid route entry is found in the routing table; if not, the packet is discarded.

NOTE   The routing mechanism should not be used to implement security policy; it should be used merely as a supporting structure designed to forward packets efficiently and reliably.

Security Appliance supports the following four ways to enable IP Routing:

- Static and default routes
- OSPF
- RIP
- EIGRP

TIP   Security Appliance supports up to three equal cost routes on the same interface for load balancing.

Static and Default Routes

The simplest option is to use static or default route(s) to forward the packets. A default route forwards all traffic for which no route is found in the routing table to the gateway address. In contrast, a static route forwards traffic for specified destination networks to the next-hop connected device that is specific in the route statement. No route is required for directly connected networks on the Security Appliance.

Static or default routes are required in transparent mode to forward traffic that originates on the Security Appliance destined for nonconnected networks.

Static Route

As the name implies, a static route provides IP routing information to the Security Appliance without the need of dynamic routing protocol. A static route has a higher precedence over any dynamic routing protocol and is always the best preference to forward traffic to the desired destination. The default administrative distance for a static route is 1, giving it precedence over other routes discovered by dynamic routing protocols, but not directly connected routes. Connected routes always take precedence over static or dynamically discovered routes. In the event of a multiple entries match for a specified destination address, the *longest match* is preferred. The longest match is the entry with the highest number of 1 bits in its Routing Mask.

Configure static routes using the **route** command from the global configuration mode to forward traffic for specified nonconnected destination network. One disadvantage of a static route is that route entry will always remain in the routing table, even if the specified gateway becomes unavailable. This is because no mechanism exists for the Security Appliance to determine that the gateway address is not reachable. (This behavior is prevented when using dynamic routing protocol.) If the specified gateway becomes unavailable, static routes need to be manually removed. However, static routes are removed automatically from the routing table if the specified physical interface goes down, and they are reinstated when the interface comes back up.

Static Route Tracking

Software Version 8.0 introduces another unique feature called Static Route Tracking. This feature supports the capability to track the status of the next-hop IP address in the static route. Prior to this feature, there was no inherent mechanism to determine whether the route was up or down, and routes remain in the routing table even if the next-hop gateway becomes unavailable. The only exception was that if the associated interface on the firewall went down, the routes were removed from the routing table.

The static route tracking feature provides the capability to install backup routes dynamically when the primary route fails.

This feature is also useful to define multiple default routes. An example is defining a primary default route to an ISP gateway and a backup default route to a secondary ISP in case the primary ISP becomes unavailable. Static route tracking can also be enabled for static or default routes obtained through Dynamic Host Configuration Protocol (DHCP) or Point-to-Point Protocol over Ethernet (PPPoE).

This feature works by associating a static route with a predefined monitoring target. The Security Appliance monitors the target by using Internet Control Message Protocol (ICMP) echo request packets. In response, if an ICMP echo-reply message is not received within a specified period, the object is considered down, and the associated static route is removed from the routing table. The backup route is installed dynamically and used in place of the removed route.

The Security Appliance can be configured to use one of the following objects as the monitoring target:

- ISP gateway address
- Next-hop gateway address
- Specific server on the target network, such as a AAA server or the web server
- Any persistent network object on the destination network

NOTE   For additional details on static route tracking, refer to the following Cisco documentation URL: http://www.cisco.com/en/US/docs/security/asa/asa80/configuration/guide/ip.html#wp1090243.

Default Route

To avoid the need to use static route entries for every possible destination network, a default route identifies the default gateway address for forwarding packets for destination network(s) not explicitly found in the routing table. Default routes are put to best use in topologies where learning all or more specific networks is not desirable, as in the case of stub networks, or networks with only a single link connecting to the external network (or Internet). A default route is simply a static route (with a destination address/mask pair of 0.0.0.0/0) that is configured using the same **route** command used to define static routes and is usually aimed toward the external network on the outside interface.

The Security Appliance has the capability to define a separate default route for encrypted traffic along with the standard default route. Use the **tunneled** option in a default route statement to define a separate gateway address for forwarding all encrypted traffic. The **tunneled** option does not support multiple equal-cost path routes. Example 6-5 shows a Security Appliance configured with two default routes, one for the non-encrypted traffic and another for encrypted traffic. Non-encrypted traffic for which there is no static or dynamically learned route is forwarded to gateway 209.165.201.1. Encrypted traffic for which there is no static or dynamically learned route is forwarded to gateway 209.165.201.2.

Example 6-5 *Configuring Separate Default Routes for Encrypted and Non-Encrypted Traffic*

```
hostname(config)# route outside 0.0.0.0 0.0.0.0 209.165.201.1
hostname(config)# route outside 0.0.0.0 0.0.0.0 209.165.201.2 tunneled
```

Figure 6-8 shows an example to configure a static and default route. A default route is configured to send all traffic to the upstream device on the outside interface. Network A and Network B are nonconnected networks; hence, two static routes are created that send traffic destined for Network A (172.16.1.0/24) to the downstream router (10.1.1.2) that is connected to the inside interface, and for Network B (192.168.1.0/24) to the downstream router (10.1.2.2) connected to the DMZ interface.

Figure 6-8 *Configuring a Static and Default Route*

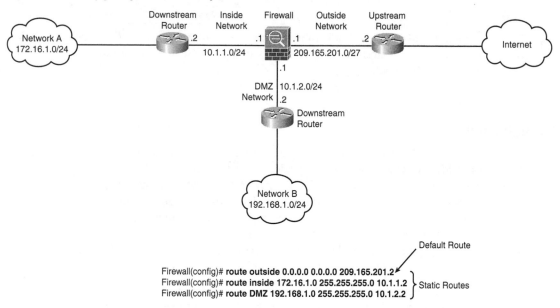

Equal Cost Multiple Path (ECMP) Forwarding

For load balancing, the Security Appliance offers the ECMP that supports up to three equal-cost routes to the same destination per interface. Based on an algorithm that hashes the source and destination IP addresses, the Security Appliance load balances the traffic among the specified gateways. Note that this does not guarantee diverting traffic equally among the gateways.

Example 6-6 shows three equal-cost static routes for destination network 10.1.1.0/24, forwarding traffic to three different gateways on the outside interface.

Example 6-6   *Configuring ECMP (Equal Cost Multiple Path) Static Routes*

```
hostname(config)# route outside 10.1.1.0 255.255.255.0 209.165.201.1
hostname(config)# route outside 10.1.1.0 255.255.255.0 209.165.201.2
hostname(config)# route outside 10.1.1.0 255.255.255.0 209.165.201.3
```

Similarly, up to three equal-cost default routes can be defined per device. Example 6-7 shows three equal-cost default routes, forwarding traffic to three different gateways on the outside interface.

Example 6-7   *Configuring ECMP (Equal Cost Multiple Path) Default Routes*

```
hostname(config)# route outside 0.0.0.0 0.0.0.0 209.165.201.1
hostname(config)# route outside 0.0.0.0 0.0.0.0 209.165.201.2
hostname(config)# route outside 0.0.0.0 0.0.0.0 209.165.201.3
```

NOTE   ECMP is not supported across multiple interfaces.

Open Shortest Path First (OSPF)

Dynamic routing occurs when devices communicate to adjacent devices, informing each other of the reachability of networks. These devices communicate using a routing protocol such as OSPF to exchange route information. Unlike static routing, the routing information populated into the routing tables is added and deleted dynamically by a dynamic routing protocol as routes change over time.

OSPF is an Interior Gateway Protocol (IGP) that distributes routing information among devices. OSPF is used over IP, and OSPF packets are transmitted with an IP data packet with the *protocol* field in the IP header set to 89. OSPF uses a link-state algorithm to build and calculate the shortest path to all known destinations. The algorithm used to calculate the shortest path is called the Dijkstra algorithm (named after its inventor Edsger W. Dijkstra).

The Security Appliance supports OSPF routing protocol in a manner similar to the IOS. The Security Appliance can run up to two OSPF processes simultaneously, for different sets of interfaces. By default, the two processes will not exchange information unless route redistribution is configured explicitly. The two processes are isolated, as in two separate routing instances in the same device. There are several reasons to have two OSPF processes on the Security Appliance. For example, two processes on the Security Appliance are useful if the Security Appliance has interfaces that use the same IP addresses. (NAT allows these interfaces to coexist, but OSPF does not allow overlapping addresses.) Or, in most cases, a separate OSPF process is enabled on the inside and the outside interfaces (as shown in

Figure 6-9), to give you the capability to control route propagation by redistributing a subset of routes between the two processes. Similarly, there could be a requirement to segregate private addresses from public addresses, making two processes necessary.

The cost (also called metric) of an interface in OSPF is inversely proportional to the bandwidth of that interface. A higher bandwidth indicates a lower cost, and a lower-cost path is the preferred route. The formula used to calculate the OSPF cost is

- OSPF Cost = 100,000,000 ÷ bandwidth (in bps)

As shown in Figure 6-9, redistribution between the two OSPF processes is supported. Static and connected routes on the Security Appliance can also be redistributed into the OSPF process, but they must be configured on OSPF-enabled interfaces.

Configuring OSPF

As per the Figure 6-9 network diagram, OSPF can be configured on the inside and outside interfaces.

NOTE   RIP and OSPF on the same firewall appliance was not supported in version 7.0 or prior. However, multiprotocol is now fully supported from v7.2 and later, as illustrated in Figure 6-9.

Example 6-8 shows how to enable two separate OSPF processes with mutual two-way redistribution to allow devices on both sides of the Security Appliance to learn networks from each other.

Figure 6-9   *IP Routing Protocols on Security Appliance*

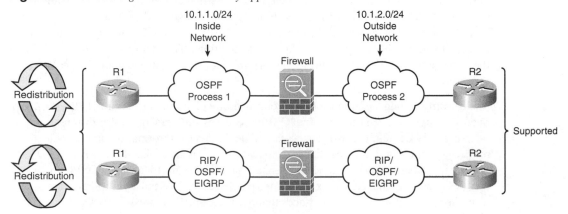

Example 6-8   *Configuring Two OSPF Processes (for Inside and Outside Interfaces) with Two-Way Redistribution*

```
hostname(config)# router ospf 1
hostname(config-router)# network 10.1.1.0 255.255.255.0 area 0
hostname(config-router)# redistribute ospf 2 metric 1 subnets
hostname(config)# router ospf 2
hostname(config-router)# network 10.1.2.0 255.255.255.0 area 0
hostname(config-router)# redistribute ospf 1 metric 1 subnets
```

Several interface-specific OSPF parameters can be configured as deemed necessary, including OSPF Hello or dead intervals, OSPF priority, and authentication keys. Example 6-9 shows some of the OSPF parameters that can be enabled under the interface.

Example 6-9   *Configuring OSPF Interface-Specific Parameters*

```
hostname(config-router)# interface inside
hostname(config-interface)# ospf cost 10
hostname(config-interface)# ospf retransmit-interval 10
hostname(config-interface)# ospf transmit-delay 5
hostname(config-interface)# ospf priority 255
hostname(config-interface)# ospf hello-interval 5
hostname(config-interface)# ospf dead-interval 20
hostname(config-interface)# ospf authentication-key cisco
hostname(config-interface)# ospf message-digest-key 1 md5 cisco
hostname(config-interface)# ospf authentication message-digest
```

Several OSPF parameters can be configured under the area that will affect the entire OSPF domain/area. Examples include authentication, route summarization, route filtering, and defining stub areas. Example 6-10 shows some of the OSPF parameters that can be enabled areawide.

Example 6-10   *Examples of Areawide OSPF Parameters*

```
hostname(config)# router ospf 1
hostname(config-router)# area 1 default-cost 10
hostname(config-router)# area 1 stub
hostname(config-router)# area 1 stub no-summary
hostname(config-router)# area 0 range 10.1.1.0 255.255.255.0
hostname(config-router)# area 0 filter-list prefix mylist in
```

Securing OSPF

Securing OSPF networks will provide protection not only from malicious attacks, but also accidental misconfigurations. The receptive nature of OSPF dictates that any router with coordinated configuration parameters (network mask, hello interval, dead interval, and the like) can participate in a given OSPF network. Because of this default behavior, any number of accidental factors (misconfigurations, lab machines, test setups, and so on) have the potential to adversely affect routing in an OSPF environment. Authentication provides password-based protection against unauthorized access to an area. The Security Appliance supports OSPF authentication to secure route exchange between the devices. OSPF supports two types of authentication: simple password (clear-text) and MD5 authentication mechanism. Security Appliance supports both.

Example 6-11 shows how to configure areawide OSPF authentication on the Security Appliance.

Example 6-11 *Configuring Area-Based OSPF Authentication*

```
hostname(config)# router ospf 1
! Enabling area-wide Simple (clear-text) authentication
hostname(config-router)# area 0 authentication
! Enabling area-wide MD5 authentication
hostname(config-router)# area 0 authentication message-digest
! Configure OSPF key on the interface
hostname(config-router)# interface inside
! Configuring Simple password authentication key
hostname(config-interface)# ospf authentication-key cisco
! Configuring MD5 authentication key
hostname(config-interface)# ospf message-digest-key 1 md5 cisco
```

Alternatively, authentication can be enabled specifically on a link basis (per-interface) and not areawide. This means that both sides of the link on the connected devices must be configured similarly. Example 6-12 shows how to configure interface-based OSPF authentication on the Security Appliance.

Example 6-12 *Configuring Interface-Based OSPF Authentication*

```
hostname(config-router)# interface inside
! Configuring Simple password authentication and key
hostname(config-interface)# ospf authentication
hostname(config-interface)# ospf authentication-key cisco
! Configuring MD5 authentication and key
hostname(config-interface)# ospf authentication message-digest
hostname(config-interface)# ospf message-digest-key 1 md5 cisco
```

Monitoring OSPF

Several useful **show** commands are available for displaying general information and other OSPF-related information, such as neighbor adjacency status, interface parameters, virtual-link status, and border-routers. The following list includes some of the common OSPF **show** commands used:

- **show ospf** [*process-id [area-id]*]**:** Displays general information about OSPF routing processes.

- **show ospf interface** [*if_name*]**:** Displays OSPF-related interface information.

- **show ospf neighbor** [*interface-name*] [*neighbor-id*] **[detail]:** Displays OSPF neighbor adjacency information on a per-interface basis.

- **show ospf** [*process-id*] **virtual-links:** Displays OSPF-related virtual links information.

- **show ospf border-routers:** Displays the internal OSPF routing table entries to the Area Border Router (ABR) and Autonomous System Boundary Router (ASBR).

- **show ospf** [*process-id* [*area-id*]] **database:** Displays lists of information related to the OSPF database for a specific device.

- **show ospf** [*process-id*] **summary-address:** Displays a list of all summary address redistribution information configured under an OSPF process.

Routing Information Protocol (RIP)

The Routing Information Protocol, or RIP as it is more commonly called, is one of the most enduring of all routing protocols. RIP was defined in RFC 1058 and Internet Standard (STD) 56. Later, the IETF (Internet Engineering Task Force) updated RIP with the release of a revised RFC 1388 in January 1993. RFC 1388 was then superseded in November 1994 by RFC 1723, which describes RIPv2 (the second version of RIP). These RFCs did not attempt to make obsolete the previous version of RIP, but proposed extensions and enhancements to the RIP capabilities. RIPv2 enabled RIP messages to carry more information and scale further with more features, such as multicast support and a next-hop router address. The next-hop router address is an authentication mechanism; its most important function is to support subnet masks and is therefore a critical feature that was not available in RIPv1. RIP is a dynamic, distance-vector routing protocol that uses UDP as the transport protocol. RIP packets are transmitted on UDP port 520 for route updates.

The Security Appliance supports both RIPv1 and RIPv2 protocols. Using RIP has advantages over using static routes, because the initial configuration for RIP is simple and does not require updating the configuration when the topology changes. The downside to RIP (or any other dynamic protocol) is that there is more network and processing overhead than with static routing.

By default, the Security Appliance sends RIPv1 updates and accepts RIPv1 and RIPv2 updates. Redistribution of routes from other routing processes into the RIP is supported in Firewall OS Version 7.2 and later. Prior to this, RIP and OSPF were not supported on the same device.

Configuring RIP

Unlike IOS, RIP is enabled differently on the Security Appliance. To enable RIP on the Security Appliance for an interface, use the **rip** command from the global configuration mode. There is no **router rip** command on the Security Appliance. Both RIP modes (passive and default) can be enabled on an interface by using the **rip** command.

Example 6-13 shows how to configure passive RIP with simple password authentication and MD5 authentication on inside and outside interfaces. Example 6-13 also shows how to propagate a default route on the inside interface, indicating that the Security Appliance will be the default gateway for the downstream devices. A default route is seldom (in most cases never) advertised out on the outside interface, because in typical network designs, the Security Appliance is not the default gateway for the upstream device.

Example 6-13   *Configuring RIP*

```
! Enabling RIPv2 with Simple Password Authentication
hostname(config)# rip outside passive version 2 authentication text cisco 1
hostname(config)# rip inside passive version 2 authentication text cisco 1
hostname(config)# rip inside default version 2 authentication text cisco 1
! Enabling RIPv2 with MD5 Authentication
hostname(config)# rip outside passive version 2 authentication md5 cisco 1
hostname(config)# rip inside passive version 2 authentication md5 cisco 1
hostname(config)# rip inside default version 2 authentication md5 cisco 1
```

Enhanced Interior Gateway Routing Protocol (EIGRP)

The Security Appliance OS Software Version 8.0 debuts the support of the Enhanced Interior Gateway Routing Protocol (EIGRP). EIGRP is a Cisco proprietary routing protocol and is available on Cisco devices only. EIGRP on Security Appliance is supported in single mode only; it is not supported in multicontext mode.

NOTE   Firewall OS supports only one EIGRP routing process on the Security Appliance.

The Security Appliance can be configured as an EIGRP stub router, which helps enhance the performance by decreasing memory and processing requirements on the Security Appliance. A firewall configured as an EIGRP stub does not require maintaining a complete EIGRP routing table, because it forwards all nonlocal traffic to a distribution router. The distribution router sends a default route to the stub router/firewall. In some occasions, only specific routes are advertised from the stub router to the distribution router. When the Security Appliance is configured as a stub router, it sends a peer information packet to all neighboring routers to report its status as a stub router. Neighbors receiving this packet will not query the stub for routes. The stub depends on the distribution router to send the proper updates to all peers.

Configuring EIGRP Stub Routing

The Security Appliance can be enabled as an EIGRP stub router through the following steps:

Step 1 Enable the EIGRP routing process from the global configuration mode as follows. The *as-num* is the Autonomous System number of the EIGRP routing process:

firewall(config)# **router eigrp** *as-num*

Step 2 Configure the interface connected to the distribution router to participate in the EIGRP process:

firewall(config-router)# **network** *ip-addr* [*mask*]

Step 3 Configure the Security Appliance for the stub routing process. Specific networks must be explicitly defined that need to be advertised by the stub routing process to the distribution router. By default, static and connected networks are not automatically redistributed into the stub routing process.

firewall (config-router)# **eigrp stub** {**receive-only** | [**connected**] [**redistributed**] [**static**] [**summary**]}

By default, EIGRP hello packets are sent as multicast packets. In a nonbroadcast environment such as a tunnel, EIGRP neighbors must be manually defined to send hello packets as unicast messages. To define a static neighbor in EIGRP, use the following command from the router configuration mode:

firewall(config-router)# **neighbor** *ip-addr* **interface** *if_name*

Multiple static neighbors can be defined using the previously outlined process.

Similar to EIGRP support in a Cisco IOS router, several other optional parameters can be configured on Security Appliance, such as the **distribute-list**, **passive-interface** and **default-information** commands.

Securing EIGRP

EIGRP supports route authentication by using MD5 authentication for all routing updates. The MD5 authentication prevents the introduction of unauthorized or false routing messages from unapproved sources.

NOTE	EIGRP route authentication is configured on a per-interface basis. All neighbors must be configured with the same authentication mode and key for EIGRP adjacencies to be established.

EIGRP authentication can be enabled on the physical interface as follows:

Step 1   Enter the physical interface configuration mode for which EIGRP authentication needs to be configured:

firewall(config)# **interface** *phy_if*

Step 2   Enable per-interface MD5 authentication as follows:

firewall(config-if)# **authentication mode eigrp** *as-num* **md5**

Step 3   Configure the secure key used by the MD5 algorithm. The *key* argument can contain up to 16 characters. The *key-id* argument is a numeric number from 0 to 255:

firewall(config-if)# **authentication key eigrp** *as-num key* **key-id** *key-id*

Network Address Translation (NAT)

NAT, also referred to as IP address masquerading, performs the translation of an IP address that is used within one network (internal network) to a different IP address known within another network (outside world). NAT technology is typically used to hide the IP addresses in an internal network (using RFC 1918 private addressing). The masquerading technique can be seen as a form of security hiding the real identity of the network.

A NAT device performs the following two processes:

  1   Substituting a real address into a mapped address, which is routable on the destination network.

  2   Undoing translation for returning traffic.

Firewall Stateful inspection tracks all connections traversing through the Security Appliance by maintaining a translation table and using this table to verify the destination of an inbound packet that matches the source of a previous outbound request.

NAT Control

The firewall has always been a device supporting and even requiring NAT for maximum flexibility and security. NAT control is available as a capability in the new software release on the Security Appliance.

NAT control dictates the firewall if the address translation rules are required for outside communications and ensures that the address translation behavior is the same as versions earlier than 7.0.

The NAT control feature works as follows:

- When NAT control is disabled, and the firewall forwards all packets from a higher-security (such as Inside) interface to a lower-security (such as Outside) interface without the configuration of a NAT rule. Traffic from a lower-security interface to a higher-security interface only requires that it be permitted in the access lists, and no NAT rule is required in this mode.

- When NAT control is enabled, this dictates the requirement of using NAT. (The NAT rule is compulsory in this case.) When NAT control is enabled, it is also required that packets initiated from a higher security-level interface (such as Inside) to a lower security-level interface (such as Outside) must match a NAT rule (**nat** command with a corresponding **global**, or a **static** command), or else processing for the packet stops. Traffic from a lower-security interface to a higher-security interface also requires a NAT and is permitted in the access lists to be forwarded through the firewall.

The default configuration is the specification of the **no nat-control** command (NAT control disabled mode). With version 7.0 and later, this behavior can be changed as required.

To enable NAT control, use the **nat-control** command in the global configuration mode, as shown next:

```
hostname(config)# nat-control
```

NOTE   The **nat-control** command is available in routed firewall mode and in single and multiple security context modes.

When the **nat-control** is enabled, each Inside address must have a corresponding Inside NAT rule. Similarly, if an Outside dynamic NAT is enabled on an interface, each Outside address must have a corresponding Outside NAT rule before communication is allowed through the Security Appliance.

By default, NAT control is disabled (**no nat-control** command). The **no nat-control** command allows Inside hosts to communicate with outside networks without the need to configure a NAT rule. In essence, with NAT control disabled, the Security Appliance does not perform an address translation function to any packets. To disable NAT control globally, use the **no nat-control** command in global configuration mode:

```
hostname(config)# no nat-control
```

The difference between the **no nat-control** command and the **nat 0** (identity NAT) command is that identity NAT requires that traffic be initiated from the higher-level interface. The **no nat-control** command does not have this requirement, nor does it require a **static** command to allow communication from the lower-level interface (from Outside to Inside); it relies only on access-policies—for example, permitting the traffic in ACL and having corresponding route entries.

To summarize, traffic traversing from a

More Secure to a Less Secure interface

- Is designated as outbound traffic.
- The firewall will allow all IP-based traffic unless restricted by access lists, authentication, or authorization.
- One or more of the following commands are required:
  - **nat**, **nat 0**, **global**, **static**

Less Secure to a More Secure interface

- Is designated as inbound traffic.
- Outside to Inside connections.
- Inbound permission is required.
- The firewall will drop all packets unless specifically allowed in the **access-list** that is applied on the arriving interface. Further restrictions apply if authentication and authorization are used.
- One or more of the following commands are required:
  - **nat 0** with ACL, **static** and inbound **access-list** on the ingress interface.

NAT Types

Several types of NAT are available. The Security Appliance can be configured to perform any of the following types:

- Dynamic NAT
- Dynamic Port Address Translation (PAT)
- Static NAT
- Static PAT

Dynamic NAT

Dynamic NAT translates a group of real (private) addresses to public IP addresses drawn from a pool of registered (public) addresses that are routable on the destination network. When a host initiates a connection to a particular destination, the Security Appliance translates the host source address to the corresponding NAT rule from the mapped pool. The translation is maintained and is valid for the duration of the connection and cleared when the session is terminated. If the same host initiates another connection, there is no guarantee it will acquire the same address from the mapped pool. Addresses from the pool are handed out on a first-come, first-served basis. Therefore, because the translated address varies, the destination-side user cannot initiate inbound connections when dynamic NAT is used. Dynamic NAT and PAT are used for unidirectional communication only. Figure 6-10 shows how dynamic NAT works.

Figure 6-10 *Dynamic NAT*

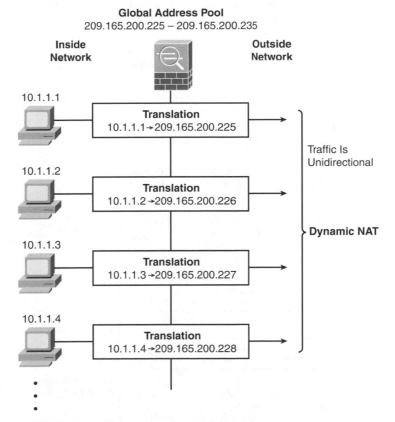

```
Firewall(config)# nat (inside) 1 10.1.1.0 255.255.255.0
Firewall(config)# global (outside) 1 209.165.200.225-209.165.200.235
```

Dynamic PAT

Dynamic PAT translates a group of real (private) addresses that are mapped to a single mapped IP address by using a combination of a mapped IP address and a source port number to create a unique session. Hence, the same IP address is used for all packets with a different source port for each session. The Security Appliance translates the source address and source port (Layer 3 and Layer 4 combination) to the mapped address and a unique port above 1024.

Each connection entails a separate translation because the source port differs for each connection. The translation is maintained and remains valid for the duration of the connection. The translation is cleared when the session is terminated. The port translation also expires after 30 seconds of inactivity. (This timeout is not configurable.) PAT lets you use a single mapped address, thus conserving routable addresses. The interface IP address of the Security Appliance can also be used as the PAT address. Similar to Dynamic NAT, the destination-side user cannot initiate an inbound connection when using dynamic PAT. Figure 6-11 shows how dynamic PAT works.

NOTE   PAT does not work for some multimedia applications that have a data stream different from the control path.

Figure 6-11 *Dynamic PAT*

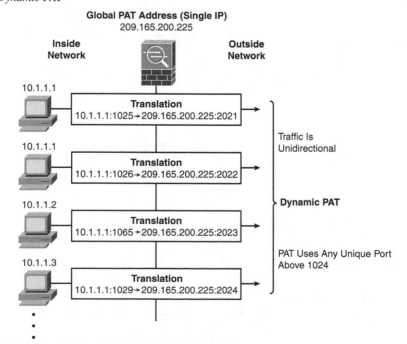

Dynamic NAT and PAT can be enabled concurrently. The Security Appliance first uses all the addresses from the global address pool. When no addresses are available in the global pool, it applies the PAT translation, as shown in Figure 6-12.

Figure 6-12 *Dynamic NAT and PAT*

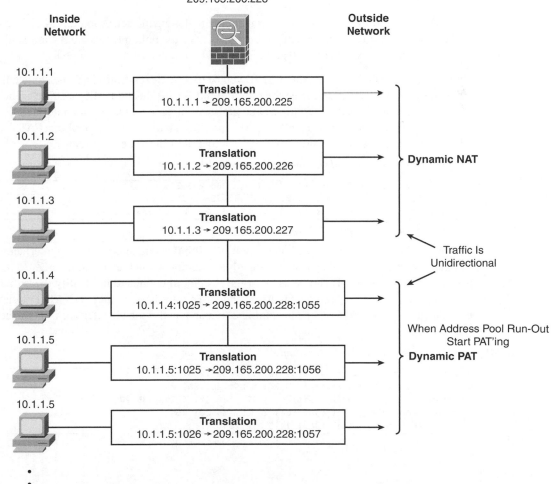

```
Firewall(config)# nat (inside) 1 10.1.1.0 255.255.255.0
Firewall(config)# global (outside) 1 209.165.200.225-209.165.200.227
Firewall(config)# global (outside) 1 209.165.200.228
```

Configure Dynamic NAT and PAT

To configure dynamic NAT and PAT, perform the following steps:

Step 1 Identify the real (private) addresses on a given interface that requires translation by using the **nat** command.

Step 2 Configure a corresponding **global** command to specify the mapped addresses pool for the egress interface. (In the case of PAT, this is one address.)

Each **nat** command matches a **global** command by matching the corresponding NAT ID, a number that is assigned in each command. NAT ID ties the **nat** and the **global** commands together. Refer back to Figure 6-10 and Figure 6-11 for demonstration examples.

When using multiple interfaces, the NAT ID can be used to tie multiple NAT rules together. For example, NAT ID 1 can be used to configure **nat** for Inside and DMZ interfaces. The same ID 1 can then be used to configure the **global** command on the outside interface. Traffic from the inside interface and the DMZ interface share a mapped pool or a PAT address when exiting the outside interface. Example 6-14 illustrates this scenario.

Example 6-14 *Configuring the Same NAT ID for the Inside and DMZ Interface*

```
hostname(config)# nat (inside) 1 10.1.1.0 255.255.255.0
hostname(config)# nat (dmz) 1 10.2.2.0 255.255.255.0
hostname(config)# global (outside) 1 209.165.201.3-209.165.201.10
```

The NAT ID can also be used to reference multiple **global** commands for exiting interfaces. For example, NAT ID 1 can be used for the **global** command on Outside and DMZ interfaces, and the same ID can be used for the Inside **nat** command to identify the traffic to be translated when going to both Outside and DMZ interfaces. Similarly, NAT ID 1 can be used on the DMZ interface, and the **global** command on the outside interface is also used for DMZ traffic.

Example 6-15 *Configuring the Same NAT ID for Multiple Global Commands*

```
hostname(config)# nat (inside) 1 10.1.1.0 255.255.255.0
hostname(config)# nat (dmz) 1 10.2.2.0 255.255.255.0
hostname(config)# global (outside) 1 209.165.201.1-209.165.201.253
hostname(config)# global (outside) 1 209.165.201.254
hostname(config)# global (dmz) 1 10.2.2.254
```

Static NAT

Static NAT creates a fixed translation (one-to-one) of real (private) addresses to mapped (public) addresses. A persistent translation rule exists (mapped address is the same) for each consecutive connection with static NAT. Because the mapped address is always the same, it allows the destination-side network to initiate traffic to a translated host. The **static** command is used to permanently associate a host address (or entire subnet) on a higher security-level interface with a host address on a lower-security level interface. Static NAT and PAT can be used for bidirectional communication. Figure 6-13 shows an example.

Figure 6-13 *Static NAT*

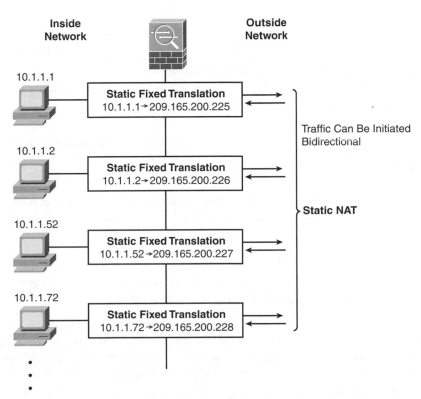

Static 1-to-1 Translation

Firewall(config)# **static (inside,outside) 209.165.200.225 10.1.1.1 netmask 255.255.255.255**
Firewall(config)# **static (inside,outside) 209.165.200.226 10.1.1.2 netmask 255.255.255.255**
Firewall(config)# **static (inside,outside) 209.165.200.227 10.1.1.52 netmask 255.255.255.255**
Firewall(config)# **static (inside,outside) 209.165.200.228 10.1.1.72 netmask 255.255.255.255**

There are several ways to configure address translation. The following examples illustrate a few scenarios.

Example 6-16 shows how to configure static NAT (persistent translation) for an Inside IP address (10.1.1.1) to an Outside IP address (209.165.200.1).

Example 6-16 *Configuring Inside NAT (1-to-1) Static Translation*

```
hostname(config)# static (inside,outside) 209.165.200.1 10.1.1.1 netmask
255.255.255.255
```

Example 6-17 shows how to configure an Outside NAT (persistent translation) using a static map for the Outside address (209.165.201.15) to an Inside address (10.1.1.6).

Example 6-17 *Configuring Outside NAT (1-to-1) Static Translation*

```
hostname(config)# static (outside,inside) 10.1.1.6 209.165.201.15 netmask
255.255.255.255
```

Example 6-18 shows how to configure a static map (persistent translation) for an entire subnet (1-to-1, host-to-host) with a 24-bit subnet mask.

Example 6-18 *Configuring Static NAT (1-to-1) for the Entire Subnet*

```
hostname(config)# static (inside,outside) 209.165.201.0 10.1.1.0 netmask
255.255.255.0
```

Static Port Address Translation (PAT)

Static PAT is similar to static NAT, with the exception that it allows for specifying the Layer 4 (TCP or UDP) port information for the real and mapped addresses.

This feature is useful for providing a single address for global users to access TFTP, HTTP, and Simple Mail Transfer Protocol (SMTP) services where the services are actually available on different servers on the local network. Define multiple static PAT statements for each server that uses the same mapped (public) IP address with ports mapped to different real IP addresses:
real_ip_A / public_ip_A / TFTP
real_ip_B / public_ip_A / HTTP
real_ip_C / public_ip_A / SMTP

Figure 6-14 shows how to configure static PAT statements for multiple services mapped to the same public IP address.

Figure 6-14 *Static PAT*

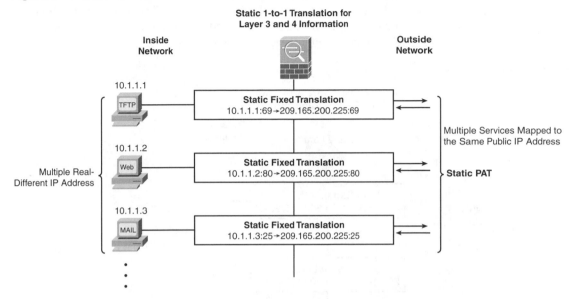

```
Firewall(config)# static (inside,outside) udp 209.165.200.225 tftp 10.1.1.1 tftp netmask 255.255.255.255
Firewall(config)# static (inside,outside) tcp 209.165.200.225 http 10.1.1.2 http netmask 255.255.255.255
Firewall(config)# static (inside,outside) tcp 209.165.200.225 smtp 10.1.1.3 smtp netmask 255.255.255.255
```

Bypassing NAT When NAT Control Is Enabled

As discussed earlier, when NAT control is enabled, each connection initiated requires a corresponding NAT rule. One of the following three methods can be used to bypass address translation for specific hosts or networks when NAT control is enabled:

- Identity NAT
- Static Identity NAT
- NAT Exemption

Identity NAT (**nat 0** Command)

Identity NAT is similar to Dynamic NAT, but it translates the real IP address to the same mapped IP address so that no need exists for a mapped global pool. Only "translated" hosts can create NAT translations, and return traffic is allowed back. Identity NAT can be used only for unidirectional communication. Even though the mapped address is the same as the real address, a connection cannot be initiated from the Outside to the Inside.

Figure 6-15 shows how to configure Identity NAT. The NAT engine will not perform address translation for the inside hosts on the 209.165.201.0/27 network, and the source address remains the same when it exits. This method can also be used when the internal network uses a public routable address and does not require address translation.

Figure 6-15 *Identity NAT*

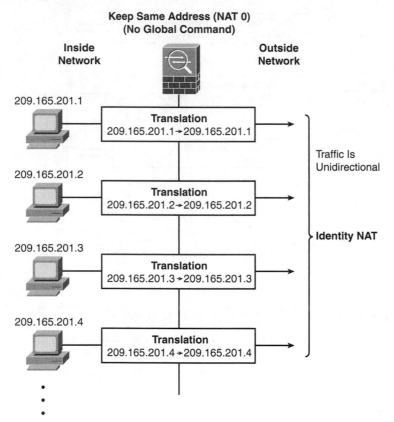

Firewall(config)# **nat (inside) 0 209.165.201.0 255.255.255.224**

Static Identity NAT (**static** Command)

Static identity NAT is similar to static NAT, but it creates a fixed translation (1-to-1) of real addresses while keeping the same mapped addresses. Static identity NAT can be used for bidirectional communication.

Figure 6-16 shows how to configure Static Identity NAT. The NAT engine will not perform address translation for the inside hosts on the 10.1.1.0/24 network, and the source address remains the same when it exits. Outside users can initiate an inbound connection to this address as long as the address is routable on the destination side network.

Figure 6-16 *Static Identity NAT*

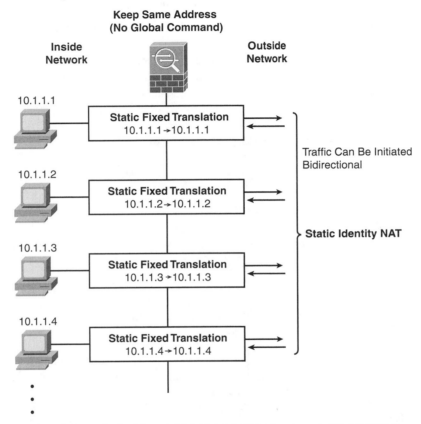

Firewall(config)# **static (inside,outside) 10.1.1.0 10.1.1.0 netmask 255.255.255.0**

Example 6-19 shows how to configure Outside Static Identity NAT. The NAT engine will not perform address translation for the Outside host 209.165.201.15 when accessed from Inside.

Example 6-19 *Configuring Outside Static Identity NAT*

```
hostname(config)# static (outside,inside) 209.165.201.15 209.165.201.15 netmask
255.255.255.255
```

NAT Exemption (**nat 0** with **ACL**)

NAT Exemption (**nat 0 access-list**) is similar to Identity NAT. The main differentiator is that NAT Exemption allows bidirectional communication. NAT Exemption allows both translated and remote hosts to initiate connections.

Figure 6-17 shows how to configure NAT Exemption. The NAT engine will not perform address translation for the inside hosts in 209.165.201.0/27 network, and they will remain the same because they exit out to another interface. Users on the Outside network (destination-side) are also able to initiate connection to a host in the 209.165.201.0/27 network.

Figure 6-17 *NAT Exemption*

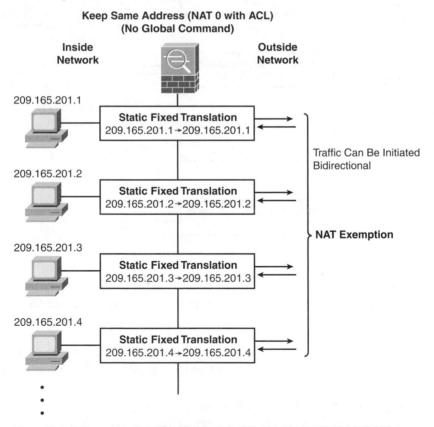

Firewall(config)# **access-list NONAT permit ip 209.165.201.0 255.255.255.224 any**
Firewall(config)# **nat (inside) 0 access-list NONAT**

Policy NAT

Policy NAT is similar to static NAT. However, it allows for defining a conditional criterion to check the source address and the destination address to determine address translation. With this feature, a source address translation can vary, subject to a different destination. For example:

Host A communicating to Server A → translate to Public_IP_A

Host A communicating to Server B → translate to Public_IP_B

Policy NAT allows identification of local traffic for address translation by specifying the combination of source and destination addresses (or ports) by using an access list. Regular NAT uses source addresses/ports only, whereas policy NAT uses both source and a combination of destination addresses/ports to identify the real address for translation.

Figure 6-18 shows how to configure Policy NAT Exemption by using the **nat/global** command. The source and destination address pair is checked, and address translation is performed accordingly. In this example, when internal hosts in network 10.1.1.0/24 initiate a connection to any host in network 172.16.1.0/24, the source address will be translated to 209.165.202.1-10.

When the same internal hosts in the network 10.1.1.0/24 initiate a connection to any host in network 192.168.1.0/24, the source address will be translated to 209.165.202.130-140 instead. Traffic flow is unidirectional when using the **nat/global** command, and bidirectional when using the **static** command.

Figure 6-18 *Policy NAT*

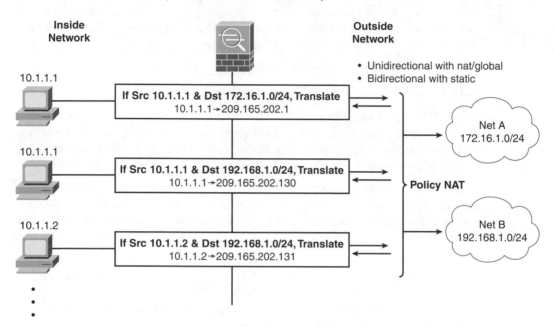

Policy NAT (Source/Destination Pair)

Firewall(config)# **access-list POLICY1 permit ip 10.1.1.0 255.255.255.0 172.16.1.0 255.255.255.0**
Firewall(config)# **access-list POLICY2 permit ip 10.1.1.0 255.255.255.0 192.168.1.0 255.255.255.0**

Firewall(config)# **nat (inside) 1 access-list POLICY1**
Firewall(config)# **global (outside) 1 209.165.202.1-209.165.202.10** ◄—— Global can be
Firewall(config)# **nat (inside) 2 access-list POLICY2**   pool or single address.
Firewall(config)# **global (outside) 2 209.165.202.130-209.165.202.140**

Order of NAT Processing

When several address translation types are configured on the firewall, there is a potential of overlap. The firewall matches real (private) addresses to corresponding NAT rules in the following order of NAT rules processing, until the first match is found.

1 NAT exemption (using **nat 0 access-list** command)

2 Policy NAT (using **static** with **access-list** command)

3 Static NAT (using **static** command)

4 Static PAT (using **static** command)

5 Policy NAT (using **nat** with **access-list** command)

    6 Dynamic NAT (using **nat** command)

    7 Dynamic PAT (using **nat** command)

Controlling Traffic Flow and Network Access

Firewall security policies are heavily based on strict access control. Network access can be controlled using access lists on the Security Appliance. Access lists can be configured to filter network traffic as it passes through the firewall.

ACL Overview and Applications on Security Appliance

Access lists specify criteria for a packet to be permitted or denied and are based on a protocol, a source and destination IP address or network, and optionally, the source and destination ports. Refer to Chapter 2, "Access Control," for more details on using access lists for traffic filtering.

Access lists have many applications and can be used in a variety of functions on the Security Appliance, including the following. The first is the most important:

- To control traffic flow and network access through the Security Appliance
- To identify addresses for NAT exemption or Policy NAT
- To identify traffic for AAA rules
- To identify traffic for a class map for MPF
- To control route redistribution
- To define traffic for IPsec VPN encryption
- To define the Webtype ACL for URL filters

ACLs can be used to control traffic flow in both routed and transparent firewall modes. The following section describes the difference between inbound and outbound ACL in the context of the Security Appliance and how to control network access through the appliance using access lists.

NOTE   Transparent mode supports two types of access lists: Extended ACLs used for Layer 3 traffic filtering and EtherType ACLs used for Layer 2 traffic filtering.

Controlling Inbound and Outbound Traffic Through the Security Appliance by Using Access Lists

Traffic can be examined in either direction on an interface, by using an inbound ACL for traffic entering into the Security Appliance and an outbound ACL for traffic exiting the Security Appliance. The main things to understand about the access list application on Security Appliance are the following:

- For traffic originating from a lower-level interface to a higher-level interface, an inbound ACL is required on the source interface to specifically allow the traffic (or else the packet will be dropped). An optional outbound ACL can be configured on the destination interface. Refer to Figure 6-19.

- For traffic originating from a higher-level to a lower-level interface, no access list is required, because traffic is permitted by default. This is also true for all returning traffic originally initiated from a higher-level to a lower-level interface, which is allowed through dynamically. An optional inbound ACL on the source interface and outbound ACL on the destination interface can be configured. Refer to Figure 6-19.

By default, traffic can exit the Security Appliance on any interface unless it is restricted through the use of an outbound ACL, which provides more granular access control in addition to the inbound ACL.

The access list architecture on the Security Appliance is similar to the IOS ACL operation.

To enable an access list for network access control on the Security Appliance, perform the following two steps. Configuring an access list on Security Appliance is similar to Cisco IOS.

Step 1—Defining an Access List

Using the **access-list** command from the global configuration mode, define access control entries (ACE) for a specific host, network, protocol, or ports. When defining an ACL on a Security Appliance, use a subnet mask rather than a wildcard mask on the IOS device. This works in a manner that is similar to the IOS, in that there is an implicit deny at the end of all access lists.

Step 2—Applying an Access List to an Interface

Apply the access list to the interface in an inbound or outbound direction by using the **access-group** {*name* | *number*} {**in** | **out**} **interface** *interface_name* command. One access list of each type (Extended and EtherType) can be applied to both directions of an interface.

Figure 6-19 *Inbound Versus Outbound ACL*

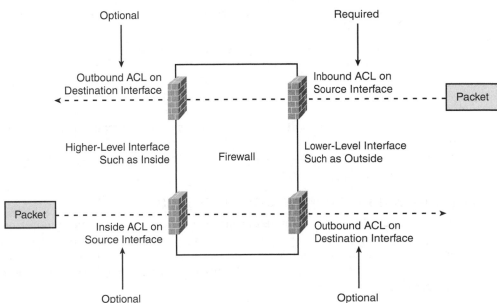

Example 6-20 shows how to configure an inbound ACL for network access from the lower level (outside interface) to a higher level (inside interface) to a web server with IP address 209.165.201.1. (This is a statically translated address that is visible on the outside interface.) ACL is applied to the outside interface filtering inbound traffic through the firewall.

Example 6-20 *Inbound ACL on the Outside Interface*

```
hostname(config)# static (inside,outside) 209.165.201.1 10.1.1.1 netmask
255.255.255.255
hostname(config)# access-list 101 extended permit tcp any host 209.165.201.1 eq www
hostname(config)# access-group 101 in interface outside
```

Example 6-21 shows how to configure an outbound ACL for granular network access control from a higher level (inside interface) to a lower level (outside interface), thereby preventing internal hosts 10.1.1.0/24 from accessing the external 209.165.202.128/27 network. All other traffic is explicitly permitted. The access list is applied on the outbound direction to the outside interface (destination interface for exiting packets). Alternatively, the same access list can be applied on the inbound to the inside interface (source interface for arriving packets) to achieve the same results.

Example 6-21 *Outbound ACL on the Outside Interface*

```
hostname(config)# access-list 102 extended deny tcp 10.1.1.0 255.255.255.0
209.165.202.128 255.255.255.224
hostname(config)# access-list 102 extended permit ip any any
hostname(config)# access-group 102 out interface outside
! or apply inbound on source interface
hostname(config)# access-group 102 in interface inside
```

TIP   Remember that configuring outbound ACL is optional and not required, as shown in Figure 6-19.

Simplifying Access Lists with Object Groups

Access lists can be long and cumbersome to create and maintain for medium-to-large enterprise networks. ACL configuration can be repetitive and difficult to troubleshoot when a problem occurs. A simpler and more effective approach is to group like objects together and reference them in the ACL. Object grouping simplifies access list creation and maintenance.

Following are four types of object groups:

- **Protocol:** A protocol-type object group is used to define the protocols (for example, ICMP, TCP, or UDP). Use the **object-group protocol** *grp_id* command and define the protocols by using the **protocol-object {*protocol*}** in the object-group submode. The *protocol* is the numeric identifier of the specific IP protocol (1 to 254) or a keyword identifier (example TCP, UDP). To include all IP protocols, use the keyword IP.

- **Network:** To add a network group, use the **object-group network grp_id** command and define the hosts or networks by using **network-object {host host_addr | net_addr mask}** in the object-group submode.

- **Service:** To add a service group, use the **object-group service** *grp_id* {**tcp** | **udp** | **tcp-udp**} command. Specify the protocol for the services (ports) you want to add, by using either **tcp**, **udp**, or **tcp-udp** keywords. Enter the **tcp-udp** keyword if your service uses both TCP and UDP with the same port number—for example, DNS (port 53). Define the ports or range of ports by using **port-object** in the object-group submode.

- **ICMP type:** To add an ICMP type group, use the **object-group icmp-type** *grp_id* command. Define the ICMP types by using **icmp-object** *icmp_type* (example, echo or echo-request) in the object-group submode.

To use object groups in an access list, replace the normal protocol (*protocol*), network (*source_address mask*, and so on), service (*operator port*), or ICMP type (*icmp_type*) parameter with **object-group** *grp_id* parameter.

It is not compulsory to use object groups for all parameters within the access list. For example, object groups can be used to group certain hosts/networks to be referenced in the source address parameter, or group like services together to reference in the operator port parameter, and so on. Object groups simplify configuration and allow easy modifications to add, update, and remove entries at a later stage.

To illustrate the benefit of using an object group, observe the access list 101 shown in Example 6-22, which has 10 lines of deny statements to web servers from selected hosts and networks. There are many repetitive entries that could be grouped together. Example 6-23 creates two object groups to cover the repetitions in these 10 lines, consolidating it into one single access list line by referencing these object groups, condensing the configuration as shown in Example 6-24.

Example 6-22   *Regular ACL with No Object Groups*

```
access-list 101 remark - ACL with no object groups
access-list 101 deny tcp host 10.1.1.52 host 209.165.201.1 eq www
access-list 101 deny tcp host 10.1.1.52 host 209.165.201.2 eq www
access-list 101 deny tcp host 10.1.1.13 host 209.165.201.1 eq www
access-list 101 deny tcp host 10.1.1.13 host 209.165.201.2 eq www
access-list 101 deny tcp host 10.1.1.15 host 209.165.201.1 eq www
access-list 101 deny tcp host 10.1.1.15 host 209.165.201.2 eq www
access-list 101 deny tcp 10.1.2.0 255.255.255.0 host 209.165.201.1 eq www
access-list 101 deny tcp 10.1.2.0 255.255.255.0 host 209.165.201.2 eq www
access-list 101 deny tcp 10.1.5.0 255.255.255.0 host 209.165.201.1 eq www
access-list 101 deny tcp 10.1.5.0 255.255.255.0 host 209.165.201.2 eq www
access-list 101 permit ip any any
```

Example 6-23 shows creating two network-type object groups named **denyhosts** that include the host and network addresses used in the source address parameter and object group named **webserver**, which defines the two web servers used in the destination address parameter.

Example 6-23   *Configuring Object Groups*

```
! Define Network Object Group denyhosts
hostname(config)# object-group network denyhosts
hostname(config-network)# description Deny Addresses
hostname(config-network)# network-object host 10.1.1.13
hostname(config-network)# network-object host 10.1.1.15
hostname(config-network)# network-object host 10.1.1.52
hostname(config-network)# network-object 10.1.2.0 255.255.255.0
hostname(config-network)# network-object 10.1.5.0 255.255.255.0
! Define Network Object Group webserver
hostname(config-network)# object-group network webserver
hostname(config-network)# description Web Servers
hostname(config-network)# network-object host 209.165.201.1
hostname(config-network)# network-object host 209.165.201.2
```

As shown in Example 6-24, you should reference these network object groups in the access list, thereby consolidating the deny statements into one single line.

Example 6-24 *Using Object Groups in the Access List*

```
hostname(config)# access-list 101 deny tcp object-group denyhosts object-group
webserver eq www
hostname(config)# access-list 101 permit ip any any
```

Use the **show object-group [protocol | network | service | icmp-type | id grp_id]** command to display a list of the currently configured object groups.

Modular Policy Framework (MPF)

Firewall software offers an adaptable and scalable modular policy framework to configure Security Appliance features in a manner similar to Cisco IOS Software QoS CLI (also known as Modular QoS CLI—MQC). For traffic flows traversing the firewall, flow-based policies can be established for any administratively defined criteria and then applied to a set of security services, such as firewall policies, inspection engine policies, Quality of Service (QoS) policies, and VPN policies, each specified traffic flow providing more granular and flexible inspection control.

The Modular Policy Framework (MPF) is supported with these features:

* TCP and general connection settings
* Protocol inspection services
* Intrusion prevention services
* QoS services
* Policing (rate limit)

Configuring MPF

To configure security features using the MPF, perform the following steps, which show an example of configuring the MPF to identify HTTP traffic and control the half-open (embryonic) TCP connection limit.

Step 1—Identifying Traffic Flow

A traffic class is a set of traffic that is identifiable by its packet content. For example, TCP traffic on port 80 is classified as an HTTP traffic class. Traffic flow is identified using a **class-map** command from the global configuration mode. Various match criteria using the **match** command can be included to define the traffic in the **class-map**. When the packet matches the specified criteria, it is subject to an action, such as application inspection or policing. Packets that do not match any of the criteria are assigned to the default traffic class. For example, create an access list to identify HTTP traffic on TCP port 80, and define it in the traffic **class-map**, as shown in Example 6-25.

Example 6-25 *Configuring Class Map to Identify Traffic (Using ACL)*

```
hostname(config)# access-list 101 permit tcp any any eq 80
hostname(config)# class-map identify_http_packets
hostname(config-cmap)# match access-list 101
```

Alternatively, the same could be achieved using the **port** command to assign the default HTTP port (as shown in Example 6-26) instead of using the ACL.

Example 6-26 *Configuring Class-Map to Identify Traffic (Using Match Port)*

```
hostname(config)# class-map identify_http_packets
hostname(config-cmap)# match port tcp eq www
```

Step 2—Creating a Policy Map

Use the **policy-map** global configuration command to create a policy map by associating the traffic class-map created in Step 1 with one or more actions that should be taken when a match occurs in a given traffic class. An action protects information or resources or performs a QoS function. Examples include specifying the maximum number of simultaneous connections, enabling inspection, or rate limiting the packets. Several types of actions are available. Example 6-27 shows how to create a **policy-map** called **mypolicy** from the global configuration mode and reference the HTTP traffic class-map **identify_http_packets** created previously by specifying an action to set the maximum number of TCP embryonic connections limit to 1000.

Example 6-27 *Configuring Policy-Map and Assigning Class-Map*

```
hostname(config)# policy-map mypolicy
hostname(config-pmap)# class identify_http_packets
hostname(config-pmap-c)# set connection embryonic-conn-max 1000
```

Step 3—Applying a Policy

Use the **service-policy** command from the global configuration mode to apply the policy globally to all the Security Appliance interfaces or on a specific interface. Associating a policy map with an interface activates the policy. Example 6-28 shows how to apply the service policy **mypolicy**, which was created in Example 6-27, to the outside interface.

Example 6-28 *Assign Policy to an Interface*

```
hostname(config)# service-policy mypolicy interface outside
```

Alternatively, the same service policy can be applied to all the interfaces globally, as shown in Example 6-29.

Example 6-29 *Assign Policy Globally to All Interfaces*

```
hostname(config)# service-policy mypolicy global
```

Here is another example showing how to use the MPF with the TCP normalization feature. As discussed earlier, TCP normalization is an advanced feature for examining TCP header information in TCP-based connections to identify and drop packets that do not appear normal. Part of the TCP normalization feature is to drop any packets that exceed the Maximum Segment Size (MSS) value set by the peer. To disable this feature and allow such packets, a TCP map needs to be created and used with the MPF to make exception to the default behavior. Example 6-30 shows how to create a TCP map that is used in the MPF to match all TCP packets and thereby allow MSS packets by setting an allow action in the advance TCP connection settings. The policy is applied to all packets entering the outside interface.

Example 6-30 *Configuring a Modular Policy Framework with the TCP Normalization Feature*

```
hostname(config)# access-list 100 permit tcp any any
hostname(config)# tcp-map permit-mss-packets
hostname(config-tcp-map)# exceed-mss allow
hostname(config-tcp-map)# exit
hostname(config)# class-map all-tcp-traffic
hostname(config-cmap)# match access-list 100
hostname(config-cmap)# exit
hostname(config)# policy-map allow-mss-packets
hostname(config-pmap)# class all-tcp-traffic
hostname(config-pmap-c)# set connection advanced-options permit-mss-packets
hostname(config-pmap-c)# exit
hostname(config-pmap)# exit
hostname(config)# service-policy allow-mss-packets interface outside
```

Use the **show service-policy** command to display the configured policies and their settings.

Cisco AnyConnect VPN Client

Security Appliance Software Version 8.0 debuts the support for Cisco AnyConnect VPN Client connections. The Cisco AnyConnect VPN Client is the next-generation VPN client, which provides remote users with secure VPN connections to the Cisco ASA 5500 Appliance by using the Secure Socket Layer (SSL) protocol.

Cisco AnyConnect VPN Client provides all the benefits of a Cisco SSL VPN client, and additionally supports applications and functions unavailable to a clientless, browser-based SSL VPN connection.

Another advantage of the Cisco AnyConnect Client is that it also supports IPv6 over an IPv4 network.

NOTE	The Cisco AnyConnect VPN Client is supported on Windows Vista, Windows XP, Windows 2000, Mac OS X, and Linux platforms.

CAUTION	The Cisco AnyConnect VPN Client is not supported on Cisco PIX appliances and Cisco VPN 3000 Concentrator series; it is supported on Cisco ASA 5500 hardware models only. PIX does not support SSL VPN connections, either clientless or AnyConnect.

TIP	For more details on the Cisco AnyConnect VPN Client, refer to the following documentation URLs:
	http://www.cisco.com/en/US/docs/security/vpn_client/anyconnect/anyconnect20/release/notes/cvcrn200.html
	http://www.cisco.com/en/US/products/ps8411/tsd_products_support_series_home.html
	http://www.cisco.com/en/US/docs/security/vpn_client/anyconnect/anyconnect20/administrative/guide/admin.html

Redundancy and Load Balancing

To achieve a high degree of availability and load-sharing capability, devices in the network must facilitate a redundancy feature and a mechanism to establish a failure and speedy recovery process. The Security Appliance offers features that increase availability and load-sharing ability to offer a fault-tolerant solution that ensures maximum uptime and maximized resource utilization. Redundancy is one of the key elements in building robust networks.

The Security Appliance offers a failover function that provides a safeguard mechanism in the event of a unit failure. When one unit fails, another immediately takes its place. The Security Appliance supports the following two types of failover setup. Both failover modes support stateful or stateless failover.

- **Active/Standby Failover Mode (Redundancy):** In this mode, only one unit (the primary, also called the Active unit) passes traffic, whereas the other unit is in a standby state. The Active/Standby failover is available in both single and multiple context modes.

- **Active/Active Failover Mode (Load Balancing):** In this mode, both devices can pass network traffic by sharing bandwidth resources on both devices. The Active/Active mode provides high-resilience, high-availability networks with load-balancing capability. The Active/Active failover mode is available on multiple contexts mode only.

Failover Requirements

Both Security Appliances in a failover pair must be identical to each other and connected through a dedicated failover link (interface) and optionally, a state link interface. To enable the failover feature on the Security Appliance, the criteria that follows must be met. *(*Note that *both units must have the same hardware and software configuration.)* In the list that follows, both units must

- Be the same model
- Have the same number and types of interfaces
- Have the same amount of Flash memory and the same amount of RAM
- Be in the same operating mode (routed or transparent, single or multiple context)
- Have same major (first number) and minor (second number) software version; for example, with version 8.0(3), the number 3, which is in the parenthesis, can vary between the two devices, but 8.0 must be the same

Failover Link

The failover link interface is used to monitor the health and operating status of each unit in a failover mode. On the PIX 500 series platform, the failover link can be either a LAN-based connection or a dedicated serial failover cable. On the ASA 5500 series platform, the failover link can only be a LAN-based connection.

State Link

The Security Appliance supports two types of failover, regular and stateful. In a regular failover mode (nonstateful), all active connections are dropped, and clients need to reestablish connections when the new active unit takes over, because the new active device has no knowledge of the previous connections. In a stateful-failover environment, active connections do not need to reestablish when a failover occurs. For example, if the client has an active connection that is transferring a file via FTP protocol, when the fail occurs, the file copying continues uninterrupted via the standby unit that has assumed an active role.

The state link interface is used to pass the state of all established connections from the active unit to the standby device. The information that is passed to the standby unit in a stateful failover setup includes the following:

- NAT translation table
- TCP connection states
- UDP connection states
- The ARP entries
- The Layer 2 bridge table when running in transparent firewall mode
- The HTTP connection states (if HTTP replication is enabled)
- The Internet Security Association and Key Management Protocol (ISAKMP) and IPsec SA table
- The connection database for GPRS Tunneling Protocol (GTP) Packet Data Protocol (PDP)

The exception to information that is not passed to the standby unit in a stateful failover setup is the following:

- The HTTP connection table (unless HTTP replication is enabled)
- The user authentication (uauth) table
- The routing tables
- Multicast traffic information
- State information for Security Service Cards

There are three options for configuring a state link when configuring failover:

1 Use any unused Ethernet interface on the Security Appliance as a dedicated state link.

2 When using LAN-based failover, use the failover link for a state link (same Ethernet for dual purpose).

3 Use the regular data Ethernet interface for the state link; however, this is not a recommended practice, although supported.

The state link interface is not configured as a normal networking interface for normal operations; it exists only for stateful failover communications and, optionally, for the failover communication when the state and failover links are shared. Connect the state link by using a dedicated hub/switch, or segment it with a VLAN with no hosts or devices on the link or by using a crossover Ethernet cable to link the units directly.

Failover Implementation

The failover implementation on the Security Appliance can be deployed in two options: the Serial Cable Failover link or LAN-based failover link modes.

Serial Cable Failover Link (PIX 500 Series Only)

The serial Failover cable, or *cable-based failover*, is available only on the PIX 500 series platform. This design is recommended for use when the two PIX units are within six feet of each other. The main advantage of using this type of cable is that it is a dedicated serial cable, which provides faster convergence. The Security Appliance can sense a power loss of the peer unit and quickly differentiate a power loss from an unplugged cable. The main drawback in this type is the distance limitation (the units cannot be separated by more than six feet). The cable that connects the two units is a six-foot modified RS-232 serial cable that transfers data at 117,760 bps (115 Kbps). One end of the cable is labeled "Primary" and is attached to the primary unit, whereas the other end is labeled "Secondary" and is attached to the secondary unit. Figure 6-20 shows a configuration example.

Figure 6-20 *Serial Cable-Based Failover (Active/Standby)*

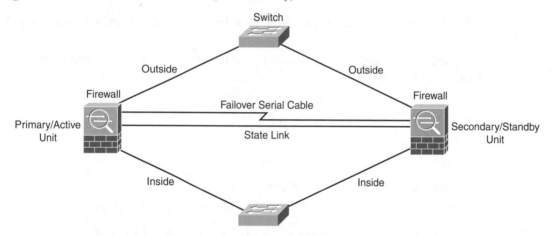

Serial Cable-Based Failover Configuration: Primary Unit
(No Configuration Required on the Secondary Unit)

Firewall(config)# **interface Ethernet0**
Firewall(config-if)# **nameif outside**
Firewall(config-if)# **ip address 209.165.201.1 255.255.255.224 standby 209.165.201.2**
Firewall(config-if)# **exit**
Firewall(config)# **interface Ethernet1**
Firewall(config-if)# **nameif inside**
Firewall(config-if)# **ip address 10.1.1.1 255.255.255.0 standby 10.1.1.2**
Firewall(config-if)# **exit**
Firewall(config)# **interface Ethernet2**
Firewall(config-if)# **description State Link**
Firewall(config-if)# **exit**
Firewall(config)# **failover link state Ethernet2**
Firewall(config)# **failover interface ip state 192.168.1.1 255.255.255.252 standby 192.168.1.2**
Firewall(config)# **failover**

LAN-Based Failover Link

Unlike the serial-cable failover implementation, the advantage of using LAN-based failover is the physical distance of the units, which can be more than six feet, and the faster configuration replication. The downside is slower convergence; the Security Appliance cannot immediately detect the loss of power of a peer, hence the firewall takes longer to failover in this case.

To replace the serial cable from the previous method, the LAN-based failover link uses the Ethernet interface on the appliance for failover link. This interface can also be used for normal network operation and can be optionally used for the state link. The failover link should be connected either via a dedicated switch or by putting in a VLAN with no other hosts/devices, or by connecting it using a crossover Ethernet cable. In multiple context mode, the failover link needs to be on the system context (admin context). Figure 6-21 shows a configuration example.

NOTE   Refer to Cisco documentation for additional failover configuration examples, such as LAN-based Active/Active: http://www.cisco.com/en/US/products/ps6120/products_configuration_guide_chapter09186a008045247e.html#wp1046980.

Asymmetric Routing Support (ASR)

The Active/Active mode additionally provisions the ASR (Asymmetric Routing Support) feature. The ASR technology allows the unit to forward the received packet for which it does not have an active connection by looking for a corresponding connection on the other interfaces in the asynchronous routing group. In regular firewall mode, if the connection originates through one device, and the ISP routes the return traffic through another device, the packet is dropped. ASR prevents the return packets from being dropped in such environments. With the ASR feature, the connection information is forwarded to the secondary pair unit, and it will forward the traffic to the unit that holds the connection information.

Figure 6-21 *LAN-Based Failover (Active/Standby)*

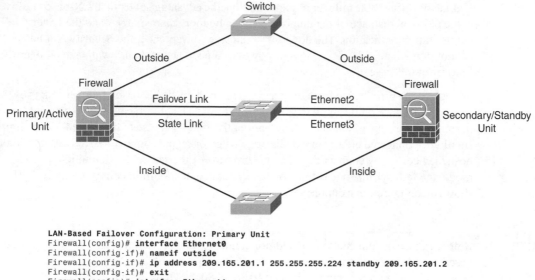

```
LAN-Based Failover Configuration: Primary Unit
Firewall(config)# interface Ethernet0
Firewall(config-if)# nameif outside
Firewall(config-if)# ip address 209.165.201.1 255.255.255.224 standby 209.165.201.2
Firewall(config-if)# exit
Firewall(config)# interface Ethernet1
Firewall(config-if)# nameif inside
Firewall(config-if)# ip address 10.1.1.1 255.255.255.0 standby 10.1.1.2
Firewall(config-if)# exit
Firewall(config)# interface Ethernet2
Firewall(config-if)# description Failover Link
Firewall(config-if)# exit
Firewall(config)# interface Ethernet3
Firewall(config-if)# description State Link
Firewall(config-if)# exit
Firewall(config)# failover lan unit primary
Firewall(config)# failover key cisco123
Firewall(config)# failover lan interface failover Ethernet2
Firewall(config)# failover link state Ethernet3
Firewall(config)# failover interface ip failover 172.16.1.1 255.255.255.0 standby 172.16.1.2
Firewall(config)# failover interface ip state 192.168.1.1 255.255.255.0 standby 192.168.1.2
Firewall(config)# failover lan enable
Firewall(config)# failover

LAN-Based Failover Configuration: Secondary Unit
Firewall(config)# failover lan unit secondary
Firewall(config)# failover key cisco123
Firewall(config)# failover lan interface failover Ethernet2
Firewall(config)# failover interface ip failover 172.16.1.1 255.255.255.0 standby 172.16.1.2
Firewall(config)# failover lan enable
Firewall(config)# failover
```

Firewall "Module" Software for Firewall Services Module (FWSM)

Catalyst 6500 Series Switch and Cisco 7600 Series Router offer high-end modules for Firewalling, IPsec VPN, WebVPN, and IPS functionality. The market-leading Firewall Services Module (commonly referred to as FWSM) is a high-performance integrated hardware and software package that delivers full firewall protection. The FWSM has its own operating system, stemming from the PIX firewall operating system that provides flow-based, stateful, and application-aware packet inspection. The FWSM software is a hardened, embedded system that eliminates security holes and performance-degrading overheads. At the heart of the system, a protection scheme based on the Adaptive Security Algorithm offers stateful connection-oriented firewalling. The main advantage of the FWSM is a modular firewall approach that leverages existing switching and routing infrastructures into a single, scalable, centrally managed solution, thereby reducing operation and deployment costs while maintaining the highest performance standards available in the industry.

Firewall Module OS Software

The FWSM has a separate operating system (OS) from the Security Appliances. In addition, the FWSM software version has a different numbering train from the appliance version numbers. The latest version that is available for the FWSM at the time of writing is version 3.x. Similar to the appliance software release, FWSM software offers all major firewall functions and features, such as multiple security contexts (virtual firewalls), transparent firewall (Layer 2) or routed firewall (Layer 3) operation, Application-Aware Inspection Services, Bidirectional NAT and Policy-based NAT, and high availability and enhanced management and monitoring services. FWSM offers several protection features to control network activity associated with specific kinds of attacks, such as ARP Inspection, DNS Guard, Flood Defender, Unicast Reverse Path Forwarding (uRPF), Frag Guard and Virtual Reassembly, Mail Guard, and UDP rate control.

Although the PIX/ASA OS is similar to the FWSM OS, there are some subtle differences. Many of the differences are enhancements that take advantage of the Catalyst 6500 Series Switch and Cisco 7600 Series Router architecture.

NOTE	FWSM does not provide VPN and IPS functionality. FWSM is a purpose-built firewall device. The following separate purpose-built products are available on the Catalyst 6500 Series Switch and Cisco 7600 Series Router: IPsec VPN Service Module (VPNSM), WebVPN Service Module, and Intrusion Detection System Module (IDSM-2).

Network Traffic Through the Firewall Module

By default, no traffic can pass through the FWSM to access the network. On PIX and ASA appliance software, traffic flow from higher-level interfaces (Inside) to lower-level interfaces (Outside) will pass unrestricted. However, the FWSM software does not allow any traffic to flow between the interfaces unless explicitly permitted with an ACL. The security level does not provide explicit permission for traffic from a high-security interface to a low-security interface. This applies to all types of FWSM implementation (routed and transparent mode). To control network traffic, access lists are applied to FWSM interfaces. ACLs determine which IP addresses and traffic can pass through the interfaces to access other networks.

Installing the FWSM

FWSM is installed in the Catalyst 6500 series switches and the Cisco 7600 series routers. The configuration on both platforms is identical, except for the basic initialization depending on the following:

- The Catalyst 6500 series switches supports two software modes:
  - Cisco IOS Software on both the switch supervisor engine and the integrated MSFC (known as Supervisor IOS or Native IOS)
  - Catalyst Operating System (CatOS) on the supervisor engine, and Cisco IOS Software on the MSFC (known as Hybrid mode—two separate OSs)
- The Cisco 7600 series routers support only Cisco IOS software.

NOTE   Refer to Cisco documentation for supported supervisor engine and software releases that support the FWSM. The version of code required to support FWSM depends on the supervisor model and whether you are running CatOS (Hybrid) or Cisco IOS (Native).

Router/MSFC Placement

The switch includes a switching processor (called the supervisor) and a router (called the MSFC–Multilayer Switch Feature Card). MSFC provides Cisco IOS-based multiprotocol routing and network services. It is important to understand the logical placement of the Router/MSFC in the network topology in relation to the FWSM. Several criteria are outlined in the subsections that follow that can be used to determine the network flow between the networks that require firewalling functions. The sections that follow explain the scenarios that are used to place the Router/MSFC in single and multiple contexts.

In Single Context

In single context mode, the Router/MSFC can be placed either in front of the firewall or behind the firewall, as shown in Figure 6-22. The placement of the Router/MSFC depends entirely on the logic and requirement of the network flow—for example, determining which

VLANs require being pushed through the firewall for inspection and/or need to bypass the firewall. If Router/MSFC is performing inter-VLAN routing between the VLANs, the firewall is not going to see that traffic.

For example, in Figure 6-22, the Router is placed behind the firewall on the left, routing packets among VLANs 10, 20, 30, and 101. In addition, inter-VLAN traffic does not go through the FWSM unless traffic is destined for the Internet. Hence, traffic flow among VLANs (inter-VLAN) is not protected. On the right-side example of Figure 6-22, the router is placed in front of the firewall, and the switch is configured to push VLANs 10, 20, and 30 traffic to the FWSM, thereby protecting all traffic among these VLANs (inter-VLAN) and traffic going to the Internet.

Figure 6-22 *Router Placement in Single Context*

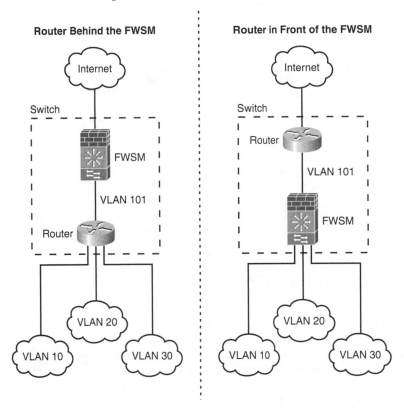

In Multiple Context Mode

In multiple context mode, the recommended placement for the router is in front of all the contexts to route traffic among the Internet and switched networks, as shown in

Figure 6-23. Placing the router behind the FWSM results in routing among the multiple contexts, which forfeits the concept of multiple context and segment isolation.

Figure 6-23 *Router Placement in Multiple Context*

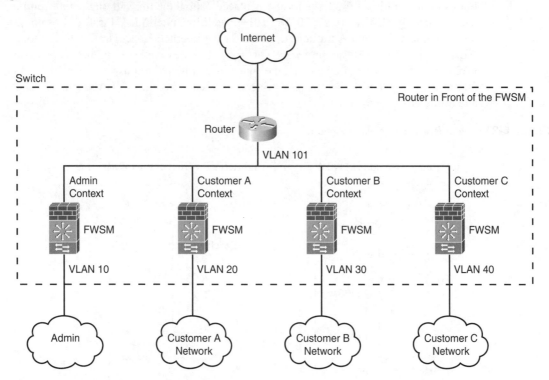

Configuring the FWSM

After the logical network flow and topology is determined, it is time to configure the switch, the Router/MSFC, and the FWSM. This section describes how to assign VLANs to the FWSM. The FWSM does not include external physical interfaces. Instead, it uses VLAN interfaces. Assigning VLANs to the FWSM is similar to assigning a VLAN to a switch port, in that the FWSM includes an internal interface to the Switch Fabric Module (if present) or the shared bus.

Perform the following basic steps to initialize the FWSM:

Step 1   Define the VLANs on the switch VLAN database and assign the VLANs to switch ports.

Step 2   Assign (push) the VLANs to the FWSM by using the **firewall vlan-group** command, and assign the firewall group to the FWSM by using the **firewall module** command.

Step 3   Create a Switched Virtual Interface (SVI) on the MSFC.

Step 4   On the FWSM, use the **nameif** command to assign the SVI to the corresponding FWSM interface, and assign an IP address on the FWSM interfaces using the **ip address** command.

Figure 6-24 shows an example of how to set up a basic firewall configuration with the router on the outside. The example creates four VLANs on the switch (VLAN 10, 20, 30, and 101), assigns the VLANs to the firewall VLAN group 1, and assigns group 1 to the FWSM in slot 5. VLAN 101 is the SVI created on the router, and the IP address 172.16.1.2 is assigned, which will be used as the default gateway on the FWSM. Only one SVI is created on the router for VLAN 101. (Do not configure SVI for VLAN 10, 20, or 30, because it will cause inter-VLAN routing, causing traffic to pass around the FWSM and thereby bypass it.) For this security reason, by default, only one SVI can exist between the router and the FWSM. Continue the configuration on the FWSM side. Corresponding VLANs are mapped with the **nameif** command, and IP addresses are assigned accordingly.

Figure 6-24 *Configuring FWSM Basic Setup*

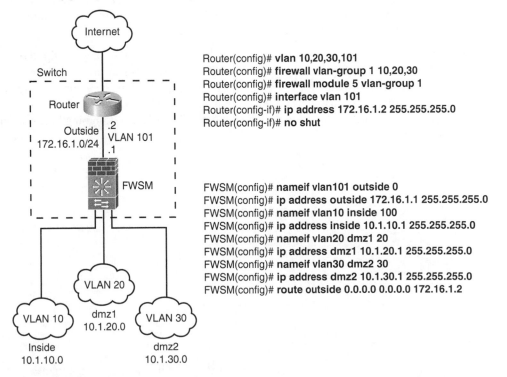

NOTE	The examples shown in this chapter are based on Cisco IOS Software output only. Refer to Cisco documentation for CatOS (Hybrid mode).

Use the **show firewall vlan-group** command to view the group configuration and the **show firewall module** to view VLAN group numbers for all modules.

After the basic configuration is finished, as shown in Figure 6-24, the FWSM can be managed in a manner that is similar to the PIX firewall. All firewall features such as mode (router or transparent), single or multiple contexts, network address translation, IP routing, failover, and all other firewall functions are more or less similar and are configured in the same way as the PIX firewall, as shown in earlier sections.

Summary

This chapter discussed Cisco industry-leading purpose-built firewall technology, highlighting the different platforms: the PIX 500 series, the ASA 5500 series, and the integrated Firewall Services Module (FWSM) for the Catalyst 6500 Series Switch and Cisco 7600 Series Router. The chapter focused on the features and solutions available on the appliance software and module software. Each section examined the technology and how to configure and effectively deploy it in the network environment.

The chapter was divided into two segments: discussion of features and configuration based on the appliance software for PIX 500 and ASA 5500 series platforms, followed by the firewall module software for FWSM. The chapter explained the core concepts, such as firewall modes, security contexts, inspection engines, various types of NAT, controlling traffic flow and network access through the firewall, MPF, and designing highly available, resilient networks.

References

http://www.cisco.com/en/US/products/hw/vpndevc/ps2030/index.html

http://www.cisco.com/en/US/products/ps6120/index.html

http://www.cisco.com/en/US/products/hw/modules/ps2706/ps4452/index.html

http://www.cisco.com/en/US/docs/security/asa/asa80/configuration/guide/conf_gd.html

http://www.cisco.com/en/US/products/ps6120/
products_installation_and_configuration_guides_list.html

http://www.cisco.com/en/US/products/ps6120/prod_configuration_examples_list.html

http://www.cisco.com/en/US/products/ps6120/prod_release_notes_list.html

http://www.cisco.com/en/US/docs/security/vpn_client/anyconnect/anyconnect20/
administrative/guide/admin.html

CHAPTER 7

Attack Vectors and Mitigation Techniques

One of the biggest problems in network security today is that network managers think of security as something to implement after a network is designed. Security, therefore, tends to be an afterthought at best and, in most cases, is often forgotten completely. This has led to many insecure network designs and solutions.

An attack vector is a vulnerability, exploit, or mode that is open to abuse. Vulnerabilities, threats, and exploits lead to network attacks and are problems that have no easy solution, mainly because they are native to the design of the TCP/IP suite. Understanding how and why these attacks are launched, coupled with the proactive prevention mechanisms, can help you protect the network from these malicious cloaking and cracking techniques.

Effective mitigation of such attacks is an especially pressing problem on the Internet, and experts have researched and proposed various methods to prevent them. This chapter provides insight into technologies and techniques available on Cisco devices to combat network attacks on Layer 3 and Layer 2 devices.

The chapter also covers details of how to use the Security Incident Response Framework to respond to a security incident and to understand and be prepared for any security event by using an incident response methodology and the formation of an Incident Response Team (IRT).

Vulnerabilities, Threats, and Exploits

It is disconcerting to realize that it is difficult, if not impossible, to track down and eliminate all possible security holes, because intruders need only one security hole to break in. In certain cases, an intruder can take advantage of the design of a particular piece of software, a misconfiguration or loosely configured device, or perhaps an inherent flaw in a protocol. The TCP/IP protocol is a good example. The protocol was developed a long time ago when designers did not pay particular attention to the security concerns we observe today. Examples of leveraging flaws in protocols include IP spoofing, source routing, SYN floods, smurf attacks, application tunneling, and much more. Before we take a closer look at the mitigation techniques, however, we will begin with a quick overview of some of the attack vectors.

Classes of Attacks

Three major types of attacks follow:

- **Reconnaissance:** Reconnaissance attacks are the first step in the process of intrusion and involve unauthorized discovery and mapping of systems, services, or vulnerabilities. These discovery and mapping techniques are commonly known as scanning and enumeration. Common tools, commands, and utilities that are used for scanning and enumeration include ping, Telnet, nslookup, finger, rpcinfo, File Explorer, srvinfo, and dumpacl. Other third-party public tools include Sniffer, SATAN, SAINT, NMAP, and netcat. In addition, custom scripts are used in this process.

- **Access:** Access attacks refer to unauthorized data manipulation that gives the attacker system access or privilege escalation on a victim or compromised host. Unauthorized data retrieval is simply the act of reading, writing, copying, or moving files that are not allowed or authorized to the intruder. Some common activities performed in this phase include exploiting passwords, accessing confidential information, exploiting poorly configured or unmanaged services, accessing a remote registry, abusing a trust relationship, and IP source routing and file sharing.

- **Denial of Service:** A DoS attack takes place when an attacker intentionally blocks, degrades, disables, or corrupts networks, systems, or services with the intent to deny the service to authorized users. The attack is geared to impede the availability of the resource to the authorized user by crashing the system or slowing it down to the point where it is unusable. Common examples of DoS attacks include TCP SYN floods, ICMP ping floods, and buffer overflow, to name a few.

A typical attack pattern consists of gaining access to a user account, escalating privilege, exploiting the victim's system, or using it as a launch platform for attacks on other systems or sites.

Attack Vectors

Attack vectors are routes or methods used to get into computer and network systems to leverage unexpected openings for misuse. Attack vectors can be generally classified as follows:

- **Viruses:** A virus is a malicious software program or piece of code that causes an unanticipated negative event and usually is capable of causing damage to data or other programs on the infected system.

- **Worms:** A computer worm is a self-replicating malicious software program, similar to a computer virus. Worms are viruses that can reside in the active memory of a system and are capable of self-duplicating and self-propagating from one computer system to the next over a network. Worms are often designed to exploit the file transmission capabilities, such as e-mail found on many computer systems.

- **Trojans:** A Trojan horse is a malicious program that pretends to be a benign application. Trojans are seemingly harmless programs that hide a malicious activity, such as a keystroke logger that could capture all passwords or any other sensitive information entered, without the knowledge of the user.

- **Password cracking:** Password attacks can be implemented using several methods, including brute force attacks, Trojan horse programs, IP spoofing, and packet sniffers. Generally, password attacks refer to repeated attempts to identify a valid user account or password. These repeated attempts are called brute force attacks.

- **Buffer overflows:** Buffers are memory locations in a system that are used to store data and generally hold a predefined amount of finite data. A buffer overflow occurs when a program attempts to store data in a buffer, when data is larger than the size of the allocated buffer. An analogy is filling an empty glass (buffer) of 1 liter capacity with 1.5 liters of liquid (data). The initial 1 liter will be held with no problem, with the 0.5 liters spilling over, just as with buffer overflow.

- **IP spoofing:** An *IP spoofing attack* occurs when an intruder attempts to disguise itself by pretending to have the source IP address of a trusted host to gain access to specified resources on a trusted network. IP spoofing is one of the most common acts of online camouflage.

- **Address Resolution Protocol (ARP) spoofing:** ARP spoofing occurs when an intruder attempts to disguise its source hardware address (MAC address) to impersonate a trusted host. This is one of the primary steps that aids many of the other attacks.

- **Man-in-the-middle attack (TCP hijacking):** The man-in-the-middle (MITM), also known as a TCP hijacking attack, is a well-known attack in which an intruder intercepts legitimate communication between two points and can modify or control the TCP session without the knowledge of either the sender or the recipient of the session. TCP hijacking is an exploit that targets the victims' TCP-based applications such as Telnet, FTP, SMTP (e-mail), or HTTP sessions. An intruder can also be "inline" in an ongoing TCP session between the sender and the receiver while using a sniffing program to watch the conversation.

- **Ping sweeps:** A ping sweep, also known as an Internet Control Message Protocol (ICMP) sweep, is a scanning technique used to determine live hosts (computers) in a network. A ping sweep, consists of ICMP ECHO requests sent to multiple hosts (one at a time, unless a broadcast IP address is used). If a given address is live, it will return an ICMP ECHO reply confirming a legitimate live host. Ping sweeps are widely used in the reconnaissance phase of the attack process.

- **Port scanning:** Port scanning is a method used to enumerate what services are running on a system. An intruder sends random requests on different ports, and if the host responds to the request, the intruder confirms that the port is active and in listening mode. The attacker can then plan exploits to any known vulnerabilities by targeting these ports. A port scanner is a piece of software designed to search a network host for open ports. Port scanning is also one of the primary reconnaissance techniques attackers use to discover services that can be exploited.

- **Sniffing:** *A packet sniffer* is software that uses a network adapter card in promiscuous mode to passively capture all network packets that are being transmitted across the network.

- **Flooding:** Flooding occurs when an excessive amount of unwanted data is sent, resulting in disruption of data availability.

- **DoS/DDoS Attacks:** In most cases, the objective of a DoS attack is to deprive legitimate user access to services or resources. DoS attacks do not typically result in intrusion or the illegal theft of information, but are geared to prevent access to authorized users by means of flooding the victim with an excessive volume of packets.

  Distributed DoS (DDoS) attacks amplify DoS attacks in that a large number of compromised systems coordinate collectively to flood the victim, thereby causing denial of service for users of the targeted systems. Common forms of DoS/DDoS attacks include SYN flood attacks, smurf attacks, land attacks, viruses, and worms.

Attackers Family

It is important to identify the attackers responsible for all computer and network abuse, as this identification assists in characterizing the attack and the level of damage it can cause. It is also useful to track them down by understanding their motives and actions. Attackers can be classified in three broad categories:

- **Script kiddies (aspiring hackers):** These are amateur members of the attacker community with no deep knowledge of the technology. They use readily available programs and tools developed by others for the purpose of intrusive activities. They are movtivated to test limits and to be noticed.

- **True hackers:** This group of attackers is well versed and has thorough knowledge of the technology with well-developed competence to perform intrusions. Hackers in this category are motivated by the pursuit of recognition and notoriety. They often see hacking as a challenge and a competition.

- **Professionals (the elite):** This type is a small group of attackers also known as the elite. Members of this group are highly motivated and in most cases remunerated for their services that include organized crime, as well as attacks on the military, intelligence organizations, law enforcement, and other groups. The main motivation for these types of hackers is remuneration.

Risk Assessment

It is imperative to audit the network and evaluate its security posture for the risks and threats in an environment to be able to preemptively determine the likelihood and ramifications of a security breach. This should be an iterative process in which you evaluate and rank each threat and identify an appropriate mitigation technique accordingly. As you face the risk assessment process, keep in mind the following facts about common network attacks:

- 75% to 80% go undetected.
- 15% to 20% are instigated by outsiders.
- 80% to 85% are launched by insiders—people with authorized trust.
- 80% to 90% are vindictive script kiddy attacks. 10% are of a more serious DDoS type.
- 1% to 5% hit the infrastructure directly.

Threat modeling involves identifying and ranking threats according to their likelihood and the damage they could potentially cause. The following steps can help identify potential attack vectors in a network.

Step 1   Identify vulnerabilities, threats, potential attack vectors, and their potential impact on the network and performance.

Step 2   Categorize each threat by criticality—that is, how much damage an attack of this nature could cause and the likelihood of occurrence. For example, assign a number between 1 and 10 for criticality, with 10 being the most severe.

Step 3   Using the following formula, calculate the assumed risk by dividing the criticality by the chance of occurrence:

Assumed Risk = Criticality / Likelihood

Step 4   Identify an appropriate technique or technology to mitigate each threat. Each threat has specific mitigation techniques with varied options. Choose the solution wisely, understanding its pros and cons.

Step 5   Repeat from Step 1 as you move on. Making only one pass through this process can potentially leave the network vulnerable to other unidentified risks and attacks.

There are no magic knobs, silver bullets, or super vendor technology features that will solve all security problems.

The fundamental law of the Internet drives the design of security into the network and how to respond to security incidents. It is all about the packet. After a packet is on the network wire, someone or something somewhere has to either deliver or drop the packet.

In the context of an intrusion or attack, the question is who will drop the packet and where will the packet be dropped?

Mitigation Techniques at Layer 3

This section highlights some of the most common mitigation techniques available on Cisco platforms and commonly applied on specific Layer 3 devices, such as routers or Layer 3 switches.

Traffic Characterization

The first and most essential step in the attack mitigation process is gathering relevant information about the characteristics of an attack to determine the type of attack and to devise a relevant threat-mitigation strategy based on attack vectors.

The Cisco IOS Access Control List (ACL) is the most commonly adopted technique to classify the packets into various attack streams, and it is valuable for characterizing both known and unknown attacks and for tracing packet streams back to their point of origin.

Other features such as debugging, logging, and IP accounting can also be used. However, with recent versions of Cisco IOS Software, access lists and access list logging are predominant in characterization and tracing network attacks.

An ACL with a series of permit statements is used to characterize traffic flows of interest. ACL extends the capability of checking packets based on various options in the packet header as more sophisticated attacks emerge. ACL counters are further used to determine which flows and protocols are potential threats because of their unexpected high volume. After the suspect flows are identified, a **logging** option can be used to capture additional packet characteristics.

Using an ACL to Characterize ICMP Flood or Smurf Attack

The smurf attack, also commonly known as ICMP flooding, has two victims: a target victim and a reflector or amplifier. The attacker sends a large number of ICMP echo requests (pings) to the broadcast address of the reflector subnet. The source addresses of these packets are forged (spoofed) to be the address of the target victim. For each packet sent by the attacker, hosts on the reflector subnet respond to the target victim, thereby flooding the victim network and causing congestion that results in a denial of service as shown in Figure 7-1.

A similar attack called *fraggle* uses directed broadcasts in the same technique, sending UDP echo requests instead of ICMP echo requests. Fraggle usually achieves a smaller amplification factor than smurf and is much less popular.

Figure 7-1 illustrates how a smurf attack works. In such an attack, a large number of ICMP echo request packets are sent to the reflectors (using the IP broadcast address) with a spoofed source IP address of the victim host. When the reflector hosts receive the ICMP echo packet, they respond with an ICMP echo-reply packet to the victim address, thereby causing an ICMP flood situation.

Figure 7-1   *Smurf Attack*

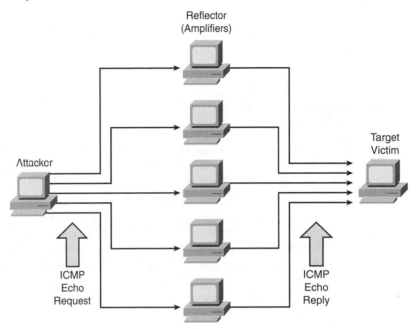

Example 7-1 shows an extended access list with permit statements to identify smurf or fraggle attacks.

Example 7-1   *Characterizing a Smurf Attack*

```
access-list 101 permit icmp any any echo
access-list 101 permit icmp any any echo-reply
access-list 101 permit ip any any
!
interface <suspected interface>
ip access-group 101 in
```

NOTE   Characterization ACLs do not filter out traffic; all the ACL entries are permit statements because the objective is to categorize the traffic.

As shown in Figure 7-1, two possible victims are affected in this attack and need to be identified accordingly:

- Possibility of being a smurf target victim
- Possibility of being a smurf reflector

Use the **show ip access-list** command to display the access-list packet match statistics to identify the potential threat.

The **show ip access-list** command output in Example 7-2 shows a large number of ICMP echo reply packets, which is an indication of a potential ICMP flood or smurf attack on the ultimate target victim rather than the reflector.

Example 7-2 *Output of Smurf Target Victim Attack*

```
Router# show ip access-list
Extended IP access list 101
    permit icmp any any echo (5 matches)
    permit icmp any any echo-reply (2198 matches)
    permit ip any any (11205 matches)
```

When the **show ip access-list** command output indicates a large number of ICMP echo requests instead of echo replies, as shown in Example 7-3, this indicates that the network is being used as a reflector (amplifier). The same output could also mean that the network is experiencing a simple ICMP ping flood, not a smurf. In either case, if the attack is successful, both the egress and the ingress interfaces will be experiencing congestion with large packet counts on the interface. Furthermore, because of the amplification factor, the egress side will be more overloaded than the ingress side.

Example 7-3 *Output of Smurf Reflector Attack*

```
Router# show ip access-list
Extended IP access list 101
    permit icmp any any echo (5432 matches)
    permit icmp any any echo-reply (2 matches)
    permit ip any any (1904 matches)
```

There are several ways to distinguish the smurf attack from the simple ping flood:

- Smurf packets are sent to a directed broadcast address, rather than to a unicast address, whereas ordinary ping floods almost always use unicast. This can be checked in the addresses with the **log-input** keyword on the appropriate access list entry.
- When experiencing a smurf reflector attack, a disproportionate number of output broadcasts in the **show interface** counters is displayed, and usually a disproportionate number of broadcasts are sent in the **show ip traffic** display. A standard ping flood does not increase the background broadcast traffic.
- When experiencing a smurf reflector attack, there is more outbound traffic toward the uplink, as compared to the inbound traffic from the uplink. In general, there are more output packets than input packets on the suspected interface.

When a smurf reflector is closer to the intruder than the ultimate target, it is much easier to trace the attack. ISPs need to be closely involved in tracing such attacks. However, in other situations, the reflector may not be closer to the attacker than the target. The target could be on your own subnet with the reflector on the other side of the network. (The broadcast address does not determine the unicast destination that has been spoofed.)

To stop Cisco routers from being reflectors in such attacks, use the **no ip directed-broadcast** interface configuration command. This should be configured on each interface of all routers. Note that **no ip directed-broadcast** is now the default on all interfaces, beginning with Cisco IOS Software Version 12.0. This command drops any packets on the router that are sent to a directed broadcast address that causes multiple hosts to respond to the ICMP echo request.

You can use several techniques to prevent or minimize the impact of smurf and similar ICMP flood attacks, such as rate limiting (Committed Access Rate [CAR]), a filter using access lists, and Unicast Reverse Path Forwarding (uRPF) and IP Source Guard features, as discussed in the "IP Spoofing Attacks" section later in this chapter.

Using an ACL to Characterize SYN Attacks

There are many variations of SYN flood attacks, with the most common being a situation in which a target machine is flooded with TCP SYN connection requests. In most cases, the source addresses and source TCP ports of the connection request packets are randomized and spoofed. The objective is to force the target host to maintain TCP state information for a large number of incomplete connections (half-open connections), also called embryonic connections, which are illustrated in Figure 7-2.

Figure 7-2 *Unfinished Half-Open TCP Connection (Also Called Embryonic Connection)*

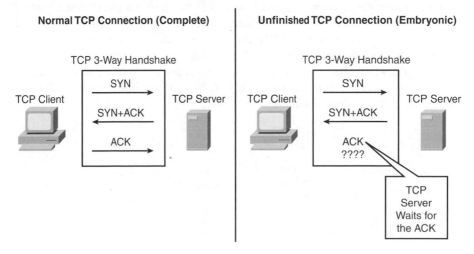

SYN flood attacks are sometimes easy to identify because the target host (such as the HTTP or SMTP server) becomes extremely slow, crashes, or hangs. SYN floods are not the only vector; several other vectors exist that are aimed in a similar flooding attack. Most people focus on SYN floods as a critical security attack vector. In reality, some SYN flood mitigation paths open the door for other TCP-based attack vectors.

TCP attack vectors are varied and include the following:

- SYN Flood
- ACK Flood
- SYN+ACK Flood
- SYN+RST Flood
- RST Flood
- Established Flood
- FIN Flood
- TCP Options Flood
- X-Tree Flood

There are two major types of SYN-flood attacks:

- **Nonspoofed source addresses:** Easy to trace, usually launched from compromised hosts (user workstations, servers, and the like)
- **Spoofed source addresses:** Difficult to trace, when spoofing invalid addresses from Bogon space (unallocated address range) or valid addresses from someone else's address blocks

SYN Round Trip Time (RTT) is the interval between the sending of SYN+ACK and reception of the corresponding ACK from the other host (receiver). A successful SYN flood occurs when the number of simultaneous SYNs exceeds the capacity of the victim's TCP Listen queue *and* the rate of SYNs exceeds the victim's ability to clear the SYN_RCVDs in an interval less than the SYN+ACK RTT. The objective of the attack is to crowd out valid SYN_RCVDs before the client's ACK has a chance to get to the server. If an ACK is received, and there is no available SYN_RCVD waiting, the connection fails and the DoS is successful, as depicted in Figure 7-3.

Figure 7-3   *SYN Flooding*

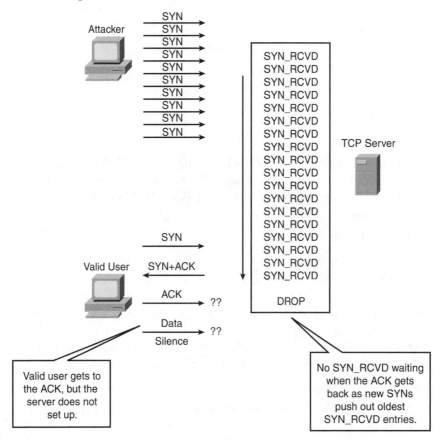

In summary, to successfully SYN-flood, the attacker must achieve the following:

- Fill and overflow the TCP server's memory so that the oldest SYN_RVCD entries are flushed.

- Fill the TCP queue faster than the typical SYN+ACK RTT so that valid customer SYN_RVCD entries are crowded out.

Example 7-4 shows an extended access list with permit statements to identify a TCP SYN attack. The TCP permit statement has several other options, such as matching FIN, URG, RST flags or established connections, or checking fragment packets.

Example 7-4 *Characterizing a TCP SYN Attack*

```
access-list 101 permit tcp any any syn
access-list 101 permit ip any any
!
interface <suspected interface>
ip access-group 101 in
```

Use the **show ip access-list** command to display the access-list packet match statistics to identify the SYN attack.

The output in Example 7-5 shows a large number of TCP SYN packets, an indication of a potential SYN flood to a target victim. The only nonattack condition that creates this signature is a massive overload of genuine TCP connection requests.

Example 7-5 *Output of Smurf Target Victim Attack*

```
Router# show ip access-list
Extended IP access list 101
   permit tcp any any syn (13174 matches)
   permit ip any any (438 matches)
```

Many features are available that you can use to reduce the impact of SYN floods. The effectiveness of these features depends on the environment; therefore, you should carefully examine these solutions. Some techniques available to prevent or minimize the impact of SYN flood attacks include the following:

- Rate-limiting (CAR).
- Context-Based Access Control (CBAC).
- TCP Intercept.
- On security appliances such as PIX firewalls, static and nat commands provide an option to monitor and control half-open embryonic connections. For more details, refer to static command in PIX documentation.
- Antispoofing: Do not allow traffic claiming to be sourced from customer IP blocks to ingress from the uplink or Internet.
- Anti-bogon: Do not allow traffic claiming to be sourced from reserved addresses or from an IPv4 block that has yet to be allocated by the Internet Assigned Numbers Authority (IANA).
- A source-based remote triggered black hole (RTBH) filtering technique can also be used as a SYN flood mitigation tool. This feature provides real-time defense against DDoS attacks by using a combination of IP routing features. To learn more about this technique, refer to the following white paper: www.cisco.com/warp/public/732/Tech/security/docs/blackhole.pdf.

IP Source Tracker

Source tracking is the process of tracing packet streams from the victim back to the point of origin to find the source of the attack through the network path. Although an ACL is a common tool and can be leveraged to trace back attacks, it has a potential performance impact when applied in a production network environment. IP source tracker provides an easier, more scalable alternative to ACLs for tracking DoS attacks, and it generates all the required information to trace the ingress point of an attack into the network with minimal performance penalty.

How IP Source Tracker Works

The following steps illustrate how IP source tracker works for tracking DoS attacks.

Step 1   After a host is identified as under attack, enable the IP source tracker feature concurrently to track multiple destination IP addresses on the router by using the **ip source-track** command from the global configuration mode.

Step 2   The router creates a special Cisco Express Forwarding (CEF) entry for the destination address being tracked.

Step 3   The CPU collects all the necessary data in the context of the traffic flow for each tracked IP address in an easy-to-use format and periodically exports this data.

Step 4   The periodically exported data can be viewed by using the **show ip source-track <ip-address>** command to display detailed information for each input interface, including detailed statistics of the traffic destined to each IP address. To display a summary of the flow information, use the **show ip source-track summary** command.

Step 5   Detailed statistics provide a breakdown of the traffic to each tracked IP address. This information allows you to determine which upstream router to analyze next and makes a hop-by-hop traceback to the attacker possible.

Step 6   These steps are repeated on each upstream router until the source of the attack is identified.

Step 7   Apply appropriate mitigation techniques to stop or minimize the attack.

Configuring IP Source Tracker

Example 7-6 shows how to enable IP source tracking on a router to collect traffic flow statistics to host address 10.1.1.1 for two minutes, create an internal system log entry, and export packet and flow information for viewing to the route processor every 30 seconds.

Example 7-6 *Configuring IP Source Tracker*

```
Router(config)# ip source-track 10.1.1.1
Router(config)# ip source-track syslog-interval 2
Router(config)# ip source-track export-interval 30
```

Example 7-7 shows detailed information of the flows per-destination IP address being tracked.

Example 7-7 *IP Source Tracker Statistics*

```
Router# show ip source-track 10.1.1.1
Address    SrcIF Bytes Pkts Bytes/s Pkts/s
10.1.1.1 PO0/0 119G2553M 5619921 156821
```

Note that the previously listed output indicates that interface POS 0/0 is the potential upstream attack path from which the attack is originating. After the next-hop is determined, it is highly recommend to disable **ip source-track** on the current router and enable it on the upstream router to track the next preceding hop.

NOTE   The IP source tracker feature was introduced in Cisco IOS Release 12.0(21)S and was integrated into Cisco IOS Release 12.3(7)T and later. Use the Feature Navigator tool to check platform support and corresponding Cisco IOS Software image at www.cisco.com/go/fn.

IP Spoofing Attacks

As discussed earlier, many network attacks rely on an intruder falsifying, forging, or spoofing the source addresses in IP datagrams. It is very important and best practice to implement antispoofing mechanisms to prevent spoofing wherever feasible.

Antispoofing measures should be taken at every point in the network where practical, but they are usually easiest to implement and most effective at the borders among large address blocks or among domains of network administration.

Apply antispoofing controls described in RFC 2827, "Network Ingress Filtering: Defeating Denial of Service Attacks Which Employ IP Source Address Spoofing," and in Best Current Practices (BCP 38). The RFC dictates that no IP packets should be sent out to the Internet with a source address other than the addresses that have been allocated to your network.

NOTE   RFC 2827 obsoletes RFC 2267.

In summary, the antispoofing implementation is used to

- Deny incoming packets if source address is allocated to your network
- Deny outbound packets if source address is not allocated to your network

Antispoofing with Access Lists

Unfortunately, there is no simple list of commands to provide as a template to configure antispoofing access lists, because networks vary and configuration depends on the network boundaries and address space allocations. However, the basic objective is to drop packets that arrive on interfaces that are not viable paths from the supposed source addresses of those packets. For example, on a two-interface router connecting a corporate network to the Internet, any datagram that arrives on the Internet interface whose source address field claims it originates from a host on the corporate network should be discarded. Similarly, any datagram exiting the corporate network whose source address field claims to be anything other than the allocated address space of the corporate network should be discarded. Figure 7-4 depicts a basic guideline to configure antispoofing access lists.

In Figure 7-4, ACL 101 is applied inbound and ACL 199 is applied outbound on the external interface. ACL 101 drops any inbound packets with forged (spoofing) source addresses as the internal allocated address space or trusted hosts. ACL 199 ensures that none of the outgoing packets change their IP addresses to one not belonging to the internal allocated address space. In addition to the antispoofing entries, Figure 7-4 shows ACL 101 with additional deny statements that drop datagrams with broadcast or multicast source addresses, and datagrams with the reserved loopback address and the RFC1918 addresses as a source address.

It is usually appropriate for an antispoofing access list to filter out all ICMP redirects regardless of source or destination address. These are just basic guidelines and can be further fine-tuned with other filtering such as anti-bogon, traffic claiming to be sourced from reserved addresses, or from an IPv4 block that has yet to be allocated by IANA.

Figure 7-4 *Preventing IP Spoofing Using ACL*

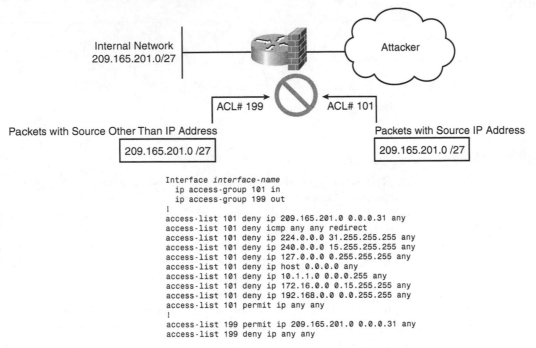

```
Interface interface-name
  ip access-group 101 in
  ip access-group 199 out
!
access-list 101 deny ip 209.165.201.0 0.0.0.31 any
access-list 101 deny icmp any any redirect
access-list 101 deny ip 224.0.0.0 31.255.255.255 any
access-list 101 deny ip 240.0.0.0 15.255.255.255 any
access-list 101 deny ip 127.0.0.0 0.255.255.255 any
access-list 101 deny ip host 0.0.0.0 any
access-list 101 deny ip 10.1.1.0 0.0.0.255 any
access-list 101 deny ip 172.16.0.0 0.15.255.255 any
access-list 101 deny ip 192.168.0.0 0.0.255.255 any
access-list 101 permit ip any any
!
access-list 199 permit ip 209.165.201.0 0.0.0.31 any
access-list 199 deny ip any any
```

In general, antispoofing filters are best deployed as input access lists; that is, packets must be filtered at the arriving interfaces, not at the interfaces through which they exit the router. The input access list also protects the router itself from spoofing attacks, whereas an output list protects only devices behind the router.

Antispoofing with uRPF

Unicast Reverse Path Forwarding (uRPF) is another common technique used to mitigate source address spoofing. When uRPF is used, the source address of IP packets is checked to ensure that the route back to the source uses the same interface that the packet arrived on. If the input interface is not a feasible path to the source network, the packet will be dropped. The uRPF feature is discussed later in this chapter.

Antispoofing with IP Source Guard

IP Source Guard is a Layer 2 security feature that prevents IP spoofing attacks by restricting IP traffic on untrusted Layer 2 ports to clients with an assigned IP address. This feature works by filtering IP traffic with a source IP address other than that assigned via Dynamic

Host Configuration Protocol (DHCP) or static configuration on the untrusted Layer 2 ports. The IP Source Guard feature works in combination with the DHCP snooping feature available on Catalyst switches and is enabled on untrusted Layer 2 ports. (DHCP snooping is discussed in Chapter 4, "Security Features on Switches" with configuration examples.)

As shown in Figure 7-5, when you are using the IP Source Guard feature in a DHCP-enabled environment, all traffic is blocked on the switch port except for the DHCP packets that are captured by the DHCP snooping process. The DHCP packets flowing between the DHCP client and the server are monitored, and the monitoring creates a binding table that lists IP-to-MAC mapping on each switch port. This allows the switch to know which port is connected with what source MAC address and the assigned IP address. If DHCP is not used, a static IP source binding map can be configured by the user. With the help of this IP-to-MAC binding table, a per-port VLAN Access Control List (PACL) is installed (PACL is a security ACL applied on Layer 2 switch ports) that denies traffic other than spoofed source, based on the binding table. This filtering mechanism protects against IP and MAC address spoofing.

Figure 7-5   *Preventing IP Spoofing Using IP Source Guard*

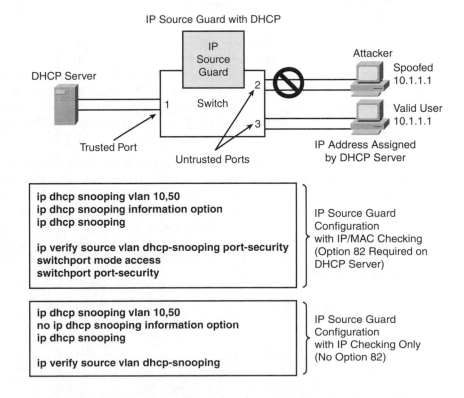

NOTE	The IP Source Guard feature will not prevent an MITM type of attack. Use Dynamic ARP Inspection (DAI) to prevent MITM, as discussed in the section "ARP Spoofing Attack" later in this chapter.

Packet Classification and Marking Techniques

Cisco IOS provides an unparalleled and comprehensive set of Quality of Service (QoS) features. These tools can be leveraged in the context of security implementations and mitigating network attacks. QoS technologies are becoming increasingly important and critical to maintaining network availability and security.

Several QoS techniques exist for various types of application protocols because not all techniques work for all protocols. These methods apply in different phases of a protocol transition; for example, packets are first characterized (classified) using classification and marking techniques, then policed and dropped, or other action is taken depending on the requirement. With the QoS technology framework, a proactive approach (explicitly protecting critical traffic) is more effective than a reactive approach (trying to identify and squelch bad traffic). It is recommended that the minimum first step when deploying QoS techniques to protect a network against DoS attacks should be to explicitly protect core routing, infrastructure devices, and mission-critical data traffic.

Traffic classification is a method used to partition traffic into groups or classes of service (CoS) dividing network traffic into different categories. Traffic classification is followed by traffic marking, which is a method of identifying certain traffic types for unique handling and allowing the marking (that is, set or change) of a value (attribute) for the traffic belonging to a specific class. Traffic classification and traffic marking are closely related and can be used together. Traffic marking can be viewed as an additional action, specified in a policy map, to be taken on a traffic class.

As mentioned earlier, various QoS techniques are available for traffic classification and marking. Examples of classification and marking techniques include Class-Based Weighted Fair Queuing (CBWFQ), Committed Access Rate (CAR), Modular QoS CLI (MQC), and Network-Based Application Recognition (NBAR). These QoS mechanisms can also be effectively used in combination. For example, MQC and NBAR with policing techniques can be used in combination to give more granular control while regulating normal traffic flows. Using tools already available in Cisco IOS Software, these solutions help provide proactive mitigation solutions.

Committed Access Rate (CAR)

CAR is a multifaceted feature that embodies a rate-limiting feature for policing traffic, in addition to its packet classification and marking feature. CAR can be used to mark packet streams, for example, setting different IP precedence for selected packets entering or exiting the network. As the packet traverses through the network, devices within the path can then use the adjusted IP precedence to determine how to treat the marked traffic.

The policing feature of CAR controls the maximum rate of traffic sent or received on an interface (bandwidth management) for a network specifying traffic handling policies, when the traffic either conforms to or exceeds the specified rate limits. This is achieved by ensuring that traffic falling within specified rate parameters is sent; however, packets that exceed the acceptable amount of traffic are dropped or sent with a different level of priority. By default, the action for traffic exceeding the specified rate limits is to drop or mark down packets.

Simple techniques such as CAR sometimes produce the best results. CAR propagates bursts. It does not perform traffic shaping, and therefore does no buffering and adds no delay. CAR can be applied to all traffic or a subset of the traffic selected by an **access-list**. CAR performs best when configured on interfaces at the edge of a network to limit traffic into or out of the network.

How CAR Works

CAR provides several fundamental capabilities, as depicted in Figure 7-6. CAR examines traffic received on an interface or a subset of selected traffic by using access list criteria, or all IP traffic, or traffic group by a classification tag such as IP precedence. It then compares the rate of the traffic to a configured token bucket and executes the action policy based on the result. For example, CAR will drop the packet or rewrite the IP precedence by resetting the type of service (ToS) bits.

CAR utilizes a token bucket measurement. Token bucket parameters include the committed rate, the normal burst size (to handle temporary bursts over the rate limit without penalty), and the excess burst size. Tokens are filled into the bucket at the committed rate; that is, if the committed rate is 1 MB, this is the number of tokens inserted into the bucket. Think of it as advance token deposit or token repository. The depth of the bucket is the burst size. When traffic arrives at the bucket and sufficient tokens are available, the traffic is said to conform, and the corresponding number of tokens are removed from the bucket (tokens spent are gone). If sufficient tokens are not available (repository is empty), the traffic is said to exceed.

Figure 7-6 *Committed Access Rate (CAR)*

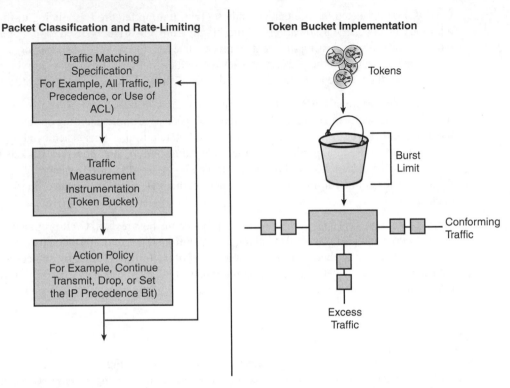

The information in Figure 7-6 is taken from Cisco security presentation on "Committed Access Rate."

Configuring Committed Access Rate (CAR)

Example 7-8 shows how CAR can be used to limit the rate for specific types of protocols to ensure sufficient capacity for other traffic, including mission-critical applications. Two access lists are created to classify the web and ICMP traffic, so that they can be handled separately by CAR. Note that multiple rate-limit statements can be configured in each direction, and they will be processed top down. The following example shows outbound rate limiting. Inbound rate limiting can also be added.

Example 7-8   *Configuring CAR*

```
Router(config)# access-list 101 permit tcp any any eq www
Router(config)# access-list 102 permit icmp any any
Router(config)# interface <interface>
Router(config-if)# rate-limit output access-group 101 10000000 24000 32000 conform-
action set-prec-transmit 5 exceed-action set-prec-transmit 0
Router(config-if)# rate-limit output access-group 102 50000 25000 30000 conform-
action set-prec-transmit 0 exceed-action drop
Router(config-if)# rate-limit output 4000000 16000 24000 conform-action continue
exceed-action drop
```

Let's look more closely at the steps involved in Example 7-8:

- The first rate-limit policy dictates that all World Wide Web traffic is sent. However, the IP precedence for web traffic that conforms to the first rate policy is set to 5. For nonconforming web traffic, the IP precedence is set to 0 (best effort).

- The second rate-limit policy dictates that ICMP traffic be sent with an IP precedence of 0 if it conforms. If the traffic exceeds the rate policy, it is dropped.

- The third rate-limit policy dictates that any remaining traffic is limited to 4 Mbps, with a normal burst size of 16,000 bytes and an excess burst size of 24,000 bytes. Traffic that conforms is transmitted, and traffic that does not conform is dropped.

Use the **show interfaces <interface> rate-limit** command to verify the configuration and monitor CAR statistics.

Modular QoS CLI (MQC)

Cisco modular QoS command-line interface (CLI), referred to as MQC, provides a modular and highly extensible framework that allows users to create hierarchical traffic policies to deliver extremely powerful and scalable solutions. A traffic policy contains a traffic class and one or more QoS features. A traffic class is used to classify (partition) traffic, whereas the QoS features determine how to treat the classified traffic. With the scalability and hierarchical policies, MQC can deliver security and attack mitigation solutions that can virtually be used for any type of attack mitigation.

MQC provides comprehensive classification and marking solutions with a complete set of capabilities to classify and mark traffic based on any Layer 2 or Layer 3 fields. MQC extends the capability to intelligently classify Layer 4 through Layer 7 protocols, using the integrated Network Based Application Recognition (NBAR) technology in the IOS. MQC offers a single-rate and two-rate policer, which allows for packet re-marking (Layer 2 and Layer 3) or dropping policies to control traffic at the network edges/aggregation points.

The MQC allows for the Unconditional Packet Discard feature in which traffic that matches certain criteria can be unconditionally dropped. This feature allows discarding (**drop** action inside a traffic class in a policy map) without any further system processing and almost no performance impact. This function is very useful in the security context because it allows the user to discard any packets for nonessential applications (such as Internet browsing applications or unauthorized file-sharing P2P applications) while allocating system resources to more essential applications.

Configuring MQC is a three-step process, which is outlined in the list that follows and depicted in Figure 7-7.

1 **Define a class-map:** The first step in MQC deployment is to identify the interesting traffic (classifying the packets). This step defines groupings of network traffic by using various classification tools, such as ACLs, IP addresses, IP precedence, IP Differentiated Services Code Point (DSCP) values, IEEE 802.1p, MPLS EXP, and Cisco Network-Based Application Recognition (NBAR) technology.

2 **Define a policy-map:** After the traffic has been identified, a **policy-map** dictates what action is to be taken. This step can be considered the actual construction of an MQC through use of a policy-map to perform specific functions. Examples of functions are queuing, dropping, policing, shaping, bandwidth control, or marking IP precedence or DSCP values.

3 **Apply the policy-map:** The final step is to apply the **policy-map** to the desired interfaces or subinterfaces. Each interface can have up to two policy-maps applied, each in one direction (inbound and outbound).

Figure 7-7   *Configuring Modular QoS CLI (MQC)*

```
1. Define a class-map
   Router(config)# class-map myclass
   Router(config-cmap)# match access-group 101
   or
   Router(config-cmap)# match protocol http url "*cmd.exe*"
   or
   Router(config-cmap)# match ip precedence [0-7]

2. Define a policy-map
   Router(config)# policy-map mypolicy
   Router(config-pmap)# class-map myclass
   Router(config-pmap-c)# drop
   or
   Router(config-pmap-c)# bandwidth [remaining | percentage]  [1-100]
   or
   Router(config-pmap-c)# police …
   or
   Router(config-pmap-c)# set ip precedence [0-7]

3. Apply the policy-map
   Router(config)# interface <interface-name>
   Router(config-if)# service-policy [input | output] mypolicy
```

The **show policy-map interface <interface-name>** command can be used to display the packet statistics of all classes that are configured for all service policies on the specified interface.

Traffic Policing

The Cisco IOS Traffic Policing features allow the control and filtering of the incoming and outgoing traffic rate on an interface, as well as network bandwidth management through the token bucket algorithm. Traffic that falls within the defined parameters is sent, whereas traffic that exceeds or violates the parameters is dropped or sent with a different priority.

Several policing techniques are available within the Traffic Policing technology:

- **Traffic Policing (Single-Rate Policer):** Single-Rate Policer controls the input or output traffic rate for class-based user-defined criteria.

- **Two-Rate Policer**: Two-Rate Policer enforces Traffic Policing according to two separate rates: committed information rate (CIR) and peak information rate (PIR). These two rates can be specified along with their corresponding values by using the **cir** and **pir** keywords in the **police** command.

- **Policer Enhancements—Multiple Actions:** This feature further extends the functionality of the Traffic Policing feature (Single-Rate Policer) and the Two-Rate Policer feature. With both features, there is a limitation to specify only one conform action, one exceed action, and one violate action. With the new Policer Enhancement "Multiple Actions" feature, multiple conform, exceed, and violate actions for the marked packets can now be specified.

- **Percentage-Based Policing and Shaping:** This feature provides the capability to configure Traffic Policing and traffic shaping based on a *percentage* of bandwidth available on the interface by using the **police** (percent) and **shape** (percent) commands.

- **Color-Aware Policer:** The Color-Aware Policer feature is a method of Traffic Policing using an enhanced "color-aware" technique. The packet color classification is based on packet-matching criteria defined for two user-specified traffic classes—the conform-color class and the exceed-color class. These two traffic classes are created using the **conform-color** command, and the metering rates are defined using the **police** command. This feature is not available on all platforms. Use Feature Navigator to check platform and IOS support.

Configuring Traffic Policing is similar to configuring MQC, as described in the previous section. The tasks of configuring each of the Traffic Policing features that are listed previously are essentially the same; that is, you configure by using the MQC (as shown in the previous section) to create a **class-map** and **policy-map**. Then, using the **police** command, you configure the various traffic-policing features previously discussed under a specific class within that policy-map, as shown in Figure 7-7, and attach the **policy-map** to the interface. Traffic Policing can be configured at any level of the **policy-map** hierarchy—

that is, at the primary level, the secondary level, or the tertiary level. Example 7-9 shows a basic configuration applying Traffic Policing (Single-Rate Policing).

Example 7-9 *Configuring Traffic Policing*

```
Router(config)# class-map myclass
Router(config-cmap)# match access-group 101
Router(config-cmap)# exit
Router(config)# policy-map mypolicy
Router(config-pmap)# class-map myclass
Router(config-pmap-c)# police 8000 1000 1000 conform-action transmit exceed-action
drop violate-action drop
Router(config-pmap-c)#exit
Router(config-pmap)#exit
Router(config)# interface <interface-name>
Router(config-if)# service-policy [input ¦ output] mypolicy
```

Network-Based Application Recognition (NBAR)

The NBAR feature adds application-level intelligent classification capability to the network infrastructures. NBAR is a classification engine that recognizes a variety of applications and protocols from Layer 4 through Layer 7, including web-based and other difficult-to-classify protocols that utilize static and dynamically assigned TCP and UDP port numbers. NBAR classification extends by looking beyond the TCP/UDP port numbers of a packet and packet headers. This capability is called subport classification. NBAR looks into the TCP/UDP payload and classifies packets on the basis of the content within the payload, such as transaction identifier, message type, or other similar data.

NBAR classifies the following three types of protocols:

- TCP and UDP protocols that use statically assigned port numbers
- TCP and UDP protocols that use dynamically assigned port numbers, requiring stateful inspection
- Non-TCP and non-UDP IP protocols such as IPsec (ESP/AH) or ICMP

Protocol Discovery

NBAR includes a special Protocol Discovery feature that provides an easy way to discover application protocols traversing a network at any given time. Protocol Discovery can be applied to interfaces by using the **ip nbar protocol-discovery** command under the interface configuration mode and can be used to monitor both input and output traffic. The Protocol Discovery feature captures important per-protocol statistics supported by NBAR, such as total number of input and output packets and bytes, and input and output bit rates. These statistics assist in developing traffic classes and policies. The **show ip nbar protocol-discovery** command displays the statistics for all interfaces on which Protocol Discovery is enabled.

Packet Description Language Module (PDLM)

An external PDLM can be loaded on the router at runtime using the **ip nbar pdlm <pdlm-name>** command from the global configuration mode, extending and enhancing the classification engine for the many existing and emerging application protocols in the NBAR list of protocols. PDLMs can also be used to enhance an existing protocol recognition capability. PDLMs allow NBAR to recognize new protocols without requiring a new Cisco IOS image or a router reload. The **show ip nbar pdlm** command displays all currently loaded PDLMs. Example 7-10 shows the current PDLM loaded from flash memory.

Example 7-10 *PDLM Loaded*

```
Router# show ip nbar pdlm
The following PDLMs have been loaded:
flash:gnutella.pdlm
flash:kazaa2.pdlm
flash:edonkey.pdlm
```

Configuring NBAR

Similar to the other techniques discussed earlier in this chapter, NBAR is configured through the MQC framework. Example 7-11 shows a **class-map** "myclass" using the NBAR technique to classify peer-to-peer (P2P) file-sharing network traffic as its matching criterion using the **match protocol** commands. P2P traffic is bandwidth intensive, and most networks would like to manage them. The example shows that P2P can be blocked using the **drop** command or policed down to the average rate of 8000 bits per second with a normal burst size of 1000 bytes and an excess burst size of 1000 bytes.

The long list of supported protocols available in the **match protocol** command includes HTTP, HTTPS, FTP, IMAP, POP3, SMTP, BGP, RIP, EIGRP, ICMP, KAZAA, NAPSTER, and PCANYWHERE.

Example 7-11 *Configuring NBAR*

```
Router(config)# class-map myclass
Router(config-cmap)# match protocol fasttrack
Router(config-cmap)# match protocol napster
Router(config-cmap)# match protocol gnutella
Router(config-cmap)# match protocol edonkey
Router(config-cmap)# match protocol kazaa2
Router(config-cmap)# exit
Router(config)# policy-map mypolicy
Router(config-pmap)# class-map myclass
! Define Drop action
Router(config-pmap-c)# drop
! OR Perform Class-based Policing
Router(config-pmap-c)# police 8000 1000 1000 conform-action transmit exceed-action
drop
Router(config-pmap-c)#exit
Router(config-pmap)#exit
Router(config)# interface <interface-name>
Router(config-if)# service-policy [input ¦ output] mypolicy
```

The **show ip nbar port-map** [*protocol-name*] command can be used to display the TCP/UDP port numbers used by NBAR to classify a given protocol.

TCP Intercept

TCP Intercept is another important security feature integrated into Cisco IOS software, which is used to protect TCP servers from SYN-flooding attacks. As discussed earlier in this chapter, a SYN-flooding attack occurs when an attacker attempts to flood a TCP server with requests for connection. Because these messages have unreachable or spoofed return addresses, the connections are not able to fully establish. The resulting volume of incomplete half-open connections eventually overwhelms the TCP server and can cause it to deny regular service to valid user requests, thereby preventing legitimate users from connecting to a website, accessing e-mail, using FTP service, or any other TCP-based application.

How TCP Intercept Works

Figure 7-8 illustrates how the TCP Intercept feature works by intercepting and validating all incoming TCP connection requests flowing between a TCP client and TCP server. In the intercept mode, the TCP Intercept engine intercepts TCP synchronization (SYN) packets from clients to servers that match an extended access list. The software establishes a connection with the client on behalf of the destination server (proxying the SYN) and, if successful, establishes the connection with the server on behalf of the client, thereby transparently knitting together the two half-connections. This mechanism protects against any connection attempts from unreachable or spoofed hosts. The software continues to intercept and forward packets (inline) throughout the duration of the connection.

In the event of illegitimate requests, the aggressive timeouts on half-open connections and thresholds on TCP connection requests protect destination servers while continuing to forward legitimate requests.

TCP intercept operates in two modes: the passive **watch** mode or the default active **intercept** mode. In **watch** mode, all connection requests are allowed to pass through the router with the software passively watching the connection that is being established. If a connection fails to establish in a configurable interval, the software then intervenes and terminates the connection attempt. Whereas in **intercept** mode, the software actively intercepts all incoming connection SYN requests and responds on behalf of the server with an SYN-ACK waiting for an ACK from the server. When an ACK is received from the TCP server, the original SYN is sent to the server and the software performs a three-way handshake with the server. When this is complete, the two half-connections are joined.

Figure 7-8   *TCP Intercept*

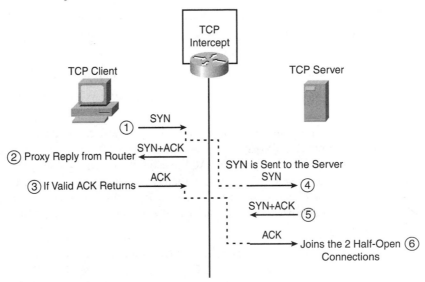

Configuring TCP Intercept

To configure the TCP Intercept feature, you need to first define an access list that instructs the intercept engine to intercept and validate either all requests or only specific networks or specific destination servers. Generally, the access list should have the source as **any** and define specific destination networks or servers. This will provide protection for destination host(s) and not the source. If no access list match is found, the router allows the request to pass with no further action.

Example 7-12 defines extended IP access list 101, instructing the TCP Intercept engine to intercept packets for all TCP servers on the 10.1.1.0/24 subnet. The example also tunes the aggressive threshold trigger values to 400 and 500 for **low** and **high** incomplete connections, respectively.

Example 7-12   *Configuring TCP Intercept on Router*

```
Router(config)# access-list 101 permit tcp any 10.1.1.0 0.0.0.255
Router(config)# ip tcp intercept list 101
Router(config)# ip tcp intercept max-incomplete low 400
Router(config)# ip tcp intercept max-incomplete high 500
```

The **ip tcp intercept mode {intercept | watch}** command in global configuration mode can be used to set the TCP intercept mode.

The **show tcp intercept connections** command displays incomplete connections and established connections, and **show tcp intercept statistics** displays TCP intercept statistics.

TCP Intercept on Firewall

The TCP Intercept feature is also available on the PIX 500, ASA 5500, and FWSM firewall software to help protect servers behind the firewall from SYN-flood attacks. The feature allows for configuring two parameters:

- The maximum number of established connections allowed to a TCP server
- The maximum number of incomplete half-open (embryonic) connections to a TCP server

When the embryonic connection limit is reached, the firewall responds to every SYN packet sent to the server with a SYN+ACK and does not pass the SYN packet to the internal server. If the external device responds with an ACK packet, the firewall knows it is a valid request and not part of a SYN attack. The firewall then establishes a connection with the internal server and joins the client connections passively. If the firewall does not get an ACK back from the server, it aggressively times out that embryonic connection. Figure 7-8 illustrates how this works.

Example 7-13 shows a **static** translation on PIX for an internal TCP server with the embryonic limit set to 100 and the Max Connection limit set to 1000. Most Windows platforms allow a maximum of 128 half-open (embryonic) connections, so when setting the embryonic limit on the **static**, use a value less than the maximum embryonic limit allowed by the server operating system.

Example 7-13 *Configuring TCP Intercept on PIX/ASA Firewall Using the **Static** Command*

```
PIX(config)# static (inside, outside) 209.165.201.1 10.1.1.1 netmask
255.255.255.255 1000 100
```

The **nat** command offers the same feature. Example 7-14 shows how configuring the **nat** command is similar to configuring the TCP Intercept.

Example 7-14 *Configuring TCP Intercept on PIX Using the **NAT** Command*

```
PIX(config)# nat (inside) 1 10.1.1.0 255.255.255.0 1000 100
```

Policy-Based Routing (PBR)

Policy-based routing (PBR) provides a method for overriding the information available in the IP routing table and can be configured to forward (route) packets based on other criteria defined in policies, such as IP addresses, port numbers, application, and the length/size of the packet. PBR can also be used for packet classification and marking with IP precedence values in the Type of Service (ToS) field of the IP header. PBR gives more granular control over routing of packets by extending and complementing the existing mechanisms provided by routing protocols.

With the capability to control a data path, in the event of an attack, PBR can be used as a security tool to divert traffic and for scrubbing or managing congestion. PBR can also be used as a mitigation tool to match the attack traffic and drop it. Example 7-15 shows sample configurations for both these scenarios.

PBR allows performing the following tasks:

- Classifying traffic based on the extended access list to identify the match criteria
- Rewriting or changing header options such as IP precedence, DF, or ToS bits, influence the next-hop address or interface
- Routing packets to specific traffic-engineered paths

Example 7-15 shows configuration of a PBR and provides details on how to route traffic from different sources to different next-hops. Traffic can be routed by overwriting the path devised by an IP routing table and setting various parameters in the packet header, such as the IP precedence or the ToS bit. All packets arriving on the specified interface matching the **match** clauses will be subject to the action defined in the **set** command.

The example shows that all packets arriving from source 1.1.1.1 are forwarded to the next-hop address at 11.11.11.11 with the Precedence bit set to priority, whereas packets arriving from source 2.2.2.2 are forwarded to a different next-hop address at 22.22.22.22 with the max-throughput TOS (4) bit set. The example also shows that all TCP packets that arrive with a minimum and maximum packet length of 100 are sent to the Null 0 interface (black holing the packets). PBR is then applied on a particular interface.

Example 7-15   *Configuring Policy-Based Routing (PBR)*

```
Router(config)# access-list 1 permit ip 1.1.1.1
Router(config)# access-list 2 permit ip 2.2.2.2
Router(config)# access-list 101 permit tcp any any
Router(config)# route-map mymap permit 10
Router(config-route-map)# match ip address 1
Router(config-route-map)# set ip precedence priority
Router(config-route-map)# set ip next-hop 11.11.11.11
Router(config-route-map)# exit
Router(config)# route-map mymap permit 20
Router(config-route-map)# match ip address 2
Router(config-route-map)# set ip tos max-throughput
Router(config-route-map)# set ip next-hop 22.22.22.22
Router(config-route-map)# exit
Router(config)# route-map mymap permit 30
Router(config-route-map)# match ip address 101
Router(config-route-map)# match length 100 100
Router(config-route-map)# set interface null 0
Router(config-route-map)# exit
Router(config)# interface <interface-name>
Router(config-if)# ip policy route-map mymap
```

Note that PBR is applicable for inbound traffic when configured on the specified interface. By default, packets generated by the router are not policy routed. To enable local PBR for such packets, the additional **ip local policy route-map <map-name>** command from the global configuration mode is required.

The **show ip policy** and **show route-map** commands can be used to verify PBR configuration and display packet statistics for each policy.

Unicast Reverse Path Forwarding (uRPF)

The uRPF feature is a security tool that helps mitigate source IP address spoofing by discarding IP packets that lack a verifiable IP source address in the IP routing table. Several DoS/DDoS attacks employ forging or rapidly altering source IP addresses to navigate around threat detection and filtering mechanisms. uRPF technique thwarts any attempts of DoS attacks by relying on IP spoofing. uRPF should be deployed at the network edge or the border/gateway device on the network.

There are two flavors of uRPF implementation:

- Strict Mode complying with RFC 2827 filters on Network Ingress Edge and Best Current Practices (BCP 38)
- Loose Mode for ISP to ISP Edge, for RTBH filtering

How uRPF Works

As illustrated in Figure 7-9, the router examines all arriving packets received on the uRPF-enabled interface and will only forward packets that pass the uRPF check; that is, the source address appears in the routing table and matches the interface on which the packet was received. In other words, source IP packets are checked to ensure that a packet's return path uses the same interface it arrived on. If the source IP address is unknown and not reachable through the interface on which the packet was received, the packet is dropped by default. Because the lookup relies on the presence of the Forwarding Information Base (FIB), this "look backward" capability works only when Cisco Express Forwarding (CEF) is enabled on the router. CEF generates the FIB as part of its operation.

Figure 7-9   *Unicast Reverse Path Forwarding (uRPF) Strict Mode*

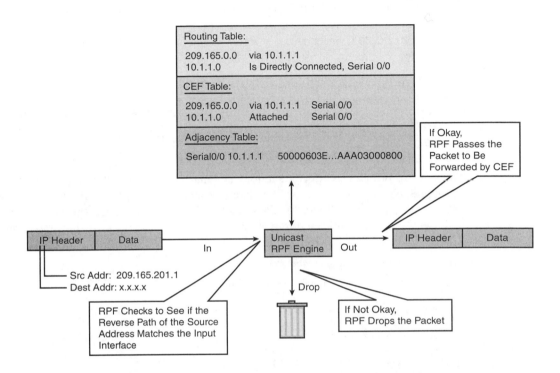

The information in Figure 7-9 is taken from the Cisco security presentation on "Unicast Reverse Path Forwarding."

NOTE   Source Address must match the FIB and Adjacency Information in the CEF Table.

The uRPF enhances with the ACL logging capability by enabling reverse path forwarding (RPF) check in a pass-through mode. In this mode, all RPF violations are logged using the ACL log-input feature. If a packet fails RPF check, the ACL is checked to determine whether the packet should be dropped (using a deny ACL) or forwarded (using a permit ACL). The ACL logging counter and match counter statistics are incremented to reflect statistics for packets with spoofed IP addresses.

Configuring uRPF

Example 7-16 shows how to configure uRPF on an interface with the ACL logging feature. Packets sourced from 10.1.1.0/24 subnet arriving at serial0/0 and failing the uRPF check are logged by the ACL log statement and dropped by the ACL deny action. Packets sourced from 172.16.1.0/24 subnet arriving at serial0/0 and failing the uRPF check are logged by the ACL log statement and forwarded by the ACL permit action.

Example 7-16 *Configuring uRPF (Strict Mode) with ACL*

```
Router(config)# access-list 101 deny ip 10.1.1.0 0.0.0.255 any log-input
Router(config)# access-list 101 permit ip 172.16.1.0 0.0.0.255 any log-input
Router(config)# interface <interface-name>
Router(config-if)# ip verify unicast reverse-path 101
```

The **show ip interface <interface-name>** command displays uRPF statistics for dropped or suppressed packets for the specified interface and can be used with the **show ip access-list** command to detect IP address spoofing. If ACL logging is enabled, the data logs can be reviewed to gather additional information about the network attack, as shown in Example 7-17.

Example 7-17 *Verifying uRPF Configuration and Statistics*

```
Router# show ip interface <interface-name>
  ...
  IP verify source reachable-via RX, allow default, ACL 101
  56 verification drops
  192 suppressed verification drops
!
Router# show ip access-lists 101
Extended IP access list 101
    deny ip 10.1.1.0 0.0.0.255 any log-input (56 matches)
    permit ip 172.16.1.0 0.0.0.255 any log-input (192 matches)
```

To verify whether uRPF is operational, use the **show cef interface <interface-name>** command, as shown in Example 7-18.

Example 7-18 *Verifying uRPF Is Operational*

```
Router# show cef interface <interface-name>
Serial0/0 is up (if_number 3)
...
  IP unicast RPF check is enabled
  IP CEF switching enabled
```

The **show ip traffic** command can be further used to display additional packet counter information for packets dropped because of uRPF checks, as shown in Example 7-19.

Example 7-19 *Verifying Drop Packet Counters*

```
Router# show ip traffic
IP statistics:
...
  Drop:  3 encapsulation failed, 0 unresolved, 0 no adjacency
         0 no route, 0 unicast RPF, 0 forced drop
```

NetFlow

NetFlow is a Cisco IOS feature that captures statistics on IP packets flowing through the router and is emerging as a primary security technology. Cisco is the pioneer in the NetFlow technology and the leader in IP traffic flow technology. NetFlow provides numerous applications and services: network traffic accounting, user and application monitoring, usage-based billing, link-usage, network planning, traffic profiling, traffic engineering, capacity planning, anomaly detection, and security and DoS monitoring capabilities.

As shown in Figure 7-10, Cisco NetFlow can be used primarily as a security analysis tool to identify and classify DoS attacks, viruses, worms, and network anomalies in real-time. The data can further be invaluable in forensic processes to gather details and comprehend security incidents. NetFlow is completely transparent to the existing network, including end stations, application software, and any devices on the network.

Figure 7-10 *Using NetFlow for Security Analysis*

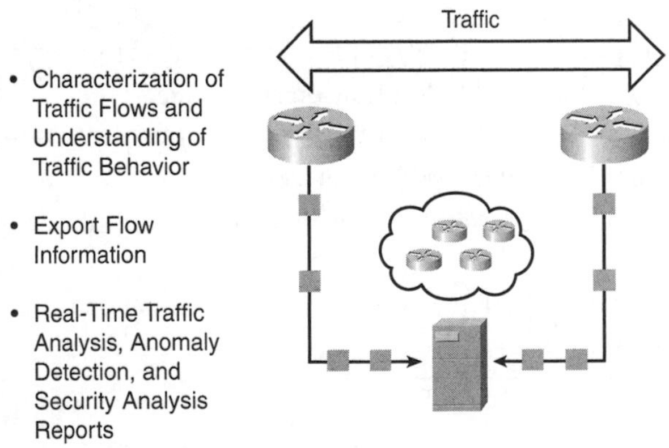

- Characterization of Traffic Flows and Understanding of Traffic Behavior

- Export Flow Information

- Real-Time Traffic Analysis, Anomaly Detection, and Security Analysis Reports

NetFlow is supported on most Cisco platforms via ASICs, Cisco IOS, and Cisco Catalyst Operating System (CatOS) software.

How NetFlow Works

NetFlow classifies packets by the direction of their flow and identifies packet flows for both ingress and egress IP packets. Each flow is defined by its unique seven-key characteristics: ingress interface, IP protocol type, type-of-service (ToS), source and destination IP addresses, and source and destination port numbers, as shown in Example 7-21. The information gathered with NetFlow is like a phone bill that provides all the required information for traffic profiling and determining the "who, what, when, where, and how" of network traffic. NetFlow is usually deployed across the edge of a network to monitor peer interfaces, because these are the potential ingress points for most attacks.

Configuring NetFlow

Example 7-20 shows you how to enable NetFlow Switching for IP on a Cisco Router.

Example 7-20   *Configuring NetFlow on a Router*

```
Router(config)# interface <interface-name>

Router(config-if)# ip flow ingress <or>
Router(config-if)# ip flow egress
```

The **ip flow ingress** command is used to capture traffic being received by the interface, whereas the **ip flow egress** command is used to capture traffic being transmitted by the interface.

NOTE   For Cisco IOS prior to releases 12.2(14)S, 12.0(22)S, or 12.2(15)T, the **ip route-cache flow** command was used to enable NetFlow on an interface.

For Cisco IOS release 12.2(14)S, 12.0(22)S, 12.2(15)T, or later, the **ip flow ingress** command is used to enable NetFlow on an interface.

If CEF is not configured, NetFlow enhances the existing switching path (optimum switching).

If CEF is configured, NetFlow becomes a flow information gatherer and feature acceleration tool.

The router maintains current NetFlow cache to track all the flows passing through the device. The **show ip cache flow** command or the **show ip flow interface** command can be used to view a snapshot of the current flows stored in the router cache.

Example 7-21 shows a sample snapshot using the **show ip cache flow** command taken from the NetFlow cache. Note the large amount of ICMP flood (Protocol 01) and other valuable flow statistics and flow details (Src/Dest interface, Src/Dest IP and port, and so on).

Example 7-21 *NetFlow Captured Statistics*

```
Router# show ip cache flow
IP packet size distribution (72014968 total packets):
   1-32   64   96  128  160  192  224  256  288  320  352  384  416  448  480
   .003 .000 .000 .118 .000 .000 .000 .000 .000 .004 .000 .005 .000 .000 .000

    512  544  576 1024 1536 2048 2560 3072 3584 4096 4608
   .013 .000 .022 .067 .231 .000 .000 .000 .000 .000 .000

IP Flow Switching Cache, 53988 bytes
  12 active, 2324 inactive, 66 added
  364 ager polls, 0 flow alloc failures
  Active flows timeout in 30 minutes
  Inactive flows timeout in 15 seconds
  last clearing of statistics never
Protocol         Total    Flows   Packets Bytes  Packets Active(Sec)  Idle(Sec)
--------         Flows     /Sec     /Flow  /Pkt     /Sec     /Flow       /Flow
TCP-Telnet           3      0.0         1    44      0.0       0.6        15.3
TCP-BGP              1      0.0         1    59      0.0       0.0        15.0
UDP-other           13      0.0        48   586      0.0     138.5        14.2
ICMP              6720    143.7        17   592    252.6       6.7        10.6

SrcIf         SrcIPaddress   DstIf       DstIPaddress    Pr SrcP DstP  Pkts
Fa0/0         10.1.1.1       Local       1.1.1.1         01 0000 0800  42K
Fa0/0         0.0.0.0        Null        255.255.255.255 11 0044 0043  360
Fa0/0         10.17.10.1     Local       192.168.5.161   01 0000 0000  423K
```

Additionally, NetFlow data can be exported from the NetFlow cache to an external collector for further analysis and can be used to map and identify the nodes under attack and also to determine the attack characteristics. To export NetFlow data, use the **ip flow-export** global configuration command.

NetFlow Ecosystem

Cisco has developed a robust ecosystem of NetFlow partners that have developed value-added functionality and reporting specialties, including accounting, traffic analysis, security, billing, network planning, and network monitoring. Many freeware tools are available that can analyze NetFlow data, including cflowd, flow-tools, and autofocus. Several GUI-based applications are available, such as Arbor, Mazu, and Adlex, which leverage NetFlow data for DoS attack detection and centralized reporting. Threat correlation tools such as Panoptis, used for anomaly detection, also take advantage of NetFlow data to detect, characterize, and mitigate DoS attacks.

Mitigation Techniques at Layer 2

One of the biggest challenges in securing the network is the OSI Layer 2—the data-link layer. The OSI reference model was built to allow different layers to work without the knowledge of each other. The data-link layer provides the functional and procedural means to transfer data among network entities with interoperability and interconnectivity to other layers, but from a security perspective, it presents its own challenges.

Layer 2 attacks are difficult to achieve from outside the network. The attacker needs to be inside the network to be able to abuse Layer 2. Some very serious Layer 2 attacks are possible that can cause damage to the network. If Layer 2 is compromised, it can in turn compromise all other layers in succession.

Network security implementations, in most cases, are highly focused on securing Layer 3 and above with firewalls, intrusion detection systems, and encryption technologies. Little to no attention is given to secure Layer 2. It is often said that network security is only as strong as the weakest link, and that may well be Layer 2 of the OSI model. Several Layer 2 attacks exist that pose major threats to other layers in the OSI layered-model (Layer 3 and above). These include MAC spoofing, MAC flooding, ARP spoofing, Spanning-Tree attacks, and VLAN hopping. These attacks and others are discussed in this section with appropriate mitigation techniques.

CAM Table Overflow—MAC Attack

Content Addressable Memory (CAM) tables are storage locations that contain lists of MAC addresses available on physical ports of the switch along with their associated VLAN parameters. CAM tables are analogous to the routing tables on a Layer 3 device.

Background

All frames arriving on the switch are checked against the CAM table. If an entry is found corresponding to the destination MAC address of the frame, the switch forwards the frame to the designated outgoing port. If the destination MAC address is not found in the CAM table, the switch forwards the frame out of every port, effectively acting like a hub. When the target device returns the frame, this knowledge is captured, and the CAM table is updated for subsequent frames with the same destination MAC address.

The Problem

Switches do not have unlimited memory; hence, the CAM table has a fixed allocated memory space. This makes the switch vulnerable to exploitation from sniffing by flooding the switch with a large number of randomly generated invalid source and destination MAC addresses, until the CAM table fills up and no new entries can be accepted. When this happens, the switch cannot handle any further frames and acts in a hub mode, in which it broadcasts all received frames to all the ports on the switch, essentially turning it into one big broadcast domain. CAM table overflow floods traffic only within the local VLAN; hence, the attacker is limited to receive traffic within the VLAN to which it is connected. Popular DoS tools such as MACOF and DSNIFF are available to launch this type of attack. The switch eventually times out older MAC address entries from the CAM table and reverts back to acting like a switch again.

CAM Table Overflow Attack Mitigation

The CAM table overflow attack can be effectively mitigated by configuring the Port Security feature on the switch. Port security can be enabled for static MAC addresses seen on a particular switch port or dynamic MAC addresses by specifying the number of MAC addresses that can be learned by a switch port. Switch ports can be configured for port violation when an invalid source MAC address is detected, to either block the offending MAC address or shut down the port.

Port security is discussed in detail in Chapter 4, with configuration examples.

MAC Spoofing Attack

MAC spoofing is a technique used to spoof source MAC addresses to impersonate other hosts or devices in a network. This is different from an ARP spoofing attack. In ARP spoofing, the switch is misguided by poisoning the ARP cache, whereas with MAC spoofing, the switch is confused to believe two ports have the same MAC address, thereby forcing the switch to attempt to forward frames destined for the trusted host to the attacker. This is illustrated in Figure 7-11.

Background

As discussed earlier, when a frame is received on the switch, the switch looks up the destination MAC address in the CAM table and forwards the frame to the corresponding egress port designated in the MAC table.

The Problem

As illustrated in Figure 7-11, the switch has built its MAC address table (also called CAM table) by mapping Host A on port 1, Host B on port 2, Host C on port 3, and Host D on port 4. An attacker crafts an Ethernet frame forging (spoofing) the source MAC address of another host (for example, Host C in the diagram), causing the switch to overwrite the CAM table entry to point the MAC address to the attacker physical port 1 instead of the port connecting the real Host C on port 3. When Host D (or any other host) sends a packet destined to the MAC address of Host C, the switch will forward all packets destined for Host C to the attacker, because the CAM table entry is poisoned, as highlighted in Figure 7-11.

When the real host sends traffic to the switch, the switch rewrites the CAM table entry, once more moving back to the original port connected to the real host. This tug-of-war continues between the intruder and the real host that is claiming the same MAC address, thereby confusing the switch CAM table and causing repetitive rewrites of MAC table entries. This not only causes a denial of service to the real host, but also has a performance impact on the switch because the intruder sends a large number of forged MAC addresses.

Figure 7-11 *MAC Spoofing Illustrated*

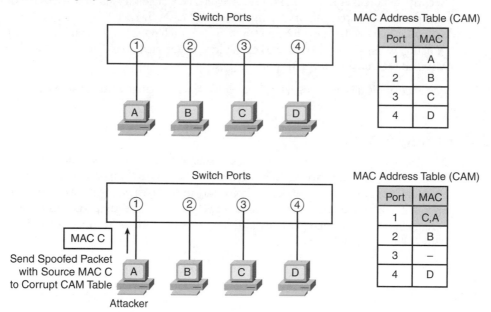

MAC Spoofing Attack Mitigation

Using a technique that is similar to the CAM table overflow mitigation technique, you use the Port Security feature to mitigate MAC spoofing attacks. Port security is discussed in detail in Chapter 4, with configuration examples.

ARP Spoofing Attack

An ARP spoofing attack is a method in which an intruder attempts to disguise its source MAC address by impersonating another host on the network. In ARP spoofing, the switch is misguided by poisoning the ARP cache. ARP spoofing is generally motivated to aid in making other DoS and MITM-type attacks possible.

Background

One of the fundamental operations of the Ethernet protocol is based on the ARP protocol for sending and receiving ARP messages. ARP is a Layer 2 protocol that is used by the IP protocol to map network addresses (32-bit IP address) to the hardware addresses (48-bit MAC address), providing IP-to-MAC resolution. When Host A needs to communicate with Host B on a network, Host A sends an ARP request, and Host B returns its MAC address with an ARP reply message. The ARP requests are broadcast requests sent to all hosts on the network.

The Problem

In the process of ARP request and reply messaging between two legitimate Host A and Host B communication systems, the intruder can inject an unsolicited fake ARP reply message with its own MAC address, sending this message to the requestor, Host A, masquerading as the victim, Host B. The requestor Host A now has a poisoned ARP entry sending all packets destined for Host B to the attacker. This technique is commonly used in many MITM-type attacks.

The ARP function can also be misused to steer traffic to the attacker host that should normally be destined for the legitimate target host. This can be accomplished with gratuitous ARP (gARP). Gratuitous ARP (gARP) is an unsolicited ARP broadcast containing the IP address of the target host and the attacker's MAC address. The gARP causes all receiving hosts to incorrectly update their ARP table (ARP poison) with an entry that pairs the target's IP address with the attacker's MAC address. Similarly, the switch will incorrectly update its MAC-address-table (CAM table); thus, when any host needs to send a packet to the target's IP, the switch will forward the packet to the attacker. This causes an MITM condition.

Tools such as the DSNIFF and ETTERCAP can be used in these types of attacks.

ARP Spoofing Attack Mitigation

A simple technique for mitigating ARP spoofing attacks is to configure the hold-down timers on the interface by specifying the duration of time (lifetime) for an ARP entry to remain in the ARP cache. This method is not scalable even in the smallest network, because all systems on the network are required to modify the ARP cache expiration time plus static ARP entries.

Another solution can be to use private VLANs to mitigate these attacks.

The best defense mechanism for mitigating these types of attacks is to enable the Dynamic ARP Inspection (DAI) feature available on Cisco Catalyst switches. The DAI security feature determines the validity of packets by performing an IP-to-MAC address binding inspection that is stored in a trusted database (the DHCP snooping binding database) before forwarding the packet to the appropriate destination. The DAI feature is discussed in detail in Chapter 4, with configuration examples.

VTP Attack

The VLAN Trunking Protocol (VTP) is a Layer 2 protocol used to distribute VLAN configuration information among switches over a trunk port. In VTP attacks, the intruder can impersonate as a trunk port and be able to receive all VLAN information via the VTP.

Background

VTP is a data link layer messaging protocol for centralized VLAN management functions, such as adding a VLAN, deleting a VLAN, or renaming a VLAN. A VTP management domain is created with all the switches joining the domain grouped together in a trusted zone to allow trusted exchange of VTP messages containing VLAN information. The switches are configured in different modems such as server, client, or transparent mode. Server mode switches are able to perform any VLAN management function, and the changes are propagated to all the switches in the VTP domain. Switches in client mode are passive switches that inherit settings from the server switch. Transparent mode does not influence changes to other nontransparent mode switches. Any VLAN changes made on a transparent mode switch are locally significant and not propagated to other switches.

The Problem

As of this writing, no known VTP vulnerabilities have been identified or published.

In theory, the intruder can send falsified VTP messages on a trunk port, posing as a VTP server, and thereby gaining privilege to add or remove VLANs from the VTP domain as well as to create Spanning Tree Protocol loops. Other malicious VTP advertisements can be sent with no VLANs configured. When a nontransparent mode switch receives such a VTP message with no VLANs defined over a trunk port, it inherits the configuration-revision number of the sending switch resulting in a DoS attack that deletes all VLANs configured in the VLAN database across the entire VTP domain.

Note that launching this type of attack is very difficult and requires high-level skills as well as inside information (such as knowledge of VTP domain name, password, and trunk port details). This information can be gained through social engineering or a network reconnaissance process. Although the difficulty of launching such an attack makes it unlikely, it can occur.

VTP Attack Mitigation

A VTP domain can be tightly secured with the built-in password functionality that is configured on all the switches in the VTP domain. VTP passwords are entered into the VTP database and used to authenticate VTP advertisements. Configure a unique VTP domain name with a strong VTP password throughout the VTP domain to prevent the possibility of forging VTP messages. However, note that the VTP password will not be shown in the switch configuration file (the password is stored in the VLAN database), and it should not be considered confidential because it can be determined using the **show vtp status** or **show vtp password** commands.

CAUTION   Do not configure passwords such as "cisco," "cisco123," or other passwords that are easily guessable and prone to brute force. In addition, create long passwords—for example, a minimum of six to eight characters in length. For guidelines on creating strong passwords, refer to Chapter 3, "Device Security," in the section titled "Creating Strong Passwords."

VLAN Hopping Attack

As the name implies, VLAN hopping attacks are methods in which an intruder tries to bypass a Layer 3 device to communicate from one VLAN to another in an attempt to compromise a device on another VLAN. VLANs are logical groups of hosts that are created to limit the broadcast domains. VLAN hopping is a network attack whereby an intruder system sends out packets destined to a host on a different VLAN that cannot normally be reached by the intruder.

Background

When a host in a particular VLAN requires communication with a host in another VLAN, a Layer 3 device is required to route packets between two different VLANs. This is commonly known as inter-VLAN routing. A VLAN hopping attack is the technique of jumping VLANs without traversing a Layer 3 device.

Dynamic Trunking Protocol (DTP) is a Layer 2 protocol used to automate ISL and 802.1Q trunk configurations between switches and supports autonegotiation of both ISL and

802.1Q trunks. DTP synchronizes the trunking mode on both sides of the link. DTP states can be configured to ON, OFF, DESIRABLE, AUTO, or NON-NEGOTIATE. Most Cisco switches default to AUTO mode.

The Problem

Two primary methods are used to perform VLAN hopping attacks:

- Switch spoofing
- Double tagging

In the switch-spoofing technique, the intruder impersonates a switch. (Note that this requires that the intruder be capable of emulating either ISL or 802.1Q signaling along with DTP signaling.) The intruder can make itself appear to be a switch with a trunk port (in AUTO mode) on the other side. If successful, the intruder's system then becomes a member of all VLANs. When the intruder learns all the VLAN information, it can take advantage of the incorrectly configured trunk port to route traffic for multiple VLANs encapsulated with ISL or 802.1Q across the same physical link, generally between switches.

In a multiple switch environment, a trunk implementation can be exploited. Trunk ports by default are implicitly set to a native VLAN-ID. (The default native VLAN-ID for a trunk is VLAN 1 on Cisco switches.) Therefore, when a user port (access port) sends a packet to a destination located in a distant switch, and that very packet is encapsulated into 802.1Q format with the native VLAN-ID, it will be successfully forwarded to the distant switch without crossing a Layer 3 device.

NOTE　Trunk ports have access to all VLANs by default unless pruning is configured.

Another variation of this attack is double tagging, also called a double encapsulated VLAN hopping attack, which involves tagging the frame with two 802.1Q headers to forward the frames to a different VLAN. The embedded hidden 802.1Q tag inside the frame allows the frame to traverse a VLAN that the outer 802.1Q tag did not specify. This attack will work even if the trunk port is set to OFF.

The first switch to encounter the double-tagged frame strips the first tag off the frame and forwards the frame. This results in the frame being forwarded with the inner 802.1Q tag out all the switch ports, including the trunk ports configured with the native VLAN-ID of the network intruder. The second switch then forwards the packet to the destination based on the VLAN identifier in the second 802.1Q header.

VLAN Hopping Attack Mitigation

Mitigating VLAN hopping attacks requires a good understanding of the Layer 2 switching and the network topology because several modifications to the VLAN configuration may be required.

To prevent a basic switch spoofing VLAN hopping attack involves explicitly turning off DTP on all user ports (by placing the port in access mode using the **switchport mode access** command) except the ports that specifically require DTP, such as the trunk ports. In addition, it involves disabling all unused switch ports by placing them in an unused VLAN (separate VLAN).

To prevent a double tagging, a double encapsulated VLAN hopping attack, ensure that the native VLAN-ID on all the trunk ports is different from the native VLAN-ID of the user ports. It is best to use a dedicated VLAN that is specific for all the trunk ports, and not the default native VLAN-ID either. Using VLAN 1 should always be avoided. Configuring the native VLAN to tag all traffic prevents the vulnerability of double dot1Q-tagged packets hopping VLANs. Enable the **vlan dot1q tag native** command from the global configuration mode on the edge switch to tag all packets on all the 802.1Q trunk ports, including the native VLAN egress traffic, and drop untagged native VLAN ingress traffic. This command was introduced in Cisco Catalyst IOS release 12.1(9)EA1. For older versions, the native VLAN should be changed to an unused VLAN number on both sides of the trunk.

PVLAN Attack

Chapter 4 discussed the details of private VLANs (PVLANs). PVLAN is a feature that prevents interhost communication by providing port-specific security between adjacent ports within a VLAN across one or more switches. PVLANs restrict communications between systems on the same logical IP subnet. A proxy-based attack can be used to bypass access restrictions that are enforced by PVLAN.

Background

Private VLANs work by restricting ports within a VLAN from communicating with other ports in the same VLAN by using the following three types of ports:

- **Promiscuous:** A promiscuous port can communicate with all interfaces, including the isolated and community ports within a PVLAN. The function of the promiscuous port is to move traffic between ports in community or isolated VLANs. Access lists can be used to identify which traffic can pass between these VLANs. Only one promiscuous port is allowed per single Private VLAN, and that one port serves the entire community as well as isolated VLANs in the Private VLAN.

- **Isolated:** An isolated PVLAN port has complete Layer 2 segregation from all other ports within the same PVLAN, but not from the promiscuous ports. Traffic from the isolated port is forwarded only to the promiscuous ports and none other.

- **Community:** Community ports are logically combined groups of ports in a common community that can pass traffic among themselves and with promiscuous ports. Ports are separated at Layer 2 from all other interfaces in other communities or isolated ports within their PVLAN.

The Problem

The Proxy Attack includes an attack against private VLANs, in which frames are forwarded to a host on the network that is connected to a promiscuous port, such as a router. Note that this attack is primarily used to defeat PVLAN configuration by avoiding the promiscuous port. Both source and destination systems are on the same IP subnet whose communications have been restricted by enforcing the PVLAN technology.

As shown in Figure 7-12, the intruder crafts the malicious packet with header parameters set as follows:

- Its own source IP and MAC address
- Destination IP address of the target victim
- Destination MAC address of the upstream router

As per the switch default behavior, the switch checks all the arriving packets' destination MAC addresses in the CAM table, and in this case, the switch forwards the frame to the router's switch port instead of the victim.

The router receives this packet, checks the destination IP address in the packet with the routing table, and in this case routes the packet to the target victim by rewriting the destination MAC address and sending the packet back out on the interface (like a U-turn), thereby making the attack successful, as shown in Figure 7-12.

This type of attack allows only for unidirectional traffic, because any attempt by the target victim to send traffic back to the intruder source IP/MAC address will be blocked by the private VLAN configuration as expected. The only way to achieve bidirectional traffic is to compromise both hosts and poisoning ARP entries or with static ARP entries. Note that this would not be considered as PVLAN vulnerability, because all the rules of PVLAN are still enforced. The ARP was poisoned by bypassing other network security mechanisms that were in place.

Figure 7-12 *Compromising PVLAN Implementation*

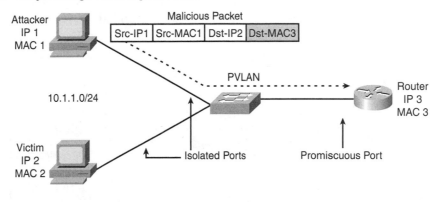

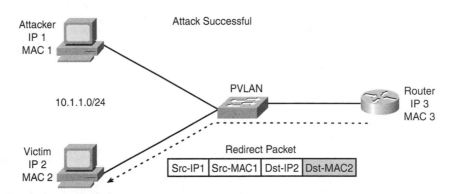

PVLAN Attack Mitigation

A simple technique to mitigate PVLAN attacks is to configure ACLs on the default gateway router facing the victim. Virtual ACLs (VACL) can also be used to mitigate the effects of PVLAN attacks. The ACL on the router can be configured to block any arriving packets that have the same source and destination IP address. (The intruder and victim are on the same IP subnet in this type of attack.)

Figure 7-13 shows how to prevent PVLAN attacks by using an Extended ACL configured inbound on the router interface facing the target victim and the intruder on IP subnet 10.1.1.0/24. The router will drop any packets arriving from the source/destination on the 10.1.1.0/24 subnet, thereby thwarting this type of attack and logging all offending packets.

Figure 7-13 *Preventing PVLAN Attacks*

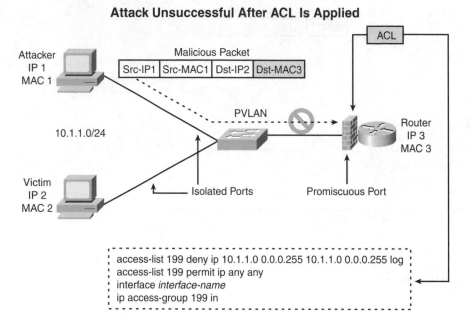

Attack Unsuccessful After ACL Is Applied

```
access-list 199 deny ip 10.1.1.0 0.0.0.255 10.1.1.0 0.0.0.255 log
access-list 199 permit ip any any
interface interface-name
ip access-group 199 in
```

Spanning-Tree Attacks

Spanning Tree Protocol attacks are methods whereby the intruder assumes the identity of a root bridge in the topology by broadcasting forged Bridge Protocol Data Unit (BPDU) messages in an attempt to force spanning-tree recalculations and thereby disrupt the network data flow.

Background

Spanning Tree Protocol (STP) is a link management protocol that provides path redundancy by preventing loops in a network of switches that are interconnected via multiple paths. Spanning Tree Protocol implements the 802.1D IEEE algorithm by exchanging BPDU messages with other switches to detect and remove any loops by shutting down selected bridge interfaces. Spanning Tree implements a unique root switch to maintain a stable network topology to guarantee that there is only one active path between two network devices.

target DHCP server, thereby exhausting the address space available for a period of time. The underlying principals of this attack are similar to the SYN flooding attack.

After successfully flooding the DHCP server, the intruder introduces a "rogue" DHCP server responding to new DHCP requests from clients with the intent of providing incorrect configuration information to the client, such as IP addresses and other falsifying network information, such as WINS, DNS, and default gateways. This forged injected information will assist the attacker in launching other types of attacks on the clients, such as man-in-the-middle. Attacking tools such as MACOF and GOBBLER can aid in the success of these types of attacks.

DHCP Spoofing and Starvation Attacks Mitigation

Similar to the CAM table overflow mitigation technique, the Port Security feature can be used to mitigate DHCP spoofing and starvation attacks by limiting the number of MAC addresses on the switch port. Port security is discussed in detail in Chapter 4.

As described in RFC 3118, "Authentication for DHCP Messages," implementation can also assist in mitigating a DHCP starvation attack.

VLAN ACLs (VACL) can also be used to mitigate "rogue" DHCP servers by preventing the rogue server from responding to DHCP requests. VACL may not completely eliminate this threat, because IP spoofed DHCP messages are still possible but more difficult to successfully implement.

The best defense mechanism to mitigate these types of attacks is to enable the DHCP Snooping feature available on Cisco Catalyst switches. The DHCP Snooping security feature filters untrusted DHCP messages by maintaining a DHCP snooping binding table. The DHCP snooping feature is discussed in detail in Chapter 4.

802.1x Attacks

The IEEE 802.1x is a framework for passing the Extensible Authentication Protocol (EAP) messages over a wired or wireless network. EAP over LAN (EAPoL) offers a framework for authentication and control of user traffic to a protected network. A critical flaw in the EAPoL protocol was identified that can be exploited by an intruder to hijack an existing session and thereby gain access to a wireless network resulting in a MITM-type of attack.

Background

The IEEE 802.1x is a device authentication standard originally targeted for use in an Ethernet LAN but that later gained widespread uptake in wireless networks when the vulnerabilities of WEP in the IEEE 802.11 standard were identified. The 802.1x framework

The Problem

The intruder can possibly force all the switches in a network to forward packets to intruder switch by injecting falsified BPDU with a priority zero and thereby forcing spanning-tree recalculations so that the intruder switch can become the new root bri priority zero bridge is the root bridge in the spanning-tree topology. When this happ traffic that should normally go through a distant link is now transmitted across the att switch.

Spanning-Tree Attacks Mitigation

Spanning Tree Protocol attacks can be mitigated using the BPDU Guard and the ROO' Guard features available on Cisco Catalyst switches. These features are designed to enfo the placement of the root bridge in the spanning-tree topology and can also be used to prevent rogue switch network extensions. BPDU Guard and the ROOT Guard features a discussed in detail in Chapter 4 with configuration examples.

DHCP Spoofing and Starvation Attacks

DHCP spoofing and starvation attacks are methods to exhaust the DHCP address pool on the DHCP server, resulting in resource starvation where no DHCP addresses are available to be assigned to legitimate users.

Background

DHCP provides a framework for offering information to clients on a network. DHCP is client-server architecture, in which designated DHCP servers allocate IP addresses and other network information (WINS, DNS, default gateway) delivering configuration parameters to dynamically configured hosts (DHCP clients) on the network.

As stated in RFC 2131, "The client collects DHCPOFFER messages over a period of time, selects one DHCPOFFER message from the (possibly many) incoming DHCPOFFER messages (for example, the first DHCPOFFER message or the DHCPOFFER message from the previously used server) and extracts the server address from the 'server identifier' option in the DHCPOFFER message. The time over which the client collects messages and the mechanism used to select one DHCPOFFER are implementation dependent."

The Problem

This is a simple resource starvation attack that works on MAC address spoofing by flooding a large number of DHCP requests with randomly generated spoofed MAC addresses to the

defines the guidelines for packaging EAP messages by using EAPoL protocol (Ethernet frames using the EAP encapsulation over LANs).

The basic framework of 802.1x has three components:

- **A supplicant:** The user or client that requires authentication on the wireless LAN
- **An authentication server:** Typically a RADIUS server
- **The authenticator:** A device that sits between the supplicant and the authentication server (such as wireless access point)

The Problem

Two critical vulnerabilities were discovered in the EAPoL 802.1x protocol:

- The first vulnerability is the injection of a forged (spoof) EAP-Success message toward the end of the EAPoL authentication sequence, resulting in an MITM attack. The EAP-Success message is sent from the authenticator to the supplicant, and this message does not have any integrity check to preserve the information before the authenticator and the supplicant transition to the next state in the authentication sequence—that is, the AUTHENTICATED state. The attacker can send an unsolicited forged EAP-Success message to the supplicant that appears to come from the authenticator, allowing the intruder to passively establish itself in the network path between the supplicant and the authenticator.

- The second vulnerability exists when an intruder can hijack an existing session that is already established. After the supplicant has successfully authenticated with the authentication server, the authenticator and the supplicant state both move to the *authenticated* state. An intruder can send a maliciously crafted *dissociate* frame to the supplicant spoofing the authenticator source MAC address. This causes the supplicant to believe that the message comes from the authenticator instructing it to terminate the session and *dissociate* from the wireless network. Note that the authenticator is still maintaining an *authenticated* and *associated* state for this session. The attacker then forges the source MAC address of the *dissociated* system to assume its identity, gaining successful access to the network impersonating the victim. The authenticator has no way to reconfirm this, and therefore the session is hijacked.

802.1x Attacks Mitigation

There is no integrity mechanism available in the EAPoL protocol that can mitigate an 802.1x attack in a wireless network. The recommended workaround is to use the Protected EAP (PEAP) protocol instead, and thereby deploy 802.1x on wireless access points. The PEAP authentication protocol was developed to address these and other concerns about

802.1x, in particular its use in a wireless network. The PEAP structure offers integrity by implementing the authentication sequence in two parts:

- A TLS session is established between the supplicant and the PEAP authentication server.
- EAP exchange is carried out over the TLS session to authenticate the supplicant that is using a defined EAP authentication protocol.

As of this writing, there are no known vulnerabilities identified in PEAP.

Security Incident Response Framework

Before wrapping up this chapter's presentation of attack vectors and mitigation techniques, it is important to consider the importance of having an incident response framework. For any organization, having such a framework is essential when dealing with attacks.

Security is a growing problem, and securing an infrastructure is a critical, complex task of balancing business needs against security risks. As we saw in the sections earlier, it is an alarming fact that gaining unauthorized access to information in an insecure heterogeneous networked environment or launching a DoS-type attack is remarkably easy, and often it is difficult to track the offenders. A network intrusion can cause a broad range of consequences, including network outage, required recovery time, decreased productivity, significant loss in revenue or man-hours, devastating loss of credibility, and legal liability. Effective response and collective actions are required to counteract security violations and activities that lead to security breaches.

This section focuses on how to respond to a security incident and how to understand and prepare for any security event using an incident response framework.

What Is a Security Incident?

A security incident is any network or system-related intrusive activity with negative security implications to the computer, network, or information systems in general. These incidents are usually in direct or indirect breach of the security policy. A security incident can originate anywhere, including the local trusted network, shared customer network, intranet, extranet, Internet, or from any other network part.

The impact of an intrusion varies depending on the damage it can cause; it can be a relatively trivial incident or a major catastrophe. Each type of attack is unique and is defined by the intent of the intruder, the level of technical sophistication, and the vulnerability exploited.

Security Incident Response Process

Security incident response is the process of building an awareness and proactive function into an organization system for managing security events, such as intrusions, cyber thefts, or denial of service (DoS).

Most organizations are not prepared when dealing with security incidents and do not test the appropriate response actions to better evaluate their safeguard options. Such organizations risk a maximum loss in an event of a security incident. A well-documented incident response procedure ensures the speedy recovery of the system and the prompt restoration of an organization's normal operations.

The International Organization for Standard (ISO) has recognized the importance of the incident response mechanism and therefore built a *code of practice* for incident response into the Information Security Management standard ISO/IEC 17799:2005. Another standard that is widely recognized and popular in Europe is the Information Technology Infrastructure Library (ITIL), which was developed in 1992 and is maintained by the United Kingdom (UK) Office of Government Commerce.

Incident Response Team (IRT)

Incident Response Team (IRT) has a number of names that are commonly used: CSIRT (Computer Security Incident Response Team); CERT (Computer Emergency Response Team); and ISIRT (Information Security Incident Response Team). IRT is a team within an organization that is charged with responding to security-related issues. Forming IRT without a goal is like implementing computer security measures without a security policy. If the goal is unclear, functions by the IRT will always be performed on an ad-hoc basis, without a clear idea of the overall security framework.

An IRT can most easily be described by using the analogy of a fire department. Just as a fire department has an emergency number that you call if you have or suspect a fire, an IRT has a number and an e-mail address that you can contact for help if you have or suspect a computer security incident. An IRT service does not necessarily provide response by showing up on your doorstep; it may provide a range of other services in addition to the incident handling service, such as vulnerability handling or the provision of an intrusion detection services.

As shown in Figure 7-14, members of the IRT team should be carefully selected. Various members from the organization across all functional groups should be involved and become part of this team, such as members from the technical security team, network operations team (NOC), operations security (OPSEC), system admin, management, legal, human resources, and public affairs. As you can see from the wide range of organizations included in the IRT, incident response involves much more than knowledge of products and technologies.

Figure 7-14 *Incident Response Team (IRT) Members*

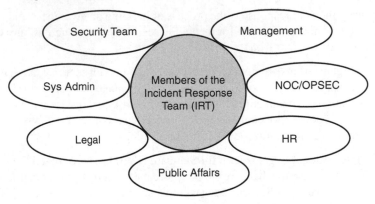

NOTE   Refer to the following comprehensive 200+ page handbook, which provides guidance on the formation and operation of an IRT:

http://www.cert.org/archive/pdf/csirt-handbook.pdf.

Security Incident Response Methodology

Effective integration of a security incident response function requires a clear methodology and an understanding of the organization's business functions, assets, teams, responsibilities, and threat modeling. A security incident framework should be approached holistically, by employing the necessary disciplines from physical, logical, and organizational security to form the best response function. As shown in Figure 7-15, an IRT reaction to a security incident can typically be categorized by five steps:

1 Planning and preparation

2 Identification and classification

3 Reaction

4 Postmortem and follow-up

5 Archiving

Figure 7-15 *Incident Response Methodology*

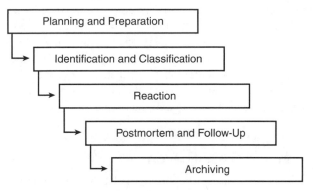

NOTE   The steps shown in Figure 7-15 are merely a guideline and should be used as a general template. You should tune the template to the organization's specific needs and requirements.

Step 1—Planning and Preparation

The most important aspect in a security incident handling is the preemptive preparation phase that handles events that can occur. An IRT must be formed with clearly defined roles and responsibilities and high-level management support.

Knowledge of the incidents that could occur and details on how they are to be handled should be developed and tested to ensure an efficient response mechanism. Ideal responses should be proactively identified and defined, and the tools used to respond should be created and validated through test scenarios. In addition, teams should be trained to deal with the security incident.

One of the major problems seen in the preparation phase is that the security operation teams do not have a security plan and procedure and are not trained in the effective use of the tools.

Another major issue is the dependence and reliance on vendors. Operators who use their vendors as Tier 2 and higher support endanger their network to a security risk. When operators today observe a problem on a device, they immediately call the vendor support center for a resolution. Vendors are partners with an operator. Note that vendors are not responsible for maintaining and troubleshooting the entire network; they facilitate and provision the network devices. The IRT of an organization armed with proper procedures and planning outlined by the security policy should drive the incident process.

In the event of a security incident, the general user community and teams that could be affected by the incident need to be informed of the incident by a predefined notification mechanism (such as e-mail notification, fax, or pager). In some cases, e-mail or other primary communication tools, such as IP phones, may not be the best communication tool, because they may have been compromised. Fax, cell phones, and other out-of-band tools are more appropriate in this situation. Clear instructions should be given to the end users on what needs to be done during the incident. Correct roles, skills, and communication techniques need to be identified to knit the notification procedures into a seamless process.

Step 2—Identification and Classification

After an incident is detected or reported, the IRT needs to conduct a detailed analysis to identify the predefined incident resolution process that should be followed. As much as possible, the organization should have agreed on an incident classification, have defined traps, and have mapped the processes that should be followed. In addition, the organization should understand the type of attack and the damage being caused.

As discussed earlier in this chapter, you should use the various classification tools and techniques available (such as NetFlow, NBAR, and MQC) to characterize the attack. In addition, monitor the CPU load, SYSLOG, and SNMP alerts, and monitor protocol and interface statistics such as Input/Output queues, drops on the device interfaces for link saturations, and other traffic flow statistics.

Step 3—Reaction

This phase represents the heart of the incident response strategy. Reaction is the response process used to counter the attack. A process that quickly and flexibly contains and eradicates the incident is executed followed by full recovery of business systems to ensure the responses have been effective. The IRT should prepare a detailed report to update both management and the staff that is managing specific security incidents to a successful conclusion. Evidence of misuse needs to be collected swiftly and accurately, with full integrity and provenance.

As discussed earlier, several techniques can be used in this phase to mitigate various types of attack vectors and restore normal business operation. Contact details for appropriate upstream providers (ISPs) need be defined and identified to block the offender.

Step 4—Postmortem and Follow-Up

After the incident is mitigated, the IRT, in conjunction with other relevant teams that were involved during the incident response process, should conduct a review on the technical components of the incident to determine what can be done to build resistance and reduce the risk of reoccurrence. This could include risk assessments, understanding the root cause, reviewing of security policies, identifying trends and patterns of the incident, as well as applying practical safeguards and compensating measures. The process should identify options to tighten or reposition security controls and enact enforcement where needed.

Based on the post-incident review findings, the organization also needs to agree on final closure actions. These could include dissemination of new policy, realignment of asset ownership, running awareness campaigns, implementing patches or new countermeasures, and also disciplinary/legal repercussions where necessary. In addition, the need to review responsibility in the organization needs to be identified to ensure an effective incident management process.

Step 5—Archiving

At this stage, all incident information should be archived and saved for future referencing, and of course that means the information related to the incident should be documented. Archiving saves you time in the future. For example, if a phone call conversation was not documented and logged, there is a good chance that a significant portion of the information is either forgotten or misinterpreted, resulting in the repetitive task of contacting the source of the information again.

In the early stages of handling an incident, it is often infeasible to determine whether prosecution of intruders is viable and if the incident is going to be prosecuted. Recording details will provide evidence for prosecution efforts, if the case moves in that direction. Therefore, gather information in a form that is submissible to law enforcement and the court of law.

Documenting an incident will also help with the final assessment of damage that can be reported back to the management; it can also be used to claim insurances where applicable.

NOTE   Refer to the following site security and incident response-related RFCs:

- RFC 2196, "Site Security Handbook" (replaces RFC 1244)
- RFC 2350, "Expectations for Computer Security Incident Response" (BCP 21)
- RFC 2504, "Users Security Handbook"
- RFC 2828, "Internet Security Glossary"
- RFC 3013, "Recommended Internet Service Provider Security Services and Procedures" (BCP 46)

Summary

Networks today are vulnerable because of security technologies being implemented as an afterthought and not during the planning and design phase of building the network. This has led to many insecure network designs and solutions.

This chapter identified some of the most common attack vectors, such as IP spoofing, SYN flooding, MAC flooding, DoS, ARP spoofing, and how an intruder can exploit these to their advantage. Several mitigation techniques, such as packet classification and marking techniques, Traffic Policing, TCP Intercept, NBAR, ARP and DHCP spoofing mitigation, Spanning Tree Protocol features, and several other Layer 2 and Layer 3 features are discussed.

The chapter concludes with a discussion on how to respond in a security incident using a set of methodological steps to prepare readiness for any security event.

References

http://www.cisco.com/en/US/tech/tk648/tk361/
technologies_tech_note09186a0080120f48.shtml

http://www.cisco.com/en/US/products/ps6350/
products_configuration_guide_chapter09186a0080465b25.html

http://www.cisco.com/en/US/products/ps6350/
products_configuration_guide_chapter09186a00808029ea.html

http://www.cisco.com/en/US/products/ps6350/
products_configuration_guide_chapter09186a008046589d.html

http://www.cisco.com/warp/public/63/car_rate_limit_icmp.html

http://www.cisco.com/en/US/tech/tk59/technologies_tech_note09186a0080149ad6.shtml

http://en.wikipedia.org/wiki/Bogon_filtering

http://www.completewhois.com/bogons/

http://www.cisco.com/warp/public/732/Tech/security/docs/blackhole.pdf

http://en.wikipedia.org/wiki/ISO/IEC_17799

http://en.wikipedia.org/wiki/ITIL

PART II

Identity Security and Access Management

CHAPTER 8

Securing Management Access

As networks grow beyond the campus, network security increases in importance and administration complexity. As identity security and access management become more complex, networks and network resources require safeguarding from unauthorized access.

An access management solution is a policy-based enforcement model that ensures that users have a secure administration model. The security of the administration model stems from providing a user with policy-based access control for all devices and services on the network, supplying audit and report functions, and giving system administrators the ability to enforce user-based privacy and security policies. Identity security and access management are essential layers in the security framework.

AAA Security Services

The AAA acronym stands for

- **Authentication:** Who is the user? (identity)
- **Authorization:** What can the user do? (services)
- **Accounting:** What did the user do? (audit)

Network access control is one of the most important measures that is often overlooked. AAA security services bring together the ability to control who is allowed access to the network devices and what services the user is allowed to access. AAA network security services provide the primary framework through which access control is set up on a network device such as a router, switch, firewall, concentrator, and other networking appliances.

AAA services can be used to control administrative access such as Telnet or Console access (also known as character mode access) to network devices and also to manage remote user network access such as dialup clients or VPN clients (also known as packet mode access).

NOTE The AAA framework is one of the most common and recommended access control methods and is available on all major Cisco IOS devices and security appliances (except IPS appliance). There are several other measures available to achieve network access control, including the following: local username authentication, enable password authentication, and line password authentication mechanisms. These features do not provide the same level of granularity in provisioning network access control that you can achieve by using AAA.

AAA services can also be administered by using local databases that are stored on the network device instead of using a security server. Username and password credentials can be stored on the router's local database and referenced by the AAA services. Local database implementation is not scalable and can be used to control network access for a small group of users for one or two devices on the network. To achieve the greatest benefit and control, use security servers that employ the authentication protocols described in this chapter. Cisco IOS Software AAA technology provides the basic framework to set up network security services and implement access control.

AAA Paradigm

AAA is an architectural framework that provisions a set of three independent security functions in a modular format to offer secure access control. AAA is a model for intelligently controlling access to network resources, enforcing policies, and auditing usage. These integrated security services are critical measures that knit together effective network management and secure implementations.

RADIUS, TACACS+, and Kerberos are the authentication protocols used to administer AAA security functions. A network device such as a router establishes a communication path to the security server by using these protocols via the AAA engine. Authentication protocols are discussed later in this chapter.

Authentication

Authentication provides the means of identifying valid users by having a user present valid credentials, such as the username and password, to get access to the network resource. Additionally, authentication offers services such as challenge and response, messaging support, and encryption, depending on the security protocol selected. In summary, authentication is a method of identifying the user before access is granted to the network and network services.

Authorization

Authorization provides the capability to enforce policies for network resources after the user gains access to the network via the authentication process. Authorization provides additional control of privileges such as downloading per-user ACL or assigning IP-addressing information. After the user successfully logs on to the device, authorization can further control the service delivery. For example, authorization can control what commands are available for the user to execute (for example, **show running-config** or **reload**).

Authorization works primarily by collating a set of authorized attributes that dictate the user capabilities. These attributes are compared to the information stored in a database. The database can either be local on the router or it can be hosted remotely on a security server using RADIUS or TACACS+ authentication protocol. The RADIUS and TACACS+ security servers validate and authorize users for specific services by associating attribute-value (AV) pairs, which define service binding with the user and provide access rights. AV pairs will be discussed in more detail later in this chapter.

Accounting

Accounting provides the means to capture resource utilization by collecting and sending to the security server information that can be used for billing, auditing, and reporting, such as user identities to check who logged in, start and stop times, report IOS commands executed, and traffic information such as number of bytes/packets transmitted and received. Accounting provides the capability to keep track of the services users are accessing as well as monitor utilization of these resources.

The network device reports user activity by sending accounting records to the security server using either RADIUS or TACACS+ authentication protocol. Each record consists of accounting AV pairs that are stored on the security server for the purposes mentioned earlier.

AAA Dependencies

The three separate functions within the AAA architecture work closely together to enforce policy with the following dependencies:

- Authentication is valid without authorization.
- Authentication is valid without accounting.
- Authorization is *not* valid without authentication.
- Accounting is *not* valid without authentication.

Authentication Protocols

As mentioned earlier, AAA services rely on the security server using authentication protocols to implement the security functions of AAA. RADIUS and TACACS+ are the predominant authentication protocols that are widely used to provide AAA security functions on Cisco devices. The sections that follow briefly discuss the features of these protocols.

RADIUS (Remote Authentication Dial-In User Service)

RADIUS is a distributed client-server protocol that is widely used to secure networks against unauthorized access. The RADIUS protocol was initially developed by Livingston Enterprises as an access server authentication and accounting protocol. RADIUS protocol gained wide acceptance and is now implemented by several vendors including Cisco. RADIUS is gaining support among a wide customer base, and most importantly the Internet service providers (ISP).

One of the main objectives of the RADIUS protocol standard is to provide interoperability and flexibility between RADIUS-based products from different vendors. For this reason, RADIUS is a fully open standard protocol, distributed in C source code format, and can be used unrestrictedly by any vendor or customer. This allows for the flexibility of being able to modify RADIUS to work with any security system currently available on the market.

As mentioned earlier, RADIUS is implemented in a client-server model, where the client is any Network Access Server (NAS) device, such as a Cisco router or a firewall, which sends an authentication request to a central RADIUS server that contains user profiles with access information for the users.

Cisco network devices support RADIUS client implementation on a wide range of products such as routers, switches, firewalls, VPN3000 concentrators, and wireless access points. RADIUS implementation provides centralized user administration, which is important to its applications. ISPs have tens of thousands of users. Because user information changes constantly, managing user databases on a regular basis can be a challenge. Centralized administration of users in this environment is a basic operational requirement.

The RADIUS protocol authentication and the accounting services are documented separately in IETF RFC 2865 and RFC 2866, which replace RFC 2138 and RFC 2139, respectively.

NOTE	A new protocol called the Diameter protocol is currently underway and is being positioned as the designated successor of RADIUS protocol. RADIUS, however, is still common and widely used in present implementations. According to the IETF, the Diameter protocol will provide a new framework for the next-generation AAA services for applications such as IP mobility. Discussion of the Diameter protocol is beyond the scope of this book and is documented in IETF RFC 3588.

RADIUS Packet

Figure 8-1 shows the header format of the RADIUS packet with descriptions of the fields in Table 8-1.

Figure 8-1 *RADIUS Packet Header Structure*

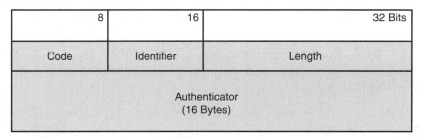

Table 8-1 *RADIUS Packet Header Structure Illustration*

Fields	Description
Code	Code is the message type of the RADIUS packet. The code is a one-octet (8-bit) value that establishes the type of the RADIUS packet. The codes are 1 = Access-Request 2 = Access-Accept 3 = Access-Reject 4 = Accounting-Request 5 = Accounting-Response 11 = Access-Challenge
Identifier	The identifier matches request and reply packets. The identifier is a one-octet (8-bit) value. The identifier is a message sequence number that allows the RADIUS client to match a RADIUS response with the correct outstanding request; that is, the value in reply is equal to the value in request.
Length	The message length is a 2-octet (16-bit) message length including the header.
Authenticator	The authenticator is a 16-octet field (16-bytes) used to authenticate the reply from the RADIUS server. The value in the request packet is randomly generated, whereas the value in the reply packet is an MD5 hash of the reply message data appended with a shared secret using a vector value from the request packet.
Attributes	The attribute field contains an arbitrary number representing sets of AV pairs.

RADIUS Communication

RADIUS uses UDP as transmission protocol to communicate between the client and the server using UDP port 1812 for authentication and authorization requests, and UDP port 1813 for accounting requests. Earlier deployments of RADIUS used UDP port 1645 for authentication and authorization requests, which conflicted with the registered "datametrics" service, and the deployments used UDP port 1646 for accounting, which conflicted with the "sa-msg-port" registered service.

As a connectionless protocol, UDP does not offer guaranteed delivery. Issues related to server availability, retransmission, and timeouts are handled by the RADIUS-enabled devices rather than the transmission protocol.

The RADIUS communication is triggered by a user login that consists of a query (packet type: **Access-Request**) that originates from the NAS and is sent to the RADIUS server. A corresponding response (packet type: **Access-Accept** or **Access-Reject**) is received back from the RADIUS server.

The Access-Request packet contains the username, encrypted password, NAS IP address, and NAS port number information. The packet also contains information on the type of session that the user wants to initiate. For example, if the query is presented in character mode (for example, when Telnet is being used), the packet will consist of a "**Service-Type = Shell**"; but if the request is presented in PPP mode, the packet will consist of "**Service-Type = Framed-User**" and "**Framed-Type = PPP**".

When the RADIUS server receives the Access-Request packet, the first thing it checks for is the shared secret key for the client that is sending the request. This ensures that only authorized clients are able to communicate with the server. If the server is not configured with the appropriate shared secret for the client or the shared secret is incorrect, the server drops the request silently without sending any response back. When the client-server communication is validated, the server continues to process the information in the Access-Request packet against the user database. Most RADIUS implementations (including the Cisco) support local database and external database systems, such as Windows Active Directory, Lightweight Directory Access Protocol (LDAP), Novell Directory Services (NDS), Open Database Connectivity (ODBC), and one-time password (OTP).

If the username is found in the database, and the password is validated, the server returns an **Access-Accept** response to the client. The Access-Accept carries a list of AV pairs that describe the parameters to be used for this session. As mentioned earlier, attributes include the service-type (Shell or Framed), protocol type, and IP address to be assigned to the user, as well as access list parameters, or static route information to be installed in the routing table of the NAS. In addition to the standard set of attributes, the RADIUS protocol specifies the vendor-specific attribute (Attribute 26), which allows vendors to support their own extended attributes that are specifically tailored to their application and are not for general use. (For details of various types of RADIUS attributes, refer to Cisco documentation.)

If the username is not found in the database, or if the password is incorrect, the RADIUS server returns an **Access-Reject** response back to the client. **Access-reject** is also sent when authorization fails.

Figure 8-2 shows RADIUS authentication and authorization communication between a RADIUS client (NAS device) and the RADIUS server. An important observation to make with this diagram is that RADIUS combines authentication and authorization information into one single Access-Request packet. For accounting, it sends information in a separate packet.

Figure 8-2   *RADIUS Authentication and Authorization Communication (Combined)*

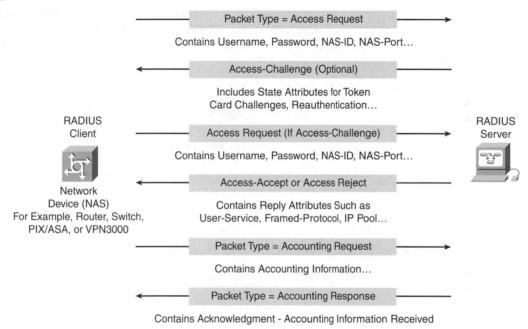

RADIUS Security

As discussed earlier, the RADIUS client generates an Access-Request packet, which contains information such as the username, password, NAS IP address, and NAS port number. The RADIUS packet lacks security, and its transmission is not completely protected. Only the password portion in the Access-Request packet is encrypted by a shared secret. The remainder of the packet is in the clear, making it vulnerable to various exploits and attack vectors. The following algorithm is used for password encryption:

The RADIUS client and server both have a common shared secret. The shared secret followed by the Request Authenticator is computed through an MD5 hash algorithm to produce a 16-octet value that is then XORed, with the password entered by the user producing the cipher text. The shared secret is used to sign RADIUS data packets to ensure that they are coming from a trusted source. The shared secret is used for message integrity, thereby ensuring that it is from a valid client and that the message has not been altered in transit.

TACACS+ (Terminal Access Controller Access Control System)

TACACS+ is a security protocol that is commonly used in the AAA framework to provide centralized authentication of users who are attempting to gain access to network devices. TACACS+ is a Cisco proprietary version of the older TACACS access protocol and is not compatible with the preceding TACACS or XTACACS protocols, which are now obsolete and deprecated by Cisco.

TACACS+ provides a modular approach in provisioning the AAA services. Separation of these services is a fundamental aspect of the AAA security model architecture. TACACS+ allows the NAS to provide each service (authentication, authorization, and accounting) independently, as shown in Figures 8-3 and 8-4.

Figure 8-3 *TACACS+ Authentication Communication*

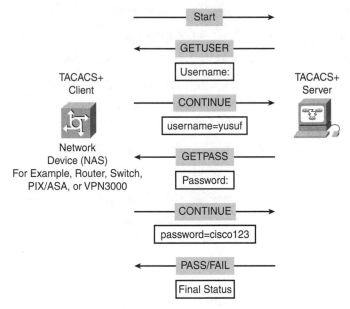

Figure 8-4 *TACACS+ Authorization Communication*

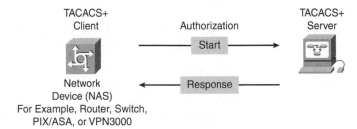

Cisco network devices support TACACS+ implementation on a wide range of products, such as routers, switches, firewalls, VPN3000 concentrators, and the TACACS+ server implementation on Cisco Secure Access Control Server (ACS) application software.

The former TACACS protocol is documented in Internet Engineering Task Force (IETF) RFC 1492. The TACACS+ protocol (developed by Cisco Systems) is a completely new version of the former TACACS protocol. Cisco makes the TACACS+ protocol specification available as a draft RFC for those customers interested in developing their own TACACS+ software.

NOTE   The draft is available at the Cisco Systems website at the following URL: www.cisco.com/warp/public/459/tac-rfc.1.76.txt.

TACACS+ Packet

Figure 8-5 shows the header format of the TACACS+ packet with illustrations in Table 8-2.

Figure 8-5   *TACACS+ Packet Header Structure*

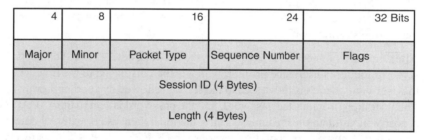

Table 8-2   *TACACS+ Packet Header Structure Illustration*

Field	Description
Major Version	Indicates major TACACS+ version number.
Minor Version	Indicates minor TACACS+ version number. This value allows for revisions to the TACACS+ protocol while maintaining backward compatibility.
Packet Type	Defines whether the packet is for authentication, authorization, or accounting. Data values in this field are TAC_PLUS_AUTHEN:= 0x01 (Authentication) TAC_PLUS_AUTHOR:= 0x02 (Authorization) TAC_PLUS_ACCT:= 0x03 (Accounting)

continues

Table 8-2 *TACACS+ Packet Header Structure Illustration (Continued)*

Field	Description
Sequence Number	Contains the sequence number for the current session. The first TACACS+ packet in a session has the sequence number 1, and each subsequent packet increments the sequence number by one. Thus, clients send packets containing only odd sequence numbers, and TACACS+ server sends packets containing only even sequence numbers.
Flags	Contains various flags in the form of bitmaps. The flag values signify whether the packet is encrypted.
Session ID	Contains the ID for this TACACS+ session.
Length	Contains the total length of the TACACS+ packet body (excluding the header).

TACACS+ Communication

TACACS+ uses TCP as the transmission protocol to communicate between the client and the server using TCP port 49.

TACACS+ authentication is normally triggered when a user attempts an ASCII login by authenticating to a TACACS+ server application. The process described in the paragraph that follows typically occurs.

After the TCP connection is established, the network device (NAS) contacts the TACACS+ server to obtain a username prompt, which is then displayed to the user. The user provides the username, which is forwarded to the server, followed by another prompt for a password. The user then provides the password, and the password is sent to the TACACS+ server. The server will validate the credentials using the local database or external database (as configured), and a corresponding response (**ACCEPT** or **REJECT**) is received from the TACACS+ server. Several other responses can be received, as follows:

- **ACCEPT:** This response states that the user was successfully authenticated and service may begin. The authorization process will begin if the NAS is configured for authorization.

- **REJECT:** This response states that the authentication process failed. Authentication failure could be because of incorrect credentials, and the user may be denied further access at this point.

- **ERROR:** This response is usually received when a communication problem occurs between the NAS and the server. This can be either at the server-side or in the client-side network connection. Several reasons can lead to an error—an incorrect secret key, a misconfigured NAS IP address, or a latency issue. When an ERROR response is received, the NAS typically attempts to use an alternative method (if configured) to continue the authentication process; this is known as a fallback process.

- **CONTINUE:** This response states that the server is expecting additional information, and the user is prompted for further input variables.

Look back at Figures 8-3 and 8-4 to see how TACACS+ authentication and authorization communication works respectively between a TACACS+ client (NAS device) and the TACACS+ server. Unlike RADIUS, the authentication and authorization communications are separated into different packets. Similarly, accounting sends information in a separate packet.

As shown in Figure 8-4, following the authentication, the user proceeds to the authorization process (if authorization has been enabled on the NAS). As the AAA dependency regulates, authorization is not valid without authentication. Authorization will follow only upon successful completion of authentication. The TACACS+ server returns an **ACCEPT** or **REJECT** authorization response. The ACCEPT response contains data in the form of attribute-values (known as AV pairs) that are used to enforce various services and functions and to determine the user access for the network resources.

TACACS+ authentication and authorization can also be triggered when a user attempts a PPP login, which is similar to an ASCII login described earlier, except that the username and password arrives at the server in a Password Authentication Protocol (PAP) packet instead of being typed in by the user, so the user is not prompted. PPP Challenge Handshake Authentication Protocol (CHAP) logins are similar in principle.

TACACS+ Security

TACACS+ protocol provides strong confidentiality by encrypting the communication between the NAS and the server. TACACS+ encrypts the entire body of the packet. The Flag field in the header of the TACACS+ packet (as shown in Figure 8-5 and Table 8-2) indicates whether the packet was encrypted.

Encryption relies on a "shared secret" key that is common on both sides—the NAS and the TACACS+ server. The "shared secret" is used to encrypt and decrypt TACACS+ packets between the two devices. The following algorithm is used for the encryption:

The TACACS+ packets are encrypted by XOR'ing with a series of MD5 hashes, each 16 bytes long. For more information on how MD5 hashing works, refer to RFC 1321.

Comparison of RADIUS and TACACS+

Table 8-3 shows a quick summary and comparison of the two protocols.

Table 8-3 *Comparison of RADIUS and TACACS+*

	RADIUS	TACACS+
Developer	Originally developed by Livingston (now industry standard)	Cisco proprietary
Transport Protocol	UDP port 1645/1646 and as per RFC 2138; 1812/1813	TCP port 49
AAA Support	Combines the authentication and authorization packet and separates the accounting packets	Uses the AAA architecture and separates the three services of AAA
Challenge Response	Unidirectional—Single challenge response	Bidirectional—Multiple challenge responses
Protocol Support	No NetBEUI	Full support
Security	Encrypts only the password in the packet	Encrypts entire packet

Implementing AAA

The AAA framework is supported on all major Cisco devices, including routers, switches, firewalls, and concentrators. This section will focus mainly on implementing AAA services on Cisco IOS devices.

AAA can be implemented on devices in three ways:

1 A self-contained AAA local security database containing usernames and passwords directly on the NAS device, such as the router. This implementation is suitable for smaller networks with a small number of users.

2 A Cisco Secure ACS for Windows application server. This can be an external server installed onto a Windows server operating system that scales well. This implementation is suitable for medium to large networks.

3 Cisco Secure ACS Solutions Engine appliance. This is a dedicated external platform offered by Cisco Systems that scales and is suitable for very large networks.

To enable AAA on a Cisco IOS device, follow these general configurable procedures:

1 Enable AAA using the **aaa new-model** global configuration command.

2 Configure the security protocol parameters, such as the IP address of the RADIUS or TACACS+ server and the shared secret key. (This does not apply if you are using a local database.)

3 Define the authentication service and the method lists by using the **aaa authentication** command set.

4 Apply the authentication method list(s) by using the **login authentication** command (under the line mode) to the corresponding interface or line, if required.

5 (Optional) Define the authorization service and method lists by using the **aaa authorization** command set.

6 (Optional) Apply the authorization method list(s) using the **authorization** command (under the line mode) to the corresponding particular interface or line, if required.

7 (Optional) Define the accounting service and method lists by using the **aaa accounting** command set.

8 (Optional) Apply the accounting method list(s) using the **accounting** command (under the line mode) to the corresponding interface or line, if required.

AAA Methods

Method lists are configured to define which of the three AAA services will be performed and the sequence in which they will be executed. The method argument refers to the actual method the authentication the algorithm tries. Method lists also allow control of the one or more security protocols to be used for the authentication, ensuring a fallback system in case the initial method fails. The AAA engine will use the first method defined in the method list, and if, for example, the TACACS+ server is not reachable, it will fall back to the next method defined in the list if there was no response from the server (known as the ERROR message), (except if the actual authentication failed with a FAIL response message). An ERROR response means that the server did not respond to the authentication request. However, if the server is reachable but the user credentials did not match, it will result in an authentication FAIL message. A FAIL response means that the user has not met the criteria required; for example, the username or password was incorrect or not found on the server. With a FAIL response, the authentication process stops and no further authentication methods are attempted in the list. The cycle continues until there is successful communication or all methods defined in the method list are exhausted.

There are two basic types of method lists:

- **Named Method:** A named method list can be configured for any AAA service—for example, for authentication or authorization—and applied to specific interfaces as required.

- **Default Method:** A default method list is configured globally and is automatically applied to all the interfaces on a device if no other method list is defined. Note that a defined method list (the same as a named method list) takes preference and will override the default method list.

All authentication methods, except local, line password, and enable authentication, must be defined through AAA.

AAA services offer a variety of methods to be performed. In the section that follows, Tables 8-4, 8-5, and 8-6 define the different types of methods available for the AAA functions.

Authentication Methods

The following methods are available in the **aaa authentication login** command. These lists are applied using the **login authentication** command under the line configuration mode.

Table 8-4   *Authentication Login Methods*

Keyword	Description
enable	Uses the enable password for authentication.
group radius	Uses the list of all RADIUS servers for authentication.
group tacacs+	Uses the list of all TACACS+ servers for authentication.
krb5	Uses Kerberos 5 authentication.
krb5-telnet	Uses Kerberos 5 Telnet authentication protocol when using Telnet to connect to the router.
Line	Uses the line password for authentication.
Local	Uses the local username database for authentication. Users can be created in the router local database using the **username** command.
local-case	The same as **local**, but uses case-sensitive local username authentication.
none	Uses no authentication when this method is processed.

Authorization Methods

The following methods are available in the **aaa authorization login** command. These lists are applied by using the **authorization** command under the line configuration mode.

Table 8-5   *Authorization Methods*

Keyword	Description
group radius	Uses the list of all RADIUS servers for authentication. The NAS device requests authorization information from the RADIUS security server. RADIUS authorization defines specific rights for users by associating attribute-value pairs, which are stored in a database on the RADIUS server, with the appropriate user.
group tacacs+	Uses the list of all TACACS+ servers for authentication. The NAS requests authorization information from the TACACS+ server. TACACS+ authorization defines specific rights for users by associating attribute-value pairs, which are stored in a database on the TACACS+ server, with the appropriate user.

Table 8-5   *Authorization Methods (Continued)*

Keyword	Description
if-authenticated	The user is allowed to access the requested function, provided he has been authenticated successfully.
local	Uses the local username database for authentication. The router will check its local database, as defined by the **username** command. The local database offers a limited set of functions with a limited control.
none	No authorization (always succeeds). The router does not request authorization information; authorization is not performed over this line/interface.

Accounting Methods

The following methods are available in the **aaa accounting** command. These lists are applied by using the **accounting** command under the line configuration mode.

Table 8-6   *Accounting Methods*

Keyword	Description
group radius	Uses the list of all RADIUS servers for accounting. The NAS reports user activity to the RADIUS server in the form of accounting records. Each accounting record contains accounting AV pairs and is stored on the server.
group tacacs+	Uses the list of all TACACS+ servers for authentication. The NAS reports user activity to the TACACS+ server in the form of accounting records. Each accounting record contains accounting AV pairs and is stored on the server.

Server Groups

Server groups can be used to group any RADIUS or TACACS+ server hosts for use in the method lists. Subsets of hosts can be specified for a particular service; for instance, for login authentication, use server1; for PPP authentication, use server2. Server groups can also include multiple host entries for the same server, as long as each entry has a unique identifier.

Example 8-1 shows two RADIUS groups configured with different server addresses. The **login authentication** is using the first server group **yusuf1**, and the **ppp authentication** is using the second group **yusuf2**. The server group also allows definition of a separate shared secret key. In Example 8-1, the first group **yusuf1** will use the default RADIUS key **cisco123** configured globally, whereas the second group **yusuf2** has its own unique secret key **cisco456**.

Example 8-1 *Configuring Server Groups*

```
aaa group server radius yusuf1
 server 172.16.1.1
aaa group server radius yusuf2
 server-private 172.16.1.2 key cisco456
 !
aaa authentication login default group yusuf1
aaa authentication ppp default group yusuf2
 !
radius-server key cisco123
```

Service Types for AAA Functions

A basic understanding of method lists and server groups enables you to effectively use the service types available for each AAA service. It is important to understand that various services are available and that the previously described methods can be used in different ways.

Authentication Services

AAA allows you to perform the types of service authentication listed in Table 8-7 by using the **aaa authentication** command.

Table 8-7 *Authentication Services*

Keyword	Description
arap	Used to enable authentication lists for AppleTalk Remote Access Protocol (ARAP)
login	Used to enable authentication lists for any ASCII-based logins, such as Telnet, SSH
enable	Used to set authentication lists for enabling access on the router
ppp	Used to enable authentication lists for any PPP-based protocol, such as ISDN, remote dial-in

Example 8-2 shows how to configure basic **login authentication** using the TACACS+ server with a default method list and a fallback method to the local user database. When using the default group, there is no need to apply it on any interface, because the command is applied to all the lines on the device.

Example 8-2 *Login Authentication Using TACACS+ Server*

```
aaa new-model
aaa authentication login default group tacacs+ local
 !
tacacs-server host 192.168.1.1
tacacs-server key cisco
```

Authorization Services

AAA allows you to perform various types of authorization for all network-related services, including IP, Serial Line Internet Protocol (SLIP), Point-to-Point Protocol (PPP), and AppleTalk Remote Access Protocol (ARAP). Service parameters are set to define a user's access to the network resources. The NAS is able to control user access to the network and network resources and allow users to perform only certain functions after successful authentication. Table 8-8 lists the types of authorization services that are available when you use the **aaa authorization** command.

Table 8-8   *Authorization Services*

Keyword	Description of Use
network	Authorizes network connections (PPP, SLIP, ARAP).
Exec	Authorizes attributes associated with a user EXEC terminal session (shell).
command	Authorizes the EXEC mode (shell) commands that a user issues. Command authorization attempts authorization for all EXEC mode commands associated with a specific privilege level.
Config-commands	Same as above; authorizes configuration mode commands.
Auth-proxy	Authorizes Authentication Proxy Service by applying specific security policies on a per-user basis.
Configuration	Downloads configurations from the AAA server.
Reverse-access	Reverses Telnet sessions.
ipmobile	Authorizes for Mobile IP services.

Authorization services can be configured to run for all network-related service requests, including IP, IPX, SLIP, PPP, Telnet, and ARAP.

Attribute-Value (AV) Pairs for Authorization

AV pairs are variable information exchanged by the RADIUS and TACACS+ server during the authorization phase to define service levels for users. AV pairs are used to define specific authentication, authorization, and accounting elements in a user profile. The attributes are stored in the server database, defined and associated with the users and groups, and sent to the NAS for enforcement, where they are applied to the user's connection.

For a list of Cisco-supported RADIUS and TACACS+ Attribute-Value pairs, refer to the Cisco technical documentation.

Accounting Service

The AAA accounting feature provides the means to track the services being used by the user and per-user resource utilization. The NAS sends accounting information in the form of accounting records to the server (RADIUS or TACACS+). Each accounting record contains accounting AV pairs, which are stored on the server and can be used for network management, reports, billing, and auditing.

Table 8-9 lists the types of accounting services available when using the **aaa accounting** command. Accounting services can be configured to run for all network-related service requests.

Table 8-9 *Accounting Services*

Keyword	Description
Network	Network accounting provides information for all network-related services, including PPP, SLIP, or ARAP sessions. This also includes the packet and byte counts for each connection.
Connection	Connection accounting provides information about all outbound connections made from the NAS, such as outbound Telnet, local-area transport (LAT), TN3270, packet assembler/disassembler (PAD), and rlogin.
Exec	EXEC accounting provides information about user EXEC terminal sessions (user shells) on the NAS, including username, date, start and stop times, the access server IP address, and (for dial-in users) the telephone number the call originated from.
System	System accounting provides information about all system-level events (for example, when the system reboots or when accounting is enabled or disabled).
Command	Command accounting provides information about the **EXEC** shell commands for a specified privilege level that are being executed on a NAS. Each command accounting record includes a list of the commands executed for that privilege level, as well as the date and time each command was executed, and the user who executed it.

NOTE For further information on implementing AAA services, refer to the AAA section in Part 1; refer also to Part 2, "Security Server Protocols" of the *Cisco IOS Security Configuration Guide* in the Cisco documentation:

www.cisco.com/en/US/products/ps6350/products_configuration_guide_book09186a008043360a.html

Configuration Examples

PPP Authentication, Authorization, and Accounting Using RADIUS

Example 8-3 shows how to configure PPP authentication, authorization, and accounting using RADIUS protocol. In this example, a default method list is used with the keyword **default** for all services and is applied to all interfaces by default. The **if-needed** keyword in the authentication indicates that if the user has already authenticated by going through the ASCII login procedure, PPP authentication is not necessary and can be skipped. The **if-authenticated** keyword in the authorization indicates that users can be given access to requested services only if they have been authenticated first.

Example 8-3 *Configuring PPP Authentication, Authorization, and Accounting Using RADIUS*

```
aaa new-model
aaa authentication ppp default if-needed group radius
aaa authorization network default group radius if-authenticated
aaa accounting network default start-stop group radius
!
radius-server host 10.1.1.1
radius-server key cisco
```

Login Authentication and Command Authorization and Accounting Using TACACS+

Example 8-4 shows how to configure login authentication and command authorization and accounting using TACACS+ protocol. In this example, named method lists are used and explicitly applied to VTY lines only. Authorization and accounting is also enabled for all IOS Exec IOS commands for privilege 1 and 15 command-sets. The example also shows a fallback method configured to the local router database in the event of an ERROR response where AAA server is not responding to the authentication and authorization requests.

Example 8-4 *Configuring Login Authentication and Command Authorization and Accounting Using TACACS+*

```
username cisco password cisco
!
aaa new-model
aaa authentication login myauthen group tacacs+ local
aaa authorization commands 1 yusuf1 group tacacs+ local
aaa authorization commands 15 yusuf15 group tacacs+ local
aaa accounting commands 1 yusuf1 start-stop group tacacs+
aaa accounting commands 15 yusuf15 start-stop group tacacs+
!
tacacs-server host 10.1.1.1
tacacs-server key cisco
!
line vty 0 4
```

continues

Example 8-4   *Configuring Login Authentication and Command Authorization and Accounting Using TACACS+ (Continued)*

```
login authentication myauthen
authorization commands 1 yusuf1
authorization commands 15 yusuf1
accounting commands 1 yusuf1
accounting commands 15 yusuf15
```

Login Authentication with Password Retry Lockout

Example 8-5 shows how to configure the Login password retry lockout feature that allows system administrators to lock out a local user account after a specified number of unsuccessful attempts to log in. This feature is available for local authentication only.

The example shows that the maximum number of failed user attempts has been set for 3.

Example 8-5   *Configuring Login Authentication Password Retry Lockout Feature*

```
username test password test123
username admin privilege 15 password cisco
!
aaa new-model
aaa local authentication attempts max-fail 3
aaa authentication login default local
```

CAUTION   A drawback of this feature is that it has no way to distinguish between an attacker who is using brute force and a legitimate authorized user who is entering the password incorrectly multiple times. Hence, a potential DoS attack is possible, in which an authorized user could be locked out by an attacker if the username of the authorized user is known to the attacker.

When the user is locked out, only the system administrator can unlock the user to resume normal service. To unlock the locked-out user, use the **clear aaa local user lockout** {**username** *username* | **all**} command from privilege exec mode.

To monitor and display a list of locked-out users, use the **show aaa local user locked** command.

NOTE	A user configured with maximum root privilege (privilege level 15) is deemed a system administrator account and cannot be locked out by using this feature. This feature is applicable to any login authentication method, such as character-based ASCII logins, CHAP, and PAP.

The login password retry lockout feature was integrated into Cisco IOS Release 12.3(14)T. Use the Feature Navigator tool to check platform support and corresponding Cisco IOS Software image at http://www.cisco.com/go/fn.

Summary

Securing access management is one of the most efficient ways to protect from unauthorized access. AAA framework offers an access-management solution that enforces a policy-based solution that controls user access to network and network resources.

This chapter illustrated essential steps in planning and implementing AAA technologies on Cisco devices. The chapter also details the basic architecture of the security protocols RADIUS and TACACS+ that are used in the AAA framework.

The chapter gave a generalized view of a Cisco-based AAA implementation, featuring a network access server (NAS, which is any Cisco device such as a router) and an AAA server using RADIUS or TACACS+ protocol.

The chapter concludes with some basic configuration examples implemented on a Cisco IOS–based device (router, switch).

References

http://www.colasoft.com/resources/protocol.php?id=TACACS

http://www.colasoft.com/resources/protocol.php?id=Radius

http://docs.hp.com/en/T1428-90025/ch01s01.html

http://www.ciscopress.com/articles/article.asp?p=25471&seqNum=6&rl=1

http://www.untruth.org/~josh/security/radius/radius-auth.html

http://www.cisco.com/en/US/products/ps6350/
products_configuration_guide_book09186a008043360a.html

http://www.cisco.com/en/US/tech/tk59/technologies_tech_note09186a0080094e99.shtml

http://www.openwall.com/advisories/OW-001-tac_plus/

CHAPTER **9**

Cisco Secure ACS
Software and Appliance

As discussed in the previous chapter, with networks growing beyond the campus, network security increases in importance and administrative complexity. Identity security and access management are essential for networks and network resources to safeguard them from unauthorized access.

Cisco Secure Access Control Server (ACS) provides a centralized access management solution for managing enterprise-wide network users and network infrastructure resources with policy-based enforcement. ACS provides a comprehensive identity-based network access control solution for intelligent information networks.

Cisco Secure ACS Software for Windows

Cisco Secure ACS software for Windows provides a scalable, centralized identity-based access control solution. ACS provides the structure to enforce user-based policies and allows granular control of user access to network and network resources.

ACS software supplies the following provisions:

- Network access user authentication
- Resource authorization and privilage levels
- Network access security policy enforcement
- Audit information
- Access and command controls
- Support for RADIUS and TACACS+ security protocols

Cisco Secure ACS is one of the key components in the integration of the Cisco trust and identity security solutions. It provides the structure for access control security by provisioning the authentication, authorization, and accounting (AAA) architecture and policy control from a centralized identity networking framework, thereby allowing greater scalability and flexibility, increased security, and user productivity gains.

ACS support spans all major Cisco devices and other network access servers (NAS), also referred to as AAA client, including

- Wired and wireless LAN
- Access points
- Edge and core routers
- Dialup and broadband connections
- Cable access solutions
- Storage devices
- Content devices
- Voice over IP (VoIP)
- Firewalls
- Virtual private networks (VPN)
- IEEE 802.1X access control
- Cisco Network Admission Control (NAC)

Figure 9-1 depicts the AAA client-server model. Note that the diagram shows the external database as optional. ACS supports local user databases and external databases, which will be discussed further in this chapter.

Figure 9-1 *AAA Client-Server Model Using ACS*

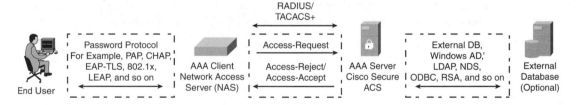

AAA Server: Cisco Secure ACS

The AAA framework implementation consists of two parts: the client side and the server side. As shown in Figure 9-1, Cisco Secure ACS serves as the AAA server side by providing authentication, authorization, and accounting services to network devices on the AAA client side. The Cisco ACS is also referred to as the network access server (NAS) or network access device (NAD). The NAS/NAD can be any Cisco device, such as the router, switch, firewall, concentrator, access point, or any other non-Cisco device. The AAA client serves as the gateway and forwards all access requests to the AAA server on behalf of the end user. The AAA server verifies the credentials by using its internal local database or optionally configured external database. The AAA server responds to the NAS with an [**access-accept**] or an [**access-reject**] message with a set of authorization attributes. Refer back to Figure 9-1 to see the basic flow.

ACS operates as a set of Windows services and can run on Microsoft Windows 2000 Server and the Windows Server 2003 operating system. ACS can be installed as a domain controller or a member server.

For further details, refer to the ACS installation and user guide:

- **Cisco ACS for Windows Installation Guide:** http://www.cisco.com/en/US/products/sw/secursw/ps2086/prod_installation_guides_list.html
- **Cisco ACS for Windows User Guide:** http://tinyurl.com/yvajyj

Protocol Compliance

ACS supports both RADIUS and TACACS+ AAA security protocols.

ACS conforms to TACACS+ protocol as defined by Cisco Systems in draft 1.78 on TCP port 49.

ACS conforms to RADIUS protocol in the following RFCs:

- RFC 2138
- RFC 2139
- RFC 2284
- RFC 2865
- RFC 2866
- RFC 2867
- RFC 2868
- RFC 2869

The RADIUS ports used in AAA have changed in RFCs. ACS supports both the older and newer RFC-defined ports in its implementation. For authentication and authorization, ACS accepts requests on UDP port 1645 and UDP port 1812. For accounting, ACS accepts requests on both UDP port 1646 and UDP port 1813.

In addition to the AAA protocol support, ACS extends support to the following common password protocols for end-user authentication (see Figure 9-1):

- ASCII
- Password Authentication Protocol (PAP)
- Challenge Handshake Authentication Protocol (CHAP)
- AppleTalk Remote Access Protocol (ARAP)

- MS-CHAP v1
- MS-CHAP v2
- Lightweight Extensible Authentication Protocol (LEAP)
- Extensible Authentication Protocol Message Digest 5 (EAP-MD5)
- Extensible Authentication Protocol Transport Layer Security (EAP-TLS)
- Protected Extensible Authentication Protocol (PEAP)

The implementation of the previously mentioned password protocol depends on the support of external databases available in ACS. Table 9-1 lists the Protocol-Database Compatibility reference supported by the various databases.

Table 9-1   *Protocol-Database Compatibility*

Database	ASCII	PAP	CHAP	ARAP	MS-CHAP v1	MS-CHAP v2	LEAP	EAP-MD5	EAP-TLS	PEAP (EAP-GTC)
Cisco Secure ACS	Yes	Yes	Yes	Yes	Yes	Yes	Yes	Yes	Yes	No
Windows SAM	Yes	Yes	No	No	Yes	Yes	Yes	No	No	Yes
Windows AD	Yes	Yes	No	No	Yes	Yes	Yes	No	Yes	Yes
LDAP	Yes	Yes	No	No	No	No	No	No	Yes	Yes
Novell NDS	Yes	Yes	No	No	No	No	No	No	No	Yes
ODBC	Yes	Yes	Yes	Yes	Yes	Yes	Yes	Yes	No	Yes
LEAP Proxy RADIUS Server	Yes	Yes	No	No	Yes	Yes	Yes	No	No	No
RSA	Yes	Yes	No	No	No	No	No	No	No	Yes
ActivCard	Yes	Yes	No	No	No	No	No	No	No	Yes
CRYPTOCard	Yes	Yes	No	No	No	No	No	No	No	Yes
PassGo	Yes	Yes	No	No	No	No	No	No	No	Yes
Safeword	Yes	Yes	No	No	No	No	No	No	No	Yes
Vasco	Yes	Yes	No	No	No	No	No	No	No	Yes
RADIUS Token Server	Yes	Yes	No	No	No	No	No	No	No	Yes

Advanced ACS Functions and Features

Cisco Secure ACS provides numerous functions and features that help secure and protect networks and resources within the network. These services are configured under various sections, as illustrated in Table 9-2, which can be found later in the chapter in the section "Configuring ACS." Some of the advanced features commonly used are discussed in the sections that follow.

Shared Profile Components (SPC)

Shared Profiles are commonly used to group sets of authorization components that can be collectively applied to many users or groups and referenced by name within their profiles. These include Downloadable IP ACL, Network Access Restrictions (NAR), Network Access Filters (NAF), RADIUS Authorization Components (RAC), Command Authorization Sets, and other options. The following sections discuss some of these commonly used features.

The advantage of using Shared Profile Components is that it offers scalability by avoiding unnecessary repetitions in configuring long lists of devices for commands and other authorization parameters.

Downloadable IP ACLs

The Downloadable IP ACLs feature is used to offer per-user based ACL functionality. This feature is compatible with any Layer 3 network device that supports Downloadable IP ACLs functionality. ACS extends per-user ACL support in conjunction with NAF to allow the application of per-device specific filtering. NAF regulates the access control on the basis of a AAA client's IP address. Hence, ACLs can be uniquely tailored on a per-user, per-device basis. Different sets of IP ACLs can be created that can be applied to various users or groups.

Before Downloadable IP ACLs were available, the RADIUS Cisco **cisco-av-pair** attribute [26/9/1] was used to achieve per-user filtering for each user or group. With Downloadable IP ACL, a single set of ACL can be defined and associated to each applicable user or group by referencing its name. This method is a more granular, easier-to-manage, and more scalable approach than configuring the RADIUS Cisco **cisco-av-pair** attribute for each user/group. RADIUS authentication is required to support the downloadable IP ACL feature.

The following Cisco devices support Downloadable IP ACL:

- PIX and ASA Firewalls
- VPN 3000 Concentrators
- Routers

Network Access Filter (NAF)

NAF is one of the newer features introduced in the ACS Shared Profile component.

Before NAF, per-device access restriction was not an option. The same level of access restrictions and ACLs were applied to all the devices in the network group. With NAF, granular application of access restrictions and downloadable ACLs is now possible, applying network-access restrictions and downloadable ACLs on network device names, network device groups (NDG), or their IP addresses. NAF can also use the IP address range and wildcards.

NAF can be defined as a named group with any combination of one or more of the following network elements:

- IP address
- AAA client (network device)
- Network device group (NDG)

Several applications of NAF exist. As discussed previously, NAF can be used in conjunction with Downloadable IP ACLs or in shared NARs to apply device-specific filtering and to regulate access control based on the AAA client's IP address.

NOTE   NAF needs to be enabled on the Advanced Options page of the Interface Configuration section before it appears as a selection on the Shared Profile Components page.

RADIUS Authorization Components

The shared RADIUS Authorization Components (RAC) function is used to group RADIUS attributes that can be dynamically assigned to user sessions based on a certain policy. Using the "Network Access Profiles (NAP)" section of this chapter, you can map various policy types to a shared RAC with set conditions, such as NDGs and posture.

Shell Command Authorization Sets

Shell command authorization sets are also part of the SPC, providing a mechanism to control the authorization of each command in various privilege levels invoked by a user on any given device in the network. AAA must be configured on each network device to support command authorization sets.

Command authorization sets are used to group the commands into varying sets. These sets can then be applied to multiple users or groups within ACS, to offer per-user granular control to enforce restriction on which commands the users are able to execute per device.

Network Access Restrictions (NAR)

The NAR function is used to define additional conditions that must be met before a user can access the network. ACS applies these conditions to a single user or a group by using information from the attributes sent by the AAA clients.

NAR can be set up in several ways, but all of them work on the same principle—that of matching the attribute information received from the AAA client. Therefore, to effectively deploy NAR, it is important to understand the format of attributes sent by the AAA client.

NAR can be configured in two ways—positive or negative filtering. NAR can either be specified to permit or deny network access. However, if a NAR does not find sufficient information, it defaults to deny access.

Two types of NAR filters are available in ACS:

- **IP-based filters:** Limit network access based on the IP address of the end-user client and the AAA client.

- **Non-IP-based filters:** Limit access based on a simple string comparison of a value sent from the AAA client. This can be the command-line interface (CLI) number, the Dialed Number Identification Service (DNIS) number, the MAC address, or any other value originating from the client.

NAR filtering is applied in the following order of precedence:

1 Shared-NAR at the user level

2 Shared-NAR at the group level

3 Nonshared-NAR at the user level

4 Nonshared-NAR at the group level

Machine Access Restrictions (MAR)

Cisco Secure ACS supports machine authentication with Active Directory in Windows 2000 and 2003. ACS extends Windows machine authentication by providing the Machine Access Restriction (MAR) feature. The MAR feature, coupled with Windows machine authentication, is used to control authorization for users connecting via various protocols such as EAP-TLS, EAP-FASTv1a, and Microsoft PEAP when authenticating with a Windows external user database. Using MAR, you can impose tighter control to prevent users from passing machine authentication within a configurable length of time, and you can deny them access to a network altogether.

Network Access Profiles (NAP)

One of the recent features introduced in Cisco Secure ACS is called Network Access Profiles (NAP), also known as a *profile*. Profiles allow classification of incoming access requests according to their network location, membership in an NDG, protocol type, or other specific RADIUS attribute values that are sent by the network access device through which the user connects. Specific profiles can be mapped to AAA policies. For example, different access policies can be applied for users connecting through wireless and remote access VPNs.

NAP is essentially a profile-based authentication and authorization technique. It is a classification tool to identify a particular network-access request and apply a common policy based on the service request. NAP has several applications. Examples include VPN, NAC, and wireless local area network (WLAN). For example, when a user connects to the network through the VPN connection, the authentication can be forwarded to an external database, whereas if the same user connects via the wireless network, a local database can be used. ACS checks incoming requests against network access profiles. When a profile is matched, ACS pushes the configuration and policies to the client according to the profile filter during packet processing.

Cisco NAC Support

Cisco Secure ACS supports the Cisco Self-Defending NAC solution. NAC is a framework of integrated technologies and solutions built on an initiative led by Cisco Systems. NAC uses the network infrastructure to enforce security policy compliance on all endpoint devices seeking access to the network and network resources, thereby limiting damage from emerging security threats. NAC restricts network access only to compliant and trusted endpoint devices (such as PCs, servers, and PDA devices) and blocks network-access requests from noncompliant devices.

ACS acts as a policy enforcement point in NAC deployments by performing posture assessment (health checks) of the endpoint devices seeking network access. Posture validation is based on credentials received from the Posture Agent (PA) related to the endpoint device-type. The Cisco Trust Agent (CTA) acts as a PA in this scenario. Examples of posture validation policy include the type of operating system, service pack, patch levels, and other attributes, such as antivirus software and data (DAT) file versions. ACS performs the posture validation and applies per-user authorization, such as policy-based ACL or VLAN assignment, to the network device.

For more details on the Cisco NAC solution, refer to Chapter 13, "Network Admission Control (NAC)."

Configuring ACS

As discussed in the previous sections, ACS incorporates many technologies to render AAA services for network-access devices, thus providing a central access-control function. The basic overview of the ACS configuration menu with screenshots that follows illustrates the various ACS functions and features.

There are two basic ways to access the ACS web interface:

- On the server itself where ACS is installed, you can browse the ACS directly by typing **http://loccalhost:2002** into the local web browser.
- You can also browse ACS remotely by typing **http://ip_address_of_the_ACS:2002** into the web browser from another computer on the network.

NOTE   Ensure that there is IP connectivity to the ACS server before browsing remotely.

HTTP port 2002 is used for remote access capability to the IP address assigned to the ACS server. Use the administrative account to log in to the server. Note that the ACS administrator accounts are unique to the ACS server only. They are not related to other administrator accounts, such as those used by Windows users with administrator privileges. ACS administrator accounts have no correlation with the internal ACS database user accounts.

NOTE   By default, no username is configured for remote administration. Upon ACS installation, configure an administrative account by granting appropriate privileges to each ACS administrator and assigning relevant privileges for ACS management purpose only. By default, no privileges are granted to a new administrator account, unless Grant All is selected.

By default, an administrator account is not required to log into the ACS application from the local server where ACS is installed. However, it is strongly recommended that you enable logon from the local server. (Otherwise, a Windows-based administrator account will have full administrative rights to the ACS application.)

TIP   When ACS is running on Windows 2003, the ACS administrator account that runs the ACS services must have a Domain Administrator account to authenticate against Windows 2003.

Figure 9-2 shows the main menu page after the login is successful. On the main menu page, the left pane shows different submenu selection options with various configuration items. The middle screen displays the menu option selected, and an additional pane on the right will display a Help screen for the selected menu. The main menu page also displays the ACS version.

Figure 9-2 *ACS Main Menu*

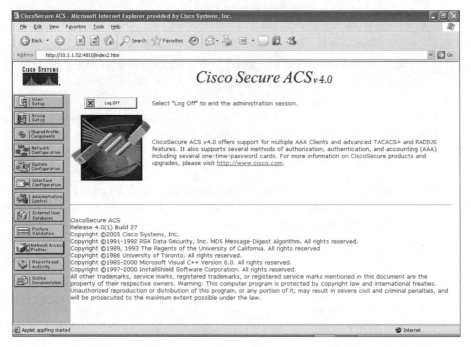

Table 9-2 illustrates the functions of the subitems available from the main menu shown in Figure 9-2.

Table 9-2 *CS Main Menu Options*

Menu Item	Description
User Setup	The User Setup section is used to configure individual user information: add users, delete users in the database, and define various privileges and settings on a per-user basis. These include password authentication, group details, IP address assignment, quotas, RADIUS and TACACS+ attribute settings, and other options.
	See Figure 9-3 for a screenshot of User Setup menu options. Note the Help pane on the right for various configurable options.

Table 9-2   *CS Main Menu Options (Continued)*

Menu Item	Description
Group Setup	The Group Setup section is used to configure individual group information, add groups, and add users to the groups in the database. The Group Setup menu applies various privileges and restrictions to all the users assigned within the group. These include NAR, Enable options, quotas, IP address assignment, RADIUS and TACACS+ attribute settings, and other options. See Figure 9-4 for a screenshot of Group Setup menu options. Note the Help pane on the right for various configurable options.
Shared Profile Components	The Shared Profile Components section is used to define shared sets of authorization components that may be applied to one or more users or groups of users and referenced by name within their profiles. These include downloadable IP access control lists (IP ACLs), NARs, NAFs, RACs, Command Authorization Sets, and other options. Shared Profile Components offers scalability for selective authorization. See Figure 9-5 for a screenshot of Shared Profile Components menu options.
Network Configuration	The Network Configuration section is used to define the NAS, also called a AAA client, with the corresponding NAS IP address, shared secret key, and security protocol (RADIUS or TACACS+). After a NAS is defined, the ACS will accept authentication requests from the corresponding NAS device. Authentication requests will not be handled by ACS for a NAS not defined under this section. NDG is a collection of AAA clients and AAA servers. See Figure 9-6 for a screenshot of Network Configuration menu options.
System Configuration	The System Configuration section is used to tune system parameters to run the ACS server. These include starting and stopping the ACS service, logging options, internal database replication, ACS backup and restore, certificate setup, and other options. See Figure 9-7 for a screenshot of System Configuration menu options.
Interface Configuration	The Interface Configuration section is used to configure the ACS web interface to display various RADIUS and TACACS+ protocol attribute options that are required to appear as a configurable option in the User Setup or Group Setup window, accordingly. It allows tailoring the interface to simplify the screens that will be used by hiding the features that are not required and adding fields for the specific configuration. See Figure 9-8 for a screenshot of Interface Configuration menu options.
Administration Control	The Administration Control section is used to control management access to the ACS by allowing you to add or edit administrative accounts and to define access, session, and audit policies to specify parameters for ACS administrative sessions. See Figure 9-9 for a screenshot of Administration Control menu options.

continues

Figure 9-4 *ACS Group Setup Menu*

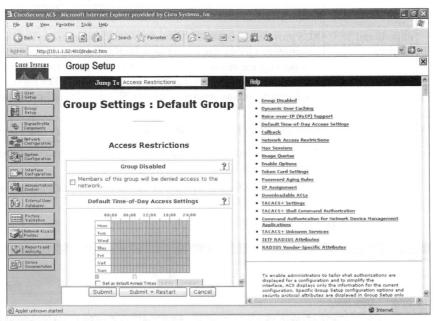

Figure 9-5 *ACS Shared Profile Components Menu*

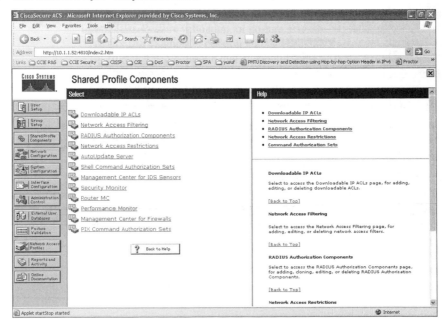

Figure 9-6 *ACS Network Configuration Menu*

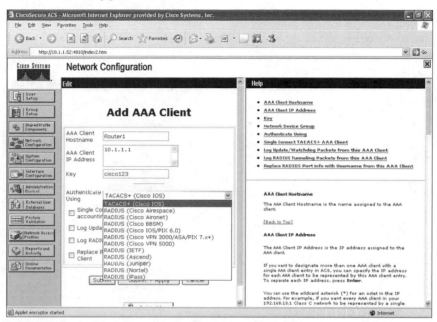

Figure 9-7 *ACS System Configuration Menu*

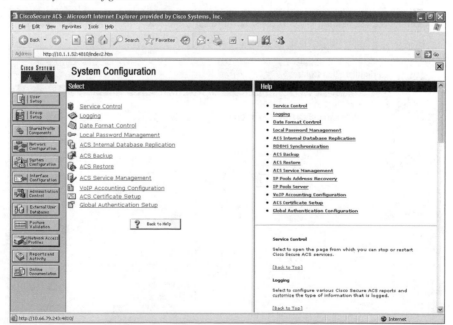

Figure 9-8 *ACS Interface Configuration Menu*

Figure 9-9 *ACS Administration Control Menu*

Figure 9-10 *ACS External User Databases Menu*

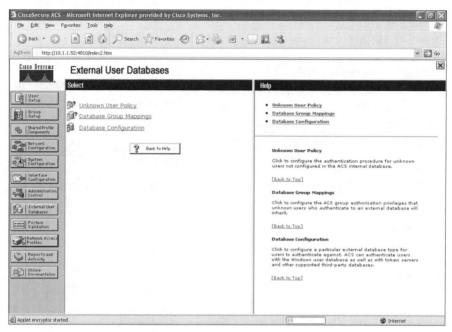

Figure 9-11 *ACS Posture Validation Menu*

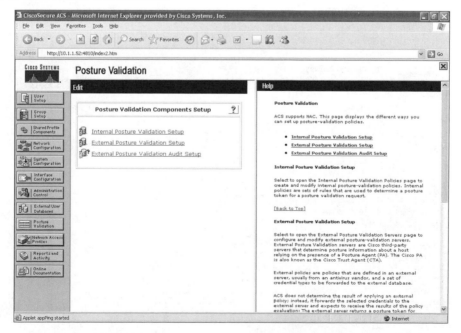

Figure 9-12 *ACS Network Access Profiles Menu*

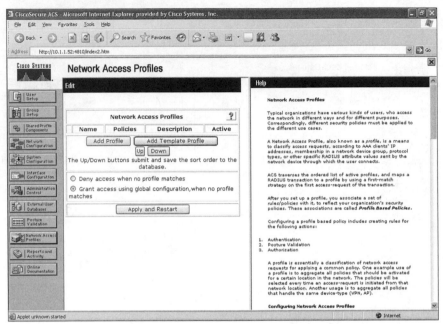

Figure 9-13 *ACS Reports and Activity Menu*

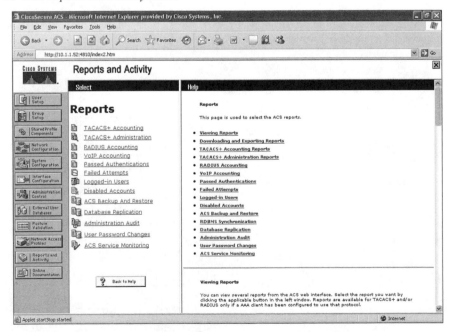

Figure 9-14 *ACS Online Documentation Menu*

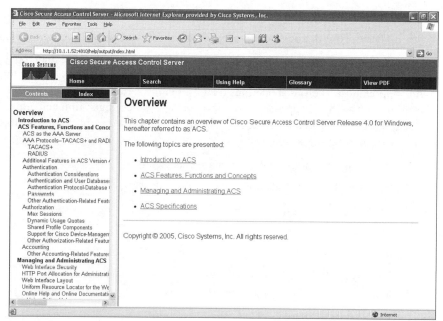

Cisco Secure ACS Appliance

Cisco Secure ACS Solution Engine (ACS SE) is a highly scalable appliance, 1U rack-mountable dedicated platform that serves as a high-performance access control server supporting centralized RADIUS and TACACS+ security protocols.

ACS SE offers the same set of functions and features as the Cisco Secure ACS software for Windows (the software product discussed earlier) in dedicated, security hardened, application-specific appliance packaging.

The underlying operating system on the ACS SE appliance is a customized and minimized version of the Windows 2000 operating system. The fact that the underlying operating system is robust Windows ensures absolute protection. ACS SE achieves this by implementing the following attributes:

- Runs only selective services required to perform the ACS core functions

- Removes all extraneous services

- Blocks all unused ports

- Does not support a keyboard or monitor

- Does not provide access to its file system

- Does not allow arbitrary applications to run
- Prevents all other access to the ACS server system
- Allows TCP/IP connections only via the ports necessary for its own operations

ACS SE includes some additional features specific to operating and managing the ACS appliance. These system administrative functions can be administered using the command-line application (shell) that operates the CLI via the serial console connection that is available on ACS SE appliance. For all other ACS SE configuration and administrative tasks, use the ACS web interface in the software described earlier. Some of these system-specific functions are as follows:

- Resetting the administrator username/password
- Resetting the system database password
- Reconfiguring the IP address
- Setting system timeouts
- Setting the system date/time/hostname/domain
- Patching rollback (removing installed patches)
- Recovering from loss of administrator credentials (password recovery)
- Reimaging the hard drive

CAUTION Powering off the ACS SE by using only the power switch may cause the loss or corruption of data. To shut down the ACS SE, log in to the ACS SE from a serial console, and at the system prompt, type **shutdown**, and then press **Enter**. The ACS SE displays the message It Is Now Safe to Turn Off the Computer. At this point, press the power switch and hold it down for four seconds to turn off the ACS SE.

Summary

Cisco Secure ACS software and appliance engine provide a centralized network access control server to safeguard the network infrastructure resources from unauthorized access. ACS offers a network-access management solution and enforces policy-based solutions that use centralized RADIUS and TACACS+ security protocols and the AAA framework.

ACS provides a comprehensive identity-based network access control solution for intelligent information networks.

The chapter illustrated basic functions provided by the ACS software and illustrations of various features available. The chapter also provided a basic overview of implementing and configuring the Cisco Secure ACS server and its web interface.

The chapter concluded with a basic overview of the ACS SE, which is a dedicated security-hardened platform appliance that offers the same set of functions and features as available in the Cisco Secure Access ACS software for Windows.

References

User Guide for Cisco Secure ACS for Windows 4.0: http://tinyurl.com/yvajyj

Cisco Secure Access Control Server for Windows: http://tinyurl.com/qfxk7

Cisco Secure Access Control Server Solution Engine: http://tinyurl.com/b9dkd

CHAPTER 10

Multifactor Authentication

Electronic data networks are becoming ubiquitous and demanding stronger secure access control and protection from unauthorized access. The changing network dynamics and increased security levels have driven new requirements in access control management solutions. Stronger forms of authentication, such as two-factor, three-factor authentication systems, and other public key infrastructure solutions are now being used to manage users who are accessing networks and controlling access to network resources.

Secure access through strong user authentication is becoming increasingly essential. Strong user authentication is typically achieved by implementing multifactor authentication technology. Examples include one-time password (OTP) solutions, hardware tokens, s/key, and smart cards.

Cisco Secure Access Control Server (ACS) provides support for two-factor authentication in a centralized access management solution for managing users and network infrastructure resources with OTP solutions.

Identification and Authentication

Identification and authentication (I&A) is a two-step process that governs user access to a network or a resource in the network.

Identification, which is the first step of the process, determines the identity of the user. The identification component of an access control system can be based on one of the following attributes:

- Username or user ID
- Computer or system name
- MAC address (Layer 2)
- IP address (Layer 3)
- Process name or process ID (PID)

Authentication is the second step in the process of verifying the identification provided earlier. The authentication component can be based on one of the following attributes:

- Simple password (one-factor)
- Multiple passwords (two-factor)
- Personal identification number (PIN)
- Shared secret key
- Certificate
- Token
- Pass-phrase
- Biometric

Two-Factor Authentication System

More often than not, static or single password (one-factor) authentication mechanisms are susceptible to brute-force attacks resulting in unauthorized access, given enough attempts and time. Authentication based on one factor does not provide adequate security, because the static password does not change between subsequent logons or is rarely altered. This risk can be greatly reduced by continually altering the password, as offered by the one-time password (two-factor) authentication mechanism.

Two-factor authentication solutions are primarily based on technologies that generate one-time passwords (OTP).

One-Time Password (OTP)

OTP technology is a system based on S/KEY but it was renamed because of trademark issues associated with the S/KEY name. S/KEY is a seminal OTP system that was developed at Bell Communications Research, Inc. or Bellcore.

The basic principle of an OTP solution is that it requires a *new* password every time a user authenticates. This effectively protects against replay attacks or any attack that attempts to use an intercepted password. The OTP system makes unauthorized access attempts more difficult.

There are three basic types of OTP technologies:

- **Mathematical algorithm:** This system uses a one-way hash function to generate a new password based on the previous password. This type of system requires an initial seed (pass phrase or PIN), which then generates subsequent passwords based on the previous password.

- **Challenge/response:** This type also uses a mathematical algorithm, but with a challenge function. The user receives a challenge (a random number or secret key) at the time of login, which needs to be entered into the password-generating token/ software to generate a one-time password. This system is very strong because it computes the new password based on a challenge mechanism instead of being based on the previous password.

- **Time-synchronized:** This system is tightly controlled by the system clock generating the password. Usually this is available on a physical hardware token, which is used to generate the password. The token has an accurate clock that is synchronized with the clock on the authentication server.

The OTP system is documented in IETF RFC 2289.

S/KEY

As mentioned earlier, S/KEY is a seminal OTP system developed for authentication at Bellcore. Using this system, the real password is never transmitted across the network. Instead, the real password is combined with a short set of characters and a decrementing counter to form a new single-use, one-time password. The S/KEY OTP system generates a password based on a seed secret pass phrase with a secure hash function such as MD5. The S/KEY server verifies the one-time password by making a pass through the secure hash algorithm and comparing the result with the previous password.

Inverting the hash function that produced the one-time single-use password is extremely difficult. However, S/KEY is sensitive to man-in-the-middle attacks. A secure transport layer protocol (SSL/TLS) can be used to counteract this.

S/KEY one-time password is documented in IETF RFC 1760.

Countering Replay Attacks Using the OTP Solution

One of the most common attacks on the network is a replay attack in which an intruder can be sniffing and eavesdropping network transmission to obtain usernames and passwords of legitimate connections. The illegitimately captured usernames and passwords can be used at a later time to gain unauthorized network access.

The OTP solution can be used to counter this type of attack because OTP generates a new password for every new user request. The captured credentials are not valid for subsequent attempts. Note that OTP does not provide confidentiality or privacy of data. After network access is granted, information is readily available to the authenticated user (legitimate or illegitimate).

NOTE   OTP does not provide nonrepudiation, because the authentication mechanism is valid only for a certain period.

Attributes of a Two-Factor Authentication System

To provide a strong authentication mechanism, the two-factor authentication system requires two elements: establishing the user identity and granting appropriate network access. The first piece consists of something you know, such as a password, and the second piece consists of something you have, such as a token or smart card. Some solutions also offer three-factor authentication, which requires an additional third piece that consists of something you are—that is, a biometric scan such as a fingerprint or an iris scan.

Authentication factors can be based on the following three most commonly recognized input attributes:

- **Something a user knows:** A password, a personal identification number (PIN), or a pass phrase.
- **Something a user has:** A smart card or token (hardware or software).
- **Something a user is:** A biometric pattern such as a fingerprint, voice, retina or iris scan, or DNA sequence.

Combinations of any two of the three methods can provide a strong, secure authentication mechanism—hence the term *two-factor* authentication solution.

Smart Cards and Tokens

Smart cards and tokens are the most common forms of the "something a user has" factor in authentication systems.

Tokens can be in the form of hardware or software. Software tokens are a weaker form of two-factor authentication, because they store tokens on a PC and are therefore vulnerable to malicious attacks and software break-ins. Another common form is USB-based tokens. The USB token has a different form factor that is not in the form of a card, but in a standard USB key type. Using a USB token is a much easier and more scalable approach because USB ports are widely available in standard equipment used today. Another advantage of using a USB token is that it has a larger storage capacity and can be used to store more numerous logon credentials than a regular smart card. Another advantage of the USB token is that it can have built-in OTP hardware. Vendors such as Booleansoft, RSA Security, VASCO, and Aladdin Knowledge Systems offer USB-based tokens as part of their two-factor authentication solution. See Figure 10-1 for samples.

A smart card resembles a normal credit card, but inside it has an embedded microprocessor and a memory chip or, in some cases, only a memory chip with nonprogrammable logic.

Many vendors offer smart card technology, some of which include RSA Security, Secure Technologies, VASCO, and ActivIdentity. Some vendors, such as ActivIdentity, HID, and RSA Security, also offer smart cards that perform the function of a proximity card in addition to network authentication. This offers proximity detection, and users can only use the cards after they enter the building or are close to the device; users then insert the card into their PC to be able to access network logon credentials. These types of solutions can also serve as employee ID badges. The downside is that these types of smart cards are bigger in size, and the card reader is an extra expense.

Figure 10-1 shows samples of various smart cards and tokens (regular and USB).

Figure 10-1 *Sample Smart Cards and Tokens*

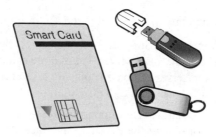

RSA SecurID

RSA SecurID is a two-factor authentication solution developed by the vendor RSA Security. RSA stands for the founders' last names: Ron Rivest, Adi Shamir, and Len Adleman, who are also the co-inventors of the RSA public key cryptography algorithm.

The RSA SecurID authentication mechanism combines multiple components to provide a two-factor authentication platform. The platform consists of a token—a piece of hardware (a USB token or other type of token)—or software ("soft token" for a PC, PDA, or mobile phone) that is assigned to a user. The platform generates an authentication code by using a built-in clock and the card's factory-encoded random key (the "seed"). The mechanism works on time-synchronized OTP technology, as discussed earlier.

Cisco Secure ACS server supports the RSA SecurID authentication solution.

Cisco Secure ACS Support for Two-Factor Authentication Systems

Cisco Secure ACS server supports the use of token servers to provide a strong security authentication mechanism using the OTP technology.

Cisco Secure ACS provides support for ASCII, Password Authentication Protocol (PAP), and Protected Extensible Authentication Protocol (PEAP)/Extensible Authentication Protocol Generic Token Card (EAP-GTC) authentication by using token servers. No other authentication protocols are supported with token server databases.

NOTE   For more information about authentication protocols and the Cisco Secure ACS external database types that support token servers, refer to the Authentication Protocol-Database Compatibility: http://tinyurl.com/2fb4nq.

Cisco Secure ACS supports two types of token server implementations:

- **RADIUS token server:** Support for token servers that provide a standard RADIUS interface built in to the token server. This feature enables Cisco Secure ACS to support a RADIUS token server database using any token server that provides an Internet Engineering Task Force (IETF) RFC 2865-compliant RADIUS interface.

- **Non-RADIUS token server:** Support for RSA SecurID token servers only. RSA SecurID does not support the RADIUS interface. ACS uses RSA proprietary client software to talk to the token server. ACS supports Point-to-Point Protocol (PPP); that is, ISDN and Async, and Telnet, for RSA SecurID token servers by acting as a token-client to the RSA SecurID token server. RSA-provided application programming interface (API) client software is installed on the computer that is running Cisco Secure ACS to communicate authentication requests with RSA token server.

How Cisco Secure ACS Works

Cisco Secure ACS acts as a client to the token server using the RADIUS-enabled interface of the token server, except in the case of RSA SecurID implementation. For RSA SecurID, Cisco Secure ACS uses RSA proprietary API client software.

When Cisco Secure ACS receives an authentication request from the AAA client (NAS), ACS forwards the authentication request to the token server. This process assumes that ACS is configured to authenticate against a token server, as configured in the external database configuration for "unknown user policy."

Figure 10-2 shows a menu option for the Cisco Secure ACS external database configuration, in which both RADIUS-enabled and non-RADIUS (RSA SecurID) token servers can be configured.

Figure 10-2 *Configuring a Cisco Secure ACS Token Server*

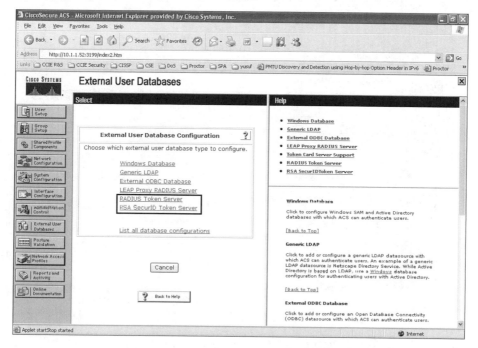

Before configuring the Cisco Secure ACS, it is important that the RADIUS-enabled token server and/or the RSA SecurID token server are installed and configured. In the case of RSA SecurID, ensure that the applicable RSA SecurID API client software is installed on the Cisco Secure ACS server.

Configuring Cisco Secure ACS for RADIUS-Enabled Token Server

Perform the following steps to configure Cisco Secure ACS for a RADIUS-enabled token server:

Step 1   Before configuring Cisco Secure ACS, ensure that the RADIUS-enabled token server is installed and configured.

Step 2   From the ACS external database configuration menu, select RADIUS token server, and create a new token server as shown in Figures 10-3, 10-4, and 10-5.

Step 3   After the token server instance is created, select Configure to add the RADIUS parameters for the token server, as shown in Figures 10-6 and 10-7.

Step 4   Configure the external database Unknown User Policy to select the RADIUS token server instance to handle authentication requests, as shown in Figures 10-8 and 10-9.

Figure 10-3 *Configuring ACS for RADIUS-Enabled Token Server (Step 2)*

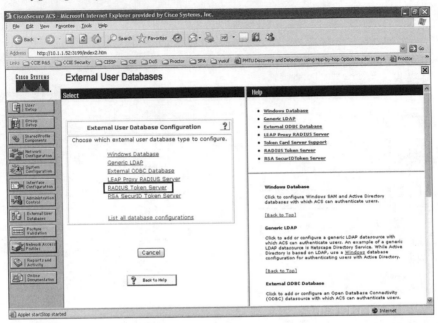

Figure 10-4 *Configuring ACS for RADIUS-Enabled Token Server (Step 2 cont)*

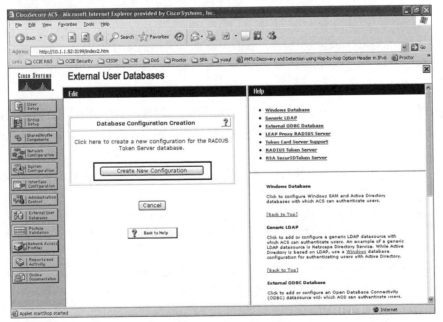

Figure 10-5 *Configuring ACS for RADIUS-Enabled Token Server (Step 2 cont)*

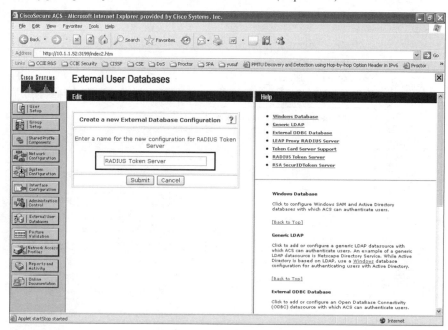

Figure 10-6 *Configuring ACS for RADIUS-Enabled Token Server (Step 3)*

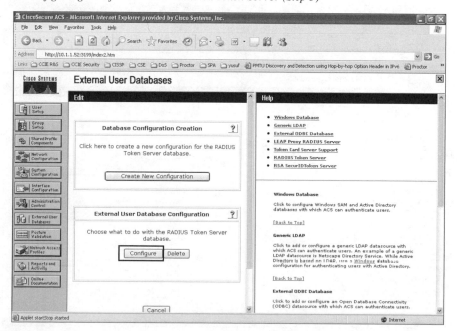

Figure 10-7 *Configuring ACS for RADIUS-Enabled Token Server (Step 3 cont)*

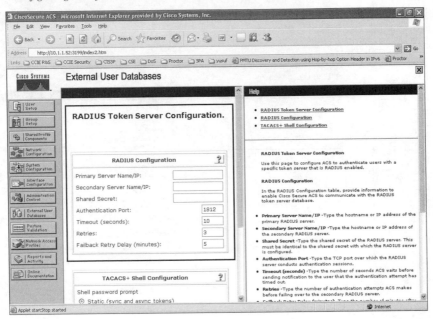

Figure 10-8 *Configuring ACS for Unknown User Policy (Step 4)*

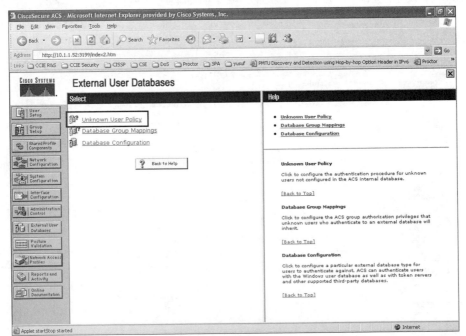

Figure 10-9 *Configuring ACS for Unknown User Policy (Step 4 cont)*

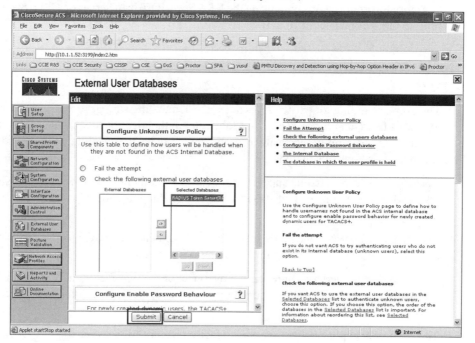

TIP	For more information on configuring a RADIUS-enabled token server on Cisco Secure ACS, refer to http://tinyurl.com/yu26nj.

Configuring Cisco Secure ACS for RSA SecurID Token Server

You can find a sample configuration available at Cisco.com to configure Cisco Secure ACS with RSA SecurID (ACE Server) implementation:

http://tinyurl.com/2xg8sr

The following options are available to install Cisco Secure ACS with RSA SecurID token server in these combinations:

- The RSA SecurID server, RSA SecurID client, and ACS can be on the same server.
- The RSA SecurID server can be on one server, and the RSA SecurID client with ACS can be on another server.

TIP	For more information on configuring the RSA SecurID Token Server on Cisco Secure ACS, refer to http://tinyurl.com/yu26nj.

Summary

The ever-expanding global networks today are demanding stronger access control methods to protect from unauthorized access. Multifactor authentication mechanisms and other PKI solutions are becoming increasing essential and popular in providing stronger and more secure access control solutions.

Cisco Secure ACS software supports the two-factor authentication mechanism using OTP technology, thereby providing stronger security to safeguard the network infrastructure from unauthorized access.

The chapter illustrated the identification and authentication (I&A) process and explained the various attributes entailed in the authentication mechanism.

The chapter provided a comprehensive overview of the two-factor authentication mechanism and details of OTP technology and how it works, including details of smart cards and tokens.

The chapter also provided an overview of Cisco Secure ACS server support for two-factor authentication mechanisms and how to implement the various types of OTP technologies in ACS.

The chapter concluded with a basic example of configuring Cisco Secure ACS for a RADIUS-enabled token server, with sample screenshots from ACS.

References

User Guide for Cisco Secure ACS for Windows 4.0: http://tinyurl.com/2xq9sg

http://en.wikipedia.org/wiki/Two-factor_authentication

http://en.wikipedia.org/wiki/One-time_password

http://en.wikipedia.org/wiki/S/KEY

CHAPTER 11

Layer 2 Access Control

The demand for comprehensive network security has never been greater. Malicious users remain a threat; they steal, manipulate, and impede information, and they interrupt network services. Numerous solutions are available to address a network's perimeter defense at the boundaries, but the greatest threat of information theft and unauthorized access remains within the internal network at the access level.

Organizations rely on networks to efficiently and securely manage *who* and *what* can access the network, and *when*, *where,* and *how* network access can occur. As threats of network service disruption by unauthorized access become more numerous, network reliability and security become more critical at each layer within the network.

The relative ease of physical and logical access to a network has been extended to enable a greater level of mobility, providing several benefits to business operations and overall productivity. However, this greater level of mobility brings concerns with it and demands more and more security solutions.

Cisco security portfolio provides an ecosystem of Cisco Trust and Identity Management solutions by offering access control at the media access level (data link Layer 2) through the implementation of the Cisco IBNS (Identity-Based Networking Services) and 802.1x technology.

NOTE   The data link layer is Layer 2 of the seven-layer OSI model. The data link layer (Layer 2) responds to service requests from the network layer (Layer 3) and issues service requests to the physical layer (Layer 1).

The Layer 2 access control solution provides secure network access and admission at any point in the network, and it isolates and controls unauthorized devices that are attempting to access the network. Layer 2 access control provides security via a user-based policy enforcement model at the port level, media access level, or logical connection.

This chapter outlines a framework and system based on technology standards that provide identity-based network access control, down to the user at the access port level at Layer 2.

Trust and Identity Management Solutions

The Cisco Trust and Identity Management Solutions offer the following essential security functions:

- **Enforcement:** Authenticates entities and determines access privileges based on policy.

- **Provisioning:** Authorizes and controls network access and pushes access policy enforcement to network devices via VLANs, ACLs, and so on.

- **Monitoring:** Accounting, auditing, and forensic tools allow system administrators to track the *who*, *what*, *when*, *where*, and *how* of network activity.

The Cisco Trust and Identity Management solution comprises three technologies:

- **Secure Identity Management:** Provides secure access control and integrity for every network device across the network by applying an access policy that uses the authentication, authorization, and accounting (AAA) framework. Various solutions addressing this domain have been covered in Chapters 8, 9, and 10.

- **Identity-Based Networking Services (IBNS):** A technology solution that expands network access security by using the 802.1x technology. IBNS provides identity-based network access control and policy enforcement at the port level. This chapter covers primarily the IBNS and 802.1x technology solutions.

- **Network Admission Control (NAC):** An integrated set of technologies and solutions built on an industry initiative led by Cisco. NAC provides policy enforcement on all devices seeking network access by allowing network access only to trusted endpoints and to those compliant with network security policies. Examples of those granted access include devices with up-to-date antivirus, OS version, or patch updates, thereby limiting damage from emerging security threats. The NAC solution is able to deny or restrict network access to any noncompliant device as well as quarantine and remediate noncompliant devices. The Cisco NAC solution will be covered in Chapter 13, "Network Admission Control (NAC)."

Building on the three types of technologies of the Cisco Trust and Identity Management solution, this chapter primarily covers how the Cisco IBNS and 802.1x combined technologies provide an important addition to the tools available for securing the network.

Figure 11-1 summarizes the Cisco Trust and Identity Management Solutions.

Figure 11-1 *Cisco Trust and Identity Management Solution Ecosystem*

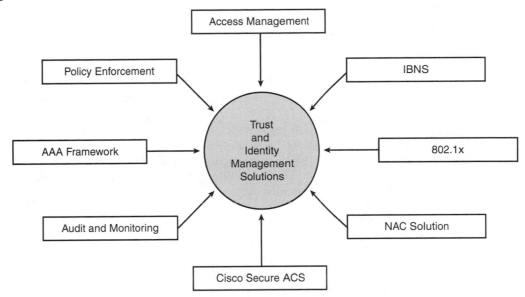

Identity-Based Networking Services (IBNS)

The Cisco Identity-Based Networking Services (IBNS) solution offers cost-effective user/ device management, flexibility and mobility, and reduced operating costs associated with granting and managing access to security network resources. Cisco IBNS provides an important addition to the tools available for securing the network.

Cisco IBNS is an integrated solution combining several Cisco products that offer authentication, access control, and user policies to secure network access and resources. The IBNS solution extends network access security based on the 802.1x technology and the Extensible Authentication Protocol (EAP). The IBNS solution provides identity-based network access control and policy enforcement at the port level.

The Cisco IBNS technology solution provides the security of physical and logical access inside the LAN. Cisco IBNS integrates all the capabilities defined in 802.1x technology. Combined with 802.1x technology, Cisco IBNS provides an integrated solution to implement identity-based network access control and policy enforcement at the port level. With IBNS, identification of both users and machines is possible through secure authentication technologies. The solution allows granular control in which policies are associated dynamically on network devices based on a user or device identity.

Cisco IBNS offers scalable and flexible access control and policy enforcement services and capabilities at the network edge as follows:

- Authentication based on per-user or per-device
- Policies mapped to network identity
- Port-based network access control based on authentication and authorization policies
- Additional policy enforcement based on access level, such as resource access

These services and capabilities are available when a Cisco end-to-end system is implemented.

As mentioned earlier, Cisco IBNS integrates all the capabilities defined in 802.1x technology. Additionally, Cisco IBNS solution offers specific services that are beyond the traditional 802.1x services. Examples include

- VLAN assignment
- Tied to port security
- Voice VLAN ID
- Guest VLAN
- ACL assignment
- High availability with redundant supervisors

Cisco IBNS solutions based on the 802.1x technology include the following components:

- Cisco Catalyst family of switches
- Wireless LAN access points
- Cisco Secure Access Control Server (ACS)
- IEEE 802.1x compliant client, such as the Windows XP operating system
- Optional X.509 PKI certificate architecture
- Interoperation of Cisco IP phones when deployed on a Cisco end-to-end infrastructure

The solution works when IEEE 802.1x-compliant client software is configured on the end device, sending requests to the Cisco Catalyst switches running IEEE 802.1x features. The switch relays the authentication request from the user or device to the back-end Cisco Secure ACS security server. The basic communication between these devices is in compliance with the IEEE 802.1x standard.

Cisco Secure ACS

The Cisco Secure ACS server is a key component of the Cisco IBNS architecture.

As mentioned earlier, Cisco IBNS is primarily a security standard for port-based access control that combines the IEEE 802.1x and the EAP to extend security AAA inside the LAN.

Before IBNS solutions were available, network access control was possible only at the perimeter of the network. Similarly, prior to 802.1x technology, *decentralized* methods of MAC existed, such as port security on the switches and MAC address filtering on the access points. However, these methods were configured statically on the devices themselves. (They had to be changed and updated individually on each port or device.) Cisco IBNS offers a *centralized* solution using the Cisco Secure ACS server and is dynamically updated.

With Cisco IBNS architecture, policy enforcement and control (such as per-user quotas, VLANs, ACLs, and identity-based session accounting and auditing) are possible within the internal LAN segment.

Several additional features are available through the Cisco Secure ACS as *the* 802.1x authentication server, such as

- Time and day restrictions
- NAS restrictions
- MAC filtering
- Per user/group VLAN assignment
- Per user/group ACL assignment

The Cisco Catalyst switches or wireless access point (AP) can be enabled as RADIUS clients, to make them capable of querying a AAA server for these controls.

External Database Support

Cisco Secure ACS RADIUS server supports internal user database and external database sources such as Microsoft Active Directory, Novell NDS, and Lightweight Directory Access Protocol (LDAP). The external database support provides the flexibility and scalability of integrating into the existing user database structure, thereby simplifying the overall deployment.

IEEE 802.1x

IEEE 802.1x is a protocol standard framework for wired and wireless LANs that authenticates users or network devices and policy enforcement at the port level to provide secure network access control.

The IEEE 802.1x protocol provides the definition to encapsulate the transport of the EAP message at the MAC layer (data link Layer 2) over any PPP or IEEE 802 media through the implementation of a port-based network access control to a network device. The 802.1x standard describes how the EAP messages are communicated between a supplicant (end device) and an authenticator (switch or access point). The authenticator relays the EAP information to the authentication server (Cisco Secure ACS) via the RADIUS protocol.

IEEE 802.1x provides not only the capability to permit or deny network access, but also provides additional policy enforcement for services and resource access in conjunction with higher layer protocols.

NOTE   330RFC 3748 replaces RFC 2284.

The IEEE 802.1x standard, combined with the capability of network devices to communicate using existing protocols such as EAP and RADIUS, provides increased security and control of access to network segments and resources by associating the identity of a network-connected entity to a corresponding set of control policies.

IEEE 802.1x Components

There are three primary components (roles) in the IEEE 802.1x authentication process, as shown in Figure 11-2 and described in the list that follows:

- **Supplicant or client:** The supplicant is an IEEE 802.1x-compliant client device such as a workstation, a laptop, or an IP Phone with software that supports the 802.1x and EAP protocols. The supplicant software may be integrated into the client, such as the Microsoft Windows XP operating system, or it can be included in the client device firmware or implemented as add-in software, such as the Meetinghouse AEGIS client. The supplicant client sends an authentication request to access the LAN via the connected authenticator (switch) using EAP, as shown in Figure 11-2.

- **Authenticator:** The authenticator is a device (such as a Cisco Catalyst switch or a wireless access point) that enforces physical access control to the network, based on the authentication status of the supplicant. The authenticator acts as a proxy to relay information between the supplicant and the authentication server, as shown in Figure 11-2. The authenticator (switch) receives the identity information from the supplicant via EAP over LAN (EAPOL) frames, which is verified and then encapsulated into the RADIUS protocol format to be forwarded to the authentication server. The EAP frames are not modified or examined during encapsulation, and the authentication server must support EAP within the native frame format. When the switch receives frames from the authentication server, the RADIUS header is removed, leaving the EAP frame, which is then encapsulated in the IEEE 802.1x format and sent back to the client.

- **Authentication server:** The authentication server is database policy software, such as the Cisco Secure ACS. The authentication server supports the RADIUS server protocol to perform the authentication of the supplicant that is relayed by the authenticator (switch) via the RADIUS client-server model. The authentication server validates the identity of the client and notifies the authenticator (switch) whether the client is allowed or denied access to the network. Based on the response from the authentication server, the authenticator relays the information back to the client. During the entire authentication process, the authentication server remains transparent to the client because the supplicant is communicating only to the authenticator, as shown in Figure 11-2. The RADIUS protocol with EAP extensions is the only supported authentication server.

Figure 11-2 *802.1x Device Components and Basic Message Exchange*

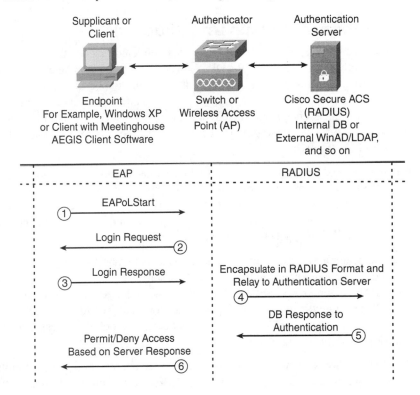

Figure 11-2 illustrates how the port-based access control solution works and shows the high-level message exchange between these three components. These messages vary depending on the EAP method selected, which will be discussed in the next section.

To understand and simplify the fundamental architecture as depicted in Figure 11-2

1 The supplicant/client sends a start message to the directly connected authenticator (switch or AP).

2 The authenticator sends a login request to the client.

3 The client replies with a login response with the user or device credentials.

4 The authenticator verifies the EAPoL frame, encapsulates it in RADIUS format, and forwards this information to the RADIUS server for validation.

5 The server verifies the client credentials and sends a response back to the authenticator for policy enforcement.

6 Based on this response, the authenticator either permits or denies network access to the client at the port level.

Port States: Authorized Versus Unauthorized

As illustrated in Step 5 of Figure 11-2, the authenticator acts on the basis of the response from the authentication server (RADIUS) to determine whether the client is granted access. This can be determined on the switch by the state of the port. The port starts in the *unauthorized* state. When in this state, no traffic is allowed through the port except for the 802.1x message exchange packets. When the client is successfully authenticated, the port changes into the *authorized* state (as shown in Step 6 of Figure 11-2), thereby allowing all traffic to flow through.

When a non-802.1x-compliant client connects to an *unauthorized* port, the switch has no way to assume that the client does not support 802.1x; hence, it sends the login request asking the client for identity credentials. Because the client does not support the 802.1x protocol, it is not able to interpret the request packet and does not respond. Therefore, the switch denies all the packets on that port, and the port remains in the *unauthorized* state.

Whereas when a 802.1x-compliant client connects to a port that is not running a 802.1x protocol, the client keeps sending the EAPoL start packet a few times and, eventually, because there is no response from the switch, the client begins sending packets assuming that 802.1x authentication is not required and continues sending the packets as if the port were in *authorized* state. The switch does not deny or block the access, because there is no 802.1x protocol running on that port.

Figure 11-3 shows the authentication process when the 802.1x port-based authentication is enabled and the supplicant client supports IEEE 802.1x-compliant client software.

Figure 11-3 *IEEE 802.1x Authentication Flowchart*

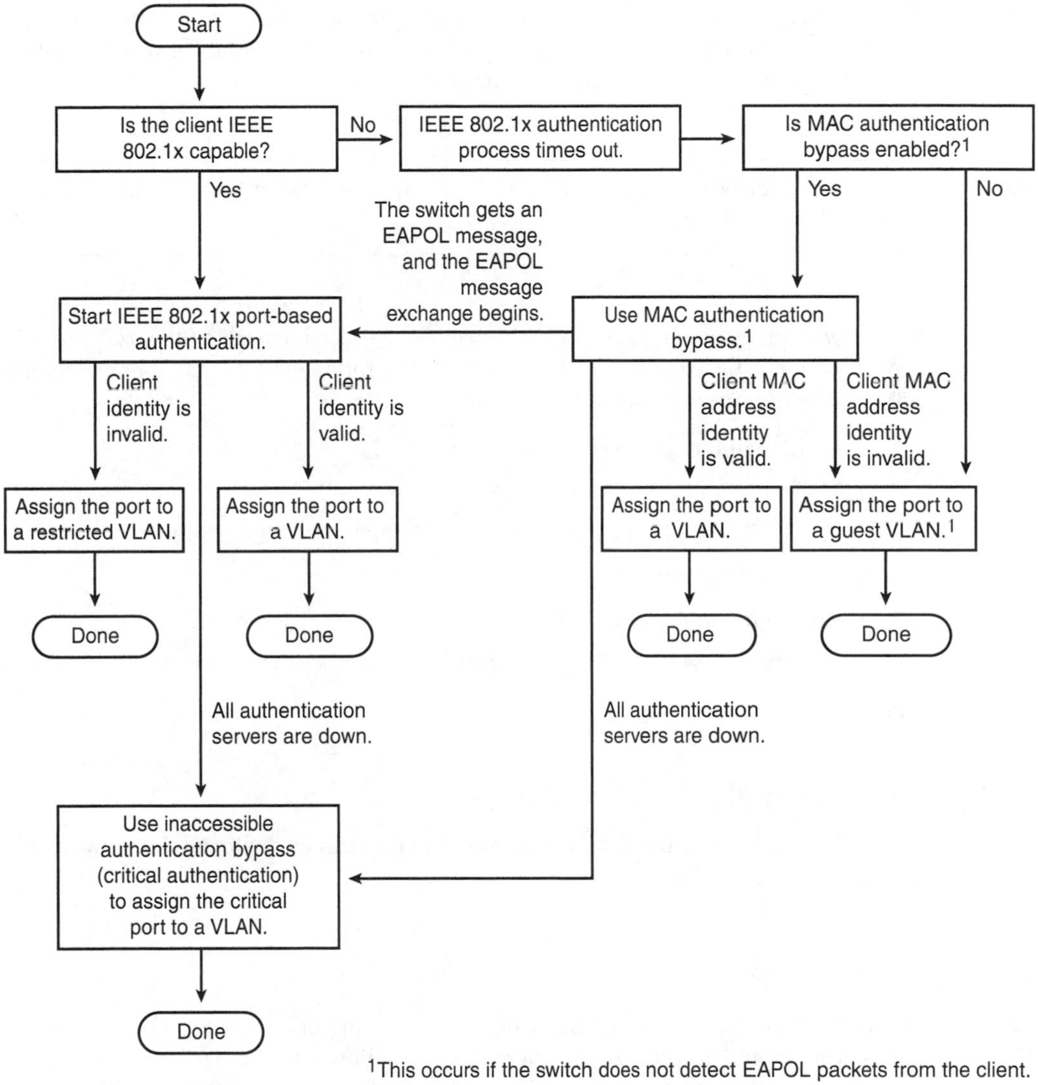

[1]This occurs if the switch does not detect EAPOL packets from the client.

NOTE The information in Figure 11-3 is taken from the "Configuring IEEE 802.1x Port-Based Authentication" section of the *Catalyst 3560 Switch Software Configuration Guide, Rel. 12.2(25)SEE*, at the following link: http://tinyurl.com/22zdyd.

EAP Methods

As discussed earlier, the Cisco IBNS solution extends network access security, based on the 802.1x technology and the EAP. Although EAP is more often used for wireless LAN networks, it can also be used for wired networks.

NOTE   RFC 4017 describes the specification and the requirements for EAP methods used in wireless LAN authentication.

Several variations are available in EAP methods that can be used in the 802.1x solution to provide identity-based network access control. The following EAP methods are commonly used in identity-based network access control solutions:

- EAP Message Digest 5 (EAP-MD5)
- EAP Transport Level Security (EAP-TLS)
- EAP Flexible Authentication via Secure Tunneling (EAP-FAST)
- Protected EAP (PEAP)
- Cisco Lightweight Extensible Authentication Protocol (Cisco-LEAP)

Chapter 12, "Wireless LAN (WLAN) Security," describes the various EAP methods in detail.

Deploying an 802.1x Solution

The IEEE 802.1x port-based authentication solution can be deployed in two ways, as described in the sections that follow.

Wired LAN (Point-to-Point)

Figure 11-4 shows a point-to-point scenario connecting one client per port. The 802.1x configuration on the switch is port based and will allow one client to authenticate. When the client is powered up, the port link changes to an *up* state, and the port state is changed to an *unauthorized* state followed by 802.1x message exchange, as shown in Figure 11-2. If the client authentication is successful, the port transitions to an *authorized* state. If the client leaves or another client connects to the port, the switch changes the port status to *down*, and the port transitions to *unauthorized* state.

Figure 11-4 *802.1x Deployment over Wired LAN*

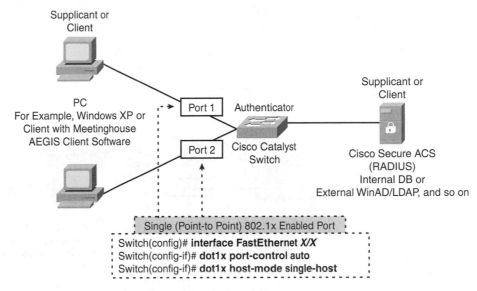

Wireless LAN (Multipoint)

Figure 11-5 and Figure 11-6 show two separate scenarios for the 802.1x port-based authentication in a wireless LAN deployment.

Figure 11-5 shows a wireless LAN access point (AP) that supports 802.1x (AP running Cisco IOS) acting as an authenticator for directly attached wireless clients.

Figure 11-5 *802.1x Deployment over Wireless LAN with Compliant Access Point*

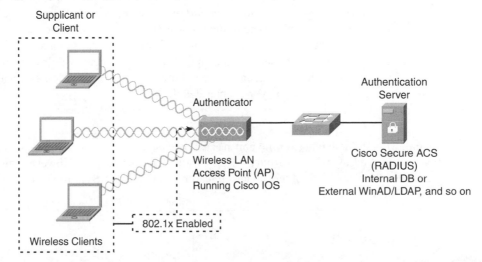

Figure 11-6 shows a wireless LAN access point that does not support the 802.1x; hence, the 802.1x is implemented on the switch just like a point-to-multipoint connection where the switch acts as an authenticator.

Figure 11-6 *802.1x Deployment over Wireless LAN with Noncompliant Access Point*

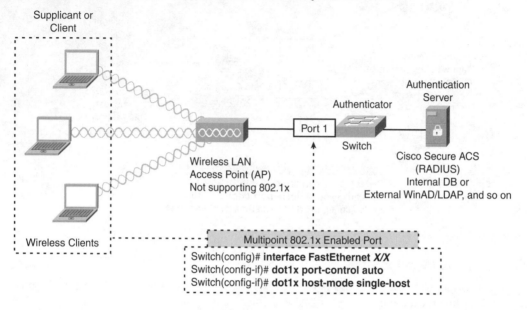

In Figure 11-6, the port on the switch connecting the AP is configured as a multihost port for the 802.1x authentication. As soon as a wireless client host is successfully authenticated, the port transitions to the *authorized* state, and all other indirectly connected wireless hosts are also granted access. If the authenticated wireless client logs out or disconnects, the port will transition to the *unauthorized* state, and all other indirect hosts will also be disconnected. In this type of deployment, the AP is responsible for authenticating the directly connected clients, and the wireless access point acts as a client to the switch. This is not a very secure method and can lead to security holes because an unauthorized wireless client may get access without having to pass valid authentication. Chapter 12 covers WLAN security in greater detail.

NOTE   It is important to note that after the port has reached an *authorized* state, any number of clients that have Layer 2 connectivity can pass traffic through that port. However, this could be changed by using some of the advanced features in Cisco IBNS solution, such as MAC address filtering.

Implementing 802.1x Port-Based Authentication

This section provides configuration examples to enable an 802.1x authentication mechanism on Cisco Catalyst switches that are running Cisco IOS and Cisco Aironet Wireless LAN Access Points running Cisco IOS.

Configuring 802.1x and RADIUS on Cisco Catalyst Switches Running Cisco IOS Software

Example 11-1 shows how to enable port-based 802.1x and RADIUS configuration on a Cisco Catalyst switch running Cisco IOS as depicted in Figure 11-4. The example also shows how to enable AAA authentication and RADIUS configuration, including the optional authorization for all network-related service requests, such as per-user ACLs, quotas, and VLAN assignment. The example also shows how to enable optional functionality or change default parameters. For example, periodic reauthentication is enabled, guest VLAN assignment is set to VLAN 10, and maximum number of times that the switch sends an EAP-request to the client is set to 3 (assuming no response is received) before restarting the authentication process.

Example 11-1   *Configuring 802.1x and RADIUS on a Catalyst Switch Running Cisco IOS*

```
hostname switch
!
aaa new-model
aaa authentication dot1x default group radius
aaa authorization network default group radius
!
dot1x system-auth-control
!
interface FastEthernet 0/1
 switchport mode access
 dot1x pae authenticator
 dot1x port-control auto
 dot1x max-req 3
 dot1x reauthentication
 dot1x guest-vlan 10
!
radius-server host 10.1.1.5 key cisco
 !
```

It is important to understand the AAA implementation and the consequences of adding the AAA commands to the Cisco IOS configuration, because they affect device access (vty and Console lines) as well. For example, by adding the AAA commands as shown in the previous example, Telnet access is restricted unless the appropriate user accounts and privilege levels are added on the RADIUS server or use separate named method lists with no authentication or line authentication for device access, which are applied to VTY and Console lines only. Refer to Chapter 8, "Securing Management Access," for configuration examples and explanation on AAA default method and named method lists.

Enabling Multiple Hosts for a Noncompliant Access Point Terminating on the Switch

This section continues the discussion of using switches as authenticators, as presented in the earlier section on the wireless LAN (multipoint) section and shown in Figure 11-6. When using an AP that is noncompliant and does not support the 802.1x authentication, the switch can act as the authenticator and authenticate the indirectly attached wireless clients.

The switch needs one additional command to support the multiple host scenario, which was explained in the section "Wireless LAN (Multipoint)" and depicted in Figure 11-6. Configure the **dot1x host-mode multi-host** command under the interface configuration mode, and in addition use the **dot1x port-control auto** command:

```
Switch(config)# interface FastEthernet 0/1
Switch(config-if)# dot1x port-control auto
Switch(config-if)# dot1x host-mode multi-host
```

RADIUS Authorization

AAA authorization must be configured on the authenticator if network-related services such as per-user VLAN assignment on 802.1x authenticated ports are required. The following vendor-specific tunnel attributes need to be configured on the RADIUS server to be passed down to the authenticator. AAA authorization must be configured for this to work, as previously shown in Example 11-1.

Two types of RADIUS server selections available in Cisco Secure ACS can be selected to achieve this purpose, and both can be used when defining the authenticator (switch or AP) as the AAA client in the network configuration on Cisco Secure ACS:

- RADIUS (IETF)

  When the RADIUS (IETF) server is selected as the NAS type in Cisco Secure ACS, the following three attributes (attribute 64, 65, and 81) must be returned to the switch for 802.1x authentication:

  — [RADIUS Attribute 64] Tunnel-Type = VLAN. RADIUS attribute [64] must contain the value "VLAN" (type 13).

> — [RADIUS Attribute 65] Tunnel-Medium-Type = 802. Attribute [65] must contain the value "802" (type 6).
>
> — [RADIUS Attribute 81] Tunnel-Private-Group-ID = VLAN NAME. Attribute [81] contains the VLAN name or VLAN ID assigned to the authenticated user.

- RADIUS (Cisco IOS/PIX 6.0)

When RADIUS (Cisco IOS/PIX 6.0) server is selected as the NAS type in Cisco Secure ACS, the vendor-specific AV-Pair (Attribute 26) must be used to download attribute 64, 65, and 81, to be returned to the switch for 802.1x authentication:

[RADIUS Attribute 26] Vendor Specific Attribute (VSA)

> — cisco-avpair= "tunnel-type(#64)=VLAN(13)"
>
> — cisco-avpair= "tunnel-medium-type(#65)=802 media(6)"
>
> — cisco-avpair= "tunnel-private-group-ID(#81)=vlan_name or vlan_id"

Figure 11-7 and Figure 11-8 show screenshots from Cisco Secure ACS that illustrate configuring RADIUS attributes for the two types of RADIUS server selection: RADIUS (IETF) and RADIUS (Cisco IOS/PIX 6.0).

Figure 11-7 *Configuring Attributes for Server Type "RADIUS IETF" on Cisco Secure ACS*

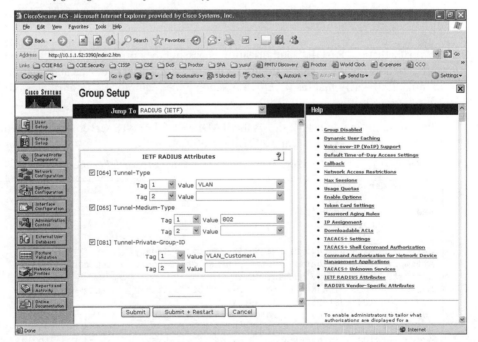

Figure 11-8 *Configuring Attributes for Server Type "RADIUS CISCO IOS" on Cisco Secure ACS*

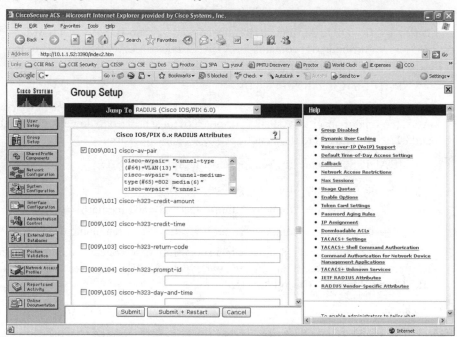

To verify that the RADIUS authorization is passing the correct attributes back to the authenticator (switch), enable **debug radius** on the Cisco IOS device and run the **test aaa** command to verify that the RADIUS is sending the required 802.1x attributes (attributes 64, 65, and 81).

The output in Example 11-2 shows the RADIUS (IETF) type server sending the three attributes (attributes 64, 65, and 81) from the ACS server.

Example 11-2 *RADIUS IETF-Based Attributes Downloaded on a Catalyst Switch Running Cisco IOS*

```
Switch# debug radius
Switch# show debug
Radius protocol debugging is on
Radius packet protocol debugging is on
!
Switch# test aaa group radius dot1xuser cisco legacy
Attempting authentication test to server-group radius using radius
User was successfully authenticated.
5d07h: RADIUS: Pick NAS IP for u=0x2080E58 tableid=0 cfg_addr=0.0.0.0
5d07h: RADIUS: ustruct sharecount=1
5d07h: Radius: radius_port_info() success=0 radius_nas_port=1
5d07h: RADIUS(00000000): Send Access-Request to 10.1.1.52:1645 id 1645/3, len 61
5d07h: RADIUS:  authenticator 58 B0 5A F7 78 0A 52 62 - 15 04 F3 A3 D7 13 CE 96
5d07h: RADIUS:  NAS-IP-Address       [4]   6    10.1.1.1
```

Example 11-2 *RADIUS IETF-Based Attributes Downloaded on a Catalyst Switch Running Cisco IOS (Continued)*

```
5d07h: RADIUS:   NAS-Port-Type       [61]  6   Async                    [0]
5d07h: RADIUS:   User-Name           [1]   11  "dot1xuser"
5d07h: RADIUS:   User-Password       [2]   18  *
5d07h: RADIUS:   Received from id 1645/3 10.1.1.52:1645, Access-Accept, len 83
5d07h: RADIUS:   authenticator BF F7 C9 3B 87 EF 45 71 - 75 75 BB 51 A5 E0 0E 50
5d07h: RADIUS:   Tunnel-Type         [64]  6   01:VLAN                  [13]
5d07h: RADIUS:   Tunnel-Medium-Type  [65]  6   01:ALL_802               [6]
5d07h: RADIUS:   Tunnel-Private-Group[81]  14  01:"VLAN_CustomerA"
5d07h: RADIUS:   Framed-IP-Address   [8]   6   255.255.255.255
5d07h: RADIUS:   Class               [25]  31
5d07h: RADIUS:    43 41 43 53 3A 30 2F 64 38 61 2F 63 61 30 32 30  [CACS:0/d8a/ca020]
5d07h: RADIUS:    31 30 66 2F 64 6F 74 31 78 75 73 65 72           [10f/dot1xuser]
5d07h: RADIUS: saved authorization data for user 2080E58 at 20CA108
```

The output in Example 11-3 shows the RADIUS (Cisco IOS/PIX 6.0) type server sending the same three attributes (attributes 64, 65, and 81) via the VSA attribute 26 from the ACS server.

Example 11-3 *RADIUS Cisco IOS-Based Attributes Downloaded on a Catalyst Switch Running Cisco IOS*

```
Switch# debug radius
Switch# show debug
Radius protocol debugging is on
Radius packet protocol debugging is on
!
Switch# test aaa group radius dot1xuser cisco legacy
Attempting authentication test to server-group radius using radius
User was successfully authenticated.
5d07h: RADIUS: Pick NAS IP for u=0x2139538 tableid=0 cfg_addr=0.0.0.0
5d07h: RADIUS: ustruct sharecount=1
5d07h: Radius: radius_port_info() success=0 radius_nas_port=1
5d07h: RADIUS(00000000): Send Access-Request to 10.1.1.52:1645 id 1645/4, len 61
5d07h: RADIUS:   authenticator 51 58 41 7D 90 6A D9 DA - 3C 59 75 F1 71 FC BE 11
5d07h: RADIUS:   NAS-IP-Address      [4]   6   10.1.1.1
5d07h: RADIUS:   NAS-Port-Type       [61]  6   Async                    [0]
5d07h: RADIUS:   User-Name           [1]   11  "dot1xuser"
5d07h: RADIUS:   User-Password       [2]   18  *
5d07h: RADIUS:   Received from id 1645/4 10.1.1.52:1645, Access-Accept, len 256
5d07h: RADIUS:   authenticator 87 FE 14 E1 4A 54 62 25 - F8 2C FC 4A C1 8C 33 B6
5d07h: RADIUS:   Vendor, Cisco       [26]  49
5d07h: RADIUS:     Cisco AVpair      [1]   43  "cisco-avpair= "tunnel-
  type(#64)=VLAN(13)""
5d07h: RADIUS:   Vendor, Cisco       [26]  60
5d07h: RADIUS:     Cisco AVpair      [1]   54  "cisco-avpair= "tunnel-medium-
  type(#65)=802 media(6)""
5d07h: RADIUS:   Vendor, Cisco       [26]  64
5d07h: RADIUS:     Cisco AVpair      [1]   58  "cisco-avpair= "tunnel-private-group-
  ID(#81)=VLAN_CustomerA""
5d07h: RADIUS:   Tunnel-Type         [64]  6   01:VLAN                  [13]
5d07h: RADIUS:   Tunnel-Medium-Type  [65]  6   01:ALL_802               [6]
5d07h: RADIUS:   Tunnel-Private-Group[81]  14  01:"VLAN_CustomerA"
5d07h: RADIUS:   Framed-IP-Address   [8]   6   255.255.255.255
```

Example 11-3 *RADIUS Cisco IOS-Based Attributes Downloaded on a Catalyst Switch Running Cisco IOS (Continued)*

```
5d07h: RADIUS:   Class                [25]  31
5d07h: RADIUS:    43 41 43 53 3A 30 2F 64 38 63 2F 63 61 30 32 30  [CACS:0/d8c/ca020]
5d07h: RADIUS:    31 30 66 2F 64 6F 74 31 78 75 73 65 72           [10f/dot1xuser]
5d07h: RADIUS: saved authorization data for user 2139538 at 2080EB0
```

Based on the 802.1x port configuration in Example 11-1 and the RADIUS attributes downloaded from the authentication server, Example 11-4 displays the **show dot1x** command being used to verify the dot1x interface on the switch. The output shows that the client has successfully passed the 802.1x authentication and the optional 802.1x parameters configured for the interface as per Example 11-1.

Example 11-4 *Verifying 802.1x Operation on a Catalyst Switch Running Cisco IOS*

```
Switch# show dot1x interface FastEthernet 0/1
Supplicant MAC 0001.2a2f.0ac2
AuthSM State= AUTHENTICATED
BendSM State= IDLE
Posture = N/A
PortStatus= AUTHORIZED
MaxReq = 3
MaxAuthReq= 2
HostMode = Single
PortContro= Auto
ControlDirection= Both
QuietPeriod= 60 Seconds
Re-authentication = Enabled
ReAuthPeriod= 3600 Seconds
ServerTimeout= 30 Seconds
SuppTimeout= 30 Seconds
TxPeriod= 30 Seconds
Guest-Vlan= 10
```

Configuring 802.1x and RADIUS on Cisco Aironet Wireless LAN Access Point Running Cisco IOS

Example 11-5 shows how to enable port-based 802.1x and RADIUS configuration on a Cisco Aironet Wireless LAN Access Point running Cisco IOS.

Example 11-5 *Configuring 802.1x and RADIUS on a Cisco Aironet Wireless LAN Access Point Running Cisco IOS*

```
aaa new-model
!
aaa authentication login myeap group radius
!
dot11 ssid cisco
authentication open eap myeap
authentication network-eap myeap
!
```

Example 11-5   *Configuring 802.1x and RADIUS on a Cisco Aironet Wireless LAN Access Point Running Cisco IOS (Continued)*

```
interface Dot11Radio0
ssid cisco
!
radius-server host 10.1.1.52
radius-server key cisco
!
```

NOTE   A named authentication method list is used in Example 11-5 in the **aaa authentication login** command on the Cisco Aironet wireless LAN access point, instead of using the default method list. The SSID configuration submode requires a list name to be referenced with the **authentication [open | network-eap]** commands, as shown in Example 11-5.

Based on the 802.1x port configuration in Example 11-5, Example 11-6 shows how to verify the dot1x interface on the access point. The output shows that the client has successfully passed the 802.1x authentication.

Example 11-6   *Verifying 802.1x Operation on a Cisco Aironet Access Point Running Cisco IOS*

```
ap# show dot11 associations
802.11 Client Stations on Dot11Radio0:
SSID [cisco] :
MAC Address IP addressDeviceNameParentState
0001.2a2f.0ac2 10.1.1.1 350-client sdelairselfEAP-Associated
```

Supplicant Settings for IEEE 802.1x on Windows XP Client

A supplicant client such as the Microsoft Windows XP operating system supports IEEE 802.1x authentication by default on all LAN-based network cards. By default, Windows XP uses the EAP-TLS authentication type; this can be changed to use another EAP method instead of the default EAP-TLS.

To configure a wireless network adapter for the IEEE 802.1X authentication on a client that is running Microsoft Windows XP, use the Authentication tab on the properties of the wireless network card, which is available from the Wireless Networks tab of the properties of a wireless connection in Network Connections.

For more details on configuring a wireless network adapter for the IEEE 802.1X authentication on a client running Microsoft Windows XP, refer to the following URL: http://tinyurl.com/28nvkt.

Summary

The Layer 2 access control solution provides secure network access control using an identity-based network solution. Cisco IBNS is a technology solution that expands network access security by using the 802.1x technology and EAP applying policy enforcement at the port level. This chapter covered details of how Cisco IBNS integrates into the network to offer cost-effective user management, with flexibility, mobility, and reduced operating costs.

The chapter outlined the IBNS and 802.1x framework and an integrated system based on technology standards that provide identity-based network access control, down to the user at the port level at Layer 2.

The chapter illustrated how the 802.1x technology works and provided comprehensive details on the components of the 802.1x solution. The chapter also provided details of various deployment scenarios in wired and wireless LAN implementations.

The chapter briefly explained the various types of EAP methods that support the 802.1x implementation. More details on various EAP types will be covered in Chapter 12.

The chapter concluded with an explanation of how to implement 802.1x technology. This explanation was supported by sample configuration examples on how to enable the 802.1x solution on Cisco Catalyst switches and Cisco Aironet Wireless LAN Access Point. The section also provided sample **show** and **debug** command outputs from the authenticator (switch and AP) to verify the configurations.

References

- http://www.cisco.com/en/US/netsol/ns463/networking_solutions_sub_solution_home.html
- http://www.cisco.com/en/US/netsol/ns340/ns394/ns171/ns75/networking_solutions_sub_sub_solution_home.html
- "Configuring IEEE 802.1x Port-Based Authentication" section of the *Catalyst 3560 Switch Software Configuration Guide, Rel. 12.2(25)SEE*: http://tinyurl.com/22zdyd
- Microsoft TechNet: The Cable Guy—April 2002, "IEEE 802.1X Authentication for Wireless and Wired Connections": http://tinyurl.com/28nvkt

Wireless LAN (WLAN) Security

Wireless LAN (WLAN) network deployments are on the rise and are becoming increasingly popular because of the ease of deployment, cost effectiveness, scalability, and significant productivity gains. This rise in the recent years has offered greater mobility to users by allowing them to move freely without tangling with wired workstations. Some of the most common WLAN deployments are not secured appropriately, thereby attracting unauthorized use of the network services. The lack of trust in the security of the wireless technology has caused increasing concern when organizations are deploying WLAN-based network solutions. Organizations now demand comprehensive and secure WLAN solutions. As the leader in providing wireless networking technology, Cisco now offers comprehensive solutions to secure wireless LAN networks.

Wireless LAN (WLAN)

WLAN is a LAN that uses radio communication to provide mobility to network users while maintaining the connectivity to the wired network.

The IEEE standardizes the security for wireless-based networks into two main components: the encryption and the authentication. The following section provides a basic overview of WLANs followed by a closer look at the security features.

Radio Waves

WLAN is a LAN that transmits over the air by using radio waves that travel between the clients and access points (AP).

WLAN uses spread-spectrum technology that is based on radio waves to enable communication between devices in a limited area, also known as the basic service set. Spread spectrum technology is used both to increase the data rate and increase its tolerance to harmful interference. Spread spectrum dictates that data transmissions are spread across numerous frequencies. This gives users the capability to avoid interference from other wireless devices.

Radio waves do not require a line of sight between sender and receiver and can send or receive signals through the walls, ceilings, floors, and so on. This means that the broadcast transmission can reach unintended recipients. Therefore, strong security measures are needed to provide the same level of security as offered by wired LAN networks.

IEEE Protocol Standards

In 1990, the IEEE standards committee established a group to develop a standard for wireless communication devices. The objective was to implement wireless LAN networks (an upper-layer feature) at the data link (Layer 2) and physical layer (Layer 1) of the OSI model because they use standard interfaces into the IP layer (Layer 3). This solution provided scalability for existing operating systems and applications to be integrated into WLAN devices without modification in the upper layers.

The IEEE introduced the 802.11 family for wireless communication devices that offered the following over-the-air modulation techniques used for the wireless-based LAN technologies:

- IEEE 802.11 (The original standard defined in 1997)
- IEEE 802.11a (Defined in 1999)
- IEEE 802.11b (Defined in 1999)
- IEEE 802.11g (Defined in 2003)
- IEEE 802.11n (Under development, expected in 2007/2008)

The Wi-Fi Alliance, on the other hand, is a nonprofit, vendor-neutral organization that provides the *branding* for 802.11-based technology known as Wi-Fi. An 802.11-based device undergoes rigorous functionality and operational testing before it can be *certified* by the Wi-Fi Alliance as a compliant device to ensure the interoperability with all other Wi-Fi certified products regardless of the vendor.

Communication Method—Radio Frequency (RF)

As pointed out earlier, the WLAN is a LAN that transmits data over the air, using radio frequencies to communicate between wireless enabled devices. The transmission frequency of a WLAN depends on the IEEE protocol standard used.

The wireless-based standards take advantage of the ISM band (Industrial, Scientific, and Medical) radio spectrum that is deemed usable by the public. The 802.11 standard specifically takes advantage of the following RF bands:

- The 2.4-GHz band is used for 802.11 and 802.11b networks, providing data rates of 1 to 2 Mbps and 11 Mbps, respectively.
- The 2.4-GHz band is also used by the 802.11g networks, providing data rates of up to 54 Mbps.

- The 5.8-GHz band is used for 802.11a networks, providing data rates of 5 Mbps, 11 Mbps, and up to 54 Mbps.

- The new 802.11n standard (which is currently under development) will also be using the 2.4-GHz or 5.8-GHz band, providing data rates of up to 540 Mbps. The 802.11n standard is projected to be up to 50 times faster than 802.11b and approximately 10 times faster than the 802.11a or 802.11g.

These bands are unlicensed frequency bands (but are regulated by authorities) and are free for use by anyone without restriction as long as they comply with the regulations.

WLAN Components

WLAN networks comprise the following basic components:

- **Wireless Access Point (WAP or AP):** An AP is often a hardware device (but it can also be software based) that connects wireless communication devices. WAPs are commonly used to relay data between the wireless and wired network devices and other wired network resources. AP is a two-way transceiver that broadcasts data within a specific frequency spectrum. AP also performs security functions such as authentication and encryption for the wireless clients and data transmission through the wireless network.

- **Wireless Network Card (NIC):** A device such as a workstation or laptop requires a NIC to connect to the wireless network through radio waves. The NIC scans the available frequency spectrum for connectivity and associates the spectrum to an AP.

- **Wireless bridge:** Wireless bridges are optional components that are used to connect multiple LANs (wired and wireless) at the MAC-layer level. Wireless bridges can be used in building-to-building wireless scenarios, because they can cover longer distances than the normal AP. A normal AP without the wireless bridge has a coverage range of up to 1 mile, as specified by the IEEE 802.11 standards. With wireless bridges, this coverage can be extended.

- **Antenna:** The function of an antenna is to radiate the modulated signal through the air so that wireless clients can send and receive transmissions. Antennas are required on both the AP and the wireless client. Access points and wireless devices such as laptops usually have built-in antennas. The range and propagation characteristics of a wireless device are determined by the antenna shape and type, which can be customized for the specific application.

Figure 12-1 shows a basic setup that includes wired and wireless LAN network connections.

Figure 12-1 *Wired and Wireless LAN Connected Clients*

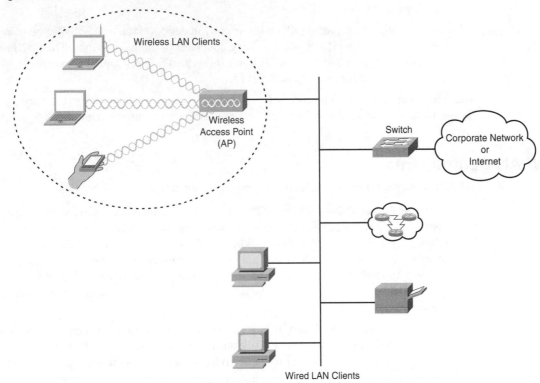

WLAN Security

Security is a top concern for all WLAN network deployments. As with any wired network, WLAN security focuses on data privacy and access control. The security of WLAN networks can be divided into two main components:

- **Authentication:** Strong authentication mechanisms enforce access control policy to allow authorized users to connect to the wireless network.

- **Encryption:** Data encryption helps ensure that only authorized recipients understand the transmitted data.

WLAN networks are widely deployed today and have become frequent targets for unauthorized access as well as a means to break into the internal network without having to connect through the wired network. WLAN networks are prone to unauthorized access as data is transmitted over the air on unlicensed frequencies, and if not encrypted, any intruder can intercept the open radio frequency range and view the data.

Using packet-sniffing software, data transmitted over the air can be easily intercepted within any unencrypted wireless network, and all contents can be viewed. In addition, the intruder can gain unauthorized access to internal networks or access to free Internet.

Most vendors are shipping wireless products with an "open-access" policy—that is, with no security features enabled by default. Although an open-access policy is suitable for public locations, such as hot spots, airports, coffee shops, and other free access zones, it is not feasible for private and enterprise networks. Wireless security features must be enabled to safeguard networks from being exposed to unauthorized access and wireless threats and attacks.

These and other security concerns have caused organizations to avoid WLAN network deployments, regardless of the numerous benefits that they provide. Securing a WLAN network is not difficult, as long as proper security solutions are selected and applied. Cisco Unified Wireless Network provides a comprehensive solution to security a WLAN network.

The following features and technologies are available to secure WLAN networks:

- Service Set Identifiers (SSID)
- MAC authentication
- Client Authentication (Open and Shared Key)
- Static WEP
- WPA, WPA2, and 802.11i (WEP enhancements)
- 802.1x and EAP
- WLAN NAC
- WLAN IPS
- VPN IPsec

Service Set Identifiers (SSID)

SSID is an arbitrary ID or name for a wireless LAN network that logically segments the subsystem. SSID provides basic access control mechanisms. All wireless devices in a specific WLAN subsystem require attachment through the SSID to bind with the WLAN network. Although SSID is not designed to be used as a security mechanism, nor does it provide data privacy or authentication, it can prevent unauthorized access to clients that do not have the valid SSID to connect to the WLAN network.

By default, an AP will broadcast its SSID in plain text to all wireless devices in the frequency range. Network sniffer tools can be used to eavesdrop on over-the-air transmission and capture SSID beacon messages to determine whether the SSID is used in the network. Therefore, it is recommended that you disable the SSID broadcast option. Network administrators should provide the SSID information to authorized wireless users to allow connection to the wireless network AP.

Although disabling the SSID broadcast may prevent someone from inadvertently connecting to your network, it is not an effective security mechanism. Disabling SSID broadcasting also breaks the Windows Wireless Zero Configuration feature. Disabling SSID does not provide complete protection from unauthorized access because some packet-sniffing software can monitor network transmission over the air to discover and learn the correct SSID in use.

MAC Authentication

Another common feature is the use of MAC address-based authentication. MAC-based authentication allows network access to known MAC addresses. The access point verifies the client MAC address against a locally configured list of allowed addresses or against an external authentication server. Access points can be preconfigured with all the wireless client MAC addresses in the MAC table that is maintained on the access point. When a client requests association to the access point, the MAC table is checked, and if the MAC address of the client matches, the authentication is successful. The client is associated to the access point and can transmit data through the AP. MAC-based authentication is very simple to configure, and most wireless vendors, including Cisco, support this feature. Note that the MAC authentication feature can be easily circumvented by using a MAC spoofing technique, in which the attacker sniffs your currently associated MAC address and spoofs it to get associated connection information, which results in an unauthorized connection. There are several techniques to combat MAC spoofing, as discussed in Chapter 7, "Attack Vectors and Mitigation Techniques."

NOTE   MAC authentication is not specified in the IEEE 802.11 standard, but many vendors, including Cisco, support it.

Client Authentication (Open and Shared Key)

The IEEE 802.11 standards support the following client authentication mechanisms that provide a rudimentary level of access control:

- **Open authentication:** In addition to SSID, open authentication can be implemented to provide an additional layer to the access control on the access point. Open authentication involves the use of wired equivalent privacy (WEP) keys, which allow authorized clients with the correct WEP key to associate with access points and transmit and receive data through the access points.

- **Shared-key authentication:** Shared-key authentication is similar to open authentication, but in this case the access point sends the client a challenge packet. The client replies to the challenge packet by encrypting it with its WEP keys. If the WEP keys are correct, the access point will be able to decrypt the packet, and the client will be associated to the access point and be able to transmit and receive data through the access point. Without the correct WEP keys, authentication will fail and the client will not be able to associate with the access point. Shared-key authentication is not considered very secure because the intruder can sniff both the clear-text challenge packet and the encrypted challenge reply with a WEP key and decipher the WEP key.

Static Wired Equivalent Privacy (WEP)

Static WEP is another common type of client authentication. A static WEP key is composed of either 40 or 128 bits that is statically defined by the user on the access point and on all individual wireless clients that need to associate with the access point. This approach is not very scalable because it requires entering the static WEP key on each wireless device in the WLAN network. A static WEP key can be sniffed using tools such as *AirSnort* and *deciphered*. The attacker must capture enough packets with a weak initialization vector to computationally compute the WEP key.

WPA, WPA2, and 802.11i (WEP Enhancements)

Enhancements are required to mitigate the WEP vulnerabilities that were discussed in the previous section. The IEEE group introduced the 802.11i standard to include two encryption enhancements for all known WEP vulnerabilities in the original 802.11 security implementation:

- **Temporal Key Integrity Protocol (TKIP):** An IEEE 802.11i standard that provides software enhancements to the RC4-based encryption algorithm used in WEP. TKIP enhances the WEP security by adding measures such as per-packet keying (PPK), message integrity check (MIC), and broadcast key rotation to address known WEP vulnerabilities.

- **Advanced Encryption Standard (AES-CCMP):** An encryption protocol in the IEEE 802.11i standard upon the Counter Mode with CBC-MAC (CCM) of the AES encryption algorithm. CCM is the algorithm providing data privacy. The Cipher Block Chaining Message Authentication Code (CBC-MAC) component of CCMP provides data integrity and authentication. AES is a stronger alternative to the RC4 encryption algorithm.

These enhancements are leveraged by the new security feature WPA and WPA2. The section that follows details the WPA, WPA2, and 802.11i standard.

IEEE 802.11i defines the core security standards for WLAN networks. The IEEE 802.11i standard provides stronger encryption, authentication, and key management approaches to secure wireless data. It includes two new confidentiality protocols as mentioned previously—the TKIP and AES. Both are used for confidentiality, with a key system for each traffic type, key caching, and preauthentication mechanisms.

Wi-Fi Protected Access (WPA) is a standard security solution from the Wi-Fi Alliance that addresses all known WEP vulnerabilities in the original IEEE 802.11 security implementation and provides protection from known WLAN attacks. WPA uses the Temporal Key Integrity Protocol (TKIP) for encryption, based on the RC4 algorithm. WPA supports the preshared key (PSK) and IEEE 802.1x/EAP modes of operation for authentication. The PSK verification works via a password or a passphrase on both the client device and the access point. If the password on the client matches with the access point, verification is successful, and the client is authenticated. WPA is supported by the Cisco Unified Wireless Network solution.

WPA2 is the next generation of wireless security. It is the Wi-Fi Alliance's interoperable implementation of the ratified IEEE 802.11i standard. WPA2 provides a stronger encryption mechanism through AES encryption algorithm using Counter Mode with Cipher Block Chaining Message Authentication Code Protocol (CCMP). WPA2 supports the PSK and IEEE 802.1x/EAP modes of operation for authentication. WPA2 is also supported by the Cisco Unified Wireless Network solution.

Both WPA and WPA2 offer a high level of assurance by providing data privacy and strong access control to restrict network access to authorized users.

WPA and WPA2 have two operation modes. Both modes provide encryption and authentication support to meet the various needs of the different market segments (refer to Table 12-1):

- **Personal Mode:** Personal Mode supports wireless products by using the PSK mode of operation for authentication. A preshared key is required to be configured manually on both the access point and clients. An authentication server is not required. Personal Mode is targeted to Small Office Home Office (SOHO) environments.

- **Enterprise Mode:** Enterprise Mode supports wireless products by using both the PSK and IEEE 802.1x/EAP modes of operation for authentication. A AAA server using the RADIUS protocol is required when using the IEEE 802.1x mode for authentication, key management, and centralized management of user credentials. (Refer to Chapter 11, "Layer 2 Access Control," for more details on implementing 802.1x solutions.) Enterprise Mode is targeted to enterprise environments.

Table 12-1 illustrates the summary of WPA, WPA2, and a comparison of the two operation modes.

Table 12-1 *Comparison of WPA, WPA2, and the Operation Mode Types*

	WPA	WPA2
Personal Mode (Recommended for SOHO, Home/Personal)	Authentication: PSK Encryption: TKIP/MIC	Authentication: PSK Encryption: AES-CCMP
Enterprise Mode (Recommended for Business, Government, Education)	Authentication: IEEE 802.1x/EAP Encryption: TKIP/MIC	Authentication: IEEE 802.1x/EAP Encryption: AES-CCMP

NOTE   The information in Table 12-1 is taken from "Cisco LAN Security - Cisco Wi-Fi Protected Access, WPA2 AND IEEE 802.11I" at http://www.cisco.com/en/US/netsol/ns339/ns395/ns176/ns178/netqa0900aecd801e3e59.html.

NOTE   The Enterprise Mode of both operation modes uses IEEE 802.1x and Extensible Authentication Protocol (EAP) for authentication.

IEEE 802.1x and EAP

As discussed in Chapter 11, the Cisco IBNS solution extends network access security based on the 802.1x technology by using EAP. EAP can be used for wired and wireless LANs, but is commonly used for wireless LAN networks. The WPA and WPA2 standard officially adopts the EAP method types for authentication.

NOTE   RFC 4017 describes the specification and the requirements for EAP methods used in WLAN authentication.

EAP is a universal authentication framework, not a specific authentication mechanism. EAP provides common functions and communication specifications for an authentication mechanism.

These varying mechanisms are called EAP methods, and there are currently about 40 different EAP methods.

Several variations in EAP methods can be used in the 802.1x solutions to provide identity-based network access control. Choosing an EAP mechanism depends on the clients, the policy, and the existing infrastructure, as illustrated in the following questions that must be answered:

- Is there a Certificate Authority PKI infrastructure available within the network?
- What client platforms are supported within the network?
- Is there any existing authentication system?
- Is there a requirement to support multiple EAP mechanisms?

The following sections describe support for some of the common EAP methods used in access control solutions:

- EAP Message Digest 5 (EAP-MD5)
- EAP Transport Level Security (EAP-TLS)

- EAP Tunneled Transport Level Security (EAP-TTLS)
- EAP Flexible Authentication via Secure Tunneling (EAP-FAST)
- Protected EAP (PEAP)
- Cisco Lightweight Extensible Authentication Protocol (Cisco-LEAP)

EAP Message Digest 5 (EAP-MD5)

EAP-MD5 (Extensible Authentication Protocol-Message Digest 5) is one of the IETF open standard, nonproprietary EAP types. EAP-MD5 is popular because of the ease of deployment. However, it is not one of the most secure EAP types because the MD5 hash function is susceptible to various attacks, such as offline dictionary attacks. EAP-MD5 does not support mutual authentication or key generation, which makes it unsuitable for use with dynamic WEP, WPA, or WPA2 environments.

EAP is defined in RFC 3748 (which replaces RFC 2284). MD5 is defined in RFC 1321.

The following list outlines the authentication process that takes place when an IEEE 802.1x supplicant connects to the wireless network using the EAP-MD5 authentication method. Figure 12-2 illustrates the EAP-MD5 message exchange between the client supplicant, the authenticator (switch or access point), and the authentication server (RADIUS), as explained in the list that follows.

Figure 12-2 *EAP-MD5 Message Exchange*

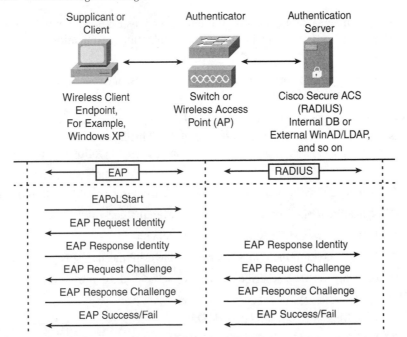

1 An IEEE 802.1x supplicant client initiates a connection request to the network by sending an EAPoL (EAP over LAN) Start message to the authenticator (Switch or Access Point).

2 The authenticator sends an EAP Identity Request message to the client.

3 The client replies with an EAP Identity Response to the authenticator.

4 The authenticator forwards the EAP Identity Response message to the authentication server encapsulated in the RADIUS protocol.

5 The authentication server sends an MD5 Challenge Request that is forwarded to the client by the authenticator.

6 The client replies with a Challenge Response message to the server.

7 The authentication server validates the user identity and sends an EAP Success or Fail message to the client.

8 Based on the authentication server reply (Pass or Fail), the authenticator enables the port connected to the client.

EAP Transport Layer Security (EAP-TLS)

Extensible Authentication Protocol-Transport Layer Security (EAP-TLS) is another open standard IETF standard, which is developed by Microsoft Corporation as an extension of Point-to-Point Protocol (PPP) to provide authentication within PPP, with TLS providing integrity of negotiation and key exchange. EAP-TLS provides greater security by using TLS, which is considered the successor of the SSL standard and therefore one of the most secure EAP methods available.

EAP-TLS offers per-packet confidentiality and integrity to protect identification and a standardized mechanism for key exchange.

EAP-TLS uses the X.509 PKI infrastructure to provide certificate-based 802.1x port-based access control. EAP-TLS addresses a number of weaknesses in other EAP protocols such as EAP-MD5.

Deployment of EAP-TLS increases in complexity because it requires mutual authentication, negotiation of encryption methods, and, most important, requires installing certificates on the client supplicant and server.

EAP-TLS is defined in RFC 2716.

The following authentication process takes place when an IEEE 802.1x supplicant connects to the wireless network by using the EAP-TLS authentication method. Figure 12-3 illustrates the EAP-TLS message exchange between the client supplicant, the authenticator (switch or access point), and the authentication server (RADIUS), as explained in the list that follows.

Figure 12-3 *EAP-TLS Message Exchange*

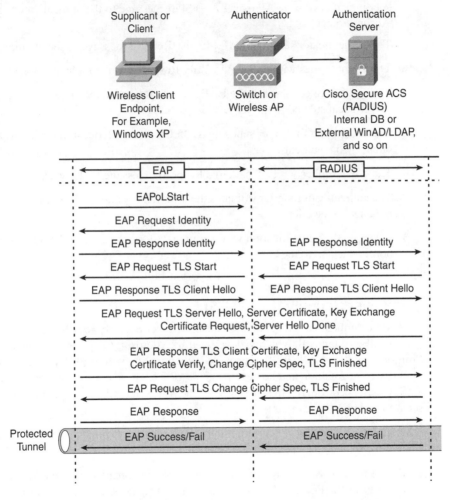

1 An IEEE 802.1x supplicant client initiates a connection request to the network by sending an EAPoL Start message to the authenticator (Switch or Access Point).

2 The authenticator sends an EAP Identity Request message to the client.

3 The client replies with an EAP Identity Response to the authenticator.

4 The authenticator forwards the EAP Identity Response message to the authentication server encapsulated in RADIUS protocol.

5 The authentication server sends an EAP-TLS Start message to the client.

6 The client replies with an EAP-TLS Client Hello message.

7 The authentication server replies with an EAP-TLS Server Hello message and includes its own server certificate and requests for the client's certificate.

8 The client verifies the server certificate using the server public key, sends the client certificate to the server, and sends the cipher trust protocol set.

9 The server verifies the client certificate, confirms the cipher trust protocol set, and validates the client credentials.

10 TLS tunnel is established and sends an EAP Success or Fail message to the client via the protected tunnel.

11 Based on the authentication server reply (Pass or Fail), the authenticator enables the port connected to the client.

EAP Tunneled Transport Layer Security (EAP-TTLS)

EAP-TTLS was codeveloped by Funk Software and Certicom. EAP-TTLS is widely supported across wireless platforms because it offers the same level of security and integrity as EAP-TLS without the overhead of installing PKI certificates on the client. EAP-TTLS requires a server-side certificate only on the authentication server. Note that despite the fact that EAP-TTLS requires only a certificate on the server side, the server is still able to authenticate the client after the secure tunnel has been established.

EAP-TTLS is described in an IETF Internet draft "draft-funk-eap-ttls-v1-01.txt." The draft can be found at http://tools.ietf.org/id/draft-funk-eap-ttls-v1-01.txt.

Here is a snippet from the abstract of the Internet draft:

"EAP-TTLS is an EAP type that utilizes TLS to establish a secure connection between a client and server, through which additional information may be exchanged. The initial TLS handshake may mutually authenticate client and server; or it may perform a one-way authentication, in which only the server is authenticated to the client."

NOTE   EAP-TTLS is an individual draft submission and is not standardized in the IETF.

EAP Flexible Authentication via Secure Tunneling (EAP-FAST)

Extensible Authentication Protocol-Flexible Authentication via Secure Tunneling (EAP-FAST) was developed by Cisco Systems, and an initial draft was submitted to the IETF in February 2004. The draft was revised and resubmitted in April 2005. EAP-FAST was developed to address the weaknesses of LEAP.

EAP-FAST uses the TLS tunnel, thereby providing a strong level of encryption. Similar to other EAP types that use the TLS approach, EAP-FAST offers confidentiality and integrity to protect user identification.

Although the concept is similar to other EAP types using TLS tunnel, the major differentiator is that EAP-FAST does not use the PKI infrastructure for user identity (server certificate is optional) to establish the tunnel. The client server architecture in EAP-FAST is based on strong shared secret keys that are unique on every client. These shared secret keys are called Protected Access Credential (PAC). The shared secret keys are distributed automatically to the client device via in-band provisioning or manually via out-band provisioning.

EAP-FAST is significantly faster because of the PAC architecture that expedites the tunnel establishment. Tunnel establishment using a shared secret key is inherently faster than using a PKI certificate-based exchange method. EAP-FAST remains popular among the other EAP-based solutions that provide encrypted EAP transactions.

EAP-FAST negotiation occurs in two phases:

- In Phase 1, the supplicant client and the authentication server perform mutual authentication using the PAC and establish the TLS tunnel.
- In Phase 2, the client exchanges the user credentials using the protected tunnel.

Figure 12-4 shows the details of the Phase 1 and 2 message exchange.

The following authentication process takes place when an IEEE 802.1x supplicant connects to the wireless network by employing EAP-FAST using the EAP-GTC (Generic Token Card) authentication method that is embedded in a TLS-protected tunnel. Figure 12-4 illustrates the EAP-FAST message exchange between the client supplicant, the authenticator (switch or access point), and the authentication server (RADIUS), as explained next:

1   An IEEE 802.1x supplicant client initiates a connection request to the network by sending an EAPoL Start message to the authenticator (Switch or Access Point).

2   The authenticator sends an EAP Identity Request message to the client.

3   The client replies with an EAP Identity Response to the authenticator.

4   The authenticator forwards the EAP Identity Response message to the authentication server, encapsulated in the RADIUS protocol.

5   The authentication server sends an EAP-TLS Start message to the client.

6   The authentication server sends an EAP-FAST Start message to the client, which includes the Authority ID.

Figure 12-4 *EAP-FAST Message Exchange*

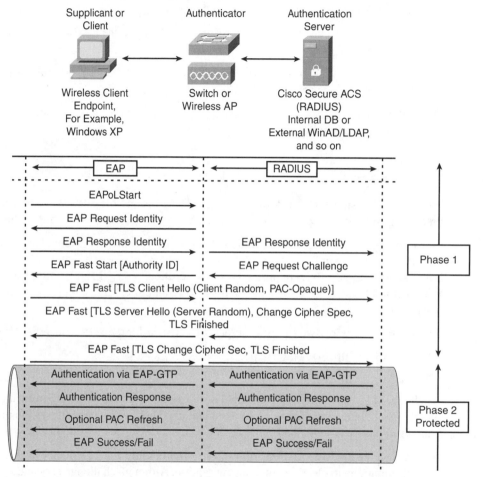

7 The client sends an EAP-TLS Client Hello message and selects a stored PAC key (a unique shared secret key based on the received Authority ID). The client also sends a PAC Opaque reply to the server (based on the PAC key selected).

8 The authentication server decrypts the PAC Opaque key by using the master key to derive the PAC key and sends an EAP-TLS Server Hello message and the cipher trust protocol set.

9 The client confirms the cipher trust protocol set.

10 When the PAC keys match on both ends, mutual authentication is successful and the TLS tunnel is established.

11 After the TLS tunnel is established, the server sends an authentication request using the EAP-GTC request via the protected tunnel.

12 The client sends an authentication response message to the EAP-GTC authentication via the tunnel.

13 The server verifies the client identity and sends an EAP Success or Fail message to the client via the protected tunnel.

14 Based on the authentication server reply (Pass or Fail), the authenticator enables the port connected to the client.

Protected EAP (PEAP)

Protected Extensible Authentication Protocol (PEAP) is another open standard EAP type that was jointly developed by Cisco Systems, Microsoft Corporation, and RSA Security.

PEAP is a hybrid authentication protocol that creates a secured TLS tunnel and design architecture that is similar to EAP-TTLS discussed earlier. To establish the TLS tunnel, both PEAP and EAP-TTLS require server-side certificates only. PEAP is unique in that any EAP method type can be encapsulated in a TLS tunnel to provide a secure connection between the client and server.

To date, the following two PEAP subtypes are certified for the WPA and WPA2 standard:

* PEAPv0 with EAP-MSCHAPv2

* PEAPv1 with EAP-GTC

As shown in Figure 12-5, PEAP establishes the TLS tunnel in Phase 1, thereby creating a secure channel that can then be used to initiate any other EAP type that uses the protected tunnel in Phase 2. Theoretically, any EAP type can be wrapped within the TLS tunnel.

As discussed in the EAP-MD5 section and shown in Figure 12-2, challenge authentication and negotiation is in clear text without encryption. Although challenge exchange provides better protection, it is still susceptible to offline dictionary attacks. With PEAP, challenge exchange is protected with the strong security of the TLS channel.

The authentication processes outlined in the steps that follow take place when an IEEE 802.1x supplicant connects to the wireless network by using the PEAP-MSCHAPv2 authentication method. Figure 12-5 illustrates the PEAP message exchange among the client supplicant, the authenticator (switch or access point), and the authentication server (RADIUS), as explained in the list that follows.

Figure 12-5 *PEAP with EAP-MSCHAPv2 Message Exchange*

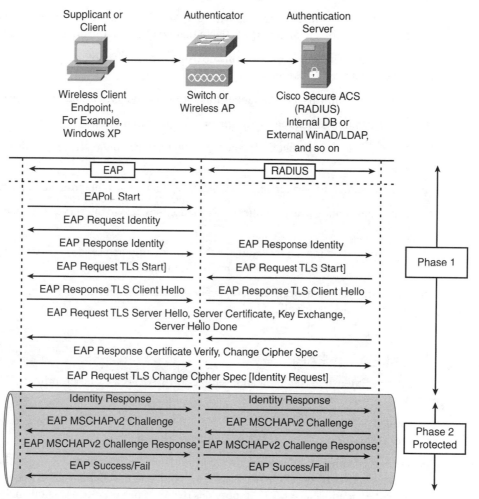

1 An IEEE 802.1x supplicant client initiates a connection request to the network by sending an EAPoL Start message to the authenticator (Switch or Access Point).

2 The authenticator sends an EAP Identity Request message to the client.

3 The client replies with an EAP Identity Response to the authenticator.

4 The authenticator forwards the EAP Identity Response message to the authentication server encapsulated in the RADIUS protocol.

5 The authentication server sends an EAP-TLS Start message to the client.

6 The client replies with an EAP-TLS Client Hello message.

7 The authentication server replies with an EAP-TLS Server Hello message and sends the server certificate to the client. (Note that no client certificate is requested.)

8 The client verifies the server certificate using the server public key and sends the cipher trust protocol set.

9 The server confirms that the cipher trust protocol and TLS tunnel is established.

10 The authenticator sends an EAP Identity Request message to the client.

11 The client replies with an EAP Identity Response to the authenticator via the protected tunnel.

12 The authentication server sends a Challenge Request via the protected tunnel.

13 The client replies with a Challenge Response message to the server via the protected tunnel.

14 The Authentication Server validates the user identity and sends an EAP Success or Fail message to the client via the protected tunnel.

15 Based on the authentication server reply (Pass or Fail), the authenticator enables the port connected to the client.

Cisco Lightweight EAP (LEAP)

Lightweight Extensible Authentication Protocol (LEAP) is a Cisco proprietary EAP method.

Cisco was a pioneer in introducing EAP support for WLAN devices. Cisco introduced LEAP in 2000 offering the first WLAN authentication method.

Cisco LEAP is a mutual authentication algorithm that uses a logon password as the shared secret that is known by the client and is used to respond to the challenges between the client and the authentication server. LEAP provides dynamic per-user, per-session encryption keys.

Most password-based authentication algorithms are susceptible to dictionary attacks, and the most effective way to safeguard against dictionary attacks is to create a strong password policy. Because Cisco LEAP uses password-based authentication, Cisco LEAP is also known to be susceptible to offline dictionary attacks, just like any other EAP type that uses a challenge response. At the DEFCON convention in 2003, a presentation was delivered that explored mechanisms that could make it easier for someone to write a tool to launch an offline dictionary attack on password-based authentications that leverage Microsoft MS-CHAP.

Cisco published a white paper, which is available on Cisco.com, to respond to the offline dictionary attacks on Cisco LEAP. EAP-FAST is one of the Cisco-suggested EAP methods to mitigate the offline dictionary attacks against MS-CHAP in LEAP.

NOTE   "Cisco Response to Dictionary Attacks on Cisco LEAP" can be found at http://www.cisco.com/en/US/products/hw/wireless/ps430/prod_bulletin09186a00801cc901.html.

Newer protocols such as EAP-TTLS and PEAP do not have this problem, because the challenge response is tunneled within a secure encrypted TLS tunnel.

EAP Comparison Chart

Table 12-2 provides a summary comparison of PEAP, EAP-FAST, Cisco LEAP, and EAP-TLS standards.

Table 12-2   *Comparison Chart of PEAP, EAP-FAST, Cisco LEAP, and EAP-TLS*

	PEAP with GTC	PEAP with MS-CHAPv2	EAP-FAST	Cisco LEAP	EAP-TLS
User Authentication Database and Server	One-time password (OTP), Lightweight Directory Access Protocol (LDAP), Novell NDS, Windows NT Domains, Active Directory	Windows NT Domains, Active Directory	Windows NT Domains, Active Directory, LDAP (limited)	Windows NT Domains, Active Directory	OTP, LDAP, Novell NDS, Windows NT Domains, Active Directory
Requires Server Certificates	Yes	Yes	No	No	Yes
Requires Client Certificates	No	No	No	No	Yes
Operating System Support	Driver: Windows XP, Windows 2000, Windows CE With third-party utility: Other OS	Driver: Windows XP, Windows 2000, Windows CE With third-party utility: Other OS	Driver: Windows XP, Windows 2000, Windows CE With third-party utility: Other OS	Driver: Windows 98, Windows 2000, Windows NT, Windows Me, Windows XP, Mac OS, Linux, Windows CE, DOS	Driver: Windows XP, Windows 2000, Windows CE With third-party utility: Other OS

continues

Table 12-2 *Comparison Chart of PEAP, EAP-FAST, Cisco LEAP, and EAP-TLS (Continued)*

	PEAP with GTC	PEAP with MS-CHAPv2	EAP-FAST	Cisco LEAP	EAP-TLS
ASD Support	No	No	Yes	Yes	No
Credentials Used	Client: Windows, NDS, LDAP password; OTP or token Server: Digital certificate	Windows password	Windows password, LDAP user ID/ password (manual provisioning required for Pac provisioning)	Windows password	Digital certificate
Single Sign On Using Windows Login	No	Yes	Yes	Yes	Yes
Password Expiration and Change	No	Yes	Yes	No	—
Works with Fast Secure Roaming	No	No	Yes	Yes	No
Works with WPA and WPA2	Yes	Yes	Yes	Yes	Yes

NOTE   The information in Table 12-2 is taken from "Cisco Aironet 1200 Series – Q&A" at http://www.cisco.com/en/US/products/hw/wireless/ps430/products_qanda_ item0900aecd801764fa.shtml.

WLAN NAC

Network Admission Control (NAC) for WLANs is a set of technologies and solutions used to enforce security policy compliance on all devices seeking network access and resources, thereby limiting damage from emerging security threats.

NAC is an industry initiative led by Cisco Systems and is part of the Cisco Self-Defending Network initiative that improves the network's capability to automatically identify, prevent, and adapt to security threats.

The WLAN NAC solution is available with the Cisco Unified Wireless Network solution.

WLAN IPS

Cisco Access Points offer an Intrusion Prevention System (IPS) for WLANs to provide intrusion detection capability while simultaneously forwarding data over the air. This allows an access point to monitor real-time wireless data, scanning for potential security threats to wireless devices. At this time, Cisco is the only vendor providing a WLAN solution that offers simultaneous wireless protection and data delivery.

WLAN IPS is part of the Cisco Self-Defending Network initiative, and is the first in the industry to offer an integrated wired and wireless IPS security solution.

A WLAN IPS solution is available with the Cisco Unified Wireless Network solution.

NOTE   Refer to the following white paper for integrating IPS to address wireless threats:

http://www.cisco.com/en/US/netsol/ns340/ns394/ns348/ns386/
networking_solutions_white_paper0900aecd804f155b.shtml

VPN IPsec

Virtual Private Network IP Security (VPN IPsec) is a framework and architecture of open standards for ensuring secure private communications over IP networks. VPN IPsec offers the confidentiality, integrity, and authenticity of data communications across shared or public networks.

IPsec can also be used as a solution (out-of-band) to secure WLAN traffic that is encapsulated in the IPsec tunnel.

Mitigating WLAN Attacks

A variety of attacks can be launched against WLAN networks. Both WPA and WPA2 devices offer protection to the network from a variety of network attacks when IEEE 802.1x, EAP types, and TKIP and AES are used. Table 12-3 shows a list of common attacks and the EAP enhancements that are used to protect against known attacks.

Table 12-3 *WLAN Attack Mitigation*

Attacks	Authentication: Open Encryption: Static WEP	Authentication: EAP-FAST, EAP-TLS, PEAP, or Cisco LEAP Encryption: Dynamic WEP	Authentication: EAP-FAST, EAP-TLS, PEAP, or Cisco LEAP Encryption: Cisco TKIP, WPA TKIP, AES
Man-in-the-Middle Attack	Vulnerable	Vulnerable	Protected
Authentication Spoofing	Vulnerable	Protected	Protected
AirSnort Attack	Vulnerable	Vulnerable	Protected
Replay Attack	Vulnerable	Vulnerable	Protected
Brute-Force Attacks	Vulnerable	Protected*	Protected*
Dictionary Attacks	Vulnerable	Protected*	Protected*

* Strong password policy is required for Cisco LEAP.

NOTE   The information in Table 12-3 is taken from "Cisco Wireless LAN Security Overview" at http://www.cisco.com/en/US/products/hw/wireless/ps430/ prod_brochure09186a00801f7d0b.html.

Cisco Unified Wireless Network Solution

The Cisco Unified Wireless Network offers a secure WLAN solution by combining the best-of-breed wireless standards and specifications to fulfill the need for scalable, reliable, and secure wireless networking and security services.

The Cisco Unified Wireless Network delivers the same level of security, scalability, reliability, ease of deployment, and management for wireless LAN networks that is offered by any other wired LAN solution.

The Cisco Unified Wireless Network solution offers all the WLAN security features that were discussed previously in this chapter and provides comprehensive WLAN attack mitigation, as described in Table 12-3.

Some of the common security features offered by Cisco Unified Wireless Network solution are

- Enterprise-ready, standards-based WLAN network
- Support of IEEE 802.11 standards
- SSID, MAC authentication, and other common techniques
- Support for WPA, WPA2, and 802.11i
- Mutual authentication mechanisms
- Support for IEEE 802.1x and various EAP methods
- Support for TKIP and AES
- Support of Wireless NAC
- Support of Wireless IPS
- Support for radio resource management (RRM) to monitor over-the-air packets and alert the network management console of different types of threats, such as rogue access points, rogue clients, ad hoc networks, and wireless DoS attacks
- Addressing of known wireless attacks and provision of mitigation techniques
- Support of Management Frame Protection (MFP) for 802.11 management attack mitigation

Components of Cisco Unified Wireless Network

The Cisco Unified Wireless Network is composed of five interconnected elements that work together to deliver a unified enterprise-class wireless solution. The five interconnected elements are

- Client devices
- Access points
- Network unification
- Network management
- Mobility services

NOTE   Cisco offers a wide range of WLAN products to support the five interconnecting elements of the Cisco Unified Wireless Network solution.

Refer to the following website for further information on the Cisco Unified Wireless Network solution, features, benefits, and in-depth details about each of the five elements: http://www.cisco.com/en/US/products/ps6521/prod_brochure09186a0080184925.html

Cisco Unified Wireless Network solution provides a comprehensive integrated security solution to protect WLAN networks.

TIP   In addition to the WLAN security features discussed in this chapter, refer to the following link on Cisco.com for white papers on WLAN Security Solutions: http://www.cisco.com/ en/US/netsol/ns340/ns394/ns348/ns386/networking_solutions_white_papers_list.html.

Summary

WLANs are increasingly deployed throughout organizations to provide greater mobility, scalability, and productivity.

Securing WLANs has always been considered difficult because of the variety of available solutions with varying standards. Cisco, one of the pioneers and leaders in providing wireless networking technology, now offers comprehensive solutions to secure WLANs.

The chapter started with a brief introduction and overview of WLAN, providing details of various IEEE 802.11 protocol standards and details of various WLAN components.

The major portion of the chapter provided detailed sections of various WLAN security features that are available to secure WLANs. Features covered include SSID, MAC authentication, Client authentication (Open and Shared Key), Static WEP, WPA/WPA2, 802.1x, EAP methods, WLAN NAC, WLAN IPS, and IPsec VPN.

The chapter provided a comparison chart of various EAP methods and another table showing a list of common attacks and the EAP enhancements used to protect against known attacks.

The chapter concluded with an overview of the Cisco Unified Wireless Network solution that provides a comprehensive integrated security solution to protect WLANs.

References

http://www.cisco.com/en/US/products/hw/wireless/ps430/
prod_brochure09186a00801f7d0b.html

http://www.answers.com/topic/wireless-lan-security

http://en.wikipedia.org/wiki/Extensible_Authentication_Protocol

http://www.cisco.com/en/US/netsol/ns339/ns395/ns176/ns178/
networking_solutions_white_paper09186a00800b469f.shtml

http://www.cisco.com/en/US/netsol/ns339/ns395/ns176/ns178/
netqa0900aecd801e3e59.html

http://www.cisco.com/en/US/products/hw/wireless/ps430/
products_qanda_item0900aecd801764f1.shtml

http://www.cisco.com/en/US/products/ps6521/prod_brochure0900aecd80355b2f.html

http://www.cisco.com/en/US/products/ps6548/
products_white_paper0900accd804f155b.shtml

http://www.cisco.com/en/US/netsol/ns340/ns394/ns348/ns337/
networking_solutions_package.html

http://www.cisco.com/en/US/products/ps6521/prod_brochure09186a0080184925.html

CHAPTER 13

Network Admission Control (NAC)

Technology is evolving every day with newer advancements bringing dynamic, amorphous security ecosystems. Today's complex network environment requires highly dynamic and scalable security solutions that can respond adaptively to different types of threats and attack vectors. Security technology solutions today are tightly integrated into the network infrastructure.

Modern researchers have found that a majority of security breaches these days originate from inside the network and often go undetected for extended periods. Security breaches can cause damage to the organization, such as interrupted services, revenue loss, cost of cleanup, loss of reputation, loss of customer satisfaction, and legal exposure.

Traditional security products and technologies working independently, such as firewalls, access control measures, and intrusion detection and prevention systems, do not provide adequate defense against insider threats because they are mainly oriented toward attacks originating from outside the network.

With the growing security challenges, perimeter defense alone that uses traditional approaches and works independently is inadequate and insufficient. The security model is rapidly evolving from a reactive to a proactive mode.

Organizations need comprehensive, pervasive, and tightly integrated information security solutions. Finding the right balance between the proactive and reactive approaches can be difficult, but it is very important to build a proactive network security model to provide pervasive and tightly integrated security solutions, safeguarding networks from both internal and external threats.

This chapter covers details on implementing a proactive, adaptable security solution using Cisco network admission control (NAC) solution to enforce policy-based compliance across the network.

Building the Self-Defending Network (SDN)

Implementing efficient, effective, and adaptable security solutions is now a baseline architecture within all network environments. Security is a vital component of every aspect of the network. The Cisco Self-Defending Network (SDN) solution is an efficient, adaptable, integrated, collaborative, and strategic systems approach to design and deploy proactive and simplified end-to-end security solutions.

The Cisco SDN is an architectural solution that provides integrated solutions to safeguard networks by using the network intelligence to identify, prevent, mitigate, and adapt to both known and unknown threats from internal and external sources.

The Cisco SDN vision encompasses three main characteristics:

- **Integrated security:** The first phase of SDN began by incorporating security features into network devices such as switches and routers, thus providing integrated security infrastructure within the network components, not as an add-on. Hence, every component in the network can act as a point of defense.

- **Collaborative security systems:** The second phase of SDN focused on building a security system that collaborates among all network and security components and policy enforcement endpoints.

- **Adaptive threat defense:** The third and final phase of SDN provides the capability for networks to evolve dynamically and intelligently to adapt and respond proactively to emerging threats at multiple layers of the network based on a new set of Anti-X technologies. Cisco offers various hardware and software products and features that compose a threat defense system, such as endpoint security, integrated firewalls, network intrusion detection and prevention systems, DDoS attack detection and mitigation, application-level content filtering, and security management and monitoring tools. The Cisco Threat Defense System offers security solutions and intelligent networking technologies to identify and prevent both known and unknown threats from internal and external network environments.

NOTE   Refer to the following URL for more information on Cisco Security Solutions for Small and Medium Businesses: http://www.cisco.com/en/US/netsol/ns643/networking_solutions_packages_list.html

Refer to the following URL for more information on Cisco Security Solutions for Large Enterprises: http://www.cisco.com/en/US/netsol/ns340/ns394/ns171/networking_solutions_packages_list.html.

Network Admission Control (NAC)

Day-zero attacks, viruses, and worms have become an increasing problem and continue to disrupt business operations. As discussed earlier, the most common issue on modern and open-standard networks is the security posture of internal endpoint devices that connect the network. Endpoints that do not comply with established security policies pose a threat and can introduce a security risk into the network. A network admission control (NAC) solution is needed to ensure that an endpoint is complying to predetermined security policies, such as the latest antivirus and operating system patches, thus preventing vulnerable and noncompliant hosts from obtaining network access.

Why NAC?

On a regular network, the hosts are trusted to join the network, without requiring authentication. In an 802.1x protected network (non-NAC 802.1x), a host is allowed on the network after authentication through a password or certificate. However, no check is made to see whether that system is compliant with a corporate security policy to ensure that the host has the latest antivirus and operating system patches. NAC takes the additional step of having a service that validates the client's security posture prior to allowing the session to go into an authorized state.

With all the firewalls and integrated security devices, the noncompliant endpoint makes its way through the network. An infected host could immediately begin to spread a virus or worm throughout the network and potentially expose the network to various threats and attacks.

Figure 13-1 illustrates this very problem, in which an infected noncompliant host connects to the network, and potential infection spreads across the network. With an automated system such as NAC in place, the network can detect endpoints that are out of policy compliance before network access is granted. A noncompliant host that is out of compliance can be denied network access or quarantined so that remedial action can be taken. A potential threat is thwarted by preventing noncompliant endpoints from joining the network.

As shown in Figure 13-1, the NAC solution uses the network access devices (NAD) to protect the infrastructure from any endpoint seeking network access. Only compliant trusted endpoints are granted access. Noncompliant devices are denied access and quarantined for remediation. This policy compliance solution limits the potential damage from known and unknown security threats.

Figure 13-1 *NAC Handling Noncompliant Host's Attempt at Network Connection*

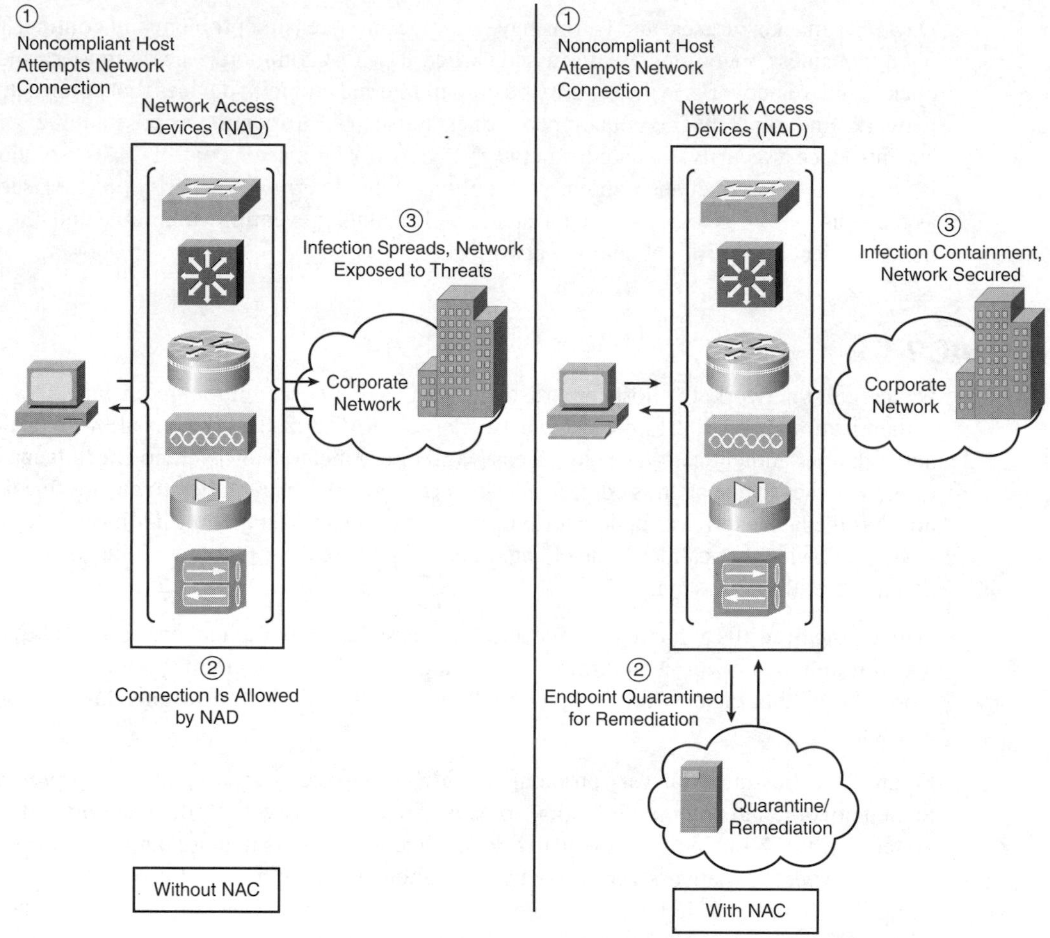

Cisco NAC

Cisco NAC is part of the Cisco SDN solution and is an initiative led by Cisco with the alliance of multiple vendors to enforce security policy compliance on all devices seeking network access. Cisco NAC enables the network to automatically identify, detect, and prevent emerging security threats. Cisco NAC is focused on proactive security solutions, thereby limiting damage from known and unknown threats from both internal and external sources.

Cisco offers NAC the solution in two forms:

- **Cisco NAC Appliance (formerly known as Cisco Clean Access):** The NAC appliance solution is the most widely deployed solution and is based on the Cisco Clean Access (CCA) dedicated NAC appliance. The NAC appliance solution does not rely on partners and vendors because it offers self-contained endpoint assessment, policy management, and remediation services. NAC appliance accommodates most common scenarios, including LAN, WAN, wireless, and remote access. The NAC appliance is a Cisco packaged solution.

- **Cisco NAC Framework:** The NAC framework solution uses the existing network infrastructure and third-party vendor solutions to enforce security policy compliance on all endpoints. The NAC framework is designed for highly specialized network environments where NAC intelligence is embedded in the network fabric. The NAC framework can be implemented on NAC-enabled network access devices (NAD) such as Cisco routers, switches, wireless access points, firewalls, and concentrators to grant access to compliant endpoints that are attempting to connect to the network. Noncompliance endpoints are placed in quarantine for remediation. The NAC framework solution does not require investment in new devices and utilizes existing investment in Cisco NADs. An overlay system is not required to perform admission control.

Figure 13-2 compares NAC appliance to NAC framework solution options.

Figure 13-2 *Cisco NAC Solution Available in Two Options*

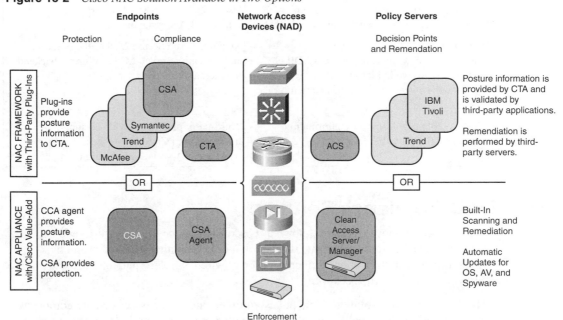

The information in Figure 13-2 is taken from the Cisco general product presentation on "Cisco NAC Solution."

Comparing NAC Appliance with NAC Framework

The multivendor NAC focuses on providing a framework for policy compliance-based access control.

Table 13-1 illustrates the different functions of a NAC environment.

Table 13-1 *NAC Appliance Versus NAC Framework Solution*

Cisco NAC Appliance	Cisco NAC Framework
Based on dedicated appliance leveraging Cisco Clean Access (CCA) products. NAC appliance is a Cisco self-sufficient package.	An embedded approach implemented on NAC-enabled network access devices (NAD) such as Cisco routers, switches, wireless access points, firewalls, and VPN concentrators.
Can identify, authenticate, scan, and remediate the endpoints without requiring other products.	Can identify, authenticate, and scan the endpoints via Cisco-enabled NAD, whereas remediation is performed by Cisco Secure ACS or third-party partner products (Trend Micro, IBM Tivoli, and so on).
Includes preconfigured checks from Microsoft for Windows updates. Most major antivirus software packages are sent regularly to the Clean Access Server.	Vendors in NAC framework solution are required to implement an API.
Uses an SNMP trap to preassign incoming users to a quarantined authentication VLAN.	Uses 802.1x and EAP to perform verification prior to VLAN assignment.
Forwards the authentication request to a backend server such as Kerberos, RADIUS, LDAP, and Active Directory. Clean Access Server does not act as the authentication server per se.	Requires Cisco Secure ACS as the AAA authentication server. ACS can further backend to external third-party servers.
CCA Agent provides posture information, whereas CSA provides protection.	Third-party plug-ins provide posture information to Cisco Trust Agent (CTA), whereas CSA provides protection.

Cisco NAC Appliance Solution

Cisco NAC appliance (formerly known as Cisco Clean Access) is an end-to-end network registration and enforcement NAC solution that offers the identification, scanning, authentication, authorization, and remediation of wired, wireless, and remote users prior to allowing users onto the network.

The NAC appliance solution offers policy enforcement to all devices that are compliant with network security policy and repairs any vulnerability before granting network access.

Mechanics of Cisco NAC Appliance

Cisco NAC appliance engages at the point of authentication:

- It recognizes an endpoint by a given device, user, and role within the network.

- It evaluates whether endpoints are compliant with security policies and enforces security policies by blocking, isolating, and repairing noncompliant endpoints. Security policies can vary by user type, device type, or operating system.

- It redirects endpoints into a quarantine area, where remediation occurs at the discretion of the administrator.

- It applies posture assessment and remediation services to all devices, regardless of device type.

- It enforces security policies on all networked devices, including Windows, Mac, and Linux laptops, desktops, PDAs, printers, and IP phones.

- It applies admission control to devices connecting through the LAN, wireless LAN, WAN, or VPN connections.

NAC Appliance Components

The Cisco NAC appliance solution consists of the following three components:

- **Clean Access Manager:** The Cisco Clean Access Manager is a web-based GUI application that is used to create security policies, establish roles, perform compliance checks, manage users, and define remediation rules.

- **Clean Access Manager:** Communicates with the Cisco Clean Access Server, which is the primary component used for enforcement in the NAC appliance architecture. The Clean Access Manager can also be used as a proxy to the backend authentication servers.

    The Cisco Clean Access Manager is available in three licensed options: the Cisco Clean Access Manager Lite, which is used to manage up to three Cisco Clean Access Servers; the standard Cisco Clean Access Manager, used to manage up to 20 Cisco Clean Access Servers; and the Cisco Clean Access Super Manager, which is used to manage up to 40 Cisco Clean Access Servers.

- **Clean Access Server:** Clean Access Server is a network layer device that triggers assessment when users attempt network access and can enforce network access privileges based on endpoint compliance. The Clean Access server is primarily used as an enforcement device and can block users at the port layer, thereby restricting access to the trusted network until they pass the inspection successfully.

The Clean Access Server can be implemented either in-band or out-of-band, in Layer 2 or Layer 3 mode, and as a virtual gateway or as a real IP gateway. The Cisco Clean Access Server can be deployed locally or globally, at the edge or centrally.

The Cisco Clean Access Server is available in five sizes based on the number of online, concurrent users: 100, 250, 500, 1500, and 2500 users.

- **Clean Access Agent (optional):** The Clean Access Agent (CAA) is a piece of lightweight read-only agent software, which runs on the client endpoint to provide posture information and streamlines remediation functions. It can perform inspection of the local host and provide information by analyzing Registry settings, services, and files. CAA can also determine whether a device has the required patches and hotfixes and whether it has the correct antivirus version and other installed security software, such as Cisco Security Agent (CSA).

Cisco Clean Access Agent is an optional component of the NAC Appliance solution and is distributed free of charge.

NAC Appliance Deployment Scenarios

The Cisco NAC appliance can be deployed in several ways to accommodate various scenarios and possibilities. Table 13-2 illustrates various NAC Appliance deployment options.

Table 13-2   *Cisco NAC Appliance Deployment Options*

Deployment Model	Options
Passing Traffic Mode	Virtual gateway (bridged mode)
	Real IP gateway/NAT gateway (routed mode)
Physical Deployment Model	Edge
	Central
Client Access Mode	Layer 2 (client is adjacent to the NAC Appliance Server)
	Layer 3 (client is multiple hops from the NAC Appliance Server)
Traffic Flow Model	In-band (NAC Appliance Server is always inline with user traffic)
	Out-of-band (NAC Appliance Server is inline only during authentication, posture assessment, and remediation)

The information in Table 13-2 is taken from "Cisco NAC Appliance" data sheet at http://www.cisco.com/en/US/products/ps6128/products_data_sheet0900aecd802da1b5.html.

Figure 13-3 illustrates the Cisco NAC Appliance deployment in in-band mode. This mode works with any 802.11 wireless access point and is the preferred mode for VPN traffic.

Figure 13-3   *Cisco NAC Appliance—Deployment in In-Band Mode*

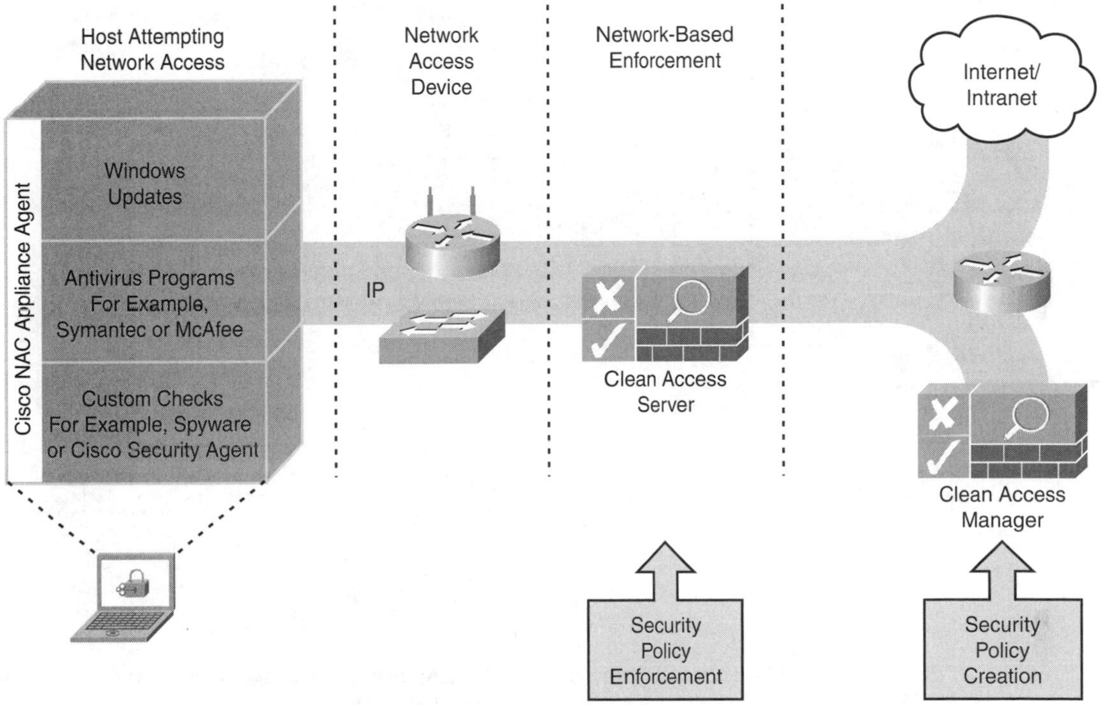

Figure 13-4 illustrates the Cisco NAC Appliance deployment in out-of-band mode. Note that the Clean Access Server will be in-band during the process of authentication, posture assessment, and remediation. After the user successfully passes these stages, all traffic traverses the switch port directly as out-of-band.

Figure 13-4 *Cisco NAC Appliance—Deployment in Out-of-Band Mode*

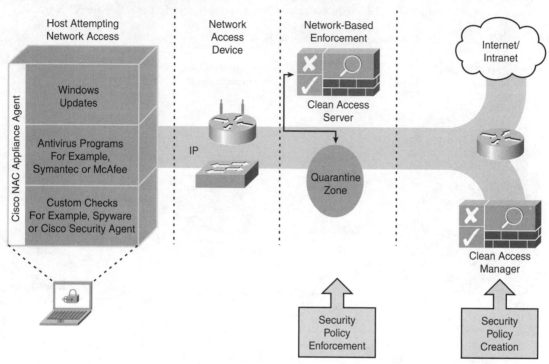

Figures 13-3 and 13-4 are taken from the "Cisco NAC Appliance" data sheet at http://www.cisco.com/en/US/products/ps6128/products_data_sheet0900aecd802da1b5.html.

<table>
<tr><td>**TIP**</td><td>Refer to the following URL for further information on the Cisco NAC Appliance solution: http://www.cisco.com/go/cca.</td></tr>
</table>

Cisco NAC Framework Solution

Cisco NAC Framework solution provides the same security policy enforcement framework as the Cisco NAC Appliance solution discussed previously. The main differentiator, which is Cisco NAC Framework, is an embedded approach that natively integrates into the existing infrastructure. It integrates using advanced security products and technologies, allowing networks to scale without making a significant investment.

Security point products only plug holes; they do not maintain network availability and resiliency. The Cisco NAC Framework solution offers proactive security architecture resulting in a resilient network infrastructure. The Cisco NAC Framework solution provides comprehensive and in-depth security defense to be built throughout the network infrastructure.

Cisco shares the NAC Framework program with third-party vendors, allowing them to integrate with Cisco NAC infrastructure to support the overall admission control solution. Participating with Cisco in this initiative are 90 leading vendors with solutions that include antivirus, remediation, client security, as well as management software manufacturers.

Partners participating in this program integrate security solutions that incorporate security features compatible with Cisco NAC infrastructure.

NOTE   Refer to the following Cisco URL for an updated list of Cisco NAC certified partners: http://www.cisco.com/web/partners/pr46/nac/partners.html.

Mechanics of the Cisco NAC Framework Solution

The Cisco NAC Framework solution provides a policy enforcement mechanism for all endpoints that request network access, regardless of their access methods, ownership, device types, application configurations, and remediation models.

The Cisco NAC Framework solution is an architecture-based framework designed to take advantage of existing Cisco-based network technologies and existing deployments of security and management solutions from other manufacturers.

The Cisco NAC Framework triggers when a host attempts network access through any of the following:

- Traffic triggers challenges on an endpoint that was installed with a Cisco Trust Agent (CTA). CTA is installed on an endpoint to gather client information, such as operating system version, patch and hotfix, and other software information.
- Cisco NAC-enabled NAD challenges for credentials.
- EAP over UDP is used to exchange identity and authentication credentials between the endpoint and the NAD.
- Credentials are forwarded to a Cisco Secure ACS (AAA server) via the RADIUS protocol.
- A AAA server can optionally proxy the credentials to backend a third-party vendor server that is using the Host Credential Authorization Protocol (HCAP) and Generic Authorization Message Exchange (GAME) protocol for further compliance validation.
- It evaluates whether endpoints are compliant with security policies (for example, antivirus DAT revision or OS patch version) and enforces security policies by blocking, isolating, and repairing noncompliant endpoints. Security policies can vary by user type, device type, antivirus type, or operating system.

- The third-party vendor replies with compliance validation and verifies the posture.

- The AAA server is configured with various authorization rule sets to respond to the respective posture validations.

- Based on the endpoint identification, enforcement is accomplished on the NAD via the posture states (refer to Table 13-3) depending on the posture verification.

- If the endpoint does not comply with the defined security policy, the Cisco NAC Framework redirects endpoints into a quarantine area, where remediation occurs at the discretion of the administrator.

- NAC can enforce security policies on all networked devices, including Windows, Mac, and Linux laptops, desktops, PDA, printers, and IP phones.

- NAC applies posture assessment and remediation services to all devices, regardless of device type.

Figure 13-5 illustrates the Cisco NAC Framework architecture and steps through the NAC flow.

Figure 13-5   *Cisco NAC Framework Architecture*

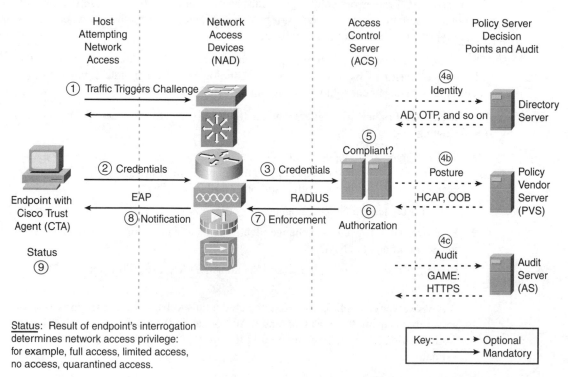

Status: Result of endpoint's interrogation
determines network access privilege:
for example, full access, limited access,
no access, quarantined access.

The information in Figure 13-5 is taken from Cisco general product presentation on "Cisco NAC Solution."

Table 13-3 lists various NAC posture states that are used for policy enforcement.

Table 13-3   *NAC Posture States*

Posture State	Description
Healthy	Endpoint is compliant; no restrictions on network access.
Checkup	Endpoint is within policy, but an update is available. Used to proactively remediate a host to the Healthy state.
Transition	Endpoint posturing is in process; give interim access pending full posture validation. Applicable during host boot up when all services may not be running or audit results are not yet available.
Quarantine	Endpoint is out of compliance; restrict network access to a quarantine network for remediation. The host is not an active threat but is vulnerable to a known attack or infection.
Infected	Endpoint is an active threat to other endpoint devices; network access should be severely restricted or totally denied.
Unknown	Endpoint posture cannot be determined. Quarantine the host and audit or remediate until a definitive posture can be determined.

There are two methods of collecting information from an endpoint to perform a posture assessment:

- **In-band:** The in-band method obtains application state via CTA, which collects state information from multiple software clients and forwards this information to the connected NAD where access control decisions are enforced.

- **Out-of-band:** The out-of-band method is mainly used for NAH (NAC agentless hosts), which does not have CTA or any other tool that can collect state information from the endpoint. Out-of-band is the dynamic assessment of the endpoint. A good example of an agentless endpoint is a printer. Agentless hosts require IP connectivity to trigger NAC.

Protocols used in the NAC Framework solution include the following:

- **EAP (Extensible Authentication Protocol):** EAP is used to exchange identity and credentials between the endpoint and the NAD. It supports a range of authentication methods. Some of the new extensions in EAP for NAC are EAP-TLV, Status Query, and EAP over UDP (EAPoUDP) (UDP port 21862), as shown in Figure 13-6.

- **RADIUS (Remote Authentication Dial-In User Service):** The RADIUS protocol is used to communicate between the NAD and a Cisco Secure ACS server.

- **HCAP (Host Credential Authorization Protocol):** HCAP is used by Cisco Secure ACS to forward client credentials to third-party vendor servers and to receive posture token responses and optional notification messages from the vendor server. It uses an HTTP(S) session between ACS and vendor servers for EAP-based credentials.

- **GAME (Generic Authorization Message Exchange):** Cisco Secure ACS triggers posture validation of NAH (NAC agentless host) by the vendor audit server and polls periodically for audit decision. The audit server responds with a posture state upon completion of the audit. It uses an HTTPS session between ACS and a vendor audit server, thereby extending Security Assertion Markup Language (SAML).

Figure 13-6 *EAP Extensions for NAC*

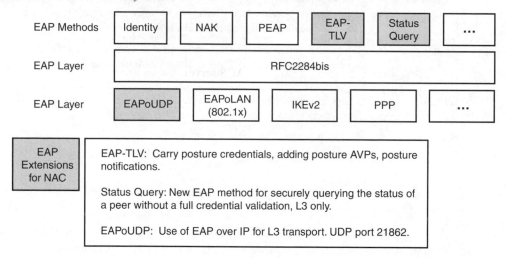

NAC Framework Components

The four primary components of the NAC Framework solution are outlined in the following list:

- **Endpoint software:** Endpoint security software includes products such as antivirus software, Cisco Security Agent (CSA), Personal Firewall, and the Cisco Trust Agent (CTA). The CTA is freely distributed software that is used to collect state information from multiple software clients, such as antivirus or any other installed security software. CTA forwards this information to the connected NAD, where access control decisions are enforced. Policy enforcement and admission control decisions are made on the basis of application and operating system status, such as antivirus and operating system patch levels. Cisco and NAC program partners integrate the CTA with their security software clients.

- **Network access devices (NAD):** NAD is a Cisco Layer 2 or Layer 3 device that is used for policy enforcement and admission control based on endpoint compliance. NAD is primarily used as the enforcement device and can block users at Layer 2 and Layer 3, thereby allowing network access to the trusted endpoint and restricting or quarantining noncompliant endpoints.

  Cisco NAC-enabled devices include Cisco routers, switches, wireless access points, and security appliances. These devices challenge endpoints for credentials and relay credential information to the access control server (AAA) and potential third-party policy servers, where admission control decisions are made. Based on the various defined policies, the NAD will enforce the appropriate posture states: permit, deny, quarantine, or restrict.

- **Access control and policy server:** The access control (Cisco Secure ACS) and third-party vendor servers are responsible for evaluating the endpoint security information that is relayed from the Cisco NAD and determine the appropriate network access policy to be applied. Cisco Secure ACS server is used as the AAA server with the RADIUS protocol. ACS can proxy backend verification functions with third-party vendor policy servers that provide deeper credential validation capabilities, such as antivirus policy servers.

- **Management system:** Cisco security management solutions provide the monitoring and reporting tools for the NAC Framework. Examples include CiscoWorks VPN/ Security Management Solution (CiscoWorks VMS), CiscoWorks Security Information Manager Solution (CiscoWorks SIMS), and Cisco Security Manager (CSM) that are used for managing varied NAC-enabled devices. Cisco NAC cosponsors also provide various management solutions for their endpoint security software.

The Cisco NAC Framework solution provides support for the following Cisco NAC-enabled devices:

- Cisco Routers—(Refer to Table 13-4)
- Cisco Catalyst switches—(Refer to Table 13-5)
- VPN 3000 Series Concentrators—(Refer to Table 13-6)
- Cisco Unified Wireless Network—(Refer to Tables 13-8 and 13-9)
- Cisco Security Agent (CSA)— v5.0 or later
- Cisco Trust Agent (CTA)—v2.0 or later
- CiscoSecure Access Control Server for Windows (ACS)—v4.0 or later
- CiscoSecure Access Control Server Solution Engine (ACS)—v4.0 or later
- Cisco Security Monitoring, Analysis, and Response System (MARS)

Table 13-4 lists Cisco routers that support the NAC L3 IP method (EAP over UDP). These are also referred to as the early NAC Release 1.0 devices.

Table 13-4 *Cisco NAC Supported Routers*

Supported Cisco Router Series	Supported Models	Operating System Image
Cisco 800 Series Routers	831, 836, 837, and 870 Series	Cisco IOS 12.3(8)T or later
Cisco 1700 Series Routers	1701, 1711, 1712, 1721, 1751, 1751-V, 1760	Cisco IOS 12.3(8)T or later
Cisco 1800 Series Routers	1841	Cisco IOS 12.3(8)T or later
Cisco 2600 Series Routers	2600XM, 2691	Cisco IOS 12.3(8)T or later
Cisco 2800 Series Routers	2801, 2811, 2821, 2851	Cisco IOS 12.3(8)T or later
Cisco 3600 Series Routers	3640/3640A, 3660-ENT Series	Cisco IOS 12.3(8)T or later
Cisco 3700 Series	3725, 3745	Cisco IOS 12.3(8)T or later
Cisco 3800 Series	3845, 3825	Cisco IOS 12.3(8)T or later
Cisco 7200 Series	All	Cisco IOS 12.3(8)T or later
Cisco 7500 Series	All	Cisco IOS 12.3(8)T or later
Cisco 7600 Series	All	Cisco IOS 12.3(8)T or later

NOTE   Cisco router models 1710, 1720, 1750, 26xx non-XM models, 3620, and 3660-CO do not support Cisco NAC. Also note that a specific Cisco IOS feature set is required to enable the Cisco NAC. Verify that the correct feature image is loaded on the supported hardware listed in Table 13-4.

NOTE   When NAC is enabled on a Cisco router, EAPoUDP is initiated from a router rather than the endpoint. Therefore, NAT issues may arise in which NAT is deployed between an endpoint and the router.

NAT implementations that depend on an endpoint having sent an EAPoUDP packet before forwarding an EAPoUDP request from the router are not supported. However, NAC and NAT can coexist on the same router.

NAC does not provide support when port address translation (PAT) is enabled between an endpoint and the router.

Table 13-5 lists Cisco switches that support either the NAC L2 IP method, which uses Extensible Authentication Protocol over User Data Protocol (EAP over UDP), or the NAC L2 802.1x (EAP over IEEE 802.1x) method. These are referred as the NAC Release 2.0 devices.

Table 13-5   *Cisco NAC Supported Switches*

Switch Models	Supported Methods	Supervisor, if Applicable	Operating System Image
Cisco Catalyst 2940	NAC-L2-802.1x	Not applicable	Cisco IOS Release 12.1(22)EA6 or later
Cisco Catalyst 2950 Cisco Catalyst 2955	NAC-L2-802.1x	Not applicable	Cisco IOS Release 12.1(22)EA6 or later
Cisco Catalyst 2960	NAC-L2-802.1x	Not applicable	Cisco IOS Release 12.2(25)SED or later
Cisco Catalyst 2970	NAC-L2- 802.1x	Not applicable	Cisco IOS Release 12.2(25)SED or later
Cisco Catalyst 3550	NAC-L2-IP NAC-L2- 802.1x	Not applicable	Cisco IOS Release 12.2(25)SED or later
Cisco Catalyst 3550	NAC-L2-802.1x	Not applicable	Cisco IOS Release 12.1(22)EA6 or later
Cisco Catalyst 3560	NAC-L2-IP NAC-L2-802.1x	Not applicable	Cisco IOS Release 12.2(25)SED or later
Cisco Catalyst 3750	NAC-L2-IP NAC-L2-802.1x	Not applicable	Cisco IOS Release 12.2(25)SED or later
Cisco Catalyst 4500	NAC-L2-IP NAC-L2-802.1x	Sup2+, 2-Plus-TS, Sup2+10GE, IV, V, V-10GE	Cisco IOS 12.2(25)SG or later
Cisco Catalyst 4900	NAC-L2-IP NAC-L2-802.1x	Not applicable	Cisco IOS 12.2(25)SG or later
Cisco 6500 Series Models: 6503, 6503-E, 6506, 6506-E, 6509, 6509-E, 6509-NEB, 6509-NEB-A, 651	NAC-L2-IP	Supervisor 32, 720	Cisco IOS 12.2(18)SXF2
Cisco 6500 Series Models: 6503, 6503-E, 6506, 6506-E, 6509, 6509-E, 6509-NEB, 6509-NEB-A, 651	NAC-L2-IP NAC-L2- 802.1x	Supervisor 2, 32, 720	Catalyst OS 8.5 or later

Table 13-6 lists the Cisco VPN 3000 series concentrator support for the NAC L3 IP method. NAC processing starts after an IPsec session is established. The VPN 3000-enabled NAC devices are referred to as the NAC Release 2.0 devices.

Table 13-6 *Cisco NAC Supported VPN 3000 Concentrators*

VPN Concentrator	Supported Models	Operating System Version
VPN 3000 series	3005 to 3080	Version 4.7 or later

NOTE At press time, the Cisco VPN 3000 concentrator supports L3 NAC IP for Remote Access sessions IPsec, SSL VPN, and L2TP over IPsec only. NAC does not apply to L2TP, PPTP, and LAN-to-LAN IPsec sessions.

The Cisco VPN 3000 Series Concentrators product is End-of-Sale and End-of-Life. For more details, refer to http://www.cisco.com/en/US/products/hw/vpndevc/ps2284/prod_eol_notice0900aecd805cd5a0.html.

Table 13-7 lists the Cisco Firewall Security Appliances that support the NAC L3 method.

Cisco NAC on the security appliances such as PIX 500 series and ASA 5500 series firewall appliances differs from NAC on Cisco IOS Layer 3 devices (such as routers) where routers trigger Posture Validation (PV) based on IP routed traffic. Cisco IOS-based NAD devices such as routers use an Intercept ACL to trigger Posture validation based on IP traffic, as shown in Example 13-1.

Cisco NAC on security appliance triggers Posture validation on IPsec VPN and SSL VPN sessions only. NAC on the security appliance does not support Layer 3 non-VPN traffic, IPv6 traffic, and security contexts.

Table 13-7 *Cisco NAC Supported Security Appliances*

Security Appliance	Operating System Version	Supported Methods
PIX 500 series	Version 7.2 or later	NAC-L3-IP
ASA 5500 series	Version 7.2 or later	NAC-L3-IP

NAC on a security appliance is supported for IPsec VPN sessions only.

Table 13-8 lists the Cisco wireless access points that support the NAC L2 802.1x method. These are referred to as the NAC Release 2.0 devices.

Table 13-8   *Cisco NAC Supported Wireless Access Points*

Cisco Wireless Access Points	Supported Models	Operating System Image
350 series	All	12.3(7)JA1 or later
1100 series	All	12.3(7)JA1 or later
1130 AG series	All	12.3(7)JA1 or later
1200 series	All	12.3(7)JA1 or later
1230 AG series	All	12.3(7)JA1 or later
1240 AG series	All	12.3(7)JA1 or later

Table 13-9 lists the Cisco wireless LAN controllers that support the NAC L2 802.1X method. These are referred to as the NAC Release 2.0 devices.

Table 13-9   *Cisco NAC Supported Airespace Appliance Devices*

Wireless LAN Controllers Models	Cisco Unified Wireless Network Software
Cisco 2000	Release 3.1 or later
Cisco 4100	Release 3.1 or later
Cisco 4400	Release 3.1 or later
Wireless Services Module (WiSM)	Release 3.1 or later
Wireless LAN Services Module (WLSM)	Release 3.1 or later
Wireless LAN Controller Module for Integrated Services Routers	Release 3.1 or later

NAC Framework Deployment Scenarios

NAC framework can be deployed on various Cisco NAC-enabled devices, as previously discussed. NADs such as Cisco routers, switches, wireless access points, firewalls, and concentrators are used for enforcement to grant access to compliant endpoints that are attempting to connect to the network. Endpoints connecting from various scenarios including LAN, wireless LAN, WAN, and through VPN connections are supported by NAC Framework.

Figure 13-7 depicts various Cisco NAC Framework deployment scenarios.

Figure 13-7 *Cisco NAC Framework—Deployment Scenarios*

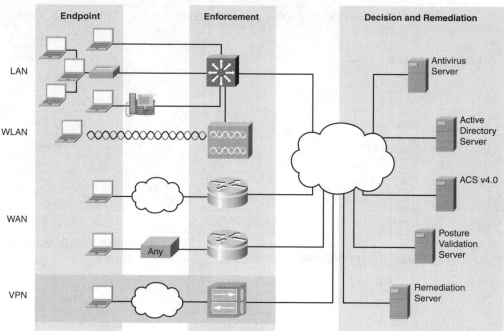

NAC Framework Enforcement Methods

As discussed earlier, the NAC Framework can be deployed on various NAC-enabled devices for policy enforcement and network admission control.

Three primary methods for enforcing a security policy and performing admission control follow:

- **NAC-L3-IP:** NAC-L3-IP is triggered on a Layer 3 device via IP packet. It uses EAPoUDP for posture and credentials. Enforcement is handled via per-host L3/L4 ACLs. The NAC-L3-IP solution can be implemented on Cisco routers, firewalls, and VPN concentrators.

- **NAC-L2-IP:** NAC-L2-IP is triggered on a Layer 2 device via a DHCP or ARP request. It uses EAPoUDP for posture and credentials. Enforcement is done via per-host L3/L4 ACLs. The NAC-L2-IP solution can be implemented on Cisco switches (L2 switch-port).

- **NAC-L2-802.1x:** NAC-L2-802.1x is triggered on a Layer 2 device via 802.1x. It leverages an existing 802.1x (EAP) L2 session to perform posture assessment and enforcement. Enforcement is done via dynamic VLAN assignment. The NAC-L2-802.1x solution can be implemented on Cisco switches (L2 switch-port) and wireless access points.

Figure 13-8 depicts various Cisco NAC Framework scenarios to perform admission control and enforcement points.

Figure 13-8 *Cisco NAC Framework—Admission Control and Enforcement Points*

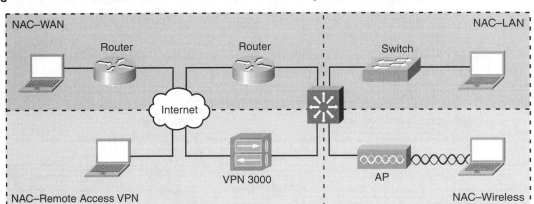

Table 13-10 shows the summary of features available in the three NAC Framework enforcement and admission control methods.

Table 13-10 *Cisco NAC Framework—Enforcement Methods*

Feature	NAC-L3-IP	NAC-L2-IP	NAC-L2-802.1x
Trigger mechanism	IP Packet	DHCP or ARP request	Data link up
Machine identity	N/A	N/A	✓
User identity	N/A	N/A	✓
Posture	✓	✓	✓
VLAN assignment	N/A	N/A	✓
URL-redirection	✓	✓	N/A
Downloadable ACLs	✓	✓	6500-only (PBACLs)
Posture status queries	✓	✓	
802.1x posture change	N/A	N/A	✓

Implementing NAC-L3-IP

Figure 13-9 shows various posture states (for example, Compliant, Noncompliant, Healthy, Quarantine) in NAC-L3-IP scenarios when a NAC-enabled device attempts a network connection:

- **NAC-Enabled:** Health endpoints evaluated and granted normal access. Endpoint will still be reassessed to ensure continued compliance.

- **NAC-Enabled:** Noncompliant endpoints placed in quarantine. This can also trigger remediation procedures. After remediation, reassessment will grant normal access.

- **NAC-Not-Enabled (Agentless):** Device assessed via out-of-band audit passes and is granted normal access.

- **NAC-Not-Enabled (Agentless):** Device assessed via out-of-band audit fails and is placed in quarantine or given no access.

Figure 13-9 *Cisco NAC Framework—NAC-L3-IP Case Scenarios*

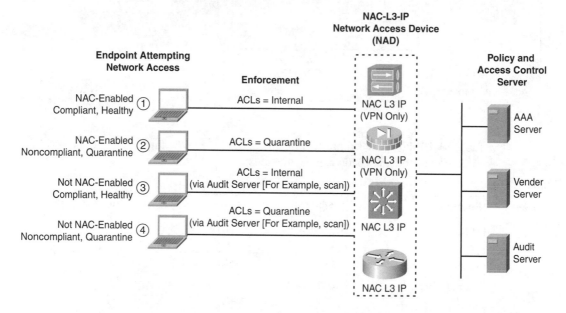

Figure 13-10 shows the topology diagram for the NAC-L3-IP sample configuration that is shown in Example 13-1, on a Cisco IOS-based device (for example, a router or Layer 3 switch) when a NAC-enabled device (with CTA) attempts network connection. NAC is triggered via an IP packet.

Figure 13-10   *Cisco NAC Framework—NAC-L3-IP Sample Configuration Topology*

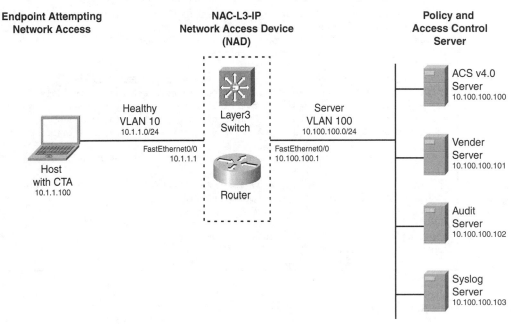

Example 13-1   *NAC-L3-IP IOS-Router Configuration*

```
aaa new-model
aaa authentication eou default group radius
aaa authorization auth-proxy default group radius
aaa session-id common
!
ip admission name NAC-L3-IP eapoudp list EoU-Trigger-ACL #Define NAC trigger
!
Interface FastEthernet0/0
 ip address 10.1.1.1 255.255.255.0
 ip access-group Interface-ACL in
 ip admission NAC-L3-IP
!
Interface FastEthernet0/1
 ip address 10.100.100.1 255.255.255.0
!
ip access-list extended EoU-Trigger-ACL    #NAC Trigger ACL
 deny udp any any eq domain            #allow DNS to bypass NAC
 deny tcp any host 10.100.100.101 eq www    #allow HTTP to bypass NAC
 permit ip any any               #all other IP traffic triggers NAC
!
ip access-list extended Interface-ACL
 permit udp any any eq 21862            #permit EAPoUDP
 permit udp any eq bootpc any eq bootps    #permit DHCP
!
```

Example 13-1 *NAC-L3-IP IOS-Router Configuration (Continued)*

```
radius-server host 10.100.100.100 auth-port 1645 acct-port 1646
radius-server key cisco123
radius-server vsa send authentication          #Enable VSAs
ip radius source-interface FastEthernet0/0
!
eou timeout hold-period 60        #Delay re-EAP after EAP failure
eou timeout revalidation 60         #Timeout to re-check all credentials
                    #ACS can override, enforces policy changes
eou timeout status-query 60        #How often check for status changes
ip auth-proxy inactivity-timer 60   #Equivalent to EoU revalidation timer
!
eou allow clientless              #Permit agentless hosts, used for auditing
!
ip http server                 #IOS web server required for URL redirection
ip http authentication aaa         #Enable auth-proxy
ip http secure-server          #SSL
!
eou logging              #Enable EAPoUDP logging
logging 10.100.100.103
!
```

Implementing NAC-L2-IP

Figure 13-11 shows various posture states (for example, Compliant, Noncompliant, Healthy, Quarantine) in NAC-L2-IP scenarios when a NAC-enabled device attempts network connection:

- **NAC-Enabled:** Health endpoints evaluated and granted normal access. Endpoint will still be reassessed to ensure continued compliance.

- **NAC-Enabled:** Noncompliant endpoints placed in quarantine. This can also trigger remediation procedures. After remediation, reassessment will grant normal access.

- **NAC-Not-Enabled (Agentless):** Device assessed via out-of-band audit passes and is granted normal access.

- **NAC-Not-Enabled (Agentless):** Device assessed via out-of-band audit fails and is placed in quarantine or given no access.

Figure 13-12 shows the topology diagram for a NAC-L2-IP sample configuration. Example 13-2 is the configuration on a Catalyst switch when a NAC-enabled device (with and without CTA) attempts network connection. NAC is triggered via ARP or DHCP packet. Layer 2 switches do not have intercept ACLs; they use port ACLs.

Figure 13-11 *Cisco NAC Framework—NAC-L2-IP Case Scenarios*

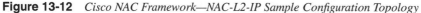

Figure 13-12 *Cisco NAC Framework—NAC-L2-IP Sample Configuration Topology*

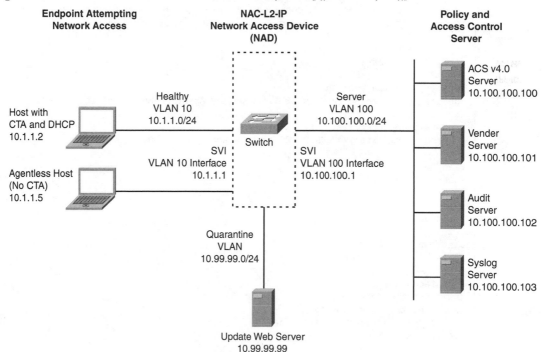

Example 13-2 *NAC-L2-IP Catalyst Switch Configuration Example*

```
hostname sw-3550
!
aaa new-model
aaa authentication eou default group radius
aaa authorization auth-proxy default group radius
aaa session-id common
!
ip subnet-zero
ip routing
no ip domain-lookup
!
ip admission name NAC-L2-IP eapoudp            #Define NAC policy
ip admission name NAC-L2-IP-Bypass eapoudp bypass
!
ip dhcp excluded-address 10.1.1.1 10.1.1.5
ip dhcp pool my_dhcp_pool
   network 10.1.1.0 255.255.255.0
   default-router 10.1.1.1
   lease 3
!
ip dhcp snooping vlan 10    #Optional—Enable DHCP snooping on VLAN 10
ip device tracking          #Build IP device table from ARP requests
!
vtp domain cisco
vtp mode transparent
!
identity profile eapoudp
 device authorize ip-address 10.1.1.5 policy AgentlessHost_Profile
identity policy AgentlessHost_Profile
 access-group AgentlessHost_ACL
 redirect url http://10.99.99.99 match Quarantine_URL_Redir_ACL
!
vlan 10
 name healthy
!
vlan 99
 name quarantine
!
vlan 100
 name server
!
interface FastEthernet0/1
 switchport mode access
 switchport access vlan 10
 ip access-group Interface-ACL in
 ip admission NAC-L2-IP
!
ip access-list extended Interface-ACL
 permit udp any any eq 21862          #permit EAPoUDP
 permit udp any eq bootpc any eq bootps    #permit DHCP
 permit udp any any eq domain          #permit DNS
 permit tcp any host 10.99.99.99 eq www    #permit HTTP access to update server
```

Example 13-2 *NAC-L2-IP Catalyst Switch Configuration Example (Continued)*

```
permit icmp any any                    #permit ICMP for testing
deny   ip any any                 #Implicit Deny
!
ip access-list extended AgentlessHost_ACL
 permit ip any any
!
ip access-list extended Quarantine_URL_Redir_ACL
 deny   tcp any host 10.99.99.99 eq www
 permit tcp any any eq www
!
radius-server attribute 8 include-in-access-req
radius-server host 10.100.100.100 auth-port 1645 acct-port 1646
radius-server key cisco123
radius-server vsa send authentication              #Enable VSAs
!
eou allow ip-station-id
eou timeout hold-period 60         #Delay re-EAP after EAP failure
eou timeout revalidation 60        #Timeout to re-check all credentials
                   #ACS can override, enforces policy changes
eou timeout status-query 60        #How often check for status changes
ip auth-proxy inactivity-timer 60   #Equivalent to EoU revalidation timer
!
eou allow clientless          #Permit agentless hosts, used for auditing
!
interface Vlan10
 ip address 10.1.1.1 255.255.252.0
!
interface Vlan99
 ip address 10.99.99.1 255.255.252.0
!
interface Vlan100
 ip address 10.100.100.1 255.255.252.0
!
ip classless
ip http server
ip http secure-server
!
eou logging                  #Enable EAPoUDP logging
logging 10.100.100.103
!
```

Implementing NAC-L2-802.1x

Figure 13-13 shows various posture states (for example, Compliant, Noncompliant, Healthy, Quarantine) in NAC-L2-802.1x scenarios when a NAC-enabled device attempts network connection:

- **NAC-Enabled:** Healthy endpoints evaluated and granted normal access. Endpoint will still be reassessed to ensure continued compliance.

- **NAC-Enabled:** Healthy endpoints evaluated and granted normal access. IP phones are not impacted when NAC is performed on endpoints when VVID is used on the switch.

- **NAC-Enabled:** Noncompliant endpoints placed in quarantine. This can also trigger remediation procedures. After remediation, reassessment will grant normal access.

- **NAC-Not-Enabled:** Known (Agentless) device. Predefined exception rules to grant access.

- **NAC-Not-Enabled:** Known (Agentless) visitor device. Visitor and Agentless devices may be given partial or no access (for example, visitor fails authentication and is placed in GUEST VLAN).

Figure 13-13 *Cisco NAC Framework—NAC-L2-802.1x Case Scenarios*

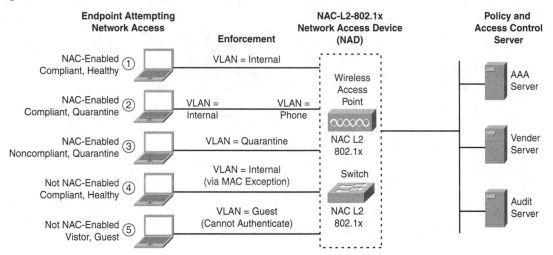

Example 13-3 shows a sample configuration for NAC-L2-802.1x on a Catalyst switch when a NAC-enabled device (with CTA) attempts network connection. NAC-L2-802.1x leverages the existing 802.1x (EAP) L2 session to perform posture assessment and enforcement. NAC is triggered when the data link state goes *up* after a host is powered on.

AAA authorization must be configured on the switch if network-related services such as a per-user VLAN assignment on 802.1x authenticated ports are required. The following three RADIUS attributes (attribute 64, 65, and 81) must be returned to the switch for 802.1x authentication:

- [RADIUS Attribute 64] Tunnel-Type = VLAN

  RADIUS attribute [64] must contain the value "VLAN" (type 13).

- [RADIUS Attribute 65] Tunnel-Medium-Type = 802

  Attribute [65] must contain the value "802" (type 6).

- [RADIUS Attribute 81] Tunnel-Private-Group-ID = VLAN NAME

  Attribute [81] contains the VLAN name or VLAN ID assigned to the authenticated user.

Example 13-3 *NAC-L2-802.1x Catalyst Switch Configuration*

```
hostname Sw-3550
!
aaa new-model
aaa authentication dot1x default group radius
aaa authorization network default group radius
aaa accounting dot1x default start-stop group radius
aaa accounting network default start-stop group radius
!
ip dhcp snooping vlan 10
ip device tracking
vtp domain cisco
vtp mode transparent
!
dot1x system-auth-control
!
vlan 10
 name healthy
!
vlan 99
 name quarantine
!
vlan 100
 name server
!
interface FastEthernet0/1
 switchport mode access
 switchport access vlan 10
 dot1x pae authenticator
 dot1x port-control auto
 dot1x reauthentication
!
radius-server host 10.100.100.100 auth-port 1645 acct-port 1646
radius-server key cisco123
radius-server vsa send authentication
!
```

The Cisco NAC Framework solution provides a scalable architecture with a centralized policy and a distributed enforcement component, with robust integration with Cisco security products and technologies.

Cisco NAC fundamentally changes how networks are secured with a strong access level that results in a proactive security model that was not available before.

NOTE Refer to the NAC Framework URL for further information on the Cisco NAC Framework solution: http://www.cisco.com/en/US/netsol/ns617/networking_solutions_sub_ solution_home.html.

Summary

The network perimeter now extends beyond geographical and organizational boundaries. Businesses require information instantly to be able to make good business decisions. With that flexibility in mind, organizations need secured solutions for the evolving security threats.

With the new generations of security threats and day-zero attack vectors, networks are relying on upper layer intelligence to be able to remain available and protect from known and unknown threats. The most common issue in the open-network policy is the security posture of internal endpoint devices seeking network access (desktop, PCs, laptops, PDAs, and so on). With network security largely built on standalone point products, it was extremely cumbersome to operate system patching and continuously install antivirus software updates. Endpoints that do not comply with established security policies pose threats, can introduce security risks into the network, and can cause considerable damage to the organization, such as interrupted services, revenue loss, cost of cleanup, loss of reputation, loss of customer satisfaction, and legal exposure.

A comprehensive NAC system is required to provide protection and ensure that all endpoints comply with the security policies in place, thus preventing vulnerable and noncompliant hosts from obtaining network access. Today, security technology solutions are tightly integrated into the network.

This chapter covered details on the Cisco-led SDN initiative, which offers proactive, adaptable security solutions via the Cisco NAC solution to enforce policy-based compliance across the network.

The chapter started with a brief introduction and overview of the Cisco SDN initiative and what the new approach of adaptive threat defense system entails.

It provided detailed information of the network admission control (NAC) solution and how the Cisco NAC solution builds a secure and proactive network approach.

The chapter provided a detailed comparison of the two available NAC solutions offered by Cisco: the Cisco NAC Appliance (formerly known as Cisco Clean Access) and the Cisco NAC Framework solutions.

The major portion of the chapter described the two Cisco NAC solutions with details on solution architecture, how it works, components, and various deployment scenarios.

The chapter provided a list of all Cisco NAC-supported devices and version information, including routers, switches, wireless, and security appliances that support the Cisco NAC Framework solution.

The chapter illustrated NAC Framework enforcement methods—namely, NAC-L3-IP, NAC-L2-IP, and NAC-L2-802.1x and provided numerous diagrams illustrating various scenarios to perform admission control and policy enforcement.

The chapter concluded with configuration examples of implementing NAC-L3-IP, NAC-L2-IP, and NAC-L2-802.1x scenarios in a Cisco NAC Framework solution.

References

http://www.cisco.com/cdc_content_elements/flash/nac/demo.htm

http://www.cisco.com/en/US/netsol/ns466/networking_solutions_package.html

http://www.cisco.com/en/US/netsol/ns617/networking_solutions_sub_solution_home.html

http://www.cisco.com/en/US/netsol/ns466/netqa0900aecd800fdd6f.html

http://www.cisco.com/en/US/netsol/ns617/networking_solutions_release_note09186a0080270825.html

http://www.cisco.com/en/US/netsol/ns617/networking_solutions_release_note09186a0080652b06.html

http://www.cisco.com/en/US/netsol/ns466/networking_solutions_white_paper0900aecd8051f9e7.shtml

http://www.cisco.com/go/cca

http://www.cisco.com/en/US/products/ps6128/products_data_sheet0900aecd802da1b5.html

http://www.cisco.com/web/partners/pr46/nac/partners.html

CHAPTER 14

Cryptography

Today, the Internet provides the most efficient and commonly used information highway for communication and information exchange. With millions of people communicating on this highway, privacy has become an extremely important issue.

Secure communication is becoming pivotal in every network design. For this reason, cryptography is one of the essential elements of today's information systems, providing secure access to information with greater reliability, authenticity, accuracy, and confidentiality.

This chapter provides an overview of cryptography solutions and various types of virtual private network (VPN) deployments. This chapter builds foundation knowledge of cryptographic algorithms and protocols for the next chapter by covering IPsec VPN that employs a cryptography approach.

Secure Communication

From the physical layer to the application layer of the OSI reference model, cryptography is the first of many steps necessary to provide secure communication solutions.

Cryptosystem

A cryptosystem—or "cryptographic system"—is a framework that involves the application of cryptography to provide secure communications.

A cryptosystem is the collection of protocols, procedures, and algorithms required to implement an encoding and decoding system using cryptography technology.

With a cryptosystem, the confidentiality and integrity of information can be achieved by using various methods that employ cryptography, such as encryption and decryption techniques, hash functions, digital signatures, key management techniques, and various other systems.

408 Chapter 14: Cryptography

Cryptography Overview

Cryptography is an ancient science. As far back as 1900 B.C., Egyptians used cryptography for ancient inscriptions. Romans used some early cryptosystems to exchange confidential messages.

The word *cryptography* comes from the Greek words *kryptos* and *graphein*. Kryptos means "hidden" and graphein means "writing." Hence, cryptography is said to be the study of hidden writing, or the science of encrypting and decrypting normal text to make it incomprehensible.

Cryptographic techniques are usually classified as

- **Traditional:** Traditional techniques date back centuries and use simple mechanisms of *transposition* (reordering of plaintext mechanisms) and *substitution* (alteration of plaintext mechanisms).

- **Modern:** Modern techniques rely on sophisticated protocols and algorithms to achieve assurance of information security.

In data and telecommunications, cryptography is necessary when communicating over untrusted or shared mediums, such as the Internet.

Cryptographic technologies and solutions help address issues related to information confidentiality, integrity, and access control. The objective is to protect the immobile and mobile (stationary or during transmission) information by using cryptographic technologies. Cryptography solutions also provide techniques for identifying unauthorized data modifications and alterations.

In the modern world of computer networks, information and information systems are digitally secured by using modern cryptographic protocols and algorithms.

Cryptographic Terminology

The following terminologies are commonly used in cryptographic context to describe a function or a role. Here are some basic terms used throughout the chapter and further:

- **Encryption:** The use of an algorithmic process that uses a secret key to transform plain data into a secret code, to prevent anyone except the intended recipient from accessing the information. Encryption is the process of obscuring information to make it unreadable to unauthorized recipients. Encryption provides a means of secure communication over an insecure communications medium. Figure 14-1 illustrates how the encryption process works.

- **Decryption:** The reverse process of encryption, converting encrypted data back into its original form.

- **Plaintext:** The original unencrypted data.

- **Ciphertext:** The product of the encryption process—the data that has been encrypted.

- **Hash:** A hash value, also known as a message digest value that is a mathematically generated unique number from a sequence of text by applying a mathematical formula. Hash is a value calculated from the original data to uniquely identify the data. Figure 14-2 illustrates how the hash function produces a unique hash value by using a mathematical algorithm, which is then appended to the original message as the unique identifier (like a fingerprint of the message).

NOTE   While explaining cryptography in various paragraphs and diagrams in this chapter, two communicating endpoints are referred to as "Alice" and "Bob" to identify the communicating parties. This is a common nomenclature in cryptographic literatures.

Figure 14-1 *Encryption Process (Data Confidentiality)*

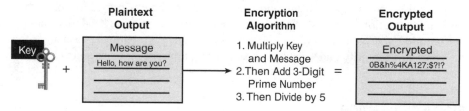

Figure 14-2 *Hash Function (Data Integrity)*

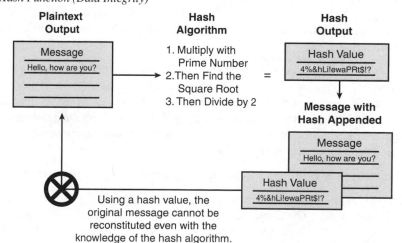

Cryptographic Algorithms

In general, there are three types of cryptographic algorithms:

- **Symmetric key cryptography (also known as secret key or preshared key cryptography):** Uses a single key for both the encryption and decryption process.

- **Asymmetric key cryptography (also known as public key cryptography):** Uses a two-key pair, one key for the encryption and another for the decryption process.

- **Hash algorithm (or hash function):** Uses a one-way mathematical function to produce an algorithmically randomized unique hash value to identify the data that is unique from other data. Using a hash value, the original message cannot be reconstituted even with the knowledge of the hash algorithm.

All three types of cryptography schemes have unique function mapping to specific applications. For example, the symmetric key cryptography approach is typically used for the encryption of data providing confidentiality, whereas asymmetric key cryptography is mainly used in key exchange and nonrepudiation, thereby providing confidentiality and authentication. The hash algorithm (noncryptic), on the other hand, does not provide confidentiality but provides message integrity, and cryptographic hash algorithms provide message integrity and identity of peers during transport over insecure channels.

Symmetric Key Cryptography

A symmetric key cryptography, also known as a secret-key or preshared key algorithm, is an approach that uses a single key for both encryption and decryption. Symmetric key cryptography is typically used to encrypt the contents of a message to provide data confidentiality.

Figure 14-3 depicts how the symmetric key encryption process works in using the same single key on both ends. The key must be known to both ends. The sender (Bob) uses a secret key to encrypt the plaintext message and thereby produce the ciphertext, and the receiver (Alice) uses the same secret key to decrypt the ciphertext, thereby producing the original plaintext message. A single key is used for both functions; hence, this method is called the symmetric encryption process.

Symmetric key cryptography ciphers are generally categorized in two modes:

- **Stream cipher:** A symmetric cipher that encrypts the plaintext digits (bits or bytes) one by one. The transformation of encrypted output varies during the encryption cycle. There are several varying types of stream ciphers, such as synchronous stream cipher and asynchronous stream cipher. RC4 is one of the most common stream cipher designs.

Figure 14-3 *Symmetric Key Encryption*

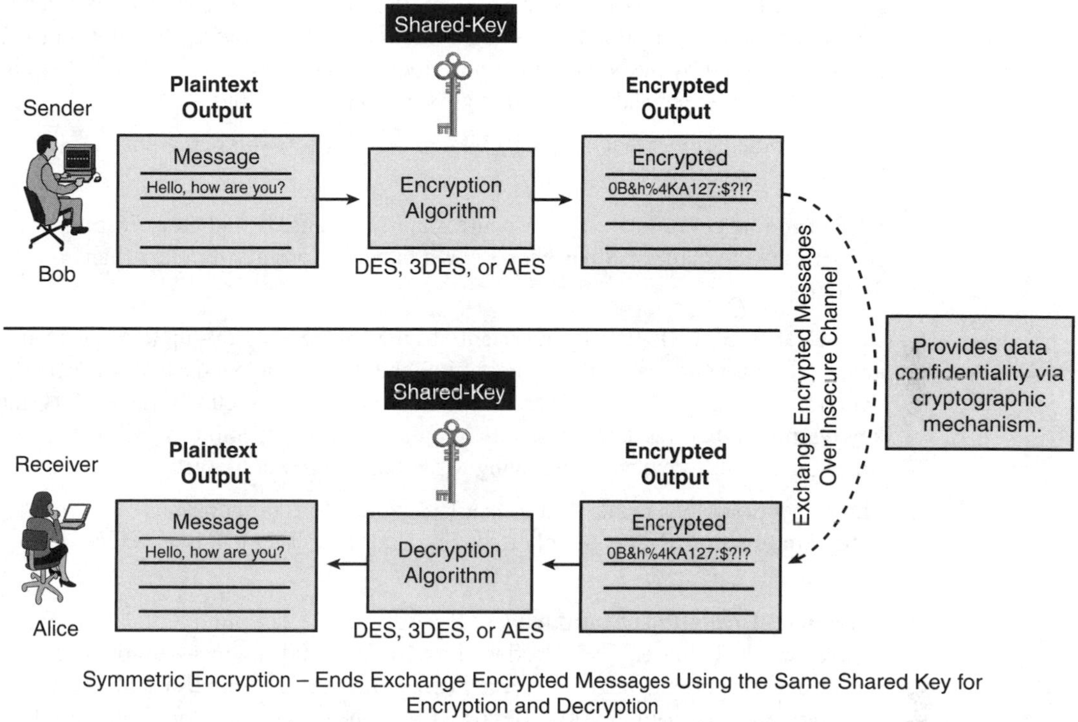

Symmetric Encryption – Ends Exchange Encrypted Messages Using the Same Shared Key for
Encryption and Decryption

- **Block cipher:** A symmetric key cipher that encrypts the plaintext on a fixed-length group of bits, with an unvarying transformation during the encryption cycle. Block ciphers encrypt blocks of data by using the same key on each block. For example, a block cipher can take a 128-bit block of plaintext as input and generate a corresponding 128-bit block of ciphertext output. DES and AES are examples of common block cipher designs.

In general, a block cipher mode yields the same ciphertext from a block of plaintext when using the same key, whereas a stream cipher mode yields different ciphertext from the same plaintext. Symmetric key cryptography algorithms are generally much less computationally intensive than asymmetric key cryptography algorithms.

Symmetric key cryptography is less computationally intensive and therefore much faster, especially for bulk data encryption such as data transfers, and can run on appliances without dedicated cryptographic hardware.

The list that follows contains some of the common symmetric key cryptography algorithms that are in use today:

- **Data Encryption Standard (DES):** DES, one of the earliest and most common symmetric key algorithms, was designed by IBM in the 1970s. DES was selected the official Federal Information Processing Standard (FIPS) for the United States in 1976 and was adopted by the National Institute for Standards and Technology (NIST) in 1977 for commercial and unclassified government applications.

  DES is a block cipher that uses a 56-bit key to encrypt 64-bit datagram blocks.

  DES is no longer considered very secure, mainly because the inherent 56-bit key size is too small. DES has been known to be compromised in less than 24 hours.

- **Triple-DES (3DES):** 3DES is a variant of DES. 3DES employs up to three 56-bit keys (168-bits) and makes three encryption and decryption passes over the same datagram block. As mentioned earlier, DES is considered insecure because of its small key length. 3DES was derived mainly to enlarge the key length to 168-bits (three times 56-bit DES key) without having to switch to a newer algorithm.

  3DES is also a block cipher that uses a 168-bit key to encrypt 64-bit datagram blocks. 3DES is mainly a recommended replacement to all DES implementations.

- **Advanced Encryption Standard (AES):** Advanced Encryption Standard (AES), also known as Rijndael, was introduced by NIST in 2001 and was announced as the new federal cryptographic standard replacing DES. AES became effectively a cryptographic standard in 2002. Today, AES is one of the most commonly used algorithms among the symmetric key cryptography implementations.

  The AES algorithm can use a variable block length and key length. Specifications indicate that any combination of key lengths of 128, 192, or 256 bits and block lengths of 128, 192, or 256 bits can be used.

  AES is a block-cipher algorithm that is capturing its share and is slowly replacing the predecessor DES and 3DES standards.

NOTE   Among the common symmetric key cryptography algorithms previously listed, several other symmetric key algorithms are available—namely, CAST-128/256, IDEA, RC4, and Blowfish.

Asymmetric Key Cryptography

Asymmetric key cryptography is also commonly known as a public-key algorithm and was first described publicly in 1976.

Asymmetric key cryptography design uses a two-key pair: one key is used to encrypt the plaintext, and the other key is used to decrypt the ciphertext. Unlike the symmetric-key approach, two parties can communicate securely over an insecure channel without having to share a secret key. Asymmetric key cryptography is typically used in digital certification and key management. Theoretically, asymmetric key cryptography could also be used to encrypt data, although this is rarely done because symmetric key cryptography is much more efficient and much less computationally intensive than asymmetric key cryptography.

Figure 14-4 depicts how the asymmetric key encryption process works using the two keys known as public and private keys. Each end user has its own pair of public and private keys. The public key from each end user is widely distributed via the key-management system to all users. The private key is never exchanged or revealed to another party.

Figure 14-4 *Asymmetric Key Encryption*

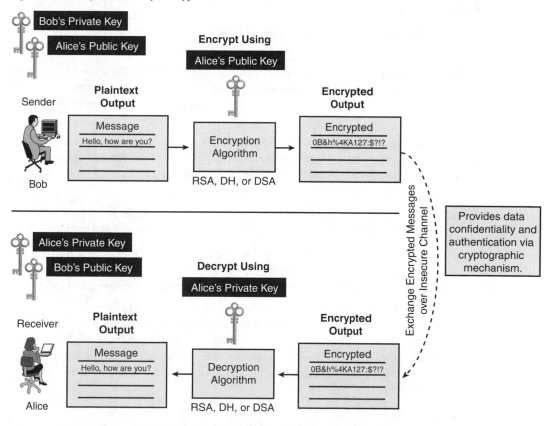

Symmetric Encryption – A Distributed Public Key Is Used to Encrypt Messages That Can Only Be Decrypted with a Private Key Held by the Publisher of the Public Key

Figure 14-4 shows that the sender (Bob) uses the receiver's (Alice) public key to encrypt the message to produce the ciphertext. When the receiver (Alice) gets the encrypted message, she uses her own private key to decrypt the ciphertext to produce the original plaintext message. This mechanism provides a secure communication exchange, assuring that only the authorized recipient (Alice, in this case) will be able to decipher the message with her own private key.

Another variation of the asymmetric key approach is used to validate the identity of the sender, whereby the sender (Bob) uses his own private key to encrypt the message, and the receiver (Alice) uses the sender's (Bob) public key to decrypt the ciphertext. This variation offers nonrepudiation, in which only the holder of the private key could have encrypted the message, thereby assuring that the sender was the one who sent the message.

Separate keys are used for both functions; therefore, this method is called the asymmetric encryption process.

The list that follows contains some of the common asymmetric key cryptography algorithms that are widely used for key exchange and digital signatures:

- **RSA:** The RSA algorithm was described publicly in 1976 by the three MIT mathematicians who developed this algorithm—Ronald Rivest, Adi Shamir, and Leonard Adleman. RSA is named after the initials from the surnames of the developers.

  The RSA algorithm was the first greatest advancement that used the asymmetric key cryptography mechanism. RSA is one of the most popular and widely implemented asymmetric key algorithms that can be used for key exchange, digital signatures, and message encryption.

  RSA algorithms are available in varying standards (RC1, RC2, RC3, RC4, RC5, and RC6), all of which use variable size block lengths and key lengths.

- **Diffie-Hellman (DH):** DH was first described publicly in 1976 by Stanford University Professor Martin Hellman and graduate student Whitfield Diffie. The DH algorithm was introduced shortly after the RSA algorithm was published in 1976.

  DH is a public-key distributing system (also known as key-exchange protocol) that employs an asymmetric key cryptography mechanism. DH allows two end users that have no prior knowledge of each other to establish a shared secret key over an insecure communications channel. The resulting secret key can be used to encrypt subsequent messages using a symmetric key algorithm.

  Contrary to the RSA algorithm, the DH algorithm is not used for authentication or digital signatures. DH is used only for secret-key key exchange.

- **Digital Signature Algorithm (DSA):** DSA is another asymmetric key algorithm proposed by the National Institute for Standards and Technology (NIST) in 1991 for their use in Digital Signature Standard (DSS). DSA is also a Federal Information Processing Standards (FIPS) standard for digital signatures.

  DSA is used mainly for digital signature capability to ensure the authentication of messages.

- **Public-Key Cryptography Standards (PKCS):** PKCS is a set of interoperable public-key cryptography standards and guidelines, designed and published by RSA Data Security Inc.

  PKCS #1: RSA Cryptography Standard (see RFC 3447).

  PKCS #2: Was withdrawn and merged into PKCS #1. It covered RSA encryption of message digests.

  PKCS #3: Diffie-Hellman Key-Agreement Standard.

  PKCS #4: Was withdrawn and merged into PKCS #1. It covered RSA key syntax.

  PKCS #5: Password-Based Encryption Standard (see RFC 2898).

  PKCS #6: Extended-Certificate Syntax Standard. It defines extensions to the old X.509v1 certificate specification, obsolete by X.509v3.

  PKCS #7: Cryptographic Message Syntax Standard (see RFC 2315). It is used to sign or encrypt messages under a PKI.

  PKCS #8: Private-Key Information Syntax Standard.

  PKCS #9: Selected Attribute Types (see RFC 2985).

  PKCS #10: Certification Request Syntax Standard (see RFC 2986). It defines the format of messages sent to a Certification Authority to request certification of a public key.

  PKCS #11: Cryptographic Token Interface Standard (cryptoki). An API defining a generic interface to cryptographic tokens.

  PKCS #12: Personal Information Exchange Syntax Standard. It defines a file format commonly used to store private keys with accompanying public-key certificates protected with a password-based symmetric key.

  PKCS #13: Elliptic Curve Cryptography (ECC) Standard.

  PKCS #14: Pseudo-Random Number Generation (PRNG) Standard. PRNG is an algorithm that generates a sequence of numbers that are not truly random.

  PKCS #15: Cryptographic Token Information Format Standard. It defines a standard allowing users of cryptographic tokens to identify themselves to applications, independent of the application's cryptoki implementation (PKCS #11) or other API.

NOTE   Among the common asymmetric key cryptography algorithms listed previously, several
          other asymmetric key algorithms are available—namely, Elliptic Curve Cryptography
          (ECC), Encrypted Key Exchange (EKE), ElGamal, and Cramer-Shoup.

Hash Algorithm

A hash algorithm has a number of names—hash function, message digest, and one-way encryption. Hash algorithms use a mathematical formula to compute a fixed-length hash value based on the original plaintext. Using a hash value, the original message cannot be reconstituted even with the knowledge of the hash algorithm. Hash functions are generally faster than encryption mechanisms.

Hash algorithms are typically used to provide a digital fingerprint of any type of data, to ensure that information has not been altered during the transmission, thus providing a measure for information integrity.

A hash value, also known as a message-digest value, is a unique number that is created from a sequence of text by applying a mathematical formula.

Figure 14-5 illustrates how the hash algorithm works. The sender (Bob) produces a unique hash value by using a mathematical algorithm, which is then appended to the original message as the unique identifier (fingerprint of the message) and transmitted to Alice. The receiver (Alice) separates the appended hash value from the original message and computes the hash locally by using the predetermined hash algorithm. If the locally computed hash equals the appended hash that was received, the data is known to be unaltered, thus providing message integrity.

Hash algorithms are commonly used for data integrity check and digital certificates.

The list that follows contains some of the common hash algorithms that are widely used for information integrity, authentication, and digital signatures:

- **Message Digest (MD) algorithms:** Message Digest algorithms are a series of byte-oriented cryptographic hash functions that produce a mathematically computed 128-bit fixed-length hash value (also called message digest or fingerprint) from an arbitrary-length input.

  MD2 (see RFC 1319): Developed by Ronald Rivest in 1989. MD2 was designed and optimized for 8-bit machines or systems with limited memory, such as smart cards. First, the message is padded to ensure that its length in bytes is divisible by 16. Then, a 16-byte checksum is appended to the message, and the resulting message is processed to compute a hash value.

Figure 14-5 *Hash Algorithm*

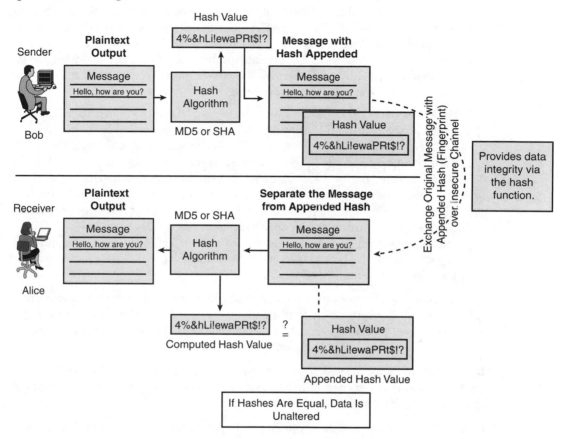

MD4 (see RFC 1320): Developed by Ronald Rivest in 1989. MD2 was designed and optimized for 32-bit machines. MD4 was similar to MD2 but designed specifically for faster processing in software. First, the message is padded to ensure that its length in bits plus 64 is divisible by 512. Then a 64-bit binary representation of the original length of the message is concatenated to the message.

MD5 (see RFC 1321): Developed by Ronald Rivest in 1991. MD5 was designed to replace MD4 after potential weaknesses were reported in MD4. MD5 is similar to MD, 4 with enhancements to provide greater security. The MD5 algorithm consists of four distinct rounds, with a slightly different design from that of MD4. Message-digest size and padding requirements remain the same. In spite of several weaknesses reported by numerous cryptographers, MD5 continues to remain popular and is widely used by various products and applications. Algorithmically, MD5 is no longer considered very secure because analytical attacks and practical collisions have been constructed in less than one hour.

- **Secure Hash Algorithm (SHA):** SHA is another series of popular cryptographic hash algorithms that produces 160-bit output. SHA was designed by the National Security Agency (NSA) and published as a U.S. government standard. The SHA algorithm is also used in NIST's Secure Hash Standard (SHS). SHA is computationally slower than MD5 but more secure. The original specification of the SHA algorithm (the first member of the family was known as SHA-0) was introduced in 1993, and two years later, its successor, SHA-1, was published.

  SHA-1 (see RFC 3174): The most commonly used hash algorithm in the SHA family, which produces a 160-bit hash value. SHA-1 was considered to be the successor to MD5 and is widely used in a variety of applications and protocols, including Transport Layer Security (TLS), Secure Sockets Layer (SSL), Pretty Good Privacy (PGP), Secure Shell (SSH), Secure Multipurpose Internet Mail Extension (S/MIME), and IPsec. Four additional variants of SHA have since been introduced—namely, SHA-224, SHA-256, SHA-384, and SHA-512 (sometimes collectively referred to as SHA-2). These variants can produce hash values that are 224, 256, 384, or 512 bits in length, respectively. These variants are described in RFC 4634. Cryptographers have reported attacks for both SHA-0 and SHA-1. However, to date, no attacks have yet been reported on the SHA-2 variants.

A traditional hash algorithm does not make use of any key mechanism to produce a hash value. However, a cryptographic hash algorithm combined with a secret key is used to calculate a keyed-hash message authentication code (HMAC). Message authentication code (MAC) provides data integrity and message authentication.

Digital signatures use the hash algorithm coupled with the asymmetric key mechanism to produce a private key encrypted hash output. Digital signatures guarantee the authenticity of the message in addition to message integrity.

Figure 14-6 illustrates how the cryptographic keyed-hash algorithm works. The sender (Bob) produces a unique hash value by using a mathematical algorithm, which is then encrypted using Bob's own private key. The encrypted hash value is appended to the original message as the unique identifier (as a fingerprint of the message) and transmitted to Alice. The receiver (Alice) separates the appended encrypted hash value from the original message and decrypts the hash with the sender's (Bob's) public key. Then the receiver takes the original message input through the predetermined hash algorithm to produce a locally generated hash value of the same text. If the locally computed hash equals the unencrypted hash received, the data is known to be unaltered, thus providing message integrity. This process provides nonrepudiation and proof of the integrity and origin of data because it proves that only the holder of the private key could have encrypted the hash, and the private key did so before sending the data. The digital signature provides data integrity and message authentication.

NOTE   Among the common hash algorithms previously listed, several other hash functions are available—RIPEMD, HAS-160, HAVAL, Whirlpool, and Tiger2.

Figure 14-6 *Digital Signature Using Keyed-Hash Algorithm*

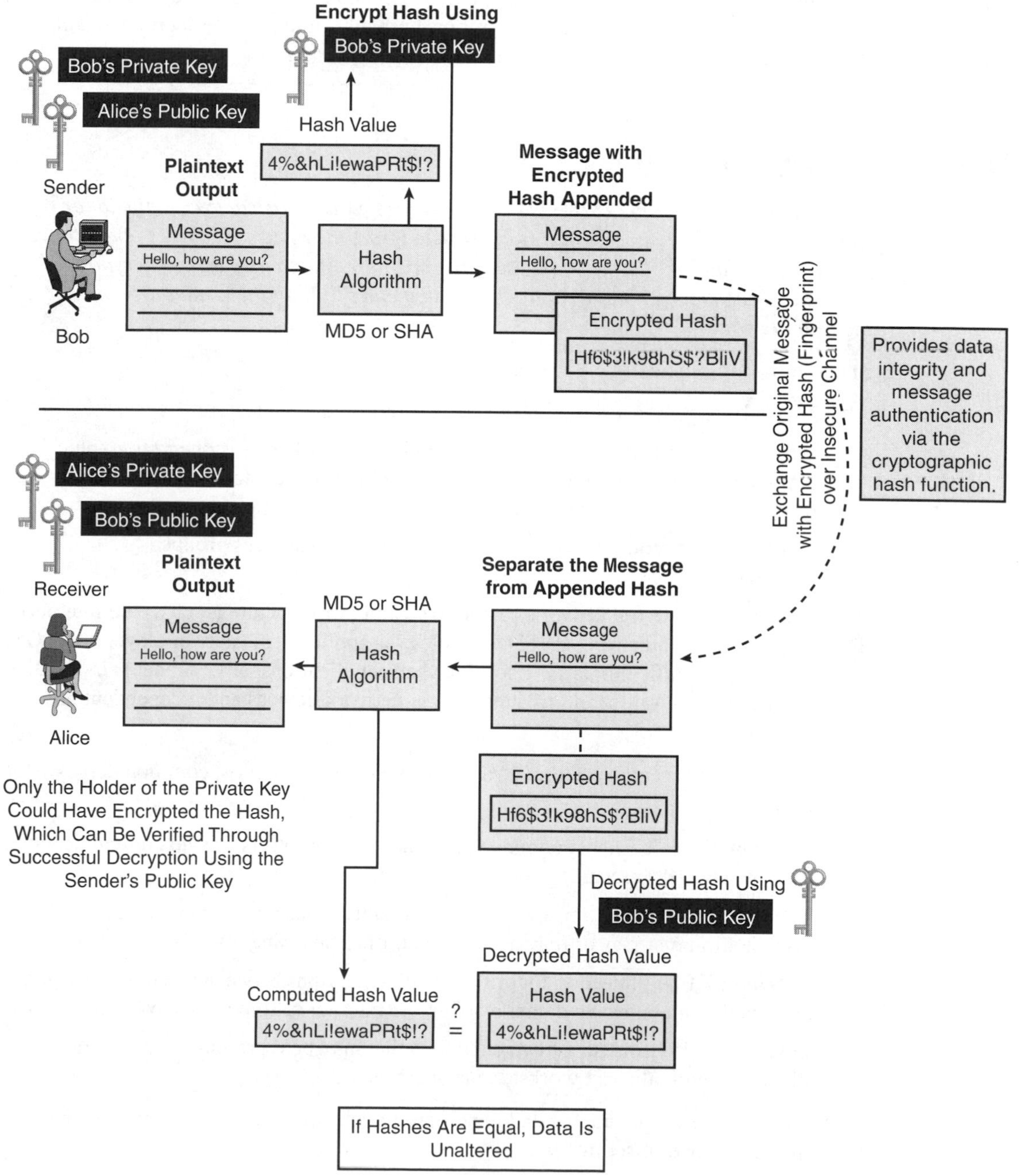

TIP	Refer to RFC 4270 (by Paul Hoffman and Bruce Schneier, November 2005) for further information on attacks on hash functions, how hash algorithms are susceptible to collision attacks, and how to thwart these known attacks.

Virtual Private Network (VPN)

By definition, as per RFC 2828—VPN is "*a restricted-use, logical (i.e., artificial or simulated) computer network that is constructed from the system resources of a relatively public, physical (i.e., real) network (such as the Internet), often by using encryption (located at hosts or gateways), and often by tunneling links of the virtual network across the real network.*"

Stated more simplistically, a VPN can be defined as

- **Virtual:** Logical networks, independent of physical architecture.
- **Private:** Independent of IP addressing and routing schemes (noncryptographic approaches). Secure confidentiality, message integrity, authentication, privacy (cryptographic approaches).
- **Network:** Interconnected computers, devices, and resources grouped to share information.

A VPN carries private traffic over a public or shared infrastructure (such as the Internet). The most common and effective VPN technology is applied at the network layer of the OSI model to encrypt traffic flow among specific users, applications, or IP subnet pairs. VPN at the network layer is transparent to intermediate network devices and independent of network topology.

VPN designs can be constructed in a variety of scenarios. The most common deployment scenarios are

- **Internet VPN:** The most common application that protects private communications over the shared (insecure) public access Internet.
- **Intranet VPN:** Protection for private communications within an enterprise or organization that may or may not involve traffic traversing a WAN.
- **Extranet VPN:** Protection for private communications between two or more separate entities that may involve data traversing the Internet or some other WAN medium.

In all cases, the VPN consists of two endpoints that may be represented by routers, firewalls, or individual client workstations or servers.

VPN employs the cryptographic and noncryptographic approaches to create a secure communication over insecure channels.

Cryptographic VPN technologies include

- IP Security (IPsec)

- Layer 2 Tunneling Protocol (L2TP): (Protected by IPsec)
- Generic Routing Encapsulation (GRE): (Protected by IPsec)
- Point-to-Point Tunneling Protocol (PPTP): (Protected by MPPE: Microsoft Point-to-Point Encryption Protocol, see RFC 3078)

Noncryptographic VPN technologies include

- Multiprotocol Label Switching (MPLS VPN): (Protected by L2VPN and L3VPN)
- Generic Routing Encapsulation (GRE) or IP-in-IP Tunneling

The next chapter will cover details of IPsec VPNs with a focus on Cisco VPN solutions that use cryptographic approaches. This chapter builds the foundation of cryptographic algorithms and protocols, which is required before moving on to the IPsec VPN solutions in the next chapter.

Summary

With the rapid growth of the Internet, secure communication is becoming critical. Using the cryptography approach to secure communication is one of the essential steps of providing secure access to information with integrity, authenticity, and confidentiality.

This chapter presented a detailed overview of the cryptography solutions and various types of VPN deployments. It started with a brief introduction to cryptosystems and an overview of cryptography, followed by an explanation of basic cryptography terminology.

The major portion of the chapter provided details of the three types of cryptographic algorithms (symmetric key cryptography, asymmetric key cryptography, and hash algorithms), giving detailed explanations using supporting diagrams and illustrations, and listed some of the most common algorithms that are in use today.

The chapter concluded with a basic description of the VPN design and deployments using cryptographic and noncryptographic approaches.

This chapter builds the foundation knowledge of cryptographic algorithms and protocols required for the next chapter, which covers IPsec VPN employing cryptography.

References

http://www.garykessler.net/library/crypto.html

http://en.wikipedia.org/wiki/Cryptography

http://en.wikipedia.org/wiki/Symmetric-key_algorithm

http://en.wikipedia.org/wiki/Public_key_cryptography

CHAPTER 15

IPsec VPN

With the growing volume of information proliferating on the Internet and data traversing insecure channel mediums, information security and data privacy are becoming imperative. Secure communication is becoming increasingly important when sensitive data traverses insecure shared channels.

IPsec VPN (Internet Protocol Security, Virtual Private Network) is a standard defined by the IETF (Internet Engineering Task Force) that provides data confidentiality, authentication, and integrity for IP traffic at the network layer of the OSI (Open System Interconnection) model. The IPsec framework is one of the essential frameworks that is used for secure communication.

This chapter provides a basic overview of various types of VPN technologies and deployments. The major component of the chapter focuses on the IPsec Secure VPN framework and its implementation.

Virtual Private Network (VPN)

As discussed in Chapter 14, "Cryptography," VPN carries private traffic over a public or shared infrastructure (such as the Internet).

VPN employs the cryptographic and noncryptographic approaches necessary to create a secure communication over insecure channels.

Types of VPN Technologies

In recent years, the term VPN has taken on many meanings. Three types of distinctly different VPN technologies available today are the following:

- Secure VPN (also known as Cryptographic VPN)
- Trusted VPN (also known as non-Cryptographic VPN)
- Hybrid VPN

Secure VPN (Cryptographic VPN)

With the rapid growth of global communication, the Internet and commonly shared mediums are now being used as the most common mode of communication. With this development, security has become a major concern for traffic traversing the shared medium. Cryptographic techniques evolved with dedicated protocols and standards to protect the privacy of traffic. These protocols and standards are rapidly growing in popularity and are increasingly being used by customers and service providers. Traffic is secured using encryption technology in a secure tunnel between the communicating peers. These are called secure VPNs.

Secure VPNs are commonly used to replace or augment existing point-to-point networks that utilize dedicated leased circuits or WAN networks over Frame Relay and ATM circuits.

Secure VPN technologies include

- IPsec
- L2TP over IPsec
- SSL encryption

This chapter primarily focuses on IPsec Secure VPN.

Trusted VPN (Non-Cryptographic VPN)

The major characteristic of Trusted VPN is that it enables the service provider to offer a dedicated leased circuit or channel to a customer. Hence, pseudo point-to-point communication occurs in this scenario, thereby allowing networks to peer directly by using a dedicated leased circuit. This technique provides a sense of security and data privacy. When traffic traverses these dedicated point-to-point circuits, you have what is called a Trusted VPN.

Security and integrity of Trusted VPN traffic relies on the fact that the circuit is not shared, thereby providing the assurance that the circuit is dedicated to a single site for point-to-point communication. Service providers today offer several types of Trusted VPN services.

Trusted VPN technologies, which can generally be categorized into Layer 2 and Layer 3 VPNs, include the following:

- MPLS VPN (Layer 3 VPN)
- BGP VPN (Layer 3 VPN)
- Multicast VPN (Layer 3 VPN)
- Transport of Layer 2 frames over MPLS and any transport over MPLS (AToM) (Layer 2 VPN)
- Virtual Private LAN Services (VPLS) (Layer 2 VPN)

NOTE	Trusted VPNs (Layer 2 and Layer 3 VPNs) will be discussed in Chapter 19, "Multiprotocol Label Switching VPN (MPLS VPN)."

Hybrid VPN

Hybrid VPN is the combination of both the Trusted and the Secure VPNs. This is an emerging concept that is slowly gaining momentum. The concept is to run a secure VPN tunnel as part of a trusted VPN—that is, a tunnel within a tunnel.

NOTE	It is important to understand that Secure VPN and Trusted VPN technologies do not technically overlay each other and can coexist in the same environment in a single service.

Types of VPN Deployment

VPN designs can be constructed in a variety of scenarios. The most common deployment scenarios are the following:

- **Internet VPN:** Internet VPN is the most common application that protects private communications over the shared (insecure) public access Internet.
- **Intranet VPN:** Intranet VPN protects private communication within an enterprise or organization that may or may not involve traffic traversing a WAN.
- **Extranet VPN:** Extranet VPN protects private communications between two or more separate entities that may involve data traversing the Internet or some other WAN medium.

IPsec VPN (Secure VPN)

IPsec (Internet Protocol Security) framework is a set of open standards developed by the IETF.

IPsec is implemented by a set of cryptographic protocols for securing IP traffic.

IPsec framework secures IP traffic operating at the Layer 3 (network layer) of the OSI model, thus securing all network applications and communications that use the IP network.

Using combinations of hashing, symmetric key, and asymmetric key cryptographic algorithms discussed in Chapter 14, the IPsec framework offers the following security services:

- Peer Authentication

- Data confidentiality
- Data integrity
- Data origin Authentication
- Replay detection
- Access control
- Traffic flow confidentiality

IPsec Request for Comments (RFCs)

As mentioned earlier, IPsec is a set of open standards that is documented in several RFCs. Originally, IPsec was defined in a series of RFCs 1825–1829, published in 1995. As technology evolved, these were updated by newer revisions and made obsolete by RFCs 2401–2412 published in 1998.

In 2005, a third-generation of RFCs 4301–4309 (superset of 2401–2412) was produced to include further advancements in this realm. IPsec VPN technology has changed significantly in the past few years.

NOTE The third-generation of RFCs 4301–4309 standardized the abbreviation of IPsec to uppercase IP and lowercase sec.

Tables 15-1 through 15-5 list IPsec-related RFCs arranged by the categories they apply to.

Generic IPsec RFCs

Table 15-1 lists the general IPsec RFCs.

Table 15-1 *IPsec General RFCs*

RFC	Description
RFC 4301	"Security Architecture for the Internet Protocol" (proposed standard)
RFC 2401	"Security Architecture for the Internet Protocol" (made obsolete by RFC 4301)
RFC 2411	"IP Security Document Roadmap (informational" RFC)
RFC 2521	"ICMP Security Failures Messages (experimental" RFC)
RFC 2709	"Security Model with Tunnel-Mode IPsec for NAT Domains" (informational RFC)
RFC 2764	"Framework for IP-Based Virtual Private Networks" (informational RFC)

Table 15-1   *IPsec General RFCs (Continued)*

RFC	Description
RFC 3102	"Realm Specific IP: Framework" (experimental RFC)
RFC 3103	"Realm Specific IP: Protocol Specification" (experimental RFC)
RFC 3104	"RSIP Support for End-to-End IPsec" (experimental RFC)
RFC 3554	"On the Use of SCTP with IPsec" (proposed standard)
RFC 3884	"Use of IPsec Transport Mode for Dynamic Routing" (informational RFC)
RFC 3723	"Securing Block Storage Protocols over IP" (proposed standard)
RFC 3706	"Traffic-Based Method of Detecting Dead IKE Peers "(informational RFC)
RFC 3776	"Using IPsec to Protect Mobile IPv6 Signaling Between Mobile Nodes and Home Agents" (proposed standard)
RFC 3756	"IPv6 Neighbor Discovery Trust Models and Threats" (informational RFC)

IPsec Protocols RFCs

Table 15-2 lists various RFCs related to Encapsulating Security Payload (ESP) and Authentication Headers (AH).

Table 15-2   *ESP and AH Headers RFCs*

RFC	Description
RFC 4302	"IP Authentication Header" (proposed standard)
RFC 4303	"Encapsulating Security Payload (ESP)" (proposed standard)
RFC 4304	"Extended Sequence Number Addendum to IPsec DOI for ISAKMP" (proposed standard)
RFC 4305	"Cryptographic Algorithm Implementation Requirements for ESP and AH" (proposed standard)

IPsec Key Exchange RFCs

Table 15-3 lists various RFCs related to key exchange.

Table 15-3   *Key Exchange RFCs*

RFC	Description
RFC 4306	"Internet Key Exchange (IKEv2) Protocol" (proposed standard)
RFC 4718	"IKEv2 Clarifications and Implementation Guidelines" (informational RFC)
RFC 4307	"Cryptographic Algorithms for Use in the Internet Key Exchange Version 2" (IKEv2) (proposed standard)

continues

Table 15-3   *Key Exchange RFCs (Continued)*

RFC	Description
RFC 4308	"Cryptographic Suites for IPsec" (proposed standard)
RFC 2407	"Internet IP Security Domain of Interpretation for ISAKMP—made obsolete by RFC 4306" (IKEv2)
RFC 2408	"Internet Security Association and Key Management Protocol (ISAKMP)—made obsolete by RFC 4306" (IKEv2)
RFC 2409	"Internet Key Exchange (IKE)—made obsolete by RFC 4306" (IKEv2)
RFC 4109	"Algorithms for IKEv1" (proposed standard)
RFC 3715	"IPsec-NAT Compatibility Requirements" (informational RFC)
RFC 3948	"UDP Encapsulation of IPsec Packets" (proposed standard)
RFC 3947	"Negotiation of NAT-Traversal in the IKE" (proposed standard)
RFC 3766	"Determining Strengths for Public Keys Used for Exchanging Symmetric Keys—Best Current Practice" (BCP 86)
RFC 2412	"OAKLEY Key Determination Protocol" (informational RFC)
RFC 2367	"PF_KEY Key Management API, Version 2" (informational RFC)
RFC 2522	"Photuris: Session-Key Management Protocol" (experimental RFC)
RFC 2523	"Photuris: Extended Schemes and Attributes" (experimental RFC)
RFC 3129	"Requirements for Kerberized Internet Negotiation of Keys" (informational RFC)
RFC 4025	"Method for Storing IPsec Keying Material in DNS" (proposed standard)
RFC 4595	"Use of IKEv2 in the Fiber Channel Security Association Management Protocol" (informational RFC)
RFC 3547	"Group Domain of Interpretation" (proposed standard)
RFC 4322	"Opportunistic Encryption Using the Internet Key Exchange (IKE)" (informational RFC)
RFC 4478	"Repeated Authentication in IKEv2" (experimental RFC)

IPsec Cryptographic Algorithm RFCs

Table 15-4 lists various RFCs related to cryptographic algorithms.

Table 15-4   *Cryptographic Algorithms RFCs*

RFC	Description
RFC 2405	"ESP DES-CBC Cipher Algorithm with Explicit IV" (proposed standard)
RFC 2451	"ESP CBC-Mode Cipher Algorithms" (proposed standard)

Table 15-4   *Cryptographic Algorithms RFCs (Continued)*

RFC	Description
RFC 2104	"HMAC: Keyed-Hashing for Message Authentication" (informational RFC)
RFC 2202	"Test Cases for HMAC-MD5 and HMAC-SHA-1" (informational RFC)
RFC 2403	"Use of HMAC-MD5-96 Within ESP and AH" (proposed standard)
RFC 2404	"Use of HMAC-SHA-1-96 Within ESP and AH" (proposed standard)
RFC 2857	"Use of HMAC-RIPEMD-160-96 Within ESP and AH" (proposed standard)
RFC 2410	"NULL Encryption Algorithm and Its Use with IPsec" (proposed standard)
RFC 1828	"IP Authentication Using Keyed MD5" (proposed standard)
RFC 1829	"ESP DES-CBC Transform" (proposed standard)
RFC 2085	"HMAC-MD5 IP Authentication with Replay Prevention" (proposed standard)
RFC 3173	"IP Payload Compression Protocol (IPComp)" (proposed standard)
RFC 2394	"IP Payload Compression Using DEFLATE" (informational RFC)
RFC 2395	"IP Payload Compression Using LZS" (informational RFC)
RFC 3051	"IP Payload Compression Using ITU-T V.44 Packet Method" (informational RFC)
RFC 3526	"More Modular Exponential (MODP) Diffie-Hellman Groups for Internet Key Exchange (IKE)" (proposed standard)
RFC 3566	"AES-XCBC-MAC-96 Algorithm and Its Use with IPsec" (proposed standard)
RFC 3602	"AES-CBC Cipher Algorithm and Its Use with IPsec" (proposed standard)
RFC 4434	"AES-XCBC-PRF-128 Algorithm for IKE" (proposed standard)
RFC 3686	"Using AES Counter Mode with IPsec ESP" (proposed standard)
RFC 4309	"Using AES CCM Mode with IPsec ESP" (proposed standard)
RFC 4196	"SEED Cipher Algorithm and Its Use with IPsec" (proposed standard)
RFC 4270	"Attacks on Cryptographic Hashes in Internet Protocols" (informational RFC)
RFC 4312	"The Camellia Cipher Algorithm and Its Use with IPsec" (proposed standard)
RFC 4106	"Use of Galois Message Authentication Code (GMAC) in IPsec ESP" (proposed standard)
RFC 4359	"Use of RSA/SHA-1 Signatures Within ESP 2 and AH" (proposed standard)
RFC 4493	"AES-CMAC Algorithm" (informational RFC)
RFC 4494	"AES-CMAC-96 Algorithm and Its Use with IPsec" (proposed standard)
RFC 4615	"AES-CMAC-PRF-128 Algorithm for IKE" (proposed standard)
RFC 4634	"US Secure Hash Algorithms (SHA and HMAC-SHA)" (Informational RFC)
RFC 4231	"Identifiers and Test Vectors for HMAC-SHA-224, HMAC-SHA-256, HMAC-SHA-384, and HMAC-SHA-512" (proposed standard)

IPsec Policy-Handling RFCs

Table 15-5 lists various RFCs related to IPsec policy handling.

Table 15-5 *IPsec Policy-Handling RFCs*

RFC	Description
RFC 3585	"IPsec Configuration Policy Information Model" (proposed standard)
RFC 3586	"IP Security Policy Requirements" (proposed standard)

IPsec Modes

IPsec has two methods of propagating the data across a network:

- **Tunnel mode:** Protects data in network-to-network or site-to-site scenarios—for example, Network A in Site1 to Network B in Site2. In tunnel mode, IPsec protects data on behalf of other network entities—that is, encrypt traffic through IPsec peers. Tunnel mode encapsulates and protects the entire IP packet—the payload including the original IP header and a new IP header. In addition, the IPsec header is added as shown in Figure 15-1.

- **Transport mode:** Protects data in host-to-host or end-to-end scenarios—for example, Host A in Site1 to Host B in Site2. Transport mode is used for peer-to-peer scenarios only—that is, encrypt traffic between IPsec peers. In transport mode, IPsec protects the payload of the original IP datagram by excluding the IP header. Unlike tunnel mode, transport mode retains the original IP header and inserts the IPsec header between the original IP header and the payload, as shown in Figure 15-2. Transport mode is available only when the IPsec endpoints are the source and destination of the original IP datagram. Transport mode is commonly used by end systems to protect individual sockets or by intermediate systems to protect already tunneled traffic.

Both tunnel mode and transport mode can be deployed with ESP or AH protocols.

Figure 15-1 depicts how IPsec tunnels are established and how packets are encapsulated in tunnel mode.

Figure 15-1   *IPsec Tunnel Mode*

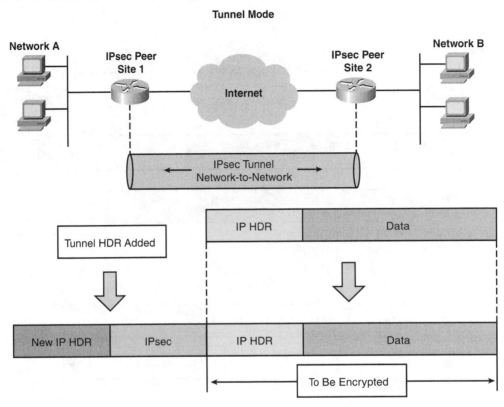

Figure 15-2 depicts how IPsec tunnels are established and how packets are encapsulated in transport mode.

Figure 15-2 *IPsec Transport Mode*

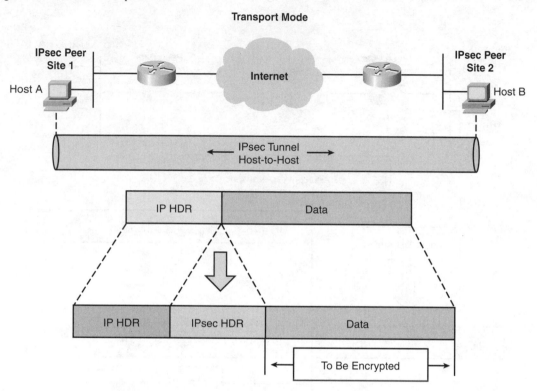

IPsec Protocol Headers

As illustrated in Figures 15-1 and 15-2, IPsec adds a new IPsec header to all IP datagrams to provide information for securing the data of the original IP datagram.

There are two types of IPsec headers:

- **Encapsulating Security Payload (ESP):** ESP is an IP-based protocol that uses IP port 50 for communication between IPsec peers. Figure 15-3 shows the ESP header format. ESP is used to protect the confidentiality, integrity, and authenticity of the data and offers anti-replay protection. ESP does not provide protection to the outer IP header, as shown in Figure 15-4. When used for data integrity, it does not include the invariant field in the IP header. ESP is documented in RFC 4303.

- **Authentication Header (AH):** AH is also an IP-based protocol that uses IP port 51 for communication between IPsec peers. Figure 15-5 shows the AH header format. AH is used to protect the integrity and authenticity of the data and offers anti-replay protection. Unlike ESP, AH provides protection to the IP header as shown in Figure 15-6. AH does not provide confidentiality protection. AH is documented in RFC 4302.

Figure 15-3 depicts the ESP header structure. Figure 15-4 shows the packet structure and the security services offered by the ESP protocol, illustrating which parts of the packet are authenticated and encrypted.

Figure 15-3 *ESP Header Structure*

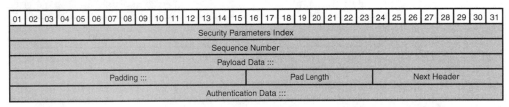

Figure 15-4 *ESP Security Services*

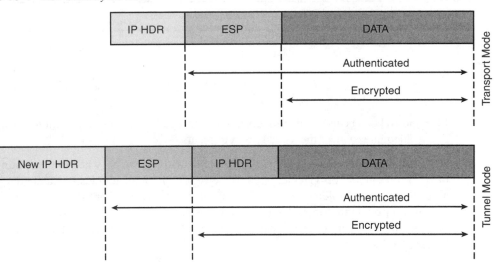

Figure 15-5 depicts the AH header structure, and Figure 15-6 shows the packet structure and the security services offered by the AH protocol, illustrating which parts of the packet are authenticated. As mentioned earlier, AH does not offer confidentiality.

Figure 15-5 *AH Header Structure*

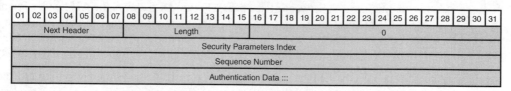

Figure 15-6 *AH Security Services*

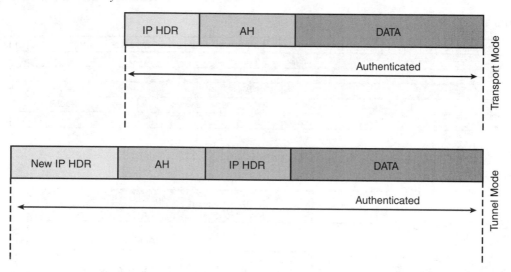

ESP and AH can be used either independently or together. In most applications, using only one is adequate to meet the security requirements.

IPsec architecture does not limit the use of individual algorithms when implementing ESP or AH protocol, but provides an open framework to implement industry standard algorithms. Most implementations of IPsec commonly use MD5 or SHA algorithms, which are used for data integrity and authentication. DES, 3DES, and AES, however, are the common protocols used for encryption. Several other algorithms are available, as discussed in Chapter 14.

IPsec Anti-Replay Service

Both ESP and AH protocols provide an anti-reply mechanism, which is mainly based on sequence numbers combined with authentication to defeat replay attacks. The sender increments the sequence number after each transmission, and the receiver can (optionally) check the sequence number and reject the packet if it is out of sequence.

Without the anti-replay mechanism, an intruder could sniff and replay intercepted encrypted packets to cause unnecessary floods, route flaps, and denial-of-service (DoS) attacks.

ISAKMP and IKE

IPsec requires secure key determination and key distribution mechanisms. The following two protocols define the framework for this:

- **Internet Security Association and Key Management Protocol (ISAKMP):** ISAKMP describes the framework for key management and defines the procedure and packet format necessary to establish, negotiate, modify, and delete security association (SA). ISAKMP offers the identification of the peers only. It does not offer a key exchange mechanism. ISAKMP is documented in RFC 2408, made obsolete by RFC 4306 (IKEv2).

- **IKE (Internet Key Exchange):** IKE is a hybrid protocol—a combination of ISAKMP, Oakley key exchange, and SKEME protocols—that defines a proper key exchange mechanism. IKE defines the mechanism for creating and exchanging keys. IKE derives authenticated keying material and negotiates SAs that are used for ESP and AH protocols. IKE uses UDP port 500. IKE is documented in RFC 2409, made obsolete by RFC 4306 (IKEv2).

NOTE   ISAKMP and IKE keywords are used interchangeably in IPsec papers. This chapter uses IKE as the standard convention.

Understanding IKE (Internet Key Exchange) Protocol

IKE is a two-phase, multimode protocol that offers three methods for authenticating a remote peer:

- **Preshared key:** Uses statically defined keys and is the most common method because of its ease of deployment; however, it is not a scalable and secure method.

- **Public key signature (rsa-signature):** The most secure method and requires Public Key Infrastructure (PKI) infrastructure.

- **Public key encryption (rsa-nonce):** Similar to public key signature, but requires prior knowledge of the peer's public key. This method has limited support.

IKE phase 1 verifies the identity of the remote peer, and two peers establish a secure, authenticated channel to communicate. IKE phase 1 also protects the negotiation of phase 2 communication.

IKE phase 1 negotiates the following:

- Techniques for protecting phase 1 itself (using crypto and hash algorithms)
- Session key generation parameters (using Diffie-Hellman groups)
- Authentication methods (using preshared, public key encryption, or digital signature)
- Keying material for IKE phase 2

At the end of phase 1 negotiation, a bidirectional ISAKMP/IKE SA (also known as phase 1 SA) is established for IKE communication.

IKE phase 1 has two modes:

- **Main mode:** The default method in most implementations. Main mode defines six message exchanges for establishing phase 1 SA. Figure 15-7 shows IKE phase 1 negotiation in main mode.
- **Aggressive mode:** A method faster than the main mode because it employs three message exchanges to establish phase 1 SA. Aggressive mode is faster but less secure, has fewer negotiation features, and does not provide identity protection. Figure 15-8 shows IKE phase 1 negotiation in aggressive mode.

Figure 15-7 *IKE Phase 1—Main Mode*

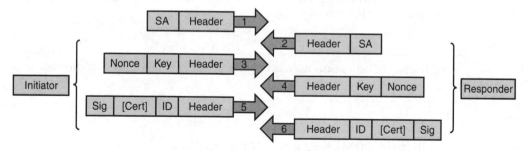

MSG 1: Initiator offers acceptable encryption and authentication algorithms (3DES, MD5, RSA)—for example the transform-set.
MSG 2: Responder presents acceptance of the proposal (or not).
MSG 3: Initiator Diffie-Helman key and nounce. (Key value is usually a number of 1024 bit length.)
MSG 4: Responder Diffie-Helman key and nounce.
MSG 5: Initiator signature, ID, and keys (maybe cert), for example authentication data.
MSG 6: Responder signature, ID and keys (maybe cert).

Figure 15-8   *IKE Phase 1—Aggressive Mode*

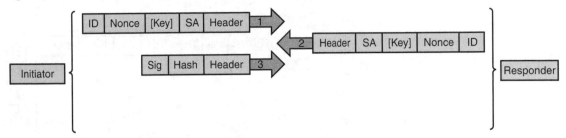

MSG 1:   Initiator key exchange, ID, nonce, parameter proposal
MSG 2:   Responder key exchange, ID, nonce, acceptable parameters
MSG 3:   Initiator signature, hash, ID

The information in Figure 15-7 and 15-8 is taken from the general Cisco security presentation on "Cisco IPsec VPN."

IKE phase 2 protects the user data and establishes SA for IPsec.

IKE phase 2 negotiates the following:

- Protection suite (using ESP and AH)

- Algorithms in the protection suite (using DES, 3DES, AES, SHA)

- Networks or IP traffic that is being protected (called proxy identities or phase 2 identities)

- Optional keying material for negotiated protocols

At the end of phase 2 negotiations, two unidirectional IPsec SAs (also known as Phase 2 SA) are established for user data—one for sending and another for receiving encrypted data.

IKE phase 2 has one mode—quick mode. Quick mode uses message exchanges to establish the phase 2 IPsec SA. Phase 2 SA is negotiated for given proxy or phase 2 identities and a given IPsec protocol (ESP). Multiple phase 2 SAs can be established under the same phase 1 SA. Figure 15-9 shows IKE phase 2 negotiation in quick mode.

Figure 15-9   *IKE Phase 2—Quick Mode*

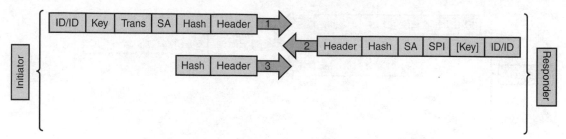

MSG 1:   Hash, SA proposal, IPsec transform, keying material, ID
          (proxy identities source and destination)
MSG 2:   Responder hash, agreed to SA proposal,
          Responder SPI, Key
MSG 3:   Hash to verify current and live peer

The information in Figure 15-9 is taken from general Cisco security presentation on "Cisco IPsec VPN."

The concept of an SA is that two devices have agreed on certain policy parameters to be used during their communications session. Therefore, SA is an agreement between two entities on a method to communicate securely. As mentioned earlier, each IKE phase has its own SAs; that is, Phase 1 has IKE/ISAKMP SA, and Phase 2 has IPsec SA. Figure 15-10 summarizes the two phases in IKE and the various modes.

IKEv2 (Internet Key Exchange—Version 2)

IKEv2 is the next version of the Internet Key Exchange protocol and is expected to be the new proposed standard. IKEv2 offers simpler message exchange with fewer complications and less overhead than its predecessor IKEv1. IKEv2 uses cryptographic mechanisms to protect its own packets that are similar to those used to protect the IP payloads in the IPsec stack ESP.

IKEv2 also uses sequence numbers and acknowledgments to provide reliability and state management and mandates few error-processing logistics.

Unlike IKEv1, which was susceptive to DoS attacks that resulted from processing bogus queries, thereby causing expensive cryptographic overhead, IKEv2 provides better attack resiliency because it addresses these issues by validating the requestor.

Figure 15-10 *IKE Two-Phase Multimode Protocol*

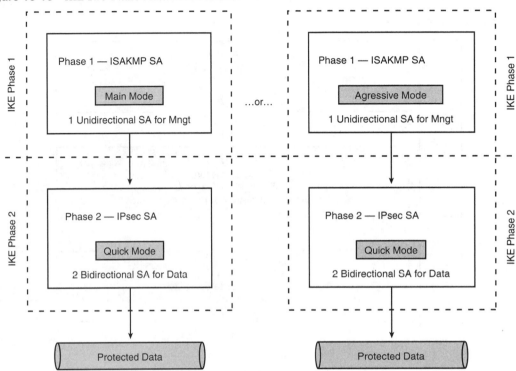

Single IPsec Tunnel = 1 IKE SA "+" 2 IPsec SAs

The following new features are included in IKEv2:

- IKE Dead Peer Detection as well as Initial Contact.

- NAT traversal support.

- No more aggressive mode; identities are always protected.

- Certs can be referenced through URL + hash to avoid fragmentation.

- EAP (MD-5, OTP, GTC) support.

- Remote address acquisition, New Config Payload (CP).

- Two kinds of SA: IKE_SA (the SA used by IKE itself) and CHILD_SA (the SA used by IPsec).

- Four kinds of message pairs: IKE_SA_INIT, IKE_AUTH, CREATE_CHILD_SA, INFORMATIONAL.

- New CP (Config Payload) payloads.

IKEv2 is documented in RFC 4306, which is coupled with other related RFCs to complete the IPsec framework.

Figure 15-11 shows how IKEv2 works, illustrating the process of the two new SA creations.

Figure 15-11 *How IKEv2 Works*

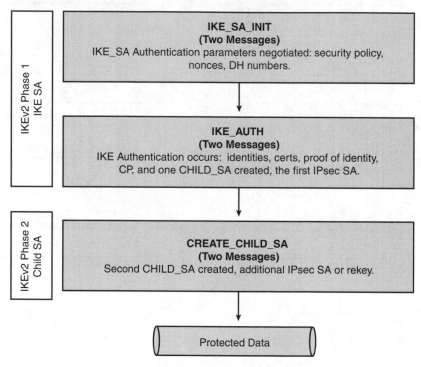

CAUTION IKEv2 does not provide downgrade protection; hence an attacker can force IKEv1 negotiation. Also note that IKEv2 is not backward compatible with IKEv1. IKEv2 does not interoperate with IKEv1.

Table 15-6 shows a summary comparison of IKEv1 and IKEv2.

Table 15-6 *IKEv1 and IKEv2 Comparison Chart*

	IKEv1	**IKEv2**
UDP port	500	500, 4500
Phases	Phase 1 (6/3 messages) Phase 2 (3 messages)	Phase 1 (4 messages) Phase 2 (2 messages)

Table 15-6 *IKEv1 and IKEv2 Comparison Chart (Continued)*

	IKEv1	**IKEv2**
Keepalives	No	Yes
Identity Hiding	Yes in main mode, No in aggressive mode	Yes
UDP/NAT	No	Yes
SA Negotiation	Responder selects initiator's proposal	Same as IKEV1, proposal structure simplified
Number of Msgs	6–9	4–8
EAP/CP	No	Yes

ISAKMP Profiles

The Internet Security Association and Key Management Protocol (ISAKMP) profile offers configuration modularity for IKE phase 1 negotiations. It allows mapping of ISAKMP parameters to IPsec tunnels. Applications of the ISAKMP profile include MPLS VPN configurations, router certificate management, and IPsec/QoS configurations.

ISAKMP profiles are commonly used when a device has two or more IPsec tunnels requiring different phase 1 parameters for different sites. The ISAKMP profile is also commonly used with Easy VPN Remote configurations and VRF-aware IPsec configurations.

An ISAKMP profile serves as a repository for IKE phase 1 and IKE phase 1.5 configurations for an individual or group of peers. The security parameters are applied to incoming IKE connections, which uniquely identify devices through the concept of "match identity" criteria. ISAKMP profiles allow you the flexibility to match parameters on a per-connection basis on various properties that are presented by incoming connections, such as a VPN client group name, a peer IP address, or a fully qualified domain name (FQDN), rather than just matching on the peer IP address. The ISAKMP profile applies parameters that are specific to each profile, such as trust points, peer identities, XAUTH AAA list, and keepalive.

Figure 15-12 shows the processing flowchart illustrating where the ISAKMP profile takes place in the IPsec tunnel establishment.

Figure 15-12 *ISAKMP Profile Flowchart*

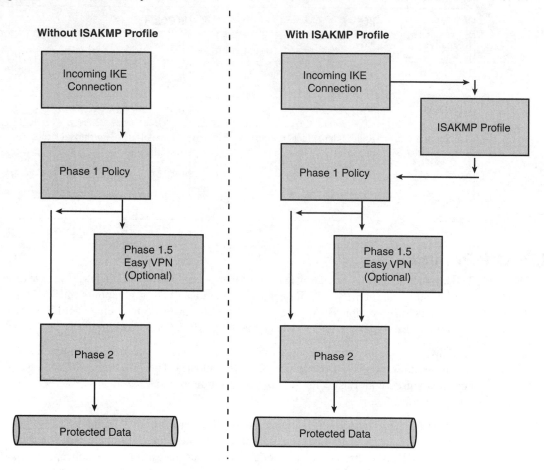

The information in Figure 15-12 is taken from the Cisco white paper on "ISAKMP Profile Overview" at http://www.cisco.com/en/US/products/ps6635/products_white_paper0900 aecd8034bd59.shtml.

NOTE The ISAKMP profile properties are applied as additional parameters to the ISAKMP policy configuration, as shown in Figure 15-12. Later sections of this chapter provide details of the ISAKMP profile parameters and configuration examples.

IPsec Profiles

The IPsec profile functionality was introduced to associate phase 2 SA parameters to a tunnel interface without using the crypto-map command. With the IPsec profile, encryption is performed after the generic routing encapsulation (GRE) is added to the tunnel packet. The **tunnel protection ipsec profile** command is used to associate an IPsec profile to a tunnel interface. The IPsec profile can be used in both of the following modes: point-to-point GRE (p-pGRE) and multipoint GRE (mGRE).

An IPsec profile can be used in various implementations; common examples include Dynamic Multipoint VPN (DMVPN) and Virtual Tunnel Interface (IPsec VTI) implementations. Configuration examples in this chapter will show how to implement IPsec profiles.

An IPsec profile concept is similar to crypto-map except that it does not require knowing its peer's address before establishing the tunnel. An IPsec profile does not use the **set peer** and **match address** commands. The IOS Software will obtain the **set peer** and **match address** parameters dynamically from the tunnel parameters and the Next Hop Resolution Protocol (NHRP) cache. For example, when a p-pGRE is used, the tunnel destination address will be used as the IPsec peer address, whereas when mGRE is used, multiple IPsec peers are possible. Hence, the corresponding NHRP mapping NBMA destination addresses will be used for the peer addresses. The profile must be applied on the tunnel interface on both sides of IPsec peers. The IPsec profile is a scalable approach and can be effectively used for varying requirements.

IPsec Virtual Tunnel Interface (IPsec VTI)

Cisco introduced the concept of using a dedicated IPsec interface called IPsec VTI (Virtual Tunnel Interface) for highly scalable IPsec-based VPNs. IPsec VTI provides a routable interface for terminating IPsec tunnels. VTI also allows the encrypting of multicast traffic with IPsec.

There are two types of IPsec VTI interfaces:

- **Static VTI (SVTI):** This can be used for site-to-site IPsec-based VPNs. SVTI is a point-to-point designated pathway across a shared media that encapsulates traffic with new packet headers and ensures encrypted packet delivery to specific destinations.

- **Dynamic VTI (DVTI):** This can be used for remote-access VPNs. The DVTI technology replaces dynamic crypto maps and the dynamic hub-and-spoke method for establishing tunnels. Dynamic VTI can be deployed for both the server and remote configurations. DVTI tunnels provide an on-demand separate virtual access interface for each VPN connection.

The router processes IPsec VTI interfaces in the same way it processes any other real interface where QoS, firewall, and other security services can be applied after the tunnel is active.

PKI consists of various protocols, services, and standards that support applications of the public key infrastructure.

The public key infrastructure assumes the use of the public key cryptography system, also known as asymmetric cryptography, which is based on two-key pairs: one key for encryption and another for decryption. Asymmetric cryptography standards and protocols are covered in greater detail in Chapter 14.

PKI Components

PKI components include the following:

- **Digital certificate (also known as identity certificate):** A digital certificate uses a digital signature to bind a public key with a user's identity to produce a public key certificate. A certificate contains information, such as the certificate validity period, peer identity information, encryption keys that are used for secure communications, and the signature of the issuing CA. A certificate is a digital equivalent of a passport.

- **Certificate Authority (CA):** A CA is the major component in the PKI system. The CA issues and verifies digital certificates. A certificate includes the public key that is bound to a user identity. A CA is also known as a trustpoint, which manages certificate requests and issues certificates to participating network devices. Many vendors offer CA Server solutions, including Cisco. The Cisco IOS Router can be configured as the certificate server. CA implementation can be either an in-house implementation or be outsourced.

- **Registration Authority (RA)(optional):** RAs provide an interface between the user and the CA. The RA acts as the verifier for the certificate authority before a digital certificate is issued to a requestor.

- **Directory service:** The certificates with their public keys are held in directory services.

- **Certificate Revocation List (CRL):** The CRL is a list of serial numbers of revoked certificates. A CA revokes certificates that are no longer used and publishes the CRL.

- **Simple Certificate Enrollment Protocol (SCEP):** SCEP is a Cisco proprietary certificate enrollment protocol used on network devices to obtain digital certificates from the CA server. SCEP uses HTTP to communicate with the CA or RA. SCEP is the most commonly used method for sending and receiving requests and certificates.

NOTE   The term PKI is interchangeably used for both the CA and CA-related components.

Certificate Enrollment

Certificate enrollment is the process of obtaining a certificate from a CA server. Each peer participating in the PKI must enroll with a CA. A number of methods are available for certificate enrollment, such as SCEP, PKCS12, IOS File System (IFS), and Manual (cut-and-paste). Figure 15-15 illustrates the certificate enrollment process.

Figure 15-15   *Certificate Enrollment Process*

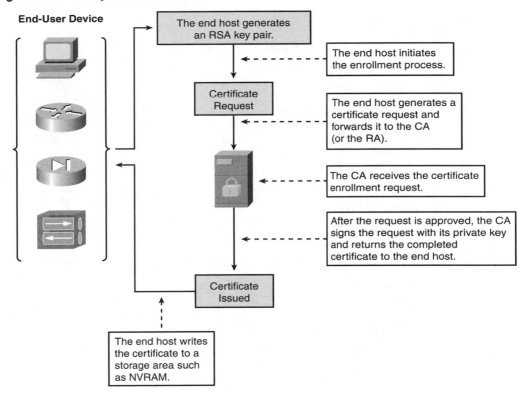

TIP   Refer to this Cisco documentation URL to learn more about certificate enrollment for a PKI and the methods available for certificate enrollment: http://www.cisco.com/en/US/ products/ps6350/products_configuration_guide_chapter09186a00804a5a17.html.

The format of a public key certificate is defined by the ITU-T based X.509 standard for a public key infrastructure. The structure format of an X.509 v3 digital certificate contains the following elements:

- Version

- Serial Number

- Algorithm ID

- Issuer

- Validity

- Subject

- Subject Public Key Info

- Issuer Unique Identifier (Optional)

- Subject Unique Identifier (Optional)

- Extensions (Optional)

- Certificate Signature Algorithm

- Certificate Signature

Example 15-1 shows a standard X.509 v3 certificate.

Example 15-1 *Standard X.509 v3 Certificate*

```
Version: 3 (0x2)
Serial Number: 2 (0x2)
Signature Algorithm: shaWithRSAEncryption
Issuer: CN=ca
Validity
    Not Before: Nov 19 02:41:41 2004 GMT
    Not After : Nov 19 02:41:41 2007 GMT
Subject: CN=myRouter.cisco.com
Subject Public Key Info:
    Public Key Algorithm: rsaEncryption
    RSA Public Key: (1024 bit)
        Modulus (1024 bit):
            00:94:a8:db:8d:f5:9b:21:c4:47:de:9e:db:84:32:
    b3:f0:ff:f2:30:dc:82:05:0e:4c:19:a8:0b:7c:d1:
    04:3e:82:b6:8d:5c:e6:59:0a:26:23:f5:23:41:78:
    75:cf:03:2e:52:45:e7:2d:4a:78:08:29:ea:8a:44:
    e5:96:ea:b6:2f:7b:71:14:3d:ec:33:b2:cd:75:01:
    49:14:da:72:9c:25:6e:72:a0:aa:60:85:37:2e:57:
    f0:2f:c5:c6:e3:57:17:b2:7a:fd:fb:58:98:2f:5f:
    9e:22:dd:62:f8:55:fa:74:fd:3e:38:66:e7:d9:78:
    df:f0:c1:a0:ae:f3:9c:e1:39
        Exponent: 65537 (0x10001)
71:b1:a5:01:ad:fb:73:20:57:57:b0:54:fc:04:2e:5e:31:ae:69:40:c0:
cf:93:b4:7a:5f:[........]
```

TIP In Chapter 14, Figure 14-4 depicts how the asymmetric key encryption process works as it uses the two keys known as public and private keys. Figure 14-6 in Chapter 14 illustrates how the cryptographic keyed-hash algorithm works.

Table 15-7 exemplifies the use of public and private keys in the PKI framework.

Table 15-7   *Public and Private Key Functions*

Function	Key-Type
To send an encrypted message	Use the receiver's public key
To decrypt an encrypted message	Use the receiver's private key
To send an encrypted signature	Use the sender's private key
To decrypt an encrypted signature (and authenticate the sender)	Use the sender's public key

Implementing IPsec VPN

The IPsec VPN framework provides network data encryption at the IP packet level (Layer 3), building scalable, highly secure, standards-based security solutions. IPsec provides data confidentiality, integrity, authentication, and anti-replay services. IPsec VPN is currently the only way to implement secure VPNs. The following sections provide guidelines for implementing IPsec VPN scenarios while using these IKE and IPsec standards.

Cisco IPsec VPN Implementations

Cisco offers extensive portfolios for IPsec VPN implementations on a wide range of products, including Cisco Routers, Catalyst 6500 Series Switches, Cisco ASA 5500 Series Adaptive Security Appliances, PIX 500 Series Firewall Appliances, and VPN3000 Concentrator Series Appliances.

The IPsec VPN is fully compliant with industry standards and best practices on all Cisco devices and can be implemented between any-to-any Cisco or non-Cisco devices.

IPsec VPN solutions can be divided into two major categories:

- Site-to-Site IPsec VPN
  - ☐ Full Mesh
  - ☐ Hub-and-Spoke
  - ☐ DMVPN
  - ☐ Static VTI
  - ☐ GET VPN
- Remote Access IPsec VPN
  - ☐ Easy VPN
  - ☐ Dynamic VTI

NOTE Dynamic Multipoint VPN (DMVPN) is discussed in Chapter 16, and Group Encrypted Transport (GET VPN) is discussed in Chapter 17.

Figure 15-16 depicts common IPsec VPN implementation scenarios.

Figure 15-16 *IPsec VPN Implementation Scenarios*

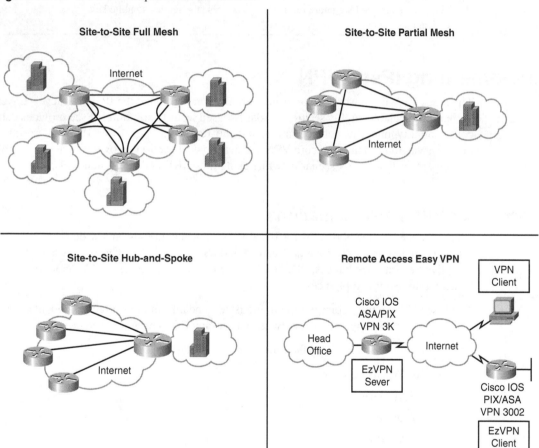

Table 15-8 is a quick comparison chart to show the various IPsec VPN implementation scenarios.

Table 15-8   *IPsec VPN Implementations Comparison Chart*

	Regular Crypto Maps	GRE/IPsec	DMVPN	Static VTI	Dynamic VTI	EzVPN
Standard	RFC compliant	Yes, but uncommon	Yes, but uncommon	Yes, but uncommon	Yes, but uncommon	No
Main advantage	Basic, simple	Reroutes, deterministic convergence	Simple to deploy	Reroutes, deterministic convergence	Per tunnel features, dial integration	Simple to deploy
Main disadvantage	Basic, simple	Peers per device	Always active (no dialup)	Peers per device	New— limited experience	Hard to debug
Best used with	Non-IOS peers	Network-to-network	Hub-and-spoke/ partial meshes	Network-to-network	Remote access	Remote access
Multicast support	No	Yes	Yes	Yes	Yes	No
IPv6 support	Not yet available	Inside only	No	Inside outside	Depends on client	No

Site-to-Site IPsec VPN

Site-to-site IPsec VPN offers integrated network intelligence and routing capabilities to deliver reliable transport mechanisms for complex mission-critical traffic, without compromising communications quality.

Site-to-site IPsec VPN provides an Internet-based WAN solution to securely connect remote offices, branch offices, home offices, or partner sites to central sites by using cost-effective Internet access rather than expensive dedicated WAN links, leased lines, or Frame Relay circuits.

Site-to-site IPsec VPN extends network resources by reducing WAN bandwidth costs while increasing connectivity speeds and maintaining quality and reliability over the Internet-based IPsec VPN solutions.

Site-to-site IPsec VPN also extends customized solutions, such as DMVPN, Routed GRE, and GET VPN technologies to cater to diverse network designs in full-mesh, hub-and-spoke, or any-to-any intersite connectivity environments.

Figure 15-17 illustrates a basic site-to-site IPsec tunnel establishment, and depicts the five-step modular flow, showing how an IPsec tunnel is established.

Figure 15-17 *Site-to-Site IPsec Tunnel (Five-Steps Model)*

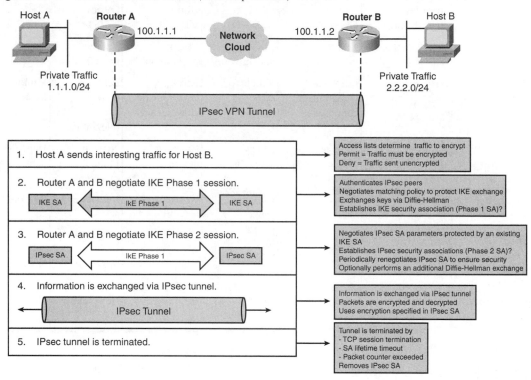

Based on Figure 15-17, Examples 15-2 and 15-3 show a basic site-to-site router-to-router IPsec configuration on Cisco IOS routers. The configuration shows the use of the ISAKMP profile with traditional crypto-map-based IPsec configurations.

Example 15-2 *Configuring Site-to-Site IPsec—Router A*

```
hostname RouterA
!
<..>
! Define Key-ring with the pre-shared key for individual spokes
crypto keyring spokes
  pre-shared-key address 100.1.1.2 0.0.0.0 key cisco123
!
! Define Phase 1 SA parameters
crypto isakmp policy 10
 encr 3des
 authentication pre-share
 group 2
```

Example 15-2 *Configuring Site-to-Site IPsec—Router A (Continued)*

```
!
! Define ISAKMP profile for Lan-to-Lan spoke connection
crypto isakmp profile isakmpprofile
   description LAN-to-LAN for spoke router connection
   keyring spokes
   match identity address 100.1.1.2
!
! Define IPsec encryption and authentication algorithms
crypto ipsec transform-set mytransformset esp-3des esp-sha-hmac
!
! Define Phase 2 SA parameters
crypto map cisco 10 ipsec-isakmp
 set peer 100.1.1.2
 set transform-set mytransformset
 set isakmp-profile isakmpprofile
 match address 101
!
! Crypto map applied to outbound interface
interface GigabitEthernet0/0
 ip address 100.1.1.1 255.255.255.0
 crypto map cisco
!
! Interface that is connected to the private side of the network for encryption
interface GigabitEthernet0/1
 ip address 1.1.1.1 255.255.255.0
!
! Define Access-list for IPsec interesting traffic, (mirrored ACL)
access-list 101 permit ip 1.1.1.0 0.0.0.255 2.2.2.0 0.0.0.255
!
! Ensure routing is configured for remote private network (static or dynamic)
ip route 2.2.2.0 255.255.255.0 100.1.1.2
<..>
```

Example 15-3 *Configuring Site-to-Site IPsec—Router B*

```
hostname RouterB
!
<..>
! Define Key-ring with the pre-shared key for individual spokes
crypto keyring spokes
   pre-shared-key address 100.1.1.1 0.0.0.0 key cisco123
!
! Define Phase 1 SA parameters
crypto isakmp policy 10
 encr 3des
 authentication pre-share
 group 2
!
! Define ISAKMP profile for Lan-to-Lan spoke connection
crypto isakmp profile isakmpprofile
   description LAN-to-LAN for spoke router connection
```

continues

Example 15-3   *Configuring Site-to-Site IPsec—Router B (Continued)*

```
      keyring spokes
      match identity address 100.1.1.1
 !
 ! Define IPsec encryption and authentication algorithms
 crypto ipsec transform-set mytransformset esp-3des esp-sha-hmac
 !
 ! Define Phase 2 SA parameters
 crypto map cisco 10 ipsec-isakmp
  set peer 100.1.1.1
  set transform-set mytransformset
  set isakmp-profile isakmpprofile
  match address 101
 !
 ! Crypto map applied to outbound interface
 interface GigabitEthernet0/0
  ip address 100.1.1.2 255.255.255.0
  crypto map cisco
 !
 ! Interface that is connected to the private side of the network for encryption
 interface GigabitEthernet0/1
  ip address 2.2.2.2 255.255.255.0
 !
 ! Define Access-list for IPsec interesting traffic (mirrored ACL)
 access-list 101 permit ip 2.2.2.0 0.0.0.255 1.1.1.0 0.0.0.255
 !
 ! Ensure routing is configured for remote private network (static or dynamic)
 ip route 1.1.1.0 255.255.255.0 100.1.1.1
 <..>
```

The ISAKMP preshared key in Examples 15-2 and 15-3 is appearing in clear text (not encrypted). Cisco IOS 12.3(2)T code introduced a new functionality that encrypts the ISAKMP preshared key in secure type 6 format in IOS Router configuration by using the Advance Encryption Standard (AES) symmetric cipher. Hence, when a **show running-config** command is executed, the ISAKMP preshared key is displayed in encrypted format.

Two new IOS commands were introduced to achieve this. Use the **key config-key password-encrypt** command and the **password encryption aes** command to configure and enable this feature. The password configured in the **key config-key password-encryption** command is the master encryption password that is used to encrypt all other keys in the router configuration. The master key is not stored in the router configuration and cannot be seen or obtained in any way while connected to the router.

Refer to the Cisco technical documentation URL that follows for more information and a configuration example of encrypting the ISAKMP preshared keys in Cisco IOS Router configuration: http://www.cisco.com/en/US/tech/tk583/tk372/ technologies_configuration_example09186a00801f2336.shtml.

Refer to the following Cisco technical documentation for additional configuration examples of configuring IPsec VPN solutions on Cisco devices:

http://www.cisco.com/en/US/tech/tk583/tk372/tech_configuration_examples_list.html

http://www.cisco.com/en/US/products/ps6635/prod_white_papers_list.html

Remote Access IPsec VPN

There are two primary methods of deploying Remote Access VPN technology:

- **Remote Access:** IPsec VPN
- **Remote Access:** Secure Sockets Layer (SSL) VPN

Both solutions can be deployed together or individually to better address the deployment requirements. Both solutions will offer access to any data, application, or network resource on the central site. Selecting the appropriate method depends on the deployment requirements and the network architecture; therefore, Remote Access VPN can be deployed using IPsec VPN, SSL VPN, or both.

Both technologies are offered by Cisco security solutions as part of the security products portfolio.

NOTE This chapter primarily covers IPsec-based VPN solutions. Non-IPsec-based SSL VPN is covered separately in Chapter 18, "Secure Sockets Layer VPN (SSL VPN)."

Remote Access IPsec VPN provides a flexible, low-cost Internet-based remote solution to connect remote users and teleworkers by providing network reachability to anyone, anyplace, and anytime. The Remote Access IPsec VPN solution extends virtually any data, voice, or video application securely to the remote desktop. Without adding complexity to the existing network, it offers access to network applications or resources when and where required.

The remote access user experiences a virtual environment that emulates a working condition of the main office with no geographical boundaries.

As discussed previously, Remote Access IPsec VPN can be implemented in two methods:

- Cisco Easy VPN
- Dynamic VTI (DVTI)

Cisco Easy VPN

Cisco Easy VPN (also referred as EzVPN) is a unified framework used to deploy simplified remote access point-to-point VPN solutions for remote users, remote offices, and teleworkers. Cisco Easy VPN offers centralized VPN management, dynamic policy distribution, and effortless provisioning, thus reducing deployment complexity and increased scalability and flexibility.

Cisco Easy VPN solution allows you to define centralized security policies at the head-end VPN device, which are then pushed to the remote site VPN device upon connection.

The Cisco Easy VPN solution is available on all Cisco security VPN devices, including Cisco IOS Routers, Cisco ASA 5500 Series Adaptive Security Appliances, PIX 500 Series Firewall Appliances, and VPN3000 Concentrator Series Appliances, with consistent policy and key management methods that simplify deployment and management.

Cisco Easy VPN can be deployed in one of the following ways:

- **Easy VPN Software Client:** This client is the traditional remote VPN implementation where remote mobile users terminate VPN connections directly to the head-end VPN server.
- **Easy VPN Hardware Client:** With this client, a pseudo site-to-site VPN connection is established between two network devices emulating a LAN-to-LAN scenario. The remote end-user client behind the LAN is unaware of the VPN setup and does not require establishment of an individual VPN connection. Traffic flows encrypted between the VPN peers.

Figure 15-18 illustrates the two types of Easy VPN implementations.

Figure 15-18   *Cisco Easy VPN Deployment Types*

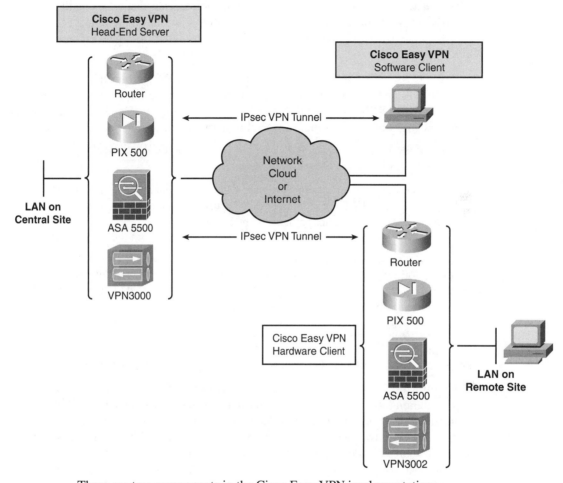

There are two components in the Cisco Easy VPN implementation:

- **Cisco Easy VPN Server**: Easy VPN Server acts as the VPN head-end device emulating a pseudo site-to-site VPN scenario, where the remote site devices are using the Cisco Easy VPN Remote client feature. The Easy VPN Server can be enabled and configured on Cisco IOS Routers (minimum Cisco IOS Software Release 12.2(8)T is required), Cisco PIX and ASA Security Appliances, and Cisco VPN 3000 Concentrators. Security policies are defined at the VPN head-end device and pushed to the remote VPN device when connected. See Figure 15-18.

Additionally, Easy VPN Server can act as the VPN head-end device terminating VPN tunnels initiated by mobile remote users that are using the Cisco VPN Client software. This flexibility allows mobile and remote workers to access any data and applications on the central site. See Figure 15-18.

- **Cisco Easy VPN Client (also referred to as Easy VPN Remote):** The Cisco Easy VPN Remote Client feature allows a remote device to receive security policies from the head-end VPN server when the tunnel is established. The Easy VPN Remote client is easy to set up, with minimal configuration required at the remote client site.

  Cisco Easy VPN Remote Software Client is available on Windows, Macintosh, Linux, and Solaris platforms.

  The Cisco Easy VPN Remote Hardware Client is available on Cisco IOS Routers, Cisco PIX 501 and 506E, ASA Security Appliances, and Cisco VPN 3002 Hardware Clients. See Figure 15-18.

TIP   Refer to the following Cisco URL to download Cisco VPN software. Note that strong cryptographic encryption access is required to download Cisco VPN Software: http://www.cisco.com/kobayashi/sw-center/sw-vpn.shtml.

The Cisco Easy VPN Remote Client has the following three modes of operation:

- **Client Mode (also known as PAT mode):** Specifies that Network Address Translation (NAT) or Port Address Translation (PAT) be employed to hide all devices behind the remote site from those on the server site. All traffic from the remote site hosts on the private network appears on the network site behind the server site with a single source IP address that is assigned to the IKE peer. This IP address is the one central server site that the VPN peer assigns to the remote site VPN peer. In client mode, traffic cannot be initiated from a host on the private network at the server site. The IPsec SA for this IP address is automatically created by the Easy VPN Remote Client device. This IP address is also commonly used for troubleshooting (by using ping, Telnet, and Secure Shell).

- **Network Extension Mode:** Specifies that the hosts at the remote site of the Easy VPN tunnel should be given IP addresses that are fully routable and reachable by the central server site network over the IPsec tunnel. These IP addresses can either be on the same subnet as the server site network or on a separate subnet, assuming that the server site routers are configured to correctly route those subnets over the IPsec tunnel. PAT is not used in this scenario, thereby allowing the remote site hosts to have direct access to the hosts on the server network.

- **Network Extension Plus+ Mode:** Is identical to the previous network extension mode, with the additional capability of being able to request an IP address via mode configuration.

All the previously described modes optionally support the Split-Tunnel feature. By default, all remote site client traffic is routed and tunneled through the VPN server. Split-tunneling allows you to control more granularly which specific hosts or subnets can traverse the IPsec tunnel. Networks and hosts defined in the Split-Tunnel ACL will be encrypted and sent via the tunnel, and all other traffic goes unencrypted in clear text (without applying IPsec) through the local egress interface based on the routing table. Example 15-4 shows how to configure split tunneling for specific subnets using an ACL.

Figure 15-19 illustrates a traditional hardware-based Cisco Easy VPN IPsec scenario that uses Cisco IOS Routers for both the client and the server.

Figure 15-19 *Implementing Hardware-Based Cisco Easy VPN on Cisco Routers*

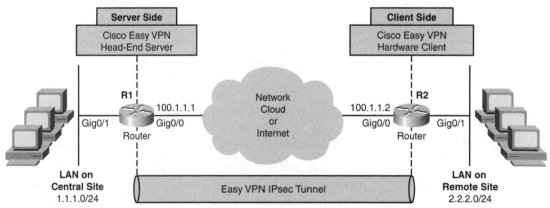

Based on Figure 15-19, Examples 15-4 and 15-5 show a traditional Cisco Easy VPN configuration on Cisco IOS Routers.

The server side configuration, hostname R1, in Example 15-4 shows the Extended Authentication (XAUTH) and Split-Tunnel features being used.

The client-side configuration, hostname R2, in Example 15-5 shows Network Extension mode being used.

Example 15-4 *Configuring Hardware-Based Cisco Easy VPN (Head-End Server Router)*

```
hostname R1
!
! Enable AAA for XAUTH
aaa new-model
aaa authentication login vpnauthen local
aaa authorization network vpnauthor local
!
```

continues

Example 15-4 *Configuring Hardware-Based Cisco Easy VPN (Head-End Server Router) (Continued)*

```
! Define Username credentials for XAUTH
username cisco password cisco
!
! Define Phase 1 SA parameters
crypto isakmp policy 10
 encr 3des
 authentication pre-share
 group 2
!
crypto isakmp client configuration address-pool local vpnpool
crypto isakmp xauth timeout 60
!
! Define Easy VPN Remote Group Parameters & Split-Tunnel ACL#
crypto isakmp client configuration group easyvpn
 key cisco123
 dns 1.2.3.4
 wins 1.2.3.4
 domain cisco.com
 pool vpnpool
 acl 101
!
!
! Define IPsec encryption and authentication algorithms
crypto ipsec transform-set mytransformset esp-3des esp-sha-hmac
!
! Define Phase 2 SA parameters
crypto dynamic-map mydynmap 10
 set transform-set mytransformset
 reverse-route
!
crypto map mydynmap client authentication list vpnauthen
crypto map mydynmap isakmp authorization list vpnauthor
crypto map mydynmap client configuration address respond
crypto map cisco 10 ipsec-isakmp dynamic mydynmap
!
!
! Crypto map applied to outbound interface
interface GigabitEthernet0/0
 ip address 100.1.1.1 255.255.255.0
 crypto map cisco
!
! Interface that is connected to the private side of the network for encryption
interface GigabitEthernet0/1
 ip address 1.1.1.1 255.255.255.0
!
! Define IP pool for VPN connected Users
ip local pool vpnpool 172.16.1.1 172.16.1.254
ip route 0.0.0.0 0.0.0.0 GigabitEthernet0/0
!
! Define ACL for Split-Tunnel
```

Example 15-4 *Configuring Hardware-Based Cisco Easy VPN (Head-End Server Router) (Continued)*

```
access-list 101 permit ip 1.1.1.0 0.0.0.255 any
!
<..>
```

Example 15-5 *Configuring Hardware-Based Cisco Easy VPN (Client Router)*

```
hostname R2
<..>
!
! Define Easy VPN Remote Group Parameters
crypto ipsec client ezvpn myeasyvpn
 connect auto
 group easyvpn key cisco123
 mode network-extension
 peer 100.1.1.1
 username cisco password cisco
 xauth userid mode local
!
! Define Easy VPN Outside Interface
interface GigabitEthernet0/0
 ip address 100.1.1.2 255.255.255.0
 crypto ipsec client ezvpn myeasyvpn outside
!
! Define Easy VPN Inside Interface
interface GigabitEthernet0/1
 ip address 2.2.2.2 255.255.255.0
 crypto ipsec client ezvpn myeasyvpn inside
!
<..>
```

TIP   Refer to the following Cisco technical documentation for additional Easy VPN configuration examples: http://www.cisco.com/en/US/products/ps6635/products_data_sheet09186a00801541d5.html#wp1067163.

Dynamic VTI (DVTI)

Cisco introduced the Dynamic Virtual Tunnel Interface (VTI) method for scalable Remote Access IPsec-based VPN. DVTI is an enhanced method and can be used in Cisco Easy VPN Server and Remote Client implementations. As mentioned previously, the DVTI technology will replace the traditional dynamic crypto maps and the dynamic hub-and-spoke method for establishing tunnels. DVTI technology combined with Cisco Easy VPN will provide highly secure connectivity for Remote Access VPN.

One of the important characteristics of the DVTI is that it provides an on-demand unique virtual access interface for each remote VPN connection that is cloned from a virtual template configuration, which inherits the IPsec configuration and any other features configured on the virtual template interface, such as NAT, QoS, NetFlow, or ACLs. This allows the configuring of varying security policies for different remote access connections. DVTI with Easy VPN provides a routable interface for forwarding traffic based on IP routing tables.

Figure 15-20 illustrates the enhanced Cisco Easy VPN with IPsec DVTI scenario using Cisco IOS Routers for both client and server.

Figure 15-20 *Implementing Cisco Easy VPN with IPsec DVTI on Cisco Routers*

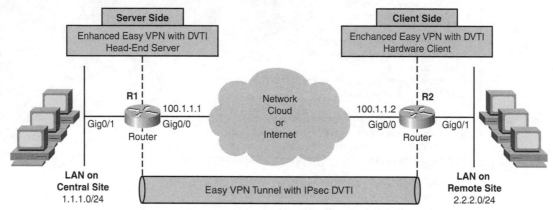

Based on Figure 15-20, Examples 15-6 and 15-7 show the enhanced Cisco Easy VPN with IPsec DVTI configuration method on Cisco IOS routers.

The server-side configuration, hostname R1, in Example 15-6 shows that ISAKMP profile, IPsec profile, Extended Authentication (XAUTH) and Split-Tunnel features are being used.

The client-side configuration in Example 15-7 shows client mode (PAT mode), hostname R2, is being used on the client router. With the enhancement in client mode operation, the dynamic IP address that is assigned to the client router from the server pool is automatically assigned to an available Loopback interface, and Easy VPN Remote Router automatically creates a corresponding IPsec SA for this IP address.

Example 15-6 *Configuring Cisco Easy VPN with IPsec DVTI (Server Router)*

```
hostname R1
!
! Enable AAA for XAUTH
aaa new-model
aaa authentication login default local
aaa authorization network default local
!
ip cef
! Define Username credentials for XAUTH
username cisco privilege 15 password 0 cisco
```

Example 15-6   *Configuring Cisco Easy VPN with IPsec DVTI (Server Router) (Continued)*

```
!
!
policy-map test123
 class class-default
  shape average 1280000
!
!
! Define Phase 1 SA parameters
crypto isakmp policy 10
 encr 3des
 authentication pre-share
 group 2
crypto isakmp key cisco123 address 0.0.0.0 0.0.0.0
crypto isakmp keepalive 10
!
! Define Easy VPN Remote Group Parameters & Split-Tunnel ACL#
crypto isakmp client configuration group cisco
 key cisco
 dns 1.2.3.4
 wins 1.2.3.4
 domain cisco.com
 pool dvtipool
 acl 101
!
! Define ISAKMP profile and bind parameters
crypto isakmp profile myisakmpprofile
 match identity group cisco
 isakmp authorization list default
 client configuration address respond
 virtual-template 1
!
!
! Define IPsec encryption and authentication algorithms
crypto ipsec transform-set mytransformset esp-3des esp-sha-hmac
!
! Define Phase 2 IPsec profile and bind parameters
crypto ipsec profile myipsecprofile
 set transform-set mytransformset
 set isakmp-profile myisakmpprofile
!
interface GigabitEthernet0/0
 ip address 100.1.1.1 255.255.255.0
!
interface GigabitEthernet0/1
 ip address 1.1.1.1 255.255.255.0
!
! Define Virtual Template for DVTI cloning & apply IPsec profile
interface Virtual-Template1 type tunnel
 ip unnumbered GigabitEthernet0/0
 tunnel source GigabitEthernet0/0
 tunnel mode ipsec ipv4
 tunnel protection ipsec profile myipsecprofile
```

continues

Example 15-6 *Configuring Cisco Easy VPN with IPsec DVTI (Server Router) (Continued)*

```
 service-policy output test123
!
! Define IP pool for VPN connected Users
ip local pool dvtipool 172.16.1.1 172.16.1.254
ip route 0.0.0.0 0.0.0.0 GigabitEthernet0/0
!
!
! Define ACL for Split-Tunnel
access-list 101 permit ip 1.1.1.0 0.0.0.255 any
!
<..>
```

Example 15-7 *Configuring Cisco Easy VPN with IPsec DVTI (Client Router)*

```
hostname R2
!
no aaa new-model
!
ip cef
username cisco privilege 15 password 0 cisco
!
policy-map test123
 class class-default
  shape average 128000
!
crypto isakmp policy 10
 encr 3des
 authentication pre-share
 group 2
!
crypto isakmp key cisco123 address 0.0.0.0 0.0.0.0
crypto isakmp keepalive 10
!
!
! Define Easy VPN Remote Group Parameters
crypto ipsec client ezvpn mydvtieasyvpn
 connect auto
 group cisco key cisco
 local-address GigabitEthernet0/0
 mode client
 peer 100.1.1.1
 username cisco password cisco
 xauth userid mode local
!
!
! Define Easy VPN Outside Interface
interface GigabitEthernet0/0
 ip address 100.1.1.2 255.255.255.0
 ip virtual-reassembly
 crypto ipsec client ezvpn mydvtieasyvpn
!
```

Example 15-7 *Configuring Cisco Easy VPN with IPsec DVTI (Client Router) (Continued)*

```
! Define Easy VPN Inside Interface
interface GigabitEthernet0/1
 ip address 2.2.2.2 255.255.255.0
 ip virtual-reassembly
 crypto ipsec client ezvpn mydvtieasyvpn inside
!
! Define Virtual Template for DVTI cloning
interface Virtual-Template1 type tunnel
 no ip address
 ip virtual-reassembly
 tunnel mode ipsec ipv4
 service-policy output test123
!
ip route 0.0.0.0 0.0.0.0 GigabitEthernet0/0
!
<..>
```

Summary

With the exponential growth and use of the Internet for IP transport, secure encrypted communication is essential to the protection of sensitive data that traverses insecure communication channels.

IPsec VPN is a standard framework that provides secure access to information with integrity, authenticity, and confidentiality. IPsec VPN provides protection for IP traffic at the network layer of the OSI model. The IPsec framework is the most common and the only available secure VPN framework solution.

The chapter provided a basic overview of various types of IPsec VPN technologies and deployments. The chapter also presented a detailed list of IPsec-related RFCs, IPsec modes, IPsec protocol headers, and a detailed understanding of ISAKMP, IKE, and IKEv2.

In addition, the chapter explained the concept of using a dedicated IPsec interface called IPsec VTI—Virtual Tunnel Interface.

The chapter also described the PKI by giving details of PKI standards, components, the certificate enrollment process, and the format of the X.509 certificate.

The major focus of the chapter is the Cisco IPsec VPN implementations. Two types of IPsec VPN implementations were discussed: the site-to-site and Remote Access VPN.

The chapter provided extensive details on how to implement site-to-site and Remote Access VPN using various illustrations, diagrams, and sample configurations.

References

http://www.vpnc.org/vpn-standards.html

http://en.wikipedia.org/wiki/IPsec

http://www.networksorcery.com/enp/protocol/ah.htm

http://www.networksorcery.com/enp/protocol/esp.htm

http://www.cisco.com/go/ipsec

http://en.wikipedia.org/wiki/Public_key_infrastructure

http://searchsecurity.techtarget.com/sDefinition/0,,sid14_gci214299,00.html

http://www.cisco.com/en/US/products/ps6635/products_white_paper0900aecd
8034bd59.shtml

http://www.cisco.com/en/US/netsol/ns340/ns394/ns171/ns142/networking_solutions_
sub_solution_home.html

http://www.cisco.com/en/US/products/sw/iosswrel/ps5207/products_feature_guide
09186a008041faef.html

http://www.cisco.com/go/easyvpn

http://www.cisco.com/en/US/netsol/ns340/ns394/ns171/ns125/
networking_solutions_sub_solution_home.html

http://www.cisco.com/en/US/products/ps6659/products_ios_protocol_option_home.html

http://www.cisco.com/en/US/products/ps6635/products_data_sheet
09186a00801541d5.html

http://www.cisco.com/en/US/netsol/ns340/ns394/ns171/ns142/
netbr09186a00801f0a72.html

http://www.cisco.com/en/US/tech/tk583/tk372/technologies_white_paper0900
aecd8029d629.shtml

http://www.cisco.com/en/US/products/ps6635 products_white_paper0900
aecd803645b5.shtml

CHAPTER 16

Dynamic Multipoint VPN (DMVPN)

VPN-based security solutions are increasingly popular and have proven to be an effective and secure technology for protecting sensitive data that is traversing insecure channel mediums, such as the Internet.

Traditional IPsec-based site-to-site, hub-to-spoke VPN deployment models do not scale well and are adequate only for small- and medium-sized networks. As demand for IPsec-based VPN implementation grows, organizations with large-scale enterprise networks require scalable and dynamic IPsec solutions that interconnect sites across the Internet with reduced latency, while optimizing network performance and bandwidth utilization.

The Dynamic Multipoint VPN (DMVPN) technology is used for scaling IPsec VPN networks by offering a large-scale IPsec VPN deployment model that allows the network to expand and realize its full potential. DMVPN offers scalability that enables zero-touch deployment models.

This chapter provides a complete overview of the DMVPN solution architecture, implementation, and various deployment scenarios.

DMVPN Solution Architecture

DMVPN allows IPsec VPN networks to better scale hub-to-spoke and spoke-to-spoke designs, thereby optimizing performance and reducing latency for communications between sites.

DMVPN offers a wide range of benefits, including the following:

- The capability to build dynamic hub-to-spoke and spoke-to-spoke IPsec tunnels
- Optimized network performance
- Reduced latency for real-time applications
- Reduced router configuration on the hub that provides the capability to dynamically add multiple spoke tunnels without touching the hub configuration
- Automatic triggering of IPsec encryption by virtue of GRE tunnel source and destination assuring zero packet loss

- Support for spoke routers with dynamic physical interface IP addresses (for example, DSL and cable connections)

- The capability to establish dynamic and direct spoke-to-spoke IPsec tunnels for communication between sites without having the traffic go through the hub; that is, intersite communication bypassing the hub

- Support for dynamic routing protocols running over the DMVPN tunnels

- Support for multicast traffic from hub to spokes

- Support for VPN Routing and Forwarding (VRF) integration extended in multiprotocol label switching (MPLS) networks

- Self-healing capability maximizing VPN tunnel uptime by rerouting around network link failures

- Load-balancing capability offering increased performance by transparently terminating VPN connections to multiple head-end VPN devices

With networks becoming geographically distributed, network availability over a secure channel is becoming a critical factor in designing scalable IPsec VPN solution designs. DMVPN solution architecture is by far the most effective and scalable solution available.

DMVPN Network Designs

DMVPN was introduced in multiple phases to address the various topological needs.

- **Phase 1—Hub-to-Spoke Designs:** Phase 1 was the first design introduced for hub-to-spoke implementation, where spoke-to-spoke traffic would traverse via the hub. Phase 1 also introduced daisy chaining of identical hubs for scaling the network, thereby providing Server Load Balancing (SLB) capability to increase the CPU power.

- **Phase 2—Spoke-to-Spoke Designs:** Phase 2 design introduced the ability for dynamic spoke-to-spoke tunnels without having the traffic go through the hub; that is, intersite communication bypassing the hub, thereby providing greater scalability and better control of traffic. In Phase 2 network design, each DMVPN network is independent of other DMVPN networks, causing spoke-to-spoke traffic from different regions to traverse through the regional hubs without the need to go through the central hub. Figure 16-1 illustrates this scenario.

- **Phase 3—Hierarchical (Tree-Based) Designs:** Phase 3 extended Phase 2 design with the capability to establish dynamic and direct spoke-to-spoke tunnels from different DMVPN network across multiple regions. In Phase 3, all regional DMVPN networks are bound together to form a single hierarchical (tree-based) DMVPN network, including the central hubs. Spoke-to-spoke traffic from different regions can establish direct tunnels with each other, thereby bypassing both the regional and central hubs, as illustrated in Figure 16-2.

Figure 16-1 depicts the DMVPN phases illustrating the various network designs that can be implemented.

Figure 16-1   *DMVPN Network Designs*

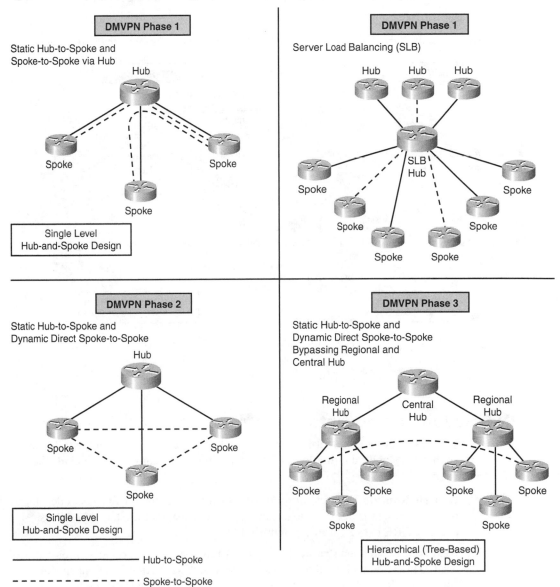

Figure 16-2 illustrates how spoke-to-spoke traffic flow in a hierarchical DMVPN (tree-based) design differs between Phase 2 and Phase 3 implementations. Before Phase 3, spoke-to-spoke tunnels were established through regional hubs. In Phase 3, spoke-to-spoke tunnels are established directly with each other, bypassing both the regional and central hubs.

Figure 16-2 *Spoke-to-Spoke Tunnel in a Hierarchical DMVPN Design (Difference Between Phase 2 and Phase 3)*

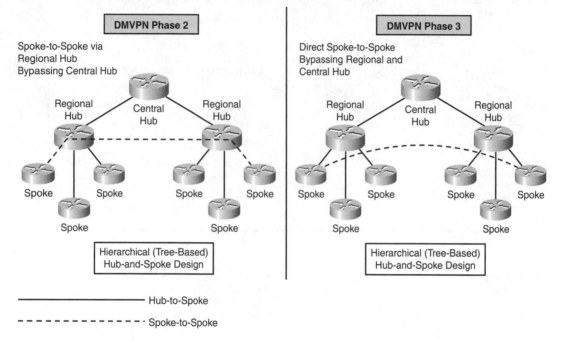

DMVPN Solution Components

The DMVPN solution is a combination of several protocols and relies on the following Cisco-enhanced standard technologies. The major functional components include the following:

- **Generic Routing Encapsulation (GRE) Protocol:** A tunneling protocol developed by Cisco, which is designed to encapsulate IP unicast, multicast, and broadcast packets. GRE uses IP protocol number 47.

- **Next Hop Resolution Protocol (NHRP):** A Layer 2 client-server resolution protocol used to map a tunnel IP address to an NBMA address. NHRP functions in a manner similar to ARP or Reverse ARP (Frame Relay). Like ARP, NHRP can have static or dynamic mappings. The hub router maintains an NHRP database of the public interface addresses for each spoke. When the spoke boots, it registers its real address with the hub and queries the NHRP database for real addresses of the destinations of other spokes so that it can build direct tunnels.

- **Dynamic Routing Protocol:** A protocol used to advertise private networks within the DMVPN networks. IP routing updates and IP multicast data packets traverse only hub-and-spoke tunnels. Unicast IP data packets traverse both hub-and-spoke and direct dynamic spoke-to-spoke tunnels. Routing adjacencies are established across the hub-to-spoke links, and the spoke-to-spoke routing logic is performed by NHRP. Routing protocol does not monitor the state of spoke-to-spoke tunnels. Protocols that are supported include RIP, EIGRP, OSPF, ODR, and BGP.

- **Standards-based IPsec Encryption Protocols:** Protocols used to protect tunnels in the DMVPN solution.

How DMVPN Works

DMVPN builds a dynamic tunnel overlay network. With the aid of Figure 16-3, the following points explain how DMVPN works:

- Initially each spoke establishes a permanent IPsec tunnel to the hub. (At this stage, spokes do not establish tunnels with other spokes within the network.) The hub address should be static and known by all of the spokes.

- Each spoke registers its real address as a client to the NHRP server on the hub. The NHRP server maintains an NHRP database of the public interface addresses for each spoke.

- When a spoke requires that packets be sent to a destination (private) subnet on another spoke, it queries the NHRP server for the real (outside) addresses of the other spoke's destination so that it can build direct tunnels.

- The NHRP server looks up the NHRP database for the corresponding destination spoke and replies with the real address for the target router. The use of NHRP prevents the need of dynamic routing protocols to discover the route to the correct spoke. (Dynamic routing adjacencies are established only from spoke to hub.)

- After the originating spoke learns the peer address of the target spoke, it initiates a dynamic IPsec tunnel to the target spoke.

- With the integration of the multipoint GRE (mGRE) interface, NHRP, and IPsec, a direct dynamic spoke-to-spoke tunnel is established over the DMVPN network.

The spoke-to-spoke tunnels are established on demand whenever traffic is sent between the spokes. Thereafter, packets can bypass the hub and use the spoke-to-spoke tunnel directly. Refer to Figure 16-3 to better understand how this feature works.

Figure 16-3 *Site-to-Site DMVPN Network*

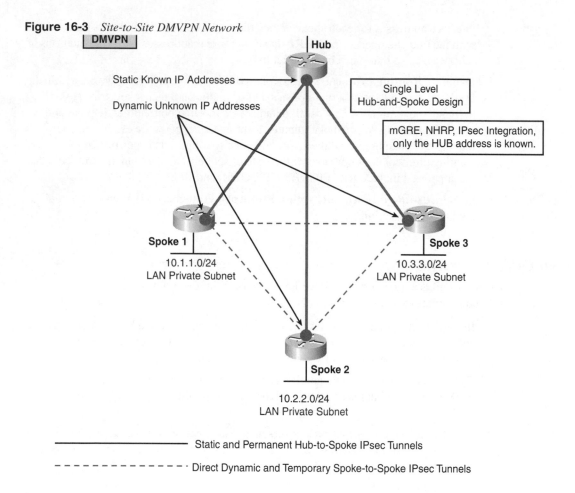

DMVPN Data Structures

The following is a list of DMVPN data structures and how the interaction works to form a complete framework, as illustrated in Figure 16-4:

- **NHRP Mapping Table:** The mapping of VPN and tunnel IP addresses to NBMA address (physical address). Use the **show ip nhrp** command to view the mapping, as shown in Figure 16-4.

- **Crypto Socket Table:** The mapping between NHRP and IPsec, as shown in Figure 16-4. The **show crypto socket** and **show crypto ipsec profile** commands can be used to display this information.

- **Crypto Map Table:** The dynamic crypto map entry for each multipoint GRE tunnel or for each IPsec profile. The **show crypto map** command can be used to display this information.

- **ISAKMP and IPsec SA Table:** The table that shows the ISAKMP Phase 1 SA and Phase 2 IPsec SA information. The **show crypto session**, **show crypto isakmp sa**, and the **show crypto ipsec sa** commands can be used to display this information.

Figure 16-4 *DMVPN Data Structures*

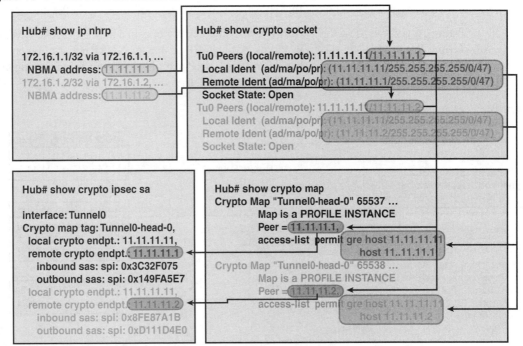

DMVPN Deployment Topologies

The following topologies can be implemented in a DMVPN network design:

- Hub-and-Spoke Designs
    - ☐ Single Hub Single DMVPN (SHSD)
    - ☐ Dual Hub Dual DMVPN (DHDD)
    - ☐ Server Load Balancing (SLB)
- Dynamic Mesh Designs
    - ☐ Dual Hub Single DMVPN (DHSD)
    - ☐ Multihub Single DMVPN (MHSD)
    - ☐ Hierarchical (Tree-Based)

Implementing DMVPN Hub-and-Spoke Designs

In a hub-and-spoke DMVPN design, one mGRE interface is required on the hub router for all spokes. Dynamically addressed spokes are supported when using the NHRP registration process. When new spokes are added, no changes are required on the hub configuration. The important thing to note is that spoke-to-spoke traffic will traverse via the hub.

Figure 16-5 shows how the NHRP registration process works in a hub-and-spoke DMVPN design. Spokes register their real address to the hub by using the NHRP registration process for dynamically addressed spokes. Using the NHRP mapping, corresponding routing table entries are created for the neighbor's private subnets.

Figure 16-5 *Hub-and-Spoke Design*

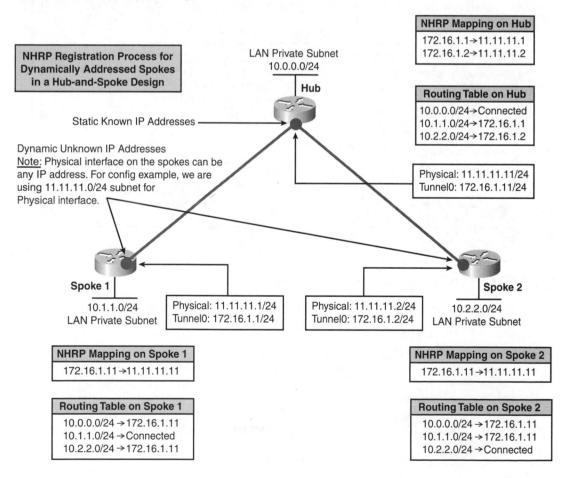

Implementing Single Hub Single DMVPN (SHSD) Topology

Based on Figure 16-5, Example 16-1 (Hub), Example 16-2 (Spoke1), and Example 16-3 (Spoke2) provide basic configuration examples using EIGRP in the implementation of a single-hub DMVPN topology scenario in a hub-and-spoke design.

Example 16-1 *Configuring a Single Hub Single DMVPN Network in a Hub-and-Spoke Design—HUB Router (See Figure 16-5)*

```
hostname Hub
<..>
! Define Phase 1 SA parameters
crypto isakmp policy 10
 encr 3des
 authentication pre-share
 group 2
crypto isakmp key dmvpnkey address 0.0.0.0 0.0.0.0
!
! Define IPsec encryption and authentication algorithms
crypto ipsec transform-set mytran esp-3des esp-sha-hmac
!
! Define Phase 2 Parameters - IPsec Profile (set peer & match ACL not required)
crypto ipsec profile vpnprof
 set transform-set mytran
!
! Interface that is connected to the private side of the network for encryption
interface Loopback0
! description LAN Private Subnet
 ip address 10.0.0.1 255.255.255.0
!
interface Tunnel0
! description DMVPN HUB
 bandwidth 1000
! Define Tunnel IP address
 ip address 172.16.1.11 255.255.255.0
 ip mtu 1400
! Define NHRP Server settings
 ip nhrp authentication cisco
 ip nhrp map multicast dynamic
 ip nhrp network-id 123
 ip nhrp holdtime 360
 no ip split-horizon eigrp 100
 delay 1000
 ip tcp adjust-mss 1360
 tunnel source GigabitEthernet0/0
! Define Multipoint GRE Type interface
 tunnel mode gre multipoint
! Define Tunnel key to Secure GRE interface
 tunnel key 12345
!Apply IPsec profile Tunnel Protection
 tunnel protection ipsec profile vpnprof
!
! Egress interface with known static IP (No ACL or Crypto map)
interface GigabitEthernet0/0
```

continues

Example 16-1 *Configuring a Single Hub Single DMVPN Network in a Hub-and-Spoke Design—HUB Router (See Figure 16-5) (Continued)*

```
ip address 11.11.11.11 255.255.255.0
<..>
! Define Dynamic Routing Protocol to advertise PRIVATE Subnets via Tunnel
router eigrp 100
 network 172.16.1.0 0.0.0.255
 network 10.0.0.0 0.0.0.255
 no auto-summary
 !
<..>
```

TIP In a hub-and-spoke design, the hub router is configured with a multipoint GRE tunnel interface, and spoke routers are configured with a point-to-point GRE (p-pGRE) tunnel interface.

Example 16-2 *Configuring a Single Hub Single DMVPN Network in a Hub-and-Spoke Design—Spoke1 Router (See Figure 16-5)*

```
hostname Spoke1
<..>
! Define Phase 1 SA parameters
crypto isakmp policy 10
 encr 3des
 authentication pre-share
 group 2
crypto isakmp key dmvpnkey address 0.0.0.0 0.0.0.0
 !
! Define IPsec encryption and authentication algorithms
crypto ipsec transform-set mytran esp-3des esp-sha-hmac
 !
! Define Phase 2 Parameters - IPsec Profile (set peer & match ACL not required)
crypto ipsec profile vpnprof
set transform-set mytran
 !
! Interface that is connected to the private side of the network for encryption
interface Loopback0
! description LAN Private Subnet
 ip address 10.1.1.1 255.255.255.0
 !
interface Tunnel0
! description DMVPN Spoke1
 bandwidth 1000
! Define Tunnel IP address
 ip address 172.16.1.1 255.255.255.0
 ip mtu 1400
! Define NHRP Spoke settings with Static Mapping
 ip nhrp authentication cisco
```

Example 16-2   *Configuring a Single Hub Single DMVPN Network in a Hub-and-Spoke Design—Spoke1 Router (See Figure 16-5) (Continued)*

```
ip nhrp map 172.16.1.11 11.11.11.11
! Network ID must match with Server
ip nhrp network-id 123
ip nhrp holdtime 360
ip nhrp nhs 172.16.1.11
delay 1000
ip tcp adjust-mss 1360
tunnel source FastEthernet0/0
! Define Point-to-Point GRE Type interface (Spoke-to-Spoke traffic will traverse via
the Hub) See the routing table of Spoke1 below
 tunnel destination 11.11.11.11
! Define Tunnel key to Secure GRE interface
 tunnel key 12345
!Apply IPsec profile Tunnel Protection
 tunnel protection ipsec profile vpnprof
!
! Egress interface with unknown IP (No ACL or Crypto map). In this example, we are
statically defining IP, but this can be dynamically obtained
interface FastEthernet0/0
ip address 11.11.11.1 255.255.255.0
!
<..>
! Define Dynamic Routing Protocol to advertise PRIVATE Subnets via Tunnel
router eigrp 100
 network 172.16.1.0 0.0.0.255
 network 10.1.1.0 0.0.0.255
 no auto-summary
!
<..>
```

Example 16-3   *Configuring a Single Hub Single DMVPN Network in a Hub-and-Spoke Design—Spoke2 Router (See Figure 16-5)*

```
hostname Spoke2
<..>
! Define Phase 1 SA parameters
crypto isakmp policy 10
 encr 3des
 authentication pre-share
 group 2
crypto isakmp key dmvpnkey address 0.0.0.0 0.0.0.0
!
! Define IPsec encryption and authentication algorithms
crypto ipsec transform-set mytran esp-3des esp-sha-hmac
!
! Define Phase 2 Parameters - IPsec Profile (set peer & match ACL not required)
crypto ipsec profile vpnprof
set transform-set mytran
!
! Interface that is connected to the private side of the network for encryption
```

continues

Example 16-3 *Configuring a Single Hub Single DMVPN Network in a Hub-and-Spoke Design—Spoke2 Router (See Figure 16-5) (Continued)*

```
interface Loopback0
! description LAN Private Subnet
 ip address 10.2.2.2 255.255.255.0
!
interface Tunnel0
! description DMVPN Spoke2
 bandwidth 1000
! Define Tunnel IP address
 ip address 172.16.1.2 255.255.255.0
 ip mtu 1400
! Define NHRP Spoke settings with Static Mapping
 ip nhrp authentication cisco
 ip nhrp map 172.16.1.11 11.11.11.11
! Network ID must match with Server
 ip nhrp network-id 123
 ip nhrp holdtime 360
 ip nhrp nhs 172.16.1.11
 delay 1000
 ip tcp adjust-mss 1360
 tunnel source GigabitEthernet0/0
! Define Point-to-Point GRE Type interface (Spoke-to-Spoke traffic will traverse via
the Hub) See the routing table of Spoke1 below
 tunnel destination 11.11.11.11
! Define Tunnel key to Secure GRE interface
 tunnel key 12345
!Apply IPsec profile Tunnel Protection
 tunnel protection ipsec profile vpnprof
!
! Egress interface with unknown IP (No ACL or Crypto map). In this example, we are
statically defining IP, but this can be dynamically obtained
interface GigabitEthernet0/0
ip address 11.11.11.2 255.255.255.0
!
<..>
! Define Dynamic Routing Protocol to advertise PRIVATE Subnets via Tunnel
router eigrp 100
 network 172.16.1.0 0.0.0.255
 network 10.2.2.0 0.0.0.255
 no auto-summary
!
<..>
```

Based on Figure 16-5 and the configuration on the hub-and-spoke routers shown in Examples 16-1, 16-2, and 16-3, Example 16-4 presents outputs that illustrate the verification of the dynamic routing table (EIGRP), the NHRP mapping, and the crypto socket table entries as explained in the "DMVPN Data Structures" section of this chapter.

Example 16-4 *Dynamic Routing Table Based on the Configuration Shown in Examples 16-1, 16-2, and 16-3*

```
Hub# show ip route ¦ include 10.
      10.0.0.0/24 is subnetted, 3 subnets
D        10.2.2.0 [90/2944000] via 172.16.1.2, 00:27:58, Tunnel0
D        10.1.1.0 [90/2944000] via 172.16.1.1, 00:33:16, Tunnel0
C        10.0.0.0 is directly connected, Loopback0
<..>
Spoke1# show ip route ¦ include 10.
      10.0.0.0/24 is subnetted, 3 subnets
D        10.2.2.0 [90/3200000] via 172.16.1.11, 00:27:41, Tunnel0
C        10.1.1.0 is directly connected, Loopback0
D        10.0.0.0 [90/2944000] via 172.16.1.11, 00:33:00, Tunnel0
<..>
Spoke2# show ip route ¦ include 10.
      10.0.0.0/24 is subnetted, 3 subnets
C        10.2.2.0 is directly connected, Loopback0
D        10.1.1.0 [90/3200000] via 172.16.1.11, 00:27:52, Tunnel0
D        10.0.0.0 [90/2944000] via 172.16.1.11, 00:27:52, Tunnel0
<..>
```

TIP   Observe the routing table entries on the spokes. All spoke LAN private subnets are routed via the hub router. That is, spoke-to-spoke communication is via the hub in this model. In hub-and-spoke design, routing information is not exchanged with the spoke router because multicast traffic has not been mapped in NHRP settings. This will be addressed in a dynamic mesh spoke-to-spoke design presented later in this chapter.

Example 16-5 *NHRP Mapping Table Based on the Configuration Shown in Examples 16-1, 16-2, and 16-3 (Refer to Figure 16-4 to Understand the Interaction)*

```
Hub# show ip nhrp
172.16.1.1/32 via 172.16.1.1, Tunnel0 created 00:41:22, expire 00:04:34
  Type: dynamic, Flags: authoritative unique registered
  NBMA address: 11.11.11.1
172.16.1.2/32 via 172.16.1.2, Tunnel0 created 00:35:17, expire 00:04:36
  Type: dynamic, Flags: authoritative unique registered
  NBMA address: 11.11.11.2
<..>
Spoke1# show ip nhrp
172.16.1.11/32 via 172.16.1.11, Tunnel0 created 00:43:02, never expire
  Type: static, Flags: authoritative
  NBMA address: 11.11.11.11
<..>
Spoke2# show ip nhrp
172.16.1.11/32 via 172.16.1.11, Tunnel0 created 00:35:46, never expire
  Type: static, Flags: authoritative
  NBMA address: 11.11.11.11
```

TIP   NHRP mapping table entries on the hub show dynamic type, whereas static type is used on the spokes because they are manually defined on the spoke routers.

Example 16-6   *Crypto Socket Table Based on the Configuration Shown in Examples 16-1, 16-2, and 16-3 (Refer to Figure 16-4 to Understand the Interaction)*

```
Hub# show crypto sockets

Number of Crypto Socket connections 2

    Tu0 Peers (local/remote): 11.11.11.11/11.11.11.2
        Local Ident  (addr/mask/port/prot): (11.11.11.11/255.255.255.255/0/47)
        Remote Ident (addr/mask/port/prot): (11.11.11.2/255.255.255.255/0/47)
        Socket State: Open
        Client: "TUNNEL SEC" (Client State: Active)
    Tu0 Peers (local/remote): 11.11.11.11/11.11.11.1
        Local Ident  (addr/mask/port/prot): (11.11.11.11/255.255.255.255/0/47)
        Remote Ident (addr/mask/port/prot): (11.11.11.1/255.255.255.255/0/47)
        Socket State: Open
        Client: "TUNNEL SEC" (Client State: Active)

Crypto Sockets in Listen state:
Client: "TUNNEL SEC" Profile: "vpnprof" Map-name: "Tunnel0-head-0"
<..>
Spoke1# show crypto sockets

Number of Crypto Socket connections 1

    Tu0 Peers (local/remote): 11.11.11.1/11.11.11.11
        Local Ident  (addr/mask/port/prot): (11.11.11.1/255.255.255.255/0/47)
        Remote Ident (addr/mask/port/prot): (11.11.11.11/255.255.255.255/0/47)
        Socket State: Open
        Client: "TUNNEL SEC" (Client State: Active)

Crypto Sockets in Listen state:
Client: "TUNNEL SEC" Profile: "vpnprof" Map-name: "Tunnel0-head-0"
<..>
Spoke2# show crypto sockets

Number of Crypto Socket connections 1

    Tu0 Peers (local/remote): 11.11.11.2/11.11.11.11
        Local Ident  (addr/mask/port/prot): (11.11.11.2/255.255.255.255/0/47)
        Remote Ident (addr/mask/port/prot): (11.11.11.11/255.255.255.255/0/47)
        Socket State: Open
        Client: "TUNNEL SEC" (Client State: Active)

Crypto Sockets in Listen state:
Client: "TUNNEL SEC" Profile: "vpnprof" Map-name: "Tunnel0-head-0"
```

Implementing Dual Hub Dual DMVPN (DHDD) Topology

The deployment of dual hub-and-spoke DMVPN is similar to the previous design of single hub DMVPN, except that there are two hub routers to achieve redundancy for the DMVPN networks. Dual hub design offers two hub-and-spoke topologies in an overlay fashion. It is also important to note that in the dual hub design, both hubs are connected through a LAN interface and should not be logically separated. (They should have the same routing table entries for connected interfaces.) The configuration is similar to previous examples, with one mGRE tunnel interface on each hub router, and two separate point-to-point GRE (p-to-pGRE) tunnel interfaces on each spoke that points to the respective hubs.

Figure 16-6 illustrates the dual hub DMVPN design.

Figure 16-6   *Dual Hub-and-Spoke Redundant DMVPN Design*

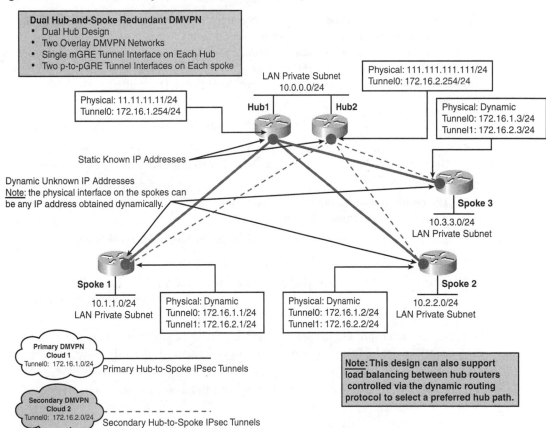

NOTE Dual hub-and-spoke dual DMVPN topology also supports the load-balancing feature for routing traffic between selected hubs. This can be controlled via the dynamic routing protocol.

Implementing Server Load-Balancing (SLB) Topology

Cisco VPN solution offers various features to provide VPN redundancy and load-balancing capabilities. For small-scale IPsec deployments, a combination of Cisco Hot Standby Router Protocol (HSRP) and Reverse Route Injection (RRI) features can be used to provide redundancy. For large-scale VPN deployments, the Cisco Server Load-Balancing (SLB) feature can be used to provide redundancy as well as load balancing.

The SLB architecture defines a virtual server that combines a group of physical (real) servers in a virtual cluster (also known as a server farm). When the spoke initiates an IPsec tunnel, the SLB server chooses an appropriate physical server for the connection based on the SLB algorithm configured. If the physical server in the cluster goes down, it is removed from the cluster, and all new IPsec connections are rerouted to an alternative physical server dynamically.

Figure 16-7, with the list that follows, explains how SLB works in a DMVPN design:

- The SLB design is transparent to the spokes. Spokes are configured with a single Next Hop Server (NHS). Spokes have an NHRP map pointing to the load balancer Virtual IP Address (VIP).

- The configuration on the spoke remains the same, as illustrated in the single hub-and-spoke design discussion earlier.

- The load balancer must be configured in forwarding mode (with no NAT).

- The load balancer owns the VIP.

- When IKE, ESP, or GRE packets are targeted at the VIP, the load balancer chooses a hub, based on a predictor policy (weighted round-robin, least-connections). All subsequent packets for that connection go to the same hub (stickiness).

- All the hub routers in the server farm have the same configuration as the same tunnel interface, and a loopback address, which is the same as the VIP address on the load balancer.

Figure 16-7 illustrates the converged Server Load Balancing (SLB) in a converged DMVPN design.

Figure 16-7 *Server Load Balancing (SLB) in a DMVPN Design*

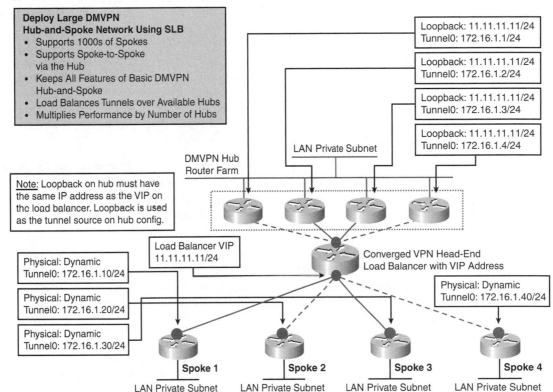

NOTE	Refer to the following Cisco white paper to learn more about Server Load Balancing (SLB) for converged DMVPN and a sample configuration example: http://www.cisco.com/en/US/products/ps6660/products_white_paper0900aecd8051bf3b.shtml.

Implementing Dynamic Mesh Spoke-to-Spoke DMVPN Designs

In a dynamic mesh spoke-to-spoke DMVPN design (also known as Phase 2 DMVPN design, as shown in Figure 16-1), a single mGRE interface is required on both the hub and the spoke routers. Dynamically addressed spokes are supported through the use of the NHRP registration process. When new spokes are added, no changes are required on the hub configuration. The main aspect of this design is that spoke-to-spoke traffic will traverse directly to another spoke (by forming Cisco Express Forwarding (CEF) adjacency), thereby bypassing the hub and reducing latency and load on the hub.

Figure 16-8 shows how the NHRP registration process works in a dynamic spoke-to-spoke DMVPN design. Spokes register their real addresses to the hub by using the NHRP registration process. When a spoke needs to send traffic to a destination (private) subnet on another spoke, it queries the NHRP server for the real (outside) addresses of the other spoke's destination so that it can build direct tunnels.

The NHRP server hub router looks up the NHRP database for the corresponding destination spoke and replies with the real address for the target router. After the originating spoke learns the peer address, it updates its NHRP mapping table for the destination spoke, and the corresponding CEF FIB table entries are created for the neighbor's private subnets. With this information, the spoke is able to build direct CEF adjacency with the target spoke and initiate a dynamic IPsec tunnel with the target spoke.

The spoke-to-spoke tunnels are established on demand whenever traffic is sent between the spokes. Thereafter, packets can bypass the hub and use the spoke-to-spoke tunnel directly, as shown in Figure 16-8.

Figure 16-8 *Dynamic Mesh Spoke-to-Spoke DMVPN Design*

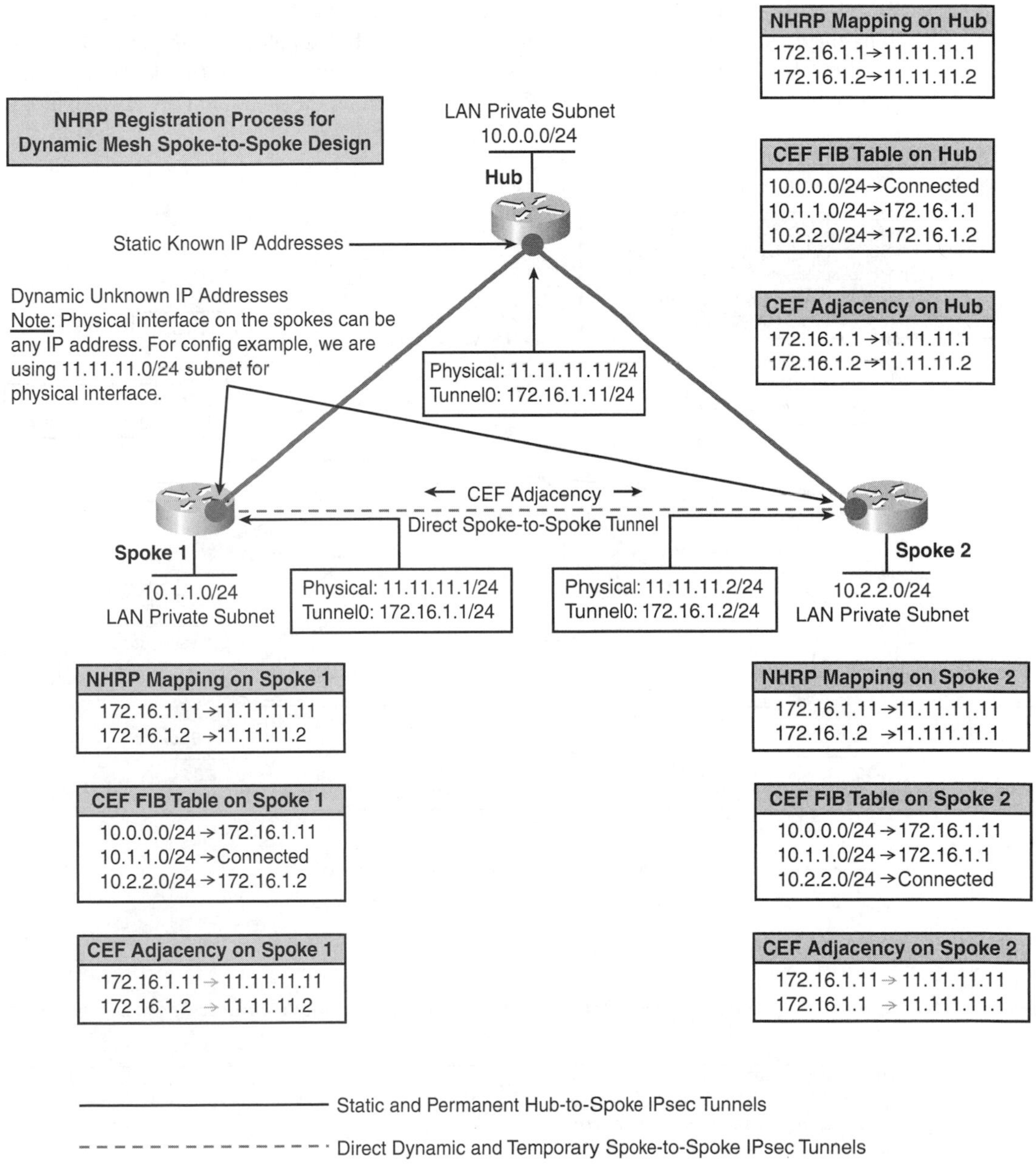

NHRP Mapping on Hub

172.16.1.1→11.11.11.1
172.16.1.2→11.11.11.2

CEF FIB Table on Hub

10.0.0.0/24→Connected
10.1.1.0/24→172.16.1.1
10.2.2.0/24→172.16.1.2

CEF Adjacency on Hub

172.16.1.1→11.11.11.1
172.16.1.2→11.11.11.2

**NHRP Registration Process for
Dynamic Mesh Spoke-to-Spoke Design**

LAN Private Subnet
10.0.0.0/24

Hub

Static Known IP Addresses

Dynamic Unknown IP Addresses
Note: Physical interface on the spokes can be
any IP address. For config example, we are
using 11.11.11.0/24 subnet for
physical interface.

Physical: 11.11.11.11/24
Tunnel0: 172.16.1.11/24

← CEF Adjacency →
Direct Spoke-to-Spoke Tunnel

Spoke 1

10.1.1.0/24
LAN Private Subnet

Physical: 11.11.11.1/24
Tunnel0: 172.16.1.1/24

Physical: 11.11.11.2/24
Tunnel0: 172.16.1.2/24

Spoke 2

10.2.2.0/24
LAN Private Subnet

NHRP Mapping on Spoke 1

172.16.1.11→11.11.11.11
172.16.1.2 →11.11.11.2

NHRP Mapping on Spoke 2

172.16.1.11→11.11.11.11
172.16.1.2 →11.111.11.1

CEF FIB Table on Spoke 1

10.0.0.0/24 →172.16.1.11
10.1.1.0/24 →Connected
10.2.2.0/24 →172.16.1.2

CEF FIB Table on Spoke 2

10.0.0.0/24 →172.16.1.11
10.1.1.0/24 →172.16.1.1
10.2.2.0/24 →Connected

CEF Adjacency on Spoke 1

172.16.1.11→ 11.11.11.11
172.16.1.2 → 11.11.11.2

CEF Adjacency on Spoke 2

172.16.1.11→ 11.11.11.11
172.16.1.1 → 11.111.11.1

———————————————— Static and Permanent Hub-to-Spoke IPsec Tunnels

– – – – – – – – – – – – – – Direct Dynamic and Temporary Spoke-to-Spoke IPsec Tunnels

Implementing Dual Hub Single DMVPN (DHSD) Topology

Based on the understanding of how NHRP registration and CEF adjacency work in a dynamic mesh design, Figure 16-9 illustrates the dual hub topology. Example 16-7 (Hub1), Example 16-8 (Hub2), Example 16-9 (Spoke1), and Example 16-10 (Spoke2) show the basic configuration examples using OSPF implementing the dual hub DMVPN topology scenario in a dynamic spoke-to-spoke design.

Figure 16-9 *Dual Hub Dynamic Mesh Spoke-to-Spoke DMVPN Design*

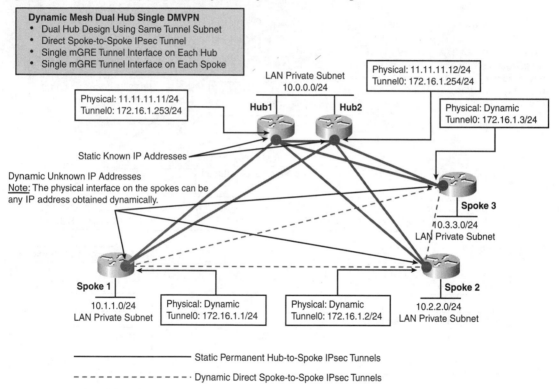

Example 16-7 *Configuring Dual Hub Single DMVPN Network in a Dynamic Mesh Spoke-to-Spoke Design—Hub1 Router (See Figure 16-9)*

```
hostname Hub1
<..>
! Define Phase 1 SA parameters
crypto isakmp policy 10
 encr 3des
 authentication pre-share
 group 2
crypto isakmp key dmvpnkey address 0.0.0.0 0.0.0.0
```

Example 16-7   *Configuring Dual Hub Single DMVPN Network in a Dynamic Mesh Spoke-to-Spoke Design—Hub1 Router (See Figure 16-9) (Continued)*

```
!
! Define IPsec encryption and authentication algorithms
crypto ipsec transform-set mytran esp-3des esp-sha-hmac
!
! Define Phase 2 Parameters - IPsec Profile (set peer & match ACL not required)
crypto ipsec profile vpnprof
 set transform-set mytran
!
! Interface that is connected to the private side of the network for encryption
interface Loopback0
! description LAN Private Subnet
 ip address 10.0.0.1 255.255.255.0
!
interface Tunnel0
! description DMVPN HUB1 Router
 bandwidth 1000
! Define Tunnel IP address
 ip address 172.16.1.253 255.255.255.0
 ip mtu 1400
! Define NHRP Server settings
 ip nhrp authentication cisco
 ip nhrp map multicast dynamic
 ip nhrp map 172.16.1.254 11.11.11.12
 ip nhrp map multicast 11.11.11.12
 ip nhrp network-id 123
 ip nhrp holdtime 360
! Define OSPF Parameters
 ip ospf network broadcast
 ip ospf cost 100
 ip ospf priority 2
 delay 1000
 ip tcp adjust-mss 1360
 tunnel source GigabitEthernet0/0
! Define Multipoint GRE Type interface
 tunnel mode gre multipoint
! Define Tunnel key to Secure GRE interface
 tunnel key 12345
! Apply IPsec profile Tunnel Protection
 tunnel protection ipsec profile vpnprof
!
! Egress interface with known static IP (No ACL or Crypto map)
interface GigabitEthernet0/0
 ip address 11.11.11.11 255.255.255.0
<..>
! Define Dynamic Routing Protocol to advertise PRIVATE Subnets via Tunnel
router ospf 1
 log-adjacency-changes
 network 10.0.0.0 0.255.255.255 area 0
 network 172.16.1.0 0.0.0.255 area 0
!
<..>
```

continues

Example 16-8 *Configuring Dual Hub Single DMVPN Network in a Dynamic Mesh Spoke-to-Spoke Design—Hub2 Router (See Figure 16-9)*

```
hostname Hub2
<..>
! Define Phase 1 SA parameters
crypto isakmp policy 10
 encr 3des
 authentication pre-share
 group 2
crypto isakmp key dmvpnkey address 0.0.0.0 0.0.0.0
!
! Define IPsec encryption and authentication algorithms
crypto ipsec transform-set mytran esp-3des esp-sha-hmac
!
! Define Phase 2 Parameters - IPsec Profile (set peer & match ACL not required)
crypto ipsec profile vpnprof
 set transform-set mytran
!
! Interface that is connected to the private side of the network for encryption
interface Loopback0
! description LAN Private Subnet
 ip address 10.0.0.2 255.255.255.0
!
interface Tunnel0
! description DMVPN HUB2 Router
 bandwidth 1000
! Define Tunnel IP address
 ip address 172.16.1.254 255.255.255.0
 ip mtu 1400
! Define NHRP Server settings
 ip nhrp authentication cisco
 ip nhrp map multicast dynamic
 ip nhrp map 172.16.1.253 11.11.11.11
 ip nhrp map multicast 11.11.11.11
 ip nhrp network-id 123
 ip nhrp holdtime 360
! Define OSPF Parameters
 ip ospf network broadcast
 ip ospf cost 105
 ip ospf priority 2
 delay 1000
 ip tcp adjust-mss 1360
 tunnel source GigabitEthernet0/0
! Define Multipoint GRE Type interface
 tunnel mode gre multipoint
! Define Tunnel key to Secure GRE interface
 tunnel key 12345
! Apply IPsec profile Tunnel Protection
 tunnel protection ipsec profile vpnprof
!
! Egress interface with known static IP (No ACL or Crypto map)
interface GigabitEthernet0/0
 ip address 11.11.11.12 255.255.255.0
```

Example 16-8   *Configuring Dual Hub Single DMVPN Network in a Dynamic Mesh Spoke-to-Spoke Design—Hub2 Router (See Figure 16-9) (Continued)*

```
<..>
! Define Dynamic Routing Protocol to advertise PRIVATE Subnets via Tunnel
router ospf 1
 log-adjacency-changes
 network 10.0.0.0 0.255.255.255 area 0
 network 172.16.1.0 0.0.0.255 area 0
 !
<..>
```

Example 16-9   *Configuring Dual Hub Single DMVPN Network in a Dynamic Mesh Spoke-to-Spoke Design— Spoke1 Router (See Figure 16-9)*

```
hostname Spoke1
<..>
! Define Phase 1 SA parameters
crypto isakmp policy 10
 encr 3des
 authentication pre-share
 group 2
crypto isakmp key dmvpnkey address 0.0.0.0 0.0.0.0
!
! Define IPsec encryption and authentication algorithms
crypto ipsec transform-set mytran esp-3des esp-sha-hmac
!
! Define Phase 2 Parameters - IPsec Profile (set peer & match ACL not required)
crypto ipsec profile vpnprof
set transform-set mytran
!
! Interface that is connected to the private side of the network for encryption
interface Loopback0
! description LAN Private Subnet
 ip address 10.1.1.1 255.255.255.0
!
interface Tunnel0
! description DMVPN Spoke1
 bandwidth 1000
! Define Tunnel IP address
 ip address 172.16.1.1 255.255.255.0
 ip mtu 1400
! Define NHRP Spoke settings with Static Mapping
 ip nhrp authentication cisco
! Define NHRP Hub1 Mapping
 ip nhrp map multicast 11.11.11.11
 ip nhrp map 172.16.1.253 11.11.11.11
! Define NHRP Hub2 Mapping
 ip nhrp map multicast 11.11.11.12
 ip nhrp map 172.16.1.254 11.11.11.12
! Network ID must match with Server
 ip nhrp network-id 123
 ip nhrp holdtime 360
```

continues

Example 16-9 *Configuring Dual Hub Single DMVPN Network in a Dynamic Mesh Spoke-to-Spoke Design—Spoke1 Router (See Figure 16-9) (Continued)*

```
! Define IP address for both Hubs
 ip nhrp nhs 172.16.1.253
 ip nhrp nhs 172.16.1.254
 delay 1000
 ip tcp adjust-mss 1360
! Define OSPF Parameters
 ip ospf network broadcast
 ip ospf priority 0
 tunnel source FastEthernet0/0
! Define Multipoint GRE Type interface
 tunnel mode gre multipoint
! Define Tunnel key to Secure GRE interface
 tunnel key 12345
!Apply IPsec profile Tunnel Protection
 tunnel protection ipsec profile vpnprof
 !
! Egress interface with unknown IP (No ACL or Crypto map). In this example, we are
statically defining IP, but this can be dynamically obtained
interface FastEthernet0/0
ip address 11.11.11.1 255.255.255.0
 !
<..>
! Define Dynamic Routing Protocol to advertise PRIVATE Subnets via Tunnel
router ospf 1
 log-adjacency-changes
 network 10.0.0.0 0.255.255.255 area 0
 network 172.16.1.0 0.0.0.255 area 0
 !
<..>
```

Example 16-10 *Configuring Dual Hub Single DMVPN Network in a Dynamic Mesh Spoke-to-Spoke Design—Spoke2 Router (See Figure 16-9)*

```
hostname Spoke2
<..>
! Define Phase 1 SA parameters
crypto isakmp policy 10
 encr 3des
 authentication pre-share
 group 2
crypto isakmp key dmvpnkey address 0.0.0.0 0.0.0.0
 !
! Define IPsec encryption and authentication algorithms
crypto ipsec transform-set mytran esp-3des esp-sha-hmac
 !
! Define Phase 2 Parameters - IPsec Profile (set peer & match ACL not required)
crypto ipsec profile vpnprof
set transform-set mytran
 !
! Interface that is connected to the private side of the network for encryption
```

Example 16-10   *Configuring Dual Hub Single DMVPN Network in a Dynamic Mesh Spoke-to-Spoke Design—*
Spoke2 Router (See Figure 16-9) (Continued)

```
interface Loopback0
! description LAN Private Subnet
 ip address 10.2.2.2 255.255.255.0
!
interface Tunnel0
! description DMVPN Spoke2
 bandwidth 1000
! Define Tunnel IP address
 ip address 172.16.1.2 255.255.255.0
 ip mtu 1400
! Define NHRP Spoke settings with Static Mapping
 ip nhrp authentication cisco
! Define NHRP Hub1 Mapping
 ip nhrp map multicast 11.11.11.11
 ip nhrp map 172.16.1.253 11.11.11.11
! Define NHRP Hub2 Mapping
 ip nhrp map multicast 11.11.11.12
 ip nhrp map 172.16.1.254 11.11.11.12
! Network ID must match with Server
 ip nhrp network-id 123
 ip nhrp holdtime 360
! Define IP address for both Hubs
 ip nhrp nhs 172.16.1.253
 ip nhrp nhs 172.16.1.254
 delay 1000
 ip tcp adjust-mss 1360
! Define OSPF Parameters
 ip ospf network broadcast
 ip ospf priority 0
 tunnel source FastEthernet0/0
! Define Multipoint GRE Type interface
 tunnel mode gre multipoint
! Define Tunnel key to Secure GRE interface
 tunnel key 12345
! Apply IPsec profile Tunnel Protection
 tunnel protection ipsec profile vpnprof
!
! Egress interface with unknown IP (No ACL or Crypto map). In this example, we are
statically defining IP, but this can be dynamically obtained
interface FastEthernet0/0
ip address 11.11.11.2 255.255.255.0
!
<..>
! Define Dynamic Routing Protocol to advertise PRIVATE Subnets via Tunnel
router ospf 1
 log-adjacency-changes
 network 10.0.0.0 0.255.255.255 area 0
 network 172.16.1.0 0.0.0.255 area 0
!
<..>
```

Based on Figure 16-9 and Examples 16-7, 16-8, 16-9, and 16-10 on the hub-and-spoke routers, the following outputs illustrate the verification of dynamic routing table (OSPF), the NHRP mapping, and the crypto socket table entries, as explained in the "DMVPN Data Structures" section.

Example 16-11 *Dynamic Routing Table Based on Examples 16-7, 16-8, 16-9, and 16-10 Configurations*

```
Hub1# show ip route | include 10.
      10.0.0.0/8 is variably subnetted, 4 subnets, 2 masks
O        10.2.2.2/32 [110/101] via 172.16.1.2, 00:13:38, Tunnel0
O        10.0.0.2/32 [110/101] via 172.16.1.254, 00:13:38, Tunnel0
C        10.0.0.0/24 is directly connected, Loopback0
O        10.1.1.1/32 [110/101] via 172.16.1.1, 00:13:38, Tunnel0
<..>
Hub2# show ip route | include 10.
      10.0.0.0/8 is variably subnetted, 4 subnets, 2 masks
O        10.2.2.2/32 [110/106] via 172.16.1.2, 00:14:03, Tunnel0
C        10.0.0.0/24 is directly connected, Loopback0
O        10.1.1.1/32 [110/106] via 172.16.1.1, 00:14:03, Tunnel0
O        10.0.0.1/32 [110/106] via 172.16.1.253, 00:14:03, Tunnel0
<..>
Spoke1# show ip route | include 10.
      10.0.0.0/8 is variably subnetted, 4 subnets, 2 masks
O        10.2.2.2/32 [110/101] via 172.16.1.2, 00:14:33, Tunnel0
O        10.0.0.2/32 [110/101] via 172.16.1.254, 00:14:33, Tunnel0
C        10.1.1.0/24 is directly connected, Loopback0
O        10.0.0.1/32 [110/101] via 172.16.1.253, 00:14:33, Tunnel0
<..>
Spoke2# show ip route | include 10.
      10.0.0.0/8 is variably subnetted, 4 subnets, 2 masks
O        10.0.0.2/32 [110/101] via 172.16.1.254, 00:15:00, Tunnel0
C        10.2.2.0/24 is directly connected, Loopback0
O        10.1.1.1/32 [110/101] via 172.16.1.1, 00:15:00, Tunnel0
O        10.0.0.1/32 [110/101] via 172.16.1.253, 00:15:00, Tunnel0
<..>
```

TIP   Observe the routing table entries on each spoke. All spokes are learning private subnet routes via OSPF with the next hop set to the corresponding spoke tunnel IP address (which should not be the hub); that is, spoke-to-spoke communication is direct in this model. In dynamic mesh spoke-to-spoke design, routing information is exchanged among the spokes as multicast traffic and mapped in NHRP settings as shown in the previous examples. In the previous section on the hub-and-spoke model, the spoke learns the private subnet routes via the hub with the next-hop address set to the hub router (as shown in Example 16-4).

Example 16-12   *NHRP Mapping Table Based on Examples 16-7, 16-8, 16-9, and 16-10 Configurations*

```
Hub1# show ip nhrp
172.16.1.1/32 via 172.16.1.1, Tunnel0 created 00:53:12, expire 00:04:17
  Type: dynamic, Flags: authoritative unique registered used
  NBMA address: 11.11.11.1
172.16.1.2/32 via 172.16.1.2, Tunnel0 created 00:45:33, expire 00:05:06
  Type: dynamic, Flags: authoritative unique registered used
  NBMA address: 11.11.11.2
172.16.1.254/32 via 172.16.1.254, Tunnel0 created 00:58:20, never expire
  Type: static, Flags: authoritative used
  NBMA address: 11.11.11.12
<..>
Hub2# show ip nhrp
172.16.1.1/32 via 172.16.1.1, Tunnel0 created 00:53:36, expire 00:05:53
  Type: dynamic, Flags: authoritative unique registered used
  NBMA address: 11.11.11.1
172.16.1.2/32 via 172.16.1.2, Tunnel0 created 00:45:57, expire 00:04:42
  Type: dynamic, Flags: authoritative unique registered
  NBMA address: 11.11.11.2
172.16.1.253/32 via 172.16.1.253, Tunnel0 created 00:57:27, never expire
  Type: static, Flags: authoritative used
  NBMA address: 11.11.11.11
<..>
Spoke1# show ip nhrp
172.16.1.2/32 via 172.16.1.2, Tunnel0 created 00:00:26, expire 00:04:08
  Type: dynamic, Flags: router
  NBMA address: 11.11.11.2
172.16.1.253/32 via 172.16.1.253, Tunnel0 created 00:52:41, never expire
  Type: static, Flags: authoritative used
  NBMA address: 11.11.11.11
172.16.1.254/32 via 172.16.1.254, Tunnel0 created 00:52:41, never expire
  Type: static, Flags: authoritative used
  NBMA address: 11.11.11.12
<..>
Spoke2# show ip nhrp
172.16.1.1/32 via 172.16.1.1, Tunnel0 created 00:00:03, expire 00:05:43
  Type: dynamic, Flags: router
  NBMA address: 11.11.11.1
172.16.1.253/32 via 172.16.1.253, Tunnel0 created 00:37:28, never expire
  Type: static, Flags: authoritative used
```

continues

Example 16-12 *NHRP Mapping Table Based on Examples 16-7, 16-8, 16-9, and 16-10 Configurations (Continued)*

```
  NBMA address: 11.11.11.11
172.16.1.254/32 via 172.16.1.254, Tunnel0 created 00:37:28, never expire
  Type: static, Flags: authoritative used
  NBMA address: 11.11.11.12
<..>
```

TIP   Observe that the NHRP mapping table entries on Hub1 show dynamic type for peer spoke1 and spoke2 and the static type for Hub2 (and vice versa); whereas spoke1 and spoke2 show static for each Hub1/Hub2, and dynamic for each peer spoke1 and spoke2. Note that these entries will populate only when traffic is initiated (on-demand tunnel).

Example 16-13 *Crypto Socket Table Based on Examples 16-7, 16-8, 16-9, and 16-10 Configurations*

```
Hub1# show crypto sockets

Number of Crypto Socket connections 3

   Tu0 Peers (local/remote): 11.11.11.11/11.11.11.12
      Local Ident  (addr/mask/port/prot): (11.11.11.11/255.255.255.255/0/47)
      Remote Ident (addr/mask/port/prot): (11.11.11.12/255.255.255.255/0/47)
      Socket State: Open
      Client: "TUNNEL SEC" (Client State: Active)
   Tu0 Peers (local/remote): 11.11.11.11/11.11.11.2
      Local Ident  (addr/mask/port/prot): (11.11.11.11/255.255.255.255/0/47)
      Remote Ident (addr/mask/port/prot): (11.11.11.2/255.255.255.255/0/47)
      Socket State: Open
      Client: "TUNNEL SEC" (Client State: Active)
   Tu0 Peers (local/remote): 11.11.11.11/11.11.11.1
      Local Ident  (addr/mask/port/prot): (11.11.11.11/255.255.255.255/0/47)
      Remote Ident (addr/mask/port/prot): (11.11.11.1/255.255.255.255/0/47)
      Socket State: Open
      Client: "TUNNEL SEC" (Client State: Active)

Crypto Sockets in Listen state:
Client: "TUNNEL SEC" Profile: "vpnprof" Map-name: "Tunnel0-head-0"
<..>
Hub2# show crypto sockets

Number of Crypto Socket connections 3

   Tu0 Peers (local/remote): 11.11.11.12/11.11.11.11
      Local Ident  (addr/mask/port/prot): (11.11.11.12/255.255.255.255/0/47)
      Remote Ident (addr/mask/port/prot): (11.11.11.11/255.255.255.255/0/47)
      Socket State: Open
      Client: "TUNNEL SEC" (Client State: Active)
   Tu0 Peers (local/remote): 11.11.11.12/11.11.11.2
      Local Ident  (addr/mask/port/prot): (11.11.11.12/255.255.255.255/0/47)
```

Example 16-13   *Crypto Socket Table Based on Examples 16-7, 16-8, 16-9, and 16-10 Configurations (Continued)*

```
              Remote Ident (addr/mask/port/prot): (11.11.11.2/255.255.255.255/0/47)
              Socket State: Open
              Client: "TUNNEL SEC" (Client State: Active)
     Tu0 Peers (local/remote): 11.11.11.12/11.11.11.1
              Local Ident  (addr/mask/port/prot): (11.11.11.12/255.255.255.255/0/47)
              Remote Ident (addr/mask/port/prot): (11.11.11.1/255.255.255.255/0/47)
              Socket State: Open
              Client: "TUNNEL SEC" (Client State: Active)

Crypto Sockets in Listen state:
Client: "TUNNEL SEC" Profile: "vpnprof" Map-name: "Tunnel0-head-0"
<..>
Spoke1# show crypto sockets

Number of Crypto Socket connections 3

     Tu0 Peers (local/remote): 11.11.11.1/11.11.11.11
              Local Ident  (addr/mask/port/prot): (11.11.11.1/255.255.255.255/0/47)
              Remote Ident (addr/mask/port/prot): (11.11.11.11/255.255.255.255/0/47)
              Socket State: Open
              Client: "TUNNEL SEC" (Client State: Active)
     Tu0 Peers (local/remote): 11.11.11.1/11.11.11.12
              Local Ident  (addr/mask/port/prot): (11.11.11.1/255.255.255.255/0/47)
              Remote Ident (addr/mask/port/prot): (11.11.11.12/255.255.255.255/0/47)
              Socket State: Open
              Client: "TUNNEL SEC" (Client State: Active)
     Tu0 Peers (local/remote): 11.11.11.1/11.11.11.2
              Local Ident  (addr/mask/port/prot): (11.11.11.1/255.255.255.255/0/47)
              Remote Ident (addr/mask/port/prot): (11.11.11.2/255.255.255.255/0/47)
              Socket State: Open
              Client: "TUNNEL SEC" (Client State: Active)

Crypto Sockets in Listen state:
Client: "TUNNEL SEC" Profile: "vpnprof" Map-name: "Tunnel0-head-0"
<..>
Spoke2# show crypto sockets

Number of Crypto Socket connections 3

     Tu0 Peers (local/remote): 11.11.11.2/11.11.11.11
              Local Ident  (addr/mask/port/prot): (11.11.11.2/255.255.255.255/0/47)
              Remote Ident (addr/mask/port/prot): (11.11.11.11/255.255.255.255/0/47)
              Socket State: Open
              Client: "TUNNEL SEC" (Client State: Active)
     Tu0 Peers (local/remote): 11.11.11.2/11.11.11.12
              Local Ident  (addr/mask/port/prot): (11.11.11.2/255.255.255.255/0/47)
              Remote Ident (addr/mask/port/prot): (11.11.11.12/255.255.255.255/0/47)
              Socket State: Open
              Client: "TUNNEL SEC" (Client State: Active)
     Tu0 Peers (local/remote): 11.11.11.2/11.11.11.1
              Local Ident  (addr/mask/port/prot): (11.11.11.2/255.255.255.255/0/47)
              Remote Ident (addr/mask/port/prot): (11.11.11.1/255.255.255.255/0/47)
```

Example 16-13 *Crypto Socket Table Based on Examples 16-7, 16-8, 16-9, and 16-10 Configurations (Continued)*

```
        Socket State: Open
        Client: "TUNNEL SEC" (Client State: Active)

Crypto Sockets in Listen state:
Client: "TUNNEL SEC" Profile: "vpnprof" Map-name: "Tunnel0-head-0"
<..>
```

Implementing Multihub Single DMVPN (MHSD) Topology

Another extension of multihub topology is to group the hub routers for large-scale, highly redundant DMVPN requirements. All hub routers can point to each other as with NHS in a daisy-chain fashion. MHSD design can be used to forward NHRP packets and data packets while dynamic spoke-spoke tunnels are being created. NHRP Resolution Request/Response always traverses the complete hub daisy chain. If any hub in the group goes down in the chain, NHRP Resolution Request/Response will dynamically converge and reroute packets to other hubs in the chain. Figure 16-10 illustrates this phenomenon.

Hub routers must use the same routing protocol for both hub-to-hub and hub-to-spoke routing neighbors to exchange routing information for DMVPN networks through mGRE tunnel interfaces.

The following list shows how to configure multiple NHS on hub routers to point to each other, thereby forming a daisy-chain setup in a multihub, spoke-to-spoke, daisy-chain topology.

- **Single daisy chain through all hubs**: Loss of hub breaks daisy chain.

  ip nhrp nhs <hub<x+1>>

- **Two layer daisy chain**: Can lose every other hub without splitting DMVPN network.

  ip nhrp nhs <hub<x+1>>
  ip nhrp nhs <hub<x+2>>

- **Three layer daisy chain**: Can handle losing more hubs, but is more complex than single and two layered.

  ip nhrp nhs <hub<x+1>>
  ip nhrp nhs <hub<x+2>>
  ip nhrp nhs <hub<x+3>>

Figure 16-10 illustrates how the hub routers are grouped in a daisy chain and shows the primary and secondary paths. It also shows the path flow if any hub (Hub3 in this case) goes down.

Figure 16-10   *Hub Daisy Chaining DMVPN Design*

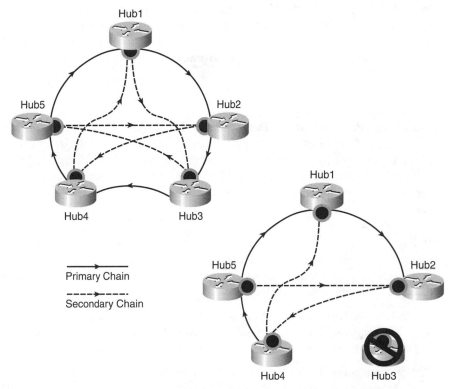

The information concept in Figure 16-10 is taken from the Cisco Networkers session presentation# SEC-2012 – "Deploying Dynamic Multipoint VPNs (DMVPN)."

Implementing Hierarchical (Tree-Based) Topology

As discussed previously, hierarchical (tree-based) DMVPN implementation was introduced in Phase 3 to replace Phase 2-based designs with the capability of spokes from different regions to establish dynamic and direct spoke-to-spoke tunnels bypassing central and regional hubs. In Phase 3, regional DMVPN networks are bound together to form a single hierarchical (tree-based) DMVPN network, including the central hubs. This allows spoke-to-spoke traffic from different regions to establish direct tunnels with each other, as illustrated in Figure 16-2.

Note that Phase 3 hierarchical topology is not daisy-chain topology as discussed earlier. Instead, it uses routing and CEF switching to forward data and NHRP packets optimally through hubs, thus reducing complexity. In addition, spokes are not required to learn individual private LAN routes from all the spokes (full routing table). Private LAN routes can be aggregated and summarized at the hub, thereby reducing the load for routing protocols and providing better convergence.

CAUTION   Phase 2 and Phase 3 DMVPN cannot coexist on the same DMVPN network. Spokes need to be migrated from Phase 2 DMVPN to Phase 3 DMVPN explicitly. Refer to the following Cisco white paper for more details on migrating from DMVPN Phase 2 to Phase 3: http://www.cisco.com/en/US/products/ps6635/products_white_paper0900. aecd8055c34e.shtml.

Summary

Cisco VPN-based security solutions are increasingly popular and have proven to be the most effective and secure technology that can be used to protect sensitive data traversing insecure channels such as the Internet.

As demand for IPsec-based VPN implementation continues to grow in today's complex VPN landscape, scalability, reduced complexity, faster convergence, and ease of deployment are becoming more important for every IPsec design.

DMVPN enhances the traditional IPsec deployment by offering scalable and dynamic IPsec environments where on-demand IPsec tunnels can be established. DMVPN offers zero-touch deployment of IPsec solutions, interconnecting sites across the Internet with reduced latency while optimizing network performance and bandwidth utilization.

DMVPN allows for scaling IPsec VPN networks to offer a large-scale IPsec VPN deployment model.

This chapter provides a comprehensive explanation of the DMVPN solution architecture, the components that make up the DMVPN solution, and how it works.

The chapter presented details of various types of DMVPN deployment topologies and extensive details on implementing various DMVPN scenarios by using numerous illustrations, diagrams, and sample configurations.

References

http://www.cisco.com/go/dmvpn

http://www.cisco.com/en/US/products/ps6635/prod_white_papers_list.html

http://www.cisco.com/en/US/tech/tk583/tk372/technologies_white_paper
09186a008018983e.shtml

http://www.cisco.com/en/US/products/ps6350/products_configuration_guide_
chapter09186a0080455c71.html

http://www.cisco.com/en/US/netsol/ns676/networking_solutions_white_paper
0900aecd805bbf96.shtml

http://www.cisco.com/en/US/products/ps6350/products_configuration_guide_
chapter09186a0080455c71.html

CHAPTER 17

Group Encrypted Transport VPN (GET VPN)

Today's highly integrated and large-scale meshed networks require a secure transport solution that provides instantaneous connectivity between sites without compromising service quality or adding complexity and overhead to the overall network.

In response to this need, Cisco introduced the innovative enhanced encryption solution—Cisco IOS GET VPN—that uses a tunnel-less VPN approach, based on the revolutionary Cisco Group Encrypted Transport (GET VPN) technology.

GET VPN technology offers global enterprise networks the capability to scale voice, video, and data applications with increased network efficiency, any-to-any encrypted connectivity, and highly scalable network environments.

This chapter provides a complete overview of the Cisco IOS GET VPN solution architecture, implementation, and deployment guidelines.

GET VPN Solution Architecture

GET VPN is a revolutionary new concept introduced by Cisco that provides a tunnel-less VPN solution. It is "tunnel-less" because it retains the original IP header of the packet and encrypts only the data payload. To retain the original IP header (including QoS markings), the original header is copied and placed before the IPsec header. GET VPN does not rely on a point-to-point VPN mechanism. By eliminating the need for traditional point-to-point tunnels, networks can further expand with the capability of scaling any-to-any intersite VPN connectivity.

GET VPN, a next-generation encryption technology, is a new category of VPN that offers a standards-based IPsec model that is based on the concept of trusted group members. Routers in a trusted group use a common security methodology that is independent of any point-to-point IPsec tunnel relationship. There is any-to-any dynamic connectivity because the group has already negotiated the security parameters by using a shared key. GET VPN provides end-to-end security for both IP unicast and multicast traffic that traverses a private WAN.

GET VPN offers a secure solution for large-scale, meshed networks by providing encrypted connectivity with higher scalability, increased network performance for latency-sensitive traffic, and always available any-to-any communications among sites.

GET VPN Features

Cisco GET VPN technology offers a wide range of benefits. Key features include the following:

- Easy-to-manage, high-scale, encrypted communications
- Always-on any-to-any intersite connectivity
- Authentication and encryption of both unicast and multicast traffic
- IP header preservation
- Secure packets that use existing routing infrastructure
- Easier distribution and management of security policies
- Prevention of overlay routing
- Provision of an anti-replay feature based on synchronization of pseudotime across group members
- Improved network performance
- Reduced latency for real-time applications
- Networkwide, advanced QoS for encrypted traffic
- Preservation of networkwide QoS and multicast capabilities for improved application performance
- Optimal multicast replication that leverages the core network
- Reduced traffic flows, because multicast is handled natively rather than having to transmit broadcast frames
- Enhanced multilevel fault isolation capabilities
- Management of encryption by either subscribers or service providers

NOTE   The Cisco GET VPN solution is available from Cisco IOS 12.4(11)T and later on Cisco Integrated Services Routers (ISR) 870, 1800, 2800, and 3800 series routers, as well as on the Cisco 7301 and 7200 series routers.

Table 17-1 shows a summary comparison between traditional point-to-point IPsec tunnel technology and the GET VPN tunnel-less technology.

Table 17-1   *Traditional Point-to-Point IPsec and GET VPN Comparison Chart*

Traditional Point-to-Point IPsec Tunnels	GET VPN
Scalability issue (N^2 problem). Individual IKE/IPsec tunnels on each pair of peers.	Scalable architecture. Single SA and key pair used for entire any-to-any group.
Not capable of any-to-any instantaneous connectivity to scale.	Any-to-any instantaneous connectivity to high-scale.
Overlay routing.	No overlay; uses native routing.
New IP header added to the original packet.	IP header preservation—keeps original IP header in IPsec packet.
Multicast replication inefficient because of tunnel overlay.	Efficient multicast replication because of IP header preservation and no tunnel overlay.

Figure 17-1 illustrates the concept of GET VPN and relationships with each other.

Figure 17-1   *Cisco GET VPN Concept*

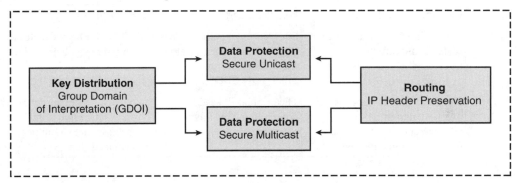

Why GET VPN?

As mentioned earlier, today's highly integrated large-scale meshed networks require a solution that provides instantaneous connectivity between sites without compromising service quality or adding complexity and overhead to the overall network.

One of the solutions commonly used to address this is MPLS VPN, which provides secure communication. However, MPLS VPN does not provide end-to-end encryption, which is critical to many applications. Other solutions are DMVPN and Easy VPN to achieve end-to-end encryption, but these solutions are overlay models using point-to-point topology that can introduce delay and suboptimal routing for large-scale meshed networks, thereby causing provisioning limitations and adding overhead to the overall network.

Another alternative solution available to address the overlay model is VRF-aware IPsec (Virtual Routing and Forwarding) on Provider Edge (PE) routers. Again, like MPLS VPN, the limitation of using this model is that it does not provide end-to-end encryption. Traffic is encrypted between the Customer Edge (CE) and PE devices only. Traffic between PE-PE is not encrypted but is secured through MPLS labels, thereby causing additional overhead on PE routes and requiring them to decrypt the traffic before forwarding it to core, and to encrypt the traffic before forwarding to the CE.

GET VPN solution is an efficient alternative to the overlay models and VRF-aware IPsec model, providing end-to-end security on CE routers without using tunnels. GET VPN offers secure encrypted communication for both IP unicast and multicast applications for any-to-any secure connectivity.

GET VPN is WAN-agnostic and can be deployed on any type of network, based on IP, MPLS, Frame Relay, or ATM.

Table 17-2 illustrates the technical advantages of Cisco GET VPN technology.

Table 17-2 *Technical Benefits of GET VPN*

Previous Limitation	New Feature	Benefit
Encrypting multicast traffic not scalable and difficult to troubleshoot	Encryption supported for native multicast and unicast traffic with Group Encrypted Transport's GDOI protocol	Allows for higher scale and simplifies troubleshooting
Overlay VPN networks created overlay routing; lack of advanced QoS; suboptimal multicast replication	The original IP header preserved; no overlay network required	Achieves optimal routing and maintains network intelligence such as efficient multicast and advanced QoS

GET VPN and DMVPN

The GET VPN and DMVPN are complementary solutions. Basic DMVPN provides hub-to-spoke and spoke-to-spoke connectivity using multipoint GRE (mGRE) and Next Hop Resolution Protocol (NHRP) functions. When a spoke needs to send packets to another spoke destination, it queries the NHRP server for real (outside) addresses of the other spoke's destination so that it can build direct tunnels, thereby bypassing the hub. Until the dynamic tunnel is built, traffic continues to pass through the hub, causing possible delays and suboptimal routing for large-scale meshed networks.

By using GET VPN together with DMVPN, the delay caused by IPsec tunnel negotiation is eliminated because connections are static.

NOTE	When group keying is applied to the tunnel in a DMVPN context, all tunnel traffic is encrypted with the group key.

GET VPN Deployment Consideration

GET VPN is an enhanced Cisco solution that enables encryption for "native" multicast packets and unicast packets over a private WAN.

GET VPN can be implemented in a variety of deployment models in a range of environments. Consider deploying Cisco GET VPN when

- Deploying latency-sensitive applications
- Deploying applications requiring any-to-any encryption
- Deploying voice or similar collaborative applications
- Securing IP unicast and multicast traffic
- Encrypting data over MPLS networks
- Encrypting data over satellite links

NOTE	The GET VPN implementation in Internet-based deployments requires DMVPN because it requires public IP addresses.

GET VPN Solution Components

GET VPN solution is a combination of some newly introduced protocols combined with current IPsec standard protocols. The major functional components in GET VPN include the following:

- **Group Domain of Interpretation (GDOI):** GDOI is a protocol that defines the ISAKMP Domain of Interpretation (DOI) for group key management to support secure group communications. GDOI is the foundation of the GET VPN solution architecture. In a trusted group model, the GDOI protocol operates between a group member and a group controller/key server (GCKS) to establish security associations (SA) among authorized group members. GDOI messages are used to create, maintain, or delete SAs for a group. GDOI protocol uses UDP port 848. GDOI is documented in IETF RFC 3547.

- **Group Controller/Key Server (GCKS):** GCKS is the router responsible for maintaining the policy and creating and maintaining the keys for the group. When a group member registers, the key server sends the policy and the keys to the group member. The key server also rekeys the group before existing keys expire. The server can send two types of keys: the traffic encryption key (TEK) and the key encryption key (KEK). The TEK becomes the IPsec SA, which is used to communicate with group members within the same group. The TEK key is essentially the group key that is shared by all the group members for secure communication with each other, whereas the KEK is used to encrypt the rekey messages and is used by the group members to decrypt the incoming rekey messages from the key server.

- **Group Member**: The Group Member is the router that registers with the key server to get the IPsec SA to communicate with other devices in the group. The group member registers with the key server to provide the group ID and receives the security policy and keys for this group from the server.

Figure 17-2 illustrates the basic components of the GET VPN solution.

Figure 17-2 *GET VPN Components*

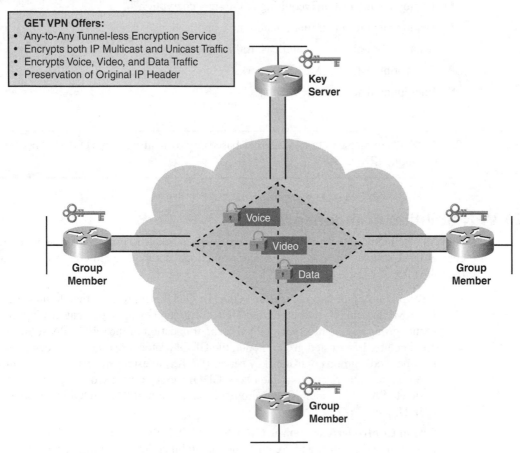

How GET VPN Works

Cisco IOS Software-based GET VPN technology is a tunnel-less solution providing end-to-end security for voice, video, and data using the core network's capability to route the packets between various sites within a fully meshed network.

GET VPN uses the keying protocol Group Domain of Interpretation (GDOI) combined with IPsec standards encryption to encrypt and decrypt the packets, thereby providing an efficient mechanism to secure native (nontunneled) IP multicast and unicast traffic. GET VPN eliminates the requirement of configuring tunnels to secure traffic. The GDOI protocol is the foundation for Cisco GET VPN architecture. GDOI is documented in RFC 3547.

Figure 17-3 illustrates the packet flow, the process of registration, and how group members participate within a group to establish a secure tunnel-less communication:

1 Each group member sends a registration request to the key server. Using the GDOI protocol, the key server authenticates and authorizes the group member and sends the IPsec policy and the keys that are required to encrypt and decrypt IP multicast and unicast packets.

2 After the group member is registered with the IPsec SA, and upon receiving the respective keys, group members can directly exchange encrypted IP multicast and unicast packets with each other, bypassing the key server, thus establishing secure communication. The traffic encryption key (TEK) is used by all the group members to communicate securely.

3 As needed, the key server sends a rekey message to all the group members within the group. The rekey message contains the new IPsec policy and keys that are used when the outdated IPsec SA expires. Rekey messages are sent in advance of the SA expiration time to ensure that valid group keys are always available.

Figure 17-3 *GDOI Registration Flow and Tunnel-less Encrypted Communication*

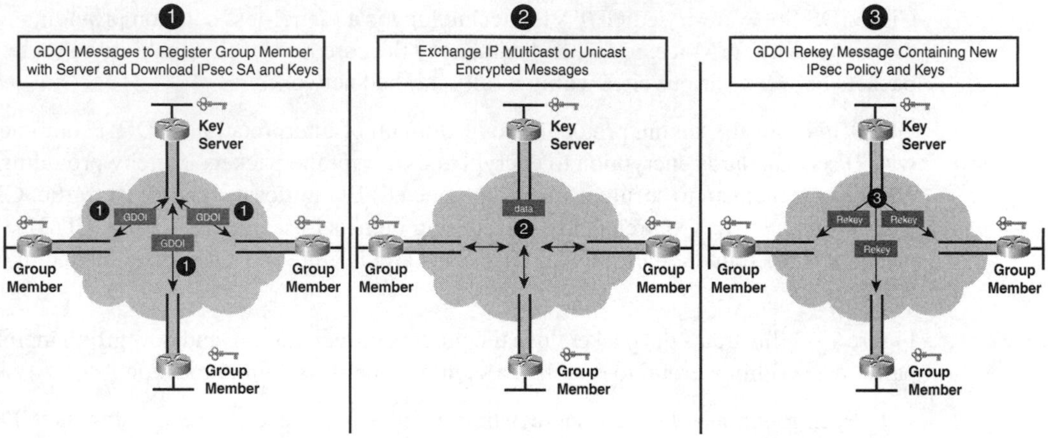

The GDOI protocol is used between the key server and a group member to distribute the security policy (IPsec SA) and keys within the group. The key server is responsible for creating and maintaining the IPsec SA and keys and downloading the IPsec SA and keys to the authenticated group members. The authenticated group members can then communicate with each other (within the same group) by using the IPsec SA received from the key server.

As shown in Figure 17-4, the GDOI protocol is protected by an ISAKMP Phase 1 exchange. The GDOI key server and the GDOI group member must have the same ISAKMP policy. Figure 17-4 shows the GDOI protocol four-message exchange that follows the Phase 1 ISAKMP policy.

Figure 17-4 *GDOI Registration Protected by ISAKMP Phase 1*

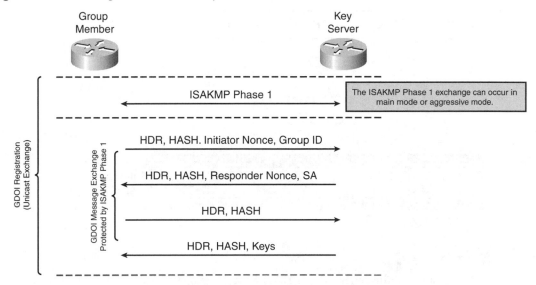

As shown in Figure 17-4, the entire GDOI registration process includes the ISAKMP Phase 1 message and the four GDOI protocol messages, which are protected by ISAKMP Phase 1.

The GDOI registration process is a unicast exchange that uses UDP port 848 (with NAT-T, it floats to port 4500).

During the GDOI registration process, each group member also receives the address of the multicast group, and each member registers with the multicast group that is required to receive the multicast rekeys. After the registration is successful, the key server sends a multicast rekey to all the group members that have registered within a group.

IP Header Preservation

One of the main attributes and advantages of using GET VPN is that it offers header preservation. Packets protected by IPsec in GET VPN retain the original source and destination addresses in the "outer" IP header, rather than replacing them with tunnel endpoint addresses. This is why this approach is called "tunnel-less" technology, because it retains the original IP header of the packet and encrypts only the data payload. To retain the original IP header, the original header is copied and placed before the IPsec header. Figure 17-5 depicts this function.

Preserving the original header is largely suited for optimal routing in an enterprise network running over a private MPLS/IP-based core network.

Figure 17-5 *IP Header Preservation*

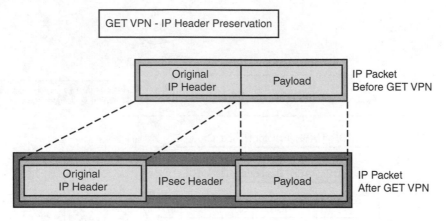

Group Member ACL

Traffic that requires encryption is statically defined on the key server through an access control list (ACL). This policy is defined for both unicast and multicast traffic. The ACL determines which traffic is encrypted. The information is sent to all authenticated group members to create a trusted domain of communication. Policies that are downloaded from the key server are appended to the locally configured ACL on the group member. Any ACL that is configured locally on the group member takes precedence over what is downloaded from the key server.

Cisco recommends using a private subnet addressing scheme from a single major network for all the inside network interfaces on the group members that require protection. For example, use a Class A major net 10.0.0.0/8 for all LAN interfaces behind the group members. Subnet the Class A into smaller chunks of /24 subnets for each member site, and so on. This will greatly reduce the complexity of defining the policy on the key server. With a contiguous network block, you can define one ACL permit statement—for example, **access-list 101 permit ip 10.0.0.0 0.255.255.255 10.0.0.0 0.255.255.255**—to represent all the private subnets in your network behind each group member. If group members use the same contiguous network block for all private LAN interfaces, they will install only one summarized SA for the 10.0.0.0/8 in the database. If different network blocks are used, separate SAs need to be installed for each subnet block.

The key server is flexible in its capability to change the policy dynamically as needed, when newer networks are introduced and group members are dynamically updated with new security policy.

Implementing Cisco IOS GET VPN

Based on the illustration shown in Figure 17-6, the following configuration examples provide deployment guidelines for implementing a Cisco IOS GET VPN solution in an any-to-any design, thereby offering end-to-end CE-CE encryption in an MPLS VPN network environment.

Figure 17-6 *Implementing Cisco IOS GET VPN*

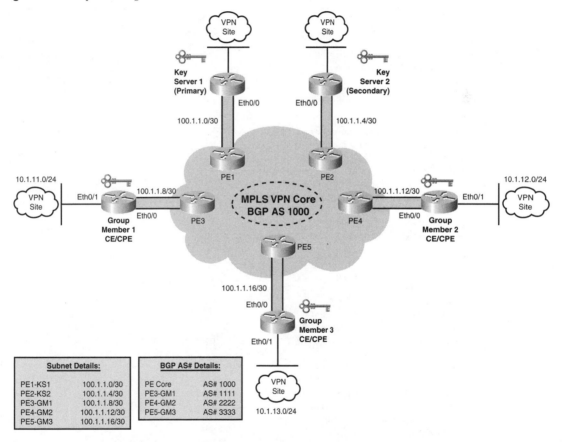

Example 17-1 shows the Key-Server-1 configuration.

Example 17-2 shows the Key-Server-2 configuration.

Example 17-3 shows the Group-Member-1 configuration.

Example 17-4 shows the Group-Member-2 configuration.

Example 17-5 shows the Group-Member-3 configuration.

The topology shown in Figure 17-6 is used in Examples 17-1 through 17-5 to demonstrate an intranet VPN scenario. The MPLS VPN core interconnects VPN sites as shown in Figure 17-6. The CE/CPE routers (Group Members 1 through 3) on each VPN site are grouped into a single GDOI group that correlates with the VPN of which these sites are a part. All the key servers and group members are part of the same VPN. Key-Server-1 is the primary key server and Key-Server-2 is the secondary key server.

Example 17-1 *Configuring Cisco IOS GET VPN Key-Server-1 Router—Primary*

```
hostname KeyServer-1
!
<..>
!
crypto isakmp policy 10
 encr 3des
 authentication pre-share
 group 2
!
crypto isakmp key cisco address 100.1.1.5
crypto isakmp key cisco address 100.1.1.9
crypto isakmp key cisco address 100.1.1.13
crypto isakmp key cisco address 100.1.1.17
!
crypto ipsec transform-set mygdoi-trans esp-3des esp-sha-hmac
!
crypto ipsec profile gdoi-profile-getvpn
 set security-association lifetime seconds 1800
 set transform-set mygdoi-trans
!
crypto gdoi group getvpn
 identity number 1234
 server local
  rekey lifetime seconds 86400
  rekey retransmit 10 number 2
  rekey authentication mypubkey rsa getvpn-export-general
  rekey transport unicast
  sa ipsec 1
   profile gdoi-profile-getvpn
   match address ipv4 199
   replay counter window-size 64
   replay time window-size 5
  address ipv4 100.1.1.1
  redundancy
   local priority 100
   peer address ipv4 100.1.1.5
   !
interface Ethernet0/0
 description Outside interface to PE1
 ip address 100.1.1.1 255.255.255.252
!
ip classless
ip route 0.0.0.0 0.0.0.0 100.1.1.2
 !
```

Example 17-1   *Configuring Cisco IOS GET VPN Key-Server-1 Router—Primary (Continued)*

```
access-list 199 remark ACL policies to be pushed to authenticated group members
access-list 199 permit ip 10.1.0.0 0.0.255.255 10.1.0.0 0.0.255.255
!
<..>
```

Example 17-2   *Configuring Cisco IOS GET VPN Key-Server-2 Router—Secondary*

```
hostname KeyServer-2
!
<..>
!
crypto isakmp policy 10
 encr 3des
 authentication pre-share
 group 2
!
crypto isakmp key cisco address 100.1.1.1
crypto isakmp key cisco address 100.1.1.9
crypto isakmp key cisco address 100.1.1.13
crypto isakmp key cisco address 100.1.1.17
!
crypto ipsec transform-set mygdoi-trans esp-3des esp-sha-hmac
!
crypto ipsec profile gdoi-profile-getvpn
 set security-association lifetime seconds 1800
 set transform-set mygdoi-trans
!
crypto gdoi group getvpn
 identity number 1234
 server local
  rekey lifetime seconds 86400
  rekey retransmit 10 number 2
  rekey authentication mypubkey rsa getvpn-export-general
  rekey transport unicast
  sa ipsec 1
   profile gdoi-profile-getvpn
   match address ipv4 199
   replay counter window-size 64
   replay time window-size 5
  address ipv4 100.1.1.5
  redundancy
   local priority 75
   peer address ipv4 100.1.1.1
   !
interface Ethernet0/0
 description Outside interface to PE2
 ip address 100.1.1.5 255.255.255.252
!
ip classless
ip route 0.0.0.0 0.0.0.0 10.1.1.6
!
```

Example 17-2 *Configuring Cisco IOS GET VPN Key-Server-2 Router—Secondary (Continued)*

```
access-list 199 remark ACL policies to be pushed to authenticated group members
access-list 199 permit ip 10.1.0.0 0.0.255.255 10.1.0.0 0.0.255.255
!
<..>
```

Example 17-3 *Configuring Cisco IOS GET VPN Group-Member-1 Router*

```
hostname GroupMember-1
!
<..>
!
crypto isakmp policy 10
 encr 3des
 authentication pre-share
 group 2
!
crypto isakmp key cisco address 100.1.1.1
crypto isakmp key cisco address 100.1.1.5
!
crypto gdoi group getvpn
 identity number 1234
 server address ipv4 100.1.1.1
 server address ipv4 100.1.1.5
!
crypto map getvpn-map 10 gdoi
 set group getvpn
!
interface Ethernet0/0
 description Outside interface to PE3
 ip address 100.1.1.9 255.255.255.252
 crypto map getvpn-map
!
interface Ethernet0/1
 description Inside interface
 ip address 10.1.11.1 255.255.255.0
!
router bgp 1111
 no synchronization
 bgp log-neighbor-changes
 network 10.1.11.0 mask 255.255.255.0
 neighbor 100.1.1.10 remote-as 1000
 no auto-summary
!
<..>
```

Example 17-4 *Configuring Cisco IOS GET VPN Group-Member-2 Router*

```
hostname GroupMember-2
!
<..>
!
```

Example 17-4 *Configuring Cisco IOS GET VPN Group-Member-2 Router (Continued)*

```
crypto isakmp policy 10
 encr 3des
 authentication pre-share
 group 2
!
crypto isakmp key cisco address 100.1.1.1
crypto isakmp key cisco address 100.1.1.5
!
crypto gdoi group getvpn
 identity number 1234
 server address ipv4 100.1.1.1
 server address ipv4 100.1.1.5
!
crypto map getvpn-map 10 gdoi
 set group getvpn
!
interface Ethernet0/0
 description Outside interface to PE4
 ip address 100.1.1.13 255.255.255.252
 crypto map getvpn-map
!
interface Ethernet0/1
 description Inside interface
 ip address 10.1.12.1 255.255.255.0
!
router bgp 2222
 no synchronization
 bgp log-neighbor-changes
 network 10.1.12.0 mask 255.255.255.0
 neighbor 100.1.1.14 remote-as 1000
 no auto-summary
!
<..>
```

Example 17-5 *Configuring Cisco IOS GET VPN Group-Member-3 Router*

```
hostname GroupMember-3
!
<..>
!
crypto isakmp policy 10
 encr 3des
 authentication pre-share
 group 2
!
crypto isakmp key cisco address 100.1.1.1
crypto isakmp key cisco address 100.1.1.5
!
crypto gdoi group getvpn
 identity number 1234
 server address ipv4 100.1.1.1
```

Example 17-5 *Configuring Cisco IOS GET VPN Group-Member-3 Router (Continued)*

```
  server address ipv4 100.1.1.5
 !
 crypto map getvpn-map 10 gdoi
  set group getvpn
 !
 interface Ethernet0/0
  description Outside interface to PE5
  ip address 100.1.1.17 255.255.255.252
  crypto map getvpn-map
 !
 interface Ethernet0/1
  description Inside interface
  ip address 10.1.13.1 255.255.255.0
 !
 router bgp 3333
  no synchronization
  bgp log-neighbor-changes
  network 10.1.13.0 mask 255.255.255.0
  neighbor 100.1.1.18 remote-as 1000
  no auto-summary
 !
 <..>
```

The following **show** commands can be used to verify functionality on key-server (ks) and group-members (gm).

- **show crypto isakmp sa**
- **show crypto gdoi**
- **show crypto gdoi ks acl**
- **show crypto gdoi ks members**
- **show crypto gdoi ks policy**
- **show crypto gdoi ks rekey**
- **show crypto gdoi ks replay**
- **show crypto gdoi ks coop**
- **show crypto session detail**
- **show crypto gdoi gm acl**
- **show crypto gdoi gm rekey**
- **show crypto gdoi gm replay**

Summary

As demand for VPN implementation grows, organizations with large-scale, full-meshed networks require scalable and instantaneous cryptographic solutions that interconnect sites with robust security, without compromising service quality or adding complexity and overhead to the overall network.

Cisco introduced the groundbreaking new category of VPN technology, which is a tunnel-less approach, based on the revolutionary Cisco IOS Group Encrypted Transport (GET VPN) solution, which provides end-to-end security for voice, video, and data in a highly scalable network environment.

Through numerous examples and diagrams that explain how it works, this chapter provides a comprehensive explanation of the Cisco IOS GET VPN solution architecture and components that make up the GET VPN solution.

The chapter presents implementation guidelines for deploying the Cisco IOS GET VPN solution that offers end-to-end encryption in an MPLS VPN network environment, providing sample configurations from key servers and group members.

References

http://www.cisco.com/go/getvpn

http://www.cisco.com/en/US/products/ps6441/products_feature_guide09186a008078e4f9.html

http://www.cisco.com/en/US/products/ps6635/products_white_paper0900aecd805cc40d.shtml

http://www.cisco.com/en/US/products/ps6635/products_qanda_item0900aecd80582072.shtml

http://www.cisco.com/application/pdf/en/us/guest/products/ps7180/c1161/cdccont_0900aecd8058203e.pdf

http://www.cisco.com/application/pdf/en/us/guest/products/ps7180/c1161/cdccont_0900aecd80582031.pdf

http://www.cisco.com/application/pdf/en/us/guest/products/ps7180/c1031/cdccont_0900aecd80582078.pdf

http://www.cisco.com/application/pdf/en/us/guest/products/ps7180/c1031/cdccont_0900aecd80582078.pdf

CHAPTER 18

Secure Sockets Layer VPN (SSL VPN)

The ubiquitous Internet fuels network access reachability and availability to users whenever and wherever needed.

Today's VPN solutions offer state-of-the-art secure technologies that extend the reach of networks to anyone, anyplace, anytime.

Remote Access VPN technology is the logical solution for remote connectivity providing secure communications with access rights tailored to individual users.

SSL-based Remote Access VPN technology provides remote-access connectivity from any Internet-enabled computer through a standard web browser and its native SSL encryption.

SSL VPN solutions offer network access at any time and any place, thereby providing the possibility of increasing productivity. SSL VPN solutions also offer greater flexibility for the remote workforce.

This chapter provides a complete overview of the SSL-based Remote Access VPN technology, describing solution architecture, deployment, and implementation guidelines. The chapter also introduces the newly released Cisco AnyConnect VPN client solution.

Secure Sockets Layer (SSL) Protocol

SSL is an application layer (Layer 7) cryptographic protocol that provides secure communications over the Internet for web browsing, e-mail, instant messaging, and other data traffic.

SSL, which was originally developed by Netscape and released in 1996, later served as the foundation for the IETF standard—Transport Layer Security (TLS) protocol.

Although SSL and TLS vary in some respects and are not interoperable, the protocol architecture largely remains the same. The primary objective of both protocols is to provide data privacy and data integrity, thereby providing secure communications between applications. By default, SSL uses TCP port 443.

NOTE   TLS was originally documented in IETF RFC 2246—"The TLS Protocol Version 1.0," and
was made obsolete by IETF RFC 4346—"The Transport Layer Security (TLS) Protocol
Version 1.1," which, as of this writing, is the current approved TLS version.

SSL VPN Solution Architecture

VPN technologies in recent years have evolved and have been widely used to provide
secure connectivity, extending the reach of networks. As discussed in Chapter 15, "IPsec
VPN," two primary methods are used to deploy Remote Access VPN technology:

- **Remote Access:** IPsec VPN (covered in Chapter 15)
- **Remote Access:** SSL VPN

Cisco IPsec VPN and SSL VPN are complementary technologies. Both solutions offer
remote access connectivity and can be deployed together or individually to better address
the deployment requirements. Selecting the appropriate method depends on the deployment
requirements and the network architecture.

Table 18-1 shows a comparison summary between IPsec VPN and SSL VPN technologies
that can assist you in evaluating the appropriate Remote Access VPN technology as needed.

Table 18-1   *IPsec and SSL VPN Comparison Chart*

	IPsec VPN	**SSL VPN**
End-User System Options	Enables access primarily from company-managed desktops.	Enables access from company-managed, employee-owned, contractor or business partner desktops, Internet cybercafés, as well as hotspots.
End-User Access Method	Initiated using a preinstalled VPN client software.	Initiated through a web browser.
End-User System Software Requirements	Requires proprietary preinstalled client software.	Requires no special-purpose desktop VPN client software; only a web browser is required.
Software Updates	Can automatically update, but is more intrusive and requires user input.	No special-purpose desktop software installed; thus no updates are required. Note that full network application access is provided through software that dynamically installs and updates without user intervention.
Customized User Access	Offers granular access policies, but no web portals.	Offers granular access policies, as well as user-customized web portals.

Note: The information in Table 18-1 is compiled from a Cisco white paper on "Remote
Access VPN for Secure Communications" at http://www.cisco.com/en/US/netsol/ns340/
ns394/ns171/ns125/networking_solutions_white_paper0900aecd804fb79a.shtml.

SSL VPN Overview

SSL VPN is an emerging technology offering a flexible, low-cost Internet-based remote solution by using the native SSL encryption of a web browser. SSL VPN does not require a special-purpose client software to be preinstalled on the system, thus enabling a user to connect from any computer, whether it is a company-managed or a non-company-managed system, such as a personal laptop, cybercafé, or home PC. SSL VPN sessions can be established from any Internet-enabled computer, thereby extending network access when and where required.

The Cisco SSL-based Remote Access VPN solution is a powerful tool that provides users with a virtual environment that emulates the working conditions of a main office with no geographical boundaries.

The Cisco Remote Access VPN solutions offer both IPsec VPN and SSL VPN technologies integrated on a single platform with unified management. The Cisco security solutions group offers the SSL VPN solution as part of the security products range. Examples include Cisco Integrated Services Routers (ISR), VPN Security, and Firewall Appliances.

NOTE   The Cisco SSL VPN solution is also commonly known as the Cisco WebVPN solution, and the two terms are interchangeably used in publications.

SSL VPN Features

SSL VPN technology offers a wide range of benefits. Key features include the following:

- Does not require special-purpose desktop VPN client software to be preinstalled on the system.
- Uses a standard web browser to establish a remote access VPN connection.
- Uses the native SSL encryption of a web browser to provide data confidentiality.
- Offers granular access control.
- Enables additional client-server applications to be downloaded dynamically with multiple delivery methods to help ensure transparent download and distribution with Java, ActiveX, or .exe files.
- Offers flexibility to establish VPN connections from any Internet-enabled system, be it a company-managed or non-company-managed system.
- Allows easy firewall and network traversal from any location.
- Allows transparent wireless roaming.
- Offers enhanced security using the integrated Cisco IOS Firewall feature.

Figure 18-1 illustrates the concept of SSL VPN and how a remote access user can access protected resources via the Internet over a secure encrypted channel.

Figure 18-1 *Cisco SSL VPN Solution*

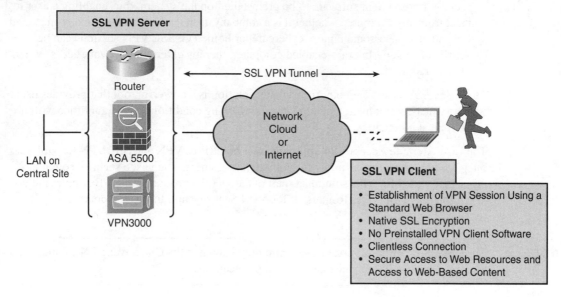

NOTE   As the industry leader in innovation, Cisco introduced the first-ever router platform to integrate the SSL VPN solution in Cisco IOS Software on Cisco Integrated Services Routers (ISR) series. The Cisco SSL VPN solution is also known as Cisco WebVPN.

SSL VPN Deployment Consideration

SSL VPN is an enhanced Cisco Remote Access VPN solution that offers data confidentiality by using the native SSL encryption technology within a web browser. Table 18-2 summarizes the characteristics that need to be considered when evaluating the SSL VPN deployment option.

Table 18-2 *SSL VPN Deployment Consideration*

Characteristics	IPsec VPN	SSL VPN
Anywhere access from non-company-managed systems, such as an employee-owned desktop, a personal laptop, cybercafés, and hotspots		X
Business partner access		X
User-customized web portals		X
Minimized desktop support and software distribution		X
Flexibility to the end users	X	X
VPN client customizability	X	
Capability to maintain existing IT deployment and support processes	X	

The information in Table 18-2 is compiled from the Cisco white paper on "Remote Access VPN for Secure Communications" at http://www.cisco.com/en/US/netsol/ns340/ns394/ ns171/ns125/networking_solutions_white_paper0900aecd804fb79a.shtml.

SSL VPN Access Methods

SSL VPN can be deployed in one of the following three access modes, as illustrated in Figure 18-2:

- **Clientless mode (Layer 7):** Clientless mode provides secure access to web resources and access to web-based content. This mode is useful for accessing content that can be accessed in a web browser, such as Internet access, databases, and online web-based tools. Clientless mode can also offer remote file sharing by using the common Internet file system (CIFS) that provides a list of file server links in the web portal page, thereby allowing the remote user to browse listings of domains, servers, and directory folders, download a file, create a new file/directory, and so on. Clientless mode is limited to web-based content only.

- **Thin client mode (Layer 7) (also known as port forwarding):** Thin client mode provides remote access to TCP-based services such as Post Office Protocol (POP3), Simple Mail Transfer Protocol (SMTP), Internet Message Access Protocol (IMAP), Telnet, and Secure Shell (SSH) applications. The thin client is delivered via a Java applet that is dynamically downloaded from the SSL VPN appliance upon session establishment. This mode extends the capability of the cryptographic functions of the web browser.

- **Thick client mode (Layer 3) (also known as tunnel mode or full tunneling client):** The thick client mode provides remote access to an extensive array of application support and is delivered dynamically by downloading SSL VPN Client (SVC) software or the Cisco AnyConnect VPN client software from the VPN server appliance. This mode delivers a lightweight, centrally configured, and easy-to-support SSL VPN tunneling client that provides full network layer (Layer 3) access to virtually any application.

Figure 18-2 illustrates the basic SSL VPN access modes that were discussed previously.

Figure 18-2 *SSL VPN Access Modes*

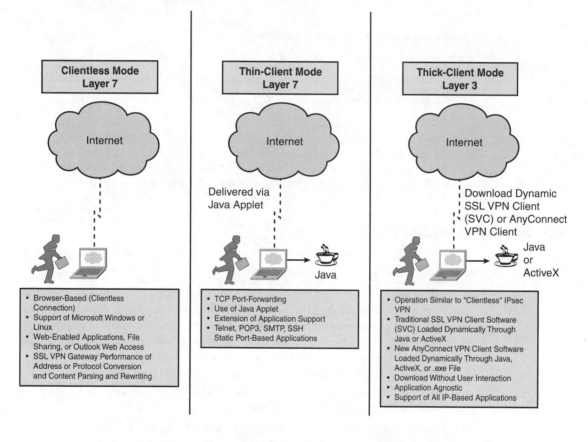

The information in Figure 18-2 is taken from the Cisco configuration guide on "Cisco IOS Software Releases 12.4T - SSL VPN" at http://www.cisco.com/en/US/products/ps6441/products_feature_guide09186a00805eeaea.html#wp1053878.

SSL VPN Citrix Support

The Cisco SSL VPN solution also offers clientless Citrix support that allows Citrix clients to use applications running on a remote Citrix server as if they were executed locally on the internal LAN.

Clientless SSL VPN is commonly used for remote access to Citrix applications. One of the major advantages of using the Cisco SSL VPN solution is that no additional helper applications are required for Citrix access over clientless SSL VPN, which helps ensure fast application initiation time and reduces the risk of desktop software conflicts. Many other SSL VPN solutions on the market require proprietary applets to be pushed down for Citrix to function.

Figure 18-3 illustrates Citrix support comparison with a traditional SSL VPN and the Cisco SSL VPN solution.

Figure 18-3 *SSL VPN Citrix Support*

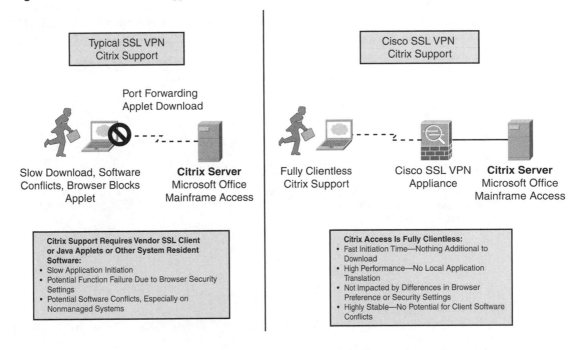

The information concept in Figure 18-3 is taken from the Cisco Networkers session presentation# SEC-2010 – "Deploying Remote Access IPSec and SSL VPNs."

Implementing Cisco IOS SSL VPN

Based on Figure 18-2, the following configuration examples provide basic deployment guidelines for implementing the Cisco IOS SSL VPN solution on the Cisco Integrated Services Routers (ISR) series.

NOTE   The Cisco SSL VPN (WebVPN) feature was introduced in Cisco IOS Software Release 12.3(14)T supporting SSL Version 3.

Example 18-1 shows a generic SSL VPN gateway configuration that includes some of the common features available.

CAUTION   There is a slight variation in command syntax between Cisco IOS version 12.3T and 12.4T when you are configuring an SSL VPN. Example 18-1 is captured from a Cisco IOS version 12.4T-based router.

Example 18-1   *Configuring Cisco IOS SSL VPN*

```
hostname SSL-Gateway
!
aaa new-model
aaa authentication login default local group radius
!
crypto pki trustpoint Gateway
 enrollment selfsigned
 ip-address 192.168.1.1
 revocation-check crl
 rsakeypair keys 1024 1024
!
crypto pki certificate chain Gateway
 certificate self-signed 02
!
interface Loopback0
 ip address 10.10.10.1 255.255.255.0
!
interface GigabitEthernet0/1
 ip address 192.168.1.1 255.255.255.0
!
ip local pool svc-pool 10.10.10.100 10.10.10.110
!
webvpn gateway ssl-vpn
 ip address 192.168.1.1 port 443
 ssl trustpoint Gateway
```

Example 18-1   *Configuring Cisco IOS SSL VPN (Continued)*

```
 inservice
 !
! The following line is required for SSLVPN Client.
webvpn install svc flash:/webvpn/svc.pkg
 !
! The following line is required for Cisco Secure Desktop.
webvpn install csd flash:/webvpn/sdesktop.pkg
 !
webvpn context ssl-vpn
 ssl authenticate verify all
 !
policy group default
 ! The following line enables SSLVPN Client.
    functions svc-enabled
 ! The following line enables clientless Citrix.
    citrix enabled
 default-group-policy default
 ! The following line maps this context to the virtual gateway and defines the domain
to use.
 gateway ssl-vpn domain sslvpn
 ! The following line enables Cisco Secure Desktop.
 csd enable
 inservice
 !
<..>
```

TIP	Refer to the following Cisco technical documentation for further details on configuring Cisco IOS SSL VPN and various other parameters:
	http://www.cisco.com/univercd/cc/td/doc/product/software/ios123/123newft/123t/123t_14/g_sslvpn.htm
	http://www.cisco.com/en/US/products/ps6441/products_feature_guide09186 a00805eeaea.html#wp1356909

The following **show** and **debug** commands can be used to verify functionality on a Cisco router (SSL VPN gateway).

- **show webvpn sessions**
- **show webvpn statistics**
- **show tcp brief all**
- **debug webvpn**

Cisco AnyConnect VPN Client

The Cisco AnyConnect VPN Client is the newly introduced SSL-based VPN client, the next generation of SSL VPN client software. Cisco AnyConnect VPN client provides remote users with secure VPN connections by using the SSL protocol.

Cisco AnyConnect VPN Client solution is available on the following:

- Cisco ASA 5500 Series security appliance running software version 8.0 and later
- Cisco IOS Software Release 12.4(15)T and later

The Cisco AnyConnect is the next-generation SSL VPN Client, replacing the older SVC software.

When using Cisco IOS Software release prior to 12.4(15)T, you should be dynamically loading the older GUI of SVC software when establishing a web-based SSL connection to the SSL server.

However, when using Cisco IOS Software Release 12.4(15)T or later, you should be dynamically loading the newer GUI of Cisco AnyConnect VPN Client software when establishing the connection.

The AnyConnect client supports Microsoft Vista, Microsoft Windows XP, Microsoft Windows 2000, Linux, or Macintosh OS, providing all the benefits of a traditional SSL VPN client and extending enhanced functions support unavailable to a regular clientless SSL VPN connection. Most notably, the AnyConnect client supports the next-generation IPv6 protocol over an IPv4 network.

As illustrated in Figure 18-2, the AnyConnect software client can be automatically downloaded to remote users with any SSL-based browser and dynamically loaded using Java, ActiveX, or .exe files.

TIP   Refer to the following Cisco technical documentation for further details on configuring Cisco AnyConnect VPN Client:

Configuring AnyConnect VPN Client on Cisco IOS Router

http://www.cisco.com/en/US/products/ps6441/products_feature_guide09186a00805eeaea.html

http://www.cisco.com/en/US/products/ps6441/products_feature_guide09186a0080806b10.html

Configuring AnyConnect VPN Client on Cisco ASA Security Appliance

http://www.cisco.com/en/US/docs/security/asa/asa80/configuration/guide/svc.html

http://www.cisco.com/en/US/docs/security/asa/asa80/getting_started/asa5500/quick/guide/ssl_vpn.html

Summary

With the increasing demand of "anywhere" remote access connectivity, using Remote Access VPN technology is the logical solution for providing secure encrypted communications.

Cisco SSL VPN is one of the Remote Access VPN technologies that offers secure remote-access connectivity from any Internet-enabled computer through a standard web browser, thus allowing networks to extend beyond geographical boundaries and providing anytime, anyplace access to a corporate network.

This chapter explained the Cisco SSL VPN solution architecture and basic deployment and implementation guidelines. The chapter also introduced the newly released Cisco AnyConnect VPN Client software.

References

http://www.cisco.com/go/sslvpn

http://www.cisco.com/en/US/products/ps6657/products_ios_protocol_group_home.html

http://www.cisco.com/web/about/security/intelligence/05_08_SSL-VPN-Security.html

http://www.cisco.com/en/US/netsol/ns340/ns394/ns171/netbr09186a00801f0a72.html

http://www.cisco.com/en/US/products/ps6441/products_feature_guide09186 a00805eeaea.html

http://www.cisco.com/en/US/netsol/ns340/ns394/ns171/ns125/networking_solutions_ white_paper0900aecd804fb79a.shtml

http://www.cisco.com/en/US/products/ps6350/prod_bulletin09186a0080457 a84.html#wp1028745

http://www.cisco.com/univercd/cc/td/doc/product/software/ios123/123newft/123t/ 123t_14/g_sslvpn.htm

http://www.cisco.com/go/iossslvpn

http://www.cisco.com/en/US/products/ps6657/products_data_sheet0900aecd80405e25.html

http://www.cisco.com/en/US/docs/security/vpn_client/anyconnect/anyconnect20/ administrative/guide/admin.html

http://www.cisco.com/en/US/docs/security/vpn_client/anyconnect/anyconnect21/release/ notes/anyconnect21.html

CHAPTER 19

Multiprotocol Label Switching VPN (MPLS VPN)

Multiprotocol Label Switching (MPLS) is a widely used transport mechanism that carries data traffic over a packet-switched network (PSN).

MPLS VPN is a service solution extension of the MPLS for providing VPN services that allows enterprises and service providers to build highly efficient, scalable, and secure next-generation intelligent networks.

This chapter provides an overview of MPLS VPN architecture and a basic understanding of the various types of MPLS VPNs. The chapter also covers the Cisco Layer 2 VPN (L2VPN) and Layer 3 VPN (L3VPN) solutions.

Multiprotocol Label Switching (MPLS)

MPLS is a transport mechanism that carries data over a packet-switched network. MPLS is widely used by service providers and large-scale enterprise networks.

MPLS framework was designed to provide flexibility to operate with virtually any Layer 3 and Layer 2 technology. MPLS-based solutions can be integrated seamlessly over any existing infrastructure.

MPLS supports several Layer 3 and Layer 2 protocols. Table 19-1 shows a list of commonly supported protocols.

Table 19-1 *MPLS Supported Protocols*

	OSI Layer 3	OSI Layer 2
MPLS can be used to carry different types of traffic	Supports IPv4, IPv6, IPX, and AppleTalk at Layer 3	Supports Ethernet, Frame Relay, PPP, Token Ring, FDDI, SONET, and ATM at Layer 2

MPLS was originally a Cisco proprietary technology called *tag switching*—a solution designed by a group of Cisco engineers. It was later handed over to the IETF for open standardization and was renamed *label switching*.

TIP   MPLS working documents, Internet-draft papers, and RFCs can be downloaded from the
following Internet Engineering Task Force (IETF)–based MPLS working group website:
http://www.ietf.org/html.charters/mpls-charter.html

MPLS Architecture Overview

The MPLS architecture defines the basic mechanism for performing label switching within
an MPLS core network.

MPLS combines the benefits of packet forwarding based on connection-oriented Layer 2
switching with connectionless Layer 3 routing.

The advantage of this architecture is that routers at the network edge can use conventional
IP forwarding, whereas routers in the network core can run MPLS and use switching
instead of conventional routing table lookup. This also simplifies the hop-by-hop data
forwarding path by replacing the Layer 3 route lookup function performed in traditional
routers with a label swapping mechanism, thus providing faster packet forwarding and
improved network performance.

MPLS architecture assigns *labels* to each packet to be able to transport them across the
MPLS core network. The concept of label is similar to other Layer 2 technologies, such as
Frame Relay or ATM. Labels are used to perform the next-hop label lookup at Layer 2 to
traverse the network. Each node within the network processes the label on the incoming
packet, swaps the label with a new label at outgoing (label swapping), and forwards the
packet to the next node.

The new advanced label-swapping technique in MPLS improves the network performance
and provides greater scalability and flexibility in the delivery of routing services.

Figure 19-1 illustrates the MPLS core architecture.

How MPLS Works

When a packet arrives on the ingress Label Switch Router (LSR), also called the Provider
Edge (PE) router, the PE router assigns a label to transport the packet through the MPLS
network.

As shown in Figure 19-2, each LSR performs a specific function; for example, the LSR at
the edge performs either label imposition (also known as the push functions) or label
removing (also known as the pop function). Other LSRs in the path simply swap the labels.

Figure 19-1 *MPLS Packet Forwarding Architecture*

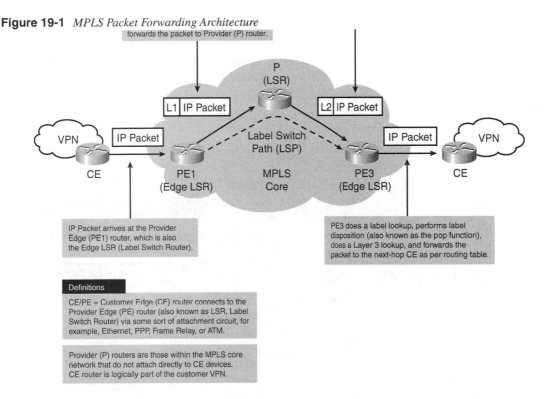

forwards the packet to Provider (P) router.

IP Packet arrives at the Provider Edge (PE1) router, which is also the Edge LSR (Label Switch Router).

PE3 does a label lookup, performs label disposition (also known as the pop function), does a Layer 3 lookup, and forwards the packet to the next-hop CE as per routing table.

Definitions

CE/PE = Customer Edge (CE) router connects to the Provider Edge (PE) router (also known as LSR, Label Switch Router) via some sort of attachment circuit, for example, Ethernet, PPP, Frame Relay, or ATM.

Provider (P) routers are those within the MPLS core network that do not attach directly to CE devices. CE router is logically part of the customer VPN.

Each LSR maintains a Label Forwarding Information Base (LFIB) table that is built using the IP routing table to determine the label binding exchange. The LFIB provides an incoming labeled packet with the outgoing interface and the new label information associated respectively with the outgoing packet.

Adjacent nodes perform a label binding exchange for individual subnets (destination-based IP routing) using the Cisco proprietary Tag Distribution Protocol (TDP) or the IETF-standard Label Distribution Protocol (LDP). If the route (prefix/mask and next hop) learned via the TDP/LDP matches the route learned via IGP in the routing table, an entry is created in the LFIB on the LSR.

Packets in the MPLS core are forwarded based on the labels that are prepended by the LSR, and not based on the IP destination address.

The LSR-to-LSR journey of this packet within the MPLS core crosses several LSR routers; this path is called the Label Switched Path (LSP). LSP is essentially a set of LSRs (similar to the AS path in BGP) through which a labeled packet must traverse to reach the edge LSR. As a packet traverses the LSP, each LSR swaps the label until it reaches the router before the last LSR (the penultimate hop), which pops the label and transmits the packet without the label to the last hop egress LSR, where the packet is out of the MPLS core and forwarded to the destination CE.

Figure 19-2 shows a detailed diagram demonstrating how the packet forwarding and label swapping works within the MPLS core network.

Figure 19-2 *MPLS Packet Forwarding and Label Switching*

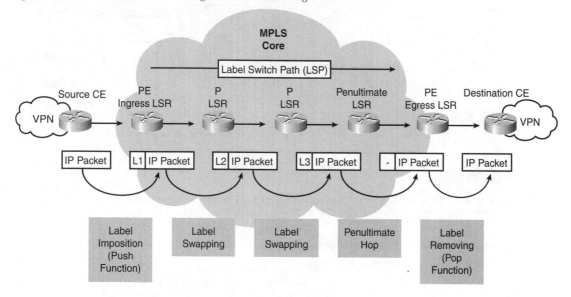

MPLS VPN and IPsec VPN

MPLS VPN and IPsec VPN are complementary technologies; both have their benefits, though in different implementations.

The MPLS VPN solution provides a pseudo point-to-point connection that allows networks to peer indirectly, providing a sense of security and data privacy. MPLS VPN creates a private data path through the MPLS core network, providing faster and more secure data paths without network overhead.

MPLS VPN does not provide data confidentiality or cryptography functions. This means that data could possibly be intercepted during transmission without sender/receiver knowledge. Thus, it will often not meet requirements for confidentiality or nonrepudiation that may be required by some of the industry standards (for example, HIPAA). The security must be provided at the network layer. To provide data confidentiality, IPsec VPN solution at the network layer can be deployed as an overlay over the MPLS network.

Table 19-2 shows a comparison between MPLS VPN and IPsec VPN technologies.

Table 19-2   *Comparison Between MPLS VPN and IPsec VPN*

	MPLS VPN	IPsec VPN
Placement	Implemented in core network (resides in service provider network).	Implemented at local loop, edge, and off-net (resides in customer network).
Scalability	Highly scalable because no site-to-site peering is required. Can support tens of thousands of VPN connections over the same network.	Scalability becomes a challenge when implementing large-scale, fully meshed IPsec VPN solutions. Requires careful planning and coordination for key management, distribution, peering configuration, and more.
Provisioning	To enable MPLS VPN connection, a one-time provisioning is required to install customer's edge (CE) and provider's edge (PE) routers to join the MPLS core.	IPsec VPN uses the IP core network provisioning, offering services with reduced operation expense through centralized network-level infrastructure. Customer edge local equipment is used to deploy IPsec end-to-end solution.
Deployment	Provider dependency, because it requires MPLS-capable network infrastructure at the core and edge of the provider network.	Does not depend on the provider and can be deployed across any existing IP network.
Authentication	Connections are authenticated via logical VPN membership during provisioning, based on logical port and unique route descriptor. Unauthorized access is denied.	Connections are authenticated via digital certificate or preshared keys. Packets that do not conform to the security policy are dropped.
Confidentiality	Logical point-to-point circuits are separated, providing a sense of security and data privacy.	Set of standard encryption and tunneling mechanisms are used at the IP network layer to protect data.
Quality of Service (QoS) and Service Level Agreement (SLA)	Provides QoS and SLAs with robust traffic-engineering capabilities.	Does not directly address QoS and SLAs, although Cisco IPsec solutions can preserve packet classification for QoS within an IPsec tunnel.
VPN client	MPLS VPN is a network-based service; hence, end users do not require VPN client software to communicate with remote networks.	Required only for Remote Access VPN solution. Cisco VPN client software is available for various platforms, including Microsoft, Linux, and MAC OS. For site-to-site network-based IPsec deployments, VPN client is not required.

Note: The information in Table 19-2 is compiled from the Cisco white paper on "VPN Architectures - Comparing MPLS and IPsec" at http://www.cisco.com/en/US/netsol/ns590/networking_solutions_white_paper09186a008009d67f.shtml.

Deployment Scenarios

There are three basic deployment scenarios for implementing MPLS solutions, as shown in Figure 19-3.

- **Shared Core and Shared Edge:** This design comprises a single MPLS core that services both the public IP and private VPN traffic. Similarly at the edge, a single PE router is used to terminate both public IP and private VPN connections.

- **Shared Core and Separate Edge:** This design also comprises a single MPLS core that services both the public IP and private VPN traffic. At the edge, dedicated, purpose-built PE routers are used to terminate public IP and private VPN connections, respectively.

- **Separate Core and Separate Edge:** This design comprises separate MPLS cores for each public IP and private VPN traffic connections, respectively. Similarly at the edge, dedicated PE routers (purpose-built) are used to terminate public IP and private VPN connections, respectively.

Figure 19-3 *MPLS Deployment Scenarios*

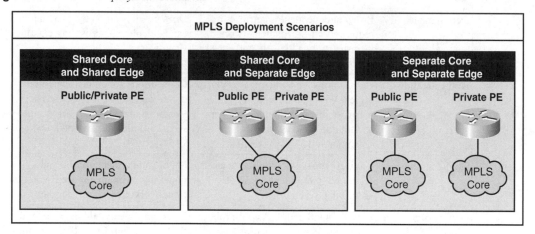

NOTE The information in Figure 19-3 is compiled from the Cisco Networkers session presentation# SEC-2100 – "MPLS-VPN Security Guidelines."

Connection-Oriented and Connectionless VPN Technologies

VPN technologies vary, and there is no fixed classification for VPN solutions. VPN can be categorized in two ways: connection-oriented and connectionless VPN. As shown in Figure 19-4, connection-oriented VPN has an end-to-end path through the core network. Examples include IPsec and generic routing encapsulation (GRE).

Connectionless VPN does not have a direct relationship with a peer site and has a virtual path joining two sites via the core network. Examples include MPLS VPN, which connects two customer sites via the MPLS core cloud.

Connectionless VPNs scale better because less information is kept at the customer edge, whereas with connection-oriented VPNs, all information is kept at the edge. Figure 19-4 illustrates the connection-oriented and connectionless VPN technologies.

Figure 19-4 *Connection-Oriented and Connectionless VPN Technologies*

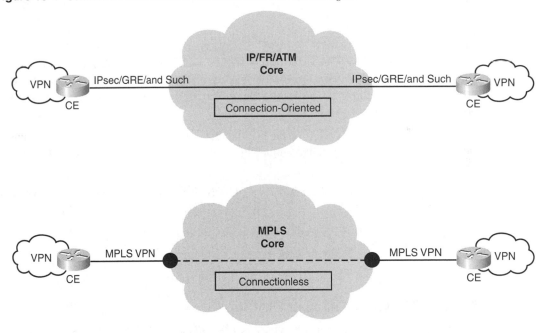

MPLS VPN (Trusted VPN)

As discussed in Chapter 15, "IPsec VPN," there are two major types of VPNs:

- **Secure VPN (also known as Cryptographic VPN):** Secure VPN technologies include IPsec, L2TP over IPsec, and Secure Sockets Layer (SSL) encryption.

- **Trusted VPN (also known as non-Cryptographic VPN):** Trusted VPN technologies include Multiprotocol Label Switching (MPLS) VPN (Layer 3 VPN), Multicast VPN (Layer 3 VPN), Transport of Layer 2 frames over MPLS, Any Transport over MPLS (AToM) (Layer 2 VPN), and virtual private LAN services (VPLS) (Layer 2 VPN).

NOTE   Secure VPN technologies are covered in Chapters 15, 16, 17, and 18. This section covers Trusted VPN technologies.

The major characteristic of Trusted VPN is based on the service provider offering a dedicated circuit or channel to a customer. Hence, pseudo point-to-point communication occurs in this scenario, allowing networks to peer directly using a dedicated circuit and providing a sense of security and data privacy. Traffic traversing this dedicated point-to-point circuit is called Trusted VPN.

In a Trusted VPN, security relies on the fact that the circuit provided by the service provider is not shared and is dedicated to a single site for point-to-point communication between specific customer sites.

Service providers today offer several Trusted VPN services. There are two major types of Trusted VPNs:

- **Layer 3 VPN (L3VPN):** Packet-based forwarding
- **Layer 2 VPN (L2VPN):** Frame-based forwarding

Comparison of L3 and L2 VPNs

Table 19-3 shows a basic comparison between L3VPN and L2VPN solutions and describes the type of data each can carry.

Table 19-3   *Comparison Between L3VPN and L2VPN*

Layer 3 VPN (L3VPN)	Layer 2 VPN (L2VPN)
Provides packet-based forwarding (for example, IP).	Provides frame-based forwarding (for example, VLAN, DLCI, VPI/VCI).
Service provider forwards customer data packets based on Layer 3 information (for example, IP).	Service provider forwards customer data packets based on Layer 2 information. Supports Multiprotocol (for example, Ethernet, Frame Relay, or ATM).
SP involvement is required to perform routing.	No SP is involved. Uses Tunnel, circuit, LSP, MAC address.
Approaches include MPLS/BGP VPN (RFC 2547), MPLS VPN over IP, GRE, virtual router.	Concept is pseudowire.

Selecting L3VPN over L2VPN depends on how much control the enterprise wants to retain within its network. With L3VPN, the service provider is involved because it performs the routing; whereas with L2VPN, the service provider is not involved, because virtual tunnels and circuits are used instead.

Subscribers have various requirements and can take advantage of L3VPN and L2VPN as needed.

- L3VPN is useful to subscribers who prefer to outsource their routing to service providers. The service provider manages routing for the customer's sites.

- L2VPN is useful to subscribers who run their own Layer 3 networks over the WAN and require Layer 2 connectivity from service providers. In this case, the subscriber manages its own routing information.

Figure 19-5 illustrates the Layer 3 and Layer 2 VPN data forwarding scenarios over the MPLS core. Both Layer 3 and Layer 2 VPN services are offered from the edge of a network.

Figure 19-5 *Layer 3 Versus Layer 2 VPN Forwarding*

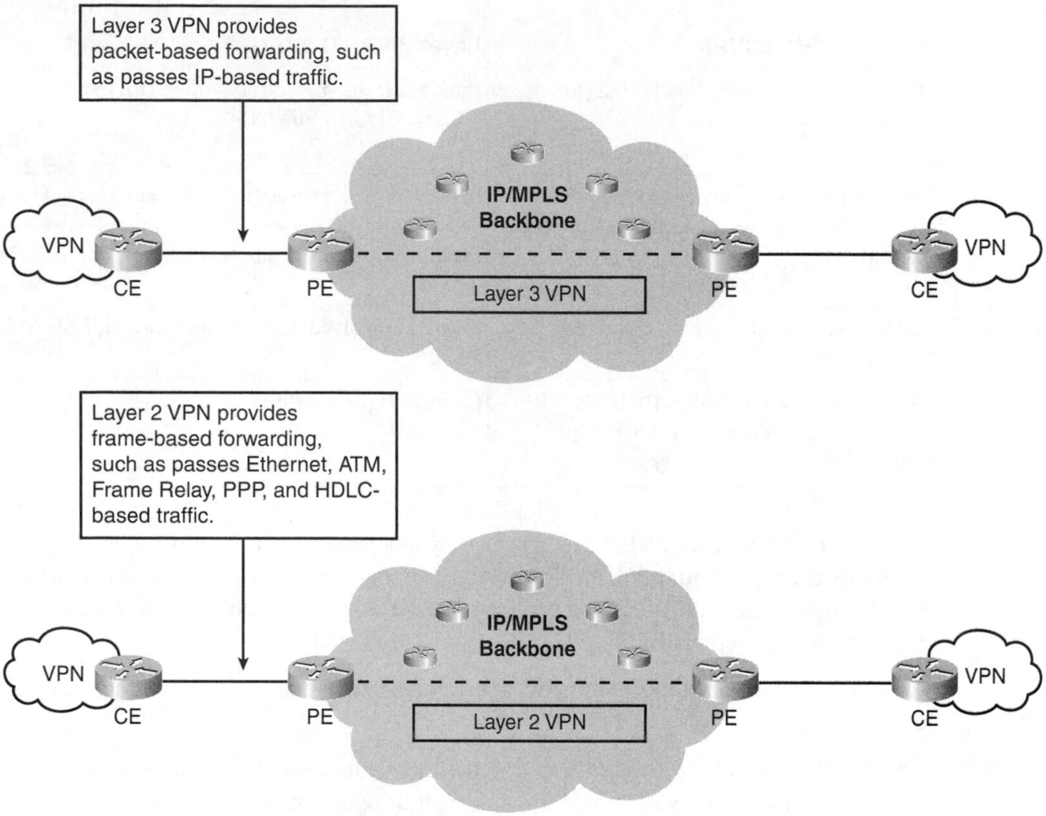

Layer 3 VPN (L3VPN)

Layer 3 VPN (L3VPN) over MPLS is one of the most widely deployed MPLS applications in service provider and large-scale enterprise networks.

Cisco IOS Software supports L3VPN architecture that uses the RFC 2547 standard implementation to provide a secure and robust VPN solution offering any-to-any connectivity that can be implemented over MPLS or IP network infrastructure.

L3VPN architecture leverages Multiprotocol Border Gateway Protocol (MP-BGP) and Virtual Routing and Forwarding (VRF) instances to constitute a peer-to-peer VPN framework via the IP/MPLS core network. This model allows enterprise networks to outsource routing table information to service providers.

L3VPN allows service providers to offer additional value-add services to the customers, such as QoS, Traffic Engineering (TE), and Fast Reroute services, thereby reducing operational costs and complexity, and increasing network performance and convergence.

Components of L3VPN

There are three major components in an L3VPN network:

- **VPN Route Target Communities:** This consists of a list of all members of the VPN community. VPN route targets need to be configured for each VPN community member.
- **Multiprotocol BGP (MP-BGP) Peering:** This is configured between all PE routers within a VPN community. MP-BGP is used to propagate VRF reachability information to all members of a VPN community.
- **MPLS Forwarding:** MPLS core transports all traffic between all VPN community members across a VPN service-provider core network.

As mentioned earlier, MPLS VPN is a connection-less technology; hence, it does not require a one-to-one relationship between customer sites and VPNs. A given customer site can be a member of multiple VPNs. However, each site can associate with only one VRF. VRF ensures a customer site gets all the routes pertaining to the site from the VPNs of which it is a member.

How L3VPN Implementation Works

L3VPN is implemented at the edge of an MPLS core network on the PE (provider's edge) router. The PE router is responsible for the following:

- Exchange routing updates with the CE (Customer's Edge) router
- Translate the CE routing information into VPNv4 routes
- Exchange VPNv4 routes with other PE routers via the MP-BGP through the MPLS core

How VRF Tables Work

Virtual Routing and Forwarding (VRF) constitutes the VPN membership of a customer site that is attached to a PE router. Each VPN can be associated with one or more VRF instances. A VRF consists of the following components:

- IP routing table
- Derived CEF table
- Set of interfaces that use the forwarding table

- Set of rules and routing protocol parameters that control the information that is included in the routing table

VRF tables are used to forward packets within a VPN. Each VRF instance maintains a separate set of routing and CEF tables. This segregation prevents leaking of routes outside a VPN and ensures that packets outside a VPN are not forwarded to any router within the VPN.

VPN routing information is distributed through the MPLS core using VPN route target communities that are implemented by MP-BGP extended communities.

Implementing L3VPN

Figure 19-6 topology demonstrates a basic L3VPN scenario using MP-BGP. The MPLS core interconnects VPN sites as shown in Figure 19-6. The customer CE router is a member of two VPNs (VPN_A and VPN_B) on each site with overlapping subnets. Intermediate System-to-Intermediate System (IS-IS) protocol is running within the MPLS core network.

Figure 19-6 *Implementing Basic L3VPN (MPLS VPN Using MP-BGP)*

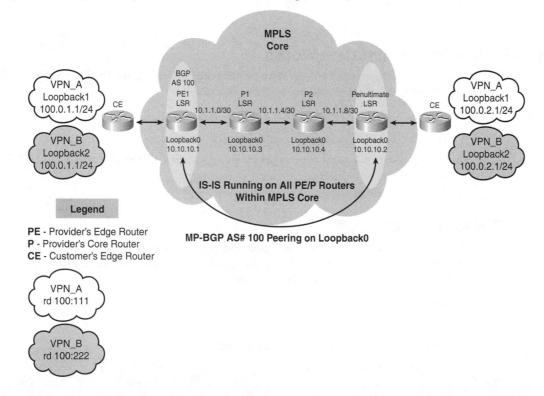

Based on the Figure 19-6 illustration, the following configuration examples provide deployment guidelines for implementing basic MPLS L3VPN solutions.

Example 19-1 shows PE-1 configuration

Example 19-2 shows PE-2 configuration

Example 19-3 shows P-1 configuration

Example 19-4 shows P-2 configuration

Example 19-1 *Configuring L3VPN on Cisco IOS Router—PE-1 LSR*

```
hostname PE1
!
ip cef
!
!--- VPN A commands.
!
ip vrf VPN_A
!--- Enables the VPN routing and forwarding (VRF) routing table.
!
 rd 100:111
!--- Route distinguisher creates routing and forwarding tables for a VRF.
 route-target export 100:111
 route-target import 100:111
!--- Creates lists of import and export route-target extended. communities for the
specified VRF.
!
!
!
!--- VPN B commands.
!
ip vrf VPN_B
 rd 100:222
 route-target export 100:222
 route-target import 100:222
!
interface Loopback0
 ip address 10.10.10.1 255.255.255.255
 ip router isis
!
!--- VPN A commands.
!
interface Looback1
ip vrf forwarding VPN_A
!--- Associates a VRF instance with an interface or subinterface.
 ip address 100.0.1.1 255.255.255.0
!--- Looback1 and Loopback2 use the same IP address 100.0.1.1
!--- Duplicate subnets are allowed because they belong to two different VRF
 no ip directed-broadcast
!
!
!
!--- VPN B commands.
```

continues

Example 19-1   *Configuring L3VPN on Cisco IOS Router—PE-1 LSR (Continued)*

```
!
interface Looback2
 ip vrf forwarding VPN_B
 ip address 100.0.1.1 255.255.255.0
!--- Looback1 and Loopback2 use the same IP address 100.0.1.1
!--- Duplicate subnets are allowed because they belong to two different VRF
 no ip directed-broadcast
!
interface Serial2/0
 no ip address
 no ip directed-broadcast
 encapsulation frame-relay
 no fair-queue
!
interface Serial2/0.1 point-to-point
 description link to P1
 bandwidth 512
 ip address 10.1.1.1 255.255.255.252
 no ip directed-broadcast
 ip router isis
 tag-switching ip
 frame-relay interface-dlci 101
!
router isis
 net 49.0001.0000.0000.0004.00
 is-type level-1
!
router bgp 100
 bgp log-neighbor-changes
 neighbor 10.10.10.2 remote-as 100
 neighbor 10.10.10.2 update-source Loopback0
!
!
!--- VPN A and B commands
 address-family vpnv4
 neighbor 10.10.10.2 activate
 neighbor 10.10.10.2 send-community both
 exit-address-family
 !
!
!
!--- VPN A commands
 address-family ipv4 vrf VPN_A
 redistribute connected
 no auto-summary
 no synchronization
 exit-address-family
!
!
!
!--- VPN B commands
 address-family ipv4 vrf VPN_B
```

Example 19-1 *Configuring L3VPN on Cisco IOS Router—PE-1 LSR (Continued)*

```
 redistribute connected
 no auto-summary
 no synchronization
 exit-address-family
 !
!
!
ip classless
!
end
```

Example 19-2 *Configuring L3VPN on Cisco IOS Router—PE-2 LSR*

```
hostname PE2
!
ip cef
!
!--- VPN A commands
!
ip vrf VPN_A
 rd 100:111
 route-target export 100:111
 route-target import 100:111
!
!--- VPN B commands.
!
ip vrf VPN_B
 rd 100:222
 route-target export 100:222
 route-target import 100:222
!
interface Loopback0
 ip address 10.10.10.2 255.255.255.255
 ip router isis
!
!--- VPN A commands
!
interface Looback1
 ip vrf forwarding VPN_A
 ip address 100.0.2.1 255.255.255.0
!--- Looback1 and Loopback2 use the same IP address 100.0.2.1
!--- Duplicate subnets are allowed because they belong to two different VRF
!
!
!--- VPN B commands
!
interface Looback2
 ip vrf forwarding VPN_B
 ip address 100.0.2.1 255.255.255.0
!--- Looback1 and Loopback2 use the same IP address 100.0.2.1
!--- Duplicate subnets are allowed because they belong to two different VRF
```

continues

Example 19-2 *Configuring L3VPN on Cisco IOS Router—PE-2 LSR (Continued)*

```
!
!
interface Serial0/0
 no ip address
 encapsulation frame-relay
 no ip mroute-cache
!
interface Serial0/0.1 point-to-point
 description link to P2
 bandwidth 512
 ip address 10.1.1.10 255.255.255.252
 ip router isis
 tag-switching ip
 frame-relay interface-dlci 403
!
router isis
 net 49.0001.0000.0000.0006.00
 is-type level-1
!
router bgp 100
 neighbor 10.10.10.1 remote-as 100
 neighbor 10.10.10.1 update-source Loopback0
 !
 !
 !
!--- VPN A and B commands
 !
 address-family vpnv4
 neighbor 10.10.10.1 activate
 neighbor 10.10.10.1 send-community both
 exit-address-family
 !
 !
!--- VPN A commands
 !
 address-family ipv4 vrf VPN_A
 redistribute connected
 no auto-summary
 no synchronization
 exit-address-family
 !
 !
!--- VPN B commands
 !
 address-family ipv4 vrf VPN_B
 redistribute connected
 no auto-summary
 no synchronization
 exit-address-family
 !
!
```

Example 19-2   *Configuring L3VPN on Cisco IOS Router—PE-2 LSR (Continued)*

```
ip classless
!
end
```

Example 19-3   *Configuring L3VPN on Cisco IOS Router—P-1 LSR*

```
hostname P1
!
ip cef
!
interface Loopback0
 ip address 10.10.10.3 255.255.255.255
 ip router isis
!
interface Serial0/0
 no ip address
 encapsulation frame-relay
 no ip mroute-cache
 tag-switching ip
 no fair-queue
!
interface Serial0/0.1 point-to-point
 description link to PE1
 bandwidth 512
 ip address 10.1.1.2 255.255.255.252
 ip router isis
 tag-switching ip
 frame-relay interface-dlci 201
!
interface Serial0/0.2 point-to-point
 description link to P2
 bandwith 512
 ip address 10.1.1.5 255.255.255.252
 ip router isis
 tag-switching ip
 frame-relay interface-dlci 203
!
router isis
 net 49.0001.0000.0000.0001.00
 is-type level-1
!
ip classless
!
end
```

Example 19-4   *Configuring L3VPN on Cisco IOS Router—P-2 LSR*

```
hostname P2
!
ip cef
!
```

continues

Example 19-4 *Configuring L3VPN on Cisco IOS Router—P-2 LSR (Continued)*

```
interface Loopback0
 ip address 10.10.10.3 255.255.255.255
 ip router isis
!
interface Serial0/0
 no ip address
 no ip directed-broadcast
 encapsulation frame-relay
 random-detect
!
interface Serial0/0.1 point-to-point
 description link to PE2
 ip address 10.1.1.9 255.255.255.252
 no ip directed-broadcast
 ip router isis
 tag-switching ip
 frame-relay interface-dlci 304
!
interface Serial0/0.2 point-to-point
 description link to P1
 ip address 10.1.1.6 255.255.255.252
 no ip directed-broadcast
 ip router isis
 tag-switching ip
 frame-relay interface-dlci 302
!
router isis
 net 49.0001.0000.0000.0003.00
 is-type level-1
!
ip classless
!
end
```

TIP   For more configuration examples on MPLS VPN, refer to following Cisco documentation URL: http://www.cisco.com/en/US/tech/tk436/tk428/tech_configuration_examples_list.html.

NOTE   IETF L3VPN is a working group responsible for standardization of Layer 3 VPN architectures, such as MPLS IP VPN, IP VPN using virtual routers, and IPsec VPN. More details can be found at http://www.ietf.org/html.charters/l3vpn-charter.html.

Layer 2 VPN (L2VPN)

Layer 2 VPN (L2VPN) over MPLS solution offers frame-based data forwarding for any Layer 2 transport technology.

Cisco IOS Software supports L2VPN architecture by encapsulating any Layer 2 traffic such as Ethernet, Frame Relay, ATM, High-Level Data Link Control (HDLC), and Point-to-Point Protocol (PPP) over MPLS or IP network infrastructures.

L2VPN architecture provides a point-to-point Pseudowire between the provider edge (PE) routers. Pseudowire emulates a point-to-point Layer 2 connection over Layer 3. The PE router encapsulates any receiving Layer 2 traffic at the sender's edge PE and decapsulated at the recipient's edge PE.

Figure 19-7 illustrates the L2VPN pseudowire end-to-end connection.

Figure 19-7 *L2VPN Pseudowire Architecture*

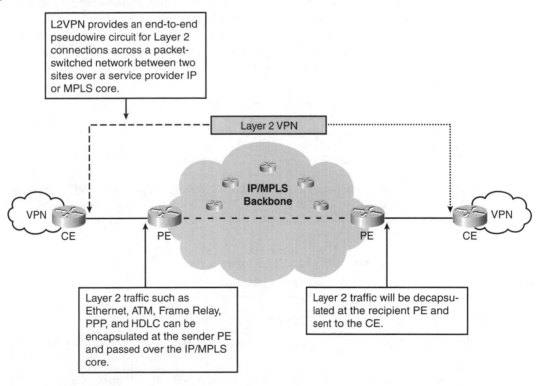

NOTE   L2VPN services are complementary to L3VPN services.

The following two emerging L2VPN service architectures are gaining momentum and generating interest among service providers and enterprises:

- **Virtual Private Wire Service (VPWS):** VPWS is a point-to-point technology that enables the transport of Layer 2 services such as Ethernet, Frame Relay, ATM, HDLC, and PPP over a packet-based infrastructure across a service provider IP/MPLS cloud. VPWS can be used to transport existing Layer 2 networks over MPLS- or IP-based networks.

  There are two common Cisco pseudowire technologies available: Any-Transport-over MPLS (AToM) for MPLS networks and L2TPv3 (Layer 2 Tunneling Protocol version 3) for native IP networks. Both AToM and L2TPv3 support the transport of Ethernet, Frame Relay, ATM, HDLC, and PPP traffic over an IP or MPLS core.

- **Virtual Private LAN Service (VPLS):** VPLS is a multipoint L2VPN technology that provides the emulation for Ethernet, connecting multiple sites over a packet-based infrastructure across a service provider IP/MPLS cloud. In essence, VPLS architecture provides multipoint Layer 2 connectivity over Layer 3 network architecture. Services in VPLS solutions appear to be on the same LAN segment regardless of the physical location.

  With VPLS, Ethernet LAN can be extended to anywhere across the provider edge network, taking local LAN beyond the physical boundaries. The provider emulates the function of a LAN switch to connect a user LAN to create a single bridge Ethernet LAN.

NOTE   The main difference between the VPLS and VPWS architecture is that VPLS provides point-to-multipoint service, whereas VPWS provides point-to-point service only.

Table 19-4 compares VPWS and VPLS technologies.

Table 19-4   *Comparison between VPWS and VPLS Technologies*

	VPWS	**VPLS**
Connection Type	Point-to-Point (at Layer 2)	Multipoint-to-Multipoint (at Layer 2)
Layer 2 Encapsulation Types	Any (Frame Relay, ATM/Cell, Ethernet/VLAN, HDLC, PPP)	Ethernet Only
Routing Involvement by Service Provider	No	No

Table 19-4 *Comparison between VPWS and VPLS Technologies (Continued)*

	VPWS	VPLS
Customer Protocol Support	Any	Any
Service Provider Core Protocol	IP and MPLS	MPLS

The information in Table 19-4 is compiled from the Cisco Networkers session presentation# AGG-1001 – "Introduction to Layer 2 Transport and Tunneling Technologies (L2VPNS)."

NOTE   IETF L2VPN is a working group responsible for standardization of Layer 2 VPN architectures, such as VPLS and VPWS. More details can be found at http://www.ietf.org/ html.charters/l2vpn-charter.html.

Implementing L2VPN

There are a number of variations in L2VPN designs and deployments, and several different technologies are available that can be used depending on different Layer 2 services. The technologies include Ethernet VLAN, Frame Relay PVC, ATM VC, HDLC, and PPP transport over a packet-based infrastructure across a service provider IP/MPLS cloud. The following sections provide some basic examples of Layer 2 service implementations, i.e., Ethernet VLAN over MPLS using VPWS- and VPLS-based architecture.

Implementing Ethernet VLAN over MPLS Service—Using VPWS Based Architecture

Figure 19-8 topology demonstrates basic VPWS (Virtual Private Wire Service) L2VPN point-to-point scenario transporting Ethernet VLAN over MPLS.

As shown in Figure 19-8, the MPLS core interconnects customer Ethernet between two sites over the MPLS core. The customer CE router on each site is configured on the same Layer 3 subnet 192.168.100.0/24, thereby establishing a virtual Layer 2 (VLAN) connection over the MPLS core network.

Figure 19-8 *Implementing Ethernet VLAN over MPLS – Basic VPWS-L2VPN*

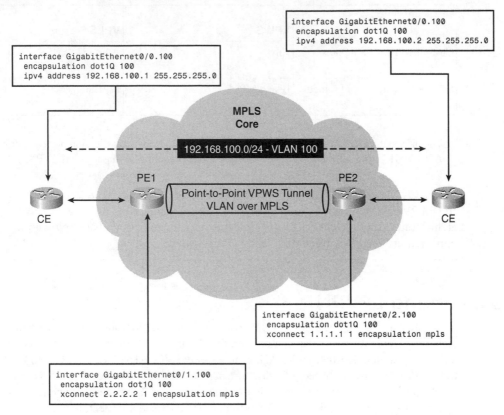

```
interface GigabitEthernet0/0.100
 encapsulation dot1Q 100
 ipv4 address 192.168.100.2 255.255.255.0
```

```
interface GigabitEthernet0/0.100
 encapsulation dot1Q 100
 ipv4 address 192.168.100.1 255.255.255.0
```

MPLS
Core

192.168.100.0/24 - VLAN 100

PE1   Point-to-Point VPWS Tunnel   PE2
      VLAN over MPLS

CE   CE

```
interface GigabitEthernet0/2.100
 encapsulation dot1Q 100
 xconnect 1.1.1.1 1 encapsulation mpls
```

```
interface GigabitEthernet0/1.100
 encapsulation dot1Q 100
 xconnect 2.2.2.2 1 encapsulation mpls
```

Implementing Ethernet VLAN over MPLS Service—Using VPLS-Based Architecture

Figure 19-9 topology demonstrates a basic VPLS (Virtual Private LAN Service) L2VPN scenario transporting Ethernet VLAN over MPLS.

The MPLS core interconnects customer Ethernet VLAN between two sites, thereby establishing a virtual Layer 2 (VLAN) connection over the MPLS core network.

Figure 19-9 *Implementing Ethernet VLAN over MPLS—Basic VPLS-L2VPN*

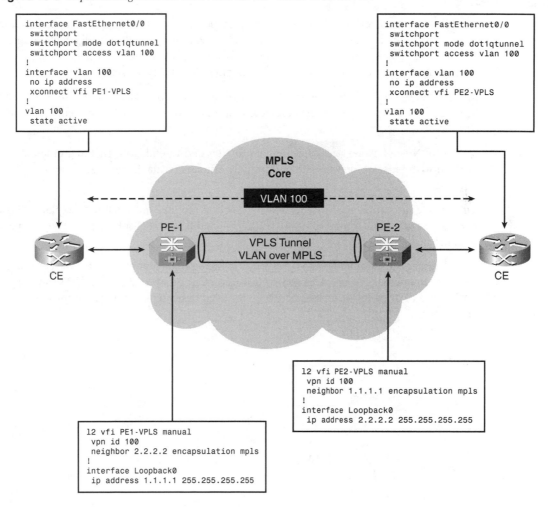

Summary

In addition to connectivity services, service providers are continually struggling to increase service offerings and differentiated end-to-end IP services with cutting edge technologies. This fast-shifting economical growth is heavily dependent on their ability to deliver managed network services along with traditional connectivity services.

Multiprotocol Label Switching (MPLS) is a widely used core transport technology that is used to carry Layer 2 and Layer 3 services that transport over a packet-switched network (PSN).

MPLS VPN is a key service solution that provides end-to-end QoS, enabling efficient utilization of existing networks to build highly efficient, scalable, next-generation networks.

This chapter provided a basic overview of the MPLS architecture and briefly explained how it works, as well as a comparison on MPLS VPN and IPsec VPN solutions and deployment scenarios.

The chapter focused mainly on MPLS VPN architecture and the two basic types of trusted VPN deployments. The chapter covered details on Cisco Layer 2 VPN (L2VPN) and Layer 3 VPN (L3VPN) solution architecture and provided basic deployment and implementation guidelines.

References

http://www.cisco.com/en/US/netsol/ns590/
networking_solutions_white_paper09186a008009d67f.shtml

http://www.cisco.com/en/US/netsol/ns589/networking_solutions_sub_sub_solution.html

http://www.cisco.com/en/US/products/ps6604/products_ios_protocol_group_home.html

http://www.cisco.com/en/US/netsol/ns588/networking_solutions_sub_sub_solution.html

http://www.cisco.com/en/US/products/ps6603/products_ios_protocol_group_home.html

http://www.cisco.com/en/US/products/sw/iosswrel/ps1829/
products_feature_guide09186a00801b2407.html#wp1050700

http://www.cisco.com/en/US/netsol/ns585/
networking_solutions_white_paper0900aecd801edd5f.shtml

http://www.cisco.com/en/US/products/ps6648/products_ios_protocol_option_home.html

http://www.cisco.com/en/US/products/ps6603/
products_white_paper09186a00801ed506.shtml

http://www.rfc-editor.org/rfc/rfc4364.txt

http://www.vpnc.org/vpn-technologies.html

http://www.cisco.com/univercd/cc/td/doc/product/software/ios124/124cg/hmp_c/part20/
mpbbk4.htm

http://www.cisco.com/en/US/tech/tk436/tk428/
technologies_configuration_example09186a0080093fcc.shtml

http://www.cisco.com/en/US/tech/tk436/tk428/
technologies_configuration_example09186a00800a6c11.shtml

http://www.cisco.com/en/US/tech/tk436/tk428/tech_configuration_examples_list.html

PART IV

Security Monitoring

CHAPTER **20**

Network Intrusion Prevention

Today, viruses, worms, and several other invading malicious codes and programs proliferate widely on the Internet. With the environment becoming increasingly hostile, networks are easy targets because the infection can spread across the network rapidly. With this growing threat, networks need to be designed and equipped with sophisticated intelligence to diagnose and mitigate threats in real-time.

Cisco Network Intrusion Prevention provides self-defending solutions that offer networkwide protection and mitigation techniques. It has the intelligence to accurately detect, analyze, classify, and mitigate malicious traffic in real-time, offering comprehensive protection for a wide range of network intrusions and attacks.

The chapter discusses various types of Cisco Network-based Intrusion Prevention solutions and takes a closer look at core concepts such as sensor architecture, packet analysis, signature and signature engines, deployment scenarios, and high availability and load-balancing techniques.

Intrusion System Terminologies

The following list outlines the major intrusion system technologies:

- **IDS (Intrusion Detection System):** The term IDS is typically limited to sensors that employ promiscuous-only monitoring based on an out-of-packet stream.

- **IPS (Intrusion Prevention System):** The term IPS is most commonly applied to sensors that reside inline within the packet stream and that can drop malicious packets, flows, or attackers.

- **IPS Feature versus IDS Feature:** The IPS feature is specifically the inline monitoring with inline response action deny-packet capability, whereas the IDS feature is promiscuous-only monitoring with post attack response actions such as TCP reset or block/shun on an external device.

NOTE	The Cisco Intrusion Prevention System (IPS) Sensor Software supports both IPS and IDS technology combined in a single box. This chapter covers mainly the IPS technology features.

Network Intrusion Prevention Overview

Networks today have grown both in size and complexity while the environment has remained highly exposed and vulnerable. Because of the evolving network landscape, networks require a security solution that works throughout the network in collaboration with all the network devices, servers, and endpoints within the network.

There are several challenges for securing modern-day networks to provide in-depth defense:

- Security incidents and evolving threats are on the rise and are increasing exponentially.
- The complexity and sophistication of malicious codes and network exploits continues to rise.
- The potential impact resulting from these attacks is significant.
- Multiple technologies are working together, in contrast to the point products deployed independently in the past.

The Cisco Network Intrusion Prevention solution is an integral part of the Cisco Self-Defending Network strategy that provides network intelligence to identify and prevent malicious traffic including network viruses, worms, spyware, adware, and application abuse. The solution offers comprehensive threat prevention and protection for a wide range of network intrusions and attacks.

The Cisco Network-based Intrusion Prevention solution protects the network from policy violations, vulnerability exploitations, and anomalous activity through detailed inspection of traffic at Layers 2 through 7, across the entire network.

Table 20-1 lists the various Cisco Network-based Intrusion Prevention solutions available on various platforms.

Table 20-1   *Cisco Network-Based Intrusion Prevention Solutions*

Solution Product	Description
Cisco IPS 4200 Series Appliance Sensor	Dedicated hardware appliance platform
Cisco IDS Services Module 2 (IDSM-2)	Security module for Cisco Catalyst 6500 Series Switches and Cisco 7600 Series Routers
Cisco Advanced Inspection and Protection Security Services Module (AIP-SSM)	Security module for Cisco ASA 5500 Series Adaptive Security Appliances
Cisco IPS Advanced Integration Module (IPS-AIM)	Network module for Cisco Integrated Services Routers (ISR), providing IPS capabilities
Cisco Internetwork Operating System (IOS) IPS	Focused set of IPS capabilities using Cisco IOS Software on the router

The following sections will briefly highlight the features and provide an overview of Cisco network-based IPS solutions.

Cisco IPS 4200 Series Sensors

The Cisco IPS 4200 Series sensors offer a broad range of solutions providing easy integration into enterprise and service provider environments.

Cisco IPS 4200 series appliance sensors offer the following:

- Detailed traffic inspection for Layers 2 through 7
- Prevention of malicious traffic, including network viruses, worms, spyware, adware, and application abuse
- Inline-ready, providing inline intrusion prevention
- Simultaneous operation in promiscuous and inline modes
- Monitoring of multiple network subnets through the support of multiple interfaces
- Signature-based and anomaly-based detection capabilities
- A wide array of transactional performance options from 65 Mbps to 2 Gbps and media-rich performance options from 80 Mbps to 4 Gbps
- Built-in web-based management solutions integrated in the sensor software

The Cisco IPS 4200 series appliance sensors shown in Figure 20-1 offer four high-performance, purpose-built appliances that range from small- and medium-sized to large enterprise and service provider environments:

- **IPS 4215:** Cisco IPS 4215 is a 1 RU appliance sensor that can deliver up to 80 Mbps of transactional performance and is suitable for multiple T1/E1 and T3 environments. The 4215 supports up to five sniffing interfaces (monitoring interfaces), which allow simultaneous protection of multiple subnets with the capability to deliver both intrusion detection and prevention (IDS/IPS) services within a single unit.

- **IPS 4240:** Cisco IPS 4240 can deliver up to 250 Mbps transactional performance providing protection in switched environments, on multiple T3 subnets. With the support of multiple 10/100/1000 interfaces, it can also be deployed on partially utilized gigabit links or fully saturated full-duplex 100 Mbps environments. Another model IPS 4240-DC is available in DC power, which is compliant with the Network Equipment Building Systems (NEBS) and can be deployed in environments that have specific requirements pertaining to NEBS Level 3 compliance.

- **IPS 4255:** Cisco IPS 4255 supports transactional performance at 600 Mbps and can be used to protect partially utilized gigabit subnets and traffic traversing switches that are being used to aggregate traffic from numerous subnets. Additionally, it delivers a high port density that allows effective mitigation of threats identified on multiple network subnets.

- **IPS 4260:** Cisco IPS 4260 can be deployed to deliver transactional performance of up to 1 Gbps of dedicated intrusion prevention protection and can be used to protect both gigabit subnets and aggregated traffic that is traversing switches from multiple subnets. This purpose-built device offers flexible deployment support for both copper and fiber network interface card (NIC) environments.

- **IPS 4270:** Cisco IPS 4270 supports unparalleled performance and can be deployed to deliver transactional performance of up to 2 Gbps of dedicated intrusion prevention protection. It can be used to protect both gigabit subnets and aggregated traffic that is traversing switches from multiple subnets. This purpose-built device offers flexible deployment support for both copper and fiber network interface card (NIC) environments with support for up to 16 monitoring interfaces.

NOTE   For further details about the Cisco IPS 4200 series appliance sensors, visit http://www.cisco.com/en/US/products/hw/vpndevc/ps4077/index.html.

Figure 20-1   *Cisco IPS 4200 Series Appliance Sensors*

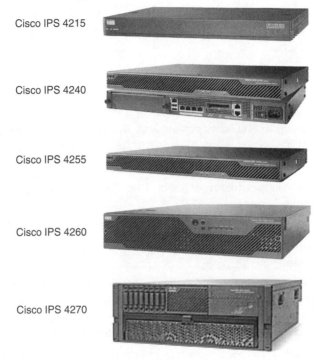

Cisco IPS 4215

Cisco IPS 4240

Cisco IPS 4255

Cisco IPS 4260

Cisco IPS 4270

Cisco IDS Services Module (IDSM-2)

Cisco Intrusion Detection System (IDSM-2) Service Module shown in Figure 20-2 is a high-speed, high-performance integrated IPS module that is installed in Cisco Catalyst 6500 switches and Cisco 7600 Series routers.

IDSM-2 can be deployed to deliver up to 600 Mbps of intrusion prevention protection in passive mode and up to 500 Mbps in inline mode.

IDSM-2 offers an intrusion prevention system (IPS) solution for safeguarding organizations from malicious attacks and network breaches, thereby ensuring stability.

IDSM-2 is the second-generation services module offering protection to switched environments by integrating full-featured IPS functionality directly into the network infrastructure. This integration allows monitoring traffic directly off the switch backplane scaling to multi-gigabit environments.

IDSM-2 offers enterprises and service providers with unparalleled intrusion security, reliability, scalability, and multi-gigabit performance.

Some of the key features in IDSM-2 are the following:

- Installs an integrated module inside a Cisco Catalyst 6500 Series Switch or Cisco 7600 Series Router. The IDSM-2 integrates intrusion security inside the network infrastructure.

- Ensures a higher Return on Investment (ROI) through flexible deployment leveraging of existing infrastructure investments.

- Provides a comprehensive inline prevention solution.

- Delivers up to 500-Mbps performance in inline mode (600 Mbps in passive mode).

- Provides multi-gigabit scalability up to eight modules per chassis, providing up to 4 Gbps of inline prevention.

- Protects your network from policy violations, vulnerability exploitations, and anomalous activity.

- Detailed multivector threat identification and traffic inspection for Layers 2 through 7.

- Prevents malicious traffic including network viruses, worms, spyware, adware, and application abuse.

- Offers accurate prevention technologies through the Cisco innovative Risk Rating and Meta Event Generator features that reduce false positives and provide confidence in data forwarded to the internal network by taking preventive actions on a wide range of threats without the risk of dropping legitimate traffic.

- Offers hot swap modules such as insertion/removal that does not affect the Cisco Catalyst switch.

- Supports the Cisco EtherChannel load balancing.

- Supports the Cisco FlexWAN module.

- Supports multiple capture techniques including Switched Port Analyzer (SPAN), Remote SPAN (RSPAN), and VLAN Access Control Lists (VACL). Cisco is the only vendor to provide an in-switch IDS/IPS solution providing access to the data stream via VACL capture.

- Offers Anti-X integrated services partnered with Trend Micro augmenting the Cisco native signature development, which provides the quickest and most complete signature updates for timely recognition and prevention of attacks.

- Offers flexible configuration by using the sensor Command Line Interface (CLI) console, which is available locally or remotely via Telnet or Secure Shell (SSH).

- Offers Cisco IPS Device Manager (IDM), which is a GUI-based, Java-enabled, built-in web-based tool for sensor configuration and management. It can be accessed through Internet Explorer, Netscape, or Mozilla and is enabled by default to use Secure Sockets Layer (SSL).

- Provides event monitoring for up to five IPS sensors through Cisco IPS Event Viewer (IEV).
- Provides through Cisco Security Manager and Cisco Security Monitoring, Analysis, and Response System (Cisco Security MARS) a world-class management and monitoring for sensor deployments of all sizes.

IDSM-2 runs the same software code as the IPS 4200 Series appliance hardware; hence, it can be integrated into the same management workflow.

Figure 20-2   *Cisco IDS Services Module (IDSM-2)*

NOTE   For further details about the Cisco Intrusion Detection System (IDSM-2) Service Module, visit http://www.cisco.com/en/US/products/hw/modules/ps2706/ps5058/index.html.

Cisco Advanced Inspection and Protection Security Services Module (AIP-SSM)

The Cisco Advanced Inspection and Prevention Security Services Module (AIP-SSM) for the Cisco ASA 5500 Series shown in Figure 20-3 provides a full-featured intrusion-prevention solution to protect against malicious traffic, including network viruses and worms.

Cisco ASA 5500 Series Adaptive Security Appliance coupled with AIP-SSM provide best-in-class firewall and intrusion prevention capabilities in a single, easy-to-deploy platform.

AIP-SSM offers multi-vector threat identification protecting the network from policy violations, vulnerability exploitations, and anomalous activity through detailed inspection of traffic in Layers 2 through 7.

AIP-SSM provides unparalleled converged protection by integrating full-featured IPS functionality directly into the network infrastructure. AIP-SSM offers comprehensive protection for the network by collaborating with other network security resources, providing a proactive approach to protecting the entire network.

Using Cisco IPS sensor software, the Cisco AIP-SSM combines inline prevention services that offer all major functions available in the traditional IPS sensor solution.

Figure 20-3 *Cisco Advanced Inspection and Prevention Security Services Module (AIP-SSM)*

NOTE   For further details about the Cisco Advanced Inspection and Prevention Security Services Module (AIP-SSM), visit http://www.cisco.com/en/US/products/ps6120/products_data_ sheet0900aecd80404916.html.

Cisco IPS Advanced Integration Module (IPS-AIM)

The Cisco IPS Advanced Integration Module (IPS-AIM) shown in Figure 20-4 can be used with Cisco Integrated Services Routers (ISR)—Cisco 2800 and 3800 series routers used for small and medium-sized business (SMB) and full service branch office environments.

IPS-AIM is part of the Cisco integrated IDS/IPS family sensor portfolio and an integral part of the Cisco Self-Defending Network solution.

IPS-AIM is attached directly to the router motherboard and does not require a separate slot, thereby saving a module slot. IPS-AIM monitoring interface is also integrated into the module directly, connecting to the router backplane. The interface can monitor incoming and outgoing packets from any router interface. IPS-AIM can deliver monitoring performance up to 45 Mbps of traffic and is suitable for T1/E1 and up to T3 environments.

The IPS-AIM provides traditional detection and prevention with enhanced capabilities such as stateful pattern matching and heuristic and anomaly detection, using the Cisco IPS Sensor Software that supports both inline and promiscuous modes.

Figure 20-4   *Cisco IPS Advanced Integration Module (IPS-AIM) for Cisco Integrated Services Routers (ISR)*

Cisco IPS-AIM has a dedicated processor and dynamic random access memory (DRAM). Note that there is no dedicated Command and Control (management) interface. However, for in-band management, an internal Gigabit Ethernet port is used, which can be accessed through the console port or SSH to connect to any router interface.

NOTE   For further details about the Cisco IPS-AIM, visit http://www.cisco.com/en/US/products/ sw/secursw/ps2113/products_data_sheet0900aecd806c4e2a.html.

Cisco IOS IPS

The Cisco IOS Intrusion Prevention System (IPS) feature set provides an integrated inline deep-packet inspection solution within the router software architecture.

IOS IPS enables the network to be able to defend itself with the intelligence to monitor, detect, identify, classify, and mitigate malicious traffic in real-time and stop malicious traffic close to its entry point.

Deploying Cisco IOS IPS in inline mode provides a unique offering that enables you to stop the attack at the point of origin. The IOS IPS solution can be deployed at various network points within the network and can be ideally situated at the network edge to protect the network from malicious and offending traffic entering into the network. Currently, Cisco is the only vendor to deliver this integrated functionality on a router.

The Cisco IOS IPS solution is available on all Cisco Integrated Services Routers (ISR) series and offers an integrated security and policy enforcement solution.

The IOS IPS feature set is a suite of intrusion prevention solutions provisioning a single point of protection at the network perimeter.

IOS IPS offers unparalleled intrusion security, reliability, scalability, and multilevel performance.

Some of the key features in IOS IPS are the following:

- Protects against network viruses, worms, and a large variety of network threats and exploits.

- Eliminates the need for a standalone IPS device.

- Provides integrated inline deep-packet inspection.

- Supports about 2,000 attack signatures similar to those available on a regular Cisco IPS sensor appliance.

- Uses Cisco IOS routing capabilities to deliver integrated functionality.

- Enables distributed networkwide threat mitigation.

- Sends a syslog message or an alarm in Secure Device Event Exchange (SDEE) format upon detecting an attack signature.

- Complements Cisco IOS Firewall and VPN solutions for superior threat protection at all entry points into the network.

NOTE   Refer to the following Cisco documentation link for further details on the Cisco IOS IPS solution: http://www.cisco.com/en/US/products/ps6634/products_data_sheet0900aecd803137cf.html.

NOTE   For complete details about the Cisco Intrusion Protection System family of products, refer to http://www.cisco.com/go/ips.

Deploying IPS

As discussed in previous sections, Cisco offers a wide range of IDS/IPS solutions that can be deployed in various network segments throughout the network architecture as required. These comprehensive deployment methods offer solutions from small- and medium-sized to large-scale enterprise and service provider network environments.

Figure 20-5 exemplifies the various areas in a network in which Cisco IDS/IPS sensors can be deployed.

Figure 20-5 *Cisco IDS/IPS Networkwide Deployment*

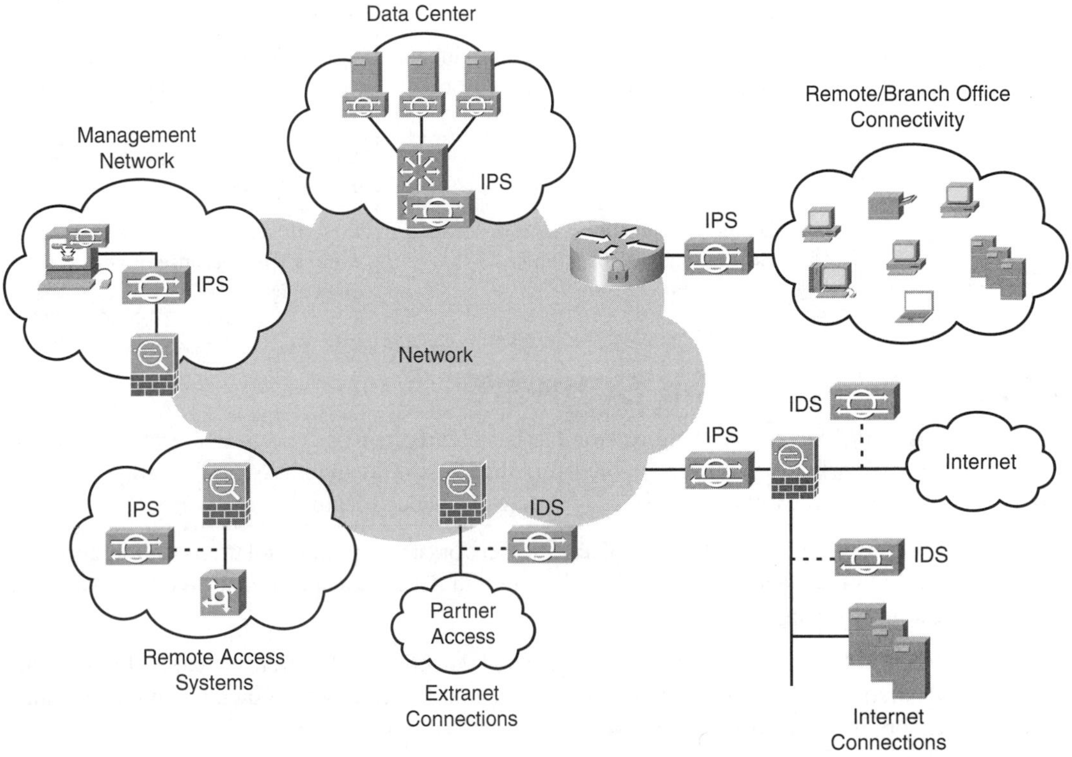

Table 20-2 lists some basic pros and cons of deploying IDS versus IPS sensors.

Table 20-2 *Deploying IDS Versus IPS*

	Pros	Cons
IDS Sensor (Intrusion Detection System)	Deploying the sensor has no impact on the network (latency, jitter, and so on).	IDS response actions cannot stop the trigger packet and cannot guarantee stopping a connection.
	Sensor is not inline; therefore, a sensor failure cannot impact network functionality.	Being out of band, IDS sensors are more vulnerable to network evasion techniques.
	Monitors traffic on a given segment promiscuously. Captures traffic by using SPAN, TAP, VACL capture, and so on.	Cannot perform inline monitoring and does not have the capability to perform inline response action (deny-packet).

continues

Table 20-2 *Deploying IDS Versus IPS (Continued)*

	Pros	Cons
IPS Sensor (Intrusion Prevention System)	Supports inline monitoring with inline response action deny-packet capability.	Packet effects (latency, and so on). Packet drops due to latency will impact traffic streams.
	TCP/IP traffic normalization.	Network effects (bandwidth, connection rate, and so on).
	Monitors all traffic traversing between two interfaces transparently.	Often, IPS cannot be implemented "everywhere" because of cost restrictions.

Cisco IPS Sensor OS Software

Cisco IPS Sensor software version 6.0 is a comprehensive, end-to-end protection solution for network-based sensors that delivers the latest IPS capabilities, enhanced performance, security improvements, and a range of new enhanced features.

Cisco IPS Sensor Software protects the network from policy violations, vulnerability exploitations, and anomalous activity through detailed inspection across the network of traffic at Layers 2 through 7.

Cisco IPS Sensor Software offers intrusion detection and prevention capabilities to shield the network from multiple threats and safeguard it from both known and unknown attacks before they can affect the network.

The new enhanced software uses a unique multi-vector threat identification algorithm that is capable of identifying an extensive range of attacks using multiple inspection and classification capabilities. The new enhanced feature has extended application intelligence to detect and prevent covert channel tunneling through common application ports such as HTTP port 80.

Cisco IPS Sensor Software supports both the IDS and IPS capabilities for hybrid operation, acting simultaneously as an IDS sensor and an IPS sensor.

Cisco IPS Sensor Software is available on Cisco IPS 4200 Series appliances and on the Cisco Catalyst 6500 Series Intrusion Detection System Services Module (IDSM-2).

The following is a brief summary of some of the advanced IPS features and capabilities in the Cisco IPS Sensor OS Software Version 6.0 release:

- Advanced and enhanced inline intrusion prevention functionality.
- Hybrid OS with detection and prevention capabilities allowing a single sensor to operate simultaneously as an IDS sensor and an IPS sensor.

- Extended application inspection technologies that allow enforcement of policy decisions based on content detected at the application layer.

- Stateful pattern recognition that helps identify vulnerability-based attacks through the use of multipacket inspection across all protocols, thwarting attacks that hide within a data stream.

- Detection and prevention of covert channel tunneling through common application ports such as HTTP port 80.

- Control of permitted traffic through user-defined policies.

- H225 VoIP engine to inspect H225 protocol for attacks on multiple H.323 gatekeepers, VoIP gateways, and endpoint terminals. Voice over IP (VoIP) engine provides deep packet inspection for call signaling messages, ensuring protocol compliance of H225 call setup messages.

- Support for the inspection and mitigation of threats in MPLS environments.

- Advanced traffic normalization algorithms, such as fragmentation and TCP session normalization.

- Enhanced visibility into IPv6 traffic to identify attacks in IPv6 environments through the inspection of IPv4 traffic being tunneled in IPv6.

- IP-in-IP detection to identify malicious traffic within mobile IP traffic.

- New risk rating feature that can be used for event action overrides that adds actions based on the risk of the alert.

- New Threat Rating (Enhanced Risk Rating), which is the extension of risk rating that has been lowered by event actions that have been taken.

- New Anomaly Detection component that creates a baseline of normal network traffic. This baseline is used to detect worm-infected hosts. Protocol Anomaly Detection identifies attacks based on observed deviations in the normal RFC behavior of a protocol or service (for example, HTTP response without an HTTP request).

- Layer 2 attack detection through identification of ARP-based attacks and man-in-the-middle attacks.

- New Passive OS Fingerprinting to determine host operating systems by inspecting characteristics of the packets exchanged on the network.

- A new Sensor Virtualization feature offering multiple virtual sensors running on the same appliance, each configured with different signature behavior and traffic feeds.

- Improved TCP session tracking modes to help inline sensors correctly track TCP sessions in complex network configurations.

Cisco IPS Sensor Software

The Cisco IPS Sensor OS Software runs on the Linux operating system. The underlying Linux OS has been secured and hardened by removing unnecessary packages from the OS, disabling unused services, restricting network access, and removing access to the shell.

Sensor Software—System Architecture

Figure 20-6 illustrates the system design and architecture of the Cisco IPS Sensor Software system.

Figure 20-6 *Cisco IPS Sensor Software System Design*

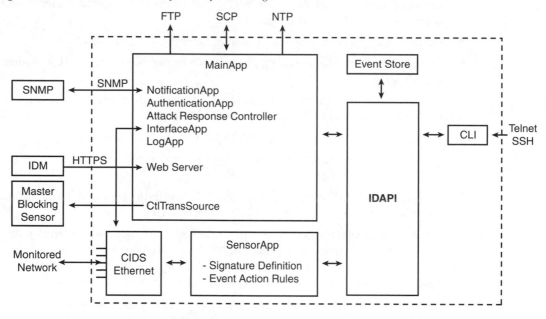

Figure 20-6, which shows the IPS system architecture, is taken from Cisco documentation on "Configuring the Cisco Intrusion Prevention System Sensor Using the Command Line Interface 6.0" at http://www.cisco.com/en/US/products/hw/vpndevc/ps4077/products_configuration_guide_chapter09186a00807517f1.html.

Cisco IPS Sensor OS Software is made up of multiple application components as shown in Figure 20-6. These components are defined with their functions in the list that follows:

- **MainApp:** The core engine of the sensor operating system. MainApp is responsible for all major functions, including managing the system processes, configuring the system, starting and stopping other applications, and performing routine maintenance. There are several subcomponents in the MainApp:

NotificationApp: Responsible for sending SNMP traps that are triggered by sensor alarms, system status, or errors. NotificationApp is also used to capture sensor health through SNMP GET.

AuthenticationApp: Responsible for validating user credentials that verify authorization status when a user is performing various configuration and management tasks.

Attack Response Controller (ARC): Provides the blocking and shunning capability to the sensor when a signature is triggered. ARC is responsible for managing network devices (routers, switches and firewalls) and can remotely log in to these network devices to dynamically apply access control lists (ACLs).

InterfaceApp: Manages sensor interface settings, such as inline pair, admin state, and bypass mechanism.

LogApp: Responsible for storing all the application logs to a log file on the sensor and all the error messages to the Event Store.

Web Server: The web-based server engine that enables the user to manage the sensor through a GUI interface. The web server engine also provides the communication interface to other IPS devices that use the RDEP2 protocol.

ctlTransSource (also known as Control Transaction server): Responsible for sending control transactions that are mainly used to enable ARC's master blocking sensor capability.

- **Event Store:** The placeholder for storing all the sensor events, including system messages, alerts, and errors.

- **SensorApp (also known as Analysis Engine):** Provides the packet capturing and analyzing capability when monitoring the traffic.

- **CLI:** The command-line interface through which a user can manage and configure the sensor. CLI can be accessed by using various methods, including direct sensor console, Telnet, or SSH connections.

Sensor Software—Communication Protocols

The sensor OS applications, illustrated in Figure 20-6, communicate with each other through a common API called IDAPI. External remote applications (such as other sensors, management applications, and third-party software) communicate with the sensor through RDEP2 and SDEE protocols. The following section describes the various communication protocols used by the Cisco IPS sensor software.

- **IDAPI:** IPS applications discussed in Figure 20-6 use an interprocess communication API called IDAPI. IDAPI is used to handle internal communications within the software architecture. Each application registers to the IDAPI to send and receive events and control transactions. IDAPI is the binding interface through which all the applications communicate.

- **RDEP2:** RDEP2 is another communication protocol used in the IPS sensor software, primarily for external communications. RDEP2 is an application-level communications protocol used to exchange IPS events, IP logs, configurations, and control messages between IPS clients and IPS servers. RDEP2 communications consist of request and response messages between RDEP2 clients and RDEP2 servers. RDEP2 uses the industry standards HTTP, Transparent Layer Security (TLS), Secure Sockets Layer (SSL), and Extensible Markup Language (XML) to provide a standardized interface between RDEP2 agents.

- **IDIOM:** IDIOM is a data format standard that defines the event messages that are reported by the IPS, as well as the operational messages that are used to configure and control intrusion-detection systems. These messages consist of XML documents that conform to the IDIOM XML schema. IDIOM supports two types of interactions: the event and control transactions. Event interactions are used to exchange IPS events such as IPS alerts. Note that in the latest sensor software OS, IDIOM for the most part has been superseded by IDCONF, SDEE, and CIDEE.

- **IDCONF:** Cisco IPS sensor software manages its configuration by using XML documents. IDCONF specifies the XML schema including IPS control transactions. The IDCONF schema does not specify the contents of the configuration documents, but rather the framework from which the configuration documents are developed. IDCONF messages are exchanged over RDEP2 and are wrapped inside IDIOM request and response messages.

- **SDEE:** IPS produces various types of events, including intrusion alerts and status events. The IPS sensor communicates events to clients and management applications by using the proprietary RDEP2. Cisco has also developed an IPS industry leading protocol, the SDEE, which is a product-independent standard for communicating security device events. SDEE is an enhancement to the current version of RDEP2 that adds extensibility features that are needed for communicating events generated by various types of security devices.

- **CIDEE:** CIDEE specifies the extensions to SDEE that are used by the Cisco IPS. The CIDEE standard specifies all possible extensions that are supported by IPS systems.

Sensor Software—User Roles

The CLI for the sensor software OS permits multiple users to connect to the sensor at the same time. Users can be created locally in the sensor configuration. Each user is associated with a specific role that controls the user privileges and an established boundary of what the user can and cannot do.

The CLI supports four user roles, described in the list that follows. Each user has a different privilege level; therefore, the menus and available commands vary for each role:

- **Administrator:** This user role has the highest level of privileges. Administrators have unrestricted view access and can perform all functions on the sensor.

- **Operator:** This user role has the second-highest level of privileges. Operators have unrestricted view access and can perform limited functions such as tuning signatures, modifying their own passwords, and assigning configuration to virtual sensors.

- **Viewer:** This user role has the lowest level of privileges. Viewers can view configuration and event data and can modify their own passwords.

- **Service:** This user role does not have direct access to the CLI. The service role is a special role that allows bypassing the CLI. Service account users are logged directly into the native operating system shell (underlying Linux OS bash shell). This account is mainly used for support and troubleshooting purposes only. Unauthorized modifications in the Linux OS are not supported and require the device to be reimaged to ensure proper operation. Only one user account can be associated with the service role privilege. Also note that only a user with Administrator privileges can edit the service account settings.

| NOTE | The service account allows switching to the Linux OS **root** user account by executing the **su-** command. The root password is synchronized to the service account password. |

Sensor Software—Partitions

The IPS sensor software has the following three partitions:

- **Application partition:** The main partition, which holds the full IPS system image.

- **Maintenance partition:** A special-purpose IPS image used to reimage the application partition of the IDSM-2 service module. Note that when the maintenance partition is reimaged, all configuration settings are lost.

- **Recovery partition:** A special-purpose image used for the recovery of the sensor. Booting into the recovery partition enables you to completely reimage the application partition. Network settings are preserved, but all other configuration is lost.

Sensor Software—Signatures and Signature Engines

Signatures and signature engines are the foundation of Cisco IPS solution architecture. The network-based IPS sensor monitors network traffic with a collection of predefined (built-in signatures) and user-defined signatures that can be grouped into various signature engines.

A signature is a description of a network traffic pattern that attackers use while conducting network-based attacks. The IPS sensor monitors network traffic and generates alerts when it detects malicious activity by matching the traffic to specific signatures. Cisco IPS Sensor Software is preloaded with a wide range of signatures for varying protocols. Cisco IPS Sensor Software Version 6.0 contains more than 1,000 built-in default signatures. The sensor software also supports the configuration of user-defined custom signatures.

A signature engine is a categorized group of a collection of like signatures, each of which inspects for a specific type of activity. The sensor software uses the signature engines to examine network traffic for intrusive activity with similar characteristics. For example, the TCP-based string engine handles signatures that search for specific textual strings in TCP traffic only. The signature engines are designed to perform a wide range of functions, such as pattern matching, stateful pattern matching, protocol decoding, deep-packet inspection, and other heuristic methods. Each signature engine has a specific set of parameters that have allowable ranges or sets of values.

Table 20-3 lists the Cisco IPS Signature Engines available in the IPS Sensor Software Version 6.0.

Table 20-3 *IPS Signature Engines*

Signature Engine	Description of the Engine
Application Inspection and Control (AIC) Engine	Provides thorough analysis of web-based traffic. The AIC engine provides granular control over HTTP sessions to prevent abuse of the HTTP protocol. It allows administrative control over applications, such as instant messaging, that try to tunnel over specified web ports, such as HTTP port 80. The AIC engine can also be used to inspect FTP traffic and control the commands being issued in FTP sessions. There are two main AIC engines: AIC FTP and AIC HTTP.
Atomic Engine	The atomic engines are now combined into two engines with multilevel selections to detect single-packet conditions. Atomic engine can combine Layer 3 and Layer 4 attributes within one signature—for example, IP and TCP. There are three basic subtypes for Atomic engine: Atomic ARP, which inspects Layer 2 ARP protocol; Atomic IP, which inspects IP protocol packets and associated Layer 4 transport protocols; and Atomic IPv6, which detects two IOS vulnerabilities that are stimulated by malformed IPv6 traffic.
Flood Engine	Detects ICMP and UDP floods directed at hosts and networks. There are two types of flood engines: Flood Host and Flood Net.

Table 20-3 *IPS Signature Engines (Continued)*

Signature Engine	Description of the Engine
Meta Engine	Meta signatures are based on multiple individual signatures that define events that occurred in a related manner within a sliding time interval. This engine processes events rather than packets.
Multistring Engine	Inspects Layer 4 transport protocols and payloads by matching several strings for one signature. This engine inspects stream-based TCP and single User Datagram Protocol (UDP) and Internet Control Message Protocol (ICMP) packets.
Normalizer Engine	Configures how the IP and TCP normalizer functions and provides configuration for signature events related to the IP and TCP normalizer. Normalizer engine allows enforcing Request for Comments (RFC) compliance.
Service Engine	Inspects services at OSI Layers 5, 6, and 7 that require detailed protocol analysis. Inspects all standard system and application-level protocols. Service engine is capable of inspecting a wide range of protocol types, such as DNS, FTP, H225, HTTP, IDENT, MSRPC, MSSQL, NTP, RPC, SMB, SNMP, SSH, and TNS.
State Engine	Stateful searches of strings in protocols such as Simple Mail Transfer Protocol (SMTP). The state engine now has a hidden configuration file that is used to define the state transitions, so new state definitions can be delivered in a signature update.
String Engine	Searches on Regex strings based on ICMP, TCP, or UDP. There are three types of string engines: String ICMP, String TCP, and String UDP.
Sweep Engine	Analyzes sweeps to detect network reconnaissance scans from a single host (Internet Control Message Protocol [ICMP] and TCP), from destination ports (TCP and UDP), and multiple ports with remote-procedure call (RPC) requests between two nodes. There are two types of sweep engines: Sweep and Sweep Other TCP.
Traffic Anomaly Engine	Inspects TCP, UDP, and other traffic for worms.
Traffic ICMP Engine	Analyzes nonstandard protocols, such as TFN2K, LOKI, and DDOS. There are only two signatures with configurable parameters in this engine.
Trojan Engine	Analyzes traffic from nonstandard protocols, such as BO2K and TFN2K. There are three types of Trojan engines: Bo2k, Tfn2k, and UDP. There are no user-configurable parameters in these engines.

<table>
<tr><td>NOTE</td><td>The information in Table 20-3 is compiled from Cisco product documentation on "Installing and Using Cisco Intrusion Prevention System Device Manager 6.0" at http://www.cisco.com/en/US/products/hw/vpndevc/ps4077/products_configuration_ guide_chapter09186a0080618a2e.html.</td></tr>
</table>

Similar to the antivirus software model, the network-based IPS sensor software must be kept up-to-date and signatures must be updated regularly. Cisco provides frequent signature updates.

Cisco has launched the Cisco Security Center, a portal that provides the latest signature updates, vendor-neutral security intelligence, exploit detection and mitigation strategies, security news, and Cisco product alerts.

The Cisco Security Center draws together the vast resources within Cisco to offer intelligence and security solutions in one location. Cisco Security Center provides around-the-clock threat and vulnerability information.

http://tools.cisco.com/security/center/home.x

<table>
<tr><td>NOTE</td><td>Use the following Cisco URL to download Cisco IPS software and signature updates: http://www.cisco.com/kobayashi/sw-center/ciscosecure/ids/crypto/.</td></tr>
</table>

<table>
<tr><td>TIP</td><td>Use the following Cisco URL to search for various types of signatures: http://tools.cisco.com/MySDN/Intelligence/searchSignatures.x.</td></tr>
</table>

<table>
<tr><td>NOTE</td><td>For more details on the signature engines and their detailed parameters, refer to the following Cisco documentation URL: http://www.cisco.com/en/US/products/hw/vpndevc/ps4077/products_configuration_guide_chapter09186a0080618a2e.html.</td></tr>
</table>

Sensor Software—IPS Events

The Cisco IPS sensor software's system applications shown in Figure 20-6 generate various IPS events to report the occurrence of some stimulus. Every event is a data representation—for example, the alerts generated by SensorApp or errors generated by any application.

IPS events are generated on demand by the application instances within the sensor OS. There is no specific request from any other application instance to generate a particular event. They usually do not have a specific destination. They are stored locally and then retrieved by one or more application instances as needed.

The following seven types of data are communicated by the various functional units in the sensor software:

- **Intrusion events:** Events produced by SensorApp. The sensor detects and reports the intrusion events.

- **Error events:** Events caused by any hardware or software malfunctions.

- **Status events:** Events reported when changes in the application's status occur; for example, the sensor configuration has been updated.

- **Control transaction log events:** Results of a control transaction logged by the sensor.

- **Attack response events:** An action for the Attack Response Controller (ARC); for example, a block request was triggered.

- **Debug events:** Events used for troubleshooting and debugging that provide detailed status.

- **Control transaction data:** Data associated with control transactions—for example, session logs and configuration data to or from an application.

These types of data are collectively referred to as *IPS data*.

These collections of IPS events can be categorized into five basic types:

- **evAlert:** Alert event messages are generated to report a signature being triggered. SensorApp writes these events into the event store. Alert events can be viewed by using the CLI and IDM Event Viewer.

- **evStatus:** Status event messages are generated to report the status and actions of the IPS applications.

- **evError:** Error event messages are generated to report errors that occurred while attempting response actions.

- **evLogTransaction:** Log transaction messages are generated to report the control transactions processed by each sensor application.

- **evShunRqst:** Block request messages are generated to report when the Attack Response Controller (ARC) issues a block request.

Each IPS event is stored in the local sensor database known as the Event Store, as shown in Figure 20-6. Each event is stored with a time stamp and a unique, monotonic, ascending ID. SensorApp is the only application that writes "alert" events into the Event Store. All other applications write log, status, and error events into the Event Store.

Sensor Software—IPS Event Actions

An IPS event action is triggered when a signature is matched and an action is required to mitigate the situation.

Table 20-4 lists the basic IPS event actions available in the sensor software OS that can be configured per individual signatures. Most of the following event actions belong to each signature engine unless they are not supported or appropriate for that particular engine. For example, the ICMP signature engine cannot be configured for TCP Reset action.

Table 20-4   *IPS Event Actions*

Event Action	Description of the Action
Deny Attacker Inline	Does not transmit this packet and future packets originating from the attacker address for a specified period. This is the most severe of the deny actions. It denies current and future packets from a single attacker address. (Available for inline mode only).
Deny Attacker Service Pair Inline	Does not transmit this packet and future packets on the attacker address victim port pair for a specified period. (Available for inline mode only).
Deny Attacker Victim Pair Inline	Does not transmit this packet and future packets on the attacker/victim address pair for a specified period of time. (Available for inline mode only).
Deny Connection Inline	Does not transmit this packet and future packets on the TCP flow. (Available for inline mode only).
Deny Packet Inline	Does not transmit this packet. (Available for inline mode only).
Log Attacker Packets	Starts IP logging packets containing the attacker address.
Log Pair Packets	Starts IP logging packets containing the attacker-victim address pair.
Log Victim Packets	Starts IP logging packets containing the victim address.
Modify Packet Inline	Modifies packet data to remove ambiguity about what the end point might do with the packet.
Produce Alert	Writes the event to the Event Store as an alert.
Produce Verbose Alert	Includes an encoded dump of the offending packet in the alert.
Request Block Connection	Sends a request to Attack Response Controller (ARC) to block this connection. Configure the blocking devices parameters appropriately for this action to work properly.
Request Block Host	Sends a request to Attack Response Controller (ARC) to block this attacker host.

Table 20-4   *IPS Event Actions (Continued)*

Event Action	Description of the Action
Request Rate Limit	Sends a rate limit request to Attack Response Controller (ARC) to perform rate limiting. Rate-limiting devices must be configured appropriately to implement this action.
Request SNMP Trap	Sends a request to NotificationApp to perform SNMP notification.
Reset TCP Connection	Sends TCP resets to hijack and terminate the TCP flow. Reset TCP Connection works only on TCP-based signatures that analyze a single connection. It does not work for sweeps or floods.

NOTE   The information in Table 20-4 is compiled from Cisco product documentation on "Installing and Using Cisco Intrusion Prevention System Device Manager 6.0" at http://www.cisco.com/en/US/products/hw/vpndevc/ps4077/products_configuration_guide_chapter09186a0080618a2e.html.

Sensor Software—IPS Risk Rating (RR)

The IPS sensor software offers a unique Risk Rating (RR) numerical integer that allows users to make informed decisions on the IPS inline drop actions and provides users with greater confidence by enhancing the reliability of the inline deployment. RR is primarily used internally and is a locally significant number (within the sensor) to determine the proper action to take on an event.

RR is a multidimensional formula that is applied on a per-signature basis. The RR is calculated from several components, some of which are configured, some collected, and some derived. RR has a value between 0 and 100; the higher the RR value, the greater the confidence that the event detected is an indication of malicious activity (and not a false positive).

RR represents a numerical quantification of the risk associated with a particular event on the network. The calculation takes into account the value of the network asset being attacked (for example, a server), so it is configured on a per-signature basis (Attack Severity Rating (ASR) and Signature Fidelity Rating (SFR)) and on a per-server basis Target Value Rating (TVR).

NOTE   The RR is associated with alerts, not signatures.

RR is a mechanism used to prioritize alerts that need user attention. These RR factors take into consideration the severity of the attack, whether it was successful, the fidelity of the signature, and the overall value of the target host. The RR is reported in the evIdsAlert.

The following values are used to calculate the RR for a particular event:

- **Signature Fidelity Rating (SFR):** A weight associated with how well this signature might perform in the absence of specific knowledge of the target. The SFR is configured per signature and indicates how accurately the signature detects the event or condition it describes. It represents to what degree of confidence the detected behavior would produce the intended effect on the target platform if the packet under analysis were allowed to be delivered.

- **Attack Severity Rating (ASR):** A weight associated with the severity of a successful exploit of the vulnerability. The ASR is derived from the alert severity parameter (informational, low, medium, or high) of a particular signature. The ASR is configured per signature and indicates how dangerous the event detected is.

- **Target Value Rating (TVR):** A weight associated with the perceived value of the target. TVR is a user-configurable value (zero, low, medium, high, or mission critical) that identifies the importance of a network asset (through its IP address). For example, assign a higher TVR value to the web server than the TVR assigned to a desktop node. TVR is configured in the Event Action Rules policy.

- **Attack Relevancy Rating (ARR):** A weight associated with the relevancy of the targeted OS. ARR is a derived value (relevant, unknown, or not relevant) is determined at alert time. The relevant OS is configured per signature.

- **Promiscuous Delta (PD):** A weight associated with the PD is in the range of 0 to 30 and is configured per signature.

- **Watch List Rating (WLR):** A weight associated with the CSA MC watch-list in the range of 0 to 100. (CSA MC only uses the range 0 to 35.) If the attacker for the alert is found on the watch list, the WLR for that attacker is added to the rating.

The formula to calculate the RR follows:

RR = ((ASR*TVR*SFR)/10000)+ARR-PD+WLR

Sensor Software—IPS Threat Rating

Threat Rating (TR) is an RR value that has been lowered by event actions that have been taken. All event actions have a specific TR adjustment. The largest TR from all of the event actions taken is subtracted from the RR.

Table 20-5 lists the event actions with the corresponding TR values.

Table 20-5   *Threat Rating Value for Event Actions*

Event Action	Threat Rating
Deny attacker inline	45
Deny attacker victim pair inline	40
Deny attacker service pair inline	40
Deny connection inline	35
Deny packet inline	35
Modify packet inline	35
Request block host	20
Request block connection	20
Reset TCP connection	20
Request rate limit	20

Sensor Software—IPS Interfaces

Cisco IPS sensor software supports the following two main types of interface roles:

- **Command and Control interface (also known as Management Interface):** As the name implies, the Command and Control interface is used for managing and configuring the sensor. It has an IP address and is permanently enabled. It receives security and status events from the sensor and queries the sensor for statistics.

  Command and Control interface is statically mapped to a specific physical interface depending on the sensor model. This mapping cannot be changed, and this interface cannot be used as a sensing interface. Table 20-6 lists the command and control interfaces for each sensor model.

Table 20-6   *Command and Control Interfaces*

Sensor Model	Command and Control Interface
IDS-4215	FastEthernet0/0
IDS-4235	GigabitEthernet0/1
IDS-4250	GigabitEthernet0/1
IPS-4240	Management0/0
IPS-4255	Management0/0
IPS-4260	Management0/0
IPS-4270	Management0/0
NM-CIDS	FastEthernet0/0

continues

Table 20-6   *Command and Control Interfaces (Continued)*

Sensor Model	Command and Control Interface
AIP-SSM-10	GigabitEthernet0/0
AIP-SSM-20	GigabitEthernet0/0
IDSM-2	GigabitEthernet0/2

- **Sensing Interface (also known as Sniffing interface):** Sensing interfaces are purpose-built interfaces used by the sensor to monitor and analyze network traffic. Each sensor has one or more sensing interfaces depending on the sensor model. Table 20-7 lists the detailed interface support providing the number and type of sensing interfaces available for each sensor model.

    Sensing interfaces can operate individually in promiscuous mode, or they can be paired to create inline interfaces for inline sensing mode.

Table 20-7   *Interface Support*

Sensor Model	Added PCI Cards	Interfaces Supporting Inline VLAN Pairs (Sensing Ports)	Combinations Supporting Inline Interface Pairs	Interfaces Not Supporting Inline (Command and Control Port)
IDS-4215	—	FastEthernet0/1	N/A	FastEthernet0/0
IDS-4215	4FE	FastEthernet0/1 FastEthernetS/0 FastEthernetS/1 FastEthernetS/2 FastEthernetS/3	1/0<->1/1 1/0<->1/2 1/0<->1/3 1/1<->1/2 1/1<->1/3 1/2<->1/3 0/1<->1/0 0/1<->1/1 0/1<->1/2 0/1<->1/3	FastEthernet0/0
IDS-4235	—	GigabitEthernet0/0	N/A	GigabitEthernet0/1
IDS-4235	4FE	GigabitEthernet0/0 FastEthernetS/0 FastEthernetS/1 FastEthernetS/2 FastEthernetS/3	1/0<->1/1 1/0<->1/2 1/0<->1/3 1/1<->1/2 1/1<->1/3 1/2<->1/3	GigabitEthernet0/1
IDS-4235	TX (GE)	GigabitEthernet0/0 GigabitEthernet1/0 GigabitEthernet2/0	0/0<->1/0 0/0<->2/0	GigabitEthernet0/1
IDS-4250	—	GigabitEthernet0/0	N/A	GigabitEthernet0/1

Table 20-7   *Interface Support (Continued)*

Sensor Model	Added PCI Cards	Interfaces Supporting Inline VLAN Pairs (Sensing Ports)	Combinations Supporting Inline Interface Pairs	Interfaces Not Supporting Inline (Command and Control Port)
IDS-4250	4FE	GigabitEthernet0/0 FastEthernetS/0 FastEthernetS/1 FastEthernetS/2 FastEthernetS/3	1/0<->1/1 1/0<->1/2 1/0<->1/3 1/1<->1/2 1/1<->1/3 1/2<->1/3	GigabitEthernet0/1
IDS-4250	TX (GE)	GigabitEthernet0/0 GigabitEthernet1/0 GigabitEthernet2/0	0/0<->1/0 0/0<->2/0	GigabitEthernet0/1
IDS-4250	SX	GigabitEthernet0/0 GigabitEthernet1/0	N/A	GigabitEthernet0/1
IDS-4250	SX + SX	GigabitEthernet0/0 GigabitEthernet1/0 GigabitEthernet2/0	1/0<->2/0	GigabitEthernet0/1
IDS-4250	XL	GigabitEthernet0/0 GigabitEthernet2/0 GigabitEthernet2/1	2/0<->2/1	GigabitEthernet0/1
IDSM-2	—	GigabitEthernet0/7 GigabitEthernet0/8	0/7<->0/8	GigabitEthernet0/2
IPS-4240	—	GigabitEthernet0/0 GigabitEthernet0/1 GigabitEthernet0/2 GigabitEthernet0/3	0/0<->0/1 0/0<->0/2 0/0<->0/3 0/1<->0/2 0/1<->0/3 0/2<->0/3	Management0/0
IPS-4255	—	GigabitEthernet0/0 GigabitEthernet0/1 GigabitEthernet0/2 GigabitEthernet0/3	0/0<->0/1 0/0<->0/2 0/0<->0/3 0/1<->0/2 0/1<->0/3 0/2<->0/3	Management0/0
IPS-4260	—	GigabitEthernet0/1	N/A	Management0/0

continues

Table 20-7 *Interface Support (Continued)*

Sensor Model	Added PCI Cards	Interfaces Supporting Inline VLAN Pairs (Sensing Ports)	Combinations Supporting Inline Interface Pairs	Interfaces Not Supporting Inline (Command and Control Port)
IPS-4260	4GE-BP	GigabitEthernet0/1		Management0/0
	Slot 1	GigabitEthernet2/0 GigabitEthernet2/1 GigabitEthernet2/2 GigabitEthernet2/3	2/0<->2/1 2/2<->2/3	
	Slot 2	GigabitEthernet3/0 GigabitEthernet3/1 GigabitEthernet3/2 GigabitEthernet3/3	3/0<->3/1 3/2<->3/3	
IPS-4260	2SX	GigabitEthernet0/1	All sensing ports can be paired together	Management0/0
	Slot 1	GigabitEthernet2/0 GigabitEthernet2/1		
	Slot 2	GigabitEthernet3/0 GigabitEthernet3/1		
IPS 4270-20	—	GigabitEthernet0/1	N/A	Management0/0 Management0/1
IPS 4270-20	4GE-BP	GigabitEthernet0/1		Management0/0 Management0/1
	Slot 1	GigabitEthernet2/0 GigabitEthernet2/1 GigabitEthernet2/2 GigabitEthernet2/3	2/0<->2/1 2/2<->2/3	
	Slot 2	GigabitEthernet3/0 GigabitEthernet3/1 GigabitEthernet3/2 GigabitEthernet3/3	3/0<->3/1 3/2<->3/3	

Table 20-7   *Interface Support (Continued)*

Sensor Model	Added PCI Cards	Interfaces Supporting Inline VLAN Pairs (Sensing Ports)	Combinations Supporting Inline Interface Pairs	Interfaces Not Supporting Inline (Command and Control Port)
IPS 4270-20	2SX	GigabitEthernet0/1	All sensing ports can be paired together	Management0/0 Management0/1
	Slot 1	GigabitEthernet2/0 GigabitEthernet2/1 GigabitEthernet2/2 GigabitEthernet2/3		
	Slot 2	GigabitEthernet3/0 GigabitEthernet3/1 GigabitEthernet3/2 GigabitEthernet3/3		
AIP-SSM-10	—	GigabitEthernet0/1 by security context instead of VLAN pair or inline interface pair	GigabitEthernet0/1 by security context instead of VLAN pair or inline interface pair	GigabitEthernet0/0
AIP-SSM-20	—	GigabitEthernet0/1 by security context instead of VLAN pair or inline interface pair	GigabitEthernet0/1 by security context instead of VLAN pair or inline interface pair	GigabitEthernet0/0

NOTE   S indicates the slot number. IDS 4FE card can be installed in either slot 1 or 2.

Table 20-7 can be found at the following Cisco documentation URL: http://www.cisco.com/en/US/products/hw/vpndevc/ps4077/products_installation_guide_chapter09186a0080757abc.html#wp522729.

Sensor Software—IPS Interface Modes

The IPS Sensor software OS expands the sensing interface roles into various modes of implementation. There are four basic types of interface modes:

- **Promiscuous mode:** Packets in promiscuous mode do not flow through the sensor. The sensor depends on a mirrored copy of the packet sent to the sensor. The sensor analyzes the copy of the packet rather than the actual packet on the wire. The packets are copied using network taps, the traffic mirroring SPAN feature, or selective mirroring using the VACL feature on the switch.

NOTE Refer to the following Cisco documentation URL to configure Catalyst Switched Port Analyzer (SPAN) Configuration: http://www.cisco.com/en/US/products/hw/switches/ps708/products_tech_note09186a008015c612.shtml.

Monitoring traffic in promiscuous mode can be seen as an advantage because the sensor does not affect the packet flow with the forwarded traffic. However, the disadvantage is that the sensor cannot stop malicious traffic from reaching its intended target for certain types of attacks, such as atomic attacks (single-packet attacks).

The IPS event response actions implemented with the promiscuous sensor devices are post-event responses and rely on other devices in the network for enforcement (such as a firewall, a switch, or a router). Such response actions can be useful to prevent some types of attacks. However, in a situation similar to an atomic attack, a single packet carrying the attack vector has a good chance of reaching the target system before the promiscuous-based sensor can apply enforcement (TCP Reset or Shun ACL on a managed device).

Figure 20-7 illustrates the network-based IDS sensor in promiscuous mode. This is typically referred to as the IDS (out-of-band detection) solution.

Figure 20-7 *Cisco IDS Sensor in Promiscuous Mode*

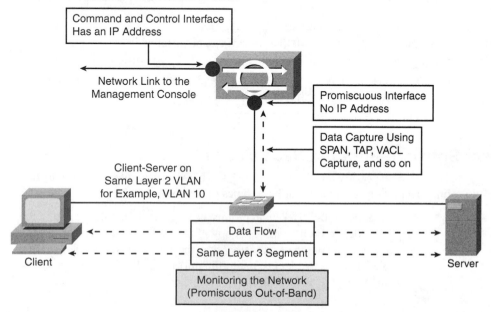

- **Inline interface mode:** This type of mode is the most effective method for detecting and preventing network intrusion. Inline interface mode puts the sensor directly in the middle of the traffic flow. Note that inline mode will affect packet-forwarding rates by making them slower and adding latency.

Inline mode gives the IPS sensor the capability to drop malicious traffic and stop attacks before they reach the intended target, thus providing a preventive protection service.

Inline mode analyzes traffic not only on Layer 3 and 4, but it also inspects upper layers within the payload of the packet for more sophisticated embedded attacks (Layers 3 to 7).

In inline interface pair mode, a packet comes in (ingress) through the first interface of the pair on the sensor and goes out (egress) the second interface of the pair. The packet is sent to the second interface of the pair unless that packet is being denied or modified by a signature.

Figure 20-8 illustrates the network-based IPS sensor in inline interface mode. This is typically referred to as the IPS (inline, within packet stream detection) solution. Note that a Layer 2 segmentation is required for inline mode to work; that is, the client and the first interface are on a separate VLAN, whereas the server and the second interface are on a separate VLAN, as shown in Figure 20-8. The Layer 3 network remains unchanged.

Figure 20-8   *Cisco IPS Sensor in Inline Interface Mode*

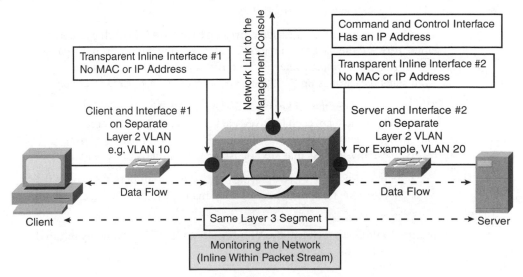

NOTE	Cisco IPS Sensor supports both inline interface pairs and inline VLAN pairs. IPS can also be deployed in an IDS mode that uses a single interface in promiscuous mode.

CAUTION	If the paired interfaces are connected to the same switch, be sure to configure them as **access** ports with a different access VLAN for the two ports. Otherwise, traffic will not flow through the inline interface.

- **Inline VLAN pair mode:** Inline VLAN pair mode is also known as Inline-on-a-Stick. This mode is similar to the inline interface mode, with an extended enhanced capability to associate VLANs in pairs on a physical interface. Therefore, it is known as inline VLAN pair mode.

  The sensing interface in the inline VLAN pair mode acts as an 802.1q trunk port, and the sensor performs VLAN bridging between pairs of VLANs on the trunk port.

  Packets received on one of the paired VLANs are analyzed and then forwarded to the other VLAN in the pair. The sensor bridges VLANs together on the same physical interface by creating, in effect, subinterfaces that allow the sensor to bring packets incoming on VLAN X and outgoing on VLAN Y, as shown in Figure 20-9.

  The sensor inspects the traffic it receives on each VLAN in each pair and can either forward the packets on the other VLAN in the pair or drop the packet if an intrusion attempt is detected. The IPS sensor can be configured to simultaneously bridge up to 255 VLAN pairs on each sensing interface.

  The sensor rewrites the packet by replacing the VLAN ID field (VLAN tag) in the 802.1q header of each received packet with the ID of the egress VLAN on which the sensor forwards the packet. The sensor drops all packets received on any VLANs that are not assigned to inline VLAN pairs.

  The advantage of inline VLAN pairing mode is that multiple VLAN pairs per physical interface reduce the need to have many physical interfaces per chassis.

  Figure 20-9 illustrates the inline VLAN pair mode. This is typically referred to as the Inline-on-a-Stick solution.

Figure 20-9 *Cisco IPS Sensor in Inline VLAN Pair Mode*

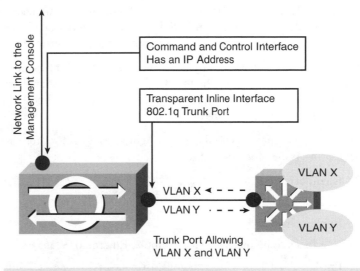

- **VLAN Group mode:** In VLAN Group mode, each physical interface or inline interface can be divided into VLAN group subinterfaces, each of which consists of a group of VLANs on that particular interface. With the introduction of multiple virtual sensors, the sensor can monitor one or more of these interfaces.

  VLAN Group mode provides the capability of applying multiple policies to the same sensor. This allows the sensor to emulate multiple interfaces; with only a few interfaces, the sensor can seem to have many interfaces.

Sensor Software—IPS Blocking (Shun)

Cisco IPS Sensor software supports dynamic response action by blocking the offending traffic during an attack. The Attack Response Controller (ARC) function in the sensor software is responsible for managing network devices to respond to suspicious events by blocking (shunning) network access from attacking hosts and networks. The ARC is part of the MainApp application, as shown in Figure 20-6.

There are three basic types of blocking:

- **Host block:** Blocks all traffic from a given IP address.
- **Connection block:** Blocks all traffic from a specific source IP address to a given destination IP address and destination port.
- **Network block:** Blocks all traffic from a given network subnet.

The ARC enforces the blocking on Cisco routers and Catalyst 6500 series switches by using ACL or VACL functions. Each ACL or VACL contains permit and deny conditions that apply to IP addresses. Other non-IOS devices and security appliances that do not support ACL or VACL use the **shun** function to enforce blocking instead.

The ARC controls the devices by using the IP address of the managed devices that are configured. It connects to all the managed devices in the list and sends the block (shun) instructions to every device. ARC will keep track of block time and undo the restrictions after the block time has expired.

The following parameters need to be configured on the sensor for ARC function to manage a device and issue block instructions:

- Login user ID.
- Login password.
- Enable password.
- Interfaces to be managed (for example, Ethernet0, Vlan5).
- Pre-Block ACL or VACL and/or Post-Block ACL or VACL information (This is to inform the sensor of any existing ACL or VACL that is already applied to this device. The sensor will append pre or post if needed.)
- Protocol (Telnet or SSH) to communicate with the device.
- Exclude address block (IP addresses or range of IP addresses that need to be excluded from blocking).
- Block time.

NOTE   In the previous IPS Sensor software versions, ARC was formerly known as Network Access Controller. The new Cisco IPS Sensor software Version 6.0 has been updated; however, IDM and the CLI may contain references to Network Access Controller, **nac**, and **network-access**.

Sensor Software—IPS Rate Limiting

In addition to blocking, which was described earlier, the Cisco IPS Sensor software also supports dynamic response action by rate limiting traffic in protected networks for specified traffic classes on network devices. Similar to blocking, the Attack Response Controller (ARC) function in the sensor software is responsible for rate limiting.

The rate limiting feature provides the capability of reducing the effect of a denial of service (DoS) attack or network attack, instead of blocking it entirely. This is similar to the Committed Access Rate (CAR) function in Cisco IOS.

Rate-limit responses are supported for the Host Flood and Net Flood engines and the TCP half-open SYN signature.

The following parameters are required to implement rate limit:

- **Layer 3 information:** Source or destination address for any rate limit
- **Layer 4 information:** Source or destination port for rate limits with TCP or UDP protocol

Rate-limit parameters can be tuned on individual signatures. To implement rate limit, select the event action type Request Rate Limit (Table 20-4) to enforce rate limiting and set the percentage for these signatures.

NOTE   Cisco IOS Software Version 12.3 or later is required for ARC to successfully implement rate limit on Cisco routers.

Sensor Software—IPS Virtualization

As discussed previously, the IPS sensor software uses the Analysis Engine to perform packet analysis and alert detection. The sensor monitors traffic that flows through specified interfaces mentioned previously.

The IPS Sensor Software OS Version 6.0 introduces the concept of virtualization, whereby virtual sensors can be created in the Analysis Engine. Version 6.0 supports up to four virtual sensors.

Virtual sensors can be effectively used to monitor multiple data streams, apply different configurations to different sets of traffic, monitor two network segments with overlapping IP spaces with one sensor, or monitor concurrently both the inside and outside of a firewall with one sensor.

Multiple virtual sensors can be hosted on the same appliance, each configured with different signature behavior and traffic feeds. Each virtual sensor has its own set of unique settings and configurations, such as a unique name with a list of interfaces, inline interface pairs, inline VLAN pairs, and VLAN groups associated with it.

Each virtual sensor is associated with a specifically named signature definition, event action rules, and anomaly detection configuration.

The sensor can receive data inputs from one or many monitored data streams. These monitored data streams can either be physical interface ports or virtual interface ports.

NOTE   For more information on the IPS Virtual Sensor feature and detailed configuration parameters, refer to the following Cisco documentation URL:http://www.cisco.com/en/US/products/hw/vpndevc/ps4077/products_configuration_guide_chapter09186 a00807517a5.html.

Sensor Software—IPS Security Policies

The IPS Sensor Software OS allows the creation of multiple security policies and the application of those multiple policies to the individual virtual sensors that were discussed previously.

A security policy configuration contains three components:

- Signature definition policy
- Event action rules policy
- Anomaly detection policy

Cisco IPS sensor software OS version 6.0 contains a default signature definition policy called **sig0**, a default event action rules policy called **rules0**, and a default anomaly detection policy called **ad0**. These default policies or customized user-defined new policies can be associated with the newly defined virtual sensor (discussed earlier) as required.

Multiple security policies can be customized and created for multiple virtual sensors based on different requirements and can be applied per VLAN or physical interface.

TIP   Refer to the following Cisco documentation URL to configure signature definition policies: http://www.cisco.com/en/US/products/hw/vpndevc/ps4077/products_configuration_guide_chapter09186a0080618a2a.html.

TIP   Refer to the following Cisco documentation URL to configure event action rules policies: http://www.cisco.com/en/US/products/hw/vpndevc/ps4077/products_configuration_guide_chapter09186a0080618a28.html.

TIP   Refer to the following Cisco documentation URL to configure anomaly detection policies: http://www.cisco.com/en/US/products/hw/vpndevc/ps4077/products_configuration_guide_chapter09186a0080618916.html.

Sensor Software—IPS Anomaly Detection (AD)

The IPS Sensor Software OS Version 6.0 introduces the revolutionary Anomaly Detection (AD) function built in to the sensor software architecture. The AD solution detects worm-infected hosts and worm-based attacks. AD detects the following two situations:

- The network starts to become congested by worm traffic.
- A single worm-infected source enters the network and starts scanning for other vulnerable hosts.

The AD works by subdividing the network into various zones, thereby enabling it to characterize the traffic patterns. This also helps reduce false negatives. A zone is a set of destination IP addresses. The following are the three zones, each with its own thresholds:

- **Internal zone:** All the traffic that comes to your IP address range. Configure the internal zone with the IP address range of the internal network. By default, the internal zone contains no IP address range.
- **Illegal zone:** The range of IP addresses that should never be seen in normal traffic—for example, unallocated IP addresses or part of your internal IP address range that is unused. Packets that do not match the set of IP addresses in the internal or illegal zone are handled by the external zone. By default, the illegal zone contains no IP address range.
- **External zone:** All the traffic that goes to the Internet. The external zone is the default zone with the default range of 0.0.0.0–255.255.255.255.

The sensor does not depend on signatures. Instead, it learns primarily normal activity and establishes the network baseline for predictable behavior patterns.

Initially, the AD conducts a learning process when the most normal state of the network is reflected. Using this baseline, AD derives a set of policy thresholds that best fit the normal network.

After a normal network baseline is established, the sensor can detect any anomalies that deviated from the normal behavior pattern and take dynamic response actions accordingly.

CAUTION AD assumes it gets traffic from both directions. If the sensor is configured to see only one direction of traffic, AD identifies all traffic as having incomplete connections—for example, scanners—and sends alerts for all such traffic flows.

The AD has the following three modes:

- **Learn mode:** As mentioned earlier, AD is in the initial learning mode for the default period of 24 hours that is required to establish the normal baseline of the network. This is assuming that during this phase (learning), no attack is being carried out, or else the baseline will be misled. The initial baseline is known as the knowledge base (KB) of the network traffic.

- **Detect mode:** This is the default mode for the AD, and for ongoing operation, the sensor should remain in detect mode 24 hours a day, 7 days a week. In this mode, the AD detects attacks based on the initial KB. AD will send alerts for any traffic flows that violate thresholds in the KB or that deviate from the normal behavior pattern. In addition, the AD records gradual changes to the KB that do not violate the thresholds and thus creates a new KB. The new KB is periodically saved and takes the place of the old KB, thus maintaining an up-to-date KB.

- **Inactive mode:** This mode is used to disable AD monitoring by putting it in the inactive mode. Under certain circumstances, AD should be in inactive mode—for example, if the sensor is running in an asymmetric environment.

NOTE   Refer to the following Cisco documentation URL for IPS Anomaly Detection (AD) technique and configuration parameters: http://www.cisco.com/en/US/products/hw/vpndevc/ps4077/products_configuration_guide_chapter09186a00807517a1.html.

IPS High Availability

Deploying an IPS sensor into the traffic stream (inline mode) introduces a new device in the data path that can possibly fail and prevent traffic from flowing.

High availability is defined as building into the network the capability of the network to cope with the loss of a component while preserving network functionality.

There are three possible solutions to resolve situations in which the inline IPS device may fail:

- **Fail-open mechanism:** A hardware or software fail-open mechanism that is able to detect problems and bypass the sensor, in the event of a device failure. Traffic stream should go uninterrupted through the device without inspection when required.

- **Failover mechanism:** A redundancy mechanism that can provide one or more data paths through the network to allow packets, in the event of a device failure. The secondary path can be set up to either go through a backup IPS sensor or through a plain wire.

- **Load-balancing mechanism:** A hardware or software load-balancing feature to split the traffic load across multiple devices; this can achieve both higher data rates and redundant paths in the event of a device failure.

The following sections take a closer look at these three solutions.

IPS Fail-Open Mechanism

One of the best case options is reliance on fail-open, but this strategy leaves the network with no protection and can bring down the entire network if intrusion is successful.

There are two possible options in fail-open—hardware and software fail-open:

- The hardware-based fail-open mechanism works by closing a circuit based on power loss, link failure, or potential software triggers. The hardware-based fail-open mechanism provides uninterrupted access to the network, thereby allowing packets to pass directly uninspected, bypassing the sensor. The hardware-based bypass is not efficient and remains a single point of failure because a physical layer failure or a problem in a device can still cause the network to shut down. This is true for all hardware bypass mechanisms.

- The software-based fail-open mechanism works by building the intelligence within the sensor software, through a built-in software feature that passes packets when a failure is detected. This feature is in most cases user configurable, allowing a user three choices: On, Off, and Auto. The Bypass Off prevents a bypass from occurring. This is designed for network instances where the flow of uninspected is not desired. The Bypass On forces the sensor to pass all packets uninspected. This is useful for troubleshooting when a network problem is detected dynamically, and the IPS device is a suspect. The Bypass Auto lets the sensor inspect packets until for some reason the sensor is not forwarding the packets. At that point, the Bypass Auto feature comes into action to ensure that traffic continues to flow uninterrupted and uninspected.

Failover Mechanism

As mentioned earlier, a good network design incorporates high availability into the network, and not into a single piece of hardware or software. Network failover allows the network to recover from a device or physical layer failure. There are two possible options in this scenario:

- **Layer 3:** PIX/ASA Failover, Cisco IOS HSRP
- **Layer 2:** Spanning Tree

Traditional IPS sensors (usually the non-Layer 3) cannot detect or control network failover. Traditional IPS sensors function like a wire, and a failure of the sensor would look like a failure of a wire. The network will respond accordingly. Fail-open capabilities may help but cannot truly solve the issue.

Fail-Open and Failover Deployments

Cisco IPS appliance sensor offers the following solutions:

- Deploy a standalone sensor in hardware bypass mode.
- Deploy redundant sensors using a spanning tree for active/passive failover.
- Deploy redundant sensors using a spanning tree for high availability (along with plain wire).

Load-Balancing Technique

Cisco IPS sensors can be deployed inline as part of an EtherChannel (EC) to provide redundancy.

- Allows up to eight sensors deployed, inspecting the same data set.
- Relies on an EC algorithm to split data flow among the different inspection detection system (IDS) modules. This cannot guarantee equal load, though.

NOTE	Refer to the following Cisco documentation URL for IPS high availability using the EtherChannel load-balancing technique: http://www.cisco.com/en/US/products/hw/vpndevc/ps4077/products_configuration_example09186a0080671a8d.shtml.

IPS Appliance Deployment Guidelines

Figure 20-10 illustrates the various deployment designs implementing the IPS appliance into the network.

Figure 20-10 *Cisco IPS Sensor Appliance Deployment*

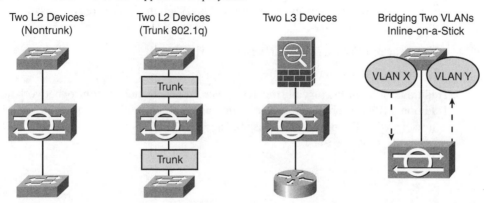

Cisco Intrusion Prevention System Device Manager (IDM)

The Cisco IPS sensor can be managed via the CLI or web-based GUI application. Cisco IPS Device Manager (IDM) is an integrated web-based, Java Web Start application available in the sensor software OS used to manage and configure the sensor. IDM can be accessed using standard web browsers such as Internet Explorer by browsing the sensor IP address configured on the Command and Control interface.

Before IDM can be used, the sensor appliance needs to be initialized (bootstrap) with basic configuration parameters. This can be done from the CLI by using the internal **setup** utility to perform basic functions, such as configuring the hostname, IP address for the command and control interface, default gateway, Telnet server, web server, ACL, and time settings.

After the sensor has been initialized and is reachable on the IP network, the IDM applet can be launched from a desktop PC to complete the remaining configuration tasks on the sensor. From the web browser, type **HTTPS** with sensor IP address to launch the IDM application;

https://sensor_ip_address

Cisco IPS Device Manager (IDM) is covered further in Chapter 24, "Security and Policy Management."

TIP   The CLI access can still be used to configure the sensor; IDM is an alternative GUI application for the same.

NOTE   Refer to the following Cisco documentation URL for more information about IDM and the system requirements to use the IDM application: http://www.cisco.com/en/US/products/hw/vpndevc/ps4077/products_configuration_guide_chapter09186a0080618948.html.

Configuring IPS Inline VLAN Pair Mode

Based on Figure 20-11, Example 20-1 shows a basic configuration example that enables an inline VLAN pair mode on the sensor appliance. The inline VLAN pair is assigned to the default virtual sensor **vs0**. IPS interface GigabitEthernet2/0 connected to Switchport FastEthernet0/5 is being used for sensing in this example. The sensor performs VLAN bridging between pairs of VLANs on the trunk port. Traffic incoming to the sensor on VLAN 10 is inspected and sent out with VLAN TAG of VLAN 20 on the same physical interface (hair-pinning).

The sample configuration also shows some basic IPS initializing parameters such as configuring the hostname, IP address, default gateway, and access list to allow trusted hosts.

Figure 20-11 *IPS Inline VLAN Pair Mode*

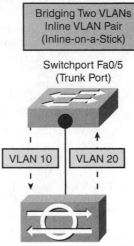

Example 20-1 *Configuring IPS Inline VLAN Pair Mode on IPS Appliance*

```
IPS# show configuration
! ----------------------------
! Current configuration last modified Mon Jul 09 11:16:02 2007
! ----------------------------
! Version 6.0(1)
! Host:
!     Realm Keys          key1.0
! Signature Definition:
!     Signature Update    S263.0    2006-12-18
!     Virus Update        V1.2      2005-11-24
! ----------------------------
service interface
physical-interfaces GigabitEthernet2/0
admin-state enabled
subinterface-type inline-vlan-pair
subinterface 1
vlan1 10
vlan2 20
<..>
service analysis-engine
virtual-sensor vs0
physical-interface GigabitEthernet2/0 subinterface-number 1
<..>
! ----------------------------
service host
```

Example 20-1   *Configuring IPS Inline VLAN Pair Mode on IPS Appliance (Continued)*

```
network-settings
host-ip 172.16.10.1/24,172.16.10.254
host-name IPS
telnet-option disabled
access-list 172.16.10.0/24
<..>
! ----------------------------
```

Based on Figure 20-11, Example 20-2 shows the basic Switch Trunk port configuration that completes the inline VLAN pair setup, allowing VLAN 10 and VLAN 20 accordingly.

Example 20-2   *Configuring Switch Trunk Port Configuration for IPS Inline VLAN Pair Mode*

```
Switch# show run interface FastEthernet0/5
Building configuration...
Current configuration : 132 bytes
!
interface FastEthernet0/5
 switchport trunk encapsulation dot1q
 switchport trunk allowed vlan 10,20
 switchport mode trunk
end
```

Example 20-3 shows a sample output from the IPS sensor appliance to verify interface configuration. Note that the interface function is "sensing" and the Inline mode is an **inline-vlan-pair**, which indicates that this is an inline VLAN pair mode setup.

Example 20-3   *Verifying IPS Inline VLAN Pair Settings*

```
IPS# show interfaces GigabitEthernet2/0
MAC statistics from interface GigabitEthernet2/0
   Statistics From Subinterface 1
      Statistics From Vlan 10
         Total Packets Received On This Vlan = 759061
         Total Bytes Received On This Vlan = 69709354
         Total Packets Transmitted On This Vlan = 292105
         Total Bytes Transmitted On This Vlan = 35889784
      Statistics From Vlan 20
         Total Packets Received On This Vlan = 292232
         Total Bytes Received On This Vlan = 35897912
         Total Packets Transmitted On This Vlan = 758907
         Total Bytes Transmitted On This Vlan = 69699312
   Interface function = Sensing interface
   Description =
   Media Type = TX
   Default Vlan = 0
   Inline Mode = Inline-vlan-pair
   Pair Status = N/A
   Hardware Bypass Capable = Yes when paired with GigabitEthernet2/1
```

continues

Example 20-3 *Verifying IPS Inline VLAN Pair Settings (Continued)*

```
     Hardware Bypass Paired = No
     Link Status = Up
     Link Speed = N/A
     Link Duplex = N/A
     Missed Packet Percentage = 0
     Total Packets Received = 1191064
     Total Bytes Received = 118989462
     Total Multicast Packets Received = 0
     Total Broadcast Packets Received = 0
     Total Jumbo Packets Received = 0
     Total Undersize Packets Received = 0
     Total Receive Errors = 0
     Total Receive FIFO Overruns = 0
     Total Packets Transmitted = 1051012
     Total Bytes Transmitted = 105589096
     Total Multicast Packets Transmitted = 0
     Total Broadcast Packets Transmitted = 0
     Total Jumbo Packets Transmitted = 0
     Total Undersize Packets Transmitted = 0
     Total Transmit Errors = 0
     Total Transmit FIFO Overruns = 0
     Dropped Packets From Vlans Not Mapped To Subinterfaces = 139771
     Dropped Bytes From Vlans Not Mapped To Subinterfaces = 13382196
```

Configuring IPS Inline Interface Pair Mode

Based on Figure 20-12, Example 20-4 shows a basic configuration example that enables an inline interface mode on the sensor appliance between two routed devices. The inline interface pair is assigned to the default virtual sensor **vs0**.

IPS interface GigabitEthernet2/0 and GigabitEthernet2/1 are being used for pairing in this example. Note that both routers are on the same Layer 3 segment, but are separated by two different Layer 2 VLANs. Note that basic IPS initializing parameters have been omitted from this sample template. Refer to Example 20-1 for basic IPS parameters.

If the paired interfaces are connected to the same switch, be sure to configure them as access ports with different access VLANs for the two ports. Otherwise, traffic will not flow through the inline interface.

Figure 20-12 *IPS Inline Interface Pair Mode*

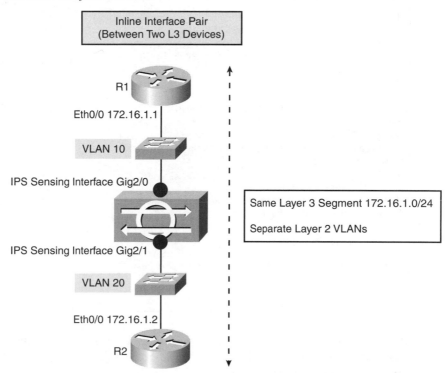

Connection	Switchport
R1 Ethernet0/0	Fa0/1
R2 Ethernet0/0	Fa0/2
IPS Gig2/0	Fa0/10
IPS Gig2/1	Fa0/20

Switchports are configured as **access** ports.

Example 20-4 *Configuring IPS Inline Interface Mode on IPS Appliance*

```
IPS# show configuration
! -----------------------------
! Current configuration last modified Mon Jul 09 11:05:35 2007
! -----------------------------
! Version 6.0(1)
```

continues

Example 20-4 *Configuring IPS Inline Interface Mode on IPS Appliance (Continued)*

```
! Host:
!     Realm Keys        key1.0
! Signature Definition:
!     Signature Update    S263.0    2006-12-18
!     Virus Update        V1.2      2005-11-24
! -----------------------------
service interface
physical-interfaces GigabitEthernet2/0
admin-state enabled
exit
physical-interfaces GigabitEthernet2/1
admin-state enabled
exit
inline-interfaces MyPair
interface1 GigabitEthernet2/0
interface2 GigabitEthernet2/1
! -----------------------------
<..>
! -----------------------------
service analysis-engine
virtual-sensor vs0
logical-interface MyPair
<..>
```

Based on Figure 20-12, Examples 20-5 and 20-6 show the sample configuration output from the two routers (R1 and R2) and a switchport configuration. Note that the switch ports must be configured as access ports.

Example 20-5 *Configuring Two Routers (R1 and R2) on the Same Layer 3 Segment*

```
R1# show run interface Ethernet0/0
Building configuration...
Current configuration : 79 bytes
!
interface Ethernet0/0
 ip address 172.16.1.1 255.255.255.0
end
<..>
R2# show run interface Ethernet0/0
Building configuration...
Current configuration : 95 bytes
!
interface Ethernet0/0
 ip address 172.16.1.2 255.255.255.0
end
```

Example 20-6 *Configuring Switch Ports for IPS Inline Interface on Separate Layer 2 VLANs*

```
Switch# show run interface FastEthernet0/1
Building configuration...
Current configuration : 84 bytes
```

Example 20-6 *Configuring Switch Ports for IPS Inline Interface on Separate Layer 2 VLANs (Continued)*

```
!
interface FastEthernet0/1
 switchport access vlan 10
 switchport mode access
end
<..>
Switch# show run interface FastEthernet0/2
Building configuration...
Current configuration : 84 bytes
!
interface FastEthernet0/2
 switchport access vlan 20
 switchport mode access
end
<..>
Switch# show run interface FastEthernet0/10
Building configuration...
Current configuration : 85 bytes
!
interface FastEthernet0/10
 switchport access vlan 10
 switchport mode access
end
<..>
Switch# show run interface FastEthernet0/20
Building configuration...
Current configuration : 85 bytes
!
interface FastEthernet0/20
 switchport access vlan 20
 switchport mode access
end
```

Example 20-7 shows a sample output from the IPS sensor appliance that verifies the interface configuration. Note that the interface function is "sensing" and the inline mode is "paired" with another interface, indicating that this is an inline interface mode setup.

Example 20-7 *Verifying IPS Inline Interface Settings*

```
IPS# show interfaces GigabitEthernet2/0
MAC statistics from interface GigabitEthernet2/0
   Interface function = Sensing interface
   Description =
   Media Type = TX
   Default Vlan = 0
   Inline Mode = Paired with interface GigabitEthernet2/1
   Pair Status = Up
   Hardware Bypass Capable = Yes when paired with GigabitEthernet2/1
   Hardware Bypass Paired = Yes
```

continues

Example 20-7 *Verifying IPS Inline Interface Settings (Continued)*

```
        Link Status = Up
        Link Speed = N/A
        Link Duplex = N/A
        Missed Packet Percentage = 0
        Total Packets Received = 208
        Total Bytes Received = 18971
        Total Multicast Packets Received = 0
        Total Broadcast Packets Received = 0
        Total Jumbo Packets Received = 0
        Total Undersize Packets Received = 0
        Total Receive Errors = 0
        Total Receive FIFO Overruns = 0
        Total Packets Transmitted = 601
        Total Bytes Transmitted = 37866
        Total Multicast Packets Transmitted = 0
        Total Broadcast Packets Transmitted = 0
        Total Jumbo Packets Transmitted = 0
        Total Undersize Packets Transmitted = 0
        Total Transmit Errors = 0
        Total Transmit FIFO Overruns = 0
<..>
IPS# show interfaces GigabitEthernet2/1
MAC statistics from interface GigabitEthernet2/1
        Interface function = Sensing interface
        Description =
        Media Type = TX
        Default Vlan = 0
        Inline Mode = Paired with interface GigabitEthernet2/0
        Pair Status = Up
        Hardware Bypass Capable = Yes when paired with GigabitEthernet2/0
        Hardware Bypass Paired = Yes
        Link Status = Up
        Link Speed = N/A
        Link Duplex = N/A
        Missed Packet Percentage = 0
        Total Packets Received = 1787
        Total Bytes Received = 129055
        Total Multicast Packets Received = 0
        Total Broadcast Packets Received = 0
        Total Jumbo Packets Received = 0
        Total Undersize Packets Received = 0
        Total Receive Errors = 0
        Total Receive FIFO Overruns = 0
        Total Packets Transmitted = 159
        Total Bytes Transmitted = 9972
        Total Multicast Packets Transmitted = 0
        Total Broadcast Packets Transmitted = 0
        Total Jumbo Packets Transmitted = 0
        Total Undersize Packets Transmitted = 0
        Total Transmit Errors = 0
        Total Transmit FIFO Overruns = 0
```

Configuring Custom Signature and IPS Blocking

Based on Figure 20-12, and building on the previous Example 20-4, Example 20-8 shows a sample configuration for creating a custom signature and IPS blocking function, thereby enabling a dynamic block request when an intrusion is detected.

A custom signature SIGID 65000 has been created in the STRING.TCP engine that defines traffic for TCP port 23 (Telnet), with an event-action **request-block-connection** to shun the offending TCP-based session.

The example shows a profile named "myprof" created to provide parameters for the managed device, where blocking is going to be enforced. Basic details such as the IP address, username, password, and communication protocol being used are defined in this profile, and the profile is associated in the managed device list.

The example also shows the exclude list, which defines the sensor IP address to be excluded from the blocking function.

Note that the inline interface parameters have been omitted in this sample output. Refer to Example 20-4 to complete this task.

Example 20-8   *Configuring Custom Signature and IPS Blocking*

```
IPS# show configuration
! ---------------------------
! Current configuration last modified Mon Jul 09 12:48:55 2007
! ---------------------------
! Version 6.0(1)
! Host:
!     Realm Keys          key1.0
! Signature Definition:
!     Signature Update    S263.0    2006-12-18
!     Virus Update        V1.2      2005-11-24
! ---------------------------
<..>
! ---------------------------
service host
network-settings
host-ip 172.16.10.1/24,172.16.10.254
host-name IPS
telnet-option disabled
access-list 172.16.10.0/24
exit
exit
! ---------------------------
<..>
! ---------------------------
service network-access
general
never-block-hosts 172.16.10.1
exit
user-profiles myprof
enable-password cisco
password cisco
```

continues

Example 20-8 *Configuring Custom Signature and IPS Blocking (Continued)*

```
username cisco
exit
router-devices 172.16.1.1
communication telnet
profile-name myprof
block-interfaces Ethernet0/0 in
exit
response-capabilities block
exit
exit
! ---------------------------
<..>
! ---------------------------
service signature-definition sig0
signatures 65000 0
sig-description
sig-name testing123
exit
engine string-tcp
event-action request-block-connection
regex-string attack
service-ports 23
direction to-service
exit
status
enabled true
<..>
```

TIP   For a complete set of IPS Sensor software configuration guides, refer to the following Cisco documentation URLs:

http://www.cisco.com/en/US/products/hw/vpndevc/ps4077/products_configuration_guide_book09186a0080751759.html

http://www.cisco.com/en/US/products/hw/vpndevc/ps4077/products_configuration_guide_book09186a00807a8a2a.html

Summary

Networks today are becoming increasingly vulnerable to hostile attacks and infections such as viruses and worms that spread rapidly, crippling the entire network. With this growing threat, networks need to be designed and equipped with the sophisticated intelligence to diagnose and mitigate these threats in real-time.

The Cisco Intrusion Prevention System (IPS) offers networkwide protection providing self-defending solutions, and threat protection through pervasive network integration. IPS defeats threats from multiple vectors and provides extensive behavioral analysis, anomaly detection, security policies, and rapid threat-response techniques.

Cisco IPS provides a comprehensive and proactive threat-prevention solution that provides end-to-end, day-zero protection of your network.

The chapter began by providing a basic overview of the Network Intrusion Prevention systems followed by a comprehensive overview of the network-based Cisco IPS solutions. The chapter listed various types of Cisco Network-based Intrusion Prevention solutions.

The chapter examined the core concepts for the Cisco IPS Sensor OS Software, such as the sensor system architecture, sensor communication protocols, signature and signature engines, IPS events and event actions, IPS Virtualization, and load-balancing techniques.

The chapter also provided basic deployment guidelines for IPS placement in network scenarios and provided sample configurations to implement IPS solutions in a network environment.

References

http://www.cisco.com/go/ips

http://www.cisco.com/en/US/products/hw/vpndevc/ps4077/index.html

http://www.cisco.com/en/US/products/hw/vpndevc/ps4077/products_data_sheet09186a008014873c.html

http://www.cisco.com/en/US/products/sw/secursw/ps2113/products_data_sheet0900aecd806c4e2a.html

http://www.cisco.com/en/US/products/ps6634/products_ios_protocol_group_home.html

http://www.cisco.com/en/US/products/ps6634/products_data_sheet0900aecd803137cf.html

http://www.cisco.com/en/US/products/hw/vpndevc/ps4077/prod_brochure0900aecd805baea7.html

http://www.cisco.com/en/US/products/hw/vpndevc/ps4077/products_data_sheet0900aecd805baef2.html

http://www.cisco.com/en/US/products/hw/vpndevc/ps4077/prod_bulletin0900aecd801e65b9.html

http://www.cisco.com/en/US/products/hw/vpndevc/ps4077/products_configuration_guide_chapter09186a00808145d3.html

http://www.cisco.com/en/US/products/hw/vpndevc/ps4077/products_configuration_guide_chapter09186a0080618a2e.html

http://www.cisco.com/en/US/products/hw/vpndevc/ps4077/products_configuration_guide_book09186a0080751759.html

CHAPTER **21**

Host Intrusion Prevention

Security enforcement evolves mainly at the network level through common techniques such as authentication, integrity mechanisms, firewalls, and encryption technologies. These techniques are adopted to provide the desired security at the network level, where data is transitional. An important area that is largely overlooked in enforcing security is the host level—the endpoint, where data resides and the potential for damage is the greatest.

The Cisco Host Intrusion Prevention solution provides self-defending solutions by deploying intelligent agents on desktops and servers that defend against the proliferation of attacks across networks.

This chapter provides details on the Cisco Host-based Intrusion Prevention solution that uses Cisco Security Agent (CSA). The chapter takes a closer look at core concepts such as CSA architecture, CSA components, CSA Policies, Rules, CSA Rule Modules, and details on managing and deploying CSA using CSA Management Center (CSA MC).

Securing Endpoints Using a Signatureless Mechanism

Today in many ways, networks are overgrown and distributed in nature. With open network policies, enforcing security at the network perimeter is insufficient. Data needs to be secured where it resides—at the endpoints.

Traditionally, endpoint security has always taken a reactive approach by implementing antivirus, scanners, personal firewalls, and other system audit programs. These products usually rely on signature-based mechanisms to detect only the known vulnerabilities and intrusions. Signatures and virus definition files are core elements of these solutions.

With endpoint security, multiple products are required to combat different aspects of the issue. For example, a desktop host may require antivirus software and a personal firewall, along with a system audit program, to cover different aspects of the intrusion. This is not a scalable solution and creates manageability issues and an administrative burden.

Figure 21-1 illustrates the five phases of the host-based attack landscape and the life cycle of activities that take place when a host intrusion occurs.

Figure 21-1 *Host-Based Attack Life Cycle*

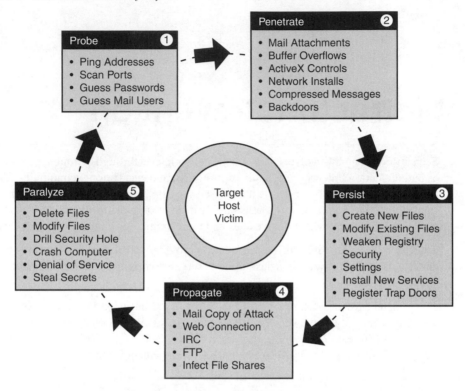

Viruses and worms take advantage of numerous vulnerabilities at the operating system and application level. New viruses and worms proliferate in no time and spread rapidly, infecting the host system. A signature-based approach cannot prevent this rapid activity of intrusions. However, taking the different approach of using a proactive, behavioral-based system can identify and dynamically prevent malicious code from interacting with a host system and therefore can prevent known and unknown (day-zero) attacks.

The most effective way to provide endpoint security is to use a signatureless approach that does not require updates or patches and yet provides a proactive mechanism to protect the host against both known and unknown (day-zero) vulnerabilities, intrusions, and attacks.

Cisco Security Agent (CSA)

Cisco Security Agent (CSA) is a unique proposition that provides proactive host-based intrusion detection and prevention solutions for endpoint systems (desktop PCs, laptops, servers, and point of service [POS] terminals) for known and unknown (day-zero) threats.

CSA goes beyond conventional security and does not rely on signature-based architecture. CSA provides endpoint security using a flexible policy-based and behavior-based architecture, thus offering defense against targeted attacks, virus, worm, spyware, adware, rootkit, and day-zero attacks that have not been discovered and new exploits and variants by taking advantage of known and unknown vulnerabilities.

CSA also provides policy compliance controls offering protection to sensitive information on the system. Examples include granular controls such as the restriction of the following: removable media storage (USB key), copy-paste sensitive information between applications, and peer-to-peer applications such as instant messaging (IM). CSA provides unique intelligence to correlate the behaviors of system functions, based on rules that define unacceptable behavior for a specific application, and it defines the necessary action to be taken. CSA is capable of implementing a wide range of granular policy-based compliance controls.

In addition, CSA provides numerous benefits:

- Endpoint system protection (desktop, server, and point of service [POS] terminals)
- Host-based intrusion prevention
- Policy-based and behavior-based architecture
- Personal firewall protection
- Day-zero attack protection
- Regulatory policy compliance enforcement
- Acceptable corporate use policy compliance
- Preventive protection against targeted attacks
- Stability and protection of the underlying operating system
- File and directory protection
- Host application visibility
- Application control
- Correlation of system calls and application functions

CSA Architecture

The architecture of CSA software is unique in that the host agent resides between the applications and the OS kernel, as shown in Figure 21-2. This provides application visibility with minimal impact to the stability and performance of the underlying operating system.

Figure 21-2 *CSA Sits Between Application and OS Kernel*

CSA works at the kernel level by controlling file system and network actions and other operating system components. CSA architecture intercepts all operating system and application-related calls when an access is requested for a certain resource, such as file access, device access, network access, Registry access, and application execution calls. CSA also intercepts dynamic runtime resources requested, such as memory pages, services, shared library modules, and any COM objects.

CSA applies unique intelligence to correlate the behavior of these system calls, based on rules that define unacceptable behavior for a specific application or for all applications. When an application attempts an operation or requests access, CSA checks the operation against the security policy, making a real-time decision to allow or deny the operation.

Security policies are collections of rules that are configurable items within CSA and can be created or modified anytime according to the corporate security policy. These rules drive application and system access to required resources. Because protection is based on blocking malicious behavior, the default policies stop both known and unknown (day-zero) threats without needing updates.

CSA Interceptor and Correlation

At the core of CSA architecture is the interceptor and correlation mechanism, which intercepts application- and system-related functions to enforce policy-based and behavior-based rules. Correlation is the enforcement engine for CSA where relationships between events are established to determine whether the behavior is acceptable and whether the event should be allowed or denied.

CSA correlation maintains the state of all system calls and application activities on the host system. For example, if an application on an endpoint creates a new file on the disk, CSA will monitor and correlate the state by checking the rules engine against a set of behavioral rules to validate the policy and act with necessary action in response (either allow the write function or deny it, depending on the rule policy).

CSA correlation enhances interoperability between applications, such as protecting the usage of a command shell from unauthorized access and ensuring that legitimate applications can invoke this without interruption. CSA achieves this by automatically creating and dynamically maintaining a whitelist of applications that are less vulnerable and allowed to invoke command shells. These applications can invoke a command shell, provided they are not vulnerable. However, if the application becomes vulnerable, the CSA whitelist will automatically update the list and remove this application, thereby denying command shell access. After the application is patched or fixed, the whitelist will dynamically update itself to reallow this application and reinstate the command shell access.

CSA can correlate numerous activities to increase the accuracy of its rules and policies and enhance its capability to make accurate decisions about what is dangerous.

Figure 21-3 illustrates the core architecture of the CSA correlation system and how it intercepts the various system and application-related functions or calls.

Figure 21-3 *CSA Interceptor and Correlation Architecture*

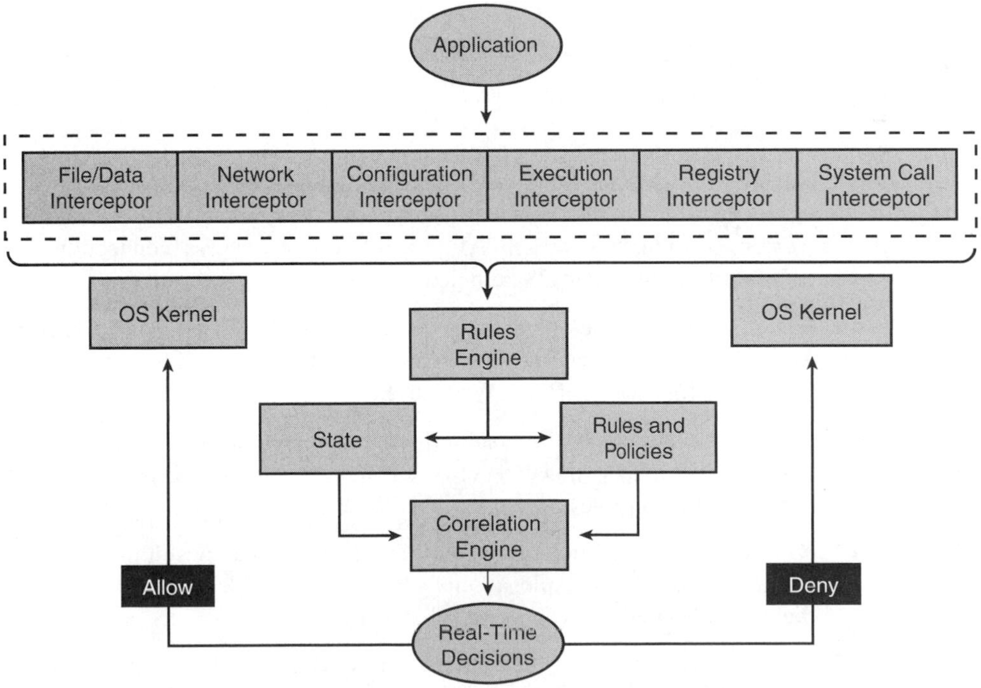

NOTE   The information in Figure 21-3 is compiled from the Cisco white paper on "Cisco Security Agent Introduction to Correlation" at http://www.cisco.com/en/US/products/sw/secursw/ ps5057/products_white_paper0900aecd8020f448.shtml.

CSA Correlation Extended Globally

The CSA correlation discussed previously occurs not only locally on the standalone host agent, but extends globally on the CSA Management Center, resulting in increased accuracy when compared to signature-based host IDS/IPS systems.

The CSA global correlation correlates events received from the network from the many desktop agents deployed throughout the network. By looking at events across the network, intrusions and attacks that went undetected on standalone systems will also be caught.

In an effort to avoid detection, smart hackers send only a few packets to selected hosts on the network, trying to map the entire network by going unnoticed and undetected. These distributed type scans will also be detected by the CSA Management Center because of the global correlation that is in place.

CSA Access Control Process

The following list outlines, in order, the access control process that the CSA agent performs:

Step 1   Identify the resource being accessed (for example, network resource, memory function calls, application execution, file access, device access, system configuration, system API control, Registry access, connection rate limit, or any other OS kernel system calls).

Step 2   Gather data about the operation (for example, if a file access operation is requested, identify and gather the process name, file path, filename, and file operation, such as Read, Write, or Erase).

Step 3   Determine the state of the system (for example, currently assigned IP address, MAC address, DNS suffix, VPN client status, NAC posture, or virus/worm detection).

Step 4   Consult the security policy by analyzing the rules and consulting the local policies (for example, anomaly based, atomic rules, pattern-based, behavioral-based, or access control matrix).

Step 5   Take action as per policy defined in the rules (for example, Allow, Deny, Query, Change Internal State, or Monitor).

Figure 21-4 illustrates the CSA access control process flowchart as previously outlined.

Figure 21-4 *CSA Access Control Process Flowchart*

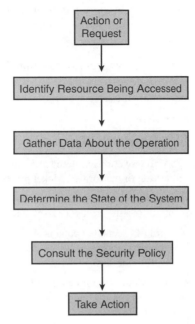

CSA Defense-in-Depth—Zero-Day Protection

A classic evidence of CSA protection was observed during the outbreak of the MyDoom worm in 2004. The MyDoom worm arrived via an e-mail message, installed itself by modifying system binaries, and then infected other systems by forwarding itself to everyone in the address book of the infected system. Host systems running CSA during this time were completely protected from the MyDoom worm because the CSA agent rules stopped the arrival and installation activities of this worm. CSA correlation tracked the worm at each stage of its life cycle and took preventive actions.

CSA Capabilities and Security Functional Roles

CSA has unique capabilities and plays many roles within the network, mainly because of its strategic positioning on the host system. With the in-depth knowledge of real-time events occurring on the system, CSA can monitor and control a wide variety of security functions and roles. CSA can control how the endpoint interacts with other surrounding systems and how users interact with the local system.

From the very beginning when CSA is first installed and launched, it begins monitoring the local system by maintaining a state table of each event and enforces security policy accordingly. As mentioned earlier, CSA monitors all system- and application-related calls, whether invoked by a user or by auto-executed malicious code that is attempting to gain unauthorized access. If the access is classified as inappropriate behavior, CSA will take real-time dynamic action and send an alert to both the local system and the CSA Management Center for global correlation.

CSA in a single agent software plays security functional roles on the host system beyond just preventing known and unknown (day-zero) attacks. Table 21-1 lists various CSA capabilities and their functional role descriptions.

Table 21-1   *CSA Capabilities and Security Roles*

CSA Capabilities	Functional Role Description
Basic security functions and controls	CSA offers various system hardening functions such as SYN-flood protection or malformed packet protection.
	Provides resource protection, including file access control, network access control, Registry access control, and COM component access control.
	Control of executable content, for example, protection against e-mail worms, protection against automatic execution of downloaded files or ActiveX controls.
	Application-related functions, such as application run control, executable file version control, protection against code injection, protection of process memory, protection against buffer overflows, and protection against keystroke logging.
	Detection capabilities, for example, packet capture and packet sniffer, unauthorized protocols, network scans, and monitoring of OS event logs.
Host integrity role	CSA is the industry standard host-based intrusion detection and prevention solution with the capability to stop zero-day malicious code without reconfiguration or updates.
	CSA has a proven track record of stopping zero-day exploits, viruses, and worms over the past several years. Examples include the following:
	In 2001—Code Red, Nimda (all variants), Pentagone (Gonner)
	In 2002—Sircam, Debploit, SQL Snake, and Bugbear
	In 2003—SQL Slammer, SoBig, Blaster/Welchia, and Fizzer
	In 2004—MyDoom, Bagle, Sasser, JPEG browser exploit (MS04-028), RPC-DCOM exploit (MS03-039), and Buffer Overflow in Workstation Service (MS03-049)
	In 2005—Internet Explorer Command Execution Vulnerability and Zotob
	In 2006—USB Hacksaw, Internet Explorer VML exploit, WMF, Internet Explorer Textrange, and RDS Dataspace
	In 2007—Rinbot, Storm Trojan, Big Yellow, MS-Word (MS07-014), Microsoft ANI 0Day, and Microsoft DNS 0Day

No configuration is required on the CSA agent. All configurations are completed on the server via the CSA MC and deployed to the CSA agent. CSA agent will have only basic viewing capabilities.

Managing CSA Hosts

In the CSA architecture, hosts are the endpoint systems that require protection. A host is any system that has installed the CSA agent kit from the CSA MC and has registered with CSA MC. The host can be a desktop computer, a laptop, or even a server. These endpoints are referred to as hosts within the CSA MC configuration. As mentioned earlier, every host on the network has to register with CSA MC to receive policy updates. The status of the host can be monitored by CSA MC.

Figures 21-6 through 21-8 show a few sample screenshots for managing a host that is using the CSA MC.

Figure 21-6 *CSA MC—Displaying List of Hosts*

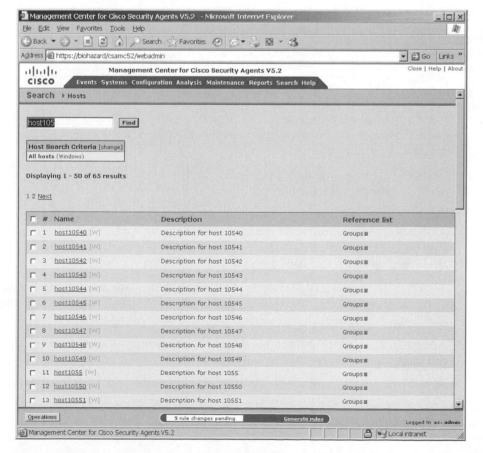

Table 21-1 *CSA Capabilities and Security Roles (Continued)*

CSA Capabilities	Functional Role Description
Application inventory feature	CSA can now track all the applications installed on a computer or group of computers across the network, which of these are actually run, which of these use the network, whether the application is a network client or a network server, and which remote IP addresses the application communicates with.
	CSA can track which applications are residing on which systems.
	Application inventory can also track unknown and unauthorized applications (that listen on a port but do not accept connections) running on a standalone system and other systems on the network, analyzing their behavior, creating patterns, grouping them into suspected spyware or adware categories, and creating rules to limit or prohibit their behavior. CSA offers this unique spyware protection at no additional cost.
Policy control	CSA can define policy controls based on the corporate security policy. Some types of behavior are not malicious but are undesired because they violate acceptable use within corporate policy—for example, music sharing via peer-to-peer (p2p) applications, instant messaging using noncorporate IM servers, external device protection, that is, devices that cannot be used (USB memory, multimedia devices, CD-ROM), or use of unauthorized applications or unauthorized versions of certain applications. CSA offers default policy control modules, including data theft prevention policy, instant messenger control policy, music download prevention policy, and network lockdown policy to enforce the previous examples.
Compliance enforcement	CSA can be used as an enforcement tool to implement controls for regulatory compliance, such as PCI, Sarbanes-Oxley, and other mandates.
User education	CSA can play the educator role. On many occasions, a user may invoke a request that may not be unauthorized from the operating system context but is restricted because of a corporate security policy. For example, a corporate policy may restrict usage of external devices, such as USB keys, and the user inserts the USB key on the system. Technically, the operating system will allow this; however, the CSA can intercept and deny this action and display a pop-up window educating the user on why this action was denied. This way, the user is educated on the corporate policy and acceptable use conditions when using the corporate equipment.

continunes

Table 21-1   *CSA Capabilities and Security Roles (Continued)*

CSA Capabilities	Functional Role Description
Traffic marking and prioritization	The host system has many applications; some are mission critical and others are normal business applications. Some applications may be tolerated, but not business related. For example, an enterprise resource planning (ERP) system should be given higher priority than other applications in the event of congestion. This can be done by assigning a unique Differentiated Services Code Point (DSCP) value that identifies the mission-critical traffic. Similarly, other business-related applications such as e-mail and browsers are important but not critical; hence, a separate unique DSCP value can be associated to them so that a relevant action can be taken accordingly.
Network integration	CSA can actively integrate with other network devices and work in close collaboration. CSA inputs can be valuable to influence actions in other solutions implemented within the network. Examples include the Network Admission Control (NAC) enforcement, Network IPS, QoS services via routers and switches, log collectors, and network correlation devices such as CS-MARS and VPN devices.

CSA Components

As shown in Figure 21-5, CSA has three basic components:

- **CSA endpoints:** Endpoints are computing desktops, servers, laptops, and point of service (POS) terminals. The CSA agent is responsible for enforcing security policies received from the management server, sending events, and interacting with the user.

- **CSA management server:** The server is the core component in the CSA deployment, a repository of configuration database. The server is responsible for deploying the security policies to the endpoints; it receives and stores all events, sends alerts to the administrator, and can deploy software to the endpoints.

- **CSA management console (CSA MC):** The management console is an administrative web-based user interface and policy configuration tool that provides event views.

NOTE   The management server can also be used as the management console for policy configuration and event views.

Figure 21-5   *CSA Components*

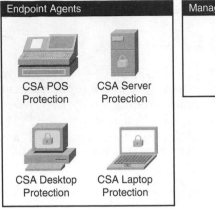

Configuring and Managing CSA Deployment by Using CSA MC

All security policies and configurations are accomplished using the CSA MC. These policies are associated with specific hosts and groups of hosts. All configurations are stored on the management server and deployed to the agents via the management server.

All communications between the CSA MC and the server are secured using Secure Sockets Layer (SSL) protocol. Similarly, communications between the CSA agent and the server database are secured using SSL.

The web-based user interface is accessed securely using SSL from any machine on the network that can connect to the management server. The web-based interface is used to deploy policies from CSA MC to all the agents across the network.

SSL protocol is also needed for the agents to periodically update the policy; therefore the network must not restrict SSL traffic on port 443. This is especially important if CSA agents are located on remote network segments that are isolated via firewalls.

The CSA MC binds with the server database which holds all the policies. All CSA endpoint agents must register with CSA MC to receive the policy. The CSA MC validates the host and deploys the respective policy pertaining to that host or group of hosts.

After the CSA agent on the local system receives the policy, it starts monitoring the system proactively and takes dynamic actions as necessary.

At regular intervals (configurable), the CSA agent polls the CSA MC for policy updates. It also sends triggered event alerts to the CSA MC global event manager.

Figure 21-7   *CSA MC—Searching a Host*

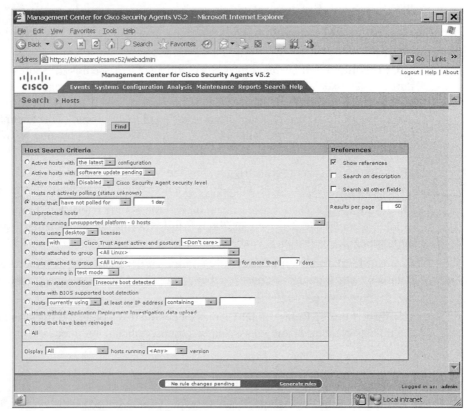

NOTE   The sample screenshots of CSA MC shown previously and in the next few sections are taken from the Cisco "Using Management Center for Cisco Security Agents 5.2" documentation pages. For more details and further information on deploying CSA using CSA MC, refer to http://www.cisco.com/en/US/products/sw/secursw/ps5057/products_configuration_guide_book09186a008080732b.html.

There is no specific configuration required to configure the host settings within the CSA MC. As mentioned earlier, hosts register dynamically with the CSA MC and inherit group membership and policy settings transparently upon successful registration. Default policies are available for implementation out of the box.

To view the details of a particular host that has registered with the CSA MC, choose Systems, Hosts. Figure 21-8 shows a sample screenshot of the host detail page for a host named biohazard with complete host details. Several types of information can be viewed from the Host Detail Page, for example:

- **Host Name and Description:** Displays the system name of the CSA endpoint and a brief description of the host.

- **Host Identification:** Displays the CSA product version, the host IP address, a numeric ID associated to this host within the CSA MC database, registration details, host operating system details, and whether the Cisco Trust Agent (CTA) is installed and the associated posture state currently assigned to this agent. (This feature is part of the Network Admission Control [NAC] of the Cisco Self-Defending Network solution.)

- **Host Status:** Displays events triggered by the host, software and policy version, the time since the policy was last updated, and a detailed status and diagnostics link.

- **Host Settings:** Displays various items such as the polling interval, test mode, learn mode, logging mode, deny actions, filtering user information, and whether application deployment investigation is enabled.

- **Group Membership and Policy Inheritance Table:** Displays group membership, details of which groups the host is a member of, the policies assigned to the groups, and the modules within the policies.

- **Combined Policy Rules Table:** Displays a complete list of all the rules running on the host as combined from all associated groups, policies, and modules.

Managing CSA Agent Kits

Every endpoint system (host) requires a CSA agent to be installed on the system. This is done via the agent kit, which is an executable installation file generated by the CSA MC for the endpoint host system. By definition, an agent kit is the CSA agent installation executable file that is installed on the endpoint system.

Agent kits can be downloaded from the CSA MC directly via the SSL-protected web page. Alternatively, the file can be transported via other media (such as a USB key or copying it across the network) and executed manually from the local system. Another alternative is to develop scripted and automated installation procedures using software installation systems.

After the agent kit is installed on the system, the host registers to the CSA MC and pulls the appropriate policies and group settings accordingly. Agent kits are associated to groups, which have appropriate policies attached to them. When a host downloads the agent kit, it dynamically associates the host to the corresponding group with the preconfigured knowledge and enforces the associated policies of that group.

Figure 21-8   *CSA MC—Host Detail Page*

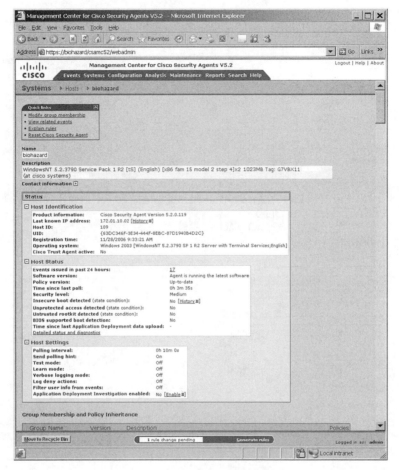

CSA MC has several built-in preconfigured agent kits available. Several default kits exist, such as kits for generic desktops, generic servers, and application servers.

Additionally, a custom agent kit can also be created by using the CSA MC. This gives you greater flexibility to define customized options to deploy to the host. Before creating a custom agent kit, other related parameters must be configured, such as initial modules, policies, and rules that the agent must use.

Figure 21-9 shows a sample screenshot from the CSA MC that was used to create an agent kit for IIS web servers.

Figure 21-9 *CSA MC—Creating Agent Kit for IIS Web Servers*

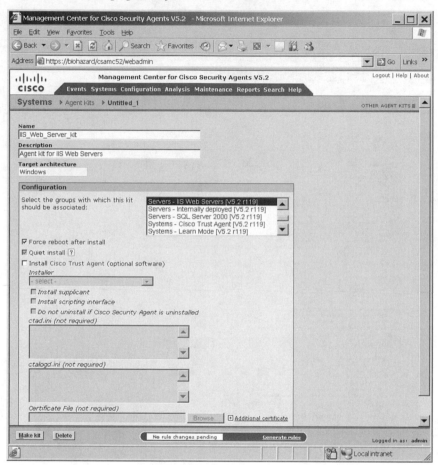

When the Make Kit button at the bottom of the page is submitted on the page shown in Figure 21-9, the kit is created, and the CSA MC produces a distribution kit for the host. The CSA MC will display a unique URL for each corresponding kit. This URL needs to be distributed to all the endpoint hosts for which the kit was created. This URL information can be sent to users via e-mail. When users receive this URL, they access the URL by using a web browser to download and install the kit. This is the most effective and recommended method for agent kit distribution.

Figure 21-10 shows a sample screenshot from the CSA MC of an agent kit URL page for IIS web servers created earlier. This URL can be distributed to all the IIS servers to be downloaded and installed on any IIS web server that needs CSA protection.

Figure 21-10 *CSA MC—Agent Kit Page for IIS Web Servers*

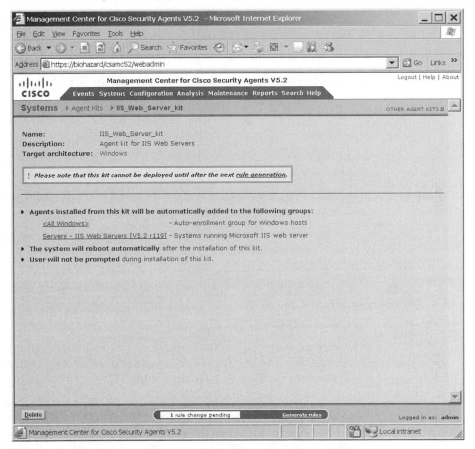

Alternatively, the default system URL for the CSA MC server can be distributed to the users. This URL lists all the available kits on the server, and users can choose the corresponding kit for their host or server and download and install it accordingly. This gives the users empowerment to make their own decisions as to which kit to download. The URL for the CSA MC is https://<system name>/csamc52/kits.

NOTE   The CSA MC URL may vary depending on the CSA MC Version number. In the previous example, it is Version 5.2, hence the URL has **/csamc52/**. If the version is 4.5, it will be **/csamc45/**.

Managing CSA Groups

Groups are logical collections of hosts. The concept is similar to Windows Active Directory Groups or any other user database system.

Grouping host systems provides the following advantages:

- Policy consistency through applying the same set of policies on multiple hosts across the network

- The capability to apply alternative mechanisms and event set parameters based on group configurations

- A test mode feature to validate policies on groups of hosts before they are actively enforced on production systems

Hosts can be grouped on logical similarities and can be bound together on any common criteria that meet the security policy requirements; for example:

- Hosts, such as web servers, can be grouped according to system function. Specific policies can be created corresponding to the web server requirements.

- Hosts can be grouped according to business units, such as sales, finance, operations, and marketing. Specific policies can be created and crafted to meet the requirements of business functions and each business unit's individual needs.

- Hosts can be grouped according to geographical or topological location.

- Hosts can be grouped according to their importance within an organization. For example, you can group mission-critical systems into a common group so that you can apply critical alert-level configurations to the group.

CSA Group simplifies configuration management by associating policy controls and other parameters into group settings. When a user is associated with the group, the host will inherit all the parameters configured within the group. The group also ensures consistency across the entire CSA deployment. All hosts have uniform settings when associated to the same group.

This scalable approach of grouping hosts allows large-scale CSA deployments to be deployed with great ease and reduced complexity.

Hosts can be members of one or more groups and will inherit all the settings merged into the host-specific policy setting from each group.

Another important advantage of having groups is that it makes creating the agent kits easier. The group parameter is the only element required to build agent kits.

CSA MC has several built-in predefined groups (in addition to the mandatory groups) that can be used according to the requirement.

Additionally, custom groups can be created using the CSA MC. This gives flexibility to define user-defined customized group options. Before creating a custom group, several parameters must be gathered, such as operating system, application information, and system user requirements to be configured for the group.

Figure 21-11 shows a sample screenshot from the CSA MC for the group setting page for the IIS web servers.

Figure 21-11 *CSA MC—Group Settings Page for IIS Web Servers*

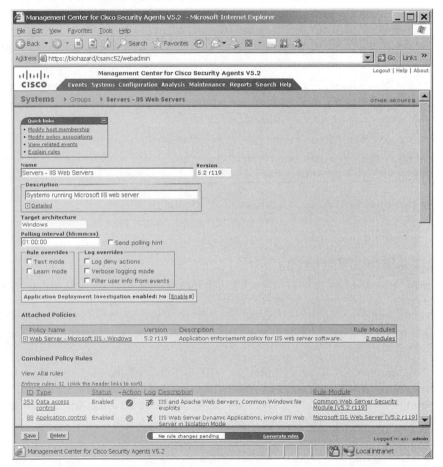

Typically, groups in CSA MC can be divided into three categories:

- Mandatory groups
- Predefined groups
- Custom groups

By default, CSA MC provides three auto-enrollment mandatory groups:

- All Windows
- All Solaris
- All Linux

One of these three mandatory groups will be associated to each endpoint host according to its OS architecture upon registration. For example, when Windows-based hosts are registered to the CSA MC, they are automatically enrolled in the "All Windows" group in addition to any other groups that are mapped to this host. Hosts cannot be removed from the mandatory groups.

Mandatory groups enforce some of the compulsory security policies to prevent critical service from being inadvertently disturbed. For example, a mandatory policy can dictate that a user cannot disable DNS or DHCP service.

CAUTION Hosts can belong to one or more groups and inherit multiple policies from these groups. However, the combined rule set will follow the rule precedence process when deciding which rules to override, if a rule conflict occurs.

CSA Agent User Interface

After the agent kit is installed on the endpoint system, the CSA is ready to monitor the system. As mentioned earlier, to run the CSA agent software, no configuration is required on the endpoint. Optionally, as the administrator, you can provide end users with an advanced user interface that allows them to control the security settings and to use other added features.

To open the CSA agent user interface (UI), double-click the CSA agent icon in the system tray. (Locate a Red Flag icon in the system tray that denotes the CSA agent.) The options available in the agent UI depend upon the options selected in the Agent UI control page that governs the agent control rules in this context, as shown in Figure 21-12.

Figure 21-12 shows a sample screenshot from the CSA MC for the Agent User Interface control setting page.

Figure 21-12   *CSA MC—Agent User Interface Control Page*

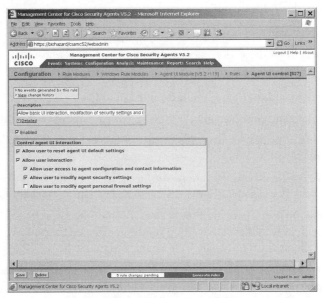

Figure 21-13 shows a sample screenshot from an endpoint host system showing the CSA Agent user interface.

Figure 21-13   *CSA Agent Host Endpoint—User Interface*

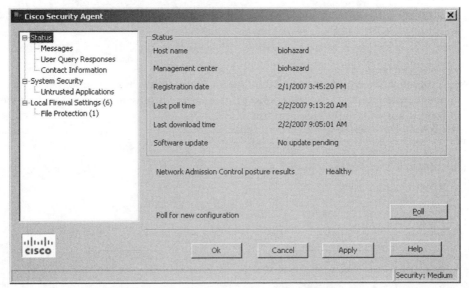

As shown in Figure 21-13, the Agent User Interface displays various status information of the endpoint host, for example:

- The hostname of the machine on which this agent is installed.

- The name of the CSA MC with which this agent is registered.

- The date and time the agent registered with CSA MC.

- The date and time the agent last polled in to CSA MC.

- The date and time the agent last downloaded data from CSA MC.

- Update information informing the user whether a software version update is available for his agent.

- Display of the NAC posture result for the agent, if the Cisco Trust Agent (CTA) is installed. For example, the display can state the status as Healthy, Quarantine, or Infected.

- When the user clicks the Poll button, it forces the agent to poll the CSA MC immediately, rather than waiting for the configured time interval to trigger a poll. This way, the agent receives any rule changes right away.

Optionally, the CSA MC for the Agent User Interface control setting page can be configured to enable the Local Firewall and File Protection feature. The local firewall settings on the endpoint allow users to manually control which applications have access permissions on their systems and define what those permissions are.

Note that these firewall settings and permissions that indicate whether the application can access the network are assigned locally by the agent by a dynamic query method via a pop-up dialog box. These permissions can also be assigned during a learning mode period.

Figure 21-14 shows a sample screenshot from an endpoint host system that shows the Local Firewall setting in the CSA Agent user interface.

CAUTION Note that this feature is intended for interactive systems, as opposed to servers that should be managed only by a central policy. If this feature is present, users must select the Enable check box to turn on firewall settings.

Figure 21-14   *CSA Agent Host Endpoint—Local Firewall Setting*

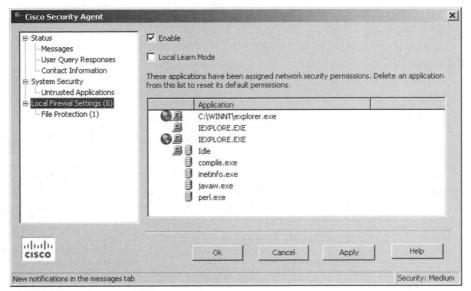

CSA Policies, Rule Modules, and Rules

As discussed in previous sections, each group is associated with a security policy that drives specific actions.

Policy is a collection of rule modules, and a *rule module* is a collection of multiple rules. The rule module acts as the container for rules, whereas the policy serves as the unit of attachment to groups. Rules provide control access to system resources. These resources can either be a system resource or a network resource.

Multiple rule modules can be attached to a single policy, and multiple policies can be attached to a single group. The rules enforce policy control actions to allow or deny specific actions. Different types of rules in a rule module can coexist, and consequently different types of rules within one policy can also exist.

CSA MC allows the creation of several types of policies in addition to the default built-in policies. An example of the three mandatory policies (Windows, Solaris, and Linux) is presented earlier in this chapter.

In principle, policies must reflect a well-planned security framework and be driven by the fundamental guidelines of the corporate security policy. Appropriate time and effort should be expended before charting these policies, because they provide network and application access to the systems.

Policies, rule modules, and rules are the enforcement tools in the CSA architecture.

TIP   For more details on building policies, refer to the following Cisco documentation URL:

http://www.cisco.com/en/US/products/sw/secursw/ps5057/products_configuration_
guide_chapter09186a00808139c0.html

For more details on rule modules and rule types, refer to the following Cisco documentation
URLs:

http://www.cisco.com/en/US/products/sw/secursw/ps5057/products_configuration_
guide_chapter09186a00808074a0.html

http://www.cisco.com/en/US/products/sw/secursw/ps5057/products_configuration_
guide_chapter09186a00808074bb.html

Several other parameters are required to be configured when you are using CSA MC to
complete the CSA deployment. For example, configure global correlation parameters,
application classes, variables, logging and alerts, and other parameters.

Refer to the following Cisco documentation for further details to implement CSA in greater
depth and additional configuration parameters: http://www.cisco.com/en/US/products/sw/
secursw/ps5057/products_configuration_guide_book09186a008080732b.html.

Summary

Endpoint systems (such as desktops, laptops, and servers) are no longer secure because the
threats from viruses, worms, adware, and spyware are on the rise. Vulnerabilities in the
operating systems and application codes are also on the rise, and exploits can compromise
endpoints in no time.

These dynamically evolving threats cannot be mitigated through traditional signature-
based tools such as antivirus software on the host systems. Endpoints need to be equipped
with the sophisticated intelligence to detect and prevent known and unknown threats in
real-time without the need of signature updates.

The trend in host intrusion prevention has shifted and evolved into a more proactive
approach that uses policy-based and behavior-based mechanisms to stop malicious
activities and unknown (day-zero) attacks.

The Cisco Host Intrusion Prevention solution using the Cisco Secure Agent (CSA) endpoint
software provides self-defending solutions by deploying intelligent agents to protect
endpoint systems (desktops, laptops, and servers) against the proliferation of known and
unknown threats and targeted attacks across networks.

The chapter began with a basic overview of the host intrusion prevention systems followed by a comprehensive overview of the Cisco host-based IPS solution that uses the Cisco Security Agent (CSA) solution.

The chapter provided in-depth details of the CSA architecture and described the workings of the CSA interceptor and correlation techniques that are equipped with the access control process.

The chapter provided a detailed list of CSA capabilities and the security functional roles that CSA can offer.

The chapter described details of CSA components, CSA hosts and groups, CSA policies, rule modules, and rules.

The chapter also provided and illustrated implementation guidelines and supporting references for configuring and managing the CSA deployment using the CSA Management Center (CSA MC).

References

http://www.cisco.com/go/csa

http://www.cisco.com/en/US/products/sw/secursw/ps5057/products_configuration_guide_book09186a008080732b.html

http://www.cisco.com/en/US/products/sw/secursw/ps5057/products_configuration_guide_chapter09186a00808074f6.html

http://www.cisco.com/en/US/products/sw/secursw/ps5057/products_data_sheet0900aecd805baf46.html

http://www.cisco.com/en/US/products/sw/secursw/ps5057/tsd_products_support_design_technotes_list.html

http://www.cisco.com/en/US/products/sw/secursw/ps5057/products_white_paper0900aecd8020f448.shtml

http://www.cisco.com/en/US/products/sw/secursw/ps5057/products_white_paper0900aecd8020f438.shtml

http://www.cisco.com/en/US/products/sw/secursw/ps5057/products_quick_installation_guide_chapter09186a00808073e5.html

http://www.ciscopress.com/title/1587052059

http://www.ciscopress.com/title/1587052520

Anomaly Detection and Mitigation

Denial-of-service (DoS) attacks and distributed denial-of-service (DDoS) attacks have become more sophisticated and prevalent over the years and are therefore major issues in service provider and large-scale network deployments.

In today's rapidly evolving networks, attackers are often one step ahead. Effective mitigation of DDoS attacks is a pressing problem. Proactive detection and prevention mechanisms can help protect the network from these malicious cloaking techniques.

The Cisco Anomaly Detection and Mitigation solution provides a self-defending preventive solution for detecting and mitigating complex and sophisticated DoS and DDoS attacks.

This chapter provides the details of the Anomaly Detection and Mitigation solution that uses the industry standard Cisco Traffic Anomaly Detectors and Cisco Guard DDoS Mitigation devices. The chapter takes a closer look at core concepts, solution architecture, solution components, and how all these are combined to demonstrate how the solution works through various illustrations and diagrams.

The chapter provides a brief overview of the configuring and managing of the Cisco Traffic Anomaly Detector and Cisco Guard Mitigation devices, showing sample configurations that use a command-line interface (CLI) and defining how to configure Zones, Filters, Policies, Learning Process parameters, and how to activate the Anomaly Detection and the Guard system.

Attack Landscape

The main objective of any DoS and DDoS attacks is to prevent authorized users from accessing network resources.

Denial-of-Service (DoS) Attack Defined

The main objective of a DoS-type attack is to prevent access to authorized users by consuming the resources such as bandwidth, memory, storage, and CPU. The attacker floods the target host(s) with unwanted packets and uses up all the resources, thus crippling the network and saturating network links, resulting in regular traffic either being slowed down, disrupted for some period, or completely interrupted.

Typically, a DoS attack is an attempt to disrupt services and prevent legitimate users from accessing certain information or services. For example, a DoS attack can be launched to prevent legitimate users from accessing e-mail, browsing Internet websites, printing services, or preventing access to any local network resources. Examples of DoS attacks include but are not limited to

- Resource removal
- Resource modification
- Resource saturation

Figure 22-1 illustrates a basic form of DoS attack showing resource saturation in which an attacker is sending a large number of unwanted TCP SYN packets, thereby filling up the target server resources, thus preventing legitimate users from establishing a valid TCP connection.

Figure 22-1 *DoS Attack Defined—How It Works*

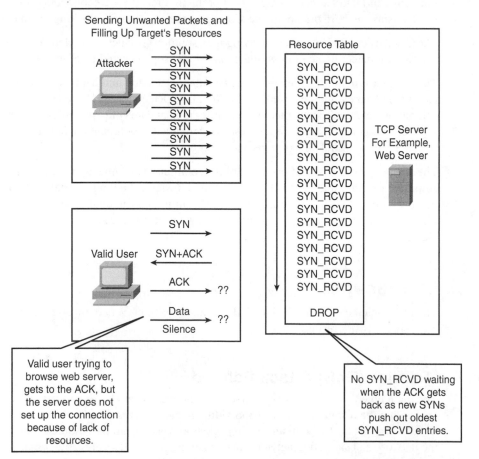

Distributed Denial-of-Service (DDoS) Attack—Defined

The objective of DDoS is similar to DoS; the major difference is that the attacker does not directly launch the attack to the target. In DDoS, the attacker compromises a multitude of systems by exploiting the security vulnerabilities and weaknesses within the systems and infects those systems with a resident Trojan, so that the attacker can take control of all compromised systems remotely.

After the compromised hosts are infected with a Trojan and ready for the attacker to use, the attacker uses them as a launch pad by sending huge amounts of unwanted traffic to the target host, thus creating a DDoS effect. This type of attack is called "distributed" because the attacker is using multiple hosts to launch the DoS attack on a single host or multiple host systems.

In DDoS, the attacker hides behind the compromised hosts, and the target victim is blindfolded so it cannot recognize the real perpetrator.

Victims of a DDoS attack consist of both the end targeted system and all systems maliciously used and controlled by the attacker in the distributed attack.

DDoS type attacks are harder to track down than DoS attacks, and they challenge defense mechanisms.

Figure 22-2 illustrates a basic form of DDoS attack in which an attacker has compromised multiple hosts with resident Trojans, thereby allowing the hosts to be remotely controlled. The attacker can use compromised hosts as a launch pad to trigger the DDoS attack to the target victims, thus preventing legitimate users from establishing connections.

Anomaly Detection and Mitigation Systems

Anomaly-based intrusion detection and mitigation is an enhanced solution that combats DoS and DDoS attacks as previously discussed.

Anomaly detection solutions provide intelligence-based intrusion prevention by monitoring system activity and categorizing the traffic as either normal or anomalous. The classification is based on heuristics or rules, rather than patterns or signatures.

Figure 22-2 *DDoS Attack Defined —How It Works*

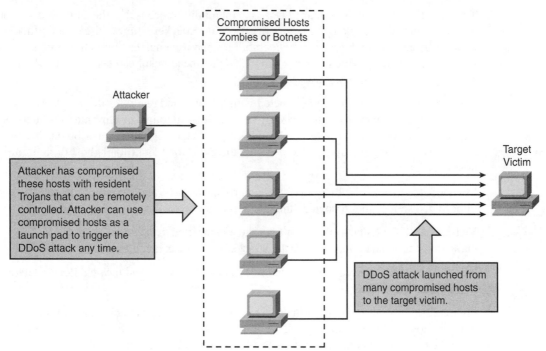

Anomaly detection systems are initially in learning mode so that they can characterize normal activity and establish a baseline for normal traffic. Anomaly detection involves defining or learning normal activity and looking for deviations from various baseline profiles. Examples include the following:

- **Protocol anomaly:** Involves looking for deviations from a standard protocol and is useful for identifying deviations from normal protocol behavior.

- **Network anomaly:** Involves watching or learning the normal traffic levels—for example, using a time-based classification of normal traffic activity. If deviation from normal traffic activity is detected, an alarm is generated. This technique is prone to false alarms but can be combined with other techniques to improve accuracy.

- **Behavioral anomaly:** Involves learning normal user behavior and detecting the relational traffic pattern activities of individual hosts or a group of hosts. If a change occurs, an alarm is generated. This technique is most useful in a very tightly controlled environment because behavior changes occur frequently in a network.

After these baselines are established, anomaly detection compares all traffic with the baseline profile, and any deviation from the profile is considered as potential attack traffic.

On many occasions and with increasing frequency, legitimate traffic is integrated with the attack traffic. Therefore, traffic patterns must be closely examined in near real-time so that the valid traffic can still be passed without interruption. Attack traffic can then be diverted to a mitigation device where scrubbing is performed to eliminate bad traffic and allow legitimate traffic to flow seamlessly.

Anomaly detection and mitigation algorithms can detect all kinds of attacks, including day-zero attacks. This is different from signature-based systems, which can only detect attacks for which a static signature has been defined.

An anomaly detection technique has the following characteristics:

- Is signatureless; it does not require use of patterns or signatures.
- Is granular, based on observed traffic pattern behavior.
- Can perform relational- and behavioral-based anomaly detection.
- Detects in real-time; anything reported is actually happening.
- Supports dynamic filtering.
- Includes sophisticated antispoofing techniques.
- Can detect day-zero and minute-zero attacks.
- Can highlight behaviors that are not indicative of attack traffic, but are still of interest.
- Includes traffic diversion architecture allowing flexibility in topological placement.

Cisco DDoS Anomaly Detection and Mitigation Solution

Cisco offers state-of-the-art solutions to protect against DDoS attacks by using the industry standard Cisco Anomaly Detection and Mitigation products.

The Cisco Anomaly Detection and Mitigation solution combats complex and sophisticated DDoS attacks. This solution can be used for service provider and enterprise environments. Some of the features are the following:

- Detect and mitigate a wide range of DDoS attacks.
- Classify legitimate traffic and attack traffic in real-time.
- Block the attack traffic by using source-based dynamic filters.
- Block large botnets and zombie attacks.
- Deliver multigigabit performance at line rate for detection and mitigation.

Figure 22-3 illustrates the packet flow through the defense modules that provides advanced DDoS protection using the Cisco Anomaly Detection and Mitigation solution.

Figure 22-3 *Advanced DDoS Protection Using the Cisco Anomaly Detection and Mitigation Solution*

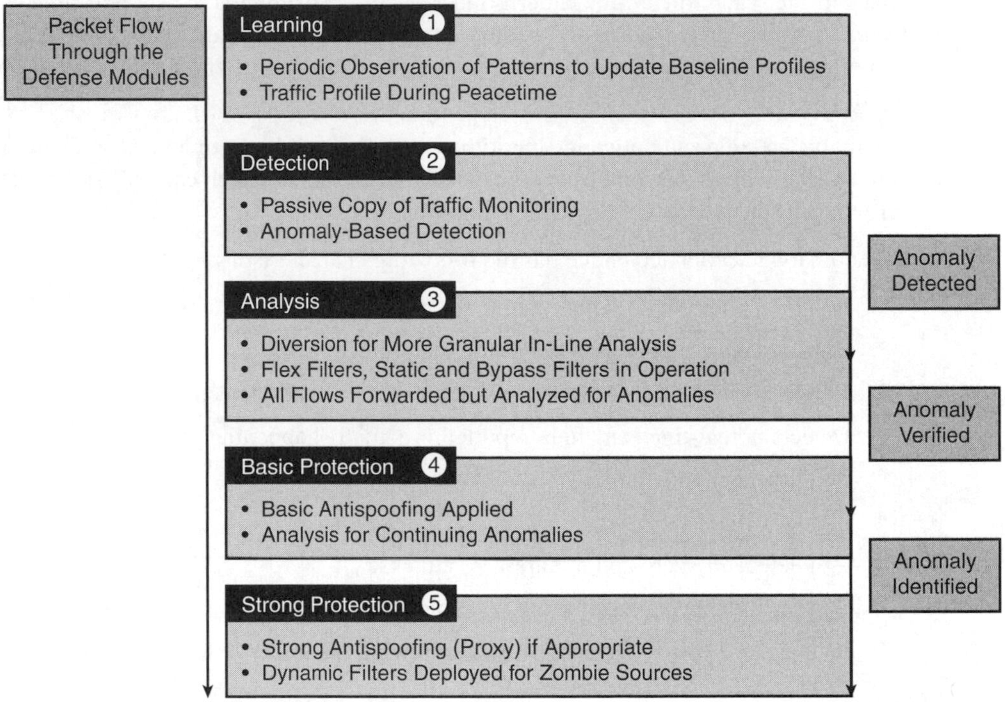

The Cisco DDoS Anomaly Detection and Mitigation solution consists of two basic deployment components:

- Cisco Traffic Anomaly Detector
- Cisco Guard DDoS Mitigation

NOTE   Both products are available as appliance-based solutions and integrated service modules for Cisco Catalyst 6500 Series Switches and Cisco 7600 Series Routers.

Cisco Traffic Anomaly Detector

The Cisco Traffic Anomaly Detector is the industry's standard solution for detecting the most complex and sophisticated DDoS attacks. The Cisco Traffic Anomaly Detector works in combination with the Cisco Guard DDoS Mitigation device.

Cisco Traffic Anomaly Detectors identify potential DDoS attacks and divert traffic destined for the targeted device to the Cisco Guard to scrub, identify, and block malicious traffic in real-time, without affecting the flow of legitimate traffic.

Cisco Traffic Anomaly Detection is based on sophisticated anomaly detection intelligence capabilities that compare current activity to profiles of known normal behavior, enabling the Traffic Anomaly Detector to identify any type of DDoS attacks including day-zero attacks. The detector has a built-in behavioral recognition engine that enables traffic pattern comparison, thus eliminating the need to manually update profiles. This also reduces the number of false alarms, in contrast to signature-based engines.

The Cisco Traffic Anomaly Detectors deliver high performance detection, diversion, and alerting capabilities for potential DDoS attacks, worms, and day-zero attacks. Without impacting legitimate flow, the Traffic Anomaly Detector triggers a mitigation service to remove malicious attack flows and blocks the attack before network resource availability is adversely affected.

The Cisco Traffic Anomaly Detector can monitor attack flows at full multigigabit line rates, by identifying more than 100,000 sources per device in a single attack, thereby providing robust protection for high-volume environments.

The Cisco Traffic Anomaly Detector is based on a unique, patented Multi-Verification Process (MVP) architecture developed by Cisco, as shown in Figure 22-5. MVP utilizes the latest behavioral analysis and attack recognition technology to proactively detect and identify all types of DDoS attacks.

Cisco Traffic Anomaly Detector products are available in two options:

- Cisco Traffic Anomaly Detector XT 5600 Series Appliance
- Cisco Traffic Anomaly Detector Module for Cisco Catalyst 6500 Series Switches and Cisco 7600 Series Routers

Cisco Traffic Anomaly Detector continuously monitors a mirrored copy of selected traffic destined for a protected host or group of hosts and compiles detailed profiles that indicate how individual hosts behave under normal operating conditions. When a traffic pattern deviation is detected, it is considered as the anomalous behavior of a potential attack, and the Detector responds based on user-configured preferences by

- Sending an operator alert to initiate a manual response
- Triggering an existing management system
- Launching the Cisco Guard XT DDoS Mitigation Appliance to immediately begin mitigation services

The Traffic Anomaly Detector performs the following tasks:

- **Traffic learning:** Classifies and categorizes the normal zone traffic pattern by using an algorithm-based process to establish a baseline. During the learning process, the Detector modifies the default zone traffic policies and policy thresholds to match the characteristics of normal zone traffic. The traffic policies and thresholds define the reference points that the Detector uses to determine when the zone traffic is normal or abnormal (indicating an attack on the zone).

- **Traffic anomaly detection:** Detects anomalies in protected zone traffic based on normal traffic characteristics.

Figure 22-4 illustrates the operation of the Cisco Traffic Anomaly Detector in which the Traffic Detector receives a mirrored copy (using SPAN/VACL) of the network traffic for analysis. If deviation is detected, it reroutes the traffic to the Cisco Guard Mitigation for analysis and mitigation services.

Figure 22-4　*Cisco Traffic Anomaly Detection and Mitigation Operation*

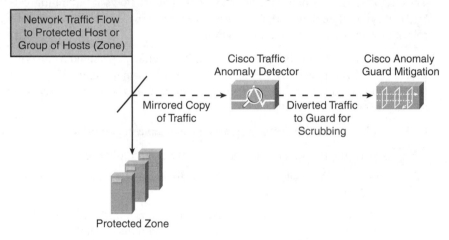

The Traffic Detector can operate as an independent DDoS detection and alarm component; however, it works optimally with the Cisco Guard to provide mitigation services completing the DDoS protection solution.

Cisco Traffic Detector device is capable of processing attack traffic at multigigabit line rates, and the recognition engine identifies the broadest range of DDoS attacks, including

- TCP-based attacks
- UDP-based attacks
- HTTP attacks
- DNS attacks

- SIP (VoIP) attacks
- Botnets and Zombie attacks

To provide the best possible implementation scenario, the Cisco Traffic Anomaly Detector can be deployed downstream, close to protected resources in the data center, or upstream adjacent to a Cisco Guard to provide more widespread coverage.

Combined with the Cisco Guard Mitigation, the Cisco Traffic Anomaly Detector provides industry's most comprehensive DDoS defense system.

Cisco Guard DDoS Mitigation

Cisco Guard DDoS Mitigation is the industry's standard solution for defeating the most complex and sophisticated DDoS attacks. Cisco Guard DDoS Mitigation works in combination with the Cisco Traffic Anomaly Detector device.

The Cisco Guard Mitigation delivers multigigabit performance to protect the service provider and large-scale enterprise environments from DDoS attacks by performing granular per-flow-level analysis and identification, and it provides blocking capabilities to stop DDoS attack traffic in real-time while allowing legitimate traffic to flow seamlessly. The guard is capable of filtering attacks from hundreds of thousands of zombies simultaneously.

Cisco Guard DDoS Mitigation products are available in two options:

- Cisco Guard DDoS Mitigation XT 5600 Series Appliance
- Cisco Guard DDoS Mitigation Guard Module for Cisco Catalyst 6500 Series Switches and Cisco 7600 Series Routers

One of the most important advantages of Cisco Guard is that it is not an inline solution. It can therefore be deployed off the critical path at any point in the network, yet achieve the in-the-traffic flow between the data stream type of scenario by using its dynamic diversion capability. This also ensures that the failure of a Cisco Guard device does not impact the traffic flow.

As shown in Figure 22-4, the Cisco Guard device receives diverted suspect traffic from the Cisco Traffic Anomaly Detector for data scrubbing and cleaning services, using its advanced statistical profiling techniques and antispoofing technologies. During the traffic-cleaning process, the Cisco Guard identifies and drops the attack packets and forwards the legitimate packets to their targeted network destinations.

The Cisco Guard is based on a unique Multi-Verification Process (MVP) architecture developed by Cisco. The diverted traffic is subjected to the MVP architecture that employs the most advanced anomaly recognition, protocol analysis, source verification, and antispoofing technologies.

Cisco Guard provides robust protection against all types of attacks with the integrated dynamic filters and active verification technologies, driven by a sophisticated profile-based anomaly recognition engine. In addition, the protocol analysis and rate limiting features ensure that only valid traffic gets through without overwhelming other downstream devices.

Figure 22-5 illustrates the innovative MVP architecture that delivers multiple interactive layers of defense, which are designed to identify and block the specific packets and flows responsible for the attack.

Figure 22-5   *Multiverification Process (MVP) Architecture*

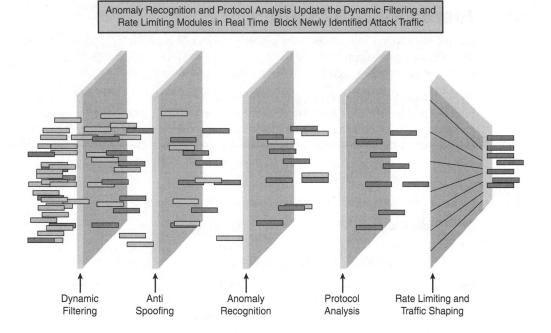

The information in Figure 22-5 is compiled from the Cisco Networkers session presentation BRKSEC-2030 on "Deploying Network IPS."

The Cisco Guard Mitigation device is capable of processing attack traffic at multigigabit line rates, and the recognition engine identifies a broad range of DDoS attacks, including

- TCP-based attacks
- UDP-based attacks
- HTTP attacks
- DNS attacks
- SIP (VoIP) attacks
- Botnets and Zombie attacks

The Guard DDoS Mitigation performs the following tasks:

- **Traffic learning:** Classify and categorize the normal zone traffic pattern using an algorithm-based process to establish a baseline. During the learning process, the Guard modifies the default zone traffic policies and policy thresholds to match the characteristics of normal zone traffic. The traffic policies and thresholds define the reference points that the Guard uses to determine when the zone traffic is normal or abnormal (indicating an attack on the zone).

- **Traffic protection:** Distinguish between legitimate and malicious traffic and filter the malicious traffic so that only the legitimate traffic is allowed to pass on to the protected zone.

- **Traffic diversion:** Divert the zone traffic from its normal network path to the Guard learning and protection processes and then return the legitimate zone traffic to the network.

To provide the best possible implementation scenario, the Cisco Guard can be deployed in a distributed upstream configuration at the backbone level, close to the network edge or ISP connection.

Cisco Guard is typically deployed off the critical path at any point in the network, from enterprise access points to peering points off an ISP backbone.

Combined with the Cisco Traffic Anomaly Detector, the Cisco Guard Mitigation provides the industry's most comprehensive DDoS defense system.

Putting It All Together for Operation

As mentioned earlier, the Cisco Traffic Anomaly Detector device works in combination with the Cisco Guard Mitigation device to provide a comprehensive anomaly protection against DDoS attacks.

Figures 22-6 through 22-10 illustrate the combination of the Cisco DDoS solution and the dynamic diversion solution.

The following steps highlight each step of the anomaly detection and mitigation process during an attack life cycle in reference to Figures 22-6 through 22-10.

NOTE It is assumed that the Traffic Anomaly Detector and the Guard Mitigation device have both completed the learning process, classifying and categorizing the normal zone traffic pattern using an algorithm-based process to establish a baseline.

Step 1   As illustrated in Figure 22-6, the Traffic Anomaly Detector device is deployed closer to the protected zone to detect anomalies and provide detection and alerting capabilities. Normal traffic flow is moving to Zone1 and Zone2 servers. The Traffic Anomaly Detector device identifies an anomaly in Zone2 and has detected an intrusion that deviates from the normal traffic policy.

Step 2   As illustrated in Figure 22-7, the Traffic Anomaly Detector device alerts the Cisco Guard Mitigation device to begin dynamic diversion, which redirects traffic destined for the targeted resources, and provides traffic flow information of the intrusion detected. This can either be triggered manually or automatically.

Step 3   As illustrated in Figure 22-8, the Cisco Guard Mitigation device triggers a redirection to the edge router for the target victim's traffic under suspicion to be redirected to the Guard. This can be achieved via routing protocol and Border Gateway Protocol (BGP) updates. All other traffic continues to flow directly to its designated destinations without interruption. Only the target victim traffic is redirected to the Guard.

Step 4   As illustrated in Figure 22-9, the edge router is now diverting all target victims' traffic (only) to the Cisco Guard Mitigation device for scrubbing. The diverted traffic is then scrutinized to classify and separate bad flows from legitimate flows filtering malicious data. The Guard performs detailed flow-level analysis to identify and mitigate the attack.

Step 5   As illustrated in Figure 22-10, the Guard filters and blocks all malicious attack traffic and forwards all legitimate traffic to its designated destination, ensuring uninterrupted network flow for valid users and legitimate transactions.

Figure 22-6   *Step 1—Anomaly Is Detected by the Cisco Traffic Detector in a Protected Zone*

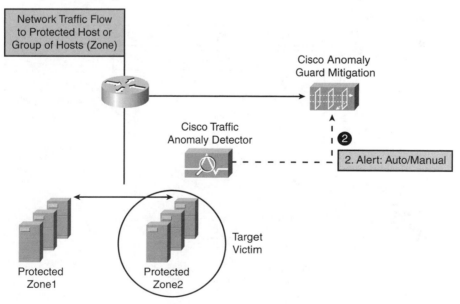

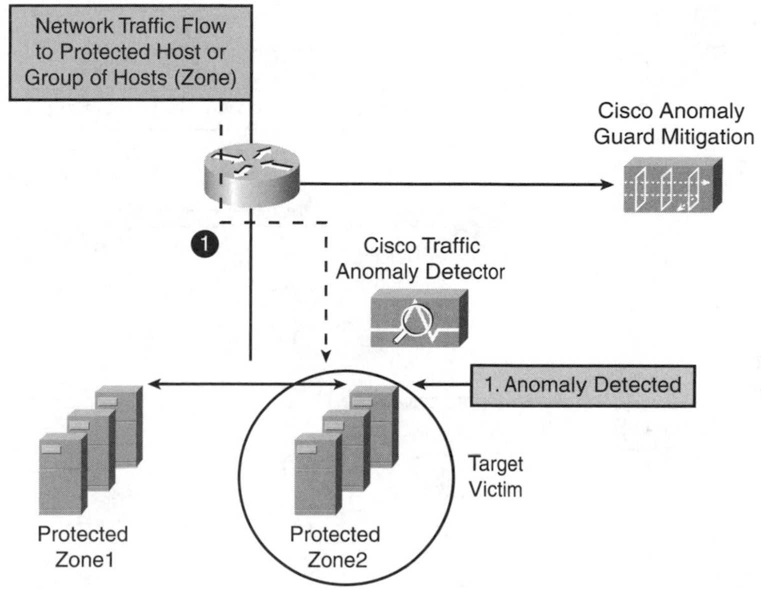

Figure 22-7   *Step 2—Cisco Traffic Detector Alerts Cisco Guard*

Figure 22-8 *Step 3—Cisco Guard Triggers Traffic Diversion*

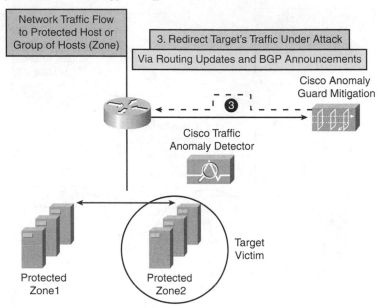

Figure 22-9 *Step 4 —Diverted Traffic Is Redirected to Cisco Guard for Scrubbing*

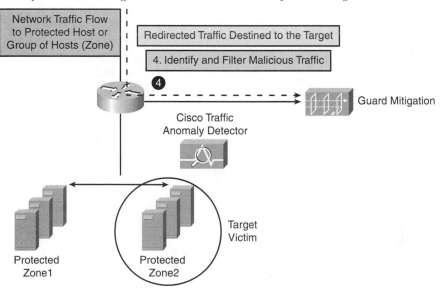

Figure 22-10   *Step 5 —Cisco Guard Forwards Legitimate Traffic to Original Destination*

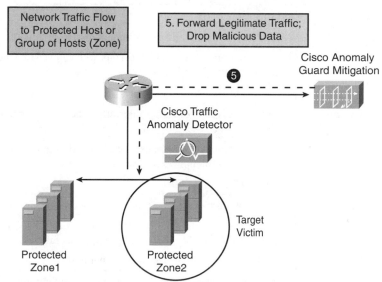

The information concept in Figures 22-6 to 22-10 is compiled from the Cisco Networkers session presentation BRKSEC-2030 on "Deploying Network IPS."

Configuring and Managing the Cisco Traffic Anomaly Detector

The following sections briefly outline the configuration parameters for the Cisco Traffic Anomaly Detector device.

Similar to the IPS sensor appliance, the Anomaly Detector can be configured by using the command-line interface (CLI) and the built-in GUI WBM user interface.

The Detector needs to be initialized using CLI for basic parameters such as the IP address, gateway, routes, and access control list (ACL). After the Detector is initialized and routable in the network, it can be accessed using the web-based GUI to configure the remaining tasks.

Several command modes on the Detector CLI are available for user access, and the access is mapped according to various CLI privilege levels, similar to the IPS Sensor software. By default, the user admin account is available with full administrative access rights to the Detector CLI.

Table 22-1 provides details of the various command and configuration modes used in the Detector CLI.

Table 22-1   *Detector Command Configuration Modes*

Mode	Description
Global	Allows connection to remote devices and listing system information. The Global prompt is the default prompt when logged into the Detector. The command prompt is as follows: user@DETECTOR#
Configuration	Allows configuration of features that affect the Detector operations and have restricted user access. To enter configuration mode, use the **configure** command in global mode. The command prompt is as follows: user@DETECTOR-conf#
Interface configuration	Allows configuration of the Detector networking interfaces. To enter interface configuration mode, use the **interface** command in configuration mode. The command prompt is as follows: user@DETECTOR-conf-if-<interface-name>#
Router configuration	Allows configuration of the Detector routing configuration. To enter router configuration mode, use the **router** command in configuration mode. The command prompt is as follows: router>
Zone configuration	Allows configuration of the zone attributes. To enter zone configuration mode, use the **zone** command in configuration mode or use the **configure** command in global mode. The command prompt is as follows: user@DETECTOR-conf-zone-<zone-name>#
Policy template configuration	Allows configuration of the zone policy templates. To enter policy template configuration mode, use the **policy-template** command in zone configuration mode. The command prompt is as follows: user@DETECTOR-conf-zone-<zone-name>-policy_template-<policy-template-name>#
Policy configuration	Allows configuration of the zone policies. To enter policy configuration mode, use the **policy** command in zone configuration mode. The command prompt is as follows: user@DETECTOR-conf-zone-<zone-name>-policy-<policy-path>#
Guard configuration	Allows configuration of the zone definitions that are unique to the Guard, such as user filters. To enter guard configuration mode, use the **guard-conf** command in zone configuration mode. The command prompt is as follows: user@DETECTOR-conf-zone-<zone-name>(guard)#

Managing the Detector

As mentioned earlier, the Detector needs to be initialized using the CLI Console access.

However, the Detector can be accessed and managed using one of the following methods:

- CLI Console access (for bootstrapping initial parameters)
- Secure Shell (SSH) session
- Built-in Web-Based Management (WBM) application
- Cisco DDoS Multi-Device Manager (MDM)

Initializing the Detector Through CLI Console Access

By default, the Detector does not have a configuration and requires basic initial parameters enabled for management via the GUI application. When the Detector boot process finishes, use the CLI console to log in to the CLI Console through the default username **admin** and password **rhadmin**.

NOTE   The Detector has four physical interfaces: eth0, eth1, giga0, and giga1. The out-of-band interfaces are eth0 and eth1 (10/100/1000 Ethernet sockets for out-of-band management). The eth0 or eth1 must be configured with an IP address and subnet mask. The in-band interfaces (copper or fiber socket) are giga0 and giga1.

Example 22-1 shows basic initial configuration parameters in the configuration mode that are used to activate the out-of-band management interface, assign the default gateway, and enable the built-in web-based GUI service for management (WBM).

By default, the Detector has restricted access and protects access for connections to the Detector, and any user trying to access the Detector must be explicitly permitted within the ACL. Example 22-1 shows a host located at IP address 10.1.1.150, which is being permitted in the ACL, so that it can manage the Detector by using the built-in WBM application and shows how to enable the MDM.

Example 22-1   *Basic Detector Initialization Parameters Using CLI Console*

```
user@DETECTOR-conf# interface eth1
user@DETECTOR-conf-if-eth1# ip address 192.168.1.1 255.255.255.0
user@DETECTOR-conf-if-eth1# no shutdown
user@DETECTOR-conf# default-gateway 192.168.1.254
user@DETECTOR-conf# service wbm
user@DETECTOR-conf# permit wbm 10.1.1.150
user@DETECTOR-conf# service mdm
user@DETECTOR-conf# mdm server 10.1.1.150
```

In addition to the previous sample configuration, other basic parameters can be configured optionally:

- Configuring Hostname, Date, and Time
- Configuring various integrated services (for example, Routing, Network Time Protocol (NTP), Simple Network Management Protocol (SNMP), WBM, MDM, and SSH)
- Configuring Access Control using AAA
- Configuring TACACS+ parameters and attributes
- Configuring keys for SSH, SSH FTP (SFTP), and SCP connections
- Configuring NTP parameters
- Configuring SNMP parameters
- Configuring Communication parameters to establish a secure session with the Guard using SSL or SSH

After configuring basic initial parameters using CLI is completed, the Detector can be managed via the standard web browser from the desktop PC (Internet Explorer) by entering the following address:

https://Detector-ip-address/

NOTE　The Detector also supports TACACS+ authentication for user authentication. If configured, the Detector uses the TACACS+ user database for user authentication instead of its local database.

Configuring the Detector (Zones, Filters, Policies, and Learning Process)

After initializing the Detector as shown in previous section, several other parameters need to be configured on the Detector to complete the configuration, such as Zones, Zone Filters, and Policies. These can either be configured using the CLI Console or are best implemented using the built-in web-based GUI manager application.

The following section highlights some of the basic concepts for configuring Zones, Zone Filters, Policies, and the Detector Learning phase, and for activating anomaly detection and the Guard device:

- **Configuring zones:** A zone is a network element that the Detector monitors for DDoS attacks. A zone can be any combination of a server, client, or router, or a subnet, or an entire network. The zone is a group of protected devices that are monitored. The Detector monitors the devices in a zone, and if an attack is identified, the Guard is activated to protect the zone. The Detector can simultaneously monitor traffic for several zones provided that their network address does not overlap. There are two ways to create a new zone: first, using one of the system-defined zone templates that allow creation of a new zone with the default policies and filters of the template; and second, duplicating an existing zone. After a zone has been created, additional zone attributes need to be configured, such as the zone IP address range.

- **Configuring zone filters:** After a zone is defined, zone filters need to be applied to enable the analysis detection level for the zone traffic flow. Zone filters also define the way the Detector handles specific traffic flows. Zone filters enable the Detector to analyze zone traffic for anomalies and bypass the Detector anomaly detection features. Zone filters can be customized for different methods that the Detector uses to detect traffic anomalies. There are several types of zone filters, such as Dynamic filters, Bypass filters, and Flex-content filters. Each of these is used for analyzing specific traffic flows and applying the required protection level to the specified traffic flow on the Detector. For example, the dynamic filter is created when the Detector identifies anomalies in the zone traffic and activates the Guard device to protect the zone. Zone filter parameters can be modified as per user requirements. Figure 22-11 illustrates the Detector zone filter system.

Figure 22-11   *Detector Zone Filter System*

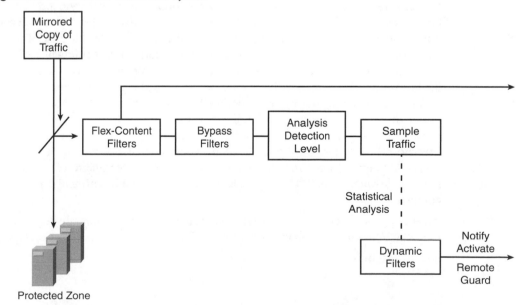

NOTE   The information in Figure 22-11 is compiled from Cisco product configuration guide on
"Cisco Traffic Anomaly Detector Configuration Guide (Software Version 6.0)" at http://
www.cisco.com/en/US/docs/security/anomaly_detection_mitigation/appliances/detector/
v6.0/configuration/guide/conffilt.html.

- **Configuring policies:** Each zone contains a set of policies that are used to perform
  statistical analysis of the zone traffic flow and enforce the policy. The Detector uses
  predefined policy templates to construct the policies for each zone. A policy template
  is a collection of policy construction rules that the Detector uses during the policy
  construction phase to create the zone policies. Several default policy templates are
  available for use. Here are three examples: First, the **ip_scan** policy template is used
  to detect scans when a client from a specific source IP address tries to access many
  destination IP addresses in the zone. Second, the **tcp_services** template is used for
  TCP services on ports other than those that are HTTP related, such as ports 80 and
  8080. Third, the **tcp_ratio** template is used for monitoring ratios between different
  types of TCP packets. For example, the ratio of SYN packets to FIN/RST packets and
  several other policy templates are available. Zone policy parameters can be modified
  after they are created. Policy triggers and the action also need to be configured to
  define the action that the policy takes when it is activated. The Detector also includes
  additional policy templates for zones designed for specific types of attacks or specific
  services—for example to monitor TCP-based WORM attacks.

- **Detector learning process and policy construction phase:** As mentioned
  previously, the Detector is initially in the learning process to establish the normal zone
  traffic patterns and threshold conditions to establish a baseline for the zone. The
  Detector creates the zone policies and its thresholds during this learning phase based
  on the normal traffic patterns. To activate the policy construction phase for zones, use
  the **learning policy-construction** command from the global configuration. For
  example, the **learning policy-construction *** command initiates the learning process
  for all zones when the asterisk (*) character is used. Alternatively, individual zones
  can also be named to initiate the learning phase separately. Similarly, use the **learning
  threshold-tuning** command from the global configuration mode to initiate the
  threshold tuning phase. After the learning is completed, accept the results from the
  policy construction phase for the respective zones using the **learning accept**
  command.

- **Activating zone anomaly detection:** Finally, to activate zone anomaly detection,
  issue the following command in the zone configuration mode.

  detect [learning]

The **learning** keyword is optional and enables the Detector to detect anomalies in the zone traffic and tune the zone policy thresholds by using detect and learn functions, as mentioned previously in the detector learning process section. Note that to enable the learning process, the switch must be configured with the port mirroring feature.

- **Activating the Guard to Protect a Zone:** As discussed previously, the Detector monitors the zone continuously for anomalies. When the Detector detects a zone traffic anomaly, it creates dynamic filters that can activate the Guards that are associated with the Detector. There are several ways to configure the Detector to activate a remote Guard: for example, the first way is to use a remote Guard list that uses SSL to enable remote activation and zone synchronization; the second way is to use SSH to enable remote activation only; the third way is to use BGP to send a BGP route update to inform the adjacent router to divert the target zone traffic to the remote Guard. The Detector can also be configured as offline to issue a notification when an attack on the zone occurs or enable manual activation to create dynamic filters to activate remote Guards.

- **Synchronizing zone configurations:** The zone synchronization process allows you to create copies of zone configuration on both the Detector and the Guard. The synchronization process can be used to create, configure, and modify a zone on the Detector and then update the same zone information to the Guard. There are two modes of synchronization: the Detector to Guard Synchronization, where the Detector copies the zone configuration from itself to the Guard, and the Guard to Detector Synchronization, where the Detector copies the zone configuration from the Guard to itself.

As discussed previously, several parameters need to be configured to complete the Cisco Traffic Anomaly Detector deployment (refer to Table 22-1).

These entire configurations can either be done via the CLI Console access or the built-in GUI WBM application.

For complete details on configuring various options, refer to the following Cisco technical documentation.

TIP   Refer to the following Cisco documentation for further details to configure the Cisco Traffic Anomaly Detector:

http://www.cisco.com/en/US/products/ps5887/products_configuration_guide_book09186a00807bfb20.html

http://www.cisco.com/en/US/products/ps5887/products_configuration_guide_book09186a00805e01e4.html

---

Configuring and Managing Cisco Guard Mitigation

This section briefly outlines the configuration parameters for the Cisco Guard Mitigation device.

Similar to the Detector software, the Guard Mitigation device can be configured by using the command-line interface (CLI) and also the built-in GUI WBM user interface.

The Guard needs to be initialized using CLI for basic parameters such as the IP address, gateway, routes, and ACL. After the Guard is initialized and routable in the network, it can be accessed using the web-based GUI to configure the remaining tasks.

Several command modes on the Guard CLI are available for user access. The access is mapped according to various CLI privilege levels, in a manner that is similar to the Detector software. By default, the user admin account is available with full administrative access rights to the Guard CLI.

Table 22-2 provides details of the various command and configuration modes used in the Guard CLI.

Table 22-2   *Guard Command Configuration Modes*

Mode	Description
Global	Allows connection to remote devices and list system information.
	The Global prompt is the default prompt when you log in to the Guard. The command prompt is as follows:
	user@GUARD#
Configuration	Allows configuration of features that affect the Guard operation and have restricted user access.
	To enter configuration mode, use the **configure** command in global mode. The command prompt is as follows:
	user@GUARD-conf#
Interface configuration	Allows configuration of the Guard networking interfaces.
	To enter interface configuration mode, use the **interface** command in configuration mode. The command prompt is as follows:
	user@GUARD-conf-if-<interface-name>#
Router configuration	Allows configuration of the Guard routing configuration.
	To enter router configuration mode, use the **router** command in configuration mode. The command prompt is as follows:
	router>
Zone configuration	Allows configuration of the zone attributes.
	To enter zone configuration mode, use the **zone** command in configuration mode or use the **configure** command in global mode. The command prompt is as follows:
	user@GUARD-conf-zone-<zone-name>#

Table 22-2 *Guard Command Configuration Modes (Continued)*

Mode	Description
Policy template configuration	Allows configuration of the zone policy templates.
	To enter policy template configuration mode, use the **policy-template** command in zone configuration mode. The command prompt is as follows:
	user@GUARD-conf-zone-<zone-name>-policy_template-<policy-template-name>#
Policy configuration	Allows configuration of the zone policies.
	To enter policy configuration mode, use the **policy** command in zone configuration mode. The command prompt is as follows:
	user@GUARD-conf-zone-<zone-name>-policy-<policy-path>#

Managing the Guard

As mentioned earlier, the Guard needs to be initialized by using the CLI Console access.

However, the Guard can be accessed and managed using one of the following methods:

- CLI Console access (for bootstrapping initial parameters)
- Secure Shell (SSH) session
- Built-in WBM application
- Cisco DDoS MDM

Initializing the Guard Using the CLI Console Access

After the Guard boot process finishes, use the CLI console to log in to the CLI Console, using the default username **admin** and password **rhadmin**.

NOTE   The Guard has four physical interfaces: eth0, eth1, giga0, and giga1. The out-of-band interfaces are eth0 and eth1 (10/100/1000 Ethernet sockets for out-of-band management). The eth0 or eth1 must be configured with an IP address and subnet mask. The in-band interfaces (copper or fiber socket) are giga0 and giga1.

Example 22-2 shows basic initial configuration parameters in the configuration mode that are used to activate the out-of-band management interface, assign the default gateway, and enable the built-in web-based GUI service for management (WBM).

By default, the Guard has restricted access and protects access for connections to the Guard, and any user trying to access the Guard must be explicitly permitted within the ACL. Example 22-2 shows a host located at IP address 10.1.1.150 that is being permitted in the ACL so that it can manage the Guard by using the built-in web-based GUI manager (WBM) application.

Example 22-2 *Basic Guard Initialization Parameters Using CLI Console*

```
user@GUARD-conf# interface eth1
user@GUARD-conf-if-eth1# ip address 192.168.10.1 255.255.255.0
user@GUARD-conf-if-eth1# no shutdown
user@GUARD-conf# default-gateway 192.168.10.254
user@GUARD-conf# service wbm
user@GUARD-conf# permit wbm 10.1.1.150
```

In addition to the previous sample configuration, other basic parameters can also be configured optionally:

- Hostname, Date, and Time
- Various integrated services (Routing, NTP, SNMP, WBM, and SSH)
- Access Control using AAA
- TACACS+ parameters and attributes
- Keys for SSH, SFTP, and SCP connections
- NTP parameters
- SNMP parameters
- Communication parameters to establish a secure session with the Detector using SSL or SSH

After the configuration of basic initial parameters using CLI is completed, the Guard can be managed via the standard web browser from the desktop PC (Internet Explorer) by entering the following address:

https://Guard-ip-address/

NOTE   The Guard also supports TACACS+ authentication for user authentication. If configured, the Guard uses the TACACS+ user database for user authentication instead of its local database.

Configuring the Guard (Zones, Filters, Policies, Learning Process)

After initializing the Guard as shown in the previous section, several other parameters need to be configured on the Guard to complete the configuration, such as zones, zone filters, and policies. These can either be configured using the CLI Console or are best implemented using the built-in web-based GUI manager application.

The following section highlights some of the basic concepts of configuring Zones, Zone Filters, Policies, Guard Learning phase, and activating anomaly detection and the Guard device.

- **Configuring zones:** A zone is a network element that the Guard monitors for DDoS attacks. A zone can be any combination of a server, client, router, subnet, or an entire network. The zone is a group of protected devices, which are monitored. The Guard monitors the devices in a zone, and if an attack is identified, the Guard is activated to protect the zone. The Guard can simultaneously monitor traffic for several zones provided that their network addresses do not overlap. There are three ways to create a new zone on the Guard: by using one of the predefined zone templates that allow creation of a new zone with the default policies and filters of the template; by duplicating an existing zone; or by copying a zone configuration from the Detector. After a zone has been created, additional zone attributes need to be configured, such as a zone IP address range.

- **Configuring zone filters:** After a zone is defined, zone filters need to be applied to enable the analysis detection level for the zone traffic flow. Zone filters also define the way the Detector handles specific traffic flows. Zone filters enable the Guard to analyze zone traffic for anomalies and apply the basic or strong level of protection to separate legitimate traffic from malicious traffic, drop malicious packets, and forward traffic directly to the zone, bypassing the Guard protection features. Zone filters can be customized for different methods that the Guard uses to detect traffic anomalies. There are several types of zone filters, including User filters, Dynamic filters, Bypass filters, and Flex-content filters. Each of these types is used for analyzing specific traffic flows and applying the required protection level to the specified traffic flow on the Guard. For example, the dynamic filter is created when the Guard identifies anomalies in the zone to protect the zone. Similarly, User filters apply the required protection level to the specified traffic flow. Most important, the User filters are the first to be enforced as an action occurs when the Guard identifies abnormal or malicious traffic. Zone filter parameters can be modified as per user requirements. Figure 22-12 illustrates the Guard Zone filter system.

Figure 22-12 *Guard Zone Filter System*

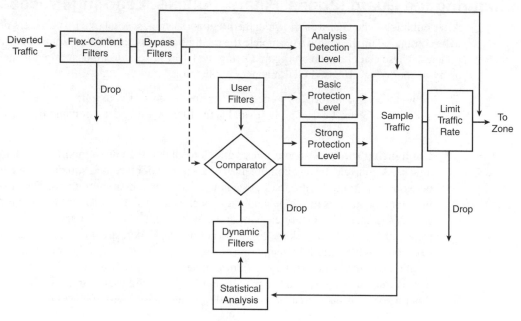

NOTE   The information in Figure 22-12 is compiled from Cisco product configuration guide on "Cisco Guard Configuration Guide (Software Version 6.0)" at http://www.cisco.com/en/ US/docs/security/anomaly_detection_mitigation/appliances/guard/v6.0/configuration/ guide/conffilt.html.

- **Configuring policies:** Each zone contains a set of policies that is used to perform statistical analysis of the zone traffic flow and enforce the policy. The Detector uses predefined policy templates to construct the policies for each zone. A policy template is a collection of policy construction rules that the Detector uses during the policy construction phase to create the zone policies. Several default policy templates are available for use, such as an **ip_scan** policy template for detecting scans when a client from a specific source IP address tries to access many destination IP addresses in the zone. Another example is the **tcp_services** template, which is used for TCP services on ports other than those that are HTTP-related, such as ports 80 and 8080. A final example is the **tcp_ratio** template, which is used for monitoring ratios between different types of TCP packets, such as the ratio of SYN packets to FIN/RST packets and several other policy templates. Zone policy parameters can be modified after being created. Policy triggers and the action also need to be configured to define the action that the policy takes when it is activated. The Guard also includes additional policy templates for zones designed for specific types of attacks or specific services— for example, to monitor VoIP applications.

- **Understanding Guard protection levels:** As shown in Figure 22-12, the Guard applies three protection levels during the zone filter system process, in which it applies different processes to the traffic flow. Three protection levels exist in the Guard: the Analysis protection level, which allows the traffic to flow monitored, but uninterrupted, during zone protection, as long as no anomalies are detected; the Basic protection level that activates antispoofing and antizombie functions to authenticate the traffic by inspecting the suspicious traffic flow to verify its source; and the most powerful strong protection level, which activates severe antispoofing functions that inspect the traffic flow packets to verify the flow legitimacy. After applying a protection function to the zone, the Guard continuously monitors the traffic for anomalies if it detects an anomaly in traffic destined to the zone, it applies a stronger protection level.

NOTE Protection levels have a static configuration and cannot be configured manually.

- **Guard learning process and policy construction phase:** As mentioned previously, the Guard is initially in the learning process to establish the normal zone traffic patterns and threshold conditions to establish a baseline for the zone. The Guard creates the zone policies and its thresholds during this learning phase based on the normal traffic patterns. For the Guard to learn the zone traffic characteristics, traffic needs to be diverted from its normal network path to the Guard. As the Guard analyzes the traffic, it injects the traffic back into the network. Note that before initiating the learning process, traffic diversion must be set up correctly. Traffic diversion can be configured using a routing protocol on the Guard. To activate the policy construction phase for zones, use the **learning policy-construction** command from the global configuration. For example, the **learning policy-construction *** command initiates the learning process for all zones when the asterisk (*) character is used. Alternatively, individual zones can be named to initiate the learning phase separately. Similarly, use the **learning threshold-tuning** command from the global configuration mode to initiate the threshold tuning phase. After the learning is done, accept the results from the policy construction phase for the respective zones using the **learning accept** command.
- **Activating zone protection:** The Guard can be configured to activate zone protection when it receives a message from the Detector; alternatively, zone protection can be manually triggered on the Guard for a zone under attack. To activate the Guard for zone protection, issue the following command in the zone configuration mode.

    protect [learning]

The **learning** keyword is optional and enables the Guard to detect anomalies in the zone traffic and tune the zone policy thresholds using the protect and learn function.

- **Synchronizing zone configurations:** The zone synchronization process allows the creation of copies of the zone configuration on both the Detector and the Guard. The synchronization process can be used to create, configure, and modify a zone on the Detector, and then update the same zone information to the Guard. There are two modes of synchronization: the Detector to Guard Synchronization, in which the Detector copies the zone configuration from itself to the Guard, and the Guard to Detector Synchronization, in which the Detector copies the zone configuration from the Guard to itself.

As discussed previously, several parameters need to be configured to complete the Cisco Guard Mitigation deployment (refer to Table 22-2).

These entire configurations can be accomplished either via the CLI Console access or the built-in GUI WBM application.

For a complete detail of configuring various options, refer to the Cisco technical documentation.

TIP   Refer to the following Cisco documentation for further details to configure the Cisco Traffic Anomaly Detector:

http://www.cisco.com/en/US/products/ps5888/products_configuration_guide_book09186a00807bfb1e.html

http://www.cisco.com/en/US/products/ps5888/products_configuration_guide_book09186a00805e01c8.html

Summary

In today's rapidly growing networks, dynamically evolving threats are on the rise. Complex DoS attacks and DDoS attacks equipped with the sophisticated intelligence are clogging the networks to immobilize traffic flow, resulting in severe network degradation and meltdown.

DDoS attacks have increased over the years and are becoming a major threat to be combated. Service providers and large-scale network deployments are struggling to find comprehensive solutions to mitigate DDoS attacks.

At the same time, the trend has also shifted and evolved from reactive detection to a more proactive detection and prevention approach that uses anomaly-based and behavioral-based systems.

The Cisco Anomaly Detection and Mitigation solution is the answer to these concerns, providing a self-defending preventive solution to detect and mitigate complex and sophisticated DoS and DDoS attacks and day-zero attacks.

The chapter gave details of the Cisco Anomaly Detection and Mitigation solution and provided core concepts of the anomaly architecture and how it works with the aid of various illustrations and diagrams.

The chapter provided a brief overview of configuring and managing the Cisco Traffic Anomaly Detector and Cisco Guard Mitigation devices through use of various sample configurations.

The chapter described and explained the important aspects of configuring Zones, Filters, Policies, and Learning Process parameters, as well as how to activate the Anomaly Detection and the Guard system.

References

http://www.cisco.com/en/US/products/ps5879/Products_Sub_Category_Home.html

http://www.cisco.com/go/detector

http://www.cisco.com/en/US/products/ps6236/index.html

http://www.cisco.com/en/US/products/ps5888/products_data_sheet0900aecd8055d170.html

http://www.cisco.com/en/US/products/hw/modules/ps2706/products_data_sheet0900aecd80220a6e.html

http://www.cisco.com/go/guard

http://www.cisco.com/en/US/products/ps6235/index.html

http://www.cisco.com/en/US/products/ps5888/products_data_sheets_list.html

http://www.cisco.com/en/US/products/ps5887/products_configuration_guide_book09186a00807bfb20.html

http://www.cisco.com/en/US/products/ps5888/products_configuration_guide_book09186a00807bfb1e.html

Security Monitoring and Correlation

The monitoring and correlation of network security infrastructure in the modern day network is becoming a challenge because each network component generates its own set of logs, events, alerts, and various notification messages, thereby creating a massive collection of event logs for analysis and investigation.

Cisco Security Monitoring, Analysis, and Response System (CS-MARS) is a comprehensive appliance-based solution providing security information and event management. CS-MARS offers network intelligence to identify and correlate events, pinpoint attack paths, and provide comprehensive security threat control and mitigation.

This chapter provides details of the appliance-based security information management (SIM) system that uses the industry standard CS-MARS solution.

The chapter takes a closer look at the core concepts of the CS-MARS appliance and its features and capabilities, and highlights the key concepts such as events, sessions, rules, and incidents.

The chapter gives an overview of the various deployment scenarios and implementation of the CS-MARS solution using the Standalone, Local Controllers (LC), and Global Controllers (GC) options. The chapter provides an overview of the CS-MARS web-based management interface and a basic overview of configuring CS-MARS appliance.

Security Information and Event Management

Security information and event management systems provide network intelligence by aggregating security events and logs from various network devices, analyzing the logs through various querying and correlation technology techniques, and generating meaningful reports regarding network anomalies and security events occurring within the network.

CS-MARS is a comprehensive security information and event management solution that identifies, manages, and mitigates security threats. CS-MARS integrates with the existing network and security infrastructure and is capable of discovering the existing network. CS-MARS can be an integral part of maintaining and enforcing the overall security policy and regulatory compliance solution.

Cisco Security Monitoring, Analysis, and Response System (CS-MARS)

CS-MARS is an appliance-based security information management (SIM) system providing security monitoring and correlation services to identify, contain, and respond to networkwide security threats.

CS-MARS is another key solution that extends the Cisco Self-Defending Network initiative and essential deployment for a security information management system.

CS-MARS offers network intelligence by using sophisticated event correlation technology to precisely identify and correlate events, validate threats, pinpoint attack paths, and provide comprehensive security threat control and mitigation solutions. Through various techniques, CS-MARS maps the entire network, thereby providing complete network visibility and reaction capability by leveraging data from all over the network.

Table 23-1 provides a summary of the common features and capabilities of the CS-MARS appliance-based security information management solution.

Table 23-1 *CS-MARS Features and Capabilities*

Feature	Capabilities
Dynamic Session-Based Correlation	• Network-based anomaly detection, including Cisco NetFlow • Behavior-based and rules-based event correlation • Comprehensive built-in and user-defined rules • Automated network address translation (NAT) normalization
Topology Discovery	• Layer 3 and Layer 2 routers, switches, and firewalls • Network intrusion detection system (IDS) blades and appliances • Manual and scheduled discovery • Secure Shell (SSH), Simple Network Protocol (SNMP), Telnet, and device-specific communications
Vulnerability Analysis	• Incident-triggered targeted network-based and host-based fingerprinting • Switch, router, firewall, and NAT configuration analysis • Automated vulnerability scanner data capture • Automated and user-tuned false positive analysis

Table 23-1   *CS-MARS Features and Capabilities (Continued)*

Feature	Capabilities
Incident Analysis and Response	• Role-based security event management dashboard • Session-based event consolidation with full-rule context • Graphical attack path visualization with detailed investigation • Attack path device profiles with endpoint MAC identification • Graphical and detailed sequential attack pattern display • Incident details, including rules, raw events, common vulnerabilities and exposures, and mitigation options • Immediate incident investigation and false positive determination • GUI rule definition in support of custom rules and keyword parsing • Incident escalation with user-based "to-do" work list • Notification, including e-mail, pager, syslog, and SNMP • Integration with existing ticketing and workflow system via Extensible Markup Language (XML) event notification
Query and Reporting	• Low-latency, real-time event query • GUI that supports numerous default queries and customized queries • More than 150 popular reports, including management, operational, and regulatory • Intuitive report generation yielding unlimited customized reports • Data, chart, and trend formats that support HTML and comma-separated vector (CSV) export • Live, batch, template, and e-mail forwarding reporting system • Easy-to-use query structure built for an effective drill down to the information in a specific incident
Administration	• Web interface (HTTPS); roles-based administration with defined privileges • Global Controller hierarchical management of multiple Cisco Security Monitoring, Analysis, and Reporting Systems • Automated, verified updates, including device support, new rules, and features • Continuous compressed raw data and incident archive to offline NFS storage

The information in Table 23-1 is compiled from *Cisco Security Monitoring, Analysis, and Response System 4.3.1 and 5.3.1* at http://www.cisco.com/en/US/products/ps6241/products_data_sheet0900 aecd80272e64.html.

Security Threat Mitigation (STM) System

CS-MARS is a state-of-the-art security threat mitigation (STM) system providing cutting-edge capabilities. New advanced STM features include data sessionization, topological awareness, and mitigation capabilities.

CS-MARS offers security countermeasures by combining state-of-the-art network intelligence, context correlation using the ContextCorrelation feature, vector analysis using the SureVector feature, anomaly detection, hotspot identification, and automated mitigation using the AutoMitigate capabilities. These are defined in the list that follows:

- **Cisco ContextCorrelation:** CS-MARS software includes an integrated ContextCorrelation feature that performs data normalization against the topology by processing the captured raw events and logs, device configurations, and same source and destination applications across Network Address Translation (NAT) boundaries. Corresponding events are grouped into sessions in real-time. System-defined and user-defined correlation rules are then applied to multiple sessions to identify meaningful incidents. CS-MARS has a default set of comprehensive predefined rules, which identify a majority of common anomaly scenarios and day-zero attacks. ContextCorrelation significantly reduces raw event data by packaging the incidents into groups, rather than individual data points.

- **Cisco SureVector:** CS-MARS software includes the integrated SureVector analysis engine that allows the processing of similar event sessions to determine whether threats are valid and have been successful in causing damage. CS-MARS validates threat information by performing endpoint scans to eliminate false positives and by using the SureVector™ engine to investigate the raw data, device logs, and third-party vulnerability assessment data. Further fine-tuning of the system can reduce additional false positives.

- **Cisco AutoMitigate:** CS-MARS software includes an integrated AutoMitigate feature that allows a real-time dynamic mitigation solution to stop the attacks. CS-MARS can identify the offending and compromised system down to the endpoint MAC address. Using the AutoMitigate feature, CS-MARS can identify available devices along the attack path and dynamically provide mitigation recommendations by suggesting the relevant device commands and configurations that can be deployed on a particular device to quickly and accurately prevent or contain an attack.

Figure 23-1 shows CS-MARS with extended security threat mitigation (STM) system capabilities of using Cisco ContextCorrelation, SureVector, and AutoMitigate features.

CS-MARS offers an automated event log collection system capturing data from various heterogeneous network devices (Layer 2 and Layer 3) across multiple devices such as routers, switches, firewalls, IDS, IPS, and server-based systems, aggregating all into a centralized database to perform intelligent correlation and to group related events of the same traffic flow.

Figure 23-1   *CS-MARS—Security Threat Mitigation (STM) System*

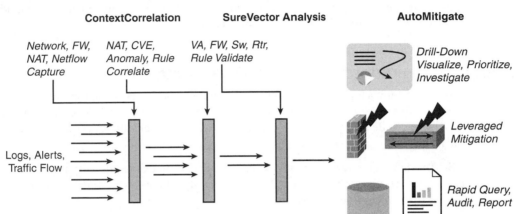

Figure 23-2 depicts how CS-MARS works by capturing raw data and configuration from various devices and processing the isolated events, performing analysis, and correlating threat information into valid incidents, thus greatly reducing false positives.

Figure 23-2   *CS-MARS—How It Works*

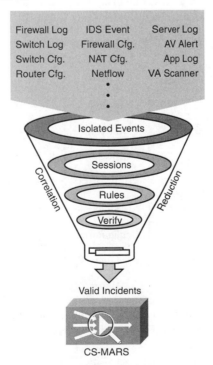

CS-MARS uses a policy-based approach to block security attacks by transforming raw data into actionable intelligence, identifying and correlating real security threats, and providing recommendations for mitigation recommendations.

Topological Awareness and Network Mapping

CS-MARS builds topological awareness and paints network maps of the entire topology by performing discovery of the network devices within the network. CS-MARS is capable of capturing a wide range of Cisco and non-Cisco devices, including Layer 2 and Layer 3 devices.

CS-MARS has an integrated network discovery function that builds a topology map containing device configuration and current security policies, which enables it to model packet flows through a network.

CS-MARS reads a network device configuration and populates into a central database, allowing the construction of a complete topological map of the network.

CS-MARS provides network behavioral analysis by profiling network traffic, capturing raw data, and aggregating and correlating from heterogeneous devices from a wide range of devices in a single CS-MARS appliance.

Figure 23-3 shows CS-MARS capturing raw data and configuration files from various heterogeneous network devices (Layer 2 and Layer 3).

Figure 23-3   *CS-MARS—Receiving Raw Data from Cisco and Non-Cisco Devices*

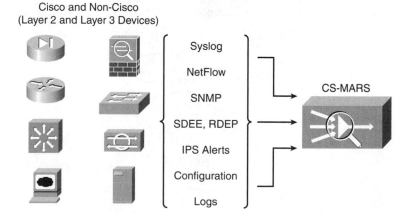

CS-MARS is capable of receiving high volumes of data with its secure and stable architecture. It can receive more than 15,000 events per second or more than 300,000 Cisco NetFlow events per second.

CS-MARS offers a high-performance aggregation and consolidation service by capturing millions of raw events and grouping them efficiently into classified incidents with unprecedented data reduction.

CS-MARS is able to deliver high-performance correlation through inline processing logic and the use of an embedded high-performance database system.

Table 23-2 is a list of supported reporting devices (Cisco and non-Cisco) that can be captured by CS-MARS appliance.

Table 23-2   *CS-MARS Device Support List*

Device Type	Cisco and Non-Cisco Devices
Network	Cisco IOS Software, Cisco Catalyst OS software, Cisco NetFlow, and Extreme Extremeware
Firewall/VPN	Cisco ASA Software, Cisco PIX Security Appliance, Cisco IOS Firewall, Cisco Firewall Services Module (FWSM), Cisco VPN 3000 Concentrator, Checkpoint Firewall-1 NG and VPN-1 versions, NetScreen Firewall, and Nokia Firewall
Intrusion Detection and Prevention	Cisco IDS and IPS Sensor, Cisco IDS Module, Cisco IOS IPS, Cisco ASA IPS Module, Enterasys Dragon NIDS, ISS RealSecure Network Sensor, Snort NIDS, McAfee Intrushield NIDS, NetScreen IDP, OS, and Symantec ManHunt
Vulnerability Assessment	eEye REM, Qualys QualysGuard, and FoundStone FoundScan
Host Security	Cisco Security Agent (CSA), McAfee Entercept, and ISS RealSecure Host Sensor
Host Logs	Windows NT, 2000, and 2003 (agent and agentless), Solaris, and Linux
Antivirus	Symantec Antivirus, Cisco Incident Control System (Cisco ICS), Trend Micro Outbreak Prevention Service (OPS), Network Associates VirusScan, and McAfee ePO
Authentication Servers	Cisco Secure Access Control Server (ACS)
Applications	Web Servers (IIS, iPlanet, and Apache), Oracle audit logs, Network Appliance NetCache, and ISS site protector
Universal	Universal device support to aggregate and monitor any application syslog
Custom	Support additional and custom devices using the custom log parser feature

The information in Table 23-2 is compiled from *Cisco Security Monitoring, Analysis, and Response System 4.3.1 and 5.3.1* at http://www.cisco.com/en/US/products/ps6241/products_data_sheet0900 aecd80272e64.html.

NOTE   CS-MARS continues to improve its device support. For a comprehensive, up-to-date list with supported version information, refer to the following URL: http://www.cisco.com/en/US/products/ps6241/products_device_support_tables_list.html.

Key Concepts—Events, Sessions, Rules, and Incidents

CS-MARS uses various terms to define contextual analysis and the process of threat investigation. These may vary from the traditional terminologies used for other systems:

- **Event:** Each log event (raw data) received by CS-MARS from any reporting device (such as syslog, SNMP trap, NetFlow, IPS alert, Security Device Event Exchange (SDEE), or Windows log) is referred to as an event in CS-MARS. Retrieved raw messages from the reporting devices are mapped into events.

- **Sessions:** Correlated events that are related to the same network flow received from one or more devices. The session is created for like events that are common to a particular criteria—for example, timestamp, source IP address, source port, destination IP address, destination port, or protocol information. Figure 23-4 depicts a CS-MARS session.

- **Rule:** Used to perform logic on events that create sessions and incidents. A rule defines patterns of normalized event types and the notification action CS-MARS will take when the rule fires. These patterns can be signatures of attacks, probes, configuration errors, or anomalous network traffic behavior. CS-MARS has two types of rules: inspection rules and drop rules.

- **Incident:** A session matched against a rule that is indicative of malicious behavior. An incident is triggered when a rule or collection of rules matched. As shown in Figure 23-5, incidents can contain one or more events detailing the event correlation, such as a complete story of an attack. Rules fire to create incidents.

Figure 23-4 depicts how a session is interpreted in CS-MARS.

Figure 23-4   *CS-MARS —Session Interpretation*

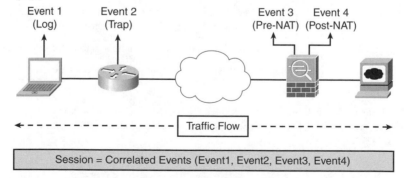

Figure 23-5 depicts how an incident is interpreted in CS-MARS.

Figure 23-5 *CS-MARS—Incident Interpretation*

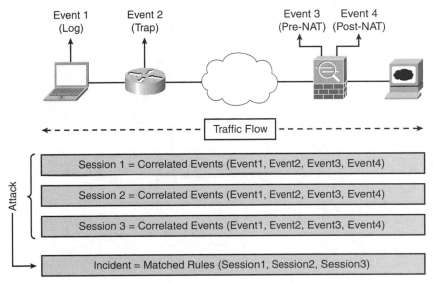

Event Processing in CS-MARS

CS-MARS uses the following steps to process events when it receives a raw message.

1 Receive raw messages from network devices either via pulling mode or listening mode

2 Parse raw messages

3 Normalize raw messages to events—statically map raw messages from different vendor devices to CS-MARS known event types

4 Sessionization/NAT correlation—identify commonality within the event, such as source IP/port, destination IP/port, protocol to sessionize events

5 Run events against rule engine

6 False positive analysis

7 Vulnerability assessment against suspected hosts

8 Traffic profiling and statistical anomaly detection

Figure 23-6 shows the event process flowchart in CS-MARS.

Figure 23-6 *CS-MARS Event Process Flowchart*

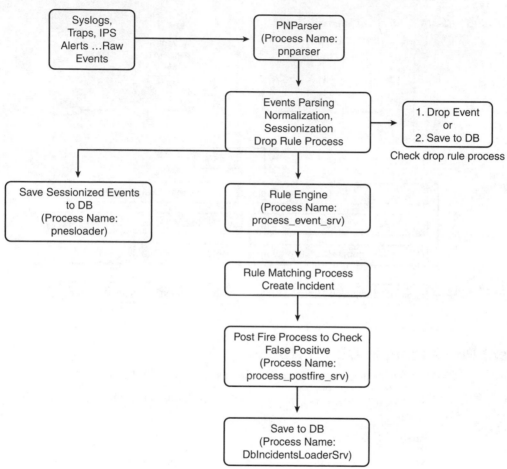

The information in Figure 23-6 is compiled from the Cisco Networkers Breakout Session presentation *#BRKSEC-3006—Network Security Monitoring and Correlation with CS-MARS.*

False Positive in CS-MARS

CS-MARS interprets false positives differently than other systems. In general terms, when a message is considered a false positive, this means that a system has incorrectly identified an attack but in reality it did not happen. However, in CS-MARS a false positive means the attack was identified correctly but it was unsuccessful against the target victim.

There are four basic types of false positives in CS-MARS:

- System Confirmed False Positive

- Unconfirmed False Positive
- User Confirmed False Positive
- User Confirmed Positive

Figure 23-7 illustrates the false positive process flowchart in CS-MARS.

Figure 23-7 *CS-MARS False Positive Process Flowchart*

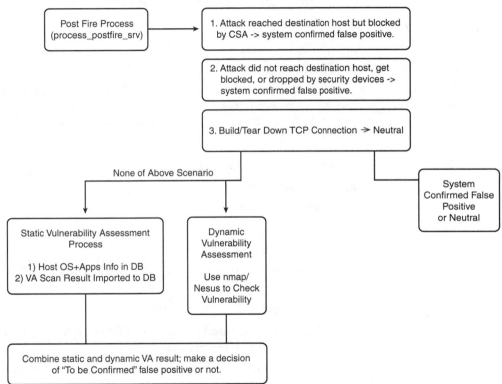

The information in Figure 23-7 is compiled from the Cisco Networkers Breakout Session presentation *#BRKSEC-3006—Network Security Monitoring and Correlation with CS-MARS.*

Deploying CS-MARS

There are several ways to deploy CS-MARS appliance into the network. Careful planning is required before considering and selecting the appropriate CS-MARS model. The decision greatly depends on the anticipated events per second (EPS) and NetFlow flows per session (FPS) for that network or segment.

The following are two types of CS-MARS deployment scenarios:

- **Standalone:** A single CS-MARS is deployed into the network collecting raw data from one or more network devices. Standalone deployment is also referred to as Local Controller (LC).

- **Global:** Two or more LCs are deployed into the network collecting raw data from various network devices. In this setup, a separate Global Controller (GC) CS-MARS appliance is required to manage the LC. The GC does not receive raw data from the reporting devices; it is only used to manage the LC and overall CS-MARS deployment.

Standalone and Local Controllers (LC)

There is no major difference between LC and standalone CS-MARS deployments. Both scenarios use the same hardware and software. The only difference is that standalone is an independent, fully operated CS-MARS deployment, whereas LC works in conjunction with GC and communicates primarily with the GC.

The LC performs the following functions:

- Collects all raw events from various devices
- Sessionizes events across different devices
- Applies inspection rules for incidents
- Performs false positive analysis
- Delivers consolidated information in diagrams, charts, queries, reports, and notifications
- Detects inactive reporting devices
- Derives set of IOS/IPS Distributed Threat Mitigation (DTM) signatures based on attacks reported by monitored Cisco IPS appliances
- Acts as a repository for the IOS/IPS DTM signatures, from which IOS/IPS devices can download current signature sets

Each LC model differs in its capability to process and store events from various reporting devices.

Table 23-3 shows a complete list of CS-MARS models and their capabilities (EPS and FPS) that can be deployed as local and standalone controllers.

Table 23-3   *CS-MARS Local and Standalone Controllers*

CS-MARS Model	Events/ Second	NetFlow/ Second	RAID Level	Power Supply
20R (CS-MARS-20R-K9)	50	1,500	None	Single
20 (CS-MARS-20-K9)	500	15,000	None	Single
50 (CS-MARS-50-K9)	1,000	30,000	0	Single
100E (CS-MARS-100E-K9)	3,000	75,000	1 + 0	Redundant
100 (CS-MARS-100-K9)	5,000	150,000	1 + 0	Redundant
110R (CS-MARS-110R-K9)	4,500	75,000	1 + 0	Redundant
110 (CS-MARS-110-K9)	7,500	150,000	1 + 0	Redundant
200 (CS-MARS-200-K9)	10,000	300,000	1 + 0	Redundant
210 (CS-MARS-210-K9)	15,000	300,000	1 + 0	Redundant

The Events per Second (EPS) listed in Table 23-3 are quoted as the maximum events per second with dynamic correlation and all other features enabled.

If high availability is required in CS-MARS deployment, begin at a CS-MARS model 100 (CS-MARS-100-K9), which has RAID 1 + 0 capabilities. The models with RAID 1 + 0 have redundant power supplies and hot swappable drives. The CS-MARS models 110 (CS-MARS-110-K9) and 210 (CS-MARS-210-K9) have special built-in battery backups for RAID cache.

LCs receive and pull raw data from a wide range of reporting devices, such as routers, switches, firewalls, IDS/IPS systems, and vulnerability assessment systems.

The LC summarizes information about the health of the network based on data it receives from the reporting devices that it monitors.

Figure 23-8 depicts a standalone LC being deployed as an independent appliance and is a fully operated CS-MARS implementation.

Figure 23-8 *CS-MARS Standalone Local Controller (LC)*

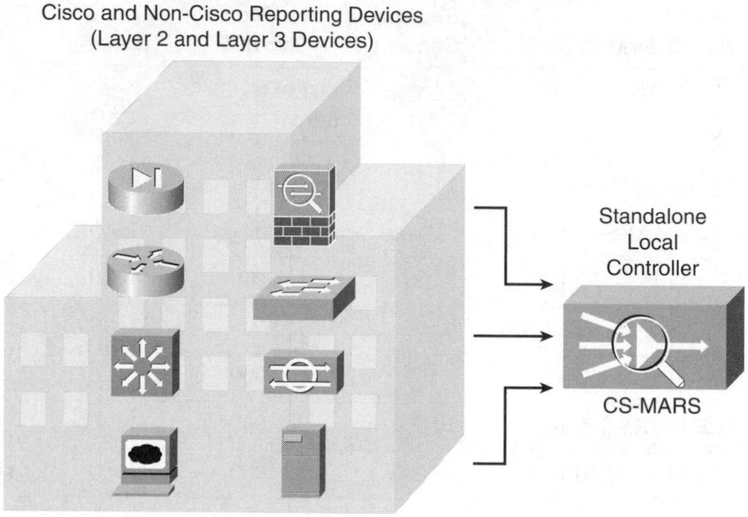

Global Controllers (GC)

The Global Controller (GC) is used to manage two or more LC zone deployments allowing scaling of the network monitoring without increasing the management burden on the LC.

The GC provides complete control and management of the LC across various sites (zones) and provides a single user interface for defining new device types, inspection rules, reports, and queries.

GC provides a central console to manage multiple LCs. It also provides additional capabilities, including

- Global authentication across all LCs
- Unified report generation across all LCs
- Unified rule generation for LC deployment
- Global view of the network
- Centralized software management
- Reduced traffic across WAN links

Three basic CS-MARS models are available for GC deployment scenarios.

Table 23-4 shows a complete list of CS-MARS models and their capabilities for GC deployments.

Table 23-4   *CS-MARS Global Controllers (GC)*

CS-MARS GC Model	Models Supported (LC Management)	Max LC	RAID Level
CS-MARS-GCM (CS-MARS-GCm-K9)	CS-MARS 20R/20/50 only	5	1 + 0
CS-MARS-GC (CS-MARS-GC-K9)	CS-MARS 20R/20/50/100/ 100e/200 only	Unlimited	1 + 0
CS-MARS-GC2R (CS-MARS-GC2R-K9)	CS-MARS 20/50 only	5	1 + 0
CS-MARS-GC2 (CS-MARS-GC2-K9)	CS-MARS 110/110R/210 only	Unlimited	1 + 0

NOTE   All CS-MARS GC models have redundant power capability.

Figure 23-9 depicts a GC scenario deployed at the central HQ Data Center managing several LCs across different sites.

Software Versioning Information

Two major software versions are available in CS-MARS deployment. There is significant feature parity across the two releases supporting different hardware platforms. The appliance model has little impact on the available features support across the two releases.

- **Software Version 4.3.x:** The 4.3.x software release supports the CS-MARS models MARS-20R, MARS-20, MARS-50, MARS-100e, MARS-100, MARS-200, MARS-GCM, and MARS-GC appliances.

- **Software Version 5.3.x:** The 5.3.x software release supports features on new appliance CS-MARS models MARS-110R, MARS-110, MARS-210, MARS-GC2, and MARS-CG2R.

NOTE   Database table structure changes between software versions; thus, an existing database cannot be restored onto a different software version, because it can cause data corruption. If you do not require preserving any configuration and event data, it is better to start with a clean system. Reimaging it can be much faster than the upgrade procedure.

Figure 23-9 *CS-MARS Global Controller*

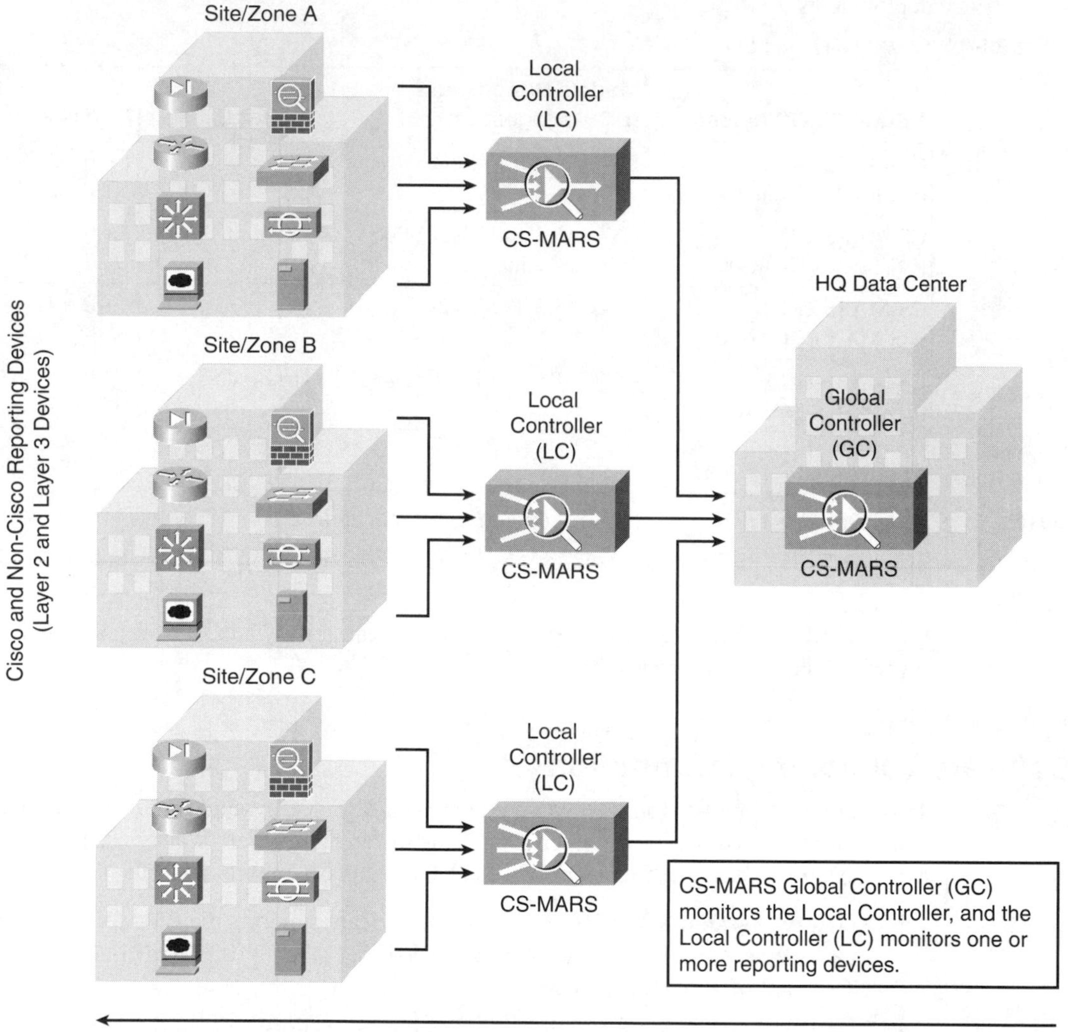

Reporting and Mitigation Devices

From a top-down deployment perspective (refer to Figure 23-9), CS-MARS GC monitors the LC, and the LC monitors one or more reporting devices.

A reporting device is any Layer 2 or Layer 3 device (Cisco or non-Cisco) that provides CS-MARS with raw data about the network from traffic flows and the configuration files, allowing CS-MARS to analyze and respond to possible attack targets.

A mitigation device is any reporting device that can deny a traffic flow within the attack path.

CS-MARS provides mitigation support in two forms:

- For supported Layer 3 devices, CS-MARS provides recommendations for a suggested Layer 3 device for mitigation and a set of corresponding commands that can be used to stop an ongoing, detected attack. This information can also be used to manually block the attack.

- For supported Layer 2 devices, CS-MARS provides recommendations for a suggested Layer 2 device for mitigation and a set of corresponding commands to stop the ongoing detected attack.

NOTE   Refer to Table 23-2 for a complete list of the supported reporting devices.

Based on the confirmed incident and correlated data, CS-MARS provides suggested mitigation rules for detected attacks and, in some cases, it can push those rules to the mitigation device, to stop the attack by restricting network access to the infected hosts.

Figure 23-10 illustrates an example of CS-MARS recommendation for enforcement that points along the attack path with a set of corresponding commands to stop the attack.

Levels of Operation

Another important consideration to be taken into account when deploying CS-MARS is the type of operation that CS-MARS will perform. This needs to be decided before CS-MARS is configured to receive raw data from reporting devices.

Three basic levels of operation exist in CS-MARS, based on the type of data it can collect from the reporting device. These levels dictate the capability of CS-MARS to identify attacks from end to end:

- **Basic:** At the basic level 1, CS-MARS performs similar to a smart Syslog server, collecting logs from the reporting devices and supporting routine queries and basic reports.

- **Intermediate:** At the intermediate level 2, CS-MARS processes isolated events and performs session-based correlation, including resolving NAT and PAT translations at the IP address layer.

- **Advanced:** At the advanced level 3, CS-MARS functions at its full potential with all its capabilities. When advanced operation is enabled, the CS-MARS appliance discovers and displays the full topology, draws attack paths, and enables MAC address lookups of the hosts involved in an attack.

Figure 23-10 *CS-MARS Mitigation Device Identified and Corresponding Commands Recommended*

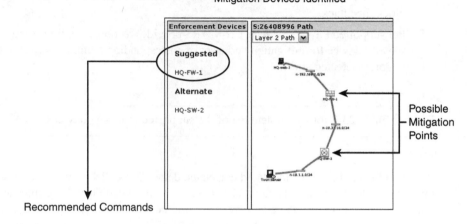

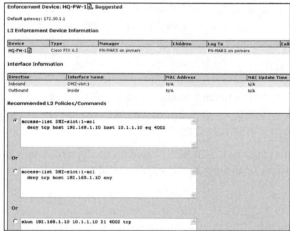

Table 23-5 summarizes the CS-MARS level of operations and the functionality enabled at each level.

Table 23-5 *CS-MARS Level of Operation and Functionality*

Level of Operation	Functionality Enabled
Basic Level 1	• Basic syslog functionality • Event correlation • Query, reports, and chart support • NetFlow anomaly detection
Intermediate Level 2	• Event and session-based correlation • NAT and PAT resolution • IP address lookup of attackers and targets
Advanced Level 3	• MAC address lookup of attackers and targets • Topologies enabled

Traffic Flows and Ports to Be Opened

Required traffic flows identify the necessary protocol and port numbers that must be allowed by gateways/firewalls/ACLs if they separate the CS-MARS appliance from a reporting device, mitigation device, or supporting device (as listed in Table 23-2). Different protocol and port numbers are used for varying functions when CS-MARS communicates with a reporting device.

Additionally, traffic flows between a GC and any monitored LCs must be allowed.

Table 23-6 identifies the various traffic flows and their associated protocol and port numbers that must be opened if there is a gateway, firewall, ACL, or any type of filtering device between CS-MARS and the reporting devices.

Table 23-6 *CS-MARS Required Traffic Flows and Ports to Be Opened*

Category	Protocols	Comments
Management GUI	HTTPS/SSL (TCP port 443)	This traffic must be enabled for GC to LC, as well as from the CS-MARS appliance to the computer used to manage the appliance.
Management CLI	SSH (TCP 22)	—
Support Servers and Services	DNS (TCP and UDP port 53) NTP (TCP/UDP port 123) SMTP (TCP port 25) ICMP (IP level service) NFS	SMTP is used for outgoing mail services. ICMP is useful for diagnostics and troubleshooting and is required by the dynamic vulnerability scanner. NFS is used for network-attached storage (NAS) servers to retain data archives for MARS. Because NFS ports are negotiated, it is recommended that the NAS server be located on the same network segment as the MARS appliance.

continues

Table 23-6 *CS-MARS Required Traffic Flows and Ports to Be Opened (Continued)*

Category	Protocols	Comments
Upgrade from GUI	HTTPS or FTP (TCP port 20 and 21)	Options from within the GUI require it.
Upgrade from CLI	HTTPS, HTTP (TCP port 80), or FTP	At the command line, the upgrade can be done from the DVD drive, which does not require extra opened ports.
Discovery of reporting device or mitigation device	Telnet (TCP port 23) SSH FTP SNMP (TCP 161)	MARS appliance periodically contacts the devices to ensure that they are operational.
Monitoring of reporting device or mitigation device	HTTPS SSH SNMP Telnet FTP PostOffice (UDP port 45000) RDEP (SSL) SDEE (SSL) syslog (UDP port 514)	
Policy query to Cisco Security Manager	HTTPS	Enable HTTPS access to the Common Services 3.0 server by the CS-MARS appliance.
Global Controller and Local Controller data synchronization	Proprietary (port 8444)	This port must remain open on the outside and inside interfaces to ensure accurate data correlation operations of the GC.
NetFlow	NetFlow (TCP port 2055)	Enable Spanning Trees between switches (distribution and access switch, not the core). Ports can be changed on which the appliance listens for NetFlow traffic on the Admin, NetFlow Config page.

Table 23-6   *CS-MARS Required Traffic Flows and Ports to Be Opened (Continued)*

Category	Protocols	Comments
Checkpoint	OPSEC-LEA (TCP port 18184) OPSEC-CA (TCP 18210) SSLCA (TCP port 18184) OPSEC-CPMI (TCP port 18190)	Used by Checkpoint devices only. CA is used for pulling a certificate for the OPSEC application.
Oracle Database	Oracle Database Listener (TCP port 1521)	Used by Oracle only.
Microsoft SQL Server	MS SQL (TCP port 1433)	Used by FoundStone and eEye.

The information in Table 23-6 is compiled from "Install and Setup Guide for Cisco Security MARS, Release 5.2.x" at http://www.cisco.com/en/US/docs/security/security_management/cs-mars/5.2/installation/guide/plan.html.

In addition to the listings in Table 23-6, if the GC and LC are separated by a firewall or any type of filtering device, the ports listed in Table 23-7 need to be allowed explicitly, on both the inside and outside interfaces of the firewall, to ensure proper operation of the GC.

Table 23-7   *CS-MARS Required Traffic Ports to Be Opened for Global Controller to Local Controller Communication*

TCP Port	Function
22	Secure Shell (SSH) used by LC for topology and device discovery
443	Hypertext Transport Protocol with Secure Sockets Layer (HTTPS) used for user interface access
8444	Cisco Proprietary data synchronization between a GC and LCs

The information in Table 23-7 is compiled from "User Guide for Cisco Security MARS Global Controller, Release 5.2.x" at http://www.cisco.com/en/US/docs/security/security_management/cs-mars/5.2/user/guide/global_controller/gccfg.html.

Web-Based Management Interface

The CS-MARS appliance can be centrally managed through a secure web-based interface supporting role-based administration.

The web-based management interface is easy to use and user friendly using a tabbed, hyperlinked, browser-based interface approach. The web-based interface can be accessed from any computer on the network that has IP reachability to the CS-MARS appliance. The web-based management interface can be used to perform all administrative functions.

Figure 23-11 shows a sample output of CS-MARS web-based management interface dashboard (Summary page).

Figure 23-11 *CS-MARS—Management Dashboard Summary Page*

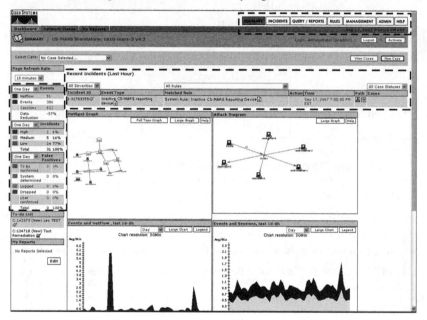

As shown in Figure 23-12, the web-based management interface offers seven menu option tabs in the right corner, which further allow navigating to the pages relevant to the tab's subtabs. Figure 23-12 shows sample outputs from each of the seven menu option tabs and their subtabs from the management interface dashboard.

Figure 23-12   *CS-MARS Web-Based Management—Seven Menu Option Tabs and Subtabs*

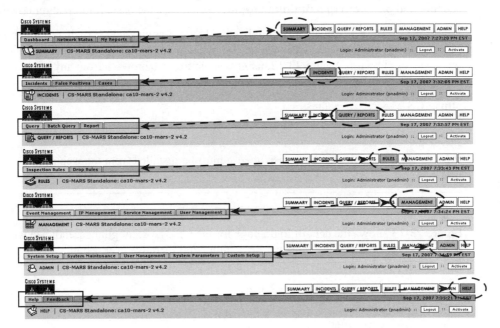

Initializing CS-MARS

Depending on the LC or GC, and whether you are using software version 4.3.x or version 5.3.x, several parameters need to be configured on the CS-MARS appliance system. These can either be configured via the CLI console or the web-based management interface.

After booting the CS-MARS appliance for the first time, you need to configure the following basic parameters as part of the initialization process using the CLI console. Basic parameters include the following:

- Hostname
- IP address and subnet mask
- Default gateway addresses
- DNS server IP addresses (if DNS is used)
- NTP server address (if NTP is used)
- Time, date, and time zone

Login via the console access to the CS-MARS system using the default administrative user account and password (**pnadmin/pnadmin**) to complete the basic initialization process.

After the CS-MARS appliance is initialized, all the remaining tasks, such as adding the reporting and mitigation devices, can be completed using the web-based management interface, as shown in Figure 23-12, using a standard web browser from any client PC on the network as follows:

https://CS-MARS_ip_address

NOTE   Prior to using the system, the device license must be installed from the web console as the first step.

Figure 23-13 shows the default login page for the CS-MARS appliance. Indicate whether it is an LC or a GC and log in using the default administrative user account and password (**pnadmin/pnadmin**) or any other user account provided by the administrator.

Figure 23-13   *Default Login Page for CS-MARS Appliance*

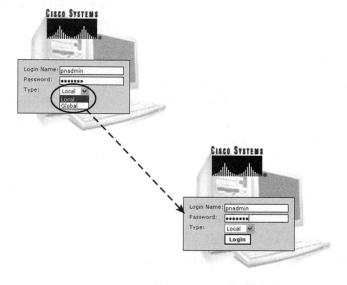

TIP	For a comprehensive list of configurations and the user guide, refer to the following Cisco documentation pages: http://www.cisco.com/en/US/products/ps6241/products_user_guide_list.html.

Summary

Because of increased security attack frequency, security monitoring and correlation of network infrastructure is extremely crucial. The result is that each component within the infrastructure is enabled to generate various logs and alerts to yield essential information to aid forensic analysis, auditing, and threat mitigation. Unfortunately, this generates a tremendous amount of raw data for the end user to analyze and effectively utilize for security threat mitigation.

The Cisco Security Monitoring, Analysis, and Response System (CS-MARS) appliance-based security information management (SIM) system offers a comprehensive solution to address this issue.

The CS-MARS offers network intelligence to precisely identify and correlate events, pinpoint attack paths, and provide a comprehensive security threat control and mitigation solution.

This chapter provided an overview of the CS-MARS solution using various illustrations.

The chapter provided the core concepts of the CS-MARS appliance and its features and capabilities, and highlighted the key concepts necessary to understanding and implementing the CS-MARS solution.

The chapter provided an overview of CS-MARS deployment scenarios and a basic overview of configuring CS-MARS appliance. For more information on CS-MARS deployment setups and configurations, refer to the following:

Security Monitoring with Cisco Security MARS
http://www.ciscopress.com/title/1587052709

Security Threat Mitigation and Response: Understanding Cisco Security MARS, Adobe Reader
http://www.ciscopress.com/title/1587054086

References

http://www.cisco.com/go/mars

http://www.cisco.com/en/US/products/ps6241/products_data_sheet0900aecd
805cae35.html

http://www.cisco.com/en/US/products/ps6241/products_data_sheet0900aecd
80272e64.html

http://www.cisco.com/univercd/cc/td/doc/product/vpn/ciscosec/mars/5_2/uglc5x/
taskflow.htm#

http://www.cisco.com/en/US/products/ps6241/prod_quick_installation_guide09186a
0080851b91.html

http://www.cisco.com/en/US/products/ps6241/products_installation_guide_book
09186a008083b016.html

http://www.cisco.com/en/US/products/ps6241/products_user_guide_book09186a
008083e365.html

http://www.cisco.com/cn/US/products/ps6241/products_user_guide_book09186a
008084ffa8.html

http://www.cisco.com/en/US/products/ps6241/products_installation_and_configuration_
guide_chapter09186a00804c4dba.html

http://www.cisco.com/en/US/products/ps6241/products_installation_guide_chapter09
186a008083b6d0.html

http://www.cisco.com/en/US/products/ps6241/prod_installation_guides_list.html

http://www.cisco.com/en/US/products/ps6241/products_user_guide_list.html

http://www.ciscopress.com/title/1587052709

http://www.ciscopress.com/title/1587053322

Networkers Breakout Session: *BRKSEC-3006—Network Security Monitoring and
Correlation with CS-MARS*

PART V

Security Management

Security and Policy Management

Today, network and network security have become vital components of the organizational operational process. In most cases, both operations are managed independently using separate network management and security management tools. Managing an integrated network security fabric requires a comprehensive and integrated management solution that can simplify the operational processes.

Cisco Security and Policy Management solutions provide the next-generation unified security management tools designed for the operational management, policy administration, and core security management functions.

The chapter provides details of the various applications available in the Cisco Security Management suite.

The chapter takes a closer look at the core concepts of the various security and policy management application tools, providing features and capabilities, and highlights some of the key concepts and functionality.

Cisco Security Management Solutions

Cisco Security and Policy Management solutions offer a suite of applications that provide the capability to view and manage the security components of the entire network while assuring complete corporate security throughout every area of the distributed network.

Cisco Security and Policy Management solutions provide easy-to-use interfaces to manage core functional areas of network and security management, including configuration, monitoring, analysis, threat identification and mitigation, and network auditing functions.

The chapter covers the following set of Cisco security and policy management applications:

- Cisco Security Manager
- Cisco Router and Security Device Manager (SDM)
- Cisco Adaptive Security Device Manager (ASDM)
- Cisco PIX Device Manager (PDM)
- Cisco IPS Device Manager (IDM)

Cisco Security Manager

Cisco Security Manager is a market-leading security and policy management software application for managing network security functions.

Cisco Security Manager is an essential tool to centrally provision all aspects of device configuration and security policies for firewalls, including PIX Security Appliance, Adaptive Security Appliance (ASA), and Firewall Services Module (FWSM), Virtual Private Networks (VPN) technologies, and Intrusion Prevention System (IPS) services across Cisco routers, security appliances, Catalyst 6500/7600 series devices, and Catalyst switch security services modules (VPNSM, FWSM).

Cisco Security Manager offers configuration, deployment, and management services across all major Cisco security devices. Cisco Security Manager can provision small networks of fewer than ten devices and scale to large-scale networks with thousands of devices.

NOTE   The Cisco Security Manager is part of the Cisco Security Management suite—a framework of products and technologies, delivering scalable policy administration and enforcement for the Cisco Self-Defending Network. The suite also includes the CS-MARS product for monitoring and mitigation. CS-MARS is covered in Chapter 23, "Security Monitoring and Correlation."

For more details about the Cisco Security Management suite, refer to the following Cisco documentation URL: http://www.cisco.com/en/US/netsol/ns647/networking_solutions_sub_solution_home.html.

Cisco Security Manager—Features and Capabilities

Cisco Security Manager provides the capability to deploy and manage security policies on Cisco security devices.

Cisco Security Manager supports integrated provisioning of firewall, VPN, and IPS services across Cisco IOS routers, PIX, and ASA security appliances, and Catalyst 6500/7600 services modules (FWSM and VPNSM).

Cisco Security Manager also supports provisioning of various platform-specific configurations—for example, Interface parameters, Routing protocols, Quality of Service (QoS), Network Address Translation (NAT), Syslog, Dynamic Host Configuration Protocol (DHCP), Multicast, Authentication, Authorization and Accounting (AAA), and so forth.

Cisco Security Manager offers various features and functions. The following are some of its common capabilities:

- A single, integrated application for managing security across all major Cisco security devices

- Integrated service-based and device-based provisioning firewall, VPN, and IPS management, all natively from a single interface
- Device configuration rollback; capability to roll back to a previous configuration if necessary
- Network visualization in the form of topology maps
- Workflow mode
- Multiple views for task optimization
- Scaling to many hundreds of remote sites
- Enforcement of corporate rules and best-practice guidelines
- Sophisticated rule analysis and optimization
- Collaboration between provisioning, configuration, monitoring, mitigation, and identity
- Integration between Cisco Security Manager and CS-MARS
- Native IPS Policy Management on IPS, Catalyst, ASA, and ISR platforms
- Advanced IOS Interface, platform settings discovery
- Transparent device manager read-only cross-launch to access Adaptive Security Device Manager (ADSM), Security Device Manager (SDM), and IPS Device Manager (IDM)
- Native IPS management in v3.1 with the same look and feel as other components, such as firewall and VPN management
- Capability to discover Cisco IOS Software-based router configurations
- Unified Management for FW/VPN/IPS security policies
- Complete VPN solution (IPsec, GRE, DMVPN, Site-to-Site, Remote Access, EasyVPN, and SSL VPN)
- VPN Discovery support—capability to discover Site-to-Site and Remote-Access VPNs
- SSL VPN support on both ASA and IOS platforms
- Native Cat6500/7600 support—router ACLs (RACL), VLAN ACLs (VACL), virtual local area networks (VLAN), and the capability to arrange them to the right FWSM and virtual context.
- Inventory report showing the managed devices with device status, OS versions, platform, and policies assigned to a particular device
- Management protocol connectivity test
- Detailed user-activity report showing exactly what the user changed during login

- Role-based access control (RBAC) and privilege-based management access integrated with Cisco Secure Access Control Server (ACS) for multiadministrator operations.

- High availability

- Scaleable deployment through the use of distributed deployment

- Automated network and security compliance audit and analysis

Cisco Security Manager provides centralized policy administration of Cisco security appliances, integrated security routers, and security service modules for

- Firewall management

- VPN management

- IPS management

- Platform management

Figure 24-1 depicts a high-level overview of Cisco Security Manager providing integrated security management provisioning functions.

Figure 24-1 *Cisco Security Manager—Integrated Security Configuration Management Application*

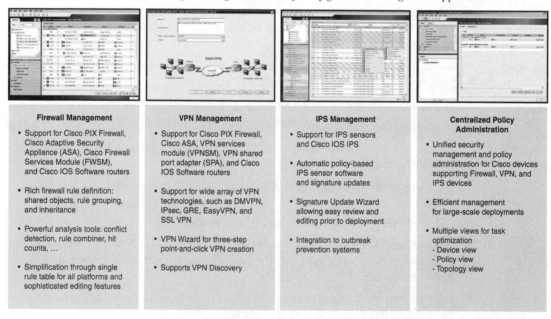

Firewall Management

- Support for Cisco PIX Firewall, Cisco Adaptive Security Appliance (ASA), Cisco Firewall Services Module (FWSM), and Cisco IOS Software routers

- Rich firewall rule definition: shared objects, rule grouping, and inheritance

- Powerful analysis tools: conflict detection, rule combiner, hit counts, ...

- Simplification through single rule table for all platforms and sophisticated editing features

VPN Management

- Support for Cisco PIX Firewall, Cisco ASA, VPN services module (VPNSM), VPN shared port adapter (SPA), and Cisco IOS Software routers

- Support for wide array of VPN technologies, such as DMVPN, IPsec, GRE, EasyVPN, and SSL VPN

- VPN Wizard for three-step point-and-click VPN creation

- Supports VPN Discovery

IPS Management

- Support for IPS sensors and Cisco IOS IPS

- Automatic policy-based IPS sensor software and signature updates

- Signature Update Wizard allowing easy review and editing prior to deployment

- Integration to outbreak prevention systems

Centralized Policy Administration

- Unified security management and policy administration for Cisco devices supporting Firewall, VPN, and IPS devices

- Efficient management for large-scale deployments

- Multiple views for task optimization
  - Device view
  - Policy view
  - Topology view

The information in Figure 24-1 is taken from the Cisco general product presentation on Cisco Security Manager.

Cisco Security Manager—Firewall Management

Cisco Security Manager supports configuration and management of Cisco firewall policies across multiple platforms, including

- Cisco IOS Software Router
- Cisco PIX appliance
- Cisco ASA appliance
- Cisco Catalyst Firewall Service Modules (FWSM)
- Cisco Catalyst 6500/7600

Following are some of the common features and capabilities in the firewall management system:

- Unified firewall service/table for all security platforms
- Native Cisco IOS Software ACL (non-CBAC) support; permit/deny traffic on interfaces through the use of access control lists (ACL)
- Inspection rules; filter TCP and UDP packets based on application-layer protocol session information
- AAA and Authentication Proxy rules; filter traffic based on authentication and authorization for users logged in to the network or that access the Internet through HTTP, HTTPS, FTP, or Telnet sessions
- Web-filtering rules, using URL-filtering software, such as Websense, to deny access to specific websites
- Transparent firewall rules, and enabling transparent firewall device to be deployed in an existing network without having to reconfigure statically defined devices
- Firewall rule sharing, inheritance, and local rules
- Reusable shared objects (for example, hosts, networks, services)
- Cross-launch of read-only Cisco Adaptive Security Device Manager (ASDM) for device status and real-time Syslog, plus the collaboration between Cisco ASDM and Cisco Security Manager
- Interface roles (apply rule to group of interfaces)
- Intelligent analysis and query of firewall policies
- Autogeneration of rules that are required by user policies
- Built-in end-to-end VLAN management for Cisco Catalyst 6500 for FWSM configurations
- Firewall security context management for Cisco FWSM and Cisco ASA
- Discovery and import of external configuration changes

Cisco Security Manager—VPN Management

The Cisco Security Manager supports configuration and management of Cisco VPN policies across multiple platforms, including

- Cisco IOS Software Router
- Cisco PIX Appliance
- Cisco ASA Appliance
- Cisco Catalyst VPN Service Modules (VPNSM)
- Cisco VPN Shared Port Adapter (SPA)

The VPN management system allows setup and configuration of IPsec Site-to-Site and Remote Access VPNs. Supported VPN technologies include

- IPsec
- GRE
- DMVPN
- Easy VPN
- SSL VPN

Some of the common features and capabilities in the VPN management system are

- Support for Site-to-Site and Remote Access VPNs
- Easy-to-use three-step wizard-based approach to create an IPsec VPN tunnel
- SSL VPN wizard
- Support of hub-and-spoke, full-mesh, and point-to-point topologies
- Capability to modify Internet Key Exchange (IKE) proposals, Internet Security Association and Key Management Protocol (ISAKMP) settings, Network Address Translation (NAT) traversal, and fragmentation settings
- Visualization of VPNs on the topology-centric map
- VPN Discovery feature, import existing VPN settings
- Virtual routing and forwarding VRF-aware IPsec VPN
- IPsec VPN high availability

Cisco Security Manager—IPS Management

Cisco Security Manager supports configuration and management of Cisco IPS policies across multiple platforms, including

- Cisco IOS Intrusion Prevention System (IPS)
- Cisco IPS 4200 series appliance

- Cisco Catalyst 6500 Series Intrusion Detection System Module (IDSM-2)
- Cisco IPS Advanced Integration Module (IPS-AIM) for router
- Cisco Advanced Inspection and Protection Security Services Module (AIP-SSM) for ASA

The IPS management system allows setup and configuration of IPS sensor management, including

- Automatic policy-based IPS sensor software and signature updates
- Signature update wizard allowing easy review and editing prior to deployment
- Integration to outbreak prevention systems

The IPS management system allows setup and configuration of IPS sensors software. Supported IPS Software versions include

- Cisco IPS Version 5.1 and 6.0
- Cisco IOS IPS 12.4(11)T2 and later

Some of the common features and capabilities in the IPS management system include

- Native IPS support with full IPS management integration into Cisco Security Manager.
- IPS device-centric signature view.
- Policy-centric signature view.
- Easy to use three-step wizard-based approach to apply signature update or sensor software update to set devices.
- Signature update automation: automatic policy-based IPS sensor software and signature updates.
- IPS subscription licensing provisioning.
- Enterprise-class operations environment: role-based access control, policy rollback, configuration archive, deployment manager, cloning and creation of signatures, policy sharing, and inheritance.
- Cross-launch for Cisco IPS Device Manager (IDM).
- Cross-launch of embedded IEV (Cisco IPS Event Viewer) to view real-time IPS events and collaborate between security events and policy management.
- Cross-launch of Cisco IEV to IPS Rule in Cisco Security Manager. Right-click IPS alert in the IEV event viewer. Click Go to CSM to bring up Cisco Security Manager with the corresponding device and IPS signature selected.

Cisco Security Manager—Platform Management

In addition to firewall, VPN, and IPS management, the Cisco Security Manager supports configuration and management of platform-specific configuration parameters, for example:

- Device settings (hostname, IP address, SNMP, NTP)
- Interface parameters and settings
- Logging setup, server setup, and syslog servers
- Multicast
- Network Address Translation (NAT), address pools, translation options, and translation rules
- IP Routing; Static, Routing Information Protocol (RIP), Open Short Path First (OSPF), Enhanced Interior Gateway Routing Protocol (EIGRP), Border Gateway Protocol (BGP)
- Service policy rules (priority queues and Quality of Service (QoS))
- IOS Security settings, antispoofing, Floodguard, fragment, and timeouts
- Manage VLANs, interfaces, and VACLs on Cisco Catalyst 6500 series

The Cisco Security Manager supports the wide range of platform settings in the previous list that supplies coverage beyond the basic firewall, VPN, and IPS services.

Cisco Security Manager—Architecture

Cisco Security Manager is built with robust architecture to centrally provision all aspects of device configuration and security policies for Cisco security devices.

Figure 24-2 illustrates the system architecture of the Cisco Security Manager.

NOTE   The information in Figure 24-2 is taken from the Cisco general product presentation on Cisco Security Manager.

Figure 24-2   *Cisco Security Manager—System Architecture*

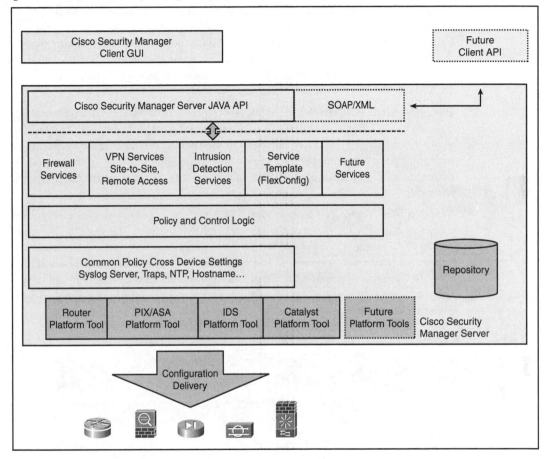

Cisco Security Manager—Configuration Views

Cisco Security Manager provides a powerful, user-friendly, easy-to-use interface. The simple and flexible user interface provides users with the capability to perform complex tasks with great ease.

Cisco Security Manager provides three feature-rich, simple-to-use views into the management system for users to manage devices and policies. Users can swap among these user views according to their needs at any time:

- **Device-centric view (DCV):** Enables users to view the properties of devices being managed, add/delete devices from the Cisco Security Manager inventory, and centrally manage all device policies, properties, interfaces, and other related device parameters. As shown in Figure 24-3, the DCV displays on a single screen all devices that are being managed. Specific devices can be selected to view their properties and define their settings and policies. DCV also allows you to define security policies locally on specific devices and further share these policies globally, making them available for assignment to other devices. DCV can be selected by clicking the Device View button from the main page. Figure 24-3 illustrates sample screen capture of a DCV from the Cisco Security Manager.

- **Policy-Centric View (PCV):** Enables users to create and manage shared reusable policies at the system level that can be shared among multiple devices for later assignments. With PCV, users can view all the shared policies that are defined for a particular policy type, and create, view, and edit policies and modify their device assignments. Figure 24-4 is a sample screen capture of a PCV from the Cisco Security Manager.

- **Map View or Topology-Centric View (TCV):** Enables users to create customized topology-based visual maps of the network, allowing users to manage the policies directly from the topology view. Within TCV, users can view network connections between devices, link topologies, and configure VPN and access control settings directly from the view maps. TCV provides a graphical view of the VPN and Layer 3 network topology. Figure 24-5 is a sample screen capture of a TCV from the Cisco Security Manager.

Figure 24-3 *Cisco Security Manager—Device-Centric View*

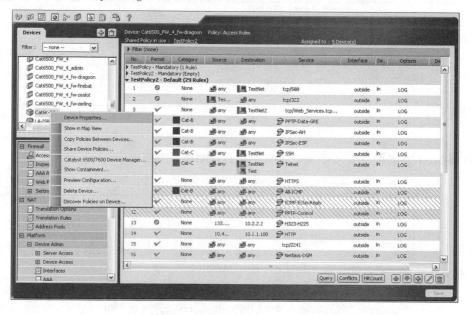

Figure 24-4 *Cisco Security Manager—Policy-Centric View*

Figure 24-5 *Cisco Security Manager—Map View*

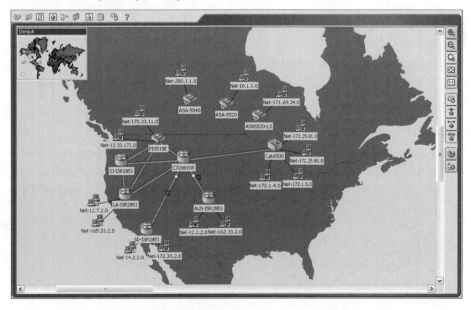

Cisco Security Manager—Managing Devices

Before Cisco Security Manager can manage a device, each device must be configured to communicate with Cisco Security Manager on the required transport protocol and the necessary settings. For example, Cisco Security Manager uses Secure Socket Layer (SSL) as the default transport protocol to communicate with PIX Firewall, Adaptive Security Appliances (ASA), Firewall Service Modules (FWSM), and Cisco IOS routers. Therefore, configure SSL settings on these devices to communicate with Cisco Security Manager before adding them to the device list.

After the device is configured and ready to be managed, add the device to the Cisco Security Manager device inventory from the Device page.

Table 24-1 summarizes the types of devices and the transport protocols used for each device to communicate with Cisco Security Manager.

Table 24-1   *Cisco Security Manager—Devices and Transport Settings*

Devices	Transport Settings
PIX Firewall, ASA, FWSM, and Cisco IOS routers (default)	SSL
Cisco IOS routers	SSH
Catalyst 6500/7600 devices (default)	SSH
PIX and ASA devices—For devices managed by an Auto Updated Server (AUS)	AUS
Cisco IOS routers—For devices managed by a CNS-Configuration Engine	CNS
Cisco IOS routers—For devices managed by a Token Management Server (TMS)	TMS

Cisco Security Manager—Workflow Mode

By default, Cisco Security Manager operates in the nonworkflow mode, which is the simplest approach; that is, select a device, make a change, and deploy the policy.

For more sophisticated and complex policy deployments, Cisco Security Manager provides a structured process for change management that complements the operational environment. For example, there can be different stages in the life cycle of a policy deployment:

- Policy definition
- Policy approval
- Deployment approval
- Actual deployment

The Cisco Security Manager workflow mode provides the capability for multiple users to be involved in the entire process.

As illustrated in Figure 24-6, the Security Operations (SecOps) officer can define the policy changes and submit them for approval to a senior authorized officer. After approval, the Network Operations (NetOps) team can generate deployment jobs, which can be approved by a senior authorized officer for deployment.

The main advantage of the workflow capability is to allow a separation of responsibilities between those who define the security policies and those who implement them.

Figure 24-6 illustrates a sample structured process for change management from defining to deploying the policy and demonstrating the collaboration across the SecOps and NetOps teams.

Figure 24-6   *Cisco Security Manager—Workflow Mode*

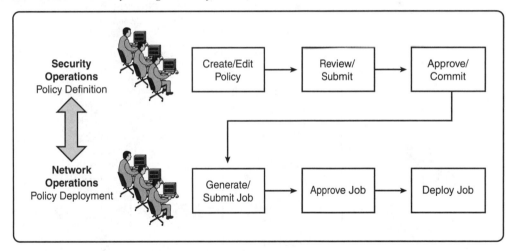

Cisco Security Manager—Role-Based Access Control (RBAC)

Cisco Security Manager provides two levels of role-based access control providing appropriate separation of ownership and controls to manage the system:

- Cisco Security Manager provides a built-in authentication mechanism to verify users and provide them with appropriate access to the management system. The user role dictates the level of permissions (also called privileges), which determine the actions that users with particular roles can perform within Cisco Security Manager. Roles are sets of tasks or operations that are authorized to be performed on a per-user basis. If the user is not authorized for certain tasks or devices, the related menu items, TOC items, and buttons are hidden or disabled. In addition, a message informs users of insufficient privilege when they view the selected item or perform a selected operation.

- Cisco Security Manager can also be integrated with Cisco Secure Access Control Server (ACS) for more granular role-based access control, and for a span of control of which devices can be viewed and managed. The integration can also determine which Cisco Security Manager functions can be exercised on those devices and related management functions. Cisco Secure ACS allows for modification of the permissions associated with each Cisco Security Manager role. Users can also be customized by creating specialized user roles with permissions that are targeted to particular tasks. Cisco Secure ACS uses TACACS+ to communicate with the Cisco Security Manager application.

Figure 24-7 illustrates the two role-based access control mechanisms used by the Cisco Security Manager.

Figure 24-7 *Cisco Security Manager—Role-Based Access Control*

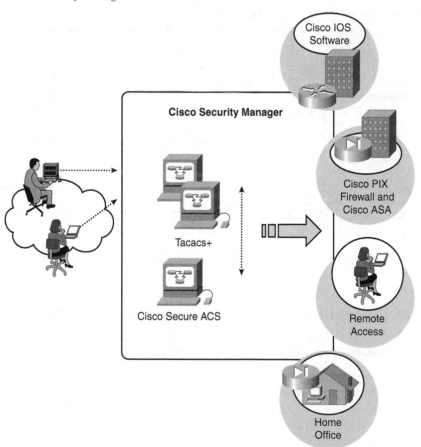

The information in Figure 24-7 is taken from the Cisco general product presentation on Cisco Security Manager.

Cisco Security Manager—Cross-Launch xDM

The Cisco Security Manager provides another unique feature—cross-launching, which supplies the capability to open connections to other device manager applications directly from the Cisco Security Manager interface.

Supported cross-launch xDMs include Cisco ASDM, Router and Security Device Manager (SDM), IPS Device Manager (IDM), and IPS Event Viewer (IEV).

This provides great flexibility and faster startup to connect to the device without having a connection from a user desktop. It also provides collaboration between security events and policy management.

Figure 24-8 illustrates an example of opening Cisco ASDM directly from the Cisco Security Manager by right-clicking the managed ASA device and selecting Device Manager to launch the Cisco ASDM application.

Figure 24-8 *Cisco Security Manager—Cross-Launch Cisco ASDM*

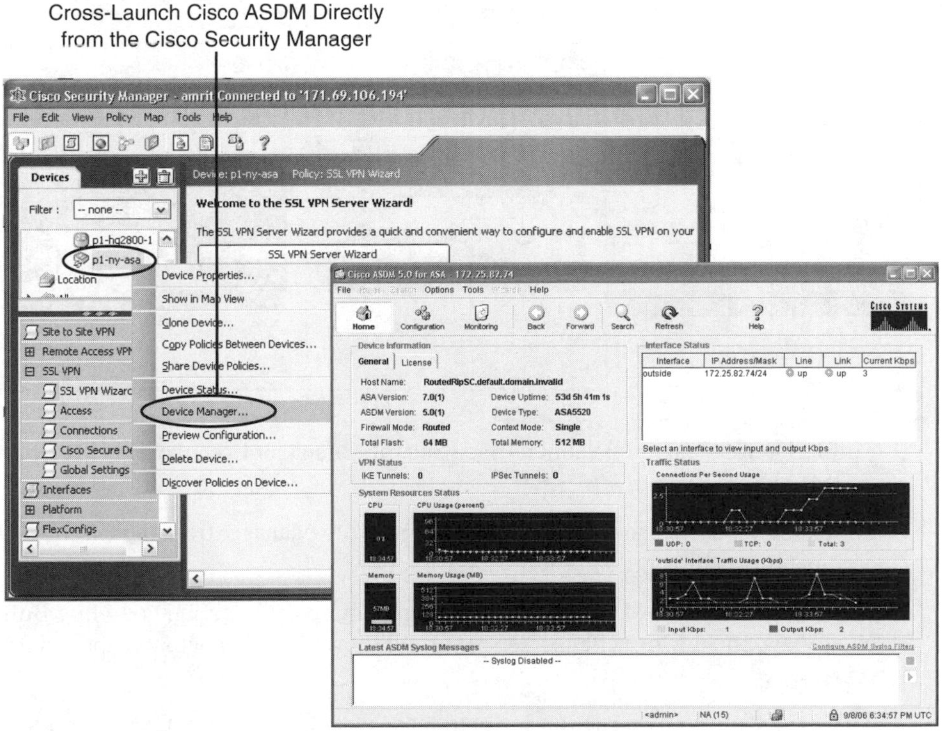

Figure 24-9 illustrates another example of opening Cisco IDM (IPS Device Manager) directly from the Cisco Security Manager by right-clicking the managed IPS device and selecting Device Manager to launch the Cisco IDM application.

Figure 24-9 *Cisco Security Manager—Cross-Launch IPS Device Manager (IDM)*

Cross-Launch Cisco IPS Device Manager (IDM)
Directly from the Cisco Security Manager

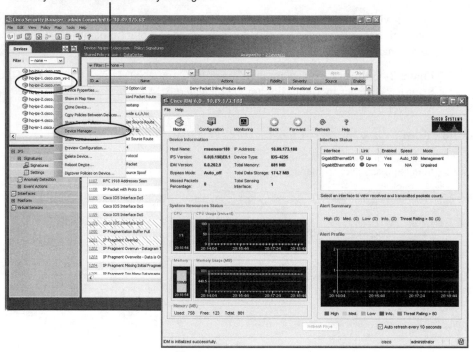

Similarly, users can cross-launch Cisco Security Manager from the d71471evice manager (xDM) and vice versa.

For example, users can cross-launch Cisco Security Manager from the Cisco ASDM application, as illustrated in Figure 24-10.

From the Cisco ASDM, select the Monitoring tab, select Logging, go to Log Buffer, and click View, and the log buffer screen panel will show all the log outputs captured from Cisco ASA.

Then, right-click any particular log entry and select Goto Rule in CSM to cross-launch Cisco Security Manager and review the corresponding Access Rule policy that triggered this log.

This feature gives enhanced power to the user to manage and correlate entries between applications without having to connect to the device directly. All this can be managed through single-click options.

Figure 24-10 shows a sample log entry output in Cisco ASDM logs. Right-click the log entry to launch the Cisco Security Manager and view the corresponding access rule that triggered the log.

Figure 24-10   *Cisco Security Manager—Cross-Launch Cisco Security Manager*

Cross-Launch Cisco Security Manager directly from the Cisco ASDM logs to view the corresponding access rule policy in Cisco Security Manager that triggered the Syslop entry.

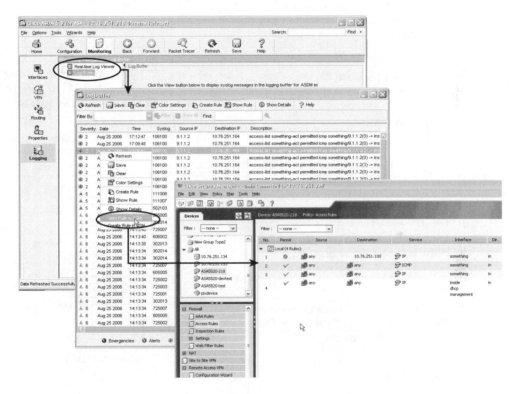

Furthermore, a packet tracer option is available in Cisco ASDM to gain more insight into the packet flow, route flow, and relevant filters pertaining to the log entries.

Cisco Security Manager—Supported Devices and OS Versions

Cisco Security Manager provides configuration and management services across multiple Cisco platforms and OS versions.

Table 24-2 provides a complete list of devices with OS versions supported by Cisco Security Manager.

Table 24-2   *Cisco Security Manager—List of Supported Cisco Devices and OS Versions*

Platforms	OS Versions
Cisco PIX Firewall and Cisco ASA Appliances • Cisco PIX 500 Series (Cisco PIX 501, PIX 506, PIX 506E, PIX 515, PIX 515E, PIX 520, PIX 525, and PIX 535) • Cisco ASA 5500 Series (Cisco ASA 5505, ASA 5510, ASA 5520, ASA 5540, and ASA 5550)	• Cisco PIX 6.3, PIX 7.0, PIX 7.1, and PIX 7.2 • Cisco ASA 7.0, ASA 7.1, and ASA 7.2
Cisco IOS Software Routers • Cisco SOHO 70, SOHO 90, Cisco 800, 1600, 1700, 1800, 2600, 2800, 3600, 3700, 3800, 7100, 7200 (VSA), 7300, 7500, and 7600	• Cisco IOS Software Releases 12.3, 12.3T, 12.4, and 12.4T. Limited support (including Layer 3 ACL, interfaces, and FlexConfig) is available for Cisco IOS Software Releases 12.1 and 12.2. • Cisco IOS IPS needs Cisco IOS Software Release 12.4(11)T2 and later.
Cisco IPS Appliances and Modules • Cisco IDS 4210, IDS 4215, IDS 4235, IDS 4240, IDS 4250 (SX and XL), IDS 4255, and IDS 4260, Cisco Catalyst 6500 Series Intrusion Detection System (IDSM-2), NM-CIDS, AIP-SSM 10 or 20	• Cisco IPS 5.1, and 6.0
Cisco Catalyst Switches and Security Modules • Cisco Catalyst 6500 (Cisco Catalyst 6503E, Catalyst 6504E, Catalyst 6506E, Catalyst 6509E, and Catalyst 6513) • Cisco FWSM • VPN-SM/VPN-SPA • IDSM-2	• Cisco IOS Software Releases 12.1S and 12.2SX; Layer 3 ACL and VLAN; VLAN ACL and FlexConfig support only on Cisco Catalyst 6500 • Cisco FWSM 2.2, 2.3, 3.1, and 3.2 • Cisco IPS 5.1 and 6.0 for IDSM

Cisco Security Manager—Server and Client Requirements and Restrictions

Cisco Security Manager can be installed on a Windows-based server that is using either one CPU or multiple CPUs.

Table 24-3 describes the minimum server requirements for installing Cisco Security Manager and highlights the restrictions.

Table 24-3   *Cisco Security Manager—Server Requirements*

Component	Minimum Requirement
System Hardware	• IBM PC-compatible with a 2 GHz or faster processor • Color monitor with at least 1024×768 resolution and a video card capable of 16-bit colors • DVD-ROM drive • 100BASE-T (100 Mbps) or faster network connection; single interface only • Keyboard • Mouse
File system	NTFS
Memory (RAM)	2 GB
System Software	One of the following: • Microsoft Windows 2003 Server: — Enterprise Edition with SP1 — Enterprise Edition Release 2 — Standard Edition with SP1 — Standard Edition Release 2 • Microsoft Windows 2000: — Advanced Server with SP4 — Server with SP4 — Professional with SP4 Note: Cisco Security Manager supports only U.S. English and Japanese versions of Windows. Microsoft ODBC Driver Manager 3.510 or later is also required so that your server can work with Sybase database files.
Browser	One of the following: • Microsoft Internet Explorer 6.0 (6.0.2600) • Microsoft Internet Explorer 6.0 with SP1 (6.0.2800) • Mozilla 1.7 or 1.7.5
Compression Software	WinZip 9.0 or compatible
Hard Drive Space	20 GB
IP Address	One static IP address. If the server has more than one IP address, disable all but one address. The Cisco Security Manager installer displays a warning if it detects any dynamic IP addresses on the target server. Dynamic addresses are not supported.

The information in Table 24-3 is taken from "Cisco Security Manager 3.1 Data Sheet" at http://www.cisco.com/en/US/products/ps6498/products_data_sheet0900aecd8062bf6e.html.

Table 24-4 describes the minimum client requirements for installing Cisco Security Manager and highlights the restrictions.

Table 24-4 *Cisco Security Manager—Client Requirements*

Component	Minimum Requirement
System Hardware	• IBM PC-compatible with a 1 GHz or faster processor • Color monitor with video card set to 24-bit color depth • Keyboard • Mouse
Memory (RAM)	1 GB
Virtual Memory/ Swap Space	512 MB
Hard Drive Space	10 GB
Operating System	One of the following: • Microsoft Windows XP Professional with SP1 or later • Microsoft Windows 2003: — Server Edition with SP1 — Enterprise Edition with SP1 • Microsoft Windows 2000: — Advanced Server with SP4 — Professional with SP4 Note: The Cisco Security Manager Client supports only U.S. English and Japanese versions of Windows. It does not support any other language version.
Browser	One of the following: • Microsoft Internet Explorer 6.0 (6.0.2600) • Microsoft Internet Explorer 6.0 with SP1 (6.0.2800) • Mozilla 1.7 or 1.7.5
Java	The Cisco Security Manager Client includes an embedded and completely isolated version of Java. This Java version does not interfere with your browser settings or with other Java-based applications. If you try to open Cisco Security Manager but do not have the required version of Java, your Cisco Security Manager server will display a message that tells you how to download and install the required Java version.

The information in Table 24-4 is taken from "Cisco Security Manager 3.1 Data Sheet" at http://www.cisco.com/en/US/products/ps6498/products_data_sheet0900aecd8062bf6e.html.

Cisco Security Manager—Traffic Flows and Ports to Be Opened

Required traffic flows identify the necessary protocol and port numbers that must be allowed by firewalls/ACLs if they separate the Cisco Security Manager from a supporting device (as listed in Table 24-2). Several protocol and port numbers are used for varying functions when the Cisco Security Manager communicates with a device. Various Internet Control Message Protocol (ICMP), Transmission Control Protocol (TCP), and User Datagram Protocol (UDP) ports need to be enabled for use by the Cisco Security Manager and its associated applications on the server to support their associated services.

Table 24-5 identifies the various traffic flows and the associated protocol and port numbers required to be opened if a gateway, firewall, ACL, or any type of filtering device exists between Cisco Security Manager and the service/device.

Table 24-5   *Cisco Security Manager—Required Traffic Flows and Ports to Be Opened*

Service	Used For/Used By	Port	Protocol	Inbound	Outbound
Ping	Resource Manager Essentials (RME)	—	ICMP	—	X
SSH	Common Services	22	TCP	—	X
	RME	22	TCP	—	X
Telnet	Common Services	23	TCP	—	X
	DM 6500/7600	23	TCP	—	X
	RME	23	TCP	—	X
TACACS+ (for ACS)	Common Services	49	TCP	—	X
	RME		TCP	—	X
Trivial File Transfer Protocol (TFTP)	Common Services	69	UDP	X	X
HTTP	Common Services	80	TCP	—	X
	DM 6500/7600		TCP	—	X
SNMP (polling)	Common Services	161	UDP	—	X
SNMP (traps)	Common Services	162	UDP	—	X

continues

Table 24-5 *Cisco Security Manager—Required Traffic Flows and Ports to Be Opened (Continued)*

Service	Used For/Used By	Port	Protocol	Inbound	Outbound
HTTPs (SSL)	Common Services	443	TCP	X	—
	Security Manager	443	TCP	—	X
	AUS	443	TCP	X	—
Syslog	Common Services	514	UDP	X	—
Remote Copy Protocol	Common Services	514	TCP	X	X
VisiBroker IIOP port for gatekeeper	Common Services	1683/1684	TCP	X	X
HTTP	Common Services	1741	TCP	X	—
	Security Manager	1741	TCP	X	—
MySQL	Security Manager	3306, 5501	MySQL	X	X
Cisco IPS Event Viewer	Security Manager server	60002, 60003	TCP	X	X
	Security Manager client	5001	TCP	X	X
HIPO port for CiscoWorks gatekeeper	Common Services	8088	TCP	X	X
Tomcat shutdown	Common Services	9007	TCP	X	—
Tomcat Ajp13 connector	Common Services	9009	TCP	X	—
Database	Security Manager	10033	TCP	X	—
License Server	Common Services	40401	TCP	X	—
Daemon Manager	Common Services	42340	TCP	X	X
Osagent	Common Services	42342	UDP	X	X
Database	Common Services	43441	TCP	X	—
DCR and OGS	Common Services	40050–40070	TCP	X	—

Table 24-5   *Cisco Security Manager—Required Traffic Flows and Ports to Be Opened (Continued)*

Service	Used For/Used By	Port	Protocol	Inbound	Outbound
Event Services	Software Service	42350/ 44350	UDP	X	X
	Software Listening	42351/ 44351	TCP	X	X
	Software HTTP	42352/ 44352	TCP	X	X
	Software Routing	42353/ 44353	TCP	X	X
Transport Mechanism (CSTM)	Common Services	50000– 50020	TCP	X	—

The information in Table 24-5 is taken from "Installation Guide for Cisco Security Manager 3.1—Requirements and Dependencies" at http://www.cisco.com/en/US/docs/security/security_management/cisco_security_manager/security_manager/3.1/installation/guide/requirem.html.

Several other features are unique to Cisco Security Manager and can be used as required.

For more details to install and configure Cisco Security Manager, refer to the following Cisco documentations:

http://www.cisco.com/en/US/products/ps6498/prod_installation_guides_list.html

http://www.cisco.com/en/US/products/ps6498/products_user_guide_list.html

Cisco Router and Security Device Manager (SDM)

Cisco Router and Security Device Manager (SDM) is a secure web-based device-management tool integrated in the Cisco IOS Software to manage Cisco routers.

Cisco SDM greatly improves productivity, simplifies router and security configuration through step-by-step smart wizards, offers proactive management through performance monitoring, and helps troubleshoot complex network and VPN connectivity issues.

The main advantage of using Cisco SDM is for the non-expert users who are not very familiar with Cisco IOS Software and its features, because it provides an easy-to-use graphical management system to aid in day-to-day operations. For the more experienced users who are familiar with Cisco IOS Software, the Cisco SDM offers advanced configuration tools to quickly configure and fine-tune their work. Users can review the commands generated by the Cisco SDM before pushing the final configuration changes to the router.

Cisco SDM can be used for day-to-day operations such as configuration tuning, monitoring, fault management, and troubleshooting.

Cisco SDM—Features and Capabilities

Cisco SDM provides an easy-to-use browser-based interface for deploying and monitoring Cisco routers without requiring advanced knowledge of the command-line interface (CLI). With Cisco SDM, users can remotely manage and configure dynamic routing, LAN, WAN, WLAN, interfaces, NAT, firewall, VPN, IPS, QoS, and various other basic and advanced IOS router and security features.

Cisco SDM offers various features and functions. The following are some of its common capabilities for configuring and deploying Cisco Routers using a web-based management interface:

- Web-based management application integrated into Cisco IOS Software.
- Secure remote management to Cisco Router using SSL and SSHv2 connections.
- Router security audit for assessing vulnerabilities and providing recommendations for best practices.
- One-step router lockdown feature to enable or disable Security and IOS configurations without requiring security expertise or knowledge of Cisco IOS Software configuration.
- Smart Wizards for frequent router and security configuration tasks.
- Capability of configuring basic to advanced level router configuration parameters.
- Support for policy-based firewall and ACL management.
- Support for IOS-based IPS.
- Cisco Easy VPN Server configuration and real-time monitoring of remote access VPN connections.
- Support of Role-Based Access Control (RBAC), leveraging the Cisco IOS Software CLI role-based access feature by providing four factory default access profiles: Administrator, Firewall-Admin, Monitor, and EasyVPN Remote.
- Real-time bandwidth and resource monitoring and traffic performance using NBAR and QoS policies.
- Network and application-level monitoring using NetFlow.
- Provisioning of digital certificates using the Cisco IOS CA server feature.
- Customized task-based wizards and an easy-to-use GUI interface to configure common router and security features such as IP Routing, Interface parameters, NAT, QoS, ACL, AAA, VPN, firewall, and IPS.
- NAC support.

- Integrated wireless management support.

- Granular protocol inspection.

- Threat control and intrusion prevention.

- Dynamic DNS support to run services without a dedicated static IP address. Supported service providers include www.justlinux.com, www.zoneedit.com, dup.hn.org, members.dyndns.org, www.dyns.cx, cgi.tzo.com, and members.easydns.com.

- Easy-to-configure wizards for VPN deployments.

- Low overhead with negligible performance impact on router dynamic random access memory (DRAM) or CPU.

- Cisco Security Device Manager (SDM) user interface and online help is available in six languages, translated into Japanese, Simplified Chinese, French, German, Spanish, and Italian.

Cisco SDM—How It Works

Cisco SDM is an integrated solution embedded within the Cisco IOS Software release. Cisco SDM communicates with routers for two purposes:

- Connects to the router to access the Cisco SDM application files for download to the local desktop PC. Cisco SDM uses HTTP/HTTPS to download the application files (sdm.tar and home.tar) to the local desktop PC.

- Connects to the router to read and write the router configuration and real-time status monitoring. Cisco SDM uses a combination of HTTP/HTTPS and Telnet/SSH to read and write the router configuration.

Cisco SDM can be launched remotely from any user desktop PC using HTTP, HTTPS, SSL, Telnet, and SSH Protocol connections. The SSL and SSH technology provides a secure connection to manage Cisco IOS Software routers remotely over the Internet or any shared network without compromising the integrity.

The preferred communication protocol used by Cisco SDM is HTTPS (using browser-based SSL) to connect to the router for secure remote management. Users can choose to use non-SSL, less secure standard HTTP-based browsing, too, but it is not recommended.

Users can launch Cisco SDM from a supported Internet browser using the router IP address as follows (HTTP or HTTPS):

https://router_ip_address

Figure 24-11 illustrates a user establishing a secure connection to launch Cisco SDM over the Internet using browser-based SSL technology.

Figure 24-11 *Cisco SDM Connection Using SSL*

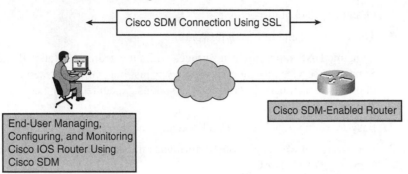

Figure 24-12 shows the Cisco SDM home page when the application is launched.

The Cisco SDM home page provides comprehensive information regarding the device, including the following:

- Hardware model of the router
- Cisco IOS Software version
- Available and total memory on the router
- Flash memory
- Features available in the IOS loaded on the router
- Totally supported and configured LAN interfaces
- Totally supported WAN connections
- IP routing status (static, RIP, OSPF, EIGRP)
- VPN deployments (Generic Routing Encapsulation [GRE], IP Security [IPsec], dynamic multipoint VPN [DMVPN], Easy VPN)
- Configuration summary

The green circles show the features supported on the router, and the red circles show the features that are not supported.

Figure 24-12 *Cisco SDM Home Page*

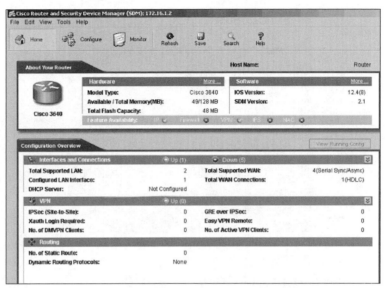

Cisco SDM—Router Security Audit Feature

Cisco SDM provides an intuitive router security audit feature with one-step security audit capability that validates router configurations against a list of common security vulnerabilities and Cisco recommended settings, and provides a summary of recommended best practices.

The audit report highlights the potential security problems identified in the router configuration and can generate corresponding configurations to correct the shortfalls.

Figure 24-13 shows a sample screen capture from the Router Security Audit report.

Figure 24-13 *Cisco SDM—Router Security Audit*

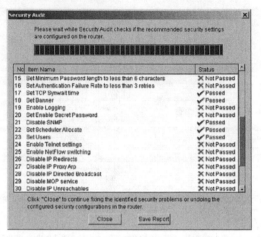

Cisco SDM—One-Step Lockdown Feature

In addition to the Router Security Audit function, Cisco SDM can perform a one-step router-lockdown function to configure the router for recommended best practices security configuration.

Table 24-6 lists features that are enabled or disabled when using the one-step lockdown feature.

Table 24-6 *Cisco SDM—One-Step Lockdown Feature*

One-Step Lock-Down Action Items	Cisco IOS Software Equivalent
Disable Finger Service	no service finger
Disable Packet Assembler/Disassembler (PAD)	no service pad
Disable Small Servers (TCP and User Datagram Protocol [UDP])	no service tcp-small-servers no service udp-small-servers
Disable BOOTP	no ip bootp server
Disable Identification Service	no ip identd
Disable Cisco Discovery Protocol	no cdp run
Disable Source Routing	no ip source-route
Enable Password Encryption	service password-encryption
Enable TCP Keepalives for Inbound and Outbound Telnet Sessions	service tcp-keepalives-in service tcp-keepalives-out

Table 24-6   *Cisco SDM—One-Step Lockdown Feature (Continued)*

One-Step Lock-Down Action Items	Cisco IOS Software Equivalent
Sequence Number and Time Stamps of All Debug and Log Messages	service timestamps debug datetime localtime show-timezone msec service timestamps log datetime localtime show-timeout msec service sequence-numbers
Enable Cisco Express Forwarding or Distributed Cisco Express Forwarding	ip cef
Cisco IOS Software Autosecure Residues	no ip gratuitous-arps
Minimum Password Length	security passwords min-length 6
Lock Access to Console or vty Line After Unsuccessful Attempts	security authentication failure rate 3 log
Tune Scheduler Interval or Allocation	scheduler interval 500 scheduler allocate 4000 1000
Set tcp synwait Time to 10 Seconds	ip tcp synwait-time 10
Text Banner	Banner—"Authorized access only. Disconnect IMMEDIATELY if you are not an authorized user!"
Enable Logging for Security and Sequence Numbers with Input for Logging Server	logging on logging console critical logging trap debugging logging buffered 51200
For Cryptographic Cisco IOS Software Images, Enable Secure Shell (SSH) Protocol and Serial Control Protocol (SCP) for Access and File Transfer Set SSH Timeouts and Retries to the Minimum Possible	ip ssh time-out 60 ip ssh authentication-retries 2 ! line vty 0 4 transport input ssh telnet !
Disable SNMP if Not Being Used	Only Disable SNMP: no snmp-server
Enable NetFlow on Software Forwarding Platforms	interface <all-interfaces> ip route-cache flow
Disable Internet Control Message Protocol (ICMP) Redirects	interface <all-interfaces> no ip redirects

continues

Table 24-6 *Cisco SDM—One-Step Lockdown Feature (Continued)*

One-Step Lock-Down Action Items	Cisco IOS Software Equivalent
Disable Proxy-arp	interface <all-interfaces> no ip proxy-arp
Disable Directed Broadcast	interface <all-interfaces> no ip directed-broadcast
Disable Maintenance Operation Protocol (MOP) Service on Ethernet Interfaces	interface <all-Ethernet-&-FastEthernet-interfaces> no mop enabled
Disable ICMP Unreachables on All Interfaces	interface <all-interfaces> no ip unreachables
Disable Mask Reply Messages	interface <all-interfaces> no ip mask-reply
Disable Sending Unreachable Messages to the Source for the Packets That Are Discarded or Routed to NULL	interface null 0 no ip unreachables

The information in Table 24-6 is taken from "Cisco Router and Security Device Manager Q&A" at http://www.cisco.com/en/US/products/sw/secursw/ps5318/products_qanda_item0900 aecd800fd11b.shtml.

Cisco SDM—Monitor Mode

Cisco SDM provides an intuitive monitor mode for router health checks. Monitor mode can provide a graphical status displaying important information related to the router's resource performance. For example, the following information can be displayed: whether the interface status is up or down, the CPU usage, and memory usage accordingly.

Using the integrated routing and security features, Cisco SDM provides in-depth diagnostics and troubleshooting of WAN and VPN connections.

Figure 24-14 shows an example of VPN troubleshooting. Cisco SDM verifies multiple items to troubleshoot the failed VPN connection, identify the fault, and provide recommendations to correct the issue. Some of the basic tasks performed include checking the interface status, IP connectivity, and complete VPN configuration from ISKAMP settings to Crypto Map parameters. At each stage, Cisco SDM provides status information for each test function performed, so that the user can easily understand and determine the root cause. Finally, Cisco SDM will provide possible reasons of failure and provide Cisco TAC recommended actions to be taken for recovery. As shown in Figure 24-14, Cisco SDM performed several checks to verify the VPN failure, has identified an IKE policy configuration issue, and recommends configuring the relevant IKE proposals on the router.

Figure 24-14   *Cisco SDM—Monitor Mode—VPN Troubleshooting*

Cisco SDM—Supported Routers and IOS Versions

Cisco SDM is supported on all major Cisco routers. Table 24-7 shows a list of Cisco routers and Cisco IOS Software versions supported by the Cisco SDM application.

Table 24-7   *Cisco SDM—Supported Router and IOS Software Revisions*

Router	Cisco IOS Software Version
Cisco Small Business 101, 106, and 107	12.3(8)YG or later
Cisco 831 and 837	12.2(13)ZH or later
	12.3(2)T or later
Cisco 836	12.2(13)ZH or later
	12.3(2)XA or later
	12.3(4)T or later
Cisco 851, 856, 871, 876, 877, and 878	12.3(8)YI or later
Cisco 1701, 1710, 1711, 1712, 1721, 1751, 1751-V, 1760, and 1870V	12.2(13)ZH or later
	12.3(13)T3 or later
	12.3(1)M or later
Cisco 1801, 1802, 1803, 1811, and 1812	12.3(8)YI or later

continues

Table 24-7   *Cisco SDM—Supported Router and IOS Software Revisions (Continued)*

Router	Cisco IOS Software Version
Cisco 1841	12.3(8)T4
Cisco 2610XM, 2611XM, 2620XM, 2621XM, 2650XM, and 2651XM Multiservice Routers, and Cisco 2691 Multiservice Routers	12.2(15)ZJ3 or later 12.2(11)T6 or later 12.3(1)M or later
Cisco 2801, 2811, 2821, and 2851	12.3(8)T4 or later
Cisco 3620, 3640, 3661, and 3662	12.2(15)ZJ3 or later 12.211)T6 or later 12.3(1)M or later
Cisco 3725 and 3745	12.2(15)ZJ3 or later 12.2(11)T6 or later 12.3(1)M or later
Cisco 3825 and 3845	12.3(11)T or later
Cisco 7204VXR, 7206VXR, and 7301	12.3(2)T or later 12.3(1)M or later No support for B, E, or S train releases on Cisco 7000 routers

The information in Table 24-7 is adapted from "Cisco Router and Security Device Manager" at http://www.cisco.com/en/US/products/sw/secursw/ps5318/products_data_sheet0900 aecd800fd118.html.

Cisco SDM is available free of charge on all major Cisco router models from Cisco 830 to Cisco 7301.

Cisco SDM ships preinstalled on all new Cisco router 850 Series, 870 Series, 1800 Series, 2800 Series, and the 3800 Series integrated services routers (ISR).

Cisco SDM—System Requirements

As mentioned earlier, Cisco SDM can be launched from any user desktop PC using a supported browser.

Table 24-8 shows the basic list of system requirements for the Cisco SDM application.

Table 24-8   *Cisco SDM—System Requirements*

Feature	Description
Router Flash Memory	Minimum of 6 MB of free Flash memory on the router for Cisco SDM files.
	Minimum of 2 MB of free Flash memory on the router for Cisco SDM Express. Wireless Management file requires additional 1.7 MB. Rest of the SDM files can be installed on PC hard disk.
PC Hardware	Pentium III or later series processor
PC Operating System	Windows XP Professional
	Windows 2003 Server (Standard Edition)
	Windows 2000 Professional
	Windows NT 4.0 Workstation (Service Pack 4)
	Windows ME
	Japanese, Simplified Chinese, French, German, Spanish, and Italian language OS support
Browser Software	Microsoft Internet Explorer 5.5 or later
	Netscape Navigator 7.1 and 7.2
	Firefox 1.0.5
Java Software	Java Virtual Machine (JVM) built-in browsers required
	Java plug-in (Java Runtime Environment Version 1.4.2_05 or later)

The information in Table 24-8 is taken from "Cisco Router and Security Device Manager" at http://www.cisco.com/en/US/products/sw/secursw/ps5318/products_data_sheet0900aecd800fd118.html.

Windows 2000 (Advanced Server) is not supported by Cisco SDM.

For more details to install and configure Cisco SDM, refer to the following Cisco documentations:

http://www.cisco.com/en/US/products/sw/secursw/ps5318/prod_installation_guides_list.html

http://www.cisco.com/en/US/products/sw/secursw/ps5318/products_user_guide_list.html

http://www.cisco.com/en/US/products/sw/secursw/ps5318/prod_configuration_examples_list.html

http://www.cisco.com/en/US/products/sw/secursw/ps5318/prod_technical_reference_list.html

Cisco Adaptive Security Device Manager (ASDM)

Cisco Adaptive Security Device Manager (ASDM) is another powerful web-based firewall management tool that is integrated into the Cisco-based firewall software.

Cisco ASDM provides support for integrated security and networking features offered by the market-leading suite of Cisco security appliances.

Cisco ASDM can be used to manage the following Cisco firewalls:

- Cisco ASA 5500 Series Adaptive Security Appliances
- Cisco PIX 500 Series Security Appliances
- Cisco Catalyst 6500 Series Firewall Services Module (FWSM)

Cisco ASDM greatly improves productivity, simplifies security policy creation through step-by-step smart wizards, and offers proactive monitoring and debugging tools.

Cisco ASDM provides firewall management and provisioning of network and application security with greater flexibility.

Cisco ASDM—Features and Capabilities

Cisco ASDM offers a state-of-the-art security management and monitoring system through an intuitive, easy-to-use, secure web-based management interface.

The following list outlines some of the common Cisco ASDM capabilities for configuring and deploying Cisco firewalls using a web-based management interface:

- Complete support for Cisco ASA 5500 series appliance software and Cisco PIX 500 series appliance software features
- Web-based management application integrated into Cisco firewall software
- Secure remote management to Cisco market-leading Cisco firewalls
- Security and policy deployments using smart wizards
- Robust administration and management tools
- Capability to configure optional features such as DHCP, NAT, administrative access
- Support of auto-update, a revolutionary secure remote-management capability that helps keep appliance configurations and software images up-to-date
- Rapid configuration support features, such as inline and drag-and-drop policy editing, autocomplete, configuration wizards, appliance software upgrades, and online help
- Integrated security policy and access control table
- Profile-based management for all application inspection and control capabilities
- Powerful troubleshooting and diagnostics tools, such as Packet Tracer, log-policy correlation, packet capture, regular expression tester, and embedded log reference

- Real-time status and monitoring information features, such as device, firewall, content security, and IPS dashboards; real-time graphing; and tabulated metrics enabling rapid response to security incidents

Cisco ASDM—How It Works

Cisco ASDM is an integrated solution embedded within Cisco firewall software release.

Cisco ASDM can be launched remotely using a web browser from any user desktop PC on the network with an enabled Java plug-in, thereby providing rapid secure access to the Cisco ASA 5500 Series Adaptive Security Appliances or Cisco PIX Security Appliances.

With the factory default configuration on the firewall, users can connect to Cisco ASDM by using the default management IP address of 192.168.1.1. By default, on the Cisco ASA 5500 series appliance, Cisco ASDM connects to the Management0/0 interface. For the PIX 500 series appliance, Cisco ASDM connects to the Ethernet1 interface. In this case, the local desktop PC must be on the same subnet as the management IP address subnet—that is, 192.168.1.0/24.

NOTE   To restore the default configuration, enter the **configure factory-default** command on the security appliance console CLI.

As with Cisco SDM, users can launch Cisco ASDM from supported Internet browser using the firewall IP address as follows:

https://firewall_ip_address

When the Cisco ASDM application is launched, it provides a dynamic dashboard that gives a complete system overview and firewall health statistics.

Figure 24-15 shows the Cisco ASDM home page when the application is launched.

The Cisco ASDM home page provides comprehensive information including the following:

- Hardware model of the firewall
- Firewall software version
- Memory usage
- License information
- Interface status
- Traffic status

Figure 24-15 *Cisco ASDM Home Page*

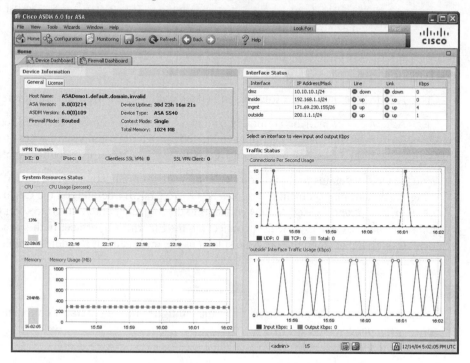

Further tabs from the home page provide comprehensive information for device configuration, monitoring, and real-time status indicators.

Figure 24-16 shows a sample screen capture of the Cisco ASDM Firewall Dashboard page that displays connection statistics, packet rate, Top 10 rules, and possible scan and network attack information.

Figure 24-16   *Cisco ASDM—Firewall Dashboard Page*

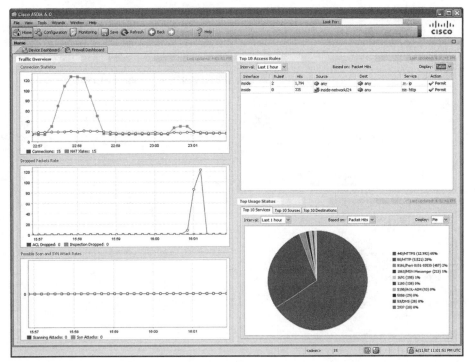

Figure 24-17 shows a sample screen capture of the Cisco ASDM Configuration page that displays firewall access rules.

Figure 24-17 *Cisco ASDM—Configuration Page Showing Access Rule Details*

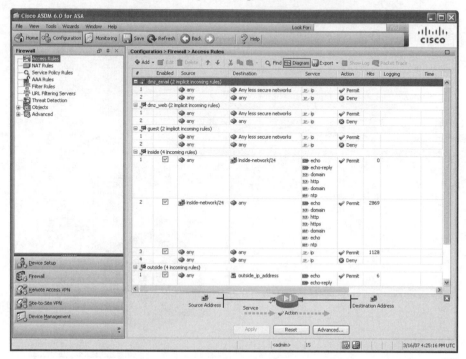

Cisco ASDM also includes a configuration search engine that helps users locate where specific features can be configured and provides convenient point-and-click access to the search results.

Cisco ASDM—Packet Tracer Utility

Cisco ASDM introduces a powerful and revolutionary Packet Tracer utility that enables rapid troubleshooting and simplifies fault finding of any nature, including the most complex policy environments, with numerous access rules, or layered security services.

The Cisco ASDM Packet Tracer is the first proactive debugging tool that is capable of determining the packet flow and charting complete details of a day-in-the-life of a packet.

The Packet Tracer utility employs an animated packet flow model, emulating a complete TCP/IP flow sequence for any given protocol or port number. It virtually passes through the entire device configuration checking all access rules, NAT rules, filter rules, and service policies. During the flows through each stage, it provides visual aids to indicate the status of each transaction and the action performed at that stage of that packet's lifetime. These visual indicators provide users the insight into the packet flow and help identify the fault and determine incorrect policies, which can be in the form of erroneous network translation policies, access rules, or inspection engines.

Figure 24-18 shows a sample screen capture of the Cisco ASDM Packet Tracer utility.

Figure 24-18   *Cisco ASDM—Packet Tracer Utility*

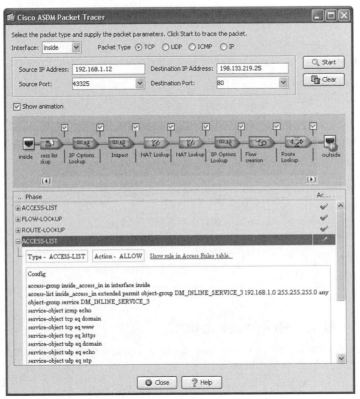

Cisco ASDM—Syslog to Access Rule Correlation

Cisco ASDM introduces yet another dynamic tool that enables Syslog to Access Rule Correlation. This dynamic feature greatly enhances day-to-day security management and troubleshooting activities to resolve common configuration issues and network connectivity problems.

The Syslog to Access Rule Correlation feature offers an intuitive view into syslog messages invoked by user-configured access rules. Users can closely inspect traffic patterns and monitor resource access behavior.

Cisco ASDM—Supported Firewalls and Software Versions

Table 24-9 lists the supported hardware and software for the Cisco ASA 5500 series security appliances.

Table 24-9 *Cisco ASDM—Cisco ASA 5500 Series System Requirements*

Hardware	Software
Platform: Cisco ASA 5505, 5510, 5520, 5540, or 5550 Adaptive Security Appliance RAM: 256 MB Flash memory: 64 MB	Cisco ASA Software: Version 7.2 Encryption: DES or 3DES enabled

Table 24-10 lists the supported hardware and software for the Cisco PIX 500 series security appliances.

Table 24-10 *Cisco ASDM—Cisco PIX 500 Series System Requirements*

Hardware	Software
Platform: Cisco PIX 515/515E, 525, or 535 Security Appliances (Cisco PIX 501 and 506/506E Security Appliances are not supported) RAM: 64 MB Flash memory: 16 MB	Cisco PIX Security Appliance Software Version 7.2 Encryption: DES or 3DES enabled

Cisco ASDM—User Requirements

Table 24-11 lists the supported operating system and web browser on the end-user PC to launch the Cisco ASDM application.

Table 24-11 *Cisco ASDM—Operating Systems and Web Browsers Supported by Cisco ASDM*

Operating Systems	Browsers (JavaScript and Java-Enabled)
Windows 2000 with Service Pack 4 (English/Japanese) Windows XP (English/Japanese)	Microsoft Internet Explorer 6.0 with Java Plug-In v1.4.2 or 1.5.0 Firefox 1.5 with Java Plug-In v1.4.2 or 1.5.0 Netscape Communicator 7.2 with Java Plug-In v1.4.2 or 1.5.0
Sun Solaris 2.8 or higher running CDE	Mozilla 1.7.3 with Java Plug-In v1.4.2 or 1.5.0
Red Hat Linux 9.0 running GNOME or KDE Red Hat Enterprise Linux WS Version 3	Firefox 1.5 with Java Plug-In v1.4.2 or 1.5.0

For more details about installing and configuring Cisco ASDM, refer to the following Cisco documentation:

http://www.cisco.com/en/US/products/ps6120/prod_installation_guides_list.html

http://www.cisco.com/en/US/products/ps6120/products_installation_and_configuration_guides_list.html

http://www.cisco.com/en/US/products/ps6120/prod_configuration_examples_list.html

http://www.cisco.com/en/US/products/ps6121/products_data_sheets_list.html

Cisco PIX Device Manager (PDM)

The Cisco PIX Device Manager (PDM) is the legacy version that predates the Cisco ASDM application. Cisco PDM also offers security management and monitoring services for the PIX Firewall series security appliances.

Cisco PDM is similar to Cisco ASDM in providing web-based firewall management services for Cisco PIX appliances running Cisco PIX Software Version 6.3 and earlier (that is, pre-version-7.x).

For Cisco PIX appliances running Cisco PIX Software Version 7.0 or later, use the Cisco ASDM application, as discussed in previous sections.

Table 24-12 provides a comprehensive software comparison chart to help you understand various xDM in the context of the Cisco PIX appliance models, Cisco FWSM models, and respective software versions.

Table 24-12 *xDM Software Version Comparison Chart*

Cisco PDM/ ASDM Version	Cisco PIX Security Appliance Software Version	Cisco FWSM Software Version	Platforms Supported
ASDM v5.0	7.0(1)	–	PIX 515, 515E, 525, 535
PDM v4.1	–	2.3	FWSM
PDM v4.0	–	2.2	FWSM
PDM v3.0(2)	6.3(4)	–	All PIX platforms
PDM v2.2	6.2	1.1	All PIX platforms/FWSM
PDM v2.0	6.2	–	All PIX platforms
PDM v1.1(2)	6.0(1), 6.1(X)	–	All PIX platforms

The information in Table 24-12 is taken from "Cisco PIX Device Manager—Software Version Comparison" at http://www.cisco.com/en/US/products/sw/netmgtsw/ps2032/prod_software_versions_comparison.html.

NOTE	Refer to the following Cisco documentation for detailed Hardware and Software Compatibility lists between the Cisco ASA 5500 Series and PIX 500 Series Security appliance model: http://www.cisco.com/en/US/docs/security/asa/compatibility/asamatrx.html.

For more details about installing and configuring Cisco PDM, refer to the following Cisco documentation:

http://www.cisco.com/en/US/products/sw/netmgtsw/ps2032/products_data_sheets_
list.html

http://www.cisco.com/en/US/products/sw/netmgtsw/ps2032/prod_installation_guides_
list.html

http://www.cisco.com/en/US/products/sw/netmgtsw/ps2032/products_user_guide_
list.html

http://www.cisco.com/en/US/products/sw/netmgtsw/ps2032/prod_presentation_list.html

Cisco IPS Device Manager (IDM)

Cisco Intrusion Prevention System Device Manager (IDM) is another powerful IPS management tool embedded in the Cisco IPS Sensor software.

Cisco IDM is a web-based, Java Web Start application that allows configuring, managing, and monitoring of a standalone Cisco IPS network appliance sensor.

Cisco IDM provides support for integrated IPS features offered by the Cisco IPS sensor appliances.

NOTE	Cisco IDM is available free of charge and is shipped with IPS sensor code at no additional cost.

Cisco IDM—How It Works

Similar to all other management tools discussed earlier, Cisco IDM is also a web-based configuration tool used primarily to manage the Cisco IPS Sensor.

The Cisco IDM has an integrated web server built in to the sensor software, preloaded on the sensor software. Each standalone Cisco IPS appliance has its own dedicated web server that provides access to the Cisco IDM application on the sensor.

To protect the communication between the client and the sensor, the web server uses Transport Layer Security (TLS) to encrypt the traffic to and from the sensor to prevent unauthorized viewing of sensitive management traffic. By default, the web server is configured to use TLS/SSL encryption. This setting can be changed, though, and the default TLS/SSL port number can also be changed.

Cisco IDM can be launched by using any user desktop PC with supported web browsers. However, the sensor needs to be initialized with basic parameters before anyone is able to browse to it using Cisco IDM. The basic IP address, mask, and gateway needs to be configured using the CLI. Alternatively, a built-in wizard configuration setup command is also available to complete the basic initialization process.

Users can use launch Cisco IDM from a supported Internet browser by using the IPS sensor IP address as follows:

https://sensor_ip_address

There are three basic built-in user roles supported to perform IPS sensor management:

- Administrator
- Operator
- Viewer

When the Cisco IDM application is launched, it provides a basic system overview and IPS health statistics.

The Cisco IDM home page provides a high-level view of the state of the sensor and provides comprehensive system information, such as

- Device information
- Cisco IPS Software version and the IDM version
- Information on whether bypass mode is enabled or disabled
- Missed packets percentage
- The number of sensing interfaces
- Displays of the CPU and memory usage of the sensor
- Interface status (management and sensing interfaces)

- Alert summary showing all event alarms from Informational, Low, Medium, and High alerts.
- Displays of a graphical view of the number of alerts at each severity level
- Other monitoring options and configuration submenus

Cisco IDM—System Requirements

Table 24-13 lists the system requirements needed to launch the Cisco IDM application.

Table 24-13 *Cisco IDM—System Requirements*

Operating System	Requirements
Windows 2000 (Service Pack 4) Windows XP (English or Japanese version)	• Internet Explorer 6.0 with Java Plug-in 1.4.2 or 1.5 or Firefox 1.5 with Java Plug-In 1.4.2 or 1.5 • Pentium IV or AMD Athlon or equivalent running at 450 Mhz or higher • 512 MB minimum • 1024 × 768 resolution and 256 colors (minimum)
Sun SPARC Solaris	• Sun Solaris 2.8 or 2.9 • Firefox 1.5 with Java Plug-in 1.4.2 or 1.5 • 512 MB minimum • 1024 × 768 resolution and 256 colors (minimum)
Linux	• Red Hat Linux 9.0 or Red Hat Enterprise Linux WS, Version 3 running GNOME or KDE • Firefox 1.5 with Java Plug-in 1.4.2 or 1.5 • 256 MB minimum, 512 MB or more strongly recommended • 1024 × 768 resolution and 256 colors (minimum)

The information in Table 24-13 is taken from "Installing and Using Cisco Intrusion Prevention System Device Manager 6.0—Getting Started" at http://www.cisco.com/en/US/products/hw/vpndevc/ps4077/products_configuration_guide_chapter09186a0080618948.html.

Other web browsers may also work with Cisco IDM, but Cisco supports and recommends only the browsers listed and system parameters mentioned in Table 24-13.

For more details on installing and using the Cisco IDM tool, refer to the following Cisco documentation:

http://www.cisco.com/en/US/products/hw/vpndevc/ps4077/products_configuration_guide_book09186a00807a8a2a.html

Summary

Network management and security management are two distinct yet closely related components within the organizational operational process. Although both can be managed independently through separate network management and security management tools, to be most effective, a comprehensive integrated solution is required to merge these two into a unified management system.

Cisco Security Management solutions provide the perfect match with sophisticated design, easy-to-deploy, and user-friendly applications that are efficient for the operational management, policy administration, and core security management functions.

This chapter provided details on the various applications available in the Cisco Security Management suite.

The chapter covered the core concepts of the Cisco Security and Policy Management application tools, providing features and capabilities, and highlighted the key concepts and functions offered by each tool.

The chapter covered the industry standard security and policy management tools; namely, Cisco Security Manager, Cisco Router and Security Device Manager (SDM), Cisco Adaptive Security Device Manager (ASDM), Cisco PIX Device Manager (PDM), and the Cisco IPS Device Manager (IDM) applications.

References

http://www.cisco.com/en/US/netsol/ns647/networking_solutions_sub_ solution_home.html

http://www.cisco.com/go/csmanager

http://www.cisco.com/en/US/products/ps6498/prod_installation_guides_list.html

http://www.cisco.com/en/US/docs/security/security_management/cisco_security_ manager/security_manager/3.1/installation/guide/ig31.html

http://www.cisco.com/en/US/docs/security/security_management/cisco_security_ manager/security_manager/3.1/user/guide/ug31.html

http://www.cisco.com/go/sdm

http://www.cisco.com/en/US/products/sw/secursw/ps5318/products_data_ sheet0900aecd800fd118.html

http://www.cisco.com/en/US/products/sw/secursw/ps5318/products_ qanda_item0900aecd800fd11b.shtml

http://www.cisco.com/en/US/products/sw/secursw/ps5318/products_configuration_ example09186a008073e067.shtml

http://www.cisco.com/en/US/products/sw/secursw/ps5318/products_user_guide_book09186a0080645da3.html

http://www.cisco.com/en/US/products/sw/secursw/ps5318/prod_installation_guides_list.html

http://www.cisco.com/en/US/products/sw/secursw/ps5318/products_user_guide_list.html

http://www.cisco.com/en/US/products/sw/secursw/ps5318/prod_configuration_examples_list.html

http://www.cisco.com/en/US/products/sw/secursw/ps5318/prod_technical_reference_list.html

http://www.cisco.com/go/asdm

http://www.cisco.com/en/US/products/ps6121/index.html

http://www.cisco.com/en/US/products/ps6121/products_data_sheet0900aecd804ba 978.html

http://www.cisco.com/en/US/products/ps6121/products_data_sheets_list.html

http://www.cisco.com/en/US/products/ps6120/prod_installation_guides_list.html

http://www.cisco.com/en/US/products/ps6120/products_installation_and_configuration_guides_list.html

http://www.cisco.com/en/US/products/ps6120/prod_configuration_examples_list.html

http://www.cisco.com/en/US/products/ps6120/products_data_sheets_list.html

http://www.cisco.com/go/pdm

http://www.cisco.com/en/US/products/sw/netmgtsw/ps2032/products_data_sheets_ list.html

http://www.cisco.com/en/US/products/sw/netmgtsw/ps2032/prod_installation_guides_list.html

http://www.cisco.com/en/US/products/sw/netmgtsw/ps2032/products_user_guide_list.html

http://www.cisco.com/en/US/products/sw/netmgtsw/ps2032/prod_presentation_list.html

http://www.cisco.com/en/US/products/hw/vpndevc/ps4077/index.html

http://www.cisco.com/en/US/products/hw/vpndevc/ps4077/products_configuration_guide_book09186a00807a8a2a.html

Security Framework and Regulatory Compliance

Today, organizations face increased pressure to comply with an array of industry regulations and legislations. Corporate governance must enforce effective controls and manage confidentiality and integrity of information. Organizations can face heavy penalties and can cause severe damage to the corporate image if they experience security breaches or are found out of compliance.

The chapter focuses on managing an effective organizational security model that provides a total security framework that includes policy compliance and risk mitigation. It provides details of various integrated pieces of the security model: security policies, industry standards, procedures, and guidelines.

This chapter highlights the two most widely used frameworks for industry best practices that are commonly employed by organizations for IT and corporate governance and for security audit compliance requirements—namely, ISO/IEC 17799 and COBIT.

In the process of reviewing the two commonly used best practices, the chapter provides details for some of the important regulatory compliance requirements, including the Gramm-Leach-Bliley Act (GLBA), HIPAA, and Sarbanes-Oxley Act (SOX) legislation, which are enforced in different types of businesses.

The chapter highlights how Cisco solutions and products help address the regulator compliance requirements and summarizes the value of the Cisco Self-Defending Network solution that is used in managing security risks and compliance.

Security Model

A security model is a framework made of many integrated entities, including logical and physical protection mechanisms, all working together to provide secure systems that comply with industry best practices and regulations.

Understanding the value of information is the first step in the development of a security model. Managing security risk and compliance audit requirements demands a policy- and system-based approach. Network and network security are fundamental elements of building a security model for business governance and compliance.

Figure 25-1 illustrates a high-level overview of the different layers in a security model that can be used as a basic template and guideline to achieve secure IT infrastructure.

Figure 25-1 *Building Blocks of Security Model*

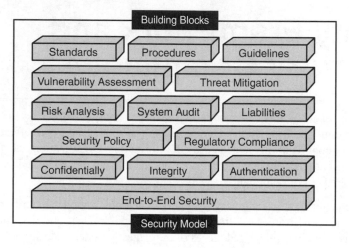

Figure 25-2 *Security Component Relationships*

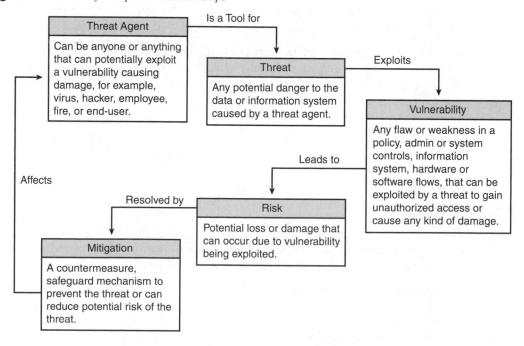

Often, security component terms are used interchangeably, although they carry different meanings in the context of different security components.

Figure 25-2 illustrates various security component associations and their relationships in the context of security framework.

Policies, Standards, Guidelines, and Procedures

Protecting and securing the information system has a fundamentally important role to play in business governance and regulatory compliance. Senior management is responsible for achieving this and providing comprehensive support for protecting information systems. This requires a complete understanding of what needs to be protected (assets) and the implications of failure (not meeting regulations).

Management needs to define a security program to fulfill this obligation by establishing appropriate security policies, following industry standards, and establishing guidelines and detailed procedures to protect the organization.

Security Policy

A security policy is a high-level document—a set of general rules, principles, and practices established by the senior management within the organization.

A security policy can comprise varying sets of rules and statements that regulate how the organization will manage, protect, and distribute sensitive information and determine how security is implemented within the organization.

Security policies are strategically defined primary frameworks that can dictate and establish the needed levels of information security to achieve the desired confidentiality goals.

Security policies can be broadly categorized into three types:

- **Regulatory policies:** Mandatory enforcements of compliance with industry regulations and legislations. These are typically driven to ensure that the organization is following industry standards as regulated by law.

- **Advisory policies:** These drive confidentiality and integrity of information systems and outline the noncompliance ramifications.

- **Informative policies:** These are non-enforceable and provide generic guidelines for best practices and acceptable behaviors.

Standards

Standards are industry-recognized best-practice frameworks and are agreed-upon principles of concepts and designs to implement, achieve, and maintain the required levels of processes and procedures.

Like security policies, standards are strategic in nature in that they define system parameters and processes.

Several available industry standards are used for various purposes. In the context of security information management and regulatory compliance, there are two notable standards—ISO 17799 and COBIT. These are discussed in the next sections.

Guidelines

Guidelines are recommended actions and operational guides for users. Similar to standards, guidelines are also tactical in nature. The major difference between standards and guidelines is that guidelines can be used as references, whereas standards are mandatory.

Procedures

Procedures are low-level documents providing systematic step-by-step instructions on completing or fulfilling a certain task. Procedures are detailed in nature to provide maximum information to users to successfully implement and enforce the security policy and apply the standards and guidelines.

Figure 25-3 depicts the relationship between security policies, standards, guidelines, and procedures.

Figure 25-3 *Security Policies, Standards, Guidelines, and Procedures*

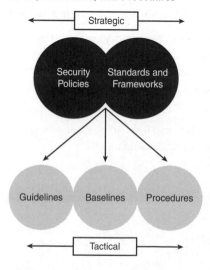

Best Practices Framework

Managing security risks and fulfilling audit requirements for regulatory compliance require an end-to-end integrated, collaborative, and adaptive approach. This allows for better manageability and ensures systemwide coverage touching every aspect of the operations and infrastructure.

Global organizations require a standard framework that not only complies with the regulations of the countries in which they operate but adheres to international regulations. This encompasses everything from privacy to security and to accountability.

With the complexity and intricate requirements laid out by various regulatory and legislations, requirements often contain overlaps, inconsistencies, and on some occasions contradictory laws and regulations. Therefore, organizations need to turn to common grounds and best practice frameworks and standards that address all the requirements of the security audit, risk management, IT governance, security controls, and meet the regulatory compliances.

There are two widely recognized and commonly deployed open standard frameworks that aim to address all individual IT governance, security controls and compliance requirements:

- ISO/IEC 17799
- COBIT

The following sections provide an overview of these two frameworks.

ISO/IEC 17799 (Now ISO/IEC 27002)

ISO/IEC 17799, titled "Code of Practice for Information Security Management," is an information security standard published by the International Organization for Standardization (ISO) and the International Electrotechnical Commission (IEC).

ISO/IEC 17799 is essentially a comprehensive set of controls composing best practices in information security.

ISO/IEC 17799 was subsequently renumbered as ISO/IEC 27002 in July 2007, bringing it inline with the other ISO/IEC 27000 series standards. ISO initiated this renaming to align the information security standards under a common naming structure—the "ISO 27000 series."

In summary, ISO/IEC 27002 provides best-practice recommendations on information security management.

To date, ISO 17799 is often used as a generic term to describe what is actually a set of two different documents:

- **ISO/IEC 27001 (formerly BS7799-2, the original British Standard):** This is the certification standard against which organizations' Information Security Management System (ISMS) may be certified. ISO 27001 represents the capability to measure, monitor, and control security management from a top-down perspective. ISO 27001 is the actual certification that can be achieved by organizations by applying the best practices outlined in ISO/IEC 27002.

- **ISO/IEC 27002 (previously ISO 17799):** This is essentially the set of security controls, measures, and safeguards for potential implementation, as well as a code of practice.

ISO/IEC 27002 has national equivalent standards in several other countries, such as

- Australia and New Zealand (AS/NZS ISO/IEC 17799:2006)
- Netherlands (NEN-ISO/IEC 17799:2002)
- Denmark (DS484:2005)
- Sweden (SS 627799)
- Japan (JIS Q 27002)
- Spain (UNE 71501)
- United Kingdom (BS ISO/IEC 27002:2005)
- Uruguay (UNIT/ISO 17799:2005)
- Estonia (EVS-ISO/IEC 17799:2003)

NOTE   For more details about the ISO/IEC 27002 (ISO/IEC 17799) framework, refer to the following documentation URLs:

http://www.iso.org/iso/iso_catalogue/catalogue_tc/catalogue_detail.htm?csnumber=39612

http://www.iso.org/iso/iso_catalogue/catalogue_ics/catalogue_detail_ics.htm?csnumber=50297

http://www.standardsdirect.org/iso17799.htm

http://www.iso-17799.com/

COBIT

COBIT, which stands for Control Objectives for Information and Related Technology, is a recognized set of best practices framework and an open standard for IT controls and security developed by the Information Systems Audit and Control Association (ISACA) and the IT Governance Institute (ITGI) in 1992.

COBIT was developed and used primarily by the IT community and has now become the internationally accepted framework for IT governance, IT security, and control practices.

COBIT provides users with a set of generally accepted measures, indicators, processes, and best practices to maximize the benefits derived through the use of IT systems and through the development of appropriate IT governance and security controls.

COBIT covers more than 300 specific control objectives categorized in four domains: Planning and Organization, Acquisition and Implementation, Delivery and Support, and Monitoring and Evaluation.

NOTE   For more details about the COBIT framework, refer to the following documentation URLs:

http://www.isaca.org/cobit

http://www.cobit.org/

http://www.controlit.org/

http://cobitcampus.isaca.org/

Comparing 17799/27002 and COBIT

These two frameworks complement each other.

In essence, COBIT covers a broader area in planning, operations, delivery, support, maintenance, and IT governance, whereas ISO/IEC 27002 mainly focuses on the area of information security management.

COBIT and ISO/IEC 27002 both allow the use of established best practices to simplify and unify both IT processes and internally defined controls.

Following are some of the distinct differences between ISO/IEC 27002 (ISO/IEC 17799) and COBIT:

- ISO/IEC 27002 is an internationally recognized and accepted standard for implementing IT security and best practices for information security management, whereas COBIT is used mainly by the IT audit community to demonstrate risk mitigation and avoidance mechanisms.
- COBIT focuses on information system processes, whereas ISO/IEC 27002 focuses on the security of the information systems.
- ISO/IEC 27002 addresses control objectives, whereas COBIT addresses information security management process requirements.

Compliance and Risk Management

Managing security controls and compliance audits requires a systematic approach, based on industry best practices that work within the requirements of standard bodies' framework, as previously discussed.

As organizations adhere to the best practices and recommended frameworks, they become prepared for security audits for regulatory compliance.

Regulatory Compliance and Legislative Acts

Several pieces of legislation for regulatory compliance are available, depending on the type of industry and businesses operated.

Organizations need to comply and participate in audits by common and regulatory bodies and get certified to be able to run and execute basic business operations with authority and control.

Depending on the type of business, organizations must comply with one of the following regulatory and legislative acts:

- **GLBA:** Gramm-Leach-Bliley Act
- **HIPAA:** Health Insurance Portability and Accountability Act
- **SOX:** Sarbanes-Oxley Act

The following sections will provide an overview of these regulatory compliance bodies.

GLBA—Gramm-Leach-Bliley Act

The Gramm-Leach-Bliley Act (GLBA), also known as the Financial Services Modernization Act, was enacted by the United States Congress in 1999.

GLBA is used primarily for organizations in the financial sector.

NOTE   The information in GLBA sections to follow is compiled from "Compliance and Risk Management: GLBA" at http://www.cisco.com/en/US/netsol/ns625/net_value_proposition0900aecd80380856.html.

Who Is Affected

Organizations that engage in financial activity or any type of activities that can be classified as financial institutions qualify for the GLBA assessments.

The GLBA defines "financial institutions" as companies that offer financial products or financial services, such as loans, investment advice, or insurance providers. Examples include the following:

- Banks
- Securities firms
- Insurance companies
- Mortgage lenders
- Brokers
- Check cashers and payday lending services
- Credit counseling service
- Financial advisors
- Medical-services providers
- Financial or investment advisory services, including tax planning, tax preparation, and individual financial management
- Companies issuing their own credit cards
- Auto dealers that lease or finance purchases
- Educational and academic institutions providing financial aid or student loans
- Collection agencies
- Government entities that provide financial products such as student loans or mortgages

GLBA Requirements

GLBA compliance is mandatory and requires United States–based financial institutions to

- Establish administrative, technical, and physical safeguard mechanisms to protect information
- Ensure the confidentiality and integrity of customer records and information
- Establish and enforce policies and controls, to protect the security and confidentiality of nonpublic information from foreseeable threats in security and data integrity
- Establish procedures for governing the collection, disclosure, and protection of consumers' nonpublic personal information and personally identifiable information
- Protect against commonly anticipated threats to information security
- Protect against unauthorized access to or use of information
- Establish a continuous risk-based information security program for ongoing monitoring, auditing, and reporting

Section 501(b) of the GLBA defines the high-level privacy and security requirements and objectives for financial institutions to comply with.

To comply with this act, organizations are required to

- Identify and assess security risks
- Plan and implement security solutions to protect sensitive information
- Establish measures to monitor and manage security systems

The internationally recognized ISO/IEC 27002 (ISO/IEC 17799) provides a best-practice framework for achieving these objectives, coupled with the Cisco Self-Defending Network solution that aligns itself with the controls recommended by ISO/IEC 27002.

Penalties for Violations

Violation of the GLBA may result in severe penalties and litigation in a civil action brought by the United States Attorney General. The penalties, as amended under the Financial Institution Privacy Protection Act of 2003, include the following:

- The financial institution shall be subject to a civil penalty of not more than $100,000 for each such violation.
- The officers and directors of the financial institution shall be subject to, and shall be personally liable for, a civil penalty of not more than $10,000 for each such violation.

The Federal Trade Commission (FTC) was authorized to execute and implement the GLBA, and a Final Rule (16 CFR Part 314) was developed in May 2002 accordingly.

The effective date of compliance for this act for all financial institutions was May 23, 2003, and May 24, 2004, for existing service contracts.

Cisco Solutions Addressing GLBA

Table 25-1 lists the Cisco products and solutions that help address the GLBA requirements.

Table 25-1 *Cisco Solutions Addressing GLBA Requirements*

Requirement	Cisco Solutions
Protect Against Unauthorized Access	• Cisco Secure Access Control Servers (ACS) • 802.1x • Network Admission Control • Cisco Integrated Services Routers (ISR) • Cisco ASA 5500 Series Adaptive Security Appliances

Table 25-1   *Cisco Solutions Addressing GLBA Requirements (Continued)*

Requirement	Cisco Solutions
Secure Data Exchange with Affiliates and Service Providers	• VPN Technologies • IPsec • DMVPN • SSL VPN
Detecting, Preventing, and Responding to Attacks and Intrusions	• Cisco Security Monitoring, Analysis, and Response System (CS-MARS) • Cisco IPS solutions • Cisco Security Agent (CSA) • Cisco Security Manager
Implement, Test, and Adjust a Security Plan on a Continuing Basis	• Cisco Security Auditor • Cisco Security Posture Assessment, and Penetration Testing Services

GLBA Summary

In summary, financial institutions need a system-based approach that is collaborative and adaptive, offering an effective governance framework to protect sensitive information and providing guidelines to meet GLBA compliance requirements.

For more details about GLBA, refer to the following documentation URLs:

http://banking.senate.gov/conf/

http://www.epic.org/privacy/glba/

http://www.ftc.gov/privacy/privacyinitiatives/glbact.html

http://www.wikipedia.org/wiki/GLBA

HIPAA—Health Insurance Portability and Accountability Act

The Health Insurance Portability and Accountability Act (HIPAA) was enacted by the United States Congress in 1996.

HIPAA is used primarily for organizations in the health care sector.

NOTE   The information in the HIPAA sections that follow is compiled from "Compliance and Risk Management: HIPAA" at http://www.cisco.com/en/US/netsol/ns625/net_value_proposition0900aecd80380862.html.

Who Is Affected

Organizations that engage in health care services or any type of activities that can be classified as a health care institution qualify for the HIPAA assessments.

HIPAA security policy applies to any entity (individual or company, public or private, government or nongovernment) that transmits any health information in electronic or print form in connection with a health care transaction. Examples include

*   Covered healthcare providers
*   Health plans
*   Health care clearing houses
*   Medicare prescription
*   Drug card sponsors

The HIPAA Requirements

HIPAA compliance is mandatory and requires health care institutions to

*   Implement security standards that protect patient data
*   Standardize on electronic data interchange (EDI)
*   Speed up the processing of medical claims
*   Implement standards for transmitting medical data
*   Protect the confidentiality of personal health information while in transit and while being stored

To comply with this act, HIPAA requires health care organizations to implement information security controls that are tightly integrated and comprehensive.

The internationally recognized ISO/IEC 27002 (ISO/IEC 17799) provides a best-practice framework for achieving these objectives, coupled with the Cisco Self-Defending Network solution that aligns itself with the controls recommended by ISO/IEC 27002.

Penalties for Violations

Violation of HIPAA may result in the following civil and criminal penalties:

*   **Civil penalties:** Violations can result in civil monetary penalties of $100 per violation, up to $25,000 per year.

- **Criminal penalties:** In June 2005, the United States Department of Justice (DOJ) clarified who can be held criminally liable under HIPAA. Covered entities and specified individuals, as explained in the sections that follow, who "knowingly" obtain or disclose individually identifiable health information in violation face a fine of up to $50,000, as well as imprisonment up to one year. Offenses committed under false pretenses allow penalties to be increased to a $100,000 fine, with up to five years in prison. Finally, offenses committed with the intent to sell, transfer, or use individually identifiable health information for commercial advantage, personal gain, or malicious harm permit fines of $250,000 and imprisonment for up to ten years.

The Department of Health and Human Services (DHHS) Office of Civil Rights (OCR) enforces the privacy standards, whereas the Centers for Medicare and Medicaid (CMS) enforce both the transaction and code set standards and the security standards (65 FR 18895).

Cisco Solutions Addressing HIPAA

Table 25-2 lists the Cisco products and solutions that help address HIPAA requirements.

Table 25-2   *Cisco Solutions Addressing HIPAA Requirements*

Requirement	Cisco Solutions
Protect Against Unauthorized Access	• Cisco Secure Access Control Servers (ACS) • 802.1x • Network Admission Control • Cisco Integrated Services Routers (ISR) • Cisco ASA 5500 Series Adaptive Security Appliances
Secure Data Exchange with Affiliates and Service Providers	• VPN Technologies • IPsec • DMVPN • SSL VPN
Detecting, Preventing, and Responding to Attacks and Intrusions	• Cisco Security Monitoring, Analysis, and Response System (CS-MARS) • Cisco IPS solutions • Cisco Security Agent (CSA) • Cisco Security Manager
Implement, Test, and Adjust a Security Plan on a Continuing Basis	• Cisco Security Posture Assessment, and Penetration Testing Services

HIPAA Summary

In summary, health care institutions need a system-based approach that is collaborative and adaptive, offering an effective security governance framework to manage information security and provide guidelines to meet HIPAA compliance requirements.

For more details about HIPAA, refer to the following documentation URLs:

http://www.hipaa.org/

http://www.hhs.gov/ocr/hipaa/

http://www.ama-assn.org/ama/pub/category/11805.html

http://www.wikipedia.org/wiki/HIPAA

SOX—Sarbanes-Oxley Act

The Sarbanes-Oxley Act, also known as the Public Company Accounting Reform and Investor Protection Act and commonly referred to as SOX or Sarbox, is a United States federal law enacted in July 2002.

Between the years 2000 and 2002, there were a series of large corporate frauds and accounting scandals, including those affecting Enron, Tyco International, Peregrine Systems, and WorldCom. These scandals and others resulted in more than $500 billion in market value declines and disbelief of public trust in accounting and reporting practices.

The SOX Act was passed in 2002 as a result of the analysis and the root causes identified that contributed to these scandals.

NOTE   The information in the SOX Act sections to follow is compiled from "Compliance and Risk Management: SOX" at http://www.cisco.com/en/US/netsol/ns625/net_value_proposition0900aecd80380886.html.

Who Is Affected

The SOX Act directly affects corporate executives of a publicly listed company who are held responsible for establishing, evaluating, and monitoring the effectiveness of internal controls over their financial reporting.

The SOX Act applies to any organization that is publicly traded in the United States and requires compliance with SOX Act mandates, including all their divisions and wholly owned subsidiaries.

The SOX Act also applies to any non-U.S. public multinational company doing business in the United States.

SOX Act Requirements

The major focus of the SOX Act is to ensure the accuracy of financial records and controls around these records related to income, expenses, accounting, and liabilities.

The SOX Act contains 11 titles, or sections, dictating specific mandates and requirements for financial reporting. Each title consists of several sections.

Table 25-3 provides a comprehensive summary of these 11 titles of the SOX Act.

Table 25-3   *SOX Act—11 Titles*

Title#	Title Name	Description
Title I	Public Company Accounting Oversight Board (PCAOB)	Requires establishing a Public Company Accounting Oversight Board (PCAOB) to provide independent oversight of public accounting firms providing audit services.
Title II	Auditors Independence	Consists of nine sections that establish standards for external auditor independence and limit conflicts of interest.
Title III	Corporate Responsibility	Mandates that senior executives take individual responsibility for the accuracy and completeness of corporate financial reports.
Title IV	Enhanced Financial Disclosures	Consists of nine sections. Describes enhanced reporting requirements for financial transactions, including off-balance sheet transactions, pro-forma figures, and stock transactions of corporate officers.
Title V	Analyst Conflicts of Interest	Consists of only one section, which includes measures designed to help restore investor confidence in the reporting of securities analysts.
Title VI	Commission Resources and Authority	Consists of four sections that define practices to restore investor confidence in securities analysts.
Title VII	Studies and Reports	Consists of five sections. These sections 701 to 705 are concerned with conducting research for enforcing actions against violations by the Securities and Exchange Commission (SEC) registrants (companies) and auditors.
Title VIII	Corporate and Criminal Fraud Accountability	Consists of seven sections and is referred to as the Corporate and Criminal Fraud Act of 2002. Describes specific criminal penalties for fraud by manipulation, destruction, or alteration of financial records or other interference with investigations, while providing certain protections for whistle blowers.

continues

Table 25-3   *SOX Act—11 Titles (Continued)*

Title#	Title Name	Description
Title IX	White Collar Crime Penalty Enhancement	Consists of two sections and is called the White Collar Crime Penalty Enhancement Act of 2002. This section increases the criminal penalties associated with white-collar crimes and conspiracies.
Title X	Corporate Tax Returns	Consists of only one section. Section 1001 states that the Chief Executive Officer should sign the company tax return.
Title XI	Corporate Fraud Accountability	Consists of seven sections. Section 1101 recommends a name for this title as Corporate Fraud Accountability Act of 2002. This also enables the Securities and Exchange Commission (SEC) to temporarily freeze large or unusual payments.

TIP   The complete and actual table of contents from the SOX Act report issued in the U.S. House of Representatives on July 24, 2002, can be found at http://www.sarbanes-oxley-101.com/sarbanes-oxley-TOC.htm.

The SOX Act does not specifically mandate information security requirements. However, security has emerged as a key component for SOX Act compliance.

For example, as part of Title 1 requirements listed in Table 25-3, a Public Company Accounting Oversight Board (PCAOB) is established for independent oversight of public accounting firms providing audit services, which is charged with overseeing, regulating, inspecting, and disciplining accounting firms in their roles as auditors of public companies. As a result of this Auditing Standard 2 of the PCAOB requirements, network security is a fundamental component of SOX compliance.

The Auditing Standard 2 states that senior management is responsible not only for financial information but also for the way that information is generated, accessed, collected, stored, processed, and transmitted, hence directly affecting network and network security domains.

Another example is SOX Section 404 in Title IV. Many organizations consider Section 404 to be the most critical part of SOX, whereby organizations must receive an annual certification of internal controls and have an independent accountant attest to the report and quarterly reviews for updates and changes required. This requires producing a new report that validates the internal controls over the financial reporting process. Because of SOX Section 404, many organizations invest heavily in networking and security systems infrastructures that ensure the confidentiality, integrity, and availability of information systems.

In addition, the SOX Act also covers issues such as auditor independence, corporate governance, internal control assessment, and enhanced financial disclosure.

To ensure compliance, the following sections are important:

- Section 302 requires the CEO and CFO to certify that the financial reports are true and accurate and that adequate controls exist over financial reporting and disclosure.

- Section 404 describes these controls, requires that certification be reasonable, and requires that outside auditors certify the existence of adequate controls over financial reporting.

- Section 409 requires prompt reporting of any changes in financial condition that might be material to investors.

- Section 802 mandates that companies and their auditors retain accounting documents and work papers for a minimum of seven years.

An internationally recognized controls-based framework, such as ISO/IEC 27002 (ISO/IEC 17799), coupled with a process-based framework, such as COBIT, can provide an organization with a comprehensive best-practices approach that underpins SOX compliance.

Many other countries have replicated the SOX Act to their localized act. They reflect similar requirements and mandates from the original SOX Act. Examples include the following:

- **Bill 198:** Ontario, Canada, version of the SOX Act
- **J-SOX:** Japanese version of the SOX Act
- **CLERP9:** Australian Corporate reporting and disclosure law
- **LSF ("Loi sur la Sécurité Financière"):** French version of the SOX Act
- **L262/2005 ("Disposizioni per la tutela del risparmio e la disciplina dei mercati finanziari"):** Italian version of the SOX Act

Penalties for Violations

To ensure compliance, the SOX Act has provisions that include both criminal and civil penalties for any violations.

Penalties for noncompliance are significant. Fines for SOX violations can go up to $500,000 and include up to 10 years in prison.

False reporting carries a huge penalty under the SOX Act. Knowingly signing false reports carries a prison sentence of up to 20 years.

These penalties ensure that businesses and government agencies treat regulatory compliance as a top priority.

Chapter 25: Security Framework and Regulatory Compliance

The Securities and Exchange Commission (SEC) and the Federal Reserve Board are charged to execute and enforce the SOX Act.

Cisco Solutions Addressing SOX

Table 25-4 lists the Cisco products and solutions that help address the SOX requirements.

Table 25-4   *Cisco Solutions Addressing SOX Requirements*

Requirement	Cisco Solutions
Intrusion Detection and Prevention	• Cisco IPS 4200 Series Sensors • Cisco Integrated Services Routers (ISR) with Security Bundle • Cisco ASA 5500 Series Adaptive Security Appliances • Cisco Catalyst Security Services Modules
Logging, Authentication, Access Control	• Cisco Secure Access Control Server (ACS) • Cisco Security Agent (CSA) • Cisco Security Mitigation, Analysis and Response System (CS-MARS)
Antivirus Policy	• Cisco ASA 5500 Series • Cisco Firewall Services Module (FWSM) • Cisco Integrated Services Routers (ISR) • Cisco IPS 4200 Series • Cisco Security Agent(CSA)
Remote-Access Policy	• Cisco ASA 5500 Series • Cisco Integrated Services Routers (ISR)
Configuration Policy	• Cisco Security Device Manager (Security Bundles) • Cisco Security Agent (CSA) • Cisco Security MARS • Cisco Security Manager • Cisco Network Admission Control (NAC)
Vulnerability Assessment	• Regular Vulnerability Assessment

SOX Summary

In summary, publicly listed companies need a system-based approach that is collaborative and adaptive, offering an effective security governance framework to manage information security as well as provide guidelines to meet SOX compliance requirements.

For more details about SOX, refer to the following documentation URLs:

http://www.sarbanes-oxley-forum.com/

http://www.wikipedia.org/wiki/SOX

http://www.whitehouse.gov/news/releases/2002/07/20020730.html

---

TIP   The actual text of the law can be downloaded in PDF format from the following URL: http://www.sec.gov/about/laws/soa2002.pdf.

Worldwide Outlook of Regulatory Compliance Acts and Legislations

As discussed previously, organizations are faced with increased pressure from governments and public shareholders demanding protection of information systems, especially those concerned with the appropriate use of information, both personal and financial.

This has resulted in increased legal and regulatory compliance demands to ensure the proper use and protection of both corporate and personal information.

There are several regulatory legislatives and acts defined to mandate information systems security covered in the previous sections. Organizations need to adhere to these frameworks and standards, depending on their region and operation in different parts of the world, facing different legislative acts. Organizations operating globally are required to comply locally and internationally in countries in which they operate or conduct business transactions.

In the United States

Within the United States, organizations are faced with public prosecutors and regulators who are equipped with a growing range of legislation and penalties, including the following:

- The U.S. Public Company Accounting Reform and Investor Protection Act of 2002 (Sarbanes-Oxley—SOX)
- The Gramm-Leach-Bliley Financial Services Modernization Act of 1999 (GLBA)
- The U.S. Health Insurance Portability and Accountability Act (HIPAA)
- The European safe harbor regulations
- California's Senate Bill 1386 (SB1386) and Online Privacy Protection Act (OPPA)

In Europe

Within Europe, organizations are faced with prosecutors and regulators at both the national and European levels who are increasingly equipped with a growing range of legislation and penalties, including those available under local implementations of the following:

- The EU Data Protection Directive of 1995
- The EU Directive on Privacy and Electronic Communications 2002
- European Human Rights Legislation
- Freedom of Information Legislation
- The Council of Europe's Convention on Cybercrime of 2001

In the Asia-Pacific Region

Within the Asia-Pacific region, organizations are faced with a complex mix of local prosecutors and regulators who are equipped with a growing range of legislation and penalties, including those available under local data protection and privacy regulations.

In addition, the Asia-Pacific Economic Cooperation (APEC) forum's privacy framework of 2004 is similar to the EU requirements on privacy, although many countries within the region have not yet passed privacy protection laws. This increases the pressure on those organizations in the Asia-Pacific region who aim to compete globally to access Western capital and commercial markets. This is particularly important for outsourcing organizations, who can be subject to the governance and regulatory requirements of their American and European customers.

NOTE   The information in the worldwide outlook of regulatory compliance and legislative act summary is compiled from Cisco documentation on regulatory compliance. For more details and full disclosure, refer to the following URLs:

- **United States**

  http://www.cisco.com/en/US/netsol/ns625/networking_solutions_white_paper0900 aecd80351e82.shtml

- **EMEA: Europe, Middle East and Africa**

  http://www.cisco.com/en/US/netsol/ns625/networking_solutions_white_paper0900 aecd80351ea6.shtml

- **Asia Pacific**

  http://www.cisco.com/en/US/netsol/ns625/networking_solutions_white_paper0900 aecd80351e9c.shtml

---

Cisco Self-Defending Network Solution

IT governance is shifting gears and becoming a corporate governance concern as senior executives focus on responding to internal and external pressures. They must establish the alignment of information systems and networks with the business strategies of the organization while managing security risks that threaten confidentiality, integrity, and availability of business processes and information.

Cisco Self-Defending Network solution is the first line of defense for the corporation, providing the foundation for all data, applications, and business processes.

Cisco Self-Defending Network is considered the foundational element of an organization's strategy for managing IT risk, providing an end-to-end system-based approach to network security that supports industry-recognized frameworks and best practices and provides the framework to meet regulatory compliance requirements.

Summary

Corporate governance depends on effective management of internal controls and on the confidentiality, integrity, and availability of the information system within an organization. Organizations are faced with increased pressure to comply with an array of industry regulations and legislation.

The chapter provided an overview of the various integrated pieces of the security model and highlighted their relationship with each of the others.

The chapter highlighted the two most important and widely used best practices framework to manage IT governance and security audit compliance requirements—namely, ISO/IEC 17799 and COBIT.

The chapter provided comprehensive details on common regulatory compliance legislations and acts that are currently being enforced around the world, including the GLBA, HIPAA, and SOX acts.

The chapter provided a summary chart of Cisco solutions and products that help meet the regulator compliance and concluded the value of Cisco's Self-Defending Network solution for managing IT risk and corporate governance.

References

http://www.cisco.com/en/US/netsol/ns625/networking_solutions_package.html

http://www.cisco.com/en/US/netsol/ns170/networking_solutions_products_generic_content0900aecd8051f36d.html

http://www.wikipedia.org/wiki/ISO_17799

http://www.wikipedia.org/wiki/COBIT

http://www.cisco.com/en/US/netsol/ns625/net_value_proposition0900aecd80380856.html

http://www.cisco.com/en/US/netsol/ns625/net_value_proposition0900aecd80380862.html

http://www.cisco.com/en/US/netsol/ns625/net_value_proposition0900aecd80380886.html

http://www.cisco.com/en/US/netsol/ns625/networking_solutions_white_paper0900aecd80351e82.shtml

http://www.cisco.com/en/US/netsol/ns625/networking_solutions_white_paper0900aecd80351ea6.shtml

http://www.cisco.com/en/US/netsol/ns625/networking_solutions_white_paper0900aecd80351e9c.shtml

H

hackers, 210
hardening devices
    Auto-Secure feature, 75–76
    BOOTP, 69
    CDP, 68
    Cisco IOS Resilient Configuration, 67
    device configuration, autoloading, 70
    DHCP, 69
    Finger, 69
    FTP servers, 70
    Gratuitous ARP, 72
    HTTP, 73
    ICMP Unreachable, 73
    infrastructure ACLs, 62
    interactive access
        via AUX port, 65
        via console port, 62
        via VTY port, 63–64
    IP directed broadcast, 72
    IP mask reply, 72
    IP source routing, 71
    NTP, 74
    PAD, 70
    physical security, 55
    privilege levels, 61
    Proxy ARP, 71
    SNMP, 75
    TCP/UDP small-servers, 69
    TFTP, 70
    user authentication, 60
    with password protection, 55
        encryption, 57
        ROMMON security, 57–60
        strong passwords, creating, 56–57
**hardware-based firewalls versus
    software-based, 140**
hash algorithms, 416–420
hash value, 409
**HCAP (Host Credential Authorization
    Protocol), 386**
**hierarchical DMVPN topology, configuring,
    499–500**

high availability, 598
    IPS fail-open mechanism, 599
    IPS failover mechanism, 599
    load balancing, 600
**HIPAA (Health Insurance Portability and
    Accountability Act), 757**
    Cisco solutions for, 759
    penaties for violations, 758
    requirements, 758
**HMAC (keyed-hash message authentication
    code), 418**
host management (CSA), 624–626
host-based attacks, life cycle, 614
HTTP (HyperText Transfer Protocol), 73
    device access from ASDM, 77
HTTP inspection engine, 127
hub-and-spoke designs (DMVPN), 476
    DHDD topology, configuring, 483
    server load-balancing topology, configuring,
        484–485
    SHSD topology, 477–482
hybrid VPNs, 425

I

I&A (identification and authentication, 311
iACLs (infrastructure protection ACLs), 47
IBNS (Identity-Based Networking Services), 326
ICMP flood attacks, characterizing, 212–215
IDAPI, 576
IDCONF, 576
identification, 311
Identity NAT, 179
IDIOM, 576
idle time, 93
**IDM (Cisco IPS Device Manager),
    78, 601, 740–742**
IDS (intrusion detection systems), 561
IEEE 802.1x, 332
    components of, 330
    EAP methods, 334
    multipoint solution, deploying, 335–336
    point-to-point solution, deploying, 334
    switch port states, 332–333
IEEE 802.11 protocol standards, 348

T

X-Y-Z

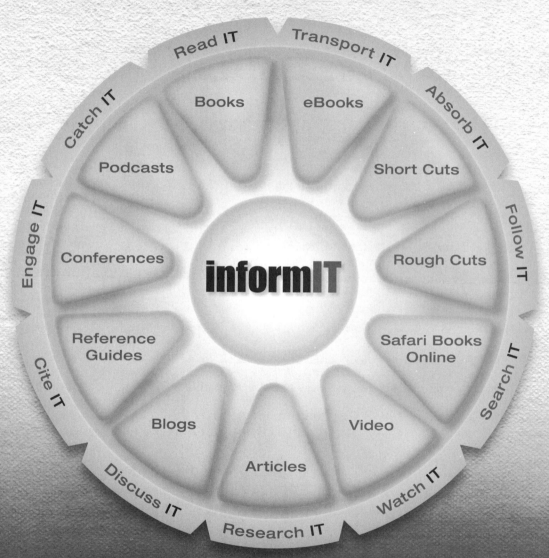

THIS BOOK IS SAFARI ENABLED

INCLUDES FREE 45-DAY ACCESS TO THE ONLINE EDITION

The Safari® Enabled icon on the cover of your favorite technology book means the book is available through Safari Bookshelf. When you buy this book, you get free access to the online edition for 45 days.

Safari Bookshelf is an electronic reference library that lets you easily search thousands of technical books, find code samples, download chapters, and access technical information whenever and wherever you need it.

TO GAIN 45-DAY SAFARI ENABLED ACCESS TO THIS BOOK:

- Go to **http://www.ciscopress.com/safarienabled**

- Complete the brief registration form

- Enter the coupon code found in the front of this book before the "Contents at a Glance" page

If you have difficulty registering on Safari Bookshelf or accessing the online edition, please e-mail customer-service@safaribooksonline.com.

To protect your network, Cisco Security Center is the Website you need, every day. Find real-time intelligence from Cisco IntelliShield analysts, the world's top network security experts, who analyze and correlate global security threats. In addition to timely threat notification, learn how to use your Cisco network to mitigate risks. Cisco Security Center: your ultimate resource for security guidance. **Bookmark cisco.com/security today**.

welcome to
the human network.

CISCO

No configuration is required on the CSA agent. All configurations are completed on the server via the CSA MC and deployed to the CSA agent. CSA agent will have only basic viewing capabilities.

Managing CSA Hosts

In the CSA architecture, hosts are the endpoint systems that require protection. A host is any system that has installed the CSA agent kit from the CSA MC and has registered with CSA MC. The host can be a desktop computer, a laptop, or even a server. These endpoints are referred to as hosts within the CSA MC configuration. As mentioned earlier, every host on the network has to register with CSA MC to receive policy updates. The status of the host can be monitored by CSA MC.

Figures 21-6 through 21-8 show a few sample screenshots for managing a host that is using the CSA MC.

Figure 21-6 *CSA MC—Displaying List of Hosts*

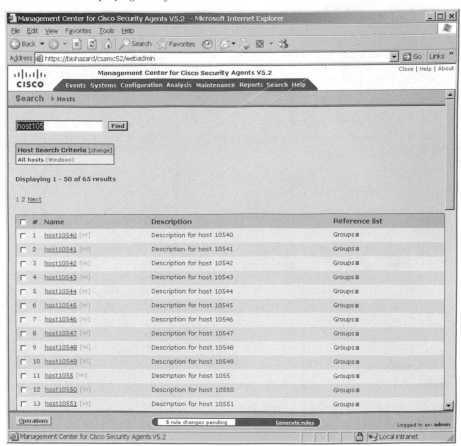

Figure 21-5 *CSA Components*

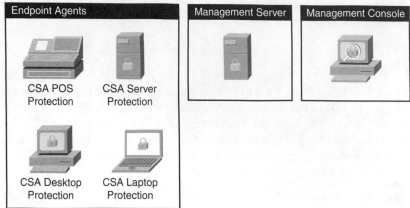

Configuring and Managing CSA Deployment by Using CSA MC

All security policies and configurations are accomplished using the CSA MC. These policies are associated with specific hosts and groups of hosts. All configurations are stored on the management server and deployed to the agents via the management server.

All communications between the CSA MC and the server are secured using Secure Sockets Layer (SSL) protocol. Similarly, communications between the CSA agent and the server database are secured using SSL.

The web-based user interface is accessed securely using SSL from any machine on the network that can connect to the management server. The web-based interface is used to deploy policies from CSA MC to all the agents across the network.

SSL protocol is also needed for the agents to periodically update the policy; therefore the network must not restrict SSL traffic on port 443. This is especially important if CSA agents are located on remote network segments that are isolated via firewalls.

The CSA MC binds with the server database which holds all the policies. All CSA endpoint agents must register with CSA MC to receive the policy. The CSA MC validates the host and deploys the respective policy pertaining to that host or group of hosts.

After the CSA agent on the local system receives the policy, it starts monitoring the system proactively and takes dynamic actions as necessary.

At regular intervals (configurable), the CSA agent polls the CSA MC for policy updates. It also sends triggered event alerts to the CSA MC global event manager.

Table 21-1 *CSA Capabilities and Security Roles (Continued)*

CSA Capabilities	Functional Role Description
Traffic marking and prioritization	The host system has many applications; some are mission critical and others are normal business applications. Some applications may be tolerated, but not business related. For example, an enterprise resource planning (ERP) system should be given higher priority than other applications in the event of congestion. This can be done by assigning a unique Differentiated Services Code Point (DSCP) value that identifies the mission-critical traffic. Similarly, other business-related applications such as e-mail and browsers are important but not critical; hence, a separate unique DSCP value can be associated to them so that a relevant action can be taken accordingly.
Network integration	CSA can actively integrate with other network devices and work in close collaboration. CSA inputs can be valuable to influence actions in other solutions implemented within the network. Examples include the Network Admission Control (NAC) enforcement, Network IPS, QoS services via routers and switches, log collectors, and network correlation devices such as CS-MARS and VPN devices.

CSA Components

As shown in Figure 21-5, CSA has three basic components:

- **CSA endpoints:** Endpoints are computing desktops, servers, laptops, and point of service (POS) terminals. The CSA agent is responsible for enforcing security policies received from the management server, sending events, and interacting with the user.

- **CSA management server:** The server is the core component in the CSA deployment, a repository of configuration database. The server is responsible for deploying the security policies to the endpoints; it receives and stores all events, sends alerts to the administrator, and can deploy software to the endpoints.

- **CSA management console (CSA MC):** The management console is an administrative web-based user interface and policy configuration tool that provides event views.

NOTE   The management server can also be used as the management console for policy configuration and event views.

Table 21-1   *CSA Capabilities and Security Roles (Continued)*

CSA Capabilities	Functional Role Description
Application inventory feature	CSA can now track all the applications installed on a computer or group of computers across the network, which of these are actually run, which of these use the network, whether the application is a network client or a network server, and which remote IP addresses the application communicates with.
	CSA can track which applications are residing on which systems.
	Application inventory can also track unknown and unauthorized applications (that listen on a port but do not accept connections) running on a standalone system and other systems on the network, analyzing their behavior, creating patterns, grouping them into suspected spyware or adware categories, and creating rules to limit or prohibit their behavior. CSA offers this unique spyware protection at no additional cost.
Policy control	CSA can define policy controls based on the corporate security policy. Some types of behavior are not malicious but are undesired because they violate acceptable use within corporate policy—for example, music sharing via peer-to-peer (p2p) applications, instant messaging using noncorporate IM servers, external device protection, that is, devices that cannot be used (USB memory, multimedia devices, CD-ROM), or use of unauthorized applications or unauthorized versions of certain applications. CSA offers default policy control modules, including data theft prevention policy, instant messenger control policy, music download prevention policy, and network lockdown policy to enforce the previous examples.
Compliance enforcement	CSA can be used as an enforcement tool to implement controls for regulatory compliance, such as PCI, Sarbanes-Oxley, and other mandates.
User education	CSA can play the educator role. On many occasions, a user may invoke a request that may not be unauthorized from the operating system context but is restricted because of a corporate security policy. For example, a corporate policy may restrict usage of external devices, such as USB keys, and the user inserts the USB key on the system. Technically, the operating system will allow this; however, the CSA can intercept and deny this action and display a pop-up window educating the user on why this action was denied. This way, the user is educated on the corporate policy and acceptable use conditions when using the corporate equipment.

continunes

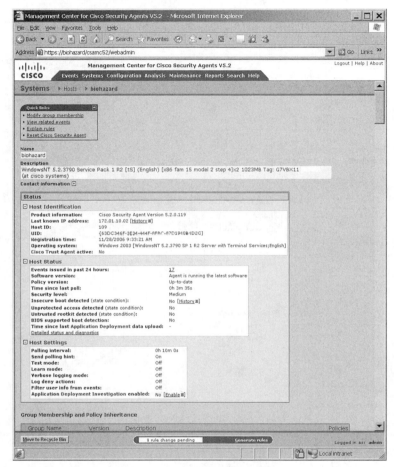

Figure 21-12 *CSA MC—Agent User Interface Control Page*

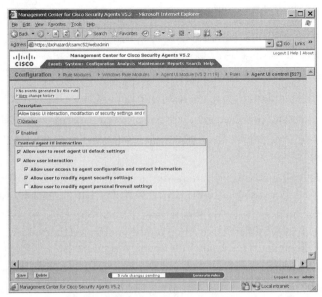

Figure 21-13 shows a sample screenshot from an endpoint host system showing the CSA Agent user interface.

Figure 21-13 *CSA Agent Host Endpoint—User Interface*

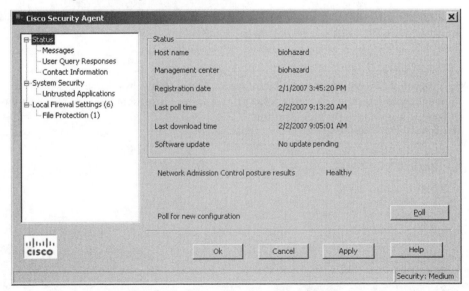

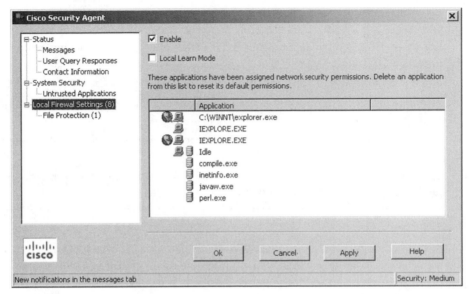

Figure 22-3   *Advanced DDoS Protection Using the Cisco Anomaly Detection and Mitigation Solution*

Packet Flow
Through the
Defense Modules

Learning   ❶
- Periodic Observation of Patterns to Update Baseline Profiles
- Traffic Profile During Peacetime

Detection   ❷
- Passive Copy of Traffic Monitoring
- Anomaly-Based Detection

Anomaly
Detected

Analysis   ❸
- Diversion for More Granular In-Line Analysis
- Flex Filters, Static and Bypass Filters in Operation
- All Flows Forwarded but Analyzed for Anomalies

Anomaly
Verified

Basic Protection   ❹
- Basic Antispoofing Applied
- Analysis for Continuing Anomalies

Anomaly
Identified

Strong Protection   ❺
- Strong Antispoofing (Proxy) if Appropriate
- Dynamic Filters Deployed for Zombie Sources

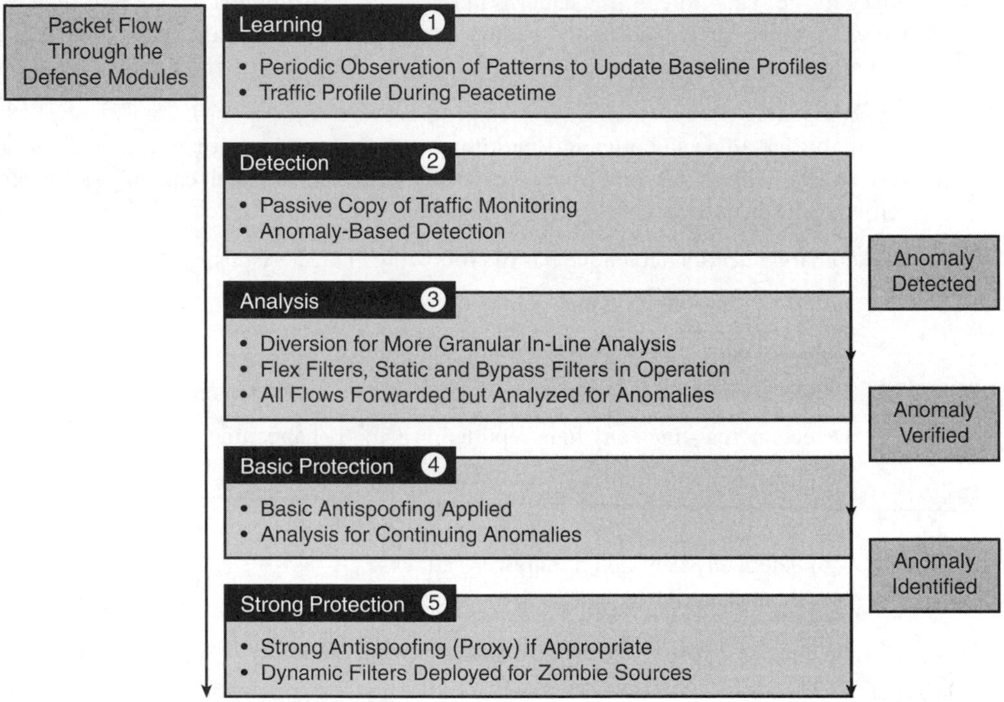

The Cisco DDoS Anomaly Detection and Mitigation solution consists of two basic deployment components:

- Cisco Traffic Anomaly Detector
- Cisco Guard DDoS Mitigation

NOTE   Both products are available as appliance-based solutions and integrated service modules for Cisco Catalyst 6500 Series Switches and Cisco 7600 Series Routers.

Cisco Traffic Anomaly Detector

The Cisco Traffic Anomaly Detector is the industry's standard solution for detecting the most complex and sophisticated DDoS attacks. The Cisco Traffic Anomaly Detector works in combination with the Cisco Guard DDoS Mitigation device.

Cisco Guard provides robust protection against all types of attacks with the integrated dynamic filters and active verification technologies, driven by a sophisticated profile-based anomaly recognition engine. In addition, the protocol analysis and rate limiting features ensure that only valid traffic gets through without overwhelming other downstream devices.

Figure 22-5 illustrates the innovative MVP architecture that delivers multiple interactive layers of defense, which are designed to identify and block the specific packets and flows responsible for the attack.

Figure 22-5 *Multiverification Process (MVP) Architecture*

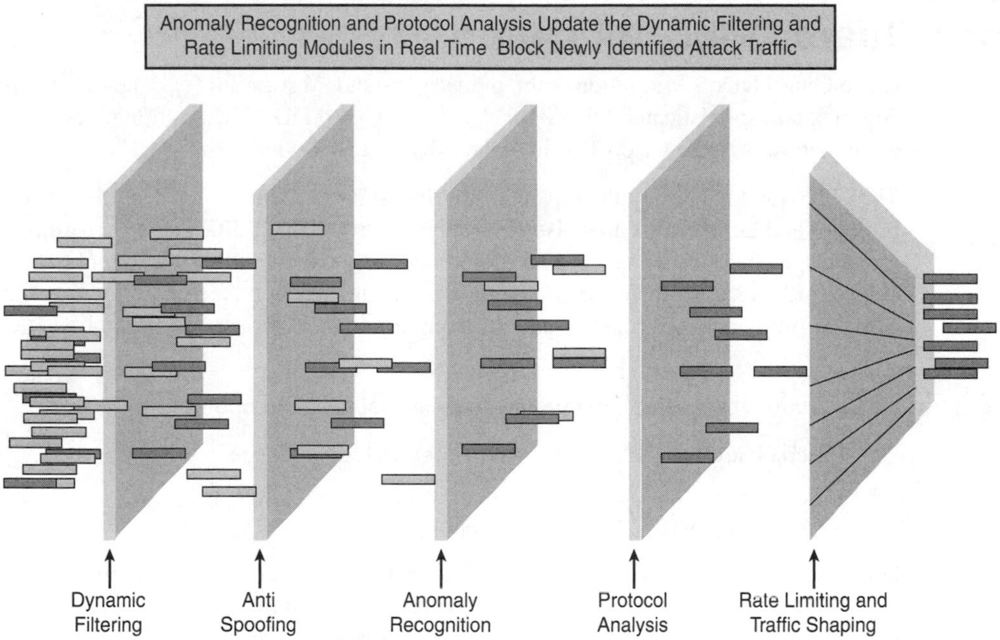

The information in Figure 22-5 is compiled from the Cisco Networkers session presentation BRKSEC-2030 on "Deploying Network IPS."

The Cisco Guard Mitigation device is capable of processing attack traffic at multigigabit line rates, and the recognition engine identifies a broad range of DDoS attacks, including

- TCP-based attacks
- UDP-based attacks
- HTTP attacks
- DNS attacks
- SIP (VoIP) attacks
- Botnets and Zombie attacks

Figure 23-8 *CS-MARS Standalone Local Controller (LC)*

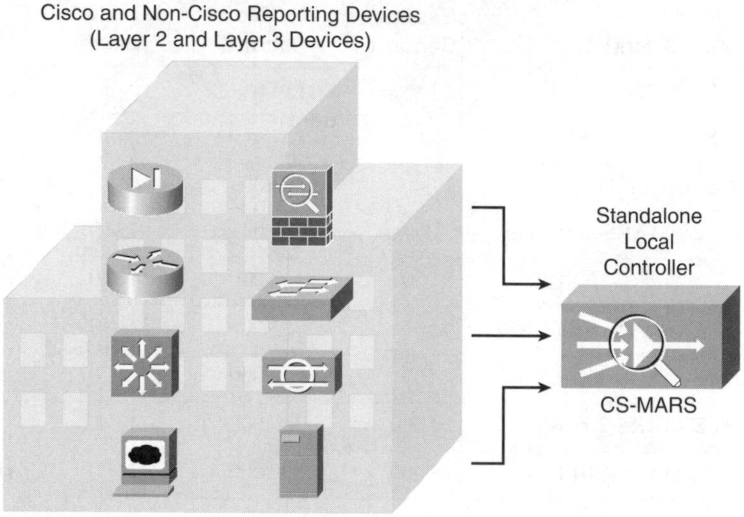

Global Controllers (GC)

The Global Controller (GC) is used to manage two or more LC zone deployments allowing scaling of the network monitoring without increasing the management burden on the LC.

The GC provides complete control and management of the LC across various sites (zones) and provides a single user interface for defining new device types, inspection rules, reports, and queries.

GC provides a central console to manage multiple LCs. It also provides additional capabilities, including

- Global authentication across all LCs
- Unified report generation across all LCs
- Unified rule generation for LC deployment
- Global view of the network
- Centralized software management
- Reduced traffic across WAN links

Three basic CS-MARS models are available for GC deployment scenarios.

Figure 23-9 *CS-MARS Global Controller*

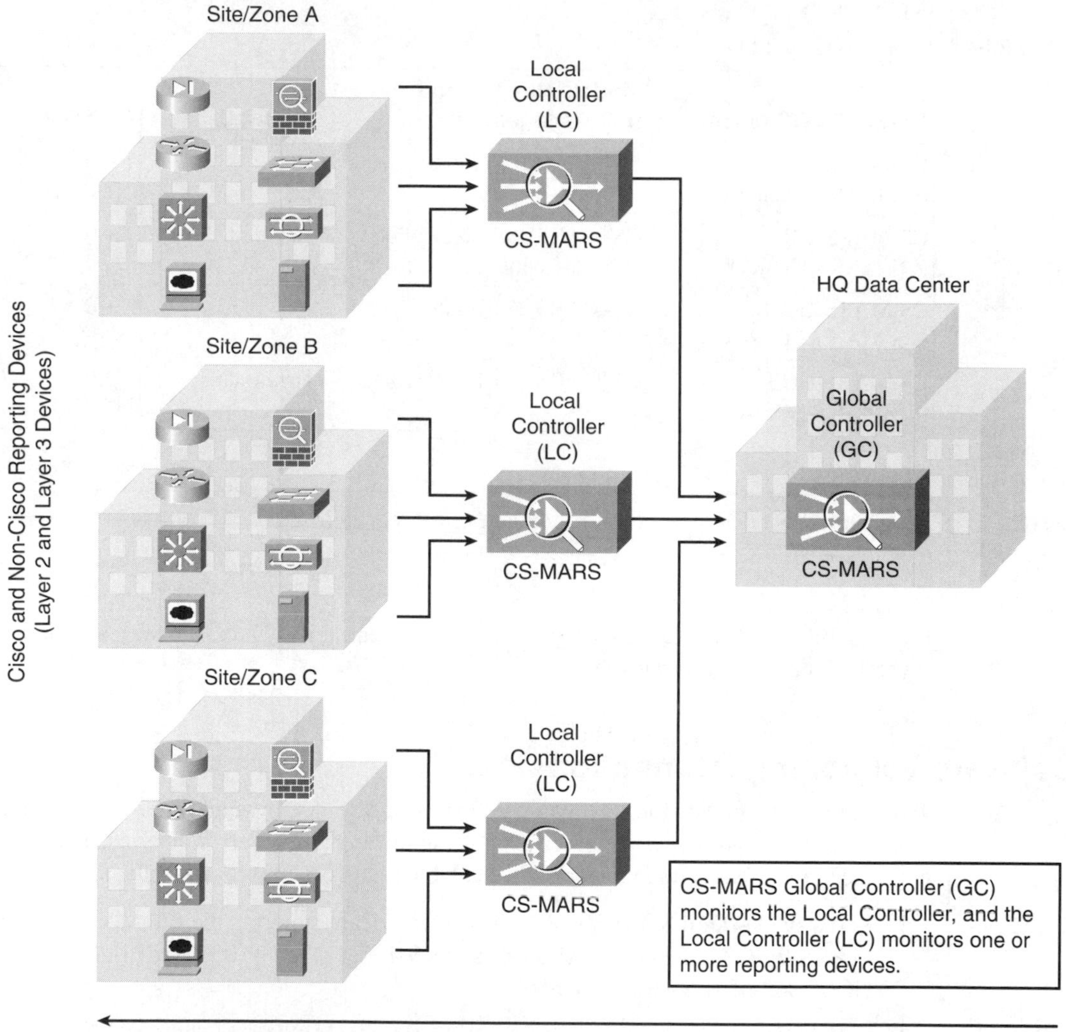

Reporting and Mitigation Devices

From a top-down deployment perspective (refer to Figure 23-9), CS-MARS GC monitors the LC, and the LC monitors one or more reporting devices.

A reporting device is any Layer 2 or Layer 3 device (Cisco or non-Cisco) that provides CS-MARS with raw data about the network from traffic flows and the configuration files, allowing CS-MARS to analyze and respond to possible attack targets.

Figure 23-12 *CS-MARS Web-Based Management—Seven Menu Option Tabs and Subtabs*

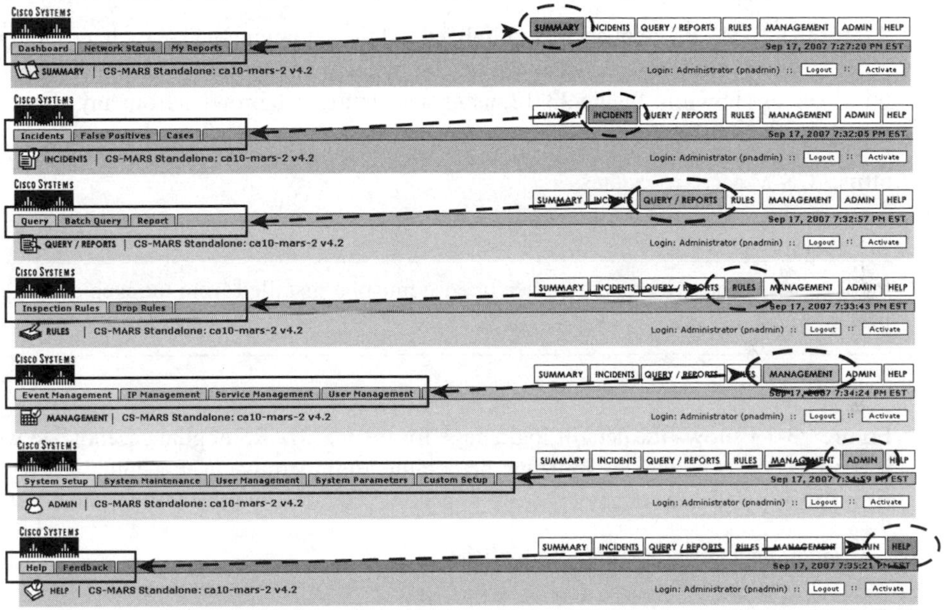

Initializing CS-MARS

Depending on the LC or GC, and whether you are using software version 4.3.x or version 5.3.x, several parameters need to be configured on the CS-MARS appliance system. These can either be configured via the CLI console or the web-based management interface.

After booting the CS-MARS appliance for the first time, you need to configure the following basic parameters as part of the initialization process using the CLI console. Basic parameters include the following:

- Hostname
- IP address and subnet mask
- Default gateway addresses
- DNS server IP addresses (if DNS is used)
- NTP server address (if NTP is used)
- Time, date, and time zone

Login via the console access to the CS-MARS system using the default administrative user account and password (**pnadmin/pnadmin**) to complete the basic initialization process.

After the CS-MARS appliance is initialized, all the remaining tasks, such as adding the reporting and mitigation devices, can be completed using the web-based management interface, as shown in Figure 23-12, using a standard web browser from any client PC on the network as follows:

https://CS-MARS_ip_address

NOTE   Prior to using the system, the device license must be installed from the web console as the first step.

Figure 23-13 shows the default login page for the CS-MARS appliance. Indicate whether it is an LC or a GC and log in using the default administrative user account and password (**pnadmin/pnadmin**) or any other user account provided by the administrator.

Figure 23-13   *Default Login Page for CS-MARS Appliance*

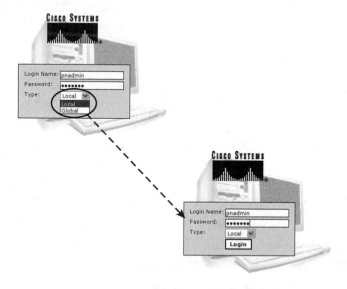

Cisco Security Manager—Cross-Launch xDM

The Cisco Security Manager provides another unique feature—cross-launching, which supplies the capability to open connections to other device manager applications directly from the Cisco Security Manager interface.

Supported cross-launch xDMs include Cisco ASDM, Router and Security Device Manager (SDM), IPS Device Manager (IDM), and IPS Event Viewer (IEV).

This provides great flexibility and faster startup to connect to the device without having a connection from a user desktop. It also provides collaboration between security events and policy management.

Figure 24-8 illustrates an example of opening Cisco ASDM directly from the Cisco Security Manager by right-clicking the managed ASA device and selecting Device Manager to launch the Cisco ASDM application.

Figure 24-8   *Cisco Security Manager—Cross-Launch Cisco ASDM*

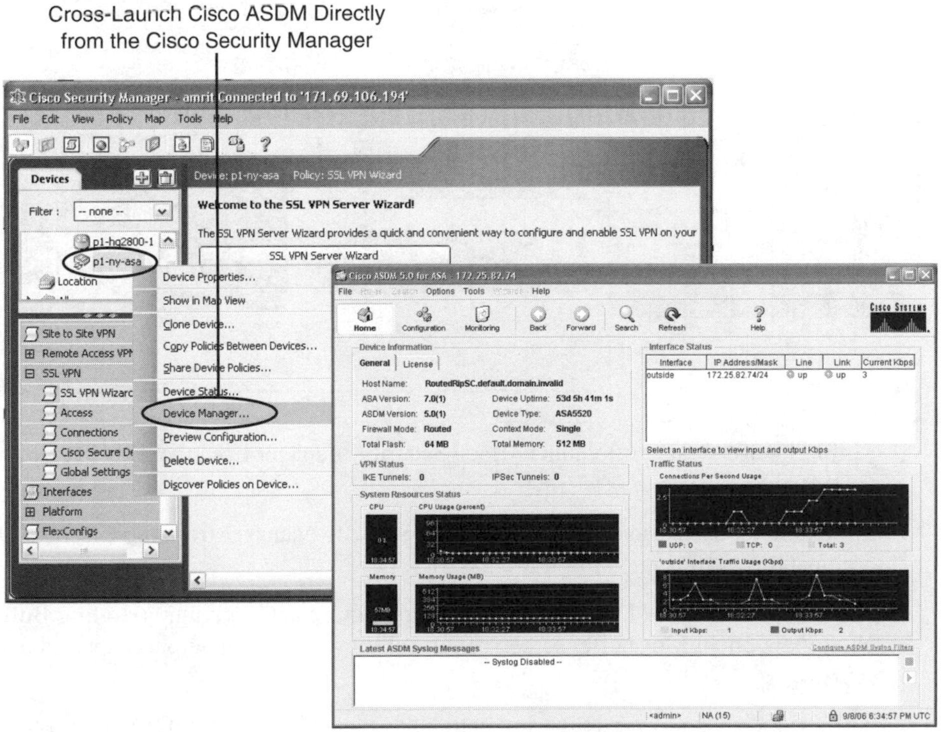

Figure 25-1 illustrates a high-level overview of the different layers in a security model that can be used as a basic template and guideline to achieve secure IT infrastructure.

Figure 25-1 *Building Blocks of Security Model*

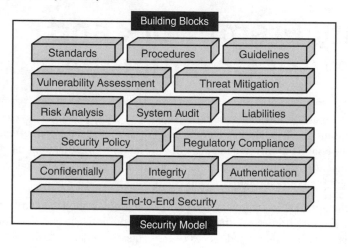

Figure 25-2 *Security Component Relationships*

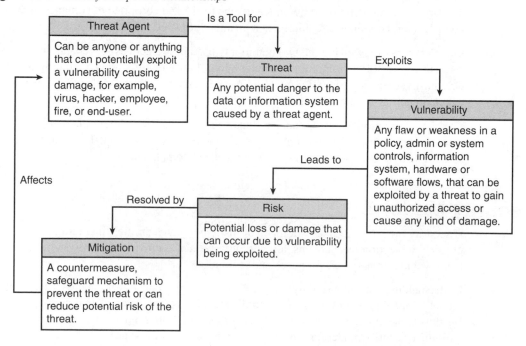

Standards

Standards are industry-recognized best-practice frameworks and are agreed-upon principles of concepts and designs to implement, achieve, and maintain the required levels of processes and procedures.

Like security policies, standards are strategic in nature in that they define system parameters and processes.

Several available industry standards are used for various purposes. In the context of security information management and regulatory compliance, there are two notable standards—ISO 17799 and COBIT. These are discussed in the next sections.

Guidelines

Guidelines are recommended actions and operational guides for users. Similar to standards, guidelines are also tactical in nature. The major difference between standards and guidelines is that guidelines can be used as references, whereas standards are mandatory.

Procedures

Procedures are low-level documents providing systematic step-by-step instructions on completing or fulfilling a certain task. Procedures are detailed in nature to provide maximum information to users to successfully implement and enforce the security policy and apply the standards and guidelines.

Figure 25-3 depicts the relationship between security policies, standards, guidelines, and procedures.

Figure 25-3 *Security Policies, Standards, Guidelines, and Procedures*

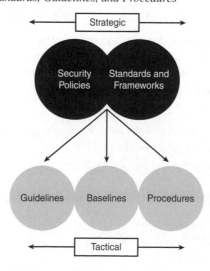

H

I

T

X-Y-Z

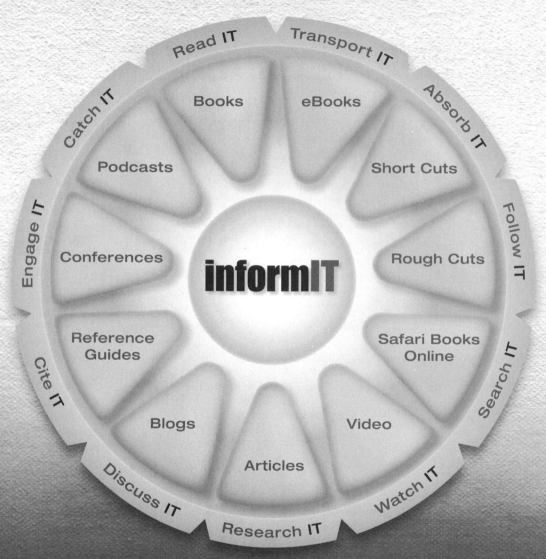